The Imperial Harem

D1246653

Studies in Middle Eastern History

BERNARD LEWIS, ITAMAR RABINOVICH,
AND ROGER SAVORY
General Editors

OTHER VOLUMES ARE IN PREPARATION

LESLIE P. PEIRCE

THE IMPERIAL HAREM

*Women and Sovereignty
in the Ottoman Empire*

New York • Oxford
OXFORD UNIVERSITY PRESS
1993

Oxford University Press

Oxford   New York   Toronto
Delhi   Bombay   Calcutta   Madras   Karachi
Kuala Lumpur   Singapore   Hong Kong   Tokyo
Nairobi   Dar es Salaam   Cape Town
Melbourne   Auckland   Madrid

and associated companies in
Berlin   Ibadan

Published by Oxford University Press, Inc.,
198 Madison Avenue, New York, New York 10016-4314

Oxford is a registered trademark of Oxford University Press

Library of Congress Cataloging-in-Publication Data
Peirce, Leslie Penn.
The imperial harem : women and sovereignty
in the Ottoman Empire / Leslie P. Peirce.
p.   cm. — (Studies in Middle Eastern history)
Includes bibliographical references and index.
ISBN-13 978-0-19-507673-8; 978-0-19-508677-5 (pbk)
ISBN 0-19-507673-7—ISBN 0-19-508677-5 (pbk.)
1. Women in politics—Turkey—History.
2. Turkey—Kings and rulers—Wives—History.
3. Women—Turkey—Social conditions. 4. Harem.
5. Favorites, Royal—Turkey—History.
6. Turkey—History—1453–1683.
I. Series: Studies in Middle
Eastern history (New York, N.Y.)
HQ1240.5.T87P45   1993
305.42'09561—dc20   93-18967

The Publisher gratefully acknowledges the financial assistance of The
Hull Memorial Publication Fund of Cornell University.

Portions of this book appeared previously in Leslie P. Peirce, "Beyond
Harem Walls: Ottoman Royal Women and the Exercise of Power," in
Gendered Domains: Rethinking Public and Private in Women's History,
Essays from the Seventh Berkshire Conference on the History of
Women, ed. Dorothy O. Helly and Susan M. Reverby. Copyright ©
1992 by Cornell University. Used by permission of Cornell University
Press.

19   18   17   16   15   14   13   12   11   10

Printed in the United States of America
on acid-free paper

Contents

Part I   The Politics of Reproduction

Part II   Women and Sovereign Power

Preface

In 1599 Sunullah Efendi, leader of the religious hierarchy of the Ottoman Empire and foremost guardian of the holy law of Islam, publicly lamented what he saw as a number of harmful and disruptive developments in Ottoman society. Among his several criticisms, he proclaimed that women should have nothing to do with "matters of government and sovereignty."[1] While other of his warnings were addressed to the general populace, this proclamation was aimed at the sultan and the dynastic family, whose senior women had come in recent decades to exercise an extraordinary degree of political influence. Sixteen years earlier, shortly before the death of Nurbanu, the mother of the sultan Murad III, the Venetian ambassador to the Ottoman court, Paolo Contarini, had commented that "all good and all bad come from the queen mother."[2] When Nurbanu died in December 1583, Contarini's successor noted:

> Some are saddened by this lady's death and others consoled, each according to his or her own interests, for just as she provided enormous benefits to many as a result of the great authority she enjoyed with her son, so conversely did she deprive others of the hopes of obtaining what they desired. But all universally admit that she was a woman of the utmost goodness, courage, and wisdom.[3]

The rise to power of the imperial harem is one of the most dramatic developments in the sixteenth-century history of the Ottoman Empire. From almost the beginning of the reign of Süleyman the Magnificent, who came to the throne in 1520, until the mid-seventeenth century, high-ranking women of the Ottoman dynasty enjoyed a degree of political power and public prominence greater than ever before or after. Indeed, this period in the empire's history is often referred to, in both popular and scholarly literature, as "the sultanate of women."[4] The women of the imperial harem, especially the mother of the reigning sultan and his leading concubines, were considerably more active than their predecessors in the direct exercise of political power: in creating and manipulating domestic political factions, in negotiating with foreign powers, and in acting as regents for their sons. Furthermore, they played a central role in what we might call the public culture of sovereignty: public rituals of imperial legitimation and royal patronage of monumental building and artistic production.

If the prominence of the imperial harem is a notable feature of the six-teenth and seventeenth centuries, it is also one of the most misunderstood. Modern historical accounts of this period have tended to represent the influence of the harem as an illegitimate usurpation of power that resulted from a weakening of the moral fiber and institutional integrity of Ottoman society and that in turn contributed to problems plaguing the empire toward the end of the sixteenth century. Difficulties in interpreting the rise of the imperial harem stem in large part from the fact that its power became manifest in the post-Süleymanic period. Traditionally, the reign of Süleyman has been re-garded as the apogee of Ottoman fortunes and the period initiated by his death in 1566 one of precipitous decline from which the empire never fully recovered (despite the fact that it survived until the end of World War I). In this view, the personal incapacity of Süleyman's successors, in contrast to the vigor and ability of their ancestors, opened the door to the "meddling" of harem women, who did not hesitate to exploit their influence over "weak-minded" sultans to satisfy their "lust" for power and wealth.

But the power of Ottoman royal women was too broadly and publicly expressed and too embedded in the structure of imperial institutions for it to be simplistically dismissed as illegitimate. Modern treatments of this period have not recognized the politically partisan nature of much of the contempo-rary critique of female power, such as the proclamation of Sunullah Efendi. Recently, new work on this period in Ottoman history has challenged the very notion of post-Süleymanic decline, bringing about a long overdue reevalua-tion of developments in the late sixteenth and early seventeenth centuries. Even some of these recent works, however, continue to repeat the unexam-ined theme of the dynasty's dissipation. In this book I seek to explain the sources of women's political power and the reasons for its prominence in the sixteenth and seventeenth centuries. I also try to answer the more difficult questions of how contemporary Ottomans viewed the influence of royal women, and why, if their reactions are not compatible with the modern cri-tique (and I believe they are not), that influence has been so misconstrued.

Perhaps the most important thing to be learned from placing royal women at the center stage of historical investigation is that they, like the men of the dynasty, gained or lost power in the context of family dynamics. Women were able to increase their influence on the conduct of government largely as a result of the shifting configurations of status and authority within the royal family during this period. The politics of the dynasty were of course condi-tioned by the larger fortunes of the Ottoman state, but it was as the premier household of the empire—a family made up of women and men, senior and junior generations, blood members, slave servants, and retainers—that the dynasty shaped its policies and public postures in reaction to external influ-ences. The roles played by royal women in the distribution and management of power within the dynastic family, as well as their roles as public exemplars of the dynasty's legitimacy, munificence, and piety, tell us a good deal about the nature of sovereignty and Ottoman claims to legitimacy. Because the political culture of the Ottoman state was formed in the matrix of its subjects' thinking about society and power, tracing the roles played by the various members of the dynasty may also tell us something about the views ordinary people held about the proper constitution of the family and relations between the sexes.

Two broad themes are developed in this book. The first is a challenge to the idea that gender segregation, so widely accepted as one of the hallmarks of traditional Islamic society, precluded women from playing anything more than a subordinate role within the household. Instead, the segregation of the sexes permitted the articulation of a hierarchy of status and authority among women, parallel to that which existed among men. The most important distinctions with regard to the distribution of power within the household appear to have been based not on a simple male/female dichotomy, but rather on other dichotomies stemming from the interaction of commonly accepted views about sexuality and authority.[5] Chief among these was a generational distinction, in which juniors were subordinated to both male and female elders. One aspect of this generational divide was the control by the senior generation of the sexual activity of the junior, reproductively active, generation. The close control of sexually active, childbearing women in traditional Islamic culture is well known, but it is important to note that the behavior of males was also scrutinized. The junior generation was subordinated not only to elder males but also, and sometimes principally, to "postsexual" female elders. Not only were elder women freed from many of the restrictions of female seclusion, but they also enjoyed the respect of males. A major error in the modern critique of royal women's power is the failure to recognize the distinction between female generations.

It should be noted that while this pattern of control of the junior generation by the senior was dominant in the dynasty for most of the period under study, it seems not to have been as pronounced in earlier stages of Ottoman dynastic history. Indeed, one of the aims of this work is to examine the factors that led to its emergence. Since so little is known about the nature of Ottoman society in the premodern period, it is hard to tell if the structure of the dynastic family reflected patterns in the larger society, or if it might have had a formative influence on them. I offer the tentative hypothesis that, at least for most of the period under study, there was continuity from the ordinary household to the dynasty in the structure and politics of the family. Indeed, the conformity of dynastic politics to the general expectations of Ottoman society may well have been one of the dynasty's lasting strengths.

The book's second theme concerns the nature of Ottoman sovereignty. One of the essential requirements of rulership in Islam, ideally conceived as successorship to the Prophet Muhammad, is that the sovereign be male. In the case of the Ottomans, rulership was conferred through a hereditary sultanate. In the legal or constitutional sense, therefore, supreme political authority was ultimately patriarchal. Practically speaking, however, the sultan's authority rested on his ability to maintain control of the ruling elites and satisfy their expectations. The sultan maintained control principally by manipulating factions and preventing any one political constellation from gaining a monopoly of power. This was accomplished primarily by means of the dynasty's control of appointment to office, but also through forms of household patronage, especially the marriage of select officials into the royal family. Women could and did play key roles in all of these sovereign functions. In the first half of the seventeenth century, when queen mothers frequently acted as regents for their minor or emotionally disturbed sons, virtually the only sultanic prerogative inaccessible to them was personal command of the Ottoman military.

Furthermore, the exercise of sovereignty was expressed in a variety of ways only some of which were "political" in the sense of the management of state affairs, such as waging war and raising revenue. Women were easily incorporated into the equally vital business of dynastic image making. Through their participation in the imperial ceremonies and progresses that stimulated the allegiance of subjects and their enhancement of the quality of urban life through charitable religious endowments and cultural patronage, royal women were living symbols of the qualities most prized in sovereignty: justice, piety, and munificence. Indeed, there were times when women of the dynasty were more publicly visible or built on a grander scale than the sultan himself.

The principal argument of the book is that changes in the nature of the Ottoman state and society in the sixteenth and seventeenth centuries were conducive to an expansion of royal women's participation in these various demonstrations of sovereignty. The major change was a gradual transition from a state geared to expansion and led by a warrior sultan to a territorially stable bureaucratic state ruled by a sedentary palace sultan. There were few radical discontinuities in this process of change, nor was it absolute: there were, for example, periods of territorial loss before the sixteenth century as well as marked gains after it, and the fifteenth century produced a sedentary sultan (Bayezid II) just as the seventeenth century produced a legendary warrior sultan (Murad IV). But there were in the late sixteenth century clearly discernible shifts of power and structural changes in many areas of administration, not least within the dynasty itself. Here two developments in particular increased the influence of women and their access to the sources of power. First, the growing importance of the imperial palace as a center of government gave women both greater physical proximity to the sultan and expanded opportunities for building networks of influence. Second, changes in the system of succession to the throne resulted in a more central role for royal mothers.

Ithaca, N.Y.   L. P.
January 1993

Acknowledgments

Many individuals and institutions have helped me over the course of the several years during which this book was researched and written. My first thanks must go to my teachers. My principal debt of gratitude is to Bernard Lewis, whose generosity in sharing his deep learning and in providing counsel and encouragement eased and cheered the long process of producing this work; he is a continuing inspiration both as teacher and scholar. I would like to thank Michael Cook, Avram Udovitch, and Jerome Clinton of Princeton University for their critical comments and their support during the dissertation stage of the work. I am grateful to Natalie Zemon Davis for her thoughtful criticisms of various stages of this project and to Halil İnalcık for his sound advice on aspects of my research. Finally, I would like to pay tribute to the memory of the late Martin B. Dickson, a very special and inspiring teacher; the questions he caused me to ask of Islamic history continue to shape my work.

To members of my family who have supported me as I worked on this book I have a deep debt of love and gratitude. My son Kerim has grown up with the book for more than half his life; in its later stages he explored dusty monuments, took photographs, and, having developed a keen intellect, helped with critical reading of the text. My cousin Richard Hamilton has been an unfailing source of advice, encouragement, and good humor; he and his wife Pinkie have contributed to this book in countless ways. My parents have supported with understanding the career changes and international comings and goings that form the backdrop to the book.

While I carried on my research in Turkey, I received help from a number of people whom I would like to thank. Aptullah Kuran, Mehmet Genç, and the late Bekir Kütükoğlu shared their knowledge of Ottoman history and culture with me. At the Topkapı Palace, Ülkü Altındağ, Filiz Çağman, and Hülya Tezcan were most generous with their knowledge and assistance, and made helpful suggestions regarding my research; Güngör Dilmen made it possible for me to explore portions of the Harem quarters closed to the public. At the Süleymaniye Library, Mine Özen provided assistance, and at the Prime Ministry Archives Veli Tola initiated a novice researcher into the mysteries of Ottoman documentary history. Cenk Alpak made it possible for me to visit a number of tombs in Istanbul closed to the public. İbrahim Manav and İsmail Erdoğan suggested works relevant to my research and found out-of-print books. The Yalçın, Ülgen, and Öztürk families provided pleasant company and helped facilitate my research. Antony Greenwood of the American Research Institute in Turkey was generous with assistance.

The contribution of friends and colleagues to the evolution of this book is profound. To Shaun Marmon I am deeply indebted for much enriching discussion and for her patient and scrupulous reading of several drafts of the work. Mary Ellen Capek, Alan Duben, and Rachel Weil asked important questions that formed critical junctures in my thinking about the issues examined herein. Dede Ruggles made numerous contributions to the book's final stages, reading drafts of its last pieces and helping with the illustrations. For helpful discussion at different stages of the work, I thank Kathryn Babayan, Linda Darling, Cornell Fleischer, Müge Göçek. Mary Harper, Leylâ Neyzi, Paula Sanders, and Amy Singer. I am grateful to Lucette Valensi, Melissa Orlie and Carol Quillen, David Powers, İsenbike Togan, Gilles Veinstein, Michael Winter, and Ross Brann for their critical comments on chapters and pieces of the book. Grace Edelman provided wisdom throughout the project.

At Oxford University Press, I am indebted to Nancy Lane, senior editor, for taking an interest in this project before its first word was even written. I thank Paul Schlotthauer for his attentive editing and shepherding of the book through its production. Edward Harcourt graciously guided a first-time author through the intricacies of book publication.

Finally, I would like to express my gratitude to the institutions and foundations whose financial assistance made possible the research and writing of the book: the Fulbright-Hays Commission and the Woodrow Wilson National Fellowship Foundation for dissertation research, the Mrs. Giles Whiting Foundation for dissertation writing, and the Institute of Turkish Studies, Cornell University (Humanities Faculty Research Grants), the American Philosophical Society, and the American Council of Learned Societies for subsequent research and writing. A grant from the Hull Memorial Publication Fund at Cornell University generously subsidized the costs of publication.

Glossary of Essential Terms

I have made a deliberate attempt in this book to minimize the use of untranslated titles and terms for Muslim and Ottoman institutions. However, the use of English equivalents or glosses, while making it easier for the nonspecialist reader, does entail the risk of imprecision. I therefore ask the reader to master the following few essential terms, which for the most part will be explained only in their initial appearance.

sultan: a formal title used by the Ottoman sovereign, as well as by other members of the royal family, male and female

padishah: the general term used by Ottomans to mean "the sovereign," "the ruler"; where English says "the sultan," Turkish says "the padishah"

valide sultan: "royal mother"—the mother of the reigning sultan

haseki: "favorite"—the principal concubine of the sultan

damad: "son-in-law"—the husband of an Ottoman princess

vezir: minister of the sultan and member of the imperial council (the highest rank in the military/administrative hierarchy of the empire); the chief minister was the grand vezir

ulema: members of the learned religious establishment, including judges (*kadı*), specialists in the interpretation of the Sharia (*müfti*), and teachers at higher institutions of Muslim education

müfti: chief *müfti* of the Ottoman Empire, and from the latter half of the sixteenth century the head of the learned religious establishment (also known as the *sheikh ül-Islam*)

ghaza: holy war, the purpose of which was to extend the domain of Islam

ghazi: one who waged *ghaza*

Sharia: the holy law of Islam

Notes on Transliteration
and Translation

In this book I have been somewhat eclectic in the transliteration of Turkish, Arabic, and Persian words. The specialist should not look for consistency. My goal has been to remain as close as possible to modern Turkish orthography without unduly straining or confusing the reader. I have used modern Turkish orthography not only for words of Turkish origin but for Arabic and Persian words used in an essentially Turkish context (both textual and cultural). Modern Turkish orthography rarely represents the long vowels represented in Ottoman Turkish, Arabic, and Persian; it sometimes uses one letter to represent two or more elements of the Arabic script, and sometimes eliminates the representation of Arabic script elements entirely.

I have sometimes chosen an English pronunciation equivalent rather than the modern Turkish script to represent an element of the Arabic script (for example, in the case of Arabic ح, I have used "j"—Hadije, jariye); on other occasions I have alternated between modern Turkish and the transliteration system used in the *International Journal of Middle East Studies* as it seems useful (for example, in the case of خ, I write khan and khatun, but Hadije, haseki and hass).

PRONUNCIATION OF MODERN TURKISH LETTERS
THAT HAVE NOT BEEN TRANSLITERATED

ç	ch, as in *church*
ş	sh, as in *ship*
ı	io, as in *motion*, or *e*, as in *women*
ö	French eu, as in *deux*
ü	French u, as in *durée*
ğ	unvocalized, lengthens preceding vowel

TRANSLATION

Unless otherwise indicated in the notes, the translations from foreign language sources are by the author.

List of Illustrations

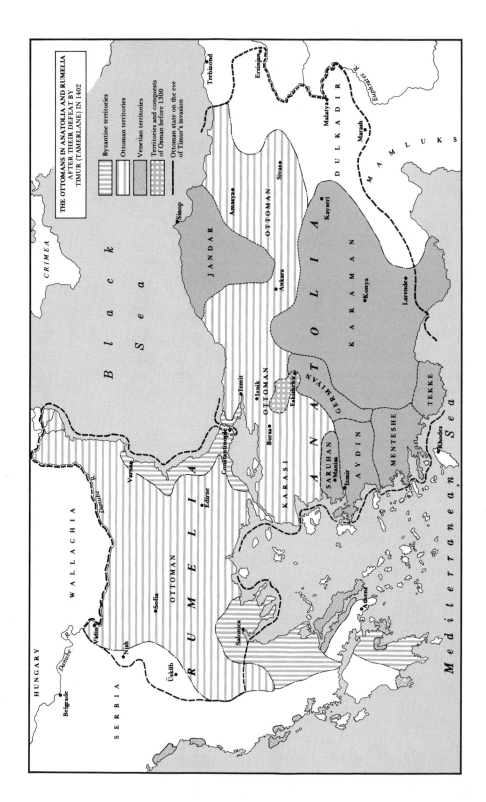

THE OTTOMANS IN ANATOLIA AND RUMELIA
AFTER THEIR DEFEAT BY
TIMUR (TAMERLANE) IN 1402

	Byzantine territories
	Ottoman territories
	Venetian territories
	Territories and conquests of Osman before 1300
---	Ottoman state on the eve of Timur's invasion

HUNGARY

Belgrade

SERBIA

Niš

Vidin

Danube

WALLACHIA

Danube

Üsküb

Sofia

R U M E L I A

OTTOMAN

Salonica

Athens

CRIMEA

B l a c k   S e a

Varna

Edirne

Constantinople

İzmit

İznik

Bursa

KARASI

OTTOMAN

İzmit

Trebizond

Erzincan

Euphrates R.

DULKADIR

Malatya

Marash

MAMLUKS

Sinop

JANDAR

Amasya

OTTOMAN

Sivas

Kayseri

Ankara

A N A T O L I A

K A R A M A N

Konya

Larende

GERMIYAN

Eskişehir

SARUHAN

Manisa

AYDIN

İzmir

MENTESHE

TEKKE

Rhodes

M e d i t e r r a n e a n   S e a

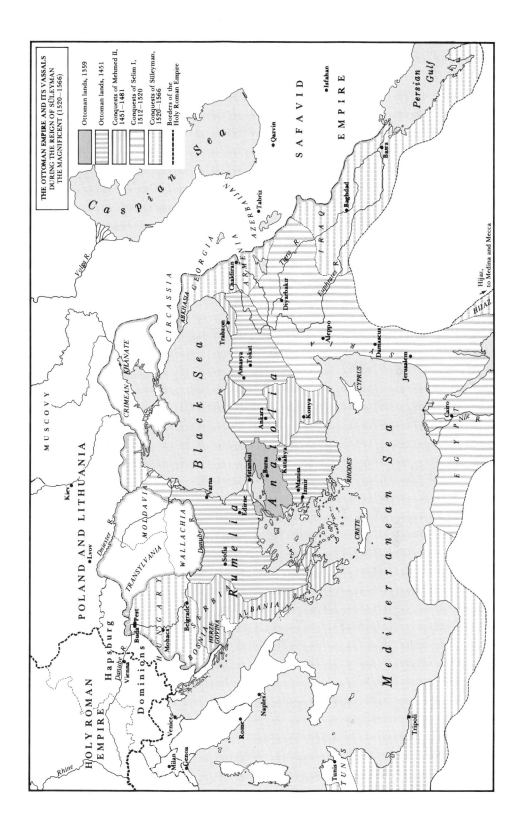

The Imperial Harem

INTRODUCTION

Myths and Realities of the Harem

We in the West are heir to an ancient but still robust tradition of obsession with the sexuality of Islamic society. The harem is undoubtedly the most prevalent symbol in Western myths constructed around the theme of Muslim sensuality. One of the most fertile periods for the production of texts and images treating this theme was the late sixteenth and the seventeenth centuries, and the most frequent subject the court of the Ottoman sultan. Preoccupied with its own forms of monarchical absolutism, Europe elaborated a myth of oriental tyranny and located its essence in the sultan's harem. Orgiastic sex became a metaphor for power corrupted (Figure 1-1).[1]

In fact, Europeans were not off the mark in fixing on the harem as a central arena of politics. It was not sex, however, that was the fundamental dynamic of the harem, but rather family politics. This is not to say that sex—sexual desire, the sexual act—was absent as an animating force within the imperial harem, but it was only one of several forces, and, for most of the period examined here, one of relatively little importance.

Sex for the Ottoman sultan, as for any monarch in a hereditary dynasty, could never be purely pleasure, for it had significant political meaning. Its consequences—the production of offspring—affected the succession to the throne, indeed the very survival of the dynasty. It was not a random activity. Sex in the imperial harem was necessarily surrounded with rules, and the structure of the harem was aimed in part at shaping, and thus controlling, the outcome of the sultan's sexual activity. Sexual relations between the sultan and chosen women of the harem were embedded in a complex politics of dynastic reproduction. This fact belies the simplistic but indefatigable notion that harem women acquired power by imprisoning sultans in the thrall of their seductiveness. In fact, their power had complex sources that stretched far beyond the walls of the imperial bedroom.

Harem: Sacred, Protected, Forbidden

To an Ottoman subject, the term "harem" did not connote a space defined exclusively by sexuality. The word *harem* is one of an important family of words in the vocabulary of Islam derived from the Arabic root *h-r-m*.[2] These words partake of one or both of two general—and obviously related—

3

Figure 1-1 Title page from M. Baudier's *Histoire genéralle du serrail*. Baudier's text, first published in 1626, is one of the most sensationalist of the seventeenth-century accounts of life within the imperial palace. (*Courtesy of Princeton University Libraries*)

meanings associated with the root: to be forbidden or unlawful, and to declare sacred, inviolable, or taboo.[3] A harem is by definition a sanctuary or a sacred precinct. By implication, it is a space to which general access is forbidden or controlled and in which the presence of certain individuals or certain modes of behavior are forbidden. That the private quarters in a domestic residence and by extension its female residents are also referred to as a "harem" comes from the Islamic practice of restricting access to these quarters, specifically access by males beyond a particular degree of consanguinity with the resident females. The word *harem* is a term of respect, redolent of religious purity and honor, and evocative of the requisite obeisance. It is gender-specific only in its reference to the women of a family.

The most sacred or exalted places in the sixteenth-century Ottoman world were harems. The holy cities of Mecca and Medina and their environs were, and remain, the two most revered harems in Islam. One of the most important titles held after 1517 by the Ottoman sultan, like the sultans of preceeding dynasties before him, was "the servant of the two noble sanctuaries" (*hadım ul-haremeyn ül-şerifeyn*), a title proudly used today by the rulers of Saudi Arabia. The central Muslim religious compound in Jerusalem, Islam's third most holy city, was also known as the "noble sanctuary" (*harem-i şerif*). In Ottoman usage, the inner courtyard of a mosque—its sanctuary—was also a harem.

While not himself divine, the sultan, "God's shadow on Earth," created a sacred space with his presence. Because the sultan lived there, the inner precinct of the royal palace, inhabited only by males, was known as "the imperial harem" (*harem-i hümayûn*). When toward the end of the sixteenth century the sultan established a second set of private quarters in the palace precinct to house women and children of the royal household, the latter area also began to be referred to as "the imperial harem" because of the presence there not of women but of the sultan. The inviolability of the imperial residence in the minds of the sultan's subjects is revealed by the fact that it was not well defended and yet was rarely assaulted, even in the seventeenth century when sultans themselves began to be forcibly deposed and even murdered. It was not in one of the great public mosques of the city but rather in the inner precinct of the palace that the holiest relics of Islam were enshrined when brought to Istanbul after the conquest in 1517 of the Mamluk sultanate. In times of crisis, the sultan manipulated these relics—especially the mantle and sacred standard of the Prophet Muhammad—to create a public aura of haremlike sanctity so that he might invoke supranormal standards of loyalty from his subjects.

Despite the multiple connotations of the term *harem,* this book will confine its use to the two meanings familiar to a non-Muslim audience: the private quarters of a family and the women of a family. These meanings of course existed in the vocabulary of contemporary Ottomans, but it is important to note that, while the institution of the household harem ultimately derived from notions of sexual propriety—specifically, the belief that unmarried women and men who might lawfully enter into a sexual relationship must be kept apart—sexuality was not the dominant ordering principle *within* the household. An Ottoman Muslim household of means included women related to the male head of the household and to each other in what could be a complex set of relationships, many of which did not include a sexual role. The harem of a prosperous household would include the wife or wives of the male head of the household, and perhaps one or more slave concubines (a Muslim male might have four wives and an unlimited number of concubines);[4] it seems, however, that polygyny was rare among the Ottoman middle and upper classes in the sixteenth and seventeenth centuries.[5] Children too, both male and female, and perhaps the widowed mother and unmarried, divorced, or widowed sisters of the husband lived in the harem. The harem would also include female slave servants, who might be the personal property of either the women or the men of the family.

The imperial harem was much like the household harem, only more extensive and with a more highly articulated structure. In our period, the head of the harem was the mother of the reigning sultan. The queen mother exercised authority over both family members—royal offspring; the consorts of the sultan, who might themselves acquire considerable power; and unmarried or widowed princesses—and the administrative/service hierarchy of the harem. During the last half of the sixteenth century this latter group grew rapidly in numbers and status, undoubtedly because of the new presence of the sultan.[6] High-ranking administrative officers of the harem—all of them women—received large stipends and enjoyed considerable prestige, especially the harem stewardess, chief of the administrative hierarchy. These women supervised the large number of servants who performed the housekeeping tasks of the harem, and, more important, managed the training of select young harem women who would wait on the sultan himself or his mother. With the exception of the reigns of one or two notoriously uxorious sultans, few women of the imperial household occupied the sultan's bed. Indeed, as the more astute and well informed of European observers commented, the imperial harem was more like a nunnery in its hierarchical organization and the enforced chastity of the great majority of its members.[7]

The Spatial Dimensions of Gender and Power

A second myth regarding the harem—and a source of serious misunderstanding about the nature of Ottoman society, at least at the level of the elite—is the erroneous assumption that the seclusion of women precluded their exercise of any influence beyond the physical boundaries of the harem itself. The harem is mistakenly seen as a woman's world—domestic, private, and parochial—and any attempt by women to influence events beyond its walls as "meddling" in an arena to which females have no rightful access. One reason for the persistence of this myth is our frequent failure, when we examine non-Western cultures, to question the relevance or validity of assumptions that have shaped Western thinking about politics, especially about gender and politics. I am thinking here particularly of modern (post-seventeenth-century) Western notions of a public/private dichotomy, in which the family is seen as occupying private, nonpolitical space. Recent feminist scholarship has challenged this assumption, emphasizing that the notion of a public/private dichotomy was historically created. Further, feminist scholars have argued that the family is indeed political, that is, that relations among its members should conform, and can be coerced by social and legal authorities to conform, to principles of justice.[8] The most superficial acquaintance with Islamic law and evidence of its application in the early modern Ottoman period demonstrates that the family was viewed as intrinsically political: individual members of the family, male and female, had socially sanctioned and legally protected rights against one another, as well as state-supervised mechanisms for obtaining legal redress when these rights were violated.[9]

There is a tendency in the West to assume that the harem institution, with its linked practice of gender segregation, is an Islamic manifestation of the Western conception of the public/private dichotomy. This assumption is a more profound obstacle to arriving at an understanding of the structure and dynamics of Muslim society than the more easily recognized myth of the harem as the site of Muslim promiscuity. The articulation of a politically based distinction between private and public was a product of late seventeenth- and eighteenth-century Western liberal thinking about how to limit absolute authority—the "private" being an arena that was not thought to need protection from arbitrary authority (in contrast to the Muslim view).[10] The problem of Western misunderstanding of the harem institution is compounded by the fact that some important modern Turkish historians, at least on the issues considered in this book, appear to have assimilated dominant Western political traditions regarding gender, space, and politics that were not shared by their sixteenth- and seventeenth-century counterparts.[11] One of the side effects of early republican state-building in modern Turkey was the discrediting of the Ottoman past after the period of its expansion, that is, after the reign of Süleyman. In this view, the "meddling" of women in government was cited as one of the causes of Ottoman decline. It is not difficult to argue, as I do below, that a dichotomy of public/commonweal/male and private/domestic/female does not work for early modern Ottoman society; a more challenging and relevant problem is determining just what the idea of private might have meant to an Ottoman man or woman.[12]

When we examine the early modern Ottoman household, we see that the segregation of the sexes created for women a society that developed its own hierarchy of authority. The larger the household, the more articulated was the power structure of its harem. Women of superior status in this female society, the matriarchal elders, had considerable authority not only over other women but also over younger males in the family, for the harem was also the setting for the private life of men.[13] Furthermore, female networks sustained through formal visiting rituals provided women with information and sources of power useful to their male relatives.[14] The authority enjoyed by female elders transcended, in both its sources and its effects, the bounds of the individual family. In a polity such as that of the Ottomans, where the empire was considered the personal domain of the dynastic family, it was natural that important women within the dynastic household—in particular, the mother of the reigning sultan—would assume legitimate roles of authority outside the royal household.

A further source of women's influence beyond the family was their ownership and exploitation of property. A woman's economic independence derived from her rights under Islamic law to the dowry provided by her husband and to fixed shares of the estates of deceased kin.[15] As property owners and litigants in property, inheritance, divorce, and other kinds of legal suits, women—or at least women of means—had access to economic and social power.[16] It must be admitted that at present we do not know the extent to which women of different social classes were able to exploit these theoretical rights to their advantage. It is clear, however, that women of means upheld the forms of Muslim noblesse oblige which required individuals of wealth and status—male and female alike—to contribute to the public welfare by endowing religious foundations, freeing their slaves, or undertaking other forms of charity. From the great mosque complexes founded by the sultans' mothers to modest neighborhood endowments created by ordinary individuals, Ottoman women left their mark on the cities, towns, and villages of the empire. An interesting feature of women's public charity was that a significant portion of it was aimed at helping other women: contemporary histories and testamentary documents show well-to-do individuals making provision not only for female family members and retainers but also for less fortunate women: orphans, paupers, prisoners, and prostitutes. Through their practice of the charity incumbent on Muslims of means, women asserted the prerogative of claiming and organizing a sector of public life for their own welfare.

We begin to see that, in the Ottoman case, conventional Western notions of public and private are not congruent with gender. In fact, when we examine the structure of male society and the interaction of male and female networks, we see that, at the highest reaches of society at least, notions of public and private tend to lose meaning altogether. In many ways, male society in the Ottoman world observed the same criteria of status and propriety as did female society. The degree of seclusion from the common gaze served as an index of the status of the man as well as the woman of means. Poor women and poor men mingled in the city streets and bazaars, for their cramped households and lack of servants prevented them from emulating the deportment of the well-to-do. Just as a woman of standing who appeared in public in the sixteenth century could maintain her reputation for virtue only if she were surrounded by a cordon of attendants,[17] so no Ottoman male of rank appeared on the streets or in the public arenas of the city without a retinue. The more powerful the individual, the greater the extent to which her or his accompanying retinue took on the aspect of a ceremonial procession. At the highest levels of government, no public buildings were set aside for the conduct of the state's or the people's affairs; instead, the household compound served as the locus of government. The highest organ of government, the imperial council, met within the walls of the imperial palace, the sultan's home.

Ottoman society of the sixteenth and seventeenth centuries was dichotomized into spheres characterized less by notions of public/commonweal/male and private/domestic/female than by distinctions between the privileged and the common, the sacred and the profane—distinctions that cut across the dichotomy of gender. We can perhaps better perceive the ill fit of a public-male/private-female dichotomy if we examine the language that Ottomans themselves used to describe divisions in their society. From centuries of Muslims before them, the Ottomans inherited the terms *hass* and *amm*.[18] The stock phrase "the *hass* and the *amm*" had both an abstract level of meaning—the private, particular, or singular versus the universal—and a sociopolitical meaning—the elite versus the common, the ruling class versus the ruled.[19] The word *hass*, however, presumably aroused a more complex range of associations because of its additional meaning of "that which is associated with or belongs to the ruler," that is, anything royal.[20] Many of the institutional manifestations of royal power were denoted by the word *hass:* for example, the sultan's privy chamber, the *has oda;* privileged attendants of the sultan, male and female, who bore the title *haseki;* and the royal domains, known simply as "hass."[21] In seventeenth-century Ottoman usage, the word *hass* appears to have had the additional meaning of "sanctity."[22]

More prevalent in the Ottomans' self-description is the dichotomy of inner and outer, the interior and the exterior. Two sets of words, one Turkish and one Persian, were commonly used to describe this division: *iç/içeri* in Turkish and *enderun* in Persian for the inner or interior, and correspondingly, *dış/dışarı* (or *taşra*) and *birun* for the outer or exterior. Bernard Lewis has pointed out that power relationships in Islamic society are represented by spatial division more horizontal than vertical, in contrast to Western metaphors: instead of moving *up,* one moves *in* toward greater authority.[23] The provinces of the empire were referred to as "taşra"—that which lay outside Istanbul, the charismatic center. In government, "iç/içeri" referred to wherever the sultan was and to things that belonged to him personally, for example his personal treasury (*iç hazine*) or the pages who served him in his private quarters (*iç oğlans,* "youths of the interior"). In this usage, "iç" is very similar to "hass" in simply meaning royal, but through its opposition to its complement, the "outer" administration, the emphasis can be seen to be slightly different: the purely sultanic or dynastic element in government, the inner household of the sultan.

The overlap among the concepts of *harem, hass,* and *iç/içeri* is not difficult to see. Each is defined by eligibility and exclusion. Each represents status and honor. As one ascends the social/political scale (to revert to a Western metaphor), authority is increasingly a phenomenon of the inner, often literally an interior, even residential, space the boundaries of which are guarded. This is an inversion of dominant modern Western notions of the politically significant as "outer" or public, and the politically marginal as "inner" or private and domestic. *Harem, hass,* and *iç/içeri* converge to place the sultan and the space he inhabits at the apex (or, in Ottoman idiom, the vortex) of the social, moral, and political order. The symbolism of the "inner" as order and security, and the vital function of the ruler in bringing about this order has been demonstrated by Walter Andrews in his study of the meaning and syntax of Ottoman poetry of this period in its relation to Ottoman society broadly considered.[24]

The importance of spatial boundaries in delimiting moral and political spheres in the Ottoman conception of the properly ordered society is revealed in a passage in the mid-seventeenth-century history of Mehmed Halife. In the 1620s, a period of political turmoil when life in the capital was frequently disrupted by the disaffected and undisciplined troops stationed there, it seemed to Mehmed Halife that "the world had lost all order and coherence." He cited a long list of crimes perpetrated by the troops: dragging women naked from public baths, smoking in the mosque of Mehmed the Conqueror, committing rape and sodomy openly on the streets, invading homes and palaces, and inviting the sultan and the queen mother to join streetcorner celebrations of a religious festival.[25] Each of these outrages caused the inversion of the inner and the outer and violated a social, religious, or political boundary. Whether these crimes all actually occurred is not important; what is significant is that Mehmed Halife was making his point about the political weakness and social chaos of the times in the most striking terms possible.

The Inner as the Source of Power

Of all Ottomans, the sultan naturally strove to surround himself with the most impenetrable barriers to his presence. Wherever he was—on the battlefield, in the inner palace—the space he occupied was visibly set off by physical or human boundaries. Even in the mosque, the most intrinsically egalitarian space in Muslim society, where the sultan was theoretically no greater than any of his subjects, he occupied a structurally isolated area. This insistence on the public display of splendid isolation was an aspect of ancient Near Eastern imperial traditions. The Ottomans were heir to these traditions through two channels: Islamic monarchy as elaborated by the various caliphates, sultanates, and principates of the Muslim past, and Christian Byzantine monarchy, itself heir to the imperial traditions of both the Roman Empire and the empires of the ancient Near East.

The centuries-long contact of Anatolian Turks with Byzantine civilization, culminating in the conquest of the Byzantine capital of Constantinople (Istanbul) in 1453, had an undeniable influence on Ottoman civilization, perhaps particularly on its imperial institutions.[26] In Ottoman historical legend, however, imperial traditions were acquired from fellow Muslim rulers: supposedly it was when told by a prince of a rival dynasty that it was not fitting for rulers to live in the midst of the masses that the sultan Mehmed II ("the Conqueror") moved from the palace he had built in the center of the newly conquered city to a new palace constructed on a more inaccessible site.[27] It is noteworthy, however, that the second palace—known today as Topkapı—was built on the site of the ancient Byzantine acropolis, and that the Ottoman sultans kept the neighboring Byzantine hippodrome as the principal arena of their public ceremonies and the adjacent basilica of Hagia Sophia as their premier imperial mosque.

The structure of the imperial palace communicated both the identity of the sovereign's residence as the central political arena of the empire and the difficulty of obtaining access to the sovereign within that arena. When understood in the context of the multiple resonances of "the inner," this was not the paradox it might seem. One consequence of the sovereign's remoteness was that the potential for enormous power lay in the hands of those who were intermediaries, formal and informal, between the sultan and those who governed in his name on the outside.

The first courtyard of the imperial palace was open to the public.[28] The second courtyard was a semipublic theater of government, where foreign ambassadors were received with elaborate ceremony and where the imperial council sat, presided over by the grand vezir and on occasion secretly observed by the sultan from a concealed cubicle. While access to this courtyard was generally limited to members of the governing elite, ordinary subjects with petitions for the sultan's justice might enter. The third, innermost, courtyard was the "imperial harem" (*harem-i hümayûn*), known also as the *enderun-ı hümayûn,* the "imperial interior." Here lived hundreds of carefully selected boys and young men who were being trained for government service, their white eunuch guards and preceptors, and, until the end of the sixteenth century, the sultan himself. The third courtyard was accessible to virtually no one from the outside, and its inhabitants were denied passage to the outside world except when accompanying the sultan. Only the sultan could freely cross the boundary isolating the inner courtyard, but when he did, he was surrounded by its eunuchs and "youths of the interior," the imperial harem transported with him.

It is well known that in the system of personal rule that is absolute monarchy, proximity to the ruler is an index of power.[29] Conversely, a principal expression of an absolute monarch's power is the control of access to his person. Manipulating political hierarchies and royal protocol was perhaps the principal means by which the Ottoman sultan both projected and protected his power. With the exception of the sultan, only those who were not considered to be fully adult males were routinely permitted in the inner worlds of the palace: in the male harem household, boys and young men, eunuchs, dwarves, and mutes; and in the family harem household, women and children. Even men in the palace who were fully adult under Islamic law—the most advanced pages in training and some princes of the dynasty—were kept in a state symbolic of adolescent dependence, for they were forbidden to grow beards or to father children. The highest officials of the empire—the grand vezir and the leader of the religious hierarchy, the *müfti* (also known as the *sheikh ül-Islam*)—might meet personally with the sultan, but only with his permission and in well-guarded areas just inside the gate separating the inner third courtyard from the semipublic second courtyard. On the rare occasion when the sultan desired or was forced to meet with members of the "outer" government or ordinary subjects, the audience was held outside this gate. Routine communication between the outside world and the inner palace was handled by the eunuch corps who guarded the two harems, white eunuchs for the male harem and black eunuchs for the female. The importance of these liminal figures in mediating the boundaries, both physical and moral, that established harems has been demonstrated by Shaun Marmon in the context of Mamluk society.[30]

One's status was marked by the extent to which one could penetrate the interior of another's household, most of all that of the sultan. A dramatic example of the desirability of proximity to the ultimate source of power is that of Gazanfer Agha, who had himself castrated so that he might remain close to the sultan, his patron. Gazanfer was a Hungarian renegade who, converted to Islam and assimilated into the Ottoman ruling class, had risen high in the service of the prince Selim, son of Süleyman the Magnificent. When Selim ascended the throne in 1566, he invited Gazanfer and his brother Jafer to join his inner household, which they could do only as eunuchs. Jafer did not survive the operation, but Gazanfer went on to hold the two most important offices of the inner service: chief white eunuch and head of the privy chamber. He was one of the most influential persons in the government for a period of more than thirty years spanning the reigns of Selim, his son, and his grandson, a tenure longer than that of any grand vezir.[31]

The more intimate one's service to the sultan in the inner world, the greater was one's standing in the outer world.[32] Those male pages of the third courtyard who held the highest ranks in the privy chamber were, upon graduation from the inner palace, destined to hold the highest military/administrative offices in the empire.[33] White eunuchs could also emerge to hold high office; indeed, there were several eunuch grand vezirs in the early modern period. When, toward the end of the sixteenth century, the sultan established private quarters in the women's precinct, its highest ranking members became the subjects closest to the empire's center of power. This new harem quickly became, in addition to the residence of the royal family, a highly structured and disciplined training institution in which female members of the royal household were prepared through personal service to the sultan and to his mother to take their places in the Ottoman ruling elite, much like the pages trained in the third courtyard. Like the pages, most would leave the harem after a term of service, and in fact marriages were frequently arranged between products of the two imperial harems. Only a very few women would remain permanent members of the dynastic household, the talented and lucky few who became the sultan's concubines or were promoted to senior administrative positions. Although they rarely crossed the harem boundary to the outside world, these high-ranking women enjoyed considerable prestige and exercised considerable influence in that world.

I

THE POLITICS
OF REPRODUCTION

1

The House of Osman

The central fact of Ottoman history is surely the extraordinary survival of the ruling dynasty, unmatched in the Islamic world. There is nothing else that gives coherence to the history of what is really several states: a local Turkish principality emerging in the late thirteenth century on the Anatolian frontier of the Byzantine Empire; a regional sultanate straddling western Anatolia and the Balkans; and a multiethnic empire spanning three continents that endured from the sixteenth to the twentieth centuries and subsumed the histories of what is today nearly a score of nations. Here we are concerned not simply with the institution of the Ottoman sultanate, but with a single dynasty: *Al-i Osman*, "the House of Osman." The founder of the state in historical legend (from whose name the European "Ottoman" was derived), Osman established a dynastic claim that was maintained by thirty-six of his descendents ruling in unbroken succession for nearly six and a half centuries.[1]

One of the most important factors in the survival of the Ottoman dynasty was the loyalty of its subjects. While they might be willing to dethrone, even execute, an individual sultan or to support the challenge of a pretender who claimed Ottoman descent, they did not question the right of the Ottoman house to rule over them. The Byzantine diplomat and historian Doukas, who observed the Ottomans at close quarters in the first half of the fifteenth century, commented that "a subject easily transfers his allegiance from one ruler to another so long as both the old and the new sovereign [are] descended from the line of Othman."[2] In 1622 the English ambassador to the Ottoman court, Sir Thomas Roe, describing the first popular deposition of a sultan in the history of Ottoman rule, noted that the rebels, before entering the palace to enthrone the new sultan, "first tooke a generall oath, not to sack the imperiall throne, which they call their house and their honor."[3] The loyalties of the Ottoman Empire's subjects were to a living family.[4] The history of the empire was the history of the dynasty, the life of the one coterminous with that of the other. Had the House of Osman died out or been overthrown, a new state would have come into existence.

The Women of the House

The enormous reverence for the Ottoman dynasty derives in large part from the two principal political traditions to which Ottoman society was heir. In the

15

Turco-Mongol traditions of pre-Islamic Central Asia, sovereignty was held to be granted by the divine power to a family chosen for earthly rule.[5] This notion was reinforced by the classical Islamic tradition that God gives to whomever he chooses a turn at sovereignty (*dawla, devlet* in Turkish, a word originally meaning "turn" or "revolution" which acquired the additional meanings of "dynasty" and then "state"). The most widely repeated historical legend regarding the inception of the Ottoman house as a ruling dynasty and its assumption of sovereignty reflected both these traditions.

According to this legend, after Osman's first local victories over neighboring Byzantine lords, he had a dream the meaning of which was obscure to him. In this dream, a moon rose from the breast of a widely revered dervish sheikh, Edebali, and entered Osman's own breast. From Osman's navel sprang a great tree, which grew to shade the entire world. Under the branches of the tree were mountains, from which flowing water served to quench the thirst of some and to irrigate the fields of others. When Osman sought Edebali to learn the meaning of the dream, the sheikh told him that it signified God's grant of sovereignty to him and his descendents. The moon, explained Edebali, represented his own daughter, to whom Osman was forthwith united in marriage (the name of this woman varies in the sources).[6] In most versions, the historical narrative continues by noting two direct outcomes of the event: Osman's solemn dedication to *ghaza,* holy war against the infidel, and the birth of Orhan, the second ruler, from the union of Osman and Edebali's daughter.

While the numerous histories of the dynasty that flourished in the late fifteenth and sixteenth centuries contain other legends justifying Ottoman rule, all of them recount this particular story of the dynasty's emergence into history.[7] The story of the dream appearance of a tree signifying hegemonic sovereignty was not unique to the Ottomans; this account of Osman's dream seems to be a variation on an old pre-Islamic Turkish theme.[8] However, a significant feature of the Ottoman version is the idea of the dynasty's foundation in a semisacred marital union: the holy man's charisma, transmitted through his daughter, figures as a necessary element in the dynasty's future success. It was not unusual in Turkish tradition to consider the mother as well as the father a source of legitimacy. In the earliest written record from a Turkish state, the sixth/seventh-century Central Asian empire of the Gökturks, the ruler presents himself as the political heir of both parents: "In order that the name and fame of the Turkish people would not perish, the heavenly god [Tanrı], who had raised my father, the khakan, and my mother, the khatun, and who had granted them the state, . . . [that heavenly god] enthroned [me]."[9]

If we were to concentrate on formal, constitutional aspects of sovereignty in the Ottoman state, which is what virtually all treatments of Ottoman political history have done, it might seem that these legends bore little relation to the reality of women's political power. In neither Islamic states nor pre-Islamic Central Asian states were rights to supreme political authority, formally exercised by men, formally inherited through women.[10] In the Ottomans' most common name for their dynasty—"the sons of Osman" (*Osmanoğulları*)—they were conforming to a naming practice, and a view of the source of political power, shared by other Anatolian Turkish states. Moreover, the Islamic tradition of relying for reproduction on slave concubinage in addition to legal marriage further emphasized the patriarchal nature of political power: slave concubines, unlike wives, had no lineage. More than any other Muslim dynasty, the Ottomans raised the practice of slave concubinage to a reproductive principle: after the generations of Osman and Orhan, virtually all offspring of the sultans appear to have been born of concubine mothers.

But to concentrate solely on the formal, legalistic expression of power is to miss the implications of an idea particularly strong in Turco-Mongol political tradition, the belief that sovereignty is invested in the whole dynastic family. This notion is usually understood to mean that all *males* enjoyed the right to rule, but when we take a close look at how power was constituted and transmitted, it is clear that women too played vital and expected political roles.[11] In the Ottoman case, princes and princesses of the blood shared in royal power simply through their birth. But members of the dynastic family whose blood carried no right to royal power—concubine mothers, women from Christian territories enslaved and converted to Islam—were also able to claim a share in the exercise of sovereign authority through their roles *within* the family. It is in the context of relations *within* the sovereign family, *among* its members, that these women exercised authority, and that their sons were seen as their political heirs.

If they were not, like males, directly endowed with sovereignty, royal mothers were its custodians. Their custodianship involved an understanding of the sources and uses of sovereign power, the duty of training its users, and the responsibility of taking necessary measures for its preservation, including exercising it themselves when suitable male rulers were unavailable. As custodians of sovereign power, royal mothers were also responsible for ensuring that the dynasty reproduced itself, a duty that gave them a legitimate interest in the sexual activity of their sons. It was simply assumed that royal mothers had a high degree of political knowledge. Ottoman sources are quite clear about their active role in preparing their sons to receive power and guiding them in its proper uses—"the duty of training and supervision," as one statesman put it.[12] In the seventeenth century it was not unusual for a royal mother to govern as regent for a minor or incompetent sultan, or for a sultan to be overthrown and his mother publicly called upon to sanction the sacrifice of her son for the broader interest of the sultanate and the state. As a result, these women came to enjoy a kind of matriarchal authority, providing the link between the dynasty's generations and symbolizing its continuity at times when it seemed perilously threatened. Nevertheless, Ottomans were ever mindful of the custodial limits of women's power: when a royal woman appeared to act in her own self-interest rather than in the interest of her son or of the dynasty as a whole—when she acted to exploit rather than to preserve sovereign power—the public did not hesitate to decry her activity as illegitimate and corrupt.

The notion that political power and legitimacy *within* the dynastic family flowed through women as well as men, through mothers as well as fathers, through nonblood as well as blood members, is reflected in the Ottomans' use of the title "sultan." *Sultan* is a word of Arabic origin, originally meaning "authority" or "dominion"; it was first used officially as a title to connote political and military supremacy over the Islamic community by the Turkish Seljuk dynasty in the eleventh century.[13] By the beginning of the sixteenth century, this title, carried by both males and females of the Ottoman dynasty, was replacing other titles by which prominent members of the royal family had been known (notably *khatun* for women and *bey* for men);[14] these old Turkish titles then began to be used for lesser members of the dynastic household. Preference for the Arabic *sultan* reflected mainly the growing attention paid to Islamic legitimating discourse as the Ottoman dynasty advanced ever-greater claims to prominence in the Islamic world. What is significant here is that the title could be used in an ungendered manner to encompass the whole royal family, male and female. This usage underlines the Ottoman conception of sovereign power as a *family* prerogative.

Western tradition knows the Ottoman ruler as "the sultan," but Ottomans themselves used other words meaning "monarch" to refer to their ruler, most commonly the Persian *padishah* or *hünkâr* (an abbreviation of *hüdaven-digâr*).[15] The *padishah*'s formal title, however, consisted of "Sultan" together with "Khan" (for example, Sultan Süleyman Khan). This dual title symbolized the Ottomans' dual legitimating heritage, Islamic and Central Asian.[16] In formal address, the sultan's children were also entitled "Sultan," with princes, like their father, carrying the title before their given name, and princesses carrying it after: for example, Sultan Mehmed and Mihrimah Sultan, brother and sister, children of Süleyman the Magnificent. Like princesses, the sultan's mother as well as favorite concubines also carried the title after their given names: for example, Hafsa Sultan, Süleyman's mother, and Hurrem Sultan, Süleyman's most cherished concubine and the mother of Mehmed and Mihrimah. The evolving usage of this title reflected power shifts among royal women, especially between female generations: as the position of favorite concubine eroded over the course of the seventeenth century, concubines lost the title "sultan," which was replaced by *kadın,* a title related to the earlier *khatun.*[17] Henceforth, the mother of the reigning sultan was the only woman of nonroyal blood to carry the title "sultan."

Controlling Power: Seniority, Sexuality, and Succession

If an important aspect of the Ottomans' heritage was the sharing of sovereign power among the family, the dynasty's amazing survival is in large part the story of its careful guard against dissipation of that power. Unlike earlier Muslim states with a discernible Turco-Mongol heritage, the Ottoman state did not fall prey to fragmentation and collapse resulting from successive divisions among male dynasts of the rule and the territory ruled. Much of this book is devoted to examining how sovereign power was allocated among the dynasty's members, and how and in favor of whom its dissipation was curtailed. Dynastic politics was in many ways a zero-sum game. The story of the changing controls the dynasty placed on its members, including the sultan, and the power that some gained from the controls placed on others is an extraordinarily complex one. Let us review this story in its broad outlines before embarking upon a detailed narrative.

Evolving conceptions of legitimate power and its bounds in the Ottoman state can be better understood if we appreciate the extent to which dynastic politics were shaped by the problem of inheritance and succession, that is, the handing down of the patrimony from one generation to the next. In many ways, the tensions inherent in this process were similar to those in an ordinary family, with the difference that the patrimony of the dynastic family consisted of the rule and the territory of a vast empire; furthermore, a very large number of people had a stake in the outcome of any dispute within the royal family. The principal tension surrounding the issue of dynastic inheritance was an intergenerational one. The need of the senior generation, male and female, to balance control of the patrimony with all its rewards against the necessity of preparing and permitting members of the junior generation to receive it was often in conflict with the junior generation's impatience to take control, especially in the event of abuse of the patrimony by the elders or their refusal to relinquish it in a timely manner. Competition among the heirs was another endemic problem (at least until the seventeenth century), one that threatened to result in loss of the family's integrity and influence and damage to or loss of the patrimony. And there was always the need to prevent dissipation of the patrimony and its control through females: solutions to this problem involved decisions about whom males of the family should marry and which outside males should be associated with the family as sons-in-law.

Political power in the premodern Ottoman state can be defined as the ability to exploit for one's own interest a piece of the patrimony. In material terms, this most often took the form of a grant of the revenues from, if not legal possession of, a piece of land. In our period, even the sultan had his allotted "pocket money." It was not only members of the dynasty whose status entitled them to such material benefits: theoretically, since the whole territory of the state was considered the patrimony of the dynasty and those employed in the service of the state members of the sultan's household, the entire ruling class could consider itself to be recompensed with a share of the patrimony. "I eat the sultan's bread," said an envoy to Europe in 1480s, attempting to convince the duke of Savoy of his status as an official of the Ottoman government.[18]

Access to the patrimony was tied to sexuality. Particularly within the dynastic family, sexual maturity and political maturity were inextricable, and political control involved control of sexuality. The dynasty bound itself to no fixed criterion of maturity, such as that found in Islamic law, which established legal majority for both males and females at puberty.[19] While the dynasty could not control the natural process of physical maturation, it could and did control reproduction, which was in turn a means of controlling the definition of political maturity, and thus the delegation of power. Here gender was clearly an issue: for males, political maturity coincided with the onset of fathering children, but for females maturity was marked by the cessation of childbearing, in other words, with a postsexual status. This did not necessarily mean that men acquired power earlier than did women, since the dynasty could manipulate the reproductive activity of an individual, postponing it, limiting it, or preventing it altogether.

Students of Ottoman history have paid insufficient attention to the increasing restrictions that the dynasty imposed on its members (we might say on itself, since the sultan too had to respect limits on his authority). Let us briefly summarize this process of control, looking first at males and then at females.

During the first generations of Osman and Orhan, the rulers shared real power and territory with their sons, and probably also with their uncles and brothers, a practice in keeping with Turco-Mongol tradition. It is difficult, however, to say much with certainty about political constellations in the nascent Ottoman state because most of our sources date from later periods and undoubtedly reflect changes in the political culture, which came increasingly to favor centralization of authority in the sultan alone.[20] What is important for our argument is that Osman's and Orhan's sons appear to have governed vital parts of the expanding state, with at least one son in each generation effectively taking over rule of the entire state during his father's lifetime and, it would seem, doing so with his father's blessing.

However, by the reign of the third sultan, Murad, not only had collateral lines (the ruler's uncles and brothers) ceased to share in the patrimony, but even the sultan's sons began to lose the right to govern with any real independence. While they continued to receive provinces to administer, they no longer had access to the European frontier, where a reputation as *ghazi* hero ("warrior for Islam") and thereby popular support might be more easily acquired than in legally dubious campaigns against fellow Muslims in Anatolia. Moreover, princes now had to answer to tutors, who were appointed by the sultan not only to supervise his sons' training but also to prevent any political challenge to his authority. Publicly visible symbols of the subordination of princes were introduced: denied permission to grow a beard, a sign of adulthood, they sent their shaved whiskers to the capital,[21] and they lost an important prerogative of wealth and power: the sponsoring of monuments and public institutions such as mosques, schools and colleges, hospitals, and markets and commercial centers.[22] Nevertheless, as provincial governors, commanders of wings of the imperial army in battle, and lieutenant sultans in the capital when their father was absent on campaign, princes continued to be public figures, whose on-the-job training was a serious business. As the primary focus, after the sultan, of imperial ritual and ceremony, princes functioned as vital and visible exemplars of the power and charisma of the dynasty. Several of them appear to have been enormously well liked and the object of widespread popular devotion.

That princes were regarded as politically competent can be seen in the process of succession to the throne. As Halil İnalcık has shown, the history of

Turkish states, the Ottomans included, demonstrates a number of options for succession, none of them regarded as illegitimate or unconstitutional: succession of the eldest son; succession of the youngest son; a system of seniority in which the succession passed to the eldest living male of the dynasty, whatever his relation to the previous ruler; or the naming by the ruler of an heir apparent, who might be anywhere in the birth order. However, the prevailing tendency in most Turkish states was to avoid restrictions on eligibility (apart from the vital qualification of being a male member of the dynasty) and to regard all males as having a claim to eligibility for the succession.[23] In theory, the will of God, who had bestowed sovereignty on the dynastic family, would determine in each generation which of its scions should emerge victorious. Sometimes the decision was based on an arbitrary contest—who could jump the highest or throw his hat the farthest. Most successions, however, were determined through violent combat and even civil war, and ultimately depended on the ability of the successful candidate to muster the support of vital constituencies.

Among the Ottomans, every succession but one from that in 1362 of Murad I, the third sultan, until that in 1574 of the twelfth sultan, Murad III, was marked by executions or challenges that were resolved through combat, sometimes not for years. The exception was the automatic accession in 1520 of Süleyman, the only surviving son of his father, Selim I; it is possible, however, that Selim had earlier executed his other sons to avoid the fate he had visited on his own father, whom he had forced from the throne in large part to preempt a bid by one of his several brothers. Even once a sultan had won the throne, the violence surrounding the process of succession was not finished, for the repression of the claims of collateral dynastic lines was made absolute through the practice, established by the mid-fifteenth century, of executing the new sultan's brothers and their sons.

In the second half of the sixteenth century a series of changes occurred that had the result within three generations of completely divesting princes of power through repression of their political and sexual maturity. Murad III was the last sultan to dispatch a son to a provincial governorate. Henceforth princes would not leave the imperial palace, nor would they be allowed to father children unless and until they became sultan. Between the public celebration of his circumcision and the public celebration of his enthronement, a prince disappeared behind the harem walls, deprived of the identity that came from possession of a piece of the patrimony and the production of heirs. A prince no longer headed a household, and therefore lacked in both real and symbolic terms the most important foundation of a political career.

This transformation of the role of princes was an intrinsic aspect of changes in the system of succession. During the three generations during which princes went from being well-known public figures to virtual unknowns, the Ottoman dynasty moved to a system of seniority (although it took several more generations before seniority ceased to be challenged). When Ahmed I, the first sultan not to have served as princely governor, died in 1617, he was succeeded by his brother. This was the first time in the fourteen generations of

Ottoman rule that a sultan was not followed by one of his sons. A necessary aspect of seniority as the new principle of succession was the restoration of the rightful claim to sovereignty of collateral dynastic lines: the practice of fratricide lapsed, and now the greatest fear of a male dynast was that he might not live long enough to take his turn on the throne. In the twenty-two generations of the Ottoman dynasty that followed Ahmed I, the throne always passed to the eldest living male Ottoman, and only three times did a son succeed his father; for the most part, sultans were followed by their brothers, less frequently by nephews, and once by a cousin.

While one could argue that these changes constituted a radical break with most of the Ottoman past, one could also argue that they did not undermine certain fundamental principles of Ottoman political culture. It is probably for this reason that these seemingly revolutionary developments provoked little comment in contempory histories. Certainly, they upheld the principle that all male members of the dynasty deserved a chance at governing. Indeed, strict limitation of the succession to a son of the previous ruler was unusual not only in states influenced by Central Asian Turco-Mongol tradition, Muslim and non-Muslim alike, but also in pre-Mongol Muslim states not influenced by that tradition (for example, the Umayyads, the Abbasids, and the Buyids).[24] In some of these states, succession passed from father to son only in the first generations, suggesting that this pattern may be associated with the consolidation of a new state. It is no coincidence that a prolonged father-son pattern of succession was not unique to the Ottomans, but was a characteristic of the more stable and long-lasting states of the post-Mongol period, notably, in addition to the Ottomans, the Safavids and the Qajars in Iran, the Mughals in India, and, if we expand the notion of son to include the fictive filiation in Islamic society of household slaves, the so-called slave dynasties of the Mamluks in Egypt. However, the Ottoman transition to seniority midway through the empire's history in no way resembled the disorganized succession characteristic of the dissolution of pre-Mongol Muslim states. The practice of seniority in the Ottoman state preserved what was the most enduring feature of Ottoman politics: absolute control by the dynasty (if not by the individual sultan) of the distribution of power.

Turning to women of the dynasty, we find that they too were both entitled to a share of the patrimony and subject to controls. The great care and deliberation given to the marriages of princesses reflected the recognition that power could flow out through them despite the fact that they themselves could not rule. Moreover, land and revenues granted to princesses were never alienated from the patrimony. Unlike some of their Anatolian contemporaries, Ottoman princesses never carried a piece of the state as their dowry,[25] and when they married into foreign dynasties the revenues of their land grants were devoted to endowments located within the Ottoman domain. By the end of the fifteenth century, the problem of stopping the outflow of power and resources through princesses was solved by the adoption of an endogamous marriage policy through which princesses married either cousins or, more often, statesmen who were considered slave members of the dynastic household.

The mothers of princes and princesses—the wives of the early sultans and the concubines who replaced them as bearers of the dynasty's progeny—also enjoyed the possession of part of the dynastic patrimony. Just as princesses might receive land grants from their sultan father or later from a brother who became sultan, a royal mother might receive grants, first from her royal consort and later from her son the sultan. Such grants began in the first Ottoman generation, when Osman bestowed the village of Kozağaç and its revenues on his wife, the daughter of Sheikh Edebali. However, royal mothers were subject to more complex controls than were their daughters. Because as custodians of sovereignty they had a greater claim to authority and greater access to the mechanisms of power, they were subject to more careful scrutiny. Moreover, they were capable of initiating the gravest threat to the integrity of the dynastic lineage (Henry VIII's execution of Anne Boleyn in 1536 for suspected adultery is a dramatic reminder of this dangerous power of queens).

With dynastic females as with males, sexuality was intimately linked with power. However, sexual maturity—and thus legitimate power—was defined for women as the absence of sexual activity. At issue was not virginity, which implied latent or repressed sexuality, but rather postsexuality. There were two essential elements to postsexuality: the cessation of childbearing, either through postmenopausal incapacity or forced sexual abstinence, and motherhood. The raising of children, especially sons, and the management of a multigenerational household conferred status and knowledge on both parents, male and female. Like princes without heirs, women without sons were women without households and therefore women of no status.

The importance of postsexuality is clearly demonstrated in the careers of royal concubines. Their public display of political power and wealth (symbolized by their assumption of the privilege of public building) began, as we shall see, only after their sexual role ended, when the sultan either ceased to have sexual contact with them or died. Postsexuality may have operated in the careers of princesses as well, although so little work has been done on them that only very tentative hypotheses can be suggested. Certainly the most prominent princesses of the early modern period were widows, for example, Seljuk Khatun (d. 1485) and Mihrimah Sultan, the daughter of Süleyman. It is surely significant that it was in 1562, the year after her husband died, that Mihrimah Sultan began the construction of her mosque complex in the Edirnekapı district of Istanbul.[26] The lesser prominence of later princesses was most likely a result of the fact that they remained in a state of active sexuality through a policy that gained momentum during the sixteenth century of remarrying a princess when her husband died.

If political status for women depended on postsexual motherhood, a problem arose in the late sixteenth century when too many royal mothers qualifying for power by this definition began to compete in a restricted arena. Before that time, the sultan's mother was an honored but not institutionally powerful person. The most politically significant roles appear to have belonged to the sultan's concubines—his own reproductive generation—in the postsexual phase of their careers as mothers of princes. From the middle of the fifteenth century, and possibly earlier, when a prince left the capital for his provincial governorate, he was accompanied by his mother, whose role was to preside over the prince's domestic household and perform her duty of "training and supervision" alongside the prince's tutor. But when the queen mother emerged as an institutionally powerful individual toward the end of the sixteenth century, there were two generations of "political mothers" related to the single politically active male of the dynasty, the sultan. The issue of household was central to the problem and to its solution. With the lapse of the princely governorate, the entire royal family was united in the capital under one roof, rather than, as previously, dispersed throughout the royal domain. There was now only one royal household, over which the senior woman, the sultan's mother, naturally took charge. Not only princes themselves but their mothers too had lost households to preside over, as a result of which they were now subordinated to the control not only of the sultan, their master, but of the queen mother as well.

In the new configuration that the royal household assumed in the late sixteenth century, the dynasty's most senior generation was represented solely by a female. The presiding role of the queen mother within the household was reflected in the physical layout of the royal living quarters of the imperial palace: her large apartments occupied a central location and connected to all parts of the harem compound, including a direct link to her son's quarters. It is no coincidence that Murad III, the sultan who moved the ruler's private quarters from the third courtyard into the harem compound, was the first sultan whose mother was presiding over the royal household at the time of his accession.

While supreme authority in the Ottoman sultanate was exercised by a male, that authority in the late sixteenth century emanated from a household that was presided over by the female elder of the dynasty. But the power dynamic within the royal household was not limited to mother and son, nor was the authority of the queen mother unchallenged. The definition of female power meant that even if princes were now nonactors on the dynastic stage, their mothers' roles could not be eliminated. As long as their sons were alive, it was difficult to deprive these women completely of status because of the political imperative that royal mothers protect their sons. The importance of women as power brokers is reflected in the fact that the greatest tension within the dynasty now existed among rival mothers. The bloodiest contest between competing mothers—the murder in 1651 of the formidable queen mother Kösem by the party of her daughter-in-law Turhan, who was impatient to take power—was reminiscent of past rebellions of princes against aging sultan fathers.

Why was it in the late sixteenth century rather than earlier that dynastic women acquired power? The causes were complex, and included internal problems of dynastic rule and control (outlined above), external problems of a military and fiscal nature, and broad sociocultural issues such as the growing importance of Islamic social norms. One factor can be isolated that encompassed all of these: the scaling down of military conquest as the organizing principle of the Ottoman state and its evolution from an expansionist, military state to an administrative, bureaucratic one. (This having been said, two caveats are in order: first, this evolution was not a steady, unbroken one, although one of its crucial periods was the late sixteenth century, and second, the military apparatus and its influence in the state diminished only in relative importance.)

The institution of seniority and its corollary, the demise of the princely governorate, are generally viewed as aspects of Ottoman decline, as both symptom and cause of dynastic weakness and loss of resolve. However, the continued strength of the Ottoman polity, indeed its creative responses to changing domestic and international conditions, requires us to reject such a view and instead analyze changes in dynastic politics in the context of broad developments in the polity as a whole. If the Ottomans had political genius, it lay in their integration of functionally effective policies into a symbolic system that satisfied their subjects, or at least those subjects whose support was necessary for the dynasty's survival.

Open succession—succession by combat—fit the ideology of the expansionist military state. This form of succession defined the monarch principally as a conqueror. It aimed at identifying the male dynast who was most skillful at mobilizing support for military victory. While dynastic continuity was assured through recognition of the sovereign right of the Ottoman house, in each generation the imperial patrimony was literally and symbolically reconquered by the victorious prince. This process of "reconquest" was recognized in the reissuing of patents to government office and foreign treaties at the beginning of each new reign. Seniority was a more stable form of succession than contest or combat. As a system of succession, it better fit the post-expansionist empire in which the ruler was more a sedentary palace sultan than a mobile *ghazi* hero. The structured nature of seniority, with its rules for automatic succession, helped to stabilize political loyalty in the postexpansionist period and to establish qualification for rule in the absence of military victory.

While open succession may have bestowed charismatic validation on the victor, it was a debilitating system for the society as a whole and one that was arguably at odds with the requirements of government in the postmedieval age of stable, long-lasting states. The often-violent competition among candidates for the throne weakened the state through internal disruption and the opportunity it provided for external enemies to take advantage of internal chaos. Moreover, in the postexpansionist sedentary sultanate, the capital of Istanbul became increasingly the focus of the empire's attention and the repository of its human resources, and the allegiance of its inhabitants thus became increasingly vital to a sultan's security on the throne. It would not do to have a prince stationed outside the capital where he might serve as a magnet for the politically discontent.

The regularization of succession can also be seen as part of a wide-ranging movement within Ottoman government, beginning under Süleyman and acquiring momentum in the later decades of the sixteenth century, to organize career paths and accommodate career aspirants by codifying, or attempting to codify, rules for recruitment, training, and promotion. This phenomenon can be traced not only in the military but in the bureaucracy and the religious establishment, structures that would gain greater institutional influence in the state during its postexpansionist period. This "rationalization" of careers in government service (including the dynastic career itself) was a better fit with an administrative state than the more fluid structures based on the personal allegiances of the military state.

In the wake of the transition to seniority came a lessened emphasis on the patriarchial bond between father and son as the fundamental axis of power. Princes now rarely inherited the throne from their father, and might not receive any political training from him. In passing on the patrimony, including the expertise of which the dynasty was assumed to be the sole possessor, the mother was the more vital representative of the elder generation. With seniority also came a subtle but palpable change in the nature of the bond between subject and sultan. It was more abstract, less personal. With their active if circumscribed public careers and their princely courts, the sultan's sons had been well-known figures, and the public, at least those persons with an active stake in the outcome of a contest for the throne, had been able to vote, so to speak, by giving their allegiance to one or another candidate. It was said that when his retainers showed concern about his dubious chances for the throne, Selim, the least popular of Süleyman's sons, quipped that of the three surviving princes, Mustafa had the support of the soldiers and Bayezid of their mother and father, but he, a poor beggar, had only the support of the clerics.[27] With seniority, the public could express its approval or lack thereof only after a sultan had acceded, and it is no coincidence that it was in the early seventeenth century, as the practice of seniority was taking root, that rulers were first forcibly deposed. More than half the sultans who came to the throne through seniority were overthrown, with depositions replacing wars of succession as the ultimate vehicle of public opinion, necessarily violent in a system of autocratic rule. Before, princes had acted as a check on their father's absolutism, perhaps unable to force a change in sultanic policy but nonetheless able to demonstrate the plausibility of alternatives through the popular support they might attract. When princes became confined to the palace, the initiative for protest necessarily shifted outside the dynasty. This is not to say that, before the advent of seniority, the loyalty of Ottoman subjects to the dynasty had inhibited them, especially the imperial troops, from demanding due recompense for their allegiance and services, or that they had hesitated to protest unpopular policies. Now, however, with the precedent of deposition, the stakes were higher. Depositions were disturbing assaults on the rights of the dynasty, even if the protesters were usually careful to obtain religious sanction for their actions. In these moments that threatened to rend the political fabric, the queen mother was the person best situated to play a mitigating or conciliatory role. Critics of the sultan might appeal to her to influence her son to remedy unpopular policies or habits of rule. If it came to deposition, the queen mother's acquiescence in the removal of her son preserved the bond between ruler and ruled in a reassuring way that all the niceties of Islamic law could not match. At such times the continuity of the dynasty could be maintained only by means of a living link between generations, and in the postexpansionist empire, it was the sultan's mother who was that link.

As we shall see, the connection between mother and son was a vital political bond throughout Ottoman history, although it became formally recognized and institutionally visible only in the late sixteenth century. Like the earlier bond between sultan and son, however, it was not an untroubled one. Especially when the queen mother became dignified as the senior member of the dynastic family, the potential for antagonism between mother and son increased.

2

Wives and Concubines: The Fourteenth and Fifteenth Centuries

The issue of marriage and reproduction is one of the most fundamental concerns of human society. Decisions regarding when to marry, whom to marry, how many children to have and when are weighty ones for ordinary families, but even weightier for royal families. Such decisions were particularly complex in a society that permitted both polygyny and concubinage, as did that of the Muslim Ottomans. Because the means by which the Ottoman dynasty reproduced itself were far from random, we can rightly speak of an Ottoman politics of reproduction. This politics was an integral, indeed fundamental, element in the broad conduct of the dynasty's and the state's affairs. Particularly during the first century and a half, it was coordinated with Ottoman strategies for meeting the challenges of rival states. Throughout the life of the empire, it was a principal means enabling the dynasty to maintain control over its own members.

Patterns of marriage, concubinage, and reproduction had symbolic as well as strategic import. How a dynasty reproduced said a good deal about how it understood power. As part of the vocabulary of Islamic monarchy, marital and reproductive choices were one of the means a dynasty utilized in constructing the image it wished to project publicly. The gravity of this aspect of royal politics may be difficult for many citizens of the world today to appreciate, but one has only to think of the intense popular interest that has been focused in this century on the alliances of British kings and queens, princes and princesses.

Marriage and Concubinage: An Overview

From the perspective of royal reproductive politics, the early Ottoman state in its first 150 years was unlike the empire it would become. Until the mid-fifteenth century the sultans took both legal wives and slave concubines. During this early period, however, there emerged certain fundamental principles that would guide the dynasty's reproductive choices over the centuries: an insistence on slave concubinage and a preference for allowing each concu-

28

bine to bear no more than one son. By the mid-fifteenth century, legal marriage had lapsed for internal as well as external reasons.

The legal marriages of Ottoman rulers and their sons in the fourteenth and
early fifteenth centuries were contracted with princesses of neighboring dynasties, both Christian powers of Rumelia and Muslim powers of Anatolia.[1] The
purpose of interdynastic marriages was tactical: to maintain favorable alliances that could strengthen the state's military and diplomatic standing in an
environment of mercurially shifting alignments. Most Ottoman marriages
were arranged as part of the negotiation of an offensive alliance or, more
often, at the conclusion of combat, to symbolize the defeated party's submission and acceptance of vassal status. The Ottomans limited their marriage
alliances to a local Rumelian-Anatolian pool of states with whom they vied for
power, potential enemies who might become allies at the next turn of events.
The dynasties in this pool with whom the Ottomans intermarried included the
Christian Byzantine and Serbian royal houses and the Anatolian Muslim principates of Germiyan, Aydın, Saruhan, Jandar, Karaman, and Dulkadır (see
map on page xviii). Obviously, the Ottomans were not alone in using marriage
as a tool of diplomacy.

While royal marriages of the fourteenth century were contracted primarily
with Christian women, those of the fifteenth century were made primarily
with Muslim women. Not only did the sultans of the fifteenth century turn to
the Anatolian principalities for marriage partners for themselves and their
sons, but they also gave their sisters and daughters to the men of these
princely houses. This shift reflects the growing importance of the Ottomans as
an Anatolian power. Marriage marked the submission of some princely
houses to the Ottomans and bonds of alliance with others. The greater propor-
tion of marriages with Muslim princesses may also reflect their increasing
availability: the Islamic sociolegal principle of *kafâ'a*—which discouraged the
marriage of women to men inferior in social status—may have provoked
unwillingness on the part of more established Muslim powers to give their
daughters in alliance to the fledgling Ottoman principality in its early decades.[2] It was this same principle that kept Ottoman royal women from marrying Christian princes, for while the status of a Muslim male was not jeopardized by marrying a non-Muslim, that of a Muslim female was.

An important reason for the cessation of interdynastic marriages after the
first half of the fifteenth century was the drying up of this pool. During the
reign of Mehmed II, known to history as "the Conqueror," (r. 1451–81),
under whom the Anatolian and Rumelian conquests of previous sultans were
finally consolidated and crowned with the capture of Constantinople, the
Ottomans eliminated the last of these neighboring dynasties. The final interdynastic marriage made by an Ottoman sultan appears to have been that in
1435 of Murad II, Mehmed's father, to Mara, the daughter of George
Brankovich, the ruler of Serbia. The dynasty contracted three more marital
alliances, but these were made for princes rather than for the sultan himself:
brides came from the southeastern Anatolian principality of Dulkadır in 1450
and 1467 and from the vassal Crimean Khanate in 1504.[3]

Claims of several marriages between Mehmed the Conqueror and women of the families of Greek petty rulers and statesmen are probably exaggerated.[4] These errors stem in part from a misconceived view of the harem as a stable of sexual partners for the sultan. A number of women taken in defeat (for example, Anna Komnenus, daughter of the last Greek ruler of Trebizond, and Thamar, daughter of George Sphrantzes, a diplomat in the service of the last Byzantine emperor) indeed entered the harem, but were not personally associated with the sultan, and frequently went on to leave as a form of sultanic bounty bestowed on Ottoman statesmen.[5]

However, it was not simply the loss of its traditional pool of marriage partners that caused the decline of marriage as an element in Ottoman reproductive politics. With the consolidation of empire, the sultan began to claim a preeminence that dictated a disdain for alliances with lesser powers. As Ottoman claims to world empire advanced, no power was seen as worthy of such an intimate bond with the mighty and august sultanate. It was doubtless this posture of superiority, in conjuction with a growing preference for concubinage, that kept the Ottomans from contracting marriages with other Sunni Muslim dynasties such as the Mamluks, the Akkoyunlu, the Mughals, and the Uzbeks.

In his account of the Ottomans, Giovanantonio Menavino, a Genoese who served in the late fifteenth and early sixteenth centuries as a page in the royal household, noted that "neither [this sultan] nor any of his ancestors has ever taken a wife."[6] Menavino's comment suggests that the memory of legal marriage faded rapidly. By the reign of Süleyman (r. 1520–66), so firmly entrenched was the principle that the Ottoman dynasty did not contract legal marriages but instead perpetuated itself solely through slave concubinage, that Süleyman's formal marriage to one of his concubines, Hurrem, greatly disturbed the public. The sultan's subjects could explain his breach of "tradition" only by attributing powers of sorcery to his wife.

Interest in the Ottoman's foreign marriage alliances has obscured the fact that concubinage was a central feature of the dynasty's reproductive politics well before the decline of interdynastic alliances.[7] The Ottomans were by no means the first or the only Muslim dynasty to practice concubinage. The second dynasty in Islam, that of the Abbasid caliphs (750–1258), had given concubinage respectability as a means of royal reproduction, which it practiced alongside legal marriage. From the point of view of dynastic succession, the son of a Muslim ruler by a concubine was in theory no less eligible for the throne than his son born of a free Muslim woman. Under Islamic law, the male owner of a female slave enjoyed lawful sexual access to her (unless she was married to another); any unmarried female slave of a male owner was thus by definition a potential concubine. The Muslim concubine, once she had borne a child, enjoyed a legally and socially enhanced position. Known as "mother of a child" (*ümm-i veled*), she could not be sold or otherwise alienated from her master's household, and she became free upon his death. If her master wished to marry her, he had first to manumit her. An *ümm-i veled*'s children were free and enjoyed equal legal and social status with the children of their father's free wife. In addition to his legal wife or wives (to the number of four), a Muslim male might have an unlimited number of concubines.[8] Since the enslavement of Muslims was forbidden, concubines, like other slaves, came from outside the Islamic lands or (although technically illegal) from non-Muslim communities in Muslim-ruled states, and were generally either taken as war booty or purchased from slave traders. Slaves were converted to Islam and frequently manumitted after several years' service, for such manumission counted as a pious act on the part of the slave owner. Slave women destined for the household of prominent or wealthy individuals were often highly trained in various arts by slave dealers, who could make large profits from the sale of talented female slaves.

If in the conduct of interdynastic marriage the Ottoman dynasty resembled its neighbors and in the practice of concubinage its Muslim forebears, in its reproductive politics it displayed a distinctly Ottoman twist. The dynasty appears to have been unique in the extent of its devotion to concubinage, even during the period when legal marriages were being contracted.[9] By the end of the fourteenth century, if not earlier, the dynasty had come to practice reproduction through concubinage to the exclusion of reproduction through legal marriage.

At this point a word must be said about the difficulty of establishing the identity of the mothers of Ottoman princes and princesses. For one thing, at present we know relatively little about the families of the sultans, at least during the medieval and early modern periods. The exact number and identity not only of their consorts but also of their children remain elusive. Moreover, the genealogical record appears to have been lost early on or perhaps deliberately disregarded. Traditions regarding the mothers of the sultans—traditions that persist today at the popular level—are striking in their divergence from historical reality. In these traditions, it is high-born Muslim women who figure as the sultans' mothers. Often the most exalted Muslim bride of a sultan is postulated as the mother of the succeeding sultan—precisely the situation that Ottoman reproductive politics sought to avoid.

These misconceptions are in part the result of the information contained in early Ottoman histories as well as of their silences. These histories rarely mention women. They do not concern themselves with recording the identity of the sultans' mothers, and they virtually ignore concubinage.[10] While the great celebrations that marked some royal weddings are recorded in considerable detail, there is a monogamizing and Islamicizing selectivity in this matrimonial record: it rarely attributes more than one wife to each sultan, and it ignores Christian alliances, although these appear to have been celebrated with as much pomp as weddings with Muslim princesses. Ottoman sources are silent, for example, on the elaborate ceremonial procession in 1346 that brought Orhan's bride, Theodora, daughter of the Byzantine usurper John VI Kantakuzenos, from Istanbul to the Ottoman capital of Bursa. Theodora was met in Silivri, on the northern coast of the Sea of Marmara, where she had been seen off by the Byzantine court in an elaborate ceremony, transported across the sea in a convoy of thirty ships, and escorted overland to the capital by a procession of prominent Ottomans led by a large cavalry detachment.[11] Maria, the Serbian bride of Bayezid I and the only foreign wife, Muslim or Christian, who appears in Ottoman histories, figures only as a force corrupting her husband and thus functions to absorb blame for the temporary collapse of the nascent empire at the feet of the Central Asian conqueror Timur (Tamerlane) in 1402 (see map on page xviii).

In all fairness, we should not look to Ottoman chronicles for the dynasty's matrimonial and reproductive record. Their goal was not historical accuracy regarding the origins and genealogy of the Ottoman house but rather its glorification. Histories celebrating the Ottoman past began to be written in the late fifteeth century as a part of the process of elaborating an imperial image made plausible by the accomplishments of Mehmed the Conqueror's reign. These histories, many of which were commissioned by the dynasty or by its leading statesmen, combined in varying proportions two genres, court panegyric and popular epic, both of which idealized the dynastic family. Early historians were perhaps impelled to provide what seemed to be the most appropriate maternal lineage for the dynasty: Muslim women of distinguished birth. The popularity of the story of Osman's divinely ordained marriage with Edebali's daughter may have stemmed in part from the fact that it provided both paternal *and* maternal origins suitable to a dynasty advancing claims to hegemonic power. It is interesting that the histories suggest a popular concern for female lineage at a time when the dynasty's policies were evolving toward its obliteration.

The account of Ottoman politics of reproduction that follows is possible because in recent decades researchers in Ottoman archives (notably İ. H. Uzunçarşılı) have turned up records of royal concubine mothers. These records allow us to attempt a reconstruction of their careers and to compare them to the careers of legal wives. Nevertheless, the conclusions reached in this book, particularly with regard to the fourteenth and fifteenth centuries, will necessarily remain tentative unless and until the documentary record becomes more nearly complete.

Toward Concubinage

Until the middle of the fourteenth century the Ottomans were not powerful enough to attract the interest of Christian powers or of well-established Anatolian dynasties in marital alliances. The first alliances of the dynasty's males were local, although no less strategically motivated than the interdynastic ties later formed. Notable in their variety, the first sultans' alliances cannot always be classified neatly into one or the other of the two categories outlined above: legal marriage and concubinage.

The marriage of Osman and the daughter of Sheikh Edebali actually occurred, if not by divine design. We know this from central government records regarding the property she received at the time of her marriage: the village of Kozağaç in the district of Bilejik, where the dervish hospice of her father was located.[12] Edebali was one of the most influential of popular religious leaders in the Ottoman territories. In Central Asian Mongol and Turkish tradition, holy men were typically the vehicle of transmission for God's choice of the bearers of sovereignty. The story of Osman's marriage to Edebali's daughter was a manifestation of the importance of this internal basis of dynastic legitimation in the early Ottoman state; hence it was encoded in the most popular of dynastic foundation myths. The success of the early Ottoman military enterprise, as well as the conversion of large numbers of Balkan Christians, were due in no small degree to the spiritual authority of dervish leaders such as Edebali. Their hostels and monasteries formed the nuclei for settlements that grew into towns and garrison centers, and they infused a religious zeal into war against the "infidel" through their participation in military campaigns.[13] Osman's marriage with Sheikh Edebali's daughter was perhaps the first example of the dynasty's attentive nurturing of its ties with these holy men. Even as the Ottoman house engaged in other forms of ideological discourse to maintain the loyalty of its increasingly diverse following, it continued to foster close relations with the sheikhly class, whose charismatic sanction was invoked to support its legitimacy.[14] The only other example of a marriage tie between the dynasty and the sheikhly class, however, was that in 1396 of Hundi Khatun, the daughter of the fourth sultan, Bayezid I, to the eminent religious scholar and sheikh Emir Bukhari.

The 1324 endowment deed for a dervish monastery built by the second sultan, Orhan, suggests that his mother was not, as popular historical tradition maintains, Edebali's daughter, but rather Mal Khatun, the daughter of one 'Umur Bey or Ömer Bey.[15] The title "bey," used by the princely dynasties of Anatolia, suggests that Mal Khatun's father was a person of some status and authority. One possibility is that he was the eponymous ruler of an "Amouri" (Umurî) principality, which was located northeast of the emerging Ottoman state and disappeared in the late thirteenth or the early fourteenth century. The Amouri are described by the Byzantine historian Pachymeres, who says that a son of 'Umur fought with Osman in one of his first raids against local Byzantine lords (the victory at Baphaion). The Ottomans, according to Pachymeres, went on to assume the role played by the Amouri until their demise as the principal aggressor against the Byzantines in northwest Anatolia.[16] If Pachymeres's report is correct, the timing and the political context are appropriate for a marriage between Osman and 'Umur Bey's daughter.

Osman, who had at least five or six sons and at least one daughter, may have had other wives in addition to Mal Khatun and Edebali's daughter.[17] A historical tradition regarding the acquisition of one of Osman's wives calls to mind the Turkish nomadic practice of acquiring women through raids on neighboring tribes. As the story goes, one day on his way to Eskişehir, Osman caught sight of a woman in the village of İtburnu, fell in love with her, and, without telling his father, sent someone to ask for her in marriage. She refused on the grounds that she was not worthy of him, although this may have been an excuse, since there were rumors that Osman intended only a brief dalliance with her. Osman was spurred to kidnap the woman when an erstwhile ally of his, listening to his description of her manifold virtues, decided to take her for himself.[18] Although the sources confuse this woman with Mal Khatun and Edebali's daughter, she was clearly a person of lesser status. The details of the story indicate that the kidnapping occurred when Osman was quite young and before he had gained more than a local reputation. Women of standing themselves, Edebali's daughter and Mal Khatun probably married a more mature and powerful Osman.

Orhan, the second ruler, was sufficiently powerful by the middle of his reign that the Byzantine emperor, John Kantakuzenos, sought his military support and rewarded him in 1346 with the hand of his daughter, Theodora, who became the mother of Orhan's youngest son, Halil. The origins of Orhan's first consorts, however, are obscure, although these women appear to be more local. The principal witnesses of the 1324 endowment deed cited above were family members; the hierarchical order of the signatories suggests that two of the four female witnesses—Melek and Efendi—were wives of Orhan (the other two were Fatma Khatun, Orhan's sister, and Mal Khatun). Efendi, identified as "Eftendize" in the record of a land grant Orhan made to her as his wife, may have been Orhan's cousin, the daughter of Osman's brother Gündüz.[19] If so, this first-cousin marriage may have functioned to seal Gündüz's loyalty to Osman. Melek appears in no histories or other documents that have come to light; if indeed she was married to Orhan, she may have been the mother of Sultan, who is known to us as one of Orhan's sons only through his appearance as a signatory to the deed and who must have died before his father.[20] Another of Orhan's wives, and the mother of his son İbrahim and two daughters, Fatma and Seljuk, was Asporça. Nothing else is known about her except that Osman granted this daughter-in-law several villages, which she then deeded to her descendents in 1323, making her son her executor.[21]

Nilüfer is the only one of Orhan's wives to appear in the histories of the late fifteenth century. According to the story of Nilüfer's origins recounted in these histories, her marriage to Orhan took place when he was a youth and his father Osman was just beginning to accrue power locally. The daughter of one local Byzantine lord, Nilüfer had been engaged to another, the lord of Bilejik, Osman's erstwhile ally. The latter had come to agree with his fellow lords that the growing power of Osman and his band of followers represented a threat that must be eliminated, and so he planned to kill them at the wedding. Osman's preemtive raid on the wedding party and the capture of Bilejik was one of the Ottomans' earliest conquests. Nilüfer was among the prisoners taken, and was presented by Osman to Orhan.[22]

This story may well recount or be based on an actual event, but it is unlikely that it is about Nilüfer. The bride from Bilejik was probably an early wife, perhaps Asporça, whose name suggests that she was of Greek origin. Nilüfer would seem to be a later wife (or concubine). Nilüfer is traditionally thought to have been the mother of two of Orhan's sons, Süleyman and Murad, the latter of whom succeeded his father. Nilüfer was indeed Murad's mother, as the inscription on the public soup kitchen he built for her in Iznik (Nicea) testifies.[23] However, it is possible, indeed likely, that she was not the mother of Süleyman, the most celebrated of Orhan's sons during the sultan's lifetime, until his untimely death through a fall from his horse. Nilüfer does not appear as a signatory to the endowment deed of 1324, and in fact she may not yet have joined Orhan's family. The traditional date for Murad's birth is ca. 1326, when Orhan already had three sons (including Süleyman), all at least in their late teens and old enough to act as legal witnesses; the age gap between Süleyman and Murad was considerable (a reliable guess is approximately twenty years). If Nilüfer was not the mother of Süleyman, we are then faced with the question of who was: a likely candidate is Efendi/Eftendize.[24]

Already by the end of the fifteenth century, historical tradition had aggrandized Nilüfer, no doubt because she was the mother of the third sultan. It is significant that she was represented also as the mother of Süleyman, the son who probably would have succeeded Orhan had he survived. Like Mal Khatun, whose name was attributed in some histories to all stories about Osman's wives, it is Nilüfer who is the featured wife for Orhan's generation. What is at work here is the historiographical privileging of the mother of the succeeding sultan. Some scholars have assumed that it was Nilüfer who received the North African traveler Ibn Battuta when he passed through the territory of the Ottomans in 1331.[25] According to Ibn Battuta's account, when he arrived in the newly conquered city of Iznik, Orhan was away, making the rounds of his various fortress cities, and his wife was in command of the soldiers stationed in the near-deserted city. Of his audience with the Khatun, whom he describes as "a pious and excellent woman," Ibn Battuta says, "she treated me honorably, gave me hospitality, and sent gifts."[26] It is unlikely that Nilüfer, the mother of a young child, would have been given such public responsibility.

It is hard to know how Orhan's Christian wives were construed, that is, whether they were considered slave concubines along Islamic lines. Certainly Asporça and Nilüfer, both of whom endowed Muslim institutions, did not resemble Christian princesses married into the Ottoman dynasty, who retained their religion. Nilüfer's name, Persian for "water lily," argues for a greater likelihood that she was a concubine, since it was typical of the mostly Persian names given to concubines in the fourteenth and fifteenth centuries, many of which were names of birds or flowers.[27] Further evidence that Nilüfer might have entered Orhan's household as a slave concubine is the fact that slaves were an abundant commodity in the Turkish principalities of western Anatolia by the time of her son Murad's birth.[28] Ibn Battuta reported that the ruler of the rival Turkish principality of Aydın had twenty Greek slaves standing at attention at the entrance to his palace; indeed, he gave the traveler a Greek slave woman as a gift.[29] The household of Osman contained slaves used in combat[30] and probably household slaves as well, although historical tradition represents the estate of the deceased ruler as modest and typically nomadic: a robe, flank armor, a saltcellar, a spoon holder, soft high houseboots, several stables of good horses, several flocks of sheep, a few wild mares, and several pairs of saddle pads.[31] By the beginning of Orhan's reign, slaves taken in conquest may have been a standard feature of soldier households in the Ottoman principality: Orhan purchased slaves from his followers in order to provide for the defense of the newly conquered fortress cities.[32] When in the early 1340s the Byzantine empress Anna sought Orhan's help against the usurper John Kantakuzenos, one of the Ottomans' rewards was permission to sell any of Kantakuzenos's followers they could capture and to carry off with them those they did not want to sell; the alliance was unsuccessful (Kantakuzenos soon made his own deal with Orhan, sealed by the marriage with Theodora), but large numbers of slaves were marched back to Ottoman territory.[33]

The endowment deed for Orhan's dervish monastery suggests that at the time of his accession (1323 or 1324), his household not only included slaves but was a well-developed one structured along typically Islamic lines. The trustee-ship of the endowment was given to his manumitted slave, the eunuch (*tavaşi*) Şerefeddin Mukbil.[34] The fact that this individual was converted to Islam, manumitted, and assigned to an important religious function suggests a close familiarity with Islamic legal and social practice; the fact that eunuchs were typically employed to guard harems suggests that Orhan's household may have been sufficiently articulated to contain a separate harem. Portrayals of Orhan as leading a simple nomadic existence with no permanent household establish-ment are misleading;[35] the fact that he moved from town to town, as Ibn Battuta noted, does not rule out the existence of a permanent household of some size in his capital or some other location. Indeed, Orhan was rapidly acquiring the trappings appropriate to his status as head of an increasingly important princely house. Ibn Battuta noted that the Ottoman prince was "the greatest of the kings of the Turkmens and the richest in wealth, lands and military forces."[36]

One obvious point about the story of Orhan's Bilejik bride is that it fits the nomadic raiding pattern. So does an oral tradition about Gülçiçek Khatun, consort of Murad, the third sultan, and mother of his son and successor, Bayezid. According to this popular tradition, Gülçiçek was the consort of Ajlan Bey, one of the princes of the Anatolian Muslim principality of Karasi, and mother of one of his sons, Yakhşi. She was captured when Orhan con-quered the principality (ca. 1344) and placed in the royal harem. Some years later, when Orhan's son Murad had reached adulthood, an attempt was made to marry Gülçiçek, but she refused several names suggested to her, until Murad suggested himself.[37] There is support for this story, or part of it at least, in the fact that the endowment deed for a dervish monastery founded by Gülçiçek indicates that she appointed her son Yakhşi trustee; Murad had no son by this name.[38] Whether Gülçiçek was Ajlan Bey's legal wife or his concubine is not clear, nor is her status as Murad's consort, although her career displayed several of the features of concubinage. Of Greek origin,[39] at some point during her career she, like Nilüfer, acquired a typically concubine name (Gülçiçek means "roseblossom" in Turkish). Her Muslim piety was publicly demonstrated by her construction of the dervish monastery as well as of a mosque in Bursa.

The stories of Osman's village wife, Orhan's bride from Bilejik, and Murad's consort Gülçiçek suggest that the practice of acquiring women through raid and conquest, familiar to the early Ottomans from their nomadic heritage, overlapped in important ways with the Muslim institution of slave concubinage. Each involved the acquisition of women of non-Ottoman origin, particularly women obtained from subjugated territories. These stories of the early rulers' captured consorts are reminiscent of episodes in the Central Asian Turkish epic tales of Dede Korkut, in which captive women were one of the prizes of nomad raids and proof of the raiders' valor.[40]

Women captured from the families of conquered rulers, especially their consorts, continued to be a valued symbol of Ottoman victory as late as the sixteenth century. The Byzantine historian Doukas tells us that Mehmed II departed from Constantinople twenty days after its conquest, "taking with him in wagons and on horseback all the [Byzantine] noblewomen and their daughters."[41] Selim I, whose conquests made the Ottoman state a world empire, captured Taçlu Khatun, the wife of the Safavid ruler of Iran, at the decisive battle of Chaldiran in 1514 and refused to return her, instead giving her to one of his leading statesmen.[42] As late as 1553, Süleyman's consort Hurrem wrote to the sultan, who was campaigning against the Safavids, lamenting the lack of a sign of victory that would content the people of Istanbul, such as the capture of the shah's wife or son.[43] As Hurrem's letter suggests, hostage sons of rival dynasties were also valued prizes of conquest, visible proof of the inability of the defeated ruler to protect his household and, by extension, his domain. These living symbols of Ottoman superiority were conspicuously displayed during public ceremonials in Istanbul. The importance of captured women in the discourse of sovereign power among states of Turkish tribal origin is underlined by a late fifteenth-century history of the eastern Anatolian Akkoyunlu dynasty, which listed as the second of six points in the dynasty's claim to "distinguished origin" the fact that "the hand of a conqueror never touched their spouses."[44]

Rather than being discontinuous modes of conjugal union, nomad raids, Islamic concubinage, and interdynastic marriage all shared important features: royal consorts came from without the tribe/state and functioned as trophies of victory. Nevertheless, there were legal considerations that suggest that a woman's status could not have been left entirely ambiguous: if she were a slave, conversion to Islam would take place and eventual manumission was a possiblity; if she were a legal wife, the issue of dowry would arise. But whatever the precise status of each harem member, the exogamous nature of these various modes of conjugal union is striking, and contrasts with the apparent absence of marriages contracted by the Ottoman sultans with Muslim daughters of the Ottoman elite. The sultans' alliances were both ethnically and religiously exogamous. Apart from the half-dozen marriages made with Muslim princesses from Anatolian Turkish principalities, all royal consorts after the first two Ottoman generations (with one exception) were neither Muslim nor Turkish by birth.[45]

Why Concubinage?

European observers of the Ottoman scene in the early modern period favored two explanations for the decline or absence of dynastic marriages. The first held that the sultans did not wish to repeat the agonizing and ignominious experience of Bayezid I: after his capture in 1402 by the Turkish-Mongol conqueror Timur (known to the West as Tamerlane), Bayezid suffered the insult of having to watch one of his wives, the Serbian Maria, forced to perform menial tasks. This unendurable shame is supposed to have contributed to the sultan's suicide in captivity, dramatized for an English audience in Christopher Marlowe's *Tamburlaine the Great,* first performed in 1590.[46] However, the unstated logic of this explanation—that it would have been less an assault on royal dignity for a slave woman than a queen to be mistreated—is perhaps more European than Ottoman. In the symbolic contest between the two Turkish Muslim monarchs, the essential point was that the sultan's harem had been violated and the female trophy carried off. Moreover, it is certainly questionable whether the Ottoman dynasty would base its marital policy on the assumption of future defeat.

The second explanation has to do with the protection afforded by Islamic law to the financial estates of legal wives. Europeans, accustomed to the absence of such legal guarantees for women in their own societies, were particularly struck by the fact that the dowry bestowed by the groom became the property of the wife.[47] It was thought that the sultans would drain Ottoman coffers if they were to contract marriages with high-born women. The proponents of this argument were obviously not aware of the enormous wealth a concubine might command.

As noted above, the ultimate preference for concubinage over dynastic marriages with foreign powers is best understood as a product of the waning political utility of such unions and the evolution of the Ottoman state along traditional Islamic lines. The first hundred years of Ottoman history were characterized by the increasing influence of classic Islamic institutions, practices, and norms. The practice of concubinage was a standard feature of Muslim dynasties.[48] While the caliphs of the Umayyad dynasty had prided themselves on the purity of their Arab lineage through marriage with noble Arab women, by the second century of Islamic history many of the caliphs of the Abbasid dynasty were sons of slave concubines.

The practice of concubinage was undoubtedly strengthened by a fundamental feature of the evolving Ottoman polity: the growing importance of slaves in the ruling elite. The presence of a military slave corps in the service of the ruling house was a classic feature of earlier Islamic states. It was believed that a corps of highly trained slaves loyal only to the ruler and dependent entirely on his good will would serve the state more reliably and efficiently than a hereditary nobility, whose interests might compete with those of the ruler. The Ottomans expanded and elaborated on this institution beyond anything that had previously existed. The systematic enslavement of Christian youths to be converted to Islam and trained for military service to the dynasty probably began under Murad I.[49] Within a hundred years the slave institution had expanded to the extent that slaves, as Ottoman Muslims and members of the ruling class, not only formed the core of the military forces but also constituted the greater part of the pool of candidates for the highest military and administrative offices in the state.[50] The elite of this slave corps was educated and trained in the inner palace, its service to the state beginning with personal service to the sultan. It should be noted that although their legal status was that of slave, these servants of the dynasty should not be thought of as analogous to chattel slaves as we know them from the history of Europe and the Americas.

Since, in its structure and the nature of its personnel, the development of the imperial harem was strikingly similar to that of the elite slave corps trained within the palace,[51] it seems likely that female slaves began to assume a significant presence in the household of the Ottoman ruler around the same time that male slaves began to assume more than a purely military role, and for much the same reason. A concubine did not carry with her either the political aspirations that the family of a foreign princess or a woman of the indigenous elite might entertain as a result of alliance with the dynasty, or the political leverage that they might attempt to exert. In theory, concubines could press few legal claims on their master and were unlikely to encumber him with pressure to favor particular interests in Ottoman society. A Muslim proverb holds that "kingship is bereft of ties."[52] Legal marriage entailed both contractual obligations and, since the legal wife was a woman of status, a certain amount of ceremonial deference to her. According to Menavino, the reason the sultan contented himself with a number of concubines and avoided taking a wife was that, were he to do so, "it would then be necessary that she be treated as Queen, just as he is the King."[53]

Childless Wives

Still, these explanations do not account for the unique features of Ottoman reproductive politics: its exclusive reliance on concubinage for producing offspring even in the presence of legal wives, and the policy of allowing each concubine to produce only one son. As we shall see, these two phenomena were linked through their relevance to the dynasty's control of succession to the throne.

After the fourteenth century or perhaps even as early as the mid-fourteenth century, virtually all royal children appear to have been born of concubines.[54] The barrenness of formal marriages was presumably accomplished through avoidance of sexual relations between the sultan and his royal wives.[55] The Byzantine statesman Sphrantzes tells us that one of the concerns in the attempt to arrange a marriage between the Serbian princess Mara, widow of Murad II, and the Byzantine emperor Constantine XI Paleologus was that Mara had already been married; this was no problem, Sphrantzes contended, since "she, it is generally believed, did not sleep with [the sultan]."[56] Birth control, sanctioned and practiced by the medieval Muslim world, may also have been employed.[57]

The fifteenth-century Ottoman historian Şükrullah asserted that all of the children of Bayezid I and of his son Mehmed I, the fourth and fifth sultans, had concubine mothers.[58] Beginning with Mehmed I, we have documentary evidence that the mothers of the sultans were concubines.[59] If, as seems possible, Nilüfer and Gülçiçek were concubines, then it may be that only the first two Ottoman rulers, Osman and Orhan, were the children of formal marriages. The concubine mothers of sultans in the pre-Süleymanic period were Devlet, mother of Mehmed I; Hüma, mother of Mehmed II; Gülbahar, mother of Bayezid II; another Gülbahar, mother of Selim I; and Hafsa, mother of Süleyman (the identity of the mother of Murad II is uncertain).

These facts contradict popular tradition, according to which it was Muslim princess wives of the sultans who bore future sultans. For example, Mehmed I's mother is often assumed to be Devletşah, whose father was Süleymanşah Bey, ruler of the Anatolian Germiyan principality, and whose mother was Mutahhare, granddaughter of Jelaleddin Rumî, founder of the Sufi order of the Mevlevis.[60] The impressive lineage of Devletşah, who was descended from powerful princes and charismatic sheikhs, probably accounts for an alternate tradition which, although acknowledging that she was not the future sultan's mother, makes her the mother of two other sons of Bayezid, İsa and Musa, who were eliminated in the decade-long succession war that followed Bayezid's defeat by Timur. If İsa and Musa had been Devletşah's sons, one would expect Germiyan support for them during the succession dispute, but in fact the Germiyan ruler Yakup delivered Musa into the hands of Mehmed, while İsa found support with several of the Anatolian principalities but not with Germiyan.[61] Other Muslim princesses popularly thought to be mothers of sultans are Emine of the Dulkadır house (supposedly mother to Murad II); Hadije Halime of the Jandar house (Mehmed II); and another Dulkadır princess, Ayşe (Selim I).[62]

In addition to silence in the genealogical record regarding royal wives, there is also silence in the record of monumental building. Beginning with Nilüfer, the mothers of princes built and endowed mosques, schools, dervish monasteries and hospices, and tombs for their sons or themselves; sometimes their sons established such structures in their mothers' names. The royal Muslim wives of the sultans are notably absent as builders and endowers of such public monuments or institutions (Christian wives did not engage in this typically Muslim activity). Only two wives appear to have left buildings, and even these may not count as Ottoman public structures. One was Hafsa Khatun, daughter of İsa Bey of the principality of Aydın, whose public works were located within her father's territory and may have been built before she married Bayezid I upon his conquest of Aydın in 1390.[63] The other was Sitti Khatun, a Dulkadır princess, married to Mehmed the Conqueror just before he became sultan. Mehmed never cared for this wife of his, who remained behind in Edirne after the court moved to Istanbul. There she built herself a palace, on whose premises she also had constructed a mosque, near which she was buried when she died in 1467.[64] This absence of public building is a powerful statement about the second-class status of royal wives, since it was virtually an imperative that Muslims of high standing, women and men alike, undertake the construction and endowment of what were considered pious works. Royal wives were deprived of this most public mark of status, presumably because they lacked the qualification that appears to have entitled royal concubines to this privilege: motherhood.

The suppression of the capacity of royal wives to bear children is an example of the Ottoman policy of manipulating sexuality and reproduction as a means of controlling power. To deny these women access to motherhood, the source of female power within the dynastic family, was to diminish the status of the royal houses from which they came. The only marriage definitely known to have produced children—that of the Byzantine princess Theodora and Orhan—was an alliance in which the Ottomans were suppliants rather than superiors. Although their careers as consorts of the sultans often began with the ceremonial of elaborate weddings, royal brides were ciphers in these events. What counted was the ceremony itself and what it symbolized: less the union of male and female than a statement of the relationship between two states. The function of the bride, particularly in view of the nonrole that awaited her as the sultan's wife, was to symbolize the subordinate status of the weaker state. The very nature of the wedding celebrations, a central feature of which was the passage of the bride from her father or brother's domain to the Ottoman capital, gave concrete expression to the vector of power. This is doubtless a reason why few Ottoman princesses married outside the dynasty.

Nothing in the Ottomans' Islamic or Turco-Mongol background suggested the policy of sterile marriage. The Ottomans' contemporaries, while they may have practiced concubinage, did not suppress the reproductive capacity of their legal wives. Ottoman princesses who married into other Anatolian princely houses bore children; for example, the eldest son of the Karaman ruler İbrahim had a concubine mother, but several other of his sons were the children of İlaldı Khatun, daughter of the Ottoman sultan Mehmed I.[65]

It may seem ironic that in pursuing a policy designed to enhance its status, the Ottoman dynasty laid itself open to accusations of base origin. The late fifteenth-century history that celebrated the Akkoyunlu dynasty's noble origin, citing the fact that its women had never been touched by a conqueror, pointed also to the fact that no member of the dynasty was disgraced by descent from a slave girl. Here, the Akkoyunlu dynasty was distinguished from its two principal rivals, the Ottomans and the Mamluks. The Ottoman dynasty's own perspective on this issue is reflected in the position taken by Bayezid II when he refused to campaign in person against the Mamluk sultanate: his argument was that it was not fitting that he equate himself with the Mamluk ruler, a slave.[66] The point would seem to be that, in the Ottoman view, honor, status, and legitimacy inhered in the dynasty, that is, in the male lineage, "the sons of Osman." Those who saw dishonor in concubinage rejected the Ottoman suppression of female lineage. In the Ottoman view, the admission of female lineage, of nobly born women, compromised the integrity and autonomy of the sultanate. In Ottoman practice, however, while concubine mothers of royal offspring were devoid of lineage, they were not devoid of status. Their standing sprang from a kind of retroactive or reverse lineage bestowed on them through having given birth to a member of the Ottoman dynasty, through the blood link to the royal family established through their offspring.

We should not, however, think of the royal wives of the Ottoman sultans as completely powerless. The symbolic statement about power issued at the time of their marriage was not the whole story. The shifting alliances among the states of Rumelia and Anatolia meant that the sultans needed to be careful about how they treated their foreign wives. It was fear that her father would raise an army of Hungarians against him that kept Mehmed II from forcing his widowed stepmother Mara to marry İshak, a prominent statesman of slave origin.[67] (The prospect of this marriage may have contributed to the failure of Sphrantzes's attempt to arrange a marriage between Mara and the Byzantine emperor, for, as he tells us, "the sultan's widow had made a vow to God and decided that if He freed her from the house of her late husband she would not remarry for the rest of her life, but would remain in His service. . . .")[68] It seems likely that the Christian wives of the sultans, because of the greater diplomatic and military force behind them, enjoyed greater independence and status at the Ottoman court than did women from the Anatolian principalities, about whom we know almost nothing after their marriages. Orhan's wife Theodora, for example, was active in encouraging Christians converted to Islam to return to their former faith (or so her father noted in his memoirs, though this may have been by way of an apology for the marriage he had fostered).[69] The blame visited by early Ottoman chroniclers on Bayezid I's wife Maria for introducing her husband to the vices of court life suggests that she was an influential figure, although she may simply have been the scape-goat for a nostalgic memory (or fantasy) in the early historiographical tradition for a time when the sultans led simple lives. As Murad II's widow, Mara exercised considerable influence as a mediator in the constant diplomatic discourse between Mehmed the Conqueror and the powers of Europe.[70]

Single-Son Concubines

Limiting the number of children a concubine woman might bear was another manifestation of the control exercised over the sexual and reproductive activity of the sultan and his consorts. The Ottoman dynasty appears to have followed a reproductive policy according to which a woman would bear no more than one son to a sultan (or prince); she might, however, bear one or more daughters before the birth of a son would put an end to her childbearing career. While there are too many gaps in the genealogical record before the mid-fifteenth century to prove this hypothesis conclusively, we can be reasonably confident that the dynasty consciously followed a one mother-one son policy from the reign of Mehmed the Conqueror, that is, from the mid-fifteenth century on. For the reigns of Mehmed and his son Bayezid II, we are fortunate in knowing the names of the concubine mothers of each of their sons. There is enough evidence regarding the family of Orhan, the second ruler, to suggest that this practice may well have been standard from the beginning, but one cannot generalize from this single reign. Other questions remain unanswered at present: whether the practice was peculiarly Ottoman or shared by other Anatolian or Turkish societies, and whether it was limited to the dynasty or observed by other elements of the society as well.

As with the practice of preventing royal wives from bearing children, the one mother-one son practice was probably managed through sexual abstinence, although here too perhaps some form of birth control was also employed. Abstinence appears to have taken the form of serial concubinage: concubines were only temporary sexual partners of a sultan, at least by the latter half of the fifteenth century. It seems likely that there was a revolving-door policy in the imperial harem that deprived a woman who had borne a son of further eligibility for the sultan's bed. Luigi Bassano, a Venetian who probably served as a page in the inner palace under Süleyman, commented that sultans before him were accustomed to having many consorts and to fathering children by all of them. Bassano emphasized the serial progression of a sultan's sexual partners: "[H]e chooses his consorts from slaves who are presented to him, and whenever it happens that one pleases him, he installs her in the palace . . . where he keeps her until he falls in love with another, then he repudiates the first and chooses the other, and this continues as long as he likes. . . ."[71] The same observation was made by Domenico Trevisano, Venetian ambassador to the Ottoman court in the early 1550s, who reported that the sultans before Süleyman "were accustomed to choosing now one, now another woman, whether to have children or for their carnal pleasure."[72]

What was the purpose of such a policy? We may find a plausible answer if we ask this question in the context of the problem of succession and the fate of the overwhelming majority of princes who lost out in the competition for the throne. During the reign of the third sultan, Murad I, there was no prince who was the chief delegate of his father as Orhan had been for Osman and Murad's elder brother Süleyman had been for Orhan. Now officials appointed by the sultan began to replace family members as the principal military commanders and administrators of the growing state. According to the historian Müneccim-başı, Murad appointed such officials because there were no family members to whom he could turn;[73] indeed, at the time of his accession in 1362, Murad's eldest son was probably no more than nineteen or so,[74] and his brothers had perished in the contest for the succession. Whatever the reasons, no uncle, brother, or son of a sultan exercised full executive power again. The fact that Murad, lacking the advantage of being the acknowledged leader during his father's lifetime, appears to have been the first ruler to fight his brothers for the throne and the first to face a revolt by one of his own sons surely contributed to the imposition of limits on the power of male dynasts other than the sultan.

Parallel to the decline of sons as the chief delegates of sovereign power, the idea of the succession as an open contest between all sons of the former sultan took stronger hold. Beginning with Murad I, each reign until the accession of Süleyman the Magnificent in 1520 opened with either violent combat among princes or the new sultan's execution of his brothers.[75] Both rulers and ruled appear to have accepted this state of affairs, if reluctantly. When, during the civil war following Bayezid I's defeat at the hands of Timur, his son Mehmed began to besiege the city of Edirne, the headquarters of his brother Musa, the inhabitants informed Mehmed that if only the two brothers would fight it out elsewhere, whomever fortune favored could freely take possession of the city.[76] One hundred fifty years later, when the two surviving sons of Süleyman the Magnificent, Selim and Bayezid, had begun to compete for the succession during their father's lifetime, the sultan admonished the latter, saying, "[Y]ou may leave all to God, for it is not man's pleasure, but God's will, that disposes of kingdoms and their government. If He has decreed that you shall have the kingdom after me, no man living will be able to prevent it."[77] Princes could not opt out of candidacy for the throne: when Korkud, one of Bayezid II's sons, requested permission to retire from political life to pursue his interests in Muslim scholarship—and to save his life, threatened by incipient civil war among his brothers—his father refused to grant his request.[78]

As open succession became acknowledged custom, so did the practice of fratricide. At first competing claimants to the throne were killed as combatants in succession wars. Murad II, who was the first sultan to secure himself on the throne with brothers safely under his control, blinded two younger brothers (blindness was considered a disqualification for sovereignty in both Islamic and Byzantine tradition). But upon his accession in 1451, Mehmed the Conqueror executed his only brother, an infant, and went on to institutionalize the practice of fratricide by incorporating it into his codification of imperial protocol. He justified royal fratricide as a means of protecting society from the threat of internecine strife: "It is proper for whichever of my sons is favored by God with the sultanate to execute his brothers for the good order of society. Most doctors of the religious law have declared this permissible."[79] By the end of the fifteenth century, the historian Neşri could call this practice an "ancient custom" of the Ottomans.[80] Until the lapse in the early seventeenth century of the pattern of succession of son to father, the sultans regularly had their brothers, as well as the latters' sons, executed. By eliminating collateral lines, they not only avoided a major source of direct challenge to their authority during their lifetime but also eliminated future challenges to their own issue from descendants of their siblings.

How did concubinage and the one mother-one son policy fit in with these developments? The point was most likely the viability of each prince's candidacy for the succession, and the key issue the role of the prince's mother in his training, the management of his princely governorate household, and the promotion of his career. If two princes shared a mother, they could not both claim this crucial member of their princely household; presumably one (or both) would have had to sacrifice a vital political ally. Hence the one mother-one son policy. Furthermore, it would have been impolitic to unfairly advantage a particular prince in the competition for the throne through the special status of his mother. A prince whose mother was the daughter or sister of an influential neighboring (and possibly rival) ruler might have had an advantage in the contest for succession because of the potential for political support from his maternal relatives. Hence the policy of denying motherhood to royal wives.

An episode in the ongoing rivalry between the Ottomans and the Karamanid dynasty is instructive in illustrating the danger of a foreign princess becoming mother to a prince (in this case, however, it was the Ottomans who were the intervening power). The Karamanid state, located in the heartland of the former Anatolian Seljuk state, was the most prestigious and powerful of the Turkish principalities absorbed by the Ottomans. İbrahim, the Karamanid ruler during the first part of Mehmed the Conqueror's reign, had seven sons, the eldest of whom, İshak, was born of a slave concubine and the others from his marriage to Sultan Khatun, daughter of the Ottoman sultan Bayezid I. According to Kemalpaşazade, author of an early sixteenth-century history and one of the most accomplished of Ottoman religious scholars, İbrahim preferred his eldest son because he was not of Ottoman descent. However, when he named İshak his heir, the sons of Sultan Khatun rebelled and marched on the capital of Konya. In Kemalpaşazade's word, when İbrahim died in 1463, "the sea of disorder overflowed in tumultuous waves, and the land of Karaman was filled with evil and sedition": that is, the domain split up into fiefs.[81] Ultimately, Mehmed the Conqueror intervened in favor of the half-Ottoman princes and placed the eldest of Sultan Khatun's sons on the throne. This Karamanid-Ottoman prince proved to be an unloyal vassal, however, and within a decade the state was completely taken over by the Ottomans.

The Princely Household

The Anatolian provincial capitals to which princes and their mothers were sent in the fifteenth and sixteenth centuries were for the most part old centers of high Islamic civilization that had served as the capitals of the principalities conquered by the Ottomans. Especially in the fifteenth century, when the Ottomans were still competing for mastery of Anatolia, it was important to maintain a royal presence in the major cities that bordered rival powers. Most popular were Amasya, the most prestigious princely post in the fifteenth century; Konya, newly captured from the Karamanids; and Manisa, an old Byzantine city and the capital to which newly dispatched princes tended to be sent because it was the closest to Istanbul.[82]

Although their authority was increasingly circumscribed, princes received real political training during their governorship. In addition to being charged with the administration of their provinces, they might be ordered to head an internal military operation or summoned to accompany their father on a major offensive against an external enemy. In 1412 the young sultan Mehmed I, fighting to reintegrate the empire after the debacle wreaked by Timur, assigned his twelve-year-old son Murad to Amasya, and a year later ordered the young prince, with the help of a trusted military commander, to quell a politico-religious rebellion that had already defeated one army sent against it.[83] At the battle of Başkent in 1473, where Mehmed the Conqueror defeated the forces of the powerful Akkoyunlu state, Bayezid, the eldest prince and governor of Amasya, commanded the right arm of the Ottoman army, while Mustafa, the sultan's second son and the governor of Konya, commanded the left arm.[84] Mehmed's third and youngest son, the fourteen-year-old Jem, was dispatched from his provincial post at Kastamonu to the Ottomans' western capital at Edirne, to serve in his father's absence as a royal presence facing down Europe.

Princely courts were models of the imperial court, consisting of the same service divisions of inner and outer household, managed by officials with the same titles as their Istanbul counterparts. The princely household was a substantial establishment, containing all the offices necessary to govern the province. Registers listing the staff and salaries of Süleyman's princely household in Manisa show that in 1513, Süleyman's fourth year out of Istanbul, there were 458 persons on his household payroll at an annual expense of 1,194,156 aspers;[85] an undated though later register indicates that the household had expanded to include a staff of 673 at an annual expense of 1,673,872 aspers.[86] Among those listed on the payroll at this later date were the prince's personal steward and treasurer; the stewards of the harem, of the kitchen, and of the scribal staff; aghas and pages of the inner household, and the latters' preceptors and eunuch guards; and divisions of houndsmen, falconers, stablemen, craftsmen, doctors, footmen, cooks, and cellarers. The military household included several divisions of cavalry, processional guards, standard-bearers, tent pitchers, and two military bands. The register also lists seventeen women as members of the princely harem. Most of these women probably served as the prince's concubines or as ladies-in-waiting to the prince and his mother, while others (including two laundrywomen) served in menial capacities. Assigned to the harem were also a female scribe and a female doctor.[87] According to the historian Peçevi, when Süleyman's great-grandson Mehmed took up his post in Manisa in 1583, a suite of nearly two thousand, drawn from the imperial palace and the households of leading statesmen, accompanied him.[88]

Should a prince gain the throne, his princely household would serve as the nucleus of the sultanic household, and the loyalties and networks established in the provinces would become the basis of future alignments at the imperial court. The prince's servants therefore had an enormous stake in the fortunes of their master in the succession struggles that marked the fifteenth and sixteenth centuries. The princely court was also a center of cultural activity and patronage to which notable religious scholars, poets, and artists were attracted. An aspiring litterateur might choose to link his career with that of a prince rather than take his chances for recognition among the stiffer competition at the imperial capital.[89] It was certainly in a prince's interest to maintain a devoted circle of poets and belletrists who would celebrate his virtues.

A prince's departure for his provincial capital was the occasion of a ceremonial celebration marking his political coming of age. He may have been the object of previous public celebrations—his circumcision and, until the lapse of foreign marriages, his wedding—but these were occasions that demonstrated the power, majesty, and beneficence of his father. The banquets, games, debating contests, and displays of martial and athletic prowess that were standard elements of circumcision and wedding festivities might last for a month or more, providing ample opportunity for the symbolic renewal of political bonds through the exchange of gifts and honors between sultan and subjects. But the sultan's role in the ceremonial marking the start of his son's official career was a private one; it was the prince who was the public figure celebrated in this event. Before leaving for his post at Manisa in 1533, Süleyman's son Mustafa was received by his father in a formal audience within the palace that was attended by the vezirs and other leading officers of the inner and outer service. After kissing his father's hand, Mustafa was escorted from the palace and publicly girded with a sword by the vezirs, one of whom held the stirrup of his horse and another his ceremonial robe.[90] In 1583 Süleyman's great-grandson Mehmed, the last prince to hold a post as provincial governor, departed for the provinces after a great public ceremony during which the vezirs, one by one, approached the prince, who was seated on horseback, to pledge their devotion and to remind him of his responsibilities regarding the execution of justice and the care of soldiers.[91]

Mother of the Prince

> When one of [the maidens] becomes pregnant by the Monarch, her salary is increased and she is honored and elevated above the others, and is served as a Lady. And if she gives birth to a son, the boy is raised by his mother until the age of 10 or 11; then the Grand Turk gives him a *sanjak* [a province] and sends his mother with him. . . . And if a girl is born, she is raised by her mother until the time she is married.

So noted Giovanni Maria Angiolello, who was in the service of Mehmed the Conqueror's eldest son Mustafa.[92] It is unclear when the practice of sending a prince's mother with him to his provincial post began. It is possible that the wife of the second sultan, Orhan, who entertained the traveler Ibn Battuta in Iznik, was present there as the mother of the prince Süleyman, since Orhan had appointed his son to the city after its conquest. Mehmed I took his mother and children with him on his 1415 campaign in western Anatolia; to be sure, his was no longer a princely but rather the sultanic household, but it is noteworthy that Mehmed did not leave his family behind in one of the capitals.[93] In addition to Angiolello's comment above, the more abundant evidence we have about the sultans' families from the mid-fifteenth century on makes clear that the practice was routine by then. Gülşah Khatun, the mother of Angiolello's master Mustafa, was with her son in Konya and in Kayseri, where he died in 1474.[94] Çiçek Khatun, the mother of Mustafa's younger brother Jem, was with her son in Konya, where he was assigned after Mustafa's death; after Jem's first defeat in the succession war following his father's death in 1481, the prince, his mother, and the rest of his household took refuge with the Mamluk sultan in Cairo.[95]

Of all the members of the prince's household, his mother was his most devoted ally. The individual perhaps most able to help him attain the throne— his *lala,* the political tutor assigned to supervise and instruct him—was also the person most able and likely to desert him if his prospects dimmed. Appointed by the sultan and ultimately loyal to him, a tutor's primary concern was not always the success of his princely charge. Gedik Ahmed Pasha, who had been tutor to Jem, failed to supply the prince with the support he confidently expected in his challenge to the enthronement of his older brother Bayezid; Ahmed Pasha was at the time the son-in-law of the grand vezir İshak Pasha, supporter of the new regime.[96]

Indeed, it was in the sultan's interest to prevent a tutor from yoking his career to that of a prince.[97] The history of earlier Turco-Islamic dynasties provided sufficient warning of the harmful consequences of overly powerful guardians (called *atabegs*) who frequently set up independent states with their princely charges as puppet rulers. Ensuring the loyalty of tutors to the central authority was a critical element in the Ottomans' attempts to accommodate Turco-Mongol principles of power shared among family members with their overriding concern for the preservation of unitary authority. The self-interest of tutors is illustrated by the quickly shifting loyalties of Kara Mustafa Pasha, tutor toward the end of Süleyman's reign first to Bayezid, then to Selim, the sultan's two surviving sons. When the grand vezir Rüstem Pasha, a partisan of Bayezid, assumed that the pasha was loyal to his first tutee and transferred him in 1556 to Selim with instructions to undermine the latter's candidacy for the succession, Mustafa Pasha proceeded to betray Bayezid in the hopes that Selim's victory would bring him the grand vezirate. Fittingly, Mustafa Pasha was known by the epithet "Lala."

A prince's mother had a vital interest in his welfare. It was not simply a desire for power that motivated her to do all she could to bring about her son's succession to the throne. If she and her son failed, the practice of fratricide sealed the prince's fate, while the fate of his mother was at best honorable exile in the former capital of Bursa. In order to strengthen the prince's position relative to that of his brothers in anticipation of the inevitable struggle for succession, it was imperative that they win the loyalty of strategic elements in the ruling class, most particularly Janissary officers and leading government officials in the capital who could manipulate affairs to their advantage. A prince's mother was presumably able to perform as an effective agent for her son through her connections with the imperial court, her wealth, and her status as a royal consort and as the most honored person at the provincial court after her son. Although Jem was deserted by his tutor Gedik Ahmed Pasha, he was well served by his mother Çiçek Khatun, who struggled on his behalf for years and served as his principal ally in his efforts to free himself from the European captivity he endured after his defeat by his brother.

Mothers of princes were responsible for the proper behavior of their sons in their provincial posts. The potential difficulties of this task are vividly illustrated in a letter to Bayezid II from Gülruh Khatun, one of his concubines and mother of the prince Alemşah. In the letter she responds to the sultan's instruction that she look to the conduct—obviously unsatisfactory—of her son. The letter begins, "My fortune-favored sultan, you instructed me to discipline my son. Since then . . . I have done everything I can to preserve order. . . ." She goes on to present her case against seven members of her son's suite—including his tutor (*lala*), his doctor, and his preceptor—to whom she attributes responsibility for the problems. It is Alemşah's tutor in particular whom she blames: "What was required was a tutor who would strive to cause my dear son's faith and government to flourish, who would ever direct him toward virtuous conduct, who would root out corrupters in his household, preserve order among the people, and honor the subjects [of the empire]. Instead, what we have is a tutor who is the author of all corruption. . . ." She accuses the tutor and his colleagues of inducing Alemşah to drink excessively so that he might be persuaded to sanction proposals "against the law of Islam and the law of the sultan" that he would ordinarily, when sober, refuse. Worried about Alemşah's ill health, she describes his difficult recovery from a month-long drinking bout (the prince was to die at forty-seven from the effects of his drinking). "Unable to bear any longer the corruption of these evil-doers," Gülruh Khatun called the tutor's shortcomings to the sultan's attention—among them the squandering of the prince's treasury to the extent that even she, the mother of the prince, had not received her stipend for a year. But the tutor had dismissed her protest as the work of the chief eunuch of the prince's private household, and unjustly denounced the latter to the sultan. Gülruh Khatun implores the sultan to remove the seven:

> My fortune-favored padishah, heed my cry for help, . . . rid us of [my son's] tutor, teacher, and doctor. They are masters of corruption. . . . Send us good Muslims, because our situation has been pitiful since these persons arrived. They have deprived me of my mother's rights. . . . If these seven do not go, they will utterly destroy the household of my son, your servant.[98]

Gülruh Khatun's letter reveals concern not only for the precariousness of her son's physical and political condition but also for the preservation of her own rights and status. The letter also suggests that the mother of a prince served as eyes and ears for the sultan, a check on his political appointees. Since she was ultimately more interested in her son's political survival than in that of his father, it might at first seem that she could not be fully trusted by the sultan. However, because her survival and that of her son during the sultan's lifetime depended upon his good will, he could rest assured that she would of necessity do all she could to ensure that her son's behavior was (outwardly at least) impeccable. Her interest in her son's survival could thus be turned to the political advantage of the sultan. Furthermore, just as the presence of a prince's mother at his provincial post provided a disincentive to self-interested behavior on the part of a tutor, the latter would presumably report to the sultan about the conduct not only of the prince but of his mother as well. The dispersal of high-ranking royal women to the provinces may well have been motivated, in part at least, by the requirements of this system of checks and balances. Furthermore, the princely governorate ensured that mothers of princes were safely removed from the center of power, where freer access to potential allies would have permitted them to engage more easily in faction building.

Even after her son's death, the mother of a prince continued to be concerned with her son and his household. The mother of a prince who either died at his provincial post or was executed in a contest for the succession did

not return to the imperial palace in Istanbul. Instead, she retired to Bursa, the
first Ottoman capital, and the place where, until the conquest of Constantinople, members of the dynastic family were buried. In retirement she occupied
herself with pious works. Often she undertook the construction of her own or
her son's tomb. Befitting her role as senior member of her son's household,
she looked after members of the deceased prince's suite and assured that they
were given appropriate new posts. Hüsnüşah Khatun, mother of Bayezid II's
son Şehinşah, corresponded with Selim I, Şehinşah's victorious brother, on
behalf of Mevlana Pir Ahmed Çelebi, a scholar who had been at Şehinşah's
court and who was neglected when the members of the prince's household
were assigned new posts.[99]

Of Mehmed the Conqueror's known concubines, only Gülbahar Khatun
returned to Istanbul as the mother of his successor. Mustafa's mother, Gülşah,
settled in Bursa after her son's death in 1474. Angiolello, who with the rest of
Mustafa's household accompanied the prince's cortege from his post in
Kayseri to Bursa, where he was buried, described the disposition of the
prince's female household:

> [T]he Grand Turk sent word that the elder Lady[100]—that is, the mother of
> Mustafa—should remain in Bursa with those maidens whom she required,
> and he had good provision made for her, that she might live there honor-
> ably. [He ordered] that the young girl [Mustafa's daughter Nergissah] and
> her mother and the rest of the maidens together with all others belonging to
> the court of his deceased son should come to Constantinople. . . . The
> women were lodged in the palace where the Grand Turk's other women and
> maidens stay, and after several days the maidens were married to courtiers
> and others. . . .[101]

Gülşah Khatun died in 1487, and was buried in Bursa in the tomb she had
built for herself near that of Mustafa. Jem's mother, Çiçek, shared her son's
exile, and died and was buried in Cairo; the prince's corpse, however, was
returned from Naples, where he died, and buried in the tomb of his elder
brother, Mustafa. Most of the concubines of Bayezid II settled in Bursa after
their sons were killed in the fierce war of succession in which Selim I emerged
victorious. For example, Bülbül Khatun, mother of Ahmed, the governor of
Amasya and Selim's principal rival, came to Bursa in 1513 when her son was
executed by Selim. She had already built and endowed a religious college in
Bursa, and now she built a tomb for Ahmed, in which she too was buried at
her death in 1515.[102]

The Iconography of Royal Tombs

The preoccupation of the mothers of princes with their own and particularly
their son's tombs is of more than incidental interest. The culture of tomb
building, the importance attached to visiting the tombs of the dead, and the
rituals connected with the latter are of pervasive significance in Islamic culture. Just as the grace and blessing of holy men and women were sought

through the rituals of visiting and worshipping at their tombs, so was the intercession of members of the Ottoman dynasty sought by their subjects. Visiting royal tombs appears to have been regarded not only as proper and requisite reverence for deceased rulers but also as a means of participating in the aura of devotion to Islam, for there was a powerful charisma associated with the sultan's role as supreme *ghazi* and upholder of the faith.[103] Indeed, the tomb personas of the early Ottomans seem to have combined both the holy man and the *ghazi* hero: for example, tradition held that on the spot where Osman's brother Saru Yatı was killed in battle, a great pine tree grew, from which blazing light would emanate from time to time.[104]

The fact that the tombs of members of the dynasty were major objects of pilgrimage and worship meant that decisions about the location and size of a tomb and particularly about who would be permitted to rest permanently beside its principal occupant were significant political statements. The changing burial pattern of the mothers of sultans and princes can thus contribute to our understanding of the changing outlines of Ottoman reproductive politics.

The concubine mothers of princes who did not attain the throne appear to have been responsible for constructing their own tombs. As we have seen, some of these women built tombs expressly for their sons, and were buried together with them. Ülkü Bates has shown that whereas royal women of the pre-Ottoman Seljuk dynasty of Anatolia primarily built tombs, Ottoman royal women turned to mosque complexes, monuments of a larger scale.[105] It may be that "defeated" concubines were encouraged to confine their endowments to tombs.

There was no fixed burial pattern for the mothers of sultans. Edebali's daughter, who predeceased her husband Osman, was buried with her father in Bilejik, perhaps because no thought had yet been given to an appropriate location for an imperial tomb. Mal Khatun, who outlived Osman, was buried in the family tomb that grew up around Osman's grave in Bursa; Osman's son Orhan and his wives Asporça and Nilüfer were also buried in this tomb.[106] The first two sultans' consorts were thus linked in death both with their husbands and with the dynastic family as a whole.

However, beginning with the reign of Murad I (and thus with the probable inception of reproduction through concubinage in the royal house) and through the reign of Süleyman, the sultans did not share their tombs with their consorts. The sultans either rested alone in their tombs or were accompanied by family members who might be their siblings, children, grandchildren, nieces or nephews. The mother of sultans rested in their own tombs, of which they were the principal occupants. However, there is change, no doubt of symbolic significance, in the location of these women's tombs, which were generally built by their sons. The tombs of the two royal mothers following Nilüfer—Gülçiçek and Devlet—stood alone in Bursa neighborhoods separate from the mosque complexes that contained the tombs of the sultans and other members of the dynasty.[107] Starting with Mehmed the Conqueror, however, the tomb of the sultan's mother not only stood within the mosque complex belonging to his father, but gradually came to assume a greater prominence within the complex. Mehmed's mother, Hüma, occupies a tomb that stands at some distance from that of Murad II but still within the lovely Muradiye mosque and tomb complex in Bursa. The mothers of succeeding sultans, however, rest in the only other tomb in addition to that of their master to be located in the latter's complex: Gülbahar, consort of Mehmed the Conqueror and mother of Bayezid II, rests beside Mehmed's tomb; Hafsa, mother of Süleyman, beside Selim I's tomb; and Hurrem, mother of Selim II, beside Süleyman's tomb.[108]

Thus, while the separate tombs of Gülçiçek and Devlet, probably the first royal concubine mothers, symbolically disassociated them from the imperial family, by the end of the fifteenth century the concubine mother of a sultan was distinguished through her visibly special tomb status and reassociated in death with the father of her son. This shift undoubtedly reflects the greater status members of the slave institution began to acquire under Mehmed. There may have been a disinclination to incorporate concubines in the royal family through the highly visible structures of funerary architecture while the sultans were still making formal marital alliances with other sovereign houses. But with the lapse of formal marriage, the field was cleared for royal concubines to assume greater public stature.

Sexuality and Power in the Princely Household

The establishment of a princely household signified the political maturity and the onset of the public political career of both the Ottoman prince and his mother. While she was presumably no longer the sultan's sexual partner after her son's birth, a concubine remained within the sultanic household during the prince's childhood. With the dispatch of the prince to his provincial post, there came into being a new household shared by son and mother, subordinate to but separate from the sultanic household. The concubine's identity was then clearly articulated as that of "mother of the prince." The seal of Hüsnüşah Khatun, one of Bayezid II's consorts, identified her as the "Mother of Sultan Şehinşah"; it was with this seal that she signed the letter she wrote to inform the sultan of his son's death in 1511.[109]

Motherhood conferred no subordinate role. At Süleyman's court in Manisa, his mother, Hafsa Khatun, received a monthly stipend of 6,000 aspers, the highest stipend of anyone on the princely payroll and triple that of the prince himself.[110] This monetary differential was symbolic of the fact that the prince's mother was present in his court as a representative of the senior generation. The prince was not the sole representation of the junior generation, for present in this household was also Hafsa's daughter, Süleyman's presumably unmarried sister; the princess received a monthly stipend of 1,200 aspers.[111] It was the prince's mother, as the elder member of the household, who enjoyed the privilege of adorning the provincial capital: until the late sixteenth century, when Murad III built a mosque complex in Manisa, the city's two most prominent mosque complexes were those built by Hüsnüşah Khatun and Hafsa Khatun (Figure 2-1).

Figure 2-1 View of Manisa in the late sixteenth century. In the center is the princely palace. The mosque of Hüsnüşah Khatun lies just above, while the mosque of Hafsa Khatun, with two minarets and an outdoor prayer courtyard, lies slightly below the larger mosque of Murad III in the upper right. From Talikizade, *Şahname-i Al-i Osman*, fs. 10b–11a. *(Courtesy of Topkapı Palace Museum Library, Istanbul)*

By the late fifteenth century, when the age of the prince's departure from the imperial household had risen to sixteen or so, the prince's assumption of his political career also signaled the onset of his reproductive career. Grooming her son's partners and ensuring the success of this aspect of his career was one of the concubine mother's roles as senior member of the domestic household. The prince's political/reproductive maturation initiated a change not only in his mother's role—to the onset of her public political career—but in one of his father's roles as well. From the reign of Mehmed the Conqueror on, and perhaps earlier, the sultan's reproductive function ceased when that of his sons began. Whereas earlier sultans tended to continue producing offspring even after their first sons were well grown, Mehmed and his descendents ceased fathering children after a healthy number of sons had survived childhood and could themselves assume the function of reproducing the dynasty.

An interesting aspect of the dynasty's monitoring of the outflow of power through princes in that is was accomplished by slaves of the sultan. *Lalas* were usually drawn from the governing slave elite. Just as the concubine mother educated and restrained the prince, the *lala* was a kind of stand-in for the sultan, performing as he did the paternal function of both training and controlling the prince in his political activities. Even when he became sultan, the prince would treat both his mother and his *lala* with filial respect; new sultans not infrequently appointed their tutors to the vezirate if they remained on good terms (upon his accession Süleyman made his tutor Kasım Pasha the fourth vezir).

There was precedent for the important role of the royal concubine as elder in a household separate from that of the ruler. It resembled in some ways the Mongol *ordu,* the separate camp or household maintained by each of the khan's wives, vividly described by Ibn Battuta in his visit to the Uzbek khan of the Crimea.[112] A crucial difference, however, is that the principal identity of the head of the *ordu* was clearly that of wife, not mother. Much struck by the power of wives in the Turkish and Mongol states he visited, Ibn Battuta commented, "Among the Turks and the Tatars [Mongols] their wives enjoy a very high position; indeed, when they issue an order they say in it 'By command of the Sultan and the Khatun.' "[113] The wife of Orhan who was in charge in Iznik when Ibn Battuta was making his way through Anatolia in the 1330s exercised some degree of sovereign power. However, the Ottomans quickly moved away from this Turco-Mongol pattern to limit the authority of both wives and sons. Slave concubinage was a key instrument in this process.

A closer parallel was the atabegate in the powerful medieval Turkish dynasty of the Seljuks, centered in Iran. The *atabeg* (Turkish for "father-governor")[114] was the Seljuk predecessor of the *lala;* in fact, the Ottomans sometimes used the two terms interchangeably. The contrast between the development of the Seljuk and the Ottoman atabegates can help us to better understand key features of Ottoman management of sovereign power. A crucial difference is that the sexuality of the Seljuk sultan's wife was not subordinated to her motherhood and truncated when her son left the paternal household: while no longer the sultan's consort, the prince's mother might marry his *atabeg.*[115] Increasingly, *atabeg*s were able to arrogate power to themselves and undermine the effective control of the sultan; indeed, the rise of *atabeg* breakaway states was a principal cause of Seljuk collapse. The household based on the relationship of *atabeg,* prince, and prince's mother might thus serve as the nucleus of a new state, with the *atabeg* deriving legitimation not only from the presence of a prince of the blood but also from the sexuality of his mother. The prince's role was the largely passive one of serving as the reason for the formation of the household, and, in the case of the Eldigüzid dynasty (a minor successor to the Seljuks), it was the children of the prince's mother by the *atabeg* who succeeded to the rule in the new state, not the Seljuk prince himself.[116] The most dramatic example of the sexuality of a royal consort as a channel of legitimation, indeed of sovereign power, was the career of the manumitted concubine Shajar al-Durr, in which the Mamluk sultanate had its birth. Shajar al-Durr briefly held the throne after the death of her Ayyubid sultan husband and his son by another woman; she was replaced as sovereign when she married one of her husband's slaves, who became the first Mamluk ("slave") ruler.[117] The Ottoman sultans were never troubled by this political constellation not only because they were able to keep tighter rein on their *lala*-administrators but also because they sealed off the sexuality of their consorts.

The consorts of the Ottoman sultans were, from the dynasty's point of view, safe political actors because their only claim to power was their motherhood. They could achieve political security only by working through their sons. The disassocation of concubine mothers from the sultan and their identification with their sons were virtually total. Once a concubine had given birth to a son, her life was devoted to ensuring the success of his, because her fate was linked to his.[118] Known officially as the "mother of the prince," she was in a sense nameless. Even in death she might not part from her son. Only the accession of her son would reassociate her with her master, and then only in death.

The Last Concubine of the Provinces: Mahidevran Khatun

This chapter concludes with a brief sketch of Mahidevran Khatun, a concubine of Süleyman the Magnificent, and mother of Mustafa, his oldest son to survive childhood. Mahidevran (Moon of Fortune) was the last royal concubine whose career fit the model described above. She is of particular interest because, in the contest with her fellow concubine Hurrem, she lost. The "sultanate of the women" begins with Hurrem, and the discontinuities between her career and that of Mahidevran are instructive.

A slave concubine of disputed origin—possibly Albanian or Circassian—Mahidevran appears among the seventeen women of the harem listed in an undated register of Süleyman's princely household at Manisa. On the basis of stipend, three women ranked above her at 5 aspers a day, while two others shared her stipend level of 4 aspers.[119] In 1515, when Mahidevran's son Mustafa was born, her status within the harem presumably rose. When in 1521 Süleyman, now sultan, lost his two other sons, nine-year-old Mahmud and the toddler Murad, Mustafa became the eldest of his princely generation. In the same year Hurrem's son Mehmed was born.

Foreign observers of the Ottomans, especially the ambassadors of the Venetian Republic, followed Ottoman dynastic politics closely. Their comments about Mahidevran provide us with glimpses of the vital role played by a prince's mother and of her necessary devotion to his welfare. Pietro Bragadin, ambassador in the early years of Süleyman's reign, reported that while both were still resident in the imperial palace in Istanbul, Mustafa was his mother's "whole joy."[120] Mustafa was sent out to his princely post at Manisa in 1533, in the formal ceremony described above. Describing his court at Kara Amid (Diyarbakır) near the Safavid border, Bassano wrote around 1540 that the prince had "a most wonderful and glorious court, no less than that of his father" and that "his mother, who is with him, instructs him in how to make himself loved by the people."[121] At some point Mustafa returned to Manisa, and in 1542 he moved to Amasya. By 1546 three more of Süleyman's sons were in the field, and the competition for the succession began among the four princes, although the sultan would live for another twenty years. The ambassador Bernardo Navagero, in a 1553 report, described Mahidevran's efforts to protect her son: "[Mustafa] has with him his mother, who exercises great diligence to guard him from poisoning and reminds him every day that he has nothing else but this to avoid, and it is said that he has boundless respect and reverence for her."[122]

Mustafa was an immensely popular prince. When he was only nine, the Venetian ambassador had reported that "he has extraordinary talent, he will be a warrior, is much loved by the Janissaries, and performs great feats."[123] In 1553, when Mustafa was thirty-eight years old, Navagero wrote, "It is impossible to describe how much he is loved and desired by all as successor to the throne." But the prince was executed that very year on charges of planning to dethrone his father; his guilt for the treason of which he was accused has since been neither proven nor disproven. Up until the very end of her son's life, Mahidevran endeavored to protect Mustafa from his political rivals, and most probably maintained a network of informants in order to do so. The ambassador Trevisano related in 1554 that on the day Mustafa was executed, Mahidevran had sent a messenger warning him of his father's plans to kill him. Mustafa unfortunately ignored the message; according to Trevisano, he had consistently refused to heed the warnings of his friends and even his mother.[124]

Mahidevran was the last concubine to retire to Bursa, where her son was buried. Less fortunate than her predecessors and presumably disgraced by her son's execution, she was unable to pay the rent on the house in which she lived, and her servants were taunted and cheated in the local markets. Mahidevran's situation improved toward the end of Süleyman's reign when her debts were paid at the sultan's order and a house was purchased for her, possibly by Süleyman's sole surviving son, Mustafa's half-brother Selim.[125] Her rehabilitation may have been possible only after the death in 1558 of her rival, Hurrem. Financially secure at last, Mahidevran had enough income to create an endowment for the upkeep of her son's tomb, which was built by Selim.[126] When she died in 1581, Mahidevran was buried in Mustafa's tomb.

3

The Age of the Favorite: 1520–1566

One of the first events of Süleyman's reign was the insurrection of Janberdi Ghazali. Janberdi had been a member of the Mamluk elite defeated by Selim I, Süleyman's father. In the words of an Ottoman historian, he was "one of those who escaped the sword" of the Ottoman conquest of the Mamluk Empire. As Selim marched back to Istanbul from Cairo, Janberdi made his submission and was rewarded with the governorship of Damascus, Jerusalem, and Ghaza. When the great conqueror died three years later in 1520, Janberdi apparently expected little from his son. "He became insubordinate and rebelled, thinking at the time of the royal accession that he had been delivered from the fear of the sword of Sultan Selim, but he was heedless of the might of the saber of Süleyman."[1] Janberdi soon lost his head to the sword of Ferhad Pasha, the commander dispatched by Süleyman to quell the uprising (the pasha was also the husband of Süleyman's sister, the princess Beyhan).

The ex-Mamluk governor may have underestimated Süleyman because the new sultan came to the throne unproven in battle. The sole heir of his father, Süleyman was the first Ottoman prince since his great-grandfather Mehmed the Conqueror to succede without undergoing armed combat. The new sultan, however, proved to be a *ghazi* in the tradition of his ancestors. Not only did he hold on to the vast lands conquered from the Mamluks but his army extended the borders of the empire to include Hungary in the west and Iraq in the east, and his navy added North Africa and the Yemen. While there were conquests after Süleyman's death, it was essentially he who carried the Ottoman Empire to its limits (see map on page xix). Süleyman was also the first Ottoman sultan to reign unquestionably as the strongest and most prestigious of Muslim monarchs.

The persistent memory of Süleyman's reign as the epitome of Ottoman glory was not the result of conquest alone, however, for it was also during his reign that the empire began to experience the political and social strains of its vast size. Süleyman was king in an age of kings. He was the contemporary of the Hapsburg emperor Charles V, reviver of the Holy Roman Empire, and of Francis I of France and Henry VIII of England, whose celebrated meeting on the Field of Cloth of Gold took place three months before his accession. In the east, Süleyman's contemporaries were the Safavid Ismail and the Mughal

Babur, conquerors and founders of two great Muslim empires. Known to his fellow monarchs in the west as "the Magnificent," Süleyman projected an image of splendor and power to an audience both European and Muslim. The Ottoman sultan was as deft as any of his royal peers at handling the politics of ceremonial monarchy—indeed, he had to be.[2]

If the sixteenth century was an age of kings, it was also an age of queens— among them Anne Boleyn, Margaret of Navarre, Elizabeth I, Catherine de Médicis, and Mary Queen of Scots. The Ottomans too produced a "queen" in Hurrem Sultan, the favorite concubine of the sultan. The long reign of Süleyman appears in many ways to constitute a break with earlier traditions of reproductive politics. Perhaps the most radical development was the intimate and intense bond between the sultan and his favorite, the *haseki,* whom he raised to a position of great prestige and influence. This new relationship, however, was at the same time a symptom of a more profound change within the dynasty.

Previously, dynastic politics had been decentralized and the dynastic family dispersed in a number of royal households. But under Süleyman the dynasty began to be centered increasingly in Istanbul, and as a result there emerged a number of new relationships and new constellations of power among members of the dynasty. Another development that paralleled the emergence of the *haseki* in its importance was the growing prestige of the husbands of Ottoman princesses. The process of accommodating these overlapping and interacting relationships to two already existing dynastic relationships of prime significance—that of the sultan and his sons and that of the prince and his mother—lasted well beyond Süleyman's lifetime and had the effect of profoundly altering the political landscape. Süleyman's own reign contained a surfeit of dynastic drama, indeed of tragedy on a Shakespearean scale. It raised many of the issues of monarchy, family, and power, of loyalty and betrayal, that preoccupied his European contemporaries.

The Concubine as Favorite

Hurrem's career as royal consort, from the birth of her first child in 1521 until her death in 1558, spanned nearly all of Süleyman's reign. It broke with the three principal features of earlier tradition: the concubine status of royal mothers, the reproductive principle of one mother-one son, and the presence of a prince's mother at her son's provincial post. Unable to comprehend these unprecedented changes, the public found a solution in blaming Hurrem for bewitching the sultan.

Exactly when Hurrem joined Süleyman's harem is not known, but she probably became his concubine just before or during the first year of his sultanate (Süleyman was a month short of his twenty-sixth birthday when he became sultan in September 1520). It is possible that she was presented to the sultan as a gift on the occasion of his accession. Hurrem was probably from the western Ukraine, then a part of Poland. According to Polish tradition, she was named Aleksandra Lisowska, and was the daughter of a Ruthenian priest, captured by

Tatar raiders from the town of Rogatin, on the Dniester near Lvov. Hurrem's name in Turkish means "joyful," but she was known to Europeans as Roxelana, perhaps from a Polish term meaning "Ruthenian maiden."[3]

Hurrem and Süleyman's first child, Mehmed, was born in 1521. At some point within the next few years, the sultan foreswore all other sexual partners. Before devoting himself exclusively to Hurrem, Süleyman had followed the precedent of his ancestors and taken a number of concubines. The Venetian ambassador Minio noted that the young sultan was "very lustful" and that he went frequently to "the palace of the women."[4] But in 1524, by which time Süleyman and Hurrem had had four children, the ambassador Zen could comment that "the Seigneur is not lustful" and that he remained constant to one woman.[5] In 1526 the ambassador Bragadin stated that the sultan no longer paid any attention to the mother of his eldest son (Mahidevran), but concentrated all his affection on Hurrem, whom the ambassador described as "young but not beautiful, although graceful and petite."[6] According to Luigi Bassano, Süleyman ignored the past custom of the sultans and did not take a succession of concubines; rather, to preserve his faithfulness to Hurrem, he married off as virgins nearly all the eligible concubines in his harem.[7]

Süleyman's willingness to put aside custom for the sake of this young concubine is underlined by a dramatic incident related by Bragadin:

> The sultan was given by a *sanjak bey* [provincial governor] two beautiful Russian maidens, one for his mother and one for him. When they arrived in the palace, his second wife [Hurrem], whom he esteems at present, became extremely unhappy and flung herself to the ground weeping. The mother, who had given her maiden to the sultan, was sorry about what she had done, took her back, and sent her to a *sanjak bey* as wife, and the sultan agreed to send his to another *sanjak bey,* because his wife would have perished from sorrow if these maidens—or even one of them—had remained in the palace.[8]

In his 1553 report, the ambassador Bernardo Navagero recounted another dramatic event as an explantion of how Hurrem had won the affection of the sultan. The incident, if accurately related, reveals the young concubine's ability to manipulate the protocol of the harem to her advantage:

> This sultan has two highly cherished women: one a Circassian, the mother of Mustafa the firstborn, the other, whom in violation of the custom of his ancestors he has married and considers as wife, a Russian, so loved by his majesty that there has never been in the Ottoman house a woman who enjoyed greater authority. It is said that she is agreeable and modest, and that she knows the nature of the sultan very well. The way in which she entered into the favor of the sultan I understand to have been the following. The Circassian, naturally proud and beautiful, and who already had a son, Mustafa, understood that [Hurrem] had pleased the sultan, wherefore she insulted her, and as she was doing so she scratched her all over her face and mussed up her clothing, saying, "Traitor, sold meat,[9] you want to compete with me?" It happened that a few days later the sultan had this Russian summoned for his pleasure. She did not let this opportunity pass, and angrily told the eunuch agha who had come to fetch her that she was not worthy to

come into the presence of the sultan because, being sold meat and with her face so spoiled and some of her hair pulled out, she recognized that she would offend the majesty of such a sultan by coming before him. These words were related to the sultan and induced in him an even greater desire to have her come to him, and he commanded again that she come. He wanted to understand why she would not come and why she had sent him such a message. The woman related to him what had happened with Mustafa's mother, accompanying her words with tears and showing the sultan her face, which still bore the scratches, and how her hair had been pulled out. The angry sultan sent for the Circassian and asked her if what the other woman had said was true. She responded that it was, and that she had done less to her than she deserved. She believed that all the women should yield to her and recognize her as mistress since she had been in the service of his majesty first. These words inflamed the sultan even more, for the reason that he no longer wanted her, and all his love was given to this other. . . .[10]

The accounts of the Venetian ambassadors, the most abundant source we have for the lives of Ottoman royal women, consist of information at best received directly from well-placed informants, at worst second- or thirdhand and embellished by rumor. Each ambassadorial report devotes several pages to an account of the dynastic family and its members; the purpose of this scrutiny was not only to monitor shifts in the power structure of the dynasty but also to identify members who might be favorable to Venetian interests.[11] It seems safe, therefore, to assume that the fundamental elements of these accounts, and possibly the details, are accurate. We may conclude that Süleyman was deeply devoted to Hurrem, that very early in her career she felt secure enough in his esteem to exert her will, and that the sultan was willing to bend protocol to preserve his relationship with her. It is also noteworthy that Süleyman's mother—custodian of the sultan's conduct—did not or perhaps could not act to prevent this unprecedented relationship.

The death in 1521 of two of Süleyman's three sons,[12] leaving alive only one male child, the six-year-old Mustafa, made it imperative that Süleyman produce more sons quickly. In his 1522 report, Minio commented that that empire would be in great confusion should Süleyman happen to die leaving only infant heirs.[13] Given the grave risks of infant and child mortality, this urgent need for heirs may explain in part the sultan's willingness to allow his new favorite to bear more than one child. Hurrem's ability to produce healthy sons certainly must have pleased the sultan, his mother, and others interested in the perpetuation of the dynasty. Although we lack precise dates for the births of Süleyman's children, it is clear that his first five children by Hurrem were born in rapid succession: Mehmed in 1521 (H. 927), Mihrimah—Süleyman's only surviving daughter—in 1522 (928),[14] Abdullah—who died three years after his birth—in 1522 (929), Selim in 1524 (930), and Bayezid in 1525 (931). In 1531 Hurrem gave birth to her last child, Jihangir, a hunchback. Süleyman was thirty-seven when Jihangir was born. By then he had five sons, the eldest of whom was sixteen and in two years would leave the imperial household to take up his provincial post, at which time he would also begin to produce offspring. With the coming of age of the next generation, Süleyman had completed the reproductive requirements of the sultanate.

Hurrem did not accompany her oldest son Mehmed when he was sent out to be governor of Manisa in 1542. Nor, after Mehmed's death a year later, did she accompany any of her other sons at a point when the youth of Jihangir was no longer a reason to prevent her from doing so. A Manisa register indicates that Hurrem did, however, make several trips to visit her sons in the provinces. In 1543 she visited Mehmed in Manisa and Selim in Konya. In 1544 she traveled to Bursa together with her daughter Mihrimah and son-in-law Rüstem Pasha and a large military escort; Selim was summoned there for a family reunion, which lasted forty days. In March 1547 Hurrem and Jihangir spent a month in Manisa, visiting Selim, who had been transferred there after Mehmed's death.[15] Presumably Hurrem went as well to visit Bayezid in his posts in Kütahya and Amasya; in a letter to Süleyman in 1553, she explains that she has had to cancel plans to visit the prince.[16]

Hurrem was the first mother of a prince since at least the mid-fifteenth century who remained behind in the capital. Süleyman's mother, Hafsa Sultan, had accompanied him to his princely posts first in Kefe and then in Manisa. Mahidevran Khatun, the mother of Mustafa, who was six years older than Mehmed, left Süleyman's harem when she accompanied her son upon his appointment in 1533 to Manisa (the assertion that Mahidevran was "exiled" from the palace to her son's provincial posts is incorrect;[17] what was unusual was not Mahidevran's absence from the imperial palace but Hurrem's presence there). Possibly Hurrem's presence in the capital was related to Jihangir's health problems. Jihangir did not receive a provincial governorate because his infirmity was seen as a disqualification for rulership[18] and perhaps also because of his need for medical treatment. In one of her letters to the sultan while he was on military campaign, Hurrem wrote of the success of an operation performed on the child's shoulder.[19] Even if compelling circumstances contributed to Hurrem's failure to follow this aspect of the concubinal career, it was nevertheless an inevitable corollary of the abandonment of the one mother-one son principle: whichever son Hurrem might have accompanied would have been advantaged over the others in the contest for the succession, which inevitably began well before the natural death of the sultan might be anticipated.

Süleyman's final breach of earlier tradition was to marry Hurrem, thus rendering her the first slave concubine in Ottoman history to be freed and made a legal wife.[20] While there were no legal barriers against the marriage, the weight of custom militated against it; custom often had the force of law in Ottoman society (the word for law, *kanun,* also meant tradition or custom). The lavish wedding festivities were described by the representative of the Genoese Bank of St. George in an undated letter:

> This week there has occurred in this city a most extraordinary event, one absolutely unprecedented in the history of the Sultans. The Grand Signior Suleiman has taken to himself as his Empress a slave-woman from Russia,

called Roxalana, and there has been great feasting. The ceremony took place in the Seraglio, and the festivities have been splendid beyond all record. There was a public procession of the presents. At night the principal streets are gaily illuminated, and there is much music and feasting. The houses are festooned with garlands and there are everywhere swings in which people swing by the hour with great enjoyment. In the old Hippodrome a great tribune is set up, the place reserved for the Empress and her ladies screened with a gilt lattice. Here Roxalana and the Court attended a great tournament in which both Christian and Moslem Knights were engaged, and tumblers and jugglers and a procession of wild beasts, and giraffes with necks so long they as it were touched the sky. . . . There is great talk about the marriage and none can say what it means.[21]

According to the ambassador of the Holy Roman Empire, Ogier Ghiselin de Busbecq, or rather according to what his sources told him, the marriage was an example of Hurrem's control of the sultan's emotions. Mistakenly believing that a concubine was freed upon the birth of a son, Busbecq stated: "Advantage was taken of this privilege by Roxolana, Soleiman's wife, when she had borne him a son while she was still a slave. Having thus obtained her freedom and become her own mistress, she refused to have anything more to do with Soleiman, who was deeply in love with her, unless he made her his lawful wife, thus violating the custom of the Ottoman Sultans."[22]

Just when this marriage occurred is not certain. It must have taken place in or before June 1534, when it was alluded to by the Venetian ambassador Daniello De'Ludovici.[23] It would seem probable that it took place only after the departure of Mahidevran and her son Mustafa from Istanbul in 1533, which removed from the harem Hurrem's most serious rival. It has been suggested that the marriage could not have occurred before the death in March 1534 of Süleyman's mother, Hafsa Sultan, one of the very few people who might have dissuaded the sultan from this unprecedented alliance.[24] However, the sultan would have been unlikely to publicly celebrate such an event during the period of mourning for his mother, and in June 1534 he departed on the great "campaign for the two Iraqs," not to return to the capital until January 1536. Moreover, we cannot automatically assume that Hafsa Sultan would have been opposed to the marriage.

Hurrem broke precedent again when she moved from the residence for royal women and children into the palace of the sultan. This move may have been related to her marriage, since De'Ludovici reported in 1534 that she and her children were living with the sultan in his palace.[25] Bassano's description of Hurrem's quarters in the New Palace, dating from the late 1530s, suggests that she was well settled by that time: "The palace of the Sultana is in that of the Grand Turk, and one can go through secret rooms from the one to the other. . . . The chambers of the Sultana are very splendid, with chapels, baths, gardens, and other amenities, not only for herself, but for her maids as well, of which she keeps as many as one hundred. . . ."[26] However, privy purse registers from the late 1550s indicate that Hurrem was resident in the Old Palace.[27] This may be an artifact of record keeping whereby the entire harem continued to be listed as resident in the Old Palace even though part of it was living in the New Palace. It may also have been because of Hurrem's ill health in the final years of her life (she died in 1558) and the presence of a hospital for women in the Old Palace.[28] According to Venetian reports, in her last years Hurrem was unwilling to let Süleyman part from her because of her constant fear of death.[29]

While contracting a legal marriage with a concubine was a radical break with past tradition, indeed a unique event, the more significant innovation of Süleyman's reign—because it underlay all other changes—was the continued ascendancy of one woman. Hurrem's title—*haseki*, the sultan's favorite—broadcast her unique status. The public was troubled by this persistent attachment of the monarch to one woman, which it considered unnatural and harmful. Describing her unpopularity, Bassano wrote:

> [S]uch love does [Süleyman] bear her that he has so astonished all his subjects that they say she has bewitched him; therefore they call her *Ziadi*, which means witch. For this reason the Janissaries and the entire court hate her and her children likewise, but because the sultan loves her, no one dares to speak. I have always heard every one speak ill of her and of her children, and well of the first-born and his mother, who has been repudiated.[30]

Confirming this view, Busbecq noted nearly twenty years later that Hurrem was "commonly reputed to retain [Süleyman's] affection by love-charms and magic arts. . . ."[31]

The Sultan's Counselor

With the favorite lodged in the capital, a new political relationship came into being: Hurrem acted as political confidante to the sultan. The letters she wrote to Süleyman when he was absent from Istanbul on military campaigns show that she was a valuable source of information.[32] In this she may have taken over a role that Hafsa Sultan had performed for her son. Süleyman was said to have been devoted to his mother. According to Bragadin's report of 1526, Hafsa was "a very beautiful woman of 48, for whom [the sultan] bears great reverence and love."[33] When, after the Ottoman defeat of Hungary at the battle of Mohacs, victory letters were dispatched to all corners of the empire, Süleyman took care to write the news to his mother personally.[34] When she died in 1534, Hafsa Sultan's funeral was the occasion for great public displays of mourning.[35]

However, in the early years of his sultanate, Süleyman may not have been able to rely on Hurrem, since her Turkish—at least her ability to read and write—was weak. In an early letter she wrote, "My sultan, you wrote that if I were able to read what you write, you would write at greater length of your longing for me."[36] Hurrem's early letters are written in high chancery style and in an elegant hand, most likely by a harem scribe. However, personal notes in less stilted Turkish are appended in which Hurrem told of her great longing for the absent sultan and of how he was missed by the children:

> My sultan, there is no limit to the burning anguish of separation. Now spare this miserable one and do not withhold your noble letters. Let my soul gain at least some comfort from a letter. . . . When your noble letters are read, your servant and son Mir Mehmed and your slave and daughter Mihrimah weep and wail from missing you. Their weeping has driven me mad, it is as if we were in mourning. My sultan, your son Mir Mehmed and your daughter Mihrimah and Selim Khan and Abdullah send you many greetings and rub their faces in the dust at your feet.[37]

In one scribe-authored letter, a postscript written by another resident of the harem supplies the sultan with information he had apparently requested from her about the state of Hurrem's finances, suggesting that Hurrem may not at that point have been able to manage her affairs herself.[38] Yet even in these early letters we observe Hurrem as a political actor: in one letter she alludes to a problem with the grand vezir İbrahim Pasha, which she has clearly mentioned before: "You asked why I am angry at the Pasha. God willing, when we are able to be together again, you will hear. For now, we send our regards to the Pasha—may he accept them."[39]

By the mid-1530s, however, if not earlier, Hurrem was writing her own letters to the sultan. The bulk of each of these letters, like the earlier ones, is taken up with expressions of Hurrem's longing for the sultan and hope that God will protect him, as well as news of the family and greetings from them. In one letter, probably written while Süleyman was absent on the eastern campaign of 1534–1535, she welcomes news of the Ottoman victory: "The good news of the conquest has arrived. My emperor, my sultan, God knows that I have died and was granted new life. Thousands upon thousands of thanks to the Lord God the Almighty! . . . My shah, my sultan, may you undertake many *ghazas,* give the enemy their due, take many lands, and conquer the seven climes!"[40]

The letters also communicate information about important events and the situation in the capital (of vital interest to any absent sultan, who feared that one of his sons might be enthroned in his place). During the eastern campaign Hurrem sent news of the admiral Barbaros Hayreddin Pasha's victorious Tunisian naval campaign.[41] During Süleyman's absence in 1537 she informed him that an epidemic illness was still affecting Istanbul, but not as severely as before, and that knowledgeable people agreed that it would end "when the autumn leaves fell." She went on to warn him of the dangerous consequences of poor communication from the front: "I ask you, I beg you, to send news quickly, very quickly, because—and I swear I am not lying—no messenger has come for the last week or two. The whole world is clamoring, all kinds of rumors are circulating. Don't think that it is just for myself that I am asking."[42] Roughly twenty years later, a similar concern about false rumor, now voiced more confidently and firmly, was expressed in a letter Hurrem wrote while Süleyman was in the midst of a campaign against the Safavids in the winter of 1553–1554. Hurrem's sense of urgency was probably caused by popular discontent over the recent execution of Mustafa:

There is great talk in the city that a messenger bearing good news is coming. Everyone is saying that he'll be here in two or three days, and they're getting ready to decorate the city with lights. I don't know if it is rumor or if it is true. Now my fortune-favored, my sultan, it is very odd that a good-news messenger should come when you yourself are wintering in Aleppo. Furthermore, my sultan, neither the son of the heretic [the Safavid shah] nor his wife has been captured, nothing has been happening. Now if a messenger arrives saying "No progress here, nothing there," no one is going to be happy, my sultan. . . . I was going to visit Bayezid soon[43] but now I'm not going to go until news comes from you.[44]

With the grand vezir and other important statesmen accompanying the sultan on campaign, Hurrem undoubtedly performed a crucial role through her vigilance over affairs in the capital. That the sultan asked her to forward letters to other members of the family suggests that she also functioned as a secure communications link.[45] After Hurrem's death, Mihrimah took her mother's place as her father's counselor, urging him to undertake the conquest of Malta and sending him news and forwarding letters for him when he was absent from the capital.[46]

The Age of the *Damad*

Hurrem and Mihrimah were not the only family members who acted as intimate and trusted advisers of the sultan. A standard feature of Süleyman's reign was the grand vezir who was at the same time royal *damad*, the husband of a princess and son- or brother-in-law of the sultan.[47] The vezirate was the highest military/administrative rank of the empire; during Süleyman's reign the number of vezirs varied between three and four, including the grand vezir, the "absolute deputy" of the sultan. Thus the highest ranking members of the male slave elite, which since the reign of Mehmed the Conqueror had been the military and administrative mainstay of the dynasty, now joined female slaves in assuming intimate roles within the dynastic family. Making an official an imperial *damad* was a means by which the sultan could bestow special favor on one of his slaves. Furthermore, in addition to enhancing the status and authority of the official, *damad*hood created a strong bond of personal loyalty and indebtedness to the sultan and to the whole dynastic family. Three of Süleyman's *damad* grand vezirs—İbrahim, Rüstem, and Sokollu Mehmed— were perhaps his most trusted personal associates.

The Ottoman bureaucrat and writer Mustafa Ali, whose late-sixteenth-century history is one of the principal sources for Süleyman's reign, attributed to Süleyman the policy of marrying princesses to statesmen of vezirial rank. Koçi Bey, political adviser to two seventeenth-century sultans, repeated this attribution.[48] But in fact this practice had its first beginnings under Süleyman's grandfather, Bayezid II (r. 1485–1512), and became the norm under his father Selim I (r. 1512–1520).[49] There was, however, under Süleyman a notable development in the politics of princess marriages: it became standard practice to link the most powerful statesman of all—the grand vezir—to the dynastic household through marriage to a princess.

Until the mid-fifteenth century or so, princesses had married rulers and princes of neighboring Muslim states or members of the Ottoman ruling class. They ceased to make interdynastic alliances around the same time that their fathers and brothers did. As for their alliances with the Ottoman ruling class, the scantiness of information on princesses' husbands before the reign of Bayezid II makes it impossible to tell if there was a preference for choosing *damad*s from the slave elite or from prominent native Turkish families.[50] From the late fifteenth century on, however, princesses made marriages exclusively with members of the slave institution or their sons, and occasionally with cousins.[51] This change under Bayezid (if indeed it was a change) probably reflected, at least initially, not so much his own decisions as those of his father, Mehmed the Conqueror, since Bayezid's daughters began to be given in marriage during his father's lifetime. The preference for avoiding marriages with native Turkish members of the ruling class was certainly consonant with Mehmed's policies of undermining their power by governing almost exclusively through the slave elite.

With very few exceptions, Bayezid's many *damad*s did not rise to the rank of vezir.[52] Selim I's *damad*s, however, tended to be statesmen who already were or who became vezirs.[53] What most likely misled Mustafa Ali and Koçi Bey into attributing the policy of vezir-princess marriages to Süleyman was the fact that he not only continued his father's practice but drew his *grand* vezirs wherever possible from among his *damad*s. Even this latter practice, however, was not without some precedent. Only one of Bayezid's seven grand vezirs—Hersekzade Ahmed, who held the post three times under Bayezid and twice under Selim—had been *damad;* married to the princess Hundi, he most likely owed this honor to the fact that he was a convert from a princely house.[54] But three of Selim's six grand vezirs were *damad*s: Hersekzade Ahmed, Dukakinzade Ahmed (like Hersekzade, a convert from a princely house), and Yunus. However, Dukakinzade Ahmed and Yunus were less directly tied to the dynasty than was Hersekzade Ahmed since they were married not to a daughter of the sultan but to daughters of princesses and their *damad* husbands.[55] The remainder of Bayezid and Selim's grand vezirs (except the four who were theoretically ineligible for *damad*hood—eunuchs or members of the native Turkish elite)[56] enjoyed a different kind of weak link to the dynasty: while not themselves *damad*s, their sons were married to princesses or princesses' daughters.[57]

Süleyman made the *damad* grand vezir a standard feature of his reign. Three of his grand vezirs—İbrahim, Lutfi, and Kara Ahmed—were married to his sisters Hadije, Şah, and Fatma.[58] Rüstem, the grand vezir who dominated the second half of Süleyman's reign, was honored with the hand of Mihrimah, the sultan's only daughter to survive infancy. Süleyman's last two grand vezirs were married to two of his granddaughters: Semiz Ali to Hümaşah Ayşe, daughter of Mihrimah and Rüstem, and Sokollu Mehmed to İsmihan, daughter of the prince Selim. Of Süleyman's nine grand vezirs, only three were not *damad*s: Piri Mehmed, inherited from the previous reign, was both elderly and of Turkish origin; Ayas, also inherited, was notorious for his sexual appetite and possessed an inappropriately large harem;[59] and Hadım Süleyman was a eunuch.

The pool of *damad* vezirs was replenished through marriages made at the three generational levels available to the dynasty: the sultan's sisters, daughters, and granddaughters. The pattern of marriages contracted during Süleyman's reign for his granddaughters is instructive. The available evidence, or rather the conspicuous lack of evidence, suggests that the daughters of Süleyman's two sons who died in disgrace, Mustafa and Bayezid, were not married to favored statesmen. In contrast, strong alliances were made for the daughters of Selim, the prince who would succeed Süleyman: İsmihan married Sokollu Mehmed, Gevherhan the admiral Piyale, and Şah the chief falconer Hasan Agha; all three *damad*s were or would become vezirs. However, these marriages did not take place until 1562,[60] the year after Selim's only remaining brother, Bayezid, was executed for insurrection, when it became clear that Selim would succeed his father. The sultan obviously did not wish to create for his sons strong alliances that might be turned against him by a prince impatient to rule and/or anxious to eliminate his brothers. On the other hand, the swiftness with which a set of *damad* alliances was put into place for Selim suggests that the aging Süleyman was building a secure political base for his heir. A good marriage was also arranged for Hüma, the only daughter of Süleyman and Hurrem's much loved son Mehmed, who died prematurely of natural causes the year after he took up his provincial governorate; in the year of her grandfather's death, Hüma married Ferhad Pasha, the third vezir.[61]

The nexus of power created through princess-vezir alliances was reinforced by the fact that a princess might make more than one match during her lifetime. Married young, she was likely to survive at least one husband and possibly more. Her spouse, who was often considerably older than she, ran the risk of death from several quarters—in battle, by political execution, or through natural cause—and the risk of career-crippling divorce should he offend his royal wife. A princess's remarriage was an attractive option for all involved, and there is evidence from the late fifteenth century on that remarriage was a common occurrence. Süleyman's grand vezirs İbrahim and Kara Ahmed were probably the second husbands of their royal wives, Hadije and Fatma.[62] However, some widowed or divorced princesses, for example, Süleyman's sister Şah and his daughter Mihrimah, chose not to marry again, returning instead to the royal palace, where it was customary for a princess to reside after the dissolution of her marriage. On a rare occasion, a princess's loyalty to her husband surpassed her loyalty to her family: Süleyman's sister Beyhan, wife of the vezir Ferhad Pasha who had quelled the rebellion of Janberdi, was alienated from her brother after Ferhad's execution in 1524 and, refusing to remarry, lived in self-exile from Istanbul.[63] Ferhad was executed on the grounds of rapacious and ruthless conduct in the provinces to which he was assigned. Through the intercession of Beyhan and Süleyman's mother, Ferhad had been pardoned after his first offenses, but when he continued to provoke complaints from his constituents, the sultan ordered him executed.

The significance of the *damad*-princess alliances of Süleyman's reign was signaled by the lavish weddings through which they were accomplished. The celebration of the marriage of İbrahim and Hadije in 1524, which lasted fifteen days, was unprecedented in its splendor. According to the historian Peçevi, "spread before the eyes was such abundance and merriment as had never before been observed at the wedding of a princess."[64] The ceremony took place at the Hippodrome (*At Meydanı*), the traditional site of imperial weddings, and was graced by the sultan's presence.[65] Mihrimah's marriage to Rüstem took place at the same time as the circumcision ceremony of her brothers Bayezid and Jihangir, the collective festivities also lasting fifteen days.[66] In 1562 Süleyman celebrated the triple wedding of his heir Selim's daughters İsmihan, Gevherhan, and Şah to Sokollu Mehmed Pasha, Piyale Pasha, and Hasan Agha. Presumably unable to cover the huge expenses necessary for an appropriately lavish ceremony and suitable gifts, the three *damad*s were granted funds by the palace: Mehmed Pasha and Hasan Agha received fifteen thousand florins each and Piyale Pasha ten thousand, while their best men (*sağdiç*) received fifteen, thirteen, and twelve thousand florins, respectively. In addition, the brides received two thousand florins each, and a further twenty-five thousand florins were allocated to cover the palace's expenditure on the wedding.[67] That these weddings were not simply publicly celebrated affairs of private consequence but also of consequence for the conduct of government is suggested by the fact that the grooms' best men were among the highest ranking statesmen of the day: İbrahim Pasha's best man was the second vezir Ayas Pasha,[68] and the best men at the triple wedding of 1562 were the vezir Ferhad Pasha (husband of Hüma), an unnamed governor-general, and the master of the stable, a leading official in the sultan's outer palace service.[69]

The weddings of princesses helped to fill the ceremonial gap left by the absence of wedding ceremonies for sultans and princes, who by the end of the fifteenth century no longer contracted marriages. While royal weddings of this period were not intended primarily to enhance the status of princesses, the latter inevitably enjoyed greater influence on their fathers, mothers, brothers, and husbands because of the vital political links forged by their marriages. The importance of princess-statesman marital alliances—and the consequent strategic interest in princesses as political contacts—is indicated by the care taken by foreign ambassadors to keep track of who was married to whom[70] and by the lavish gifts they bestowed on these politically key members of the dynasty.

These unions could be very happy ones: Şah Sultan, daughter of Selim II, and her second husband, Zal Mahmud Pasha, were so suited to each other, it was said, that they fell ill at the same time, lay in their deathbeds together, and expired at the very same moment. After the triple wedding described above, Mihrimah Sultan pushed assiduously for a naval campaign against Malta, enlisting the help of her son-in-law, the grand vezir Semiz Ali Pasha, and promising to outfit four hundred ships at her own expense; however,

Süleyman and his son Selim prevented the campaign from going forward so that the admiral, Piyale Pasha, might remain in Istanbul with his new wife, Gevherhan Sultan, Selim's daughter.[71] On the other hand, becoming a royal *damad* was not always an unmixed blessing for an Ottoman statesman. Princesses made expensive wives, and their husbands were required to divorce any wives they might already have. After the death of the grand vezir Sokollu Mehmed Pasha, husband of İsmihan Sultan, the princess's first choice for a new husband, Özdemiroğlu Osman Pasha, was not interested. Her next choice, Kalaylıkoz Ali Pasha, the governor of Buda, agreed to the marriage, but when the imperial order came demanding his divorce, his wife's sorrow and suffering were said to have caused the city to revolt.[72]

The prestige of Süleyman's *damad*s, like that of other members of the royal family, gained public expression through the structures associated with them. They built or were given sumptuous palaces that would provide suitable lodging for their princess wives. The palaces of İbrahim Pasha and Sokollu Mehmed Pasha were located on the Hippodrome, the most popular site for imperial ceremonies; that of Ferhad Pasha and Hüma Sultan was located in the precincts of the Old Palace. The number and scale of the public works of the royal *damad*s also reflected both their status and their enormous incomes. Rüstem Pasha and Sokollu Mehmed Pasha in particular left a large number of monuments in the capital and in various cities and towns elsewhere in the empire.[73]

While not of imperial scale, the mosques of Süleyman's *damad*s are among the grandest and most opulent mosques in the capital. I am grateful to Aptullah Kuran for drawing my attention to the special character of the *damad* mosques. Like the imperial mosques of Süleyman's reign, they were scattered about Istanbul. The mosque of Piyale Pasha was in the hills above the eastern shore of the Golden Horn. That of Zal Mahmud Pasha, the second husband of Süleyman's granddaughter Şah Sultan, stood on the opposite side of the Golden Horn, near the town of Eyüp, the holiest place of pilgrimage in Istanbul.[74] The mosque of Rüstem Pasha, famous for its splendid tile panels, was located in the busy commercial and industrial area along the lower Golden Horn. The mosque bearing Sokollu Mehmed Pasha's name, located near the Hippodrome, was built for him by his wife, İsmihan, while he was responsible for the religious college and dervish hostel associated with it.[75] The site of a *damad*'s tomb might also emphasize his special status as adjunct to the royal family: Rüstem Pasha was buried near the tomb of Mehmed, Süleyman's favorite son, in the complex built to memorialize him. Near him was later buried another celebrated sixteenth-century *damad*, İbrahim, grand vezir of Mehmed III and husband of his sister Ayşe Sultan.

According to Koçi Bey, Süleyman's practice of choosing his vezirs from the royal *damad*s was one of the defects of his reign. Koçi Bey argued that the earlier practice of keeping *damad*s from rising above the rank of provincial governor was aimed at ensuring that they would remain away from the capital and thus be prevented from interfering in important matters of state. Vezirs were politicians of the capital. Although they might be assigned to command military operations, vezirs were known as "those who sit under the dome" (*kubbenişin*), a reference to the fact that their weighty duties were executed in the imperial council hall, located within the very walls of the sultan's residence. The talents and energies of *damad*s, argued Koçi Bey, were better devoted to the improvement of the provinces to which they had earlier been assigned and to the protection of the borders of the empire.[76]

Until the reign of Selim I, the Ottoman dynasty in fact followed the policy described by Koçi Bey, with all but very few royal *damad*s holding the rank of provincial governor (*sanjakbeyi*) and perhaps rising to the rank of governor-general (*beylerbeyi*). This practice of assigning royal *damad*s to the provinces was consonant with the overall conduct of dynastic politics in the fifteenth century, which was characterized by the decentralization of the royal family. Princes, consorts, princesses, and *damad*s played their political roles away from the capital. The center stage of politics was reserved for the sultan, his vezirs and other officials of the central administration, and important members of the sultanic household.

Implicit in Koçi Bey's criticism was the correct assumption that marriage to a princess placed a *damad* in a position to influence the sultan. But in his simplistic and static view of the empire's political structure, Koçi Bey ignored another dynamic inherent in the relations between dynasty and ruling class, one that had plagued earlier Muslim states: the potential for powerful members of the elite to build factions in their own interest and to challenge, even defy, sovereign authority. It was not the dynasty alone that might employ the technique of consolidating political power through marriage alliance. One of the goals in the dynasty's *damad* marriage policy may well have been to undermine the ability of the elite to build its own marriage networks. During the reign of Mehmed the Conqueror, there was ample evidence that the ruling elite itself could form powerful internal alliances: for example, Mehmed's *lala* and later vezir Zaganos Mehmed Pasha was the *damad* of Timurtaşoğlu Oruç Pasha, goveror-general of Anatolia under Murad II and scion of an influential native Turkish family; in turn, Zaganos had as his own *damad* the most celebrated grand vezir of Mehmed's reign, Mahmud Pasha. Two other of Mehmed's grand vezirs were related through a *damad* tie: Gedik Ahmed Pasha was married to a daughter of İshak Pasha (who was himself a freed slave of Pasha Yiğit, an important member of the Turkish aristocracy in the reigns of Mehmed's father and grandfather).[77] The tenacity of such alliances was demonstrated at Mehmed's death, when Gedik Ahmed abandoned the party of Mehmed's son Jem, whose principal supporter he was widely considered to be, when his father-in-law was appointed grand vezir to the new sultan, Jem's brother and rival Bayezid.

The politics of princess marriages forms a prism through which the evolution of the politics of the elite is reflected. When interdynastic marriage was abandoned as a useful marriage policy, the dynasty turned to its own ruling class for suitable husbands for its daughters. But it appears with few exceptions to have avoided alliances with native-born Muslims either from the dynasties of military lords, such as the Evrenos and the Mihaloğulları, or from the *ulema*-administrator class, such as the Çandarlı dynasty of vezirs.[78] In other words, the dynasty held aloof from the indigenous nobility. When, in 1621, the sultan Osman II married the daughter of the *müfti* Esad Efendi, scion of the most prestigious *ulema* family in Ottoman history, there was popular opposition to what was perceived to be a harmful violation of political protocol.

Roy Mottahedeh has argued in the context of tenth- and eleventh-century Islamic society that kingship was effective because it was perceived to be independent of and above indigenous social hierarchies. The king maintained social and political order not "by virtue of his position at the top of the social hierarchy [but rather] as an outsider, the man who was above categories and their associated hierarchies." Hence, Mottahedeh argues, the importance of slave armies, the army being the only category in which the king participated; the army "had to consist of men who were, like the king, detached from special interests and not identified with the categories present in the population."[79]

Mottahedeh's analysis would seem to hold for early modern Ottoman society. The dynasty developed the slave institution in large part as a bulwark against the political pretensions of the native Turkish aristocracy who had contributed so much to the empire's expansion. But the history of Muslim states, which the Ottomans knew well, showed that the slave institution tended to become the most intractible of political forces. When the Ottoman sultan's household troops, especially the Janissaries, threatened to become the dominant force in the polity, the dynasty had to take measure to protect itself. One of the means by which it contained the administrative hold of the military elite over society was to make judges, members of the *ulema,* a second arm of the central administration by endowing them with the power to apply both religious and customary law, that is, with the responsibility of enforcing both the Sharia and imperial commands. The policy of binding the most powerful of slave statesmen to the dynasty through marriage was another means of control, aimed primarily at curbing the potential centrifugal power of the slave elite. This policy not only prevented this elite of the elite from allying itself with other interests in the society but also diverted its primary loyalty from its own group, the slave institution, to the dynasty. Moreover, the policy of princess-*damad* marriage also helped to curb the ever-present problem of the dissipation of dynastic power through family members: the power that princesses carried with them was contained within the elite of the ruling elite. The fact that the policy was encouraged under Selim I, perhaps the most autocratic of Ottoman sultans, adds weight to the argument that it was perceived, at least initially, as a tool of sovereign control rather than, as Koçi Bey saw it, a manifestation of sultanic weakness.

From the perspective of dynastic reproduction, the central household had become a self-sufficient unit: female partners of sultans and male partners of princesses were slaves raised within the household. By the reign of Süleyman, a ruling clan had formed within the ruling class, composed of the royal family and its slave clients. For a large part of his reign, Süleyman governed through a kind of family cabal. When his heir was identified, Süleyman helped him establish his own circle of political intimates through the marriage of budding statesmen to Selim's daughters. Upon his accession, Selim did not disturb this arrangement, allowing his son-in-law Sokollu Mehmed Pasha to continue in charge of government throughout his reign. What may not have been immediately apparent, however, was the potential of the family cabal for spawning factions *within* rather than outside the dynastic household.

The *Damad* as Favorite

From the reign of Mehmed the Conqueror, vezirs were drawn with few exceptions from the slave elite[80] and were thus in many respects the male parallels of the sultan's concubines, the women who rose to the top of the female slave hierarchy. A brief look at the careers of the two most powerful of Süleyman's *damad* grand vezirs, especially at the sources and limits of their power, may cast some light on the extraordinary career of Hurrem. İbrahim Pasha—Süleyman's second grand vezir and the first he appointed himself—held the post from 1523 until his execution in 1536; İbrahim was married to the sultan's sister Hadije. Rüstem Pasha, married to Mihrimah, Süleyman and Hurrem's daughter, held the post from 1544 until his death in 1561, except for a two-year interval when he was dismissed to assuage popular outrage following the execution of the prince Mustafa in 1553.

During the reigns of Süleyman and his predecessors, promotion to the vezirate was the culmination of a well-defined career path.[81] The most talented and favored graduates of the inner palace service would begin their formal career with promotion to one of the prestigious offices in the outer palace service, for example, Agha of the Janissaries, Bearer of the Imperial Standard, Master of the Stable, Chief Falconer, Head Doorkeeper, or Chief Taster. After holding one or more of these offices, the official received a provincial governorate, whence he would rise to more prestigious governorates or perhaps (after the mid-sixteenth century) the admiralty. He might then go on to hold one or both of the highest ranks below that of vezir, the governor-generalships of Rumelia and Anatolia. After attaining the high station of vezir, he progressed along the vezirial hierarchy, from fourth to third vezir, third to second, and then, upon the retirement, dismissal, natural death, or execution of the incumbent, to the grand vezirate. According to the historian Mustafa Ali, it took roughly thirty years to advance to this highest office. In Ali's words, the military/administrative career was considered to be "like a craft that had to be learned through observation and experience no matter how bright the individual might be."[82] There was, however, some flexibility in this arrangement: for example, one might move directly to a governor-generalship from the outer service, or one might hold the rank of vezir simultaneously with a governor-generalship or the admiralty or command of a particular campaign.

İbrahim Pasha's dual appointment to the grand vezirate and the governor-generalship of Rumelia defied customary sultanic observance of this career path.[83] In 1523, three years after Süleyman's accession, İbrahim was promoted to the empire's highest office directly from the inner service, albeit as the most senior of its statesmen-in-training (he held the offices of Chief of the Privy Chamber and Head Falconer of the Inner Service). Süleyman's boon companion since the days of his princely governorate, İbrahim might well have expected promotion to the outer palace service at the sultan's accession, but Süleyman would seem to have been reluctant to part with him. By appointing İbrahim grand vezir, Süleyman was able to maintain his intimate relationship with his favorite, for the grand vezir was the only official of the outer government who enjoyed the privilege of regular contact with the sultan.

Despite the fact that, unlike either his predecessors or successors in office, İbrahim had held no outer government post before his appointment, he was far from being a political novice. Koçi Bey, who a century later criticized İbrahim's appointment on the grounds of his inexperience,[84] missed the important point that a high-ranking inner palace official and favorite such as İbrahim, because he accompained the sultan wherever he went, had not only received military and administrative training, but also, like other of the sultan's palace favorites, enjoyed a kind of hands-on political experience that was not accessible to statesmen in the field, no matter how much they might learn of their craft. İbrahim had participated in the first military campaigns that established the new sultan's standing as a *ghazi* hero in the tradition of his forebears, and his influence on political decisions was evident in the fact that people sought his favor and advice over that of the ranking vezirs.[85]

Contemporary histories attribute İbrahim's appointment to the grand vezirate to a number of factors: Süleyman's affection for him; his useful talents; the sultan's discomfort with his first grand vezir, Piri Mehmed Pasha, whom he had inherited from his father; and the general dislike for the second vezir, Ahmed Pasha.[86] Süleyman reportedly felt bashful and reluctant to put forward his own ideas in the presence of Piri Mehmed,[87] whose very nickname, "the venerable elder," projected the weight of experience under which the young sultan felt constrained. The historian Peçevi's account of the dismissal of Piri Mehmed suggests Süleyman's uneasy deference to the grand vezir:

> The sultan's affection for [İbrahim] had increased to the point that it was even rumored that he wanted to make him grand vezir. This rumor had reached the ear of [Piri] Mehmed Pasha. One day the sultan said to Mehmed Pasha, "I want to promote to the outer service a slave for whose service I am infinitely grateful, but I just don't know what office I should appoint him to." When [the sultan] asked this of Mehmed Pasha, the latter answered, "It is my office that should be given to such a close and esteemed slave." And so the sultan made İbrahim, who was head [page] of the privy chamber, grand vezir, and promoted him to the outer service.[88]

With Piri Mehmed retired from government on a handsome stipend, the sultan could now pay the elder statesman the respect that was his due without hampering his own freedom of action, by, for example, seating the pasha beside him on ceremonial occasions.

With his favorite as partner in government, Süleyman celebrated his power with great exuberance. Described by Bragadin as greatly interested in the history of ancient kings and the circumstances of present monarchs of the world, İbrahim was a skilled architect of the sultan's public image.[89] During İbrahim's grand vezirate, the imperial theater reached from Vienna to Baghdad and the theme of Ottoman power and legitimate sovereignty was played in two symbolic languages. Gülru Necipoğlu has shown that İbrahim's talents were well suited to selecting the iconographic representations of Ottoman power that would speak to a European audience.[90] İbrahim probably also had a hand in staging the message of Ottoman hegemony for the sultan's Muslim subjects. Ottoman supremacy was graphically represented at his own wedding in 1523 and at Süleyman's celebration of his sons' circumcision in 1530 through the symbolic display of the captured households of defeated Muslim sovereigns: the imperial tents of Akkoyunlu, Mamluk, and Safavid rulers were prominently deployed on both occasions,[91] and hostage princes of the former Akkoyunlu, Dulkadır, and Mamluk dynasties were seated conspicuously on the sultan's left at the circumcision festivities.[92]

From the beginning, İbrahim's power was enormous. The grant of the grand vezirate together with the governor-generalship of Rumelia gave him a clear monopoly of power. The Venetian ambassadors during his tenure uniformly reported that whatever he wanted was done and that nothing was done without his advice.[93] In the celebration of Ottoman power, İbrahim's own august status was not neglected, for the first of the lavish public ceremonies of Süleyman's reign was his wedding. In later years, sultan and grand vezir debated the question of whose wedding had been the more splendid (the princes' circumcision celebration was called by the same Turkish word as that for "wedding"); İbrahim's clever riposte was that the answer was clearly his own, since only he had had the sultan as guest. Despite his many public honors, however, İbrahim was not popular. Bragadin reported in 1526 that he "was much hated at first, but now that they see that the sultan likes him so well, all have been made to be friendly to him, including the mother and the wife of the sultan and the other two pashas [vezirs]."[94]

The sultan could destroy a favorite as swiftly and seemingly arbitrarily as he had created him. İbrahim was cut down at the apparent height of his fortunes shortly after returning from the victorious two-year campaign he had led against the Safavids. Süleyman ordered İbrahim executed as he slept in his room in the inner palace on March 15, 1536. İbrahim fell ostensibly because his overweening ambition exceeded the generous arena granted him by the sultan. The former favorite's obliteration was symbolized by the fact that the site of his grave was obscure and dishonored by the lack of a tomb.[95] In 1614 another *damad* grand vezir, Nasuh Pasha, was buried beside İbrahim, having been executed for similar reasons: excessive pride, failure to defer to the sultan, and designs on the sultanate.[96] The choice of Nasuh's burial site was surely intended to remind the public of the crimes and ignominious end of İbrahim and repeated the object lesson of the fate of the overly ambitious.

The parallels between the careers of İbrahim and Hurrem are striking.

Both acquired unprecedently high status that depended solely on the sultan's favor. Their status was achieved through disregard, even flouting, of the traditional constraints on the sultan's choice of his highest-ranking male and female associates. Also notable is the swiftness of their rise. Both İbrahim and Hurrem had acquired a monopoly of power within their respective spheres by 1523, three years after the sultan's accession. Their simultaneous rise suggests the impatience of the young ruler to escape from the restraints inherited from the previous generation and to assert the implacability of his own will. Lacking the opportunity before his accession to prove his personal qualifications for rulership, Süleyman may have felt a greater need at the outset of his reign to impress his authority upon his subjects, especially the ruling elite.

Although Süleyman confounded public expectations by breaking the rules governing both the veziral and the concubinal careers, his subjects, rather than placing blame on the revered sultan, focused their discontent on his favorites. Süleyman's relationship with his favorites disordered the hierarchy of inner and outer and blurred the boundaries that defined sovereignty. Süleyman took the unprecedented step of leaving the palace to honor his male servant on at least two occasions: he attended the wedding of İbrahim and Hadije in 1524, and later that year he publicly saw the grand vezir off with an open display of affection when he left to settle affairs in Egypt. Although the head of the outer government, İbrahim frequently entered the inner palace to spend the night in a bedroom that was maintained for him near that of the sultan, a breach of traditional protocol. Not only did Hurrem fail to leave the capital with her son, but by moving into the royal palace, she quite literally crossed the boundary that had isolated the sultan from the rest of the dynastic family. It was this blurring of boundaries that caused popular resistance to Süleyman's two favorites.

The paradox of Hurrem's and İbrahim's power was that while it was a manifestation of the sultan's absolute authority, it was perceived as a compromise of that authority. Expressed here was perhaps the essential feature of the Ottoman political constitution: too much strength in the sultanate was weakness in the polity because it altered the balance of power. Although there were no legal restraints on the Ottoman sultan's exercise of the rights of controlling appointments to office and of summary execution, by no means did he exercise absolute power. The influence of the military, especially the imperial infantry—the famed Janissaries—and of the *ulema* were the principal checks on the arbitrary use of power at the center. It was really only in the nineteenth century, as a result of the "reforms" of Mahmud II that weakened the checks of these ancient institutions on the sultanate, that the sultan could exercise arbitrary authority.[97]

İbrahim's execution may have been necessary to restore the boundaries of power. According to Mustafa Ali, the grand vezirs following İbrahim achieved their office "in accordance with the promotional hierarchy."[98] It is likely, however, that considerations in addition to İbrahim's pretensions contributed to his downfall. Two years before his death, the ambassador De'Ludovici described the grand vezir's neglect of the army and administration.[99] Further-more, significant shifts in the orientation of government were beginning to be perceptible. In 1537, the year after İbrahim's death, several important devel-opments occurred, signaling a greater emphasis on Muslim piety. In this year Süleyman began the refurbishment of Jerusalem, the third holiest city in Islam, improving the water supply system and reconstructing the great wall surrounding the city, which, in Peçevi's words, was "so perfect it induced jealousy in the walls of China and sat like a matchless crown atop all the [sultan's] public works."[100] In Istanbul, construction began on the first of the dynasty's mosque complexes built under Süleyman, that constructed in Hurrem's name. Finally, Ebussuud Efendi, the great jurist remembered for bringing common law into line with the Sharia, acquired the influential post of chief justice of Rumelia, an event that initiated a period in which the sultan began to shape his imperial orders with more deliberate and careful reference to the holy law of Islam.[101]

By the end of the 1530s the great conquests of Süleyman's reign had been completed. The Ottoman army and navy continued to campaign—Süleyman in fact died while on the fifteenth campaign of his career—but military activ-ity, particularly on land, was directed more at maintaining borders than at pushing them forward. The achievement of the sultan and his advisers now lay more in the domains of administrative consolidation and legal codification. Later generations of Ottomans remembered Süleyman not as "the Magnifi-cent," but as "*Kanunî*," "the legislator," "the upholder of law and tradition." New emphases required different skills in the grand vezir.

Rüstem Pasha, the dominant figure of the second half of Süleyman's reign, had been, like İbrahim, long a favorite of the sultan before his appointment to the grand vezirate.[102] In fact, De'Ludovici noted in 1534 that upon learning that the sultan often sought the advice of Rüstem (who at that time held the outer palace office of Master of the Stable), İbrahim jealously dispatched the new favorite to a distant provincial governorate (Diyarbakır).[103] According to a story related by Mustafa Ali, Süleyman was frustrated in his desire to make Rüstem a vezir and marry him to his daughter Mihrimah: according to a rumor circulated by Rüstem's enemies, he had leprosy. Luckily, the doctor dispatched to Diyarbakır to examine him found proof that he was not leprous: there was a flea in his clothing, despite the fact that the fastidious Rüstem changed his garments daily.[104] Rüstem and Mihrimah were married in 1539 at the same time that the circumcision of Süleyman's two youngest sons, Bayezid and Jihangir, was celebrated. Five years later the *damad* became grand vezir.

The Venetian ambassadors consistently commented that Rüstem's consid-erable influence in government was secured by his marriage to the princess.[105] Yet once he left the sultan's personal service, he did not again approach the intimate status İbrahim had enjoyed, but was kept at a distance from the royal presence. Navagero described the failure of efforts by Mihrimah and her mother Hurrem to promote Rüstem as an intimate of the sultan: "I have learned through a reliable channel that they have tried many times to bring it about that Rustan might enter the palace of the sultan on such a familial basis as İbrahim used to; the sultan has responded that committing folly once is enough."[106]

Nevertheless, foreign ambassadors believed that Rüstem exercised authority at least as great as that of İbrahim. The Hapsburg ambassador Busbecq, who was on familiar terms with Rüstem, commented: "Of all the Pashas Roostem enjoyed most influence and authority with the Sultan. A man of keen and far-seeing mind, he had been largely instrumental in promoting Soleiman's fame."[107] According to Navagero, the sultan permitted Rüstem more power than he had allowed İbrahim because he filled rather than emptied the treasury.[108] This virtue did not, however, gain Rüstem public favor. He was associated with unpopular fiscal policies, for example, administrative innovations such as the granting of state sources of income to officials as tax farms (*iltizam*) rather than the traditional usufruct land grants (*timar*), and the attachment of what might be called a "bestowal tax" (bribery to its critics) to the grant of high office.[109] According to Navagero's successor, Rüstem was liked by no one and hated in particular for his avarice.[110] The empire's financial stability in Süleyman's later reign, however, owed much to the grand vezir's "avarice." Busbecq commented that "yet even this vice was employed in his master's interest, since he was entrusted with the privy purse and the management of his finances, which were a cause of considerable difficulty to Soleiman."[111]

The Family as Faction

It was inevitable that Süleyman's male and female favorites would either clash or combine. Rooted in the immediate vicinity of the sultan, their spheres of power overlapped. The direct political influence of harem women begins with Hurrem, the first high-ranking female of the dynasty to pursue her career in the capital. The joining of women in the contest for power at the heart of government was a prominent feature of politics in the reigns of Süleyman and his successors. But it was not, at it has been so often represented, a simple contest between harem and outer government. The harem was by no means a political monolith. Coalitions cut across the division of inner and outer government, and factions composed of both men and women vied with each other.

As Eric Ives has noted in his biography of Anne Boleyn, faction was the natural political unit in an absolute monarchy.[112] It was through the formation of factions including members of the royal family that developments in dynastic politics in the reign of Süleyman—the concubine favorite and the *damad* favorite—intersected most significantly. Obviously, every *damad* had a mother-in-law as well as a father-in-law, and every princess wife of a statesman a concubine mother as well as a sultan father. The natural tendency was for the unit of concubine mother, her daughter, and the latter's grand vezir husband to favor the candidacy of the concubine's son (the princess's full brother). The effective formation of such a political unit was not possible until the reign of Süleyman. Before then, the mother of a princess either had a son as well, whom she accompanied to the provinces, or if she only had daughters, she presumably enjoyed relatively low status and little power. In either case, no significant political constellation could be based on the mother-daughter relationship. Moreover, before Süleyman, only one *damad* grand vezir, Hersekzade Ahmed Pasha, was married to a daughter of the sultan (Bayezid II's daughter Hundi Khatun) and had a concubine mother-in-law (Bülbül Khatun). It may be significant that toward the end of his long reign, as the contest between princes for the succession began, Bayezid II favored the prince Ahmed, son of Bülbül, full brother of Hundi, and brother-in-law of Hersekzade Ahmed.[113] On the other hand, there is evidence that this grouping did not form an overtly partisan faction—or at least not an effective one: Ahmed did not win the contest among the princes, and a year after taking the throne the victor, Selim I, appointed Hersekzade Ahmed grand vezir for the fourth time in his career.

During Süleyman's reign there were at least two family factions. The first existed between İbrahim Pasha and Hadije, on the one hand, and the prince Mustafa and his mother Mahidevran, on the other. İbrahim's kindly patience in soothing the child Mustafa's jealousy of his father's affection for his favorite is illustrated by the following story in Bragadin's report: "The sultan sent İbrahim the gift of a beautiful saddle for his horse with jewels and all; and Mustafa, aware of this, sent word to İbrahim to have one like it made for him; [İbrahim] understood this and sent him the said saddle, and said to him, 'now listen, if the sultan learns of this, he will make you send it back.' "[114] As time passed, the relationship between the two seems to have consolidated, no doubt in part because Mustafa realized that it was not the grand vezir but his half-brothers against whom he ultimately needed to be on guard. Letters exchanged between İbrahim and Hadije and the prince and his mother in the provinces indicate that a strong and warm relationship existed between these two branches of the dynastic family. In 1534 the grand vezir wrote to Mustafa acknowledging receipt of a letter the prince had sent regarding affairs in the Aegean and informing him of his father's victories in the Baghdad campaign. In the letter İbrahim refers to himself as Mustafa's "sincere friend" and expresses the wish to see him soon, to "take profit from and be gladdened by [his] noble and blessed grace." Mahidevran, writing a note asking after the well-being of Hadije, makes long reference to the two families' "sisterhood and brotherhood, and the truly sincere kind friendship and tender compassion" that the princess and her husband have shown.[115]

It is hard to know how politically active this faction was in furthering the interests of Mustafa. It would have been natural for İbrahim to back Mustafa, for, had Süleyman died prematurely, it is likely that the prince would have become sultan and İbrahim Pasha his grand vezir. The tension between Hurrem and İbrahim reflected in the letter cited earlier may lend some truth to the contention that İbrahim was actively pro-Mustafa. On the other hand, it may simply reflect some other affair or a personal rivalry between the sultan's two favorites for his affections.

It is often asserted that Hafsa, mother of both Süleyman and Hadije, was a member of the putatively partisan grouping of İbrahim-Hadije-Mustafa-Mahidevran. However, I have found no clear evidence to support this contention. Letters that İbrahim sent to Hadije while he was away from the capital reveal no particular closeness to Hafsa Sultan.[116] The grand vezir routinely sent greetings to all female members of Süleyman's family living in the imperial harem: his mother-in-law, his wife's two sisters, and Hurrem. Indeed, a letter İbrahim wrote to Hadije after learning of the death of Hafsa in March 1534 indicates that, at least while he was absent from Istanbul, he had severely restricted his wife's ability to visit her mother and other family members (despite the sultan's urging otherwise).[117] It is tempting to cast Hafsa as İbrahim's protector since the grand vezir was executed at the first reasonable opportunity after her death (after his return from leading the successful two-year eastern campaign of 1534–1535); on the other hand, it was in part İbrahim's excessive arrogation of executive power during the campaign that contributed to his downfall. Even if Hafsa *did* act as his protector, it may have been less a manifestation of factional partisanship than an instance of the royal mother's traditional role in tempering her son's behavior and protecting her daughters' interests. Earlier, for example, Hafsa had tried to protect the vezir husband of Süleyman's sister Beyhan from execution. Nevertheless, even if there is no strong available evidence that Hafsa, Hadije, and İbrahim formed an overtly political alliance, close ties among the three would have been natural. It is certainly worthy of note that the two most powerful and longest tenured grand vezirs of Süleyman's reign had influential mothers-in-law at court.

The more publicly evident and partisan of family factions under Süleyman, and the first clear instance of the many concubine-daughter-*damad* alliances of the sixteenth and seventeenth centuries, was that of Hurrem, Mihrimah, and Rüstem. Although there is no proof of Hurrem's or Mihrimah's direct involvement, Ottoman sources and foreign accounts indicate that it was widely believed that the three worked first to eliminate Mustafa so as to ensure the throne to a son of Hurrem, and then to strengthen the position of Bayezid, the younger of Hurrem's two surviving sons (it was in fact Selim who succeeded).

Because of the nature of the succession system, it was in the interest of all three to work against Mustafa's candidacy. His victory would undoubtedly spell disaster for each: the end of Rüstem's career because of his family links to the rival faction, and perhaps his execution; the execution of all Hurrem's sons, Mihrimah's brothers; and loss of status for Hurrem and Mihrimah, and perhaps the impoverishment that was ultimately the lot of Mahidevran.[118] Hurrem and her allies were competing against considerable odds on account of Mustafa's enormous popularity, especially among the imperial troops. But, as Navagero noted several months before Mustafa's death, while it was the universal opinion that the prince would succeed, the course of events could be changed by "all the schemes of the mother . . . and of Rustan."[119]

The Problem of Succession

In evaluating the succession crises of Süleyman's reign, a certain amount of skepticism is necessary, since they tend to be burdened with partisan reaction to the failure or success of the various princes. Furthermore, the sources give contradictory evidence regarding Süleyman's preferences, asserting variously that he preferred Mustafa to Hurrem's sons, as well as the opposite; that he named Hurrem's firstborn, Mehmed, his heir apparent; and, contrary to the accepted tradition, that he preferred Selim to Bayezid when only the two sons remained. What seems likely is that the passage of time and evolving circumstances changed Süleyman's views of his sons and their relative merits. It is probable that his thinking about the qualities that would best suit the ruler who succeeded him and indeed about the very process of succession and ways in which it might be changed, evolved over the course of his long reign. In any event, solving the problem of Süleyman's view of the succession is beyond the scope of this work, although, given the close relation between reproductive choices and the issue of succession, an answer might help us to better understand Hurrem's place in the evolution of dynastic politics.

Some histories assert that Süleyman favored the sons of Hurrem and considered abandoning the tradition of open succession in favor of his second eldest and much-loved son Mehmed, Hurrem's firstborn.[120] It is difficult, however, to find conclusive support for Süleyman's privileging of Mehmed. Often cited as proof of Mehmed's special status is the fact that when he was sent out from the palace in 1542, he was assigned to Manisa, until then Mustafa's provincial post, while Mustafa was transferred to Amasya. The argument goes that Manisa was the most prized because the closest of princely posts to Istanbul; it was strategically advantageous in the event of a rush to take the capital at the sultan's death. While there may be some validity to this argument, other factors were also at play in the princes' appointments. Traditionally, Manisa had been the *first* post to which a prince was sent, probably because of its relative proximity to Istanbul and because it was not a center from which military campaigns were mounted. Amasya, on the other hand, closer to the vital eastern front, was a post of greater military and political significance. The historian Kemalpaşazade relates an incident suggesting that Amasya was the most desirable post, at least in the time of Bayezid II: when Mehmed the Conqueror asked his several grandsons (the sons of Bayezid) if they loved him or their father more, only Ahmed answered that he preferred his father to his grandfather, the sultan; for this he suffered his grandfather's displeasure during Mehmed's lifetime, but when Bayezid became sultan, Ahmed was rewarded for his loyalty by being appointed to Amasya.[121] Furthermore, Mustafa's move to Amasya, which occurred in June 1541, may not have been directly connected to Mehmed's assignment to Manisa, which did not occur until fourteen months later. While Mustafa's transfer was cast as a promotion, with a large increase in stipend, its purpose may have been to enable the grand vezir, stationed in Anatolia, to keep a closer eye on the prince during his father's absence on campaign (Süleyman departed for Hungary in June of that year).[122]

Whatever Süleyman's plans for Mehmed, they were dashed when the prince died, probably of smallpox, only a year after his appointment. Süleyman's grief at his son's death was symbolized in the sumptuous mosque and tomb that he constructed in Mehmed's memory in Istanbul. Burying the prince in the capital was another break with dynastic tradition for the sake of a favorite, for until Süleyman's reign princes of the dynasty had been buried in Bursa.[123] The two sons who died in disgrace for allegedly challenging their father's sovereignty, Mustafa and Bayezid, were deprived of this new honor of burial in the capital.[124]

Following Mehmed's death, Süleyman appears to have upheld the tradition of open succession rather than favoring either of Hurrem's two sons, Selim and Bayezid, over Mustafa. Even had he preferred one of the latter, he would have had little choice in the matter. At midcentury Mustafa's ultimate victory seemed a probability. In the words of the historian Peçevi, Mustafa was "the envy of all the princes in his gloriousness, lofty titles, and learning, and in his liberality, justice and munificence; nearly all the soldiers were of one heart and mind in their love of him."[125] Shortly before the prince's execution, Navagero reported that Mustafa was in such great favor that there was no suspicion he might attempt a coup against his father; furthermore, he did not worry that he had brothers closer to Istanbul than he and one even resident in the palace.[126] That the sultan acknowledged the probability of Mustafa's success is reflected in a conversation related by Navagero: when Jihangir, his father's constant companion, ventured that his physical deformity would allow him to escape the princely fate of fratricide, Süleyman responded, "My son, Mustafa will become the sultan and will deprive you all of your lives."[127]

It is difficult to assess the degree to which Mustafa's execution may have been warranted. While the efforts of Rüstem Pasha were undoubtedly instrumental in Mustafa's downfall,[128] the prince's fate was not simply the result of a partisan conspiracy. The not-so-distant events surrounding the end of Süleyman's grandfather's reign were a memory that framed the tensions of Süleyman's relations with his own sons. Sixty-four years old and well past the age when earlier sultans had died, Bayezid II had been repeatedly challenged and ultimately "retired" by his son Selim in 1512.[129] The former sultan died on the way to his retirement post in Dimetoka, possibly poisoned by Selim's agents, while Selim proceeded to counter the resistance of his brothers with the most violent enactment of the law of fratricide on record. Eighteen when these events began, Süleyman had been not only an observer but an element in his father Selim's strategy.

Forty years later, given Süleyman's advancing age (he was sixty the year Mustafa was executed), the prospect of Mustafa's "retiring" his father and initiating a war for the succession was not implausible. Mustafa's popularity can only have exacerbated this threat in the eyes of his rivals. Indeed, when Mustafa was only eleven, people seemed already to be concerned about the threat that an active son presented to his father: after describing the youngster's talents, strong sense of self, and popularity among the Janissaries, Bragadin had commented, "they say that if he lives, he will bring great fame to the Ottoman House, and this also is said, that if it happens that the sultan lives long, it is inevitable that he [Mustafa] will create much disorder."[130]

Figure 3-1 Süleyman receiving his eldest son Mustafa. Süleyman, on his way to fight the Safavids in 1548, enjoys a quiet moment with Mustafa. Mustafa's striking resemblance to his father, bearded and dressed in identical colors of green, orange and blue, is unusual in representations of the sultan and his sons. The artist may have wished to suggest Mustafa's rumored intention to usurp his father's place, or perhaps, though less likely, the prince's qualifications to succeed his father. From Arifi, *Süleymanname*, f. 477b. *(Courtesy of Topkapı Palace Museum Library, Istanbul)*

Displacing a sovereign father was a deed fraught with ambiguity, with taboos as well as potential legitimacy. The fact that the survival of the House of Osman, its fate inextricably bound to that of the state, was a higher good than the survival of an individual sultan meant that the father's overthrow could be presented as a virtuous and politically warranted act. Selim had justified his actions on the grounds that the aged and ill Bayezid's inability to govern effectively threatened the survival of the state, particularly in view of the success of Safavid propaganda in undermining the loyalty of Anatolians to the Ottoman dynasty. Justifiable patricide opens the epic of Oghuz Khan, the ancestral hero of the Central Asian Turkish tribes from whom the Ottomans claimed descent: in the initial sequence of a thirteenth-century Muslim version of the epic, which enjoyed a revival among the Ottomans in the second half of the fifteenth century, Oghuz kills his father and uncles upon hearing that they plan to eliminate him for having abandoned the ancestral religion in favor of Islam.[131]

It was the possibility that Mustafa was planning a move similar to Selim's that was the ostensible cause of his execution. Mustafa's supporters supposedly misled him into believing that, while Süleyman was ready to retire to Dimetoka and relinquish the throne to him, the grand vezir Rüstem was determined to eliminate him.[132] At first, the sultan discounted the seriousness of charges against the prince. According to an eyewitness account, he refused to believe Rüstem's charge of treason against Mustafa:

> When the *padishah* read the grand vezir's dispatch, he said, "God forbid that my Mustafa Khan should dare such insolence and should commit such an unwise move during my lifetime! It is trouble-makers trying to obtain the rule for the prince they support who are responsible for such slander. Beware that you never again repeat such a thing and that you do not believe such maliciousness."[133]

Nevertheless, in a matter of months, Mustafa was dead.

Süleyman may have been convinced of Mustafa's guilt. He may also have recognized that the prince, even if innocent of any plotting against his father, might nevertheless compromise his ability to rule effectively. Mustafa's enormous popularity with the army was certainly cause for unease. A few years after the prince's death, Busbecq reported a conversation in which Rüstem spoke of the sultan's fears of the Janissaries:

> "[I]t was a time of war, during which [the Janissaries] were masters to such an extent that not even Soleiman himself could control them and was actually afraid of personal harm at their hands." And these were no idle words from Roostem's lips, for he was well aware of his master's uneasiness. There was nothing which the Sultan so much dreaded as that there might be some secret disaffection among the Janissaries, which might break out when it was impossible to apply any remedy.[134]

Compounding this potential for disorder, virtually as old as the Janissary organization itself, was the ever-present fear that the sultan's prolonged absence on military campaign would invite one of his sons to make a preemptive bid against his brothers. It is noteworthy that Mustafa was executed while his father was on the way to war. Even after the elimination of Mustafa, the tension between the surviving brothers, Selim and Bayezid, continued to constrain Ottoman foreign policy. As Busbecq ruefully noted, the death of Bayezid in 1561 resolved the succession crisis and thereby released the energies of the sultan and his advisers, who proceeded to adopt a more aggressive stance vis-à-vis Europe.[135]

Whatever the sultan's view of the matter and degree of responsibility for decisions taken, Hurrem and Rüstem were widely perceived as responsible. According to Busbecq, Rüstem's dismissal from the grand vezirate on the day of Mustafa's death was a sacrifice to the latter's partisans (Busbecq surmised that Rüstem had instigated his own dismissal): "This change soothed the grief and calmed the feelings of the soldiers, who, with the usual credulity of the vulgar, were easily led to believe that Soleiman had discovered the crimes of Roostem and the sorceries of his wife and had learnt wisdom, though it was too late, and had therefore deposed Roostem and would not spare even his wife on his return to Constantinople."[136] But less than two years later, Rüstem was again grand vezir, having spent the interim in Mihrimah's palace in Istanbul. Rüstem's return to office may not have been a foregone conclusion. After his dismissal, Hurrem had written to Süleyman to plead for his mercy: "Rüstem Pasha is your slave. Do not withhold your noble favor from him, my fortune-favored. Do not listen to what anyone says. Just this once, let it be for the sake of your slave Mihrimah, my fortune-favored, my emperor, for your own sake, and for my sake too, my prosperous sultan."[137]

Writing at the end of the sixteenth century, Mustafa Ali, one of the greatest and most influential of Ottoman historians, openly blamed the execution of Mustafa on "the plotting of women and the deceit of the dishonest son-in-law."[138] While he did not name the "women" and the "son-in-law," it was clear to his readers that he was referring to the coalition of Hurrem, Mihrimah, and Rüstem. Furthermore, in the introduction to his history, Ali presented this alleged coup instigated by the coalition as a symbol of the victory of disruptive forces and as the moment from which the decline of the empire could be dated.[139] The Hurrem-Rüstem-Mihrimah coalition was also blamed for the execution in 1555 of the grand vezir Kara Ahmed Pasha, whose elimination cleared the way for Rüstem's return. According to Ali, the Safavid ruler Tahmasp commented that Süleyman had committed two errors in judgment because of the "scheming of women": the execution of Mustafa and that of Kara Ahmed.[140] Contemporary Ottoman histories described Ahmed Pasha, husband of Süleyman's sister Fatma, as a paragon of martial and political virtue, most probably in part at least to add weight to the burden of the coalition's guilt. Busbecq, however, thought he was "a man of greater courage than judgment."[141]

The question of the succession was a major preoccupation of Süleyman's sultanate. On the basis of the available evidence, it does not seem that Süleyman had a deliberate or comprehensive plan for change or reform. It is more likely that each step taken over his long reign was a response to an immediate problem, or as suggested above, that Süleyman's views on how best to address this issue changed over time. Nevertheless, the broader questions raised by this problem in the dynasty's internal politics were doubtless never far from the minds of the sultan, his advisers, and the members of his family, or indeed, from the minds of his subjects.

Süleyman's father's legacy in this area was problematic. For one thing, Selim had deposed his father. For another, there was the question of his disposition of the succession issue in his own reign, a problem that is strangely ignored in both contemporary and modern sources. Süleyman was the only son sent out to the provinces, and the only son mentioned in contemporary accounts of Selim's reign. According to Venetian ambassadorial reports in 1514 and 1518, the sultan avoided sexual contact with women so that he would produce no more sons.[142] However, it is highly unlikely that Selim had only one son, since he had six daughters who survived into adulthood.[143] His other sons may have died while young, although no such deaths are mentioned in the Ottoman historical or genealogical record. There is a tradition that Selim's other sons were executed on the eve of the 1514 campaign against Iran, with the presumed aim of preventing a coup in favor of one of these princes in the absence from the capital of both Selim, who faced the possibility of death during the campaign, and the heir presumptive, Süleyman.[144] Whatever the truth concerning Selim's sons, it was no doubt known to Süleyman.

In its general outline—securing the succession through privileging a single son, and thus avoiding both potential challenge during the sultan's lifetime and civil war among his heirs—Selim's policy was followed by Süleyman's heirs. Looking back over the sixteenth century, we see that Süleyman was the only sultan to permit open succession. The question, then, is why he chose not to follow his father's precedent, since it avoided the enormous costs to the dynasty and society of open succession. Indeed, the next chapter raises the possibility that Süleyman may have urged a variation of Selim's solution on his own sons. In trying to answer this question, we can only speculate.

Let us assume, first, that Selim's solution involved the execution of innocent princes. Süleyman may have rejected this course of action as too extreme. It violated Ottoman custom and would probably have met with the disapproval of the guardians of the holy law. In the interests of sovereign integrity, Ottoman royal custom had sanctioned fratricide and the killing of nephews. But it did not extend the underlying principle—the killing of the few to preserve domestic peace and order for the many—to the killing of the sultan's own sons or, in the case of the sultan's incompetence, his death at the hands of one of his sons. The father-son bloodline was, so to speak, sacred. Selim may well have been doubly guilty of violating that taboo.

Let us now assume that the death of Selim's other sons somehow did not involve violence. Süleyman could then have followed his father and adopted a policy of privileging his eldest son and producing other sons only as insurance against the death of the eldest. It would then have fallen to his successor to deal with his brothers, presumably through application of the law of fratricide (this was the practice of Süleyman's successors). The problem here was that it was the sons of Hurrem who would be sacrificed. The affection Süleyman developed for her and the influence she and her allies wielded would presumably have made this a difficult option to pursue.

Whatever his thinking in the early years of his sultanate, by dispatching Mehmed, his second son, to a provincial governorate Süleyman committed himself to a policy of open succession and the ultimate death by execution of all but one of his sons. A prince with a court was invested with sovereign, if limited, power, and could not without extreme justification be eliminated from candidacy for the throne. The policy of open succession did not, however, preclude a sultan from publicly indicating a preferred heir—Mehmed the Conqueror supposedly preferred his younger son Jem, who was ultimately defeated by his brother Bayezid—but such a preference never had a binding effect in practice.

Conclusion

In attempting to make sense of the developments described in this chapter, we need to take into account certain historiographic issues. With the reign of Süleyman, the sources offer us more and varied information. Histories of the dynasty composed in the sixteenth and seventeenth centuries are less often than in the fifteenth century celebratory accounts commissioned by or composed expressly for members of the elite. Written from varied perspectives and sometimes consciously attempting to incorporate multiple points of view, these accounts permit us to reconstruct a more balanced and nuanced representation of this period. Furthermore, Ottoman documentary sources become more abundant in the sixteenth century: not only did the expansion of empire and the elaboration of administrative structures produce more records, but such records stood a better chance of surviving than those from earlier centuries. Documents—letters and salary registers, for example—provide us with an inside view of relationships and structures (for example, the harem) that would otherwise be inaccessible to us. In addition, largely because ambassadorial accounts become relatively abundant from the sixteenth century on, we learn more about the personalities of members of the dynasty and of the ruling elite as well as the relationships among them.

One of the most important problems that confronts us, then, is integrating contemporary judgments of individuals into the larger frame of sixteenth-century political and social change as we in the late twentieth century reconstruct it. Were we unreflectingly to accept the opinions related by our sixteenth- and seventeenth-century sources (as has happened with Hurrem), we would know little more than popular reaction to contemporary developments. Even that we would understand imperfectly. People reacted to powerful figures like Hurrem and İbrahim not simply as individuals but as intimate associates of the sultan. And so we must consider how Süleyman's contemporaries understood the sovereign's relationship to sovereign power and to his associates.

Ancient Near Eastern wisdom on the subject of absolute monarchy—incorporated into Islamic culture largely from pre-Islamic Persian imperial traditions—recognized that a monarch, no matter how exalted his status, needed companions for relaxation. Manuals written to advise sultans, vezirs, and other important figures of government stress that the companions of kings (*nedim*) must not be allowed any influence on the conduct of public affairs.[145] An unstated corollary to this principle is that the sultan should neither allow himself emotional attachments to those persons upon whom he has bestowed public office nor permit those to whom he has emotional attachments to exercise undue influence on affairs of state. While this was largely an ideal paradigm of monarchical conduct, it seems to have been alive in the minds of Süleyman's subjects, who were troubled by personal attachments which they saw as compromising his sovereignty.

In seeking to explain Süleyman's relationship with his closest associates, contemporaries looked to his temperament. In 1555 Busbecq wrote that "even his bitterest critics can find nothing more serious to allege against him than his undue submission to his wife. . . ."[146] Navagero concurred with this view, commenting that Hurrem "has the bridle of the sultan's will in her hands," but also noted a tendency on Süleyman's part to allow himself to be "the prey" of almost all his counselors.[147] Indeed, Süleyman appears to have been a person who formed many close personal relationships: to his mother Hafsa, to Hurrem and İbrahim, to his youngest son and constant companion Jihangir, to his daughter Mihrimah, and to his grandson Murad. In his style of governing, he was unlike his father Selim, about whom the Venetian ambassador Bartolomeo Contarini had said, "he reflects constantly; no one dares to say anything, not even the pashas who are there with him; he governs alone, on the basis of his own thinking."[148] Rather, Süleyman preferred to govern with the close association of those who enjoyed his personal trust and affection, including, in addition to most of those just mentioned, Rüstem, his last grand vezir and former palace favorite Sokollu Mehmed, and the *müfti* Ebussuud Efendi. Süleyman heaped Sokollu Mehmed and Ebussuud with favors and honors, as he did his other favorites.[149]

However, Süleyman did not lag in the exercise of *siyaset,* that imperative of sovereignty that required the just ruler to mete out summary punishment whenever and wherever it was warranted.[150] He executed three of his *damad*s—Ferhad, İbrahim, and Kara Ahmed—and two of his sons, Mustafa and Bayezid. Süleyman was only the second Ottoman sultan to execute an adult son and the first to do so in nearly two centuries.[151] Four years before the sultan's death, the Venetian ambassador Andrea Dandolo noted that he was "held by all to be very wise and very just but extraordinarily cruel toward those who attempt, or who in his judgment might attempt, anything against either his sovereignty or his person."[152] The historian Peçevi labeled Mustafa's execution "a manifestation of sultanic ire."[153]

In these representations of the sultan, we notice two poles of behavior: the sultan is easily swayed or quick to punish. Moreover, in contemporary Ottoman historical narratives, Süleyman is sometimes curiously absent as the rational decision maker, the ultimate arbiter of events that he obviously was. In the affair of Mustafa, for example, Süleyman is represented as naively allowing himself to be the tool of conspirators. This tendency to assign responsibility to the sultan's associates for unpopular actions or seeming breaches of proper monarchical conduct is typical of the attitude of Ottomans toward their sovereign. They preferred to see him as blameless, and if the author of harmful policy, then the victim of self-seeking and treacherous intimates. Sultans were more easily and comfortably judged misguided than unwise or cruel. It was not only rulers who benefited from this attitude: the impolitic behavior of both İbrahim and Mustafa, for example, was attributed to the harmful influence of their associates.

Let us assume, then, that Süleyman exerted a more deliberate control on events than some representations suggest. Given that his reign lasted forty-six years, he appears to have been astute at managing faction and exacting expert service from his officials. The question, then, is how the developments described in this chapter might have benefitted Süleyman or, on a larger scale, fitted into the changing dynamics of dynastic politics. Unfortunately, we probably will never be able to determine the extent to which the innovations in the concubinal career introduced for Hurrem and the vezirial career for İbrahim were deliberate structural changes or, as contemporaries saw them, the indulgence of a bewitched lover and an imprudently fond friend. The two, however, are not necessarily incompatible in a polity where the will of the ruler is absolute and decisions of a personal nature can easily affect the structures and alignments of politics.[154] We need only remember the complex relationship between the roving eye of Süleyman's contemporary, Henry VIII, his difficulty in producing a male heir, and the English Reformation.

It was of course in the interest of the sultan and the dynasty to encourage the popular view of the fallibility and corruptibility of the sultan's associates. Exploiting satellites of the ruler as scapegoats for criticism and failure is a universal tactic of absolutist government (indeed, even of democracy). Süleyman's favorites were useful means for accomplishing ends from which the sultan himself was better off maintaining a discreet distance. İbrahim could be blamed for the excessive influence of Europeans and European influence at court.[155] He was discarded when his particular talents were no longer useful and had in fact become a liability. Rüstem took the heat for tightening the royal pursestrings. He also shielded the sultan from direct responsibility for the elimination of Mustafa. In fact, with regard to the prince's death, it is hard to see how Rüstem or Hurrem could escape a negative judgment in the Ottoman historical record since, if they had been allowed to be presumed innocent, Süleyman would have been guilty of a ruthless and heinous act unprecedented in the House of Osman.

But while there was nothing new in this function of favorites, there were other areas where significant structural change in the politics of the dynasty was taking place. The changes become apparent particularly when we consider the phenomenon of the *haseki* together with that of the *damad* vezir. As we have seen, the conjunction of these two roles resulted in a powerful new configuration, that of concubine, princess, and *damad* vezir. This was only one manifestation, however, of a broader and more fundamental change: the consolidation of the dynastic family in the capital and the formation of new political networks based on the royal household. Beginning with Hurrem, royal concubines spent their entire career within the imperial residence, and the routinization of the princess-vezir marriage alliance meant that princesses and royal *damad*s were more regularly figures of the capital. Only princes continued to pursue traditional careers in the provinces, and even this would change in the generation after Süleyman. The sultanic household was considerably enlarged during the reign of Süleyman through the presence of the *haseki* and her suite. By the end of the century, with the incorporation of the suites of princes and their mothers, the royal household would become a vast and complex institution. Moreover, the number of satellite family units in the capital multiplied. The establishments maintained by *damad* vezirs were very large: İbrahim Pasha was said to own 1,300 slaves and Rüstem Pasha 1,700.[156]

As the constitution of the royal family changed, so did the distribution of power within it. With the growth in complexity of the central sultanic household, more of the sovereign power delegated or shared by the sultan remained confined within it. In terms of political control, this development was probably no more than a trade-off. While it may have enabled the dynasty to maintain control over the slave elite, the problem remained of controlling the vast bulk of the slave institution, especially the Janissaries. In addition, the consolidation of the royal family in Istanbul increased the number of powerful actors in the immediate orbit of the sultan. Already under Süleyman the effect of this density of political activity at the heart of government was evident in the politics of the succession.

In the near-universal view of Ottoman society that regards the influence of harem women as illegitimate, Hurrem has always been a hated figure.[157] She has been presented as a powerful schemer selfishly manipulating the sultan to secure the succession for one of her sons, and thereby jeopardizing the welfare of the empire. Rather, I argue that, in trying to eliminate Mustafa from the succession and enlist allies in her efforts, Hurrem was fulfilling the expected role of a prince's mother in protecting her son. Her attempts to subvert the candidacy of Mustafa were paralleled by those of Mahidevran to ensure her son's success. But while Mahidevran was praised for her efforts on behalf of her son, Hurrem was reviled. Hurrem's dilemma, and the principal source of her unpopularity, was that she was caught between two conflicting loyalties: mother to the prince and wife to the sultan.

It was the ambivalence of Hurrem's role that was principally responsible for her negative reputation among her contemporaries. Even her legal status would seem to be uncertain: she became the sultan's legal wife and in the process, one presumes, was manumitted. Yet her identity as it was recorded in formal acts of state, like that of concubines before her, continued to be mother of the prince.[158] No matter how much the old career was dismantled for Hurrem and a new one created, this fundamental relationship of Ottoman reproductive politics was inescapable so long as the combination of polygyny and open succession prevailed. But unlike the mothers of princes before her, Hurrem was made visible as the sultan's favorite (even the mosque built for her by Süleyman proclaimed this identity: it was known as the *Haseki* Mosque). Consequently, Hurrem's role as maternal advocate of the prince was also visible, a role that had previously been played discreetly in the provinces. The image of Mahidevran relayed by foreign ambassadors was that of a woman performing her maternal and political duty, honorably devoted to her son and his success. Hurrem could not enjoy that image because she was caught in conflicting roles. For the sultan's favorite, to foster the son's success was to undermine the husband's authority.

The gap between popular perceptions of Hurrem and Mahidevran must have been exacerbated by the fact that the contest between the two was so unequal. Hurrem's position as the sultan's favorite gave her access to sources of power no other mother of a prince had enjoyed. She disposed of enormous wealth, and her residence in the capital gave her greater access to information and more opportunities to form political alliances. Hurrem's closeness to the sultan—both emotional and physical—gave her great power of suasion over him. Busbecq observed that she tried to "counteract Mustapha's merits and his rights as the eldest son by asserting her authority as a wife."[159]

Insofar as the current state of research permits generalization, it would seem that it is only in the Ottoman tradition (with the exception of the early generations) that the functions of mother and of wife were delineated separately, in contrast, for example, to the Mongols, the Timurids, and the Safavids. It was with Hurrem that these two functions were collapsed for the first time in the career of one woman. The result was an untenable role that was never repeated. But the position of *haseki* did not disappear with Hurrem, although its assimilation to earlier traditions of reproductive politics would be achieved only in the generations following Süleyman.

4

The Age of the Queen Mother:
1566–1656

According to the Venetian ambassador Paulo Contarini, the dismissal of the grand vezir Sinan Pasha in 1582 was due in large part to the efforts of the queen mother, Nurbanu Sultan, who wanted her own candidate in the post. In addition, observed Contarini, she was motivated by a desire "to avenge herself for the words that Sinan had dared to speak, that empires are not governed with the counsel of women, and moreover that authority did not rest with her, even though she might try to make it seem so, but rather with the sultana consort."[1] It was perhaps at that moment, a year before the death of Nurbanu, that the combined power of the queen mother and the favorite was the greatest. The affair of Sinan Pasha's dismissal reveals the rivalry not only between influential individuals in the inner and outer government (exemplified here in the tension between queen mother and grand vezir) but between female generations (queen mother and favorite).

The first *haseki*, Hurrem, pursued the greater part of her career free from the restraints imposed by a mother-in-law, and she died before she could act as queen mother, *valide sultan*, to her own daughter-in-law, Selim II's *haseki*, Nurbanu. Thus it was for the first time in the reign of Murad III, who ascended the throne in 1574, that *valide sultan* and *haseki* competed for influence over the sultan and over factions in government. The broad arena of power enjoyed by Hurrem could not easily be reoccupied by a concubine *haseki* in the presence of the *valide sultan*, the dynastic family's eldest member. It is in this period that we observe the emergence of a hierarchy of female royal power, with the *valide sultan* at the top.

This tension among female generations existed not in a vacuum but rather in a political environment that was experiencing a number of interrelated shifts in the distribution of power. The late sixteenth century was a time of great flux in the constitution of the royal family and in the relationships among its members. The most notable changes were the demise of the princely governorate and the evolution of the system of succession from open contest through a period resembling primogeniture to a system based on seniority (the succession of the eldest male dynast). This period was also characterized by the consolidation into a single unit of the dynastic household, until then composed of the central sultanic household and the satellite princely households. During this process princes and their mothers surrendered to the sultan and his mother the autonomy, albeit limited, that had earlier been permitted them.

Hasekis and Favorite Sons

Nurbanu Sultan, the *haseki* of Selim II and the first of the great *valide sultans*, was born Cecelia Venier-Baffo, the illegitimate daughter of two Venetian noble families. Captured in 1537 by the Ottoman admiral Barbarossa Hayreddin Pasha when she was twelve, Nurbanu entered the imperial palace as a slave.[2] She probably accompanied Selim as a member of his household when he left Istanbul in 1543 for his princely governorate in Konya, where she soon gave birth to the prince's first child, a daughter. Selim seems to have confined his reproductive activity during the years of his princedom to this single concubine, although as sultan he fathered children by a number of concubines. Only one son, Murad, was born to Selim in the twenty-three years between his departure for his princely governorate and his accession in 1566, at the age of forty-two.

During Selim's princedom the Venetian ambassadors reported consistently that he was "lustful."[3] If Selim had more than one sexual partner as prince, however, measures must have been taken to ensure that only Nurbanu would bear children. The fact that she gave birth in rapid succession to four children—three daughters (Şah, Gevherhan, and İsmihan) followed by Murad in 1546—and then produced no other sons, suggests that Selim's goal was to produce his· heir by this particular concubine.[4] Another daughter, Fatma, was born during Selim's principate, probably around 1559; claims have been made that Nurbanu was her mother, although no conclusive evidence of this has come to light.[5]

When Selim came to the throne, his son Murad, twenty years old, had held the post of provincial governor for eight years. (In 1558 Süleyman had assigned provincial posts to two grandsons, Murad and Bayezid's son Orhan, both of whom were about twelve years old; Orhan and his younger brothers died by imperial order following their father's execution in 1561).[6] By the time of Selim's accession, Murad was acknowledged as his father's heir, and Selim was thus protected from the specter of a succession war during his lifetime. But the survival of the dynasty was again at risk, since it was reduced to two adult males and one infant (Murad had two daughters and a newly-born son at the time of his father's accession). Selim now addressed the vital issue of producing more sons to carry on the dynasty in the event that Murad and his infant son should die—and given the ravages of infectious disease, such a prospect was not unimaginable. As sultan, Selim produced six sons during the eight years of his reign (one predeceased his father).[7] In the process he probably observed the one mother-one son principle, since a privy purse register from the final days of his reign lists four women, each a mother of one of Selim's young sons.[8]

Selim solved the problem of avoiding civil strife among male dynasts through what we might call temporary reproductive monogamy *cum* primogeniture, a pattern followed by his son Murad. In singling out his eldest son as heir to the sultanate, Selim resembled his grandfather Selim I, who had made Süleyman his only heir. However, the temporary nature of Selim II's concubinal monogamy helped avoid repetition of the risk taken by Selim I in pinning the future of the dynasty on a single son and his offspring. But Selim II's successor was still faced with the problem of eliminating his brothers at his accession. As Murad's reign opened, the dynasty's subjects mourned not only the death of Selim but also the deaths of the five small princes whose coffins followed that of their father to his tomb. Selim was the first Ottoman sultan to die in Istanbul, and his five sons the first princes to be executed in the capital since the execution of Murad II's infant son Ahmed at the accession of Mehmed the Conqueror in 1451.

The fact that, like Selim, Süleyman's eldest son Mustafa had only one son and two daughters in what was presumably a sexually productive career of approximately twenty years suggests that the two brothers deliberately chose to limit to one the number of sons born during their princedom. Since their reproductive choices were made during their father's reign, one must wonder if Süleyman and/or the princes' mothers Mahidevran and Hurrem encouraged their sons to produce only one potential heir and to accomplish this through the practice of reproductive monogamy. That such a policy was not forced on the princes, however, is suggested by the fact that Bayezid chose to form a household different from those of his brothers. Bayezid's family was large: he had several sons at the time of his death and several daughters as well.[9] Whatever the reason, Bayezid did not emulate the reproductive continence of his elder brothers.

How did the changes made by Selim in the management of dynastic reproduction affect the women involved? So far as we know, Nurbanu was not the mother of any of the children born during Selim's sultanate, and it is likely that she ceased to be Selim's sexual partner after his accession, if not earlier. Her position as premiere concubine was assured, however, by the fact that her son had already been singled out as the heir. Moreover, because her mother-in-law Hurrem had remained in Istanbul and had not presided over the harem of her son at his provincial posts, Nurbanu had no doubt been recognized and honored as the head of Selim's princely harem. When she arrived in Istanbul in 1566 to become head of the imperial harem at Selim's accession, the Venetian ambassador Jacopo Soranzo commented that "the *Chassechi* [*haseki*]. . . . is said to be extremely well loved and honored by His Majesty both for her great beauty and for being unusually intelligent."[10] Nurbanu's prestige persisted even after Selim began to take other concubines, for in 1573 the ambassador Andrea Badoaro was still reporting that "she is called the *cassachi* and is much loved by his majesty."[11]

Following his father's precedent, Selim appears to have taken his *haseki* as legal wife. According to the 1571 report of the ambassador Jacopo Ragazzoni, this marriage was related to the sultan's esteem for his son Murad:

> Sultan Amurat [is] twenty-two, talented and well-educated, and very obser-
> vant of his religion, and therefore very much loved by all and by his father the
> Grand Signor, contrary to the custom of the Ottomans; six months ago his
> father the Signor, as a great token of his love, made a *Chebin,* which means
> that he took as legal wife [the prince's] mother, a Circassian woman, and
> bestowed upon her a dowry of 110,000 ducats, wishing to outdo his father,
> who had bestowed a dowry of only 100,000 ducats on the mother of Selim.[12]

This wedding, like that of Süleyman and Hurrem, is not mentioned in Ottoman sources.

When Selim died in 1574, Murad (III) began his twenty-one-year reign at
the age of twenty-eight. Like his father, Murad had only a single concubine
during his princedom (or at least reproduced only with one woman), and
publicly honored only his eldest son by that concubine. But unlike his father,
he continued his monogamous relationship with his *haseki* several years into
his sultanate. Murad's favorite was Safiye, a concubine said to be of Albanian
origin, from the village of Rezi in the Ducagini mountains.[13] It was with great
difficulty that Murad was persuaded by his mother Nurbanu to take other
concubines. Finally he accepted as a gift from his sister İsmihan, wife of the
grand vezir Sokollu Mehmed Pasha, two beautiful slave women, each skilled
at dance and musical performance. Murad's reluctance to take concubines
may have been due to the impotence he suffered during this period of his life:
Ottoman histories openly describe his inability to perform sexually with the
concubines offered to him.[14] Once cured, however, Murad commenced his
legendary preoccupation with a record number of consorts: at his death he left
twenty sons and twenty-seven daughters.

According to Venetian reports, Safiye maintained her dignity and status by
evincing no jealousy of Murad's concubines, although it was with bitterness
that she initially tolerated her displacement. Turning adverse circumstances to
political advantage, she even procured beautiful slaves for the sultan's pleasure, an effort that earned his gratitude.[15] Murad continued to esteem his first
concubine, consulting her on political matters, especially after the death in
1583 of his mother Nurbanu Sultan, on whom he had relied greatly.[16] Giovanni Moro reported in 1590 that "with the authority she enjoys as mother of
the prince, she intervenes on occasion in affairs of state, although she is much
respected in this, and is listened to by His Majesty, who considers her sensible
and wise."[17] In later years when Murad no longer occupied himself with other
concubines, Safiye again became the sultan's sole companion, and enjoyed
great honor and reputation.[18]

Unlike Hurrem and Nurbanu, however, Safiye probably did not become
the sultan's legal wife. Although Mustafa Ali refers to Safiye as the sultan's
wedded wife in his history,[19] foreign sources maintain that Murad did not
marry his *haseki.* The ambassador Morosini reported in 1585 that "while he
did not make her a marriage settlement, which is the equivalent of freeing her,
and assign her an appropriate dowry, she was nevertheless called by all his
wife."[20] According to "Salomone the Jew," author of a report prepared at the
time of Murad's death for the English ambassador Edward Barton, Murad did

not marry Safiye—"give her the dowry"—because of "the advice given him by some malicious enemies of his mother, that if he gave it, he would die soon, like his father, who did not live long after giving it."[21]

The reproductive politics of Murad's reign differed from those of his father in that Safiye bore more than one son. At the time of Murad's accession, there were two princesses: Ayşe and Fatma, and two princes: Mehmed, the first-born, and Mahmud; possibly other children had been born who did not survive.[22] Sometime before or during 1581 Mahmud died, placing the dynasty in the perilous situation of having a single male heir, the fifteen-year-old Mehmed, whose ability to reproduce had not yet been tested.[23] According to Salomone's report, "the . . . Sultana gave the said King many sons and daughters, most of whom having died, there remained only one son, the present Sultan Mehemet."[24] No wonder, then, that Nurbanu was anxious for her son to take other concubines.

Ambassadorial comments regarding Nurbanu and Safiye suggest the power of Hurrem's career in establishing a model that influenced the expectations of the generations following her. They also illustrate the swiftness with which innovation became accepted tradition. Within two generations, the once-disturbing *haseki* and even the marriage of the sultan had become expected features of dynastic life. This shortness of the historic memory is reminiscent of Menavino's comment at the end of the fifteenth century that the Ottoman sultans had never taken legal wives, when in fact marriages had been contracted only thirty or so years before then. There was, however, a crucial difference between Hurrem and her successors. The reputations of Nurbanu and Safiye as *haseki* were established in the provinces. Once in the capital, they moved out of their role as the sultan's favorite, a sexual role, into a postsexual political role: as mothers of the heir apparent, they acted as advisers to their husbands. Their careers combined features of the pre-Süleymanic concubinal career, with its reproductively and sexually differentiated phases, and the career of Hurrem, which was innovative in its privileging of a single concubine. The unease caused by Murad III's prolonged monogamous relationship with Safiye may have been due not only to concern about the production of heirs but also to the perception that had damaged Hurrem's reputation, namely, that the *sultan's* devotion to a single woman in a relationship that endowed her with monopoly of his sexual attention was a compromise of his autonomy.

A key element in the acceptance of the *haseki,* her legitimation, was the privileging of a single son, who was thus in an optimal position to succeed his father. While Süleyman's intention in honoring Hurrem as *haseki* is unclear—at the time it seemed a structural anomoly, one that therefore troubled his subjects—under Selim and Murad the position of favorite acquired a kind of institutional logic. The *haseki* was special because she was the mother of the honored son, the heir. The political influence of the *haseki*s Nurbanu and Safiye was more tolerable than that of Hurrem because it was not tied to partisan advocacy that appeared to challenge the sultan's autonomy. However, the reverse was perhaps also true, if not openly expressed: the effect of Hurrem's career in establishing the notion of a favorite consort facilitated the precedent-breaking move to primogeniture; it was a natural progression from favoring a consort to favoring her son.

The practice of honoring a single son, the eldest prince, in the reigns of Selim II and Murad III functioned as a transition to the system of seniority, which institutionalized the notion that sovereignty belonged to the eldest, not only of the generation, but of the entire dynastic family. In the search for precedents or influences behind this move toward privileging the eldest, two are worth considering, one indigenous, one foreign. The Ottomans' heritage did not rule out the possibility of favoring the eldest. In the first two Ottoman generations, a single son of the ruler (in the second reign, the eldest prince) had played a special role, acting as his father's delegate in government and warfare. Even after the pattern of succession began to limit the preeminence of a single prince in favor of more equal opportunity and his political role passed to the grand vezir, the eldest son often enjoyed a pragmatic advantage in the contest for the throne. It was not, however, absolute: after the death of Mehmed the Conqueror, his son Bayezid claimed a greater right to the sultanate because he was the elder of the two princes, while the younger brother, Jem, claimed preeminence because he had been born during his father's sultanate rather than during his princedom. The privileging of the eldest prince in the late sixteenth century, rather than constituting a radical innovation, involved a resumption of an earlier Ottoman pattern in which one element in the Turco-Mongol heritage, the greater status of the elder, received more emphasis than another, the equal opportunity of all to compete for the throne.

It is also tempting to consider the possibility of European influence on the Ottoman polity in the sixteenth century, when the expansion of ambassadorial networks gave monarchs greater awareness of one another. Certainly, the Ottoman dynasty displayed a propensity toward eclecticism in its reproductive politics, for example, participating in Balkan-Anatolian Christian-Muslim marriage diplomacy in its first 150 years while at the same time evolving an idiosyncratic practice of concubinage. It may have appeared to the sultans of the sixteenth century that primogeniture reduced the danger of internal dynastic disorder. As princes, Murad III and Mehmed III resembled the heirs apparent of European royalty, and the *haseki*s Hurrem, Nurbanu, and Safiye were more like queens than royal concubines (and were perceived as such by European observers, who called them "royne"). Even in his illicit affairs (if the allegations of the Venetian ambassadors are accurate), Selim II resembled the kings of Europe, exercising his *droit du seigneur* with a number of women.[25] Yet even if it was influenced by its Christian peers during the sixteenth century, the Ottoman dynasty was unable for long, or indeed really ever, to abandon a tenacious feature of its constitution: the idea that all princes were candidates for the throne, no matter how slim the odds of their becoming sultan. The fact that both Murad and his successor Mehmed felt compelled at their accession to eliminate young brothers born during their father's sultanates indicates that primogeniture as it was known in European dynasties, where cadet sons were not perceived as a threat to their elder brother, could not displace the Turkish belief that all sons were heir to the family legacy of sovereignty.

Lapse of the Princely Governorate

Since the changes in reproductive politics described above took place in conjunction with the transformation of the system of succession to the throne, we must now turn to the latter phenomenon. The major features of this process were the lapse of the princely governorate, the move to seniority (the succession of the eldest male dynast), and the lapse of royal fratricide. In this transformation the role of dynastic accident was considerable.

Like his father Murad, Mehmed III gained the throne with no opposition, having been the only son of the sultan to hold a provincial post during his father's reign. An interesting if unanswerable question is what sort of princely career Mehmed's younger brother Mahmud would have had had he lived, and what shape the succession would have taken with two princes born to the *haseki*. At any rate, Mehmed's nineteen brothers—the princes born during Murad's sultanate—were virtual unknowns outside the imperial palace where they were confined. They were executed the day the new sultan arrived in Istanbul.

With the reign of Mehmed begins the total confinement of princes to the palace. None of Mehmed's sons was assigned a provincial post, nor did the sultan single out one son as heir apparent. We cannot know if this was the result of deliberate policy or of the sultan's early death, since Mehmed died (at age thirty-seven) just as his sons were reaching the age for posting to provincial governorates. Although his eldest son Mahmud (and perhaps others) had reached late teenhood,[26] the sultan reportedly did not want to circumcise the princes (a preliminary to provincial posting) until the conclusion of the protracted war over Hungary.[27] It made sense to postpone the great festivities that princely circumcision entailed: they would serve either to celebrate victory, or, more likely, to counteract public disappointment at stalemate or defeat (just as the great circumcision festivities of 1530 had come on the heels of the Ottoman failure to take Vienna). However, the war perhaps also furnished the sultan with a convenient excuse for postponing or preventing his sons from assuming public careers. Mehmed was no doubt wary of reproducing the threat that he himself, as prince, had posed to his father. Venetian ambassadors consistently reported that during Mehmed's princedom, Murad had been extremely jealous of the public popularity of his son; indeed, fear of overthrow in favor of his son was one reason Murad so rarely left the palace.[28] According to a report of 1594, a year before Mehmed's accession, his mother Safiye had advised him to keep a low profile: "[S]eeing that his too powerful and ruthless nature did not please his father, who doubted that with these qualities [his son] could avoid winning the hearts of the soldiers, she advised him to devote himself to pleasure, as he does continually."[29]

It was probably to avoid a similar threat that Mehmed executed his eldest son Mahmud just a few months before his own death in 1603. The sultan was disturbed by Mahmud's eagerness to leave the palace and take up the role of warrior prince, especially since he himself had grown so fat that he could not campaign. Mahmud was very popular with the Janissaries, and was remembered after his death as "courageous and zealous."[30] The historian Peçevi gave an account of the affair which he learned from a confidant of Mahmud's younger brother Ahmed (who would become the next sultan). Hoping to dispel his father's worries over provincial rebellions and Safavid advances, Mahmud would say, "My lord, why are you upset, why are you angry? Send *me,* give *me* command of the army—with God's grace I'll subdue all those obstinate rebels and force them to submit to you." "Whenever he spoke like that," related Ahmed, "I would try to stop him because I could see the sultan becoming distressed, but I was unsuccessful."[31] Furthermore, Mehmed feared that the youth intended to mount a rebellion against him from within the palace.[32]

It is not difficult to see that, if the sultans of the late sixteenth century had solved the problem of avoiding a contest among their sons during their lifetime, a problem that had plagued Süleyman and his grandfather Bayezid II, they had not solved the equally serious problem of the threat of a son unseating his father. There persisted a kind of constitutional ambiguity regarding the point at which a prince had the right to claim sovereignty in the name of the welfare of the polity, or, as the Ottomans put it, "the order of the world." In contemporary biographical sketches of princes, the phrase "he was much loved by the Janissaries" is so frequently encountered as to form a topos, employed even for child princes. The Janissaries preferred assertive and activist princes, for example, Süleyman's son Mustafa and Mehmed III's son Mahmud. In the case of the latter, even confining the prince to the palace did not dispel the danger, from the sultan's point of view, that the public would prefer the son to the father. While Murad III's anxiety over the prince Mehmed in Manisa severely limited the freedom of action of both father and son (it led to the encouragement of the prince's quiescence and was a major factor in Murad's reluctance to leave his palace), Mehmed III's fears of his son led to the extreme solution of executing a prince despite the lack of any overt justification. Starting in the reign of the third Ottoman ruler, Murad I, the security of the sultan was thought to require ever-greater controls on princes, until their identity was virtually denied, although their right to the throne was never suppressed. Succession by seniority was the optimal and perhaps the only solution to this paradox of Ottoman sovereignty.

Mehmed III was the last sultan to enjoy a public role as prince. The lapse of the princely governorate during his reign, whether by design or as a result of his early death, became institutionalized largely through a subsequent series of dynastic accidents. During the next five reigns—those of Ahmed I, Osman II, Mustafa I, Murad IV, and İbrahim, spanning the half century from 1603 to 1648—no son of the reigning sultan reached the traditional age at which princes were sent to the provinces. Henceforth all male members of the dynasty spent their lives within the palace, to emerge only if and when they ascended the throne. Princes continued to be assigned provincial governorships, but this was merely a formality: stewards were dispatched in their place to oversee the affairs of the assigned province and collect its revenues. Until the time that a prince became sultan, the only public role that remained to him was to provide an opportunity for the display of royal pomp on the occasion of his circumcision. No longer an apprentice ruler, a prince had minimal status even within the palace. His official stipend of one hundred aspers a day was the lowest received by members of the sultan's immediate family, matched only by those of his unmarried sisters.[33] His lack of political status was emphasized by the fact that he was not permitted to father children when he became sexually mature (although he was given concubines).

The Transition to Seniority

The abandonment of the principle of succession of son to father came about through the combination of trends set in motion in the three generations succeeding Süleyman and a series of untimely deaths in the seventeenth century. The transition to seniority (*ekberiyet*)—the automatic succession of the eldest male member of the dynasty, be he the brother, cousin, nephew, or son of the previous sultan—was linked to the demise of the princely career. If there were no contestants for the public competition among potential heirs to identify the fittest, then there was no contest.

A necessary element in the transition to seniority was the lapse of the practice of royal fratricide. When Mehmed III's son Ahmed ascended the throne in 1603 at the age of thirteen, his nine-year-old brother Mustafa was not executed. The reason generally stated for the sparing of Mustafa is that he presented no threat to his elder brother's rule because of his mental infirmity. However, the fact that Mustafa was later considered sane enough to be enthroned raises the question of the degree to which his infirmity could have been obvious at this early stage. A more plausible explanation for Mustafa's survival is that his execution would have entailed a great risk, pinning the survival of the dynasty on a single male child whose ability to father children was untested. Ahmed seems not to have been entirely reconciled to his brother's survival and to have contemplated Mustafa's execution more than once. According to the 1612 report of the Venetian ambassador Simon Contarini, Ahmed ordered his brother strangled on two occasions, but quickly rescinded his command when he experienced violent stomach pains on the first occasion and a terrible thunderstorm suddenly developed on the second.[34] Although Ahmed left a number of male children when he died in 1617 at the age of twenty-seven, Mustafa was made sultan.

This break with the principle of succession of son to father, which had endured for three centuries, is lightly passed over in the histories of this period.[35] When explanation *is* given, it is the youth of Ahmed's children that is cited (though his eldest son Osman was fourteen, no younger than his father had been at the time of his accession). This suggests that the interlude of primogeniture, with its stress on the privilege of age, may have prepared the way for what was to come. The longest account of Mustafa's accession appears in the history of Peçevi. A contemporary of these events, Peçevi wrote that when Ahmed died, "his sons being still young but his brother Sultan Mustafa being older and having reached the age of manhood, he ascended the imperial throne." Peçevi went on to relate that leading statesmen were hesitant to take the oath of loyalty (*bi'at*) to Mustafa but that they were persuaded by the chief black eunuch Mustafa Agha that the sultan's eccentric behavior was attributable to his long confinement and that it would improve once he was in normal contact with society. Further argument by which the deputy grand vezir and the *müfti* were persuaded, according to Peçevi, emphasized Osman's youth: "It was thought that, because bringing a child prince to the throne when there was a fully grown prince available would cause public rumor and would create numerous potential dangers, the times required that the throne of the sultanate, by way of succession, be Sultan Mustafa's. Otherwise they would be the target of all the people's arrows of censure and reviling." Peçevi implies that an additional factor was the interest of Mustafa Agha, "to whose management all affairs of state had been committed during the reign of Ahmed Khan," in maintaining his power.[36]

It was this rationale of the right of the elder, or rather the danger of the rule of the younger, that was put forward in a letter sent by Osman II to the English king James I three months later. The letter informed James of Mustafa's removal from the throne (he proved to be embarrassingly incompetent) and proclaimed Osman's accession: "This paternall Empire and Monarchicall Kingdome hath almost untill this present blessed time beene alwaies hereditarie, from Grandfather to Father, from Father to Sonne, and so cursively in that manner: but having regard unto the age and yeeres of Our Great and Noble Uncle, Sultan Mustafa, hee was preferred and honoured to sit on the Ottoman Throne. . . ."[37] As might be expected, Osman resented the interpolation of his uncle into the line of succession. He dismissed the lieutenant grand vezir and limited the prerogatives of the *müfti,* both of whom he held responsible for Mustafa's enthronement.[38] In a formal decree to military forces stationed in the east, he referred to Mustafa's sultanate as a harmful breach (*bid'at*) of "an ancient tradition."[39]

The death without male heirs of the three sultans following Ahmed I was another key factor in the transition to seniority. When Osman was deposed and executed in 1622, he left no sons (one died in infancy); even if he had, the eldest would have been no more than three. The only other male members of the dynasty were Osman's five brothers (the sons of Ahmed I)—the eldest of whom, Murad, was only twelve. Mustafa was therefore returned to the throne. The fact that Mustafa was reinstalled despite his proven incompetence suggests that the statesmen of the time considered it necessary to avoid placing a child on the throne if at all possible, although the circumstances of Mustafa's enthronement—he was literally dragged to the throne from his quarters in the palace by rebel soldiers—suggest that there may have been little choice in Osman's successor. Mustafa could not be persuaded to take concubines and thus provide an heir, and so when a year later he was again deposed, Murad (IV) perforce ascended the throne. He too left no male heirs; all his sons appear to have died in infancy.[40] When Murad died at the age of twenty-eight in 1640, he was succeeded by his brother İbrahim, the only surviving male member of the dynasty. Dethroned eight years later, İbrahim left three sons, the eldest of whom, Mehmed IV, was only seven.

At Mehmed's deposition in 1687, after a reign of thirty-nine years, there was for the first time since 1617 a potential choice between the son and the brother of the ex-sultan. While some discussion took place as to whether the deceased sultan should be succeeded by one of his two brothers or by his eldest son, the principle of seniority prevailed.[41] It was by no means a foregone conclusion, however. Süleyman II, who succeeded Mehmed, had lived in such fear of execution that when he was summoned to the throne for his accession, he was convinced that the executioners had come, and remarked that death itself was better than the fear of death he had lived with every day for forty years.[42] The fact that Süleyman II had no children provided further opportunity for consolidation of the principle of seniority.

The seventeenth century was one of dynastic disorganization. Old assumptions about succession and the role of princes were no longer valid, but it took several generations for new patterns to emerge and gain consensual support. Uncertainty regarding succession was compounded by the fact that the six sultans who came to the throne in the first half of the seventeenth century were, at the time of their accession, either children or mentally incompetent, and could not rule effectively, at least at the outset of their reigns. The problem of succession was a vicious circle: uncertainty exacerbated by the frequent weakness of the throne led to a willingness on the part of subjects to depose one sultan and raise another in his place. While no sultan before the seventeenth century had been deposed by his subjects, only two of the five sultans of the first half of the seventeenth century—Ahmed I and Murad IV— died on the throne. As a result, princes did not have an opportunity to grow to adulthood before being catapulted to the throne, nor were they able to produce heirs who might reach maturity before their own accession. In this unstable environment, the political involvement of mothers was the glue that held the dynasty together.

Lapse of Dynastic Fratricide

The intermittent practice of fratricide during this half-century underlined the uncertainties of the transition to a new pattern of legitimate succession. Significantly, the only sultans in this period who executed their brothers—Osman II and Murad IV—were the only sultans to go on military campaign and thus to experience prolonged absence from the capital. Fratricide appears therefore to be linked to the possibility of a real threat to a sultan's tenure on the throne. Osman executed Mehmed, the eldest of his younger brothers, when he set out on the Hotin (Polish) campaign in 1621; he obtained the official sanction of the chief justice of Rumelia (the second highest ranking member of the *ulema*) for the execution on the grounds of preventing civil disorder.[43] Mehmed was at the time sixteen, only a year and a half younger than the sultan and thus a plausible candidate for the throne.[44] Murad executed three of his brothers, using the celebration of his victorious campaign against the Savafids in 1635 to mask the death of two, and the celebration of the reconquest of Baghdad in 1638 to do away with the other. He was persuaded to spare his last brother, İbrahim, only because of the entreaties of their mother Kösem to the effect that İbrahim's infirmities rendered him harmless (all Murad's brothers except İbrahim had been, in terms of age and mental competence, plausible candidates for the throne). Although future sultans attempted on occasion to bypass their brothers and secure the throne for their sons, the principle of seniority was sufficiently entrenched by the second half of the seventeenth century that it could be invoked as custom to prevent them from doing so. When Mehmed IV tried to do away with his brothers so that his sons might accede directly, his mother Turhan Sultan took the princes under her protection, even though they were not her own sons.[45]

The lapse of fratricide resulted to a considerable degree from the increasing power of kingmakers, leading members of the military/administrative and religious hierarchies as well as troops stationed in the capital. High-ranking statesmen had always been influential in the resolution of succession disputes. Their role in choosing among candidates derived not only from sheer political power but also the presence of an electoral principle in the Ottomans' political heritage: acceptance of the legitimate role of leading members of the community in the selection of the ruler stemmed from early Islamic tradition as well as from the Turco-Mongol tradition of the election of khans by an assembly of members of the royal family and nobles.[46] Enjoying an even greater say in this period in who would occupy the throne, these "binders and releasers" of the sultan to his throne were themselves often overwhelmed by unofficial kingmakers: the combined forces of the rank and file of the Janissary and imperial cavalry troops stationed in İstanbul, as well as the city's merchants, university students, and others who hoped to improve their lot with a change of ruler. It was in the interest of these subjects of the sultan to have close at hand a number of replacements for his office. The lapse of the practice of fratricide was due in considerable degree to this political interest in the survival of princes.[47] Lacking overt political power, princes were neverthless able to constrain the sultan through their function as figures around whom competing factions might coalesce.

The practice of fratricide was also becoming increasingly unpopular. Originally tolerated in the interest of unitary authority as a means of preventing challenges to the throne, fratricide may have seemed more justifiable as the empire was expanding and the sultans' presence on military campaigns at more distant frontiers left the capital and throne vulnerable to usurpation for more extended periods of time. After the reign of Süleyman, however, the practice of fratricide frequently involved the execution of powerless infants and young boys, and was often undertaken to protect sultans who were rarely absent from the capital. Not until 1574 did the populace of the capital witness the drama of fratricide in its own midst.

The simultaneous execution of all the brothers of a new sultan and the sight of several coffins being carried out of the palace, some of them very small, must have made fratricide seem an anachronistic practice. Pilgrims to the tombs of Selim II and Murad III, located in the courtyard of Aya Sofya, Istanbul's premier mosque, could not fail to be reminded of the sorrowful executions upon seeing the coffins of the princes, some of them doll-sized, ranged at the foot of their father's casket. According to Salomone's report for the English ambassador, a crowd of mourners twice the size of that which had come out for the funeral of Murad III appeared the next day for the funeral of his nineteen sons, who were buried "amidst the tears of all the people."[48] The Venetian ambassador reported that before their execution, the nineteen had been brought before the new sultan shortly after his arrival in the palace from Manisa: "They say that the eldest [Mahmud] a most beautiful lad and of excellent parts, beloved by all, when he kissed the Sultan's hand exclaimed, 'My Lord and brother, now to me as my father, let not my days be ended thus in this my tender age.' The Sultan tore his beard with every sign of grief, but answered never a word. They were all strangled, all the nineteen."[49] According to the historian Naima, the overthrow and violent death of Osman II was God's punishment for his unjust execution of his brother Mehmed. Writing nearly a century after the event, when royal fratricide had finally become an artifact of dynastic history, Naima condemned the sultan and his allies for the death of "the beloved prince of the Ottoman house, Mehmet Khan of noble lineage": "showing no mercy toward the blameless prince, they committed an act of tyrannical cruelty in this unjustifiable martyrdom." Less mild, or perhaps less politic, than Murad III's younger brother, Mehmed cursed the sultan: "Osman! I beseech God that your life and your reign be full of dread, and as you have deprived me of my life, may the same fate be yours." According to Naima, "his curse was accepted by God and [Osman's] punishment was soon visited upon him."[50]

Finally, fratricide was incompatible with the practice initiated in this period whereby princes confined to the palace were not allowed to father children.[51] A sultan came to the throne childless, either because he was too young to produce children or because he had been prevented from doing so. To permit a childless sultan to execute his brothers when his own ability to father children was unproven was to risk extinction of the dynasty. High rates of infant mortality exacerbated this situation. The fate of the sons of Ahmed I illustrates the perils of fratricide: of the seven princes, four were executed by their brothers Osman II and Murad IV, neither of whom produced sons who survived their fathers. The Ottoman house was fortunate that the mentally infirm İbrahim, the sole remaining prince and the only Ottoman male still alive when he ascended the throne in 1640, was able to achieve reproductive competence, unlike his uncle Mustafa, who refused sexual contact with women.

Decline of the *Haseki:*
Reproductive Politics From Mehmed III to Mehmed IV

One outcome of all these changes was that the position of *haseki* lost its traditional logic. Since the dynasty was never able to give up the notion of all sons having a right to rule, it could control delegation of power to the junior generation only by controlling the timing of a prince's assumption of public identity. A prince's right to exercise a share of sovereignty came with the establishment of an independent household. Over the course of the fifteenth and sixteenth centuries, the age at which princes were assigned to provincial posts gradually increased: Murad II had been approximately twelve, Mehmed II five, and Bayezid II eight or nine, while Süleyman's sons ranged in age from eighteen to twenty-one.

A mother's political role traditionally began with the creation of a separate household for her son. The establishment of her public political identity entailed her separation from the sultan and his household. As noted above, this kind of functional division appears to have occurred with Nurbanu and Safiye, in spite of the fact that they never left the sultan's household; the shift in their roles—that is, their assumption of a candidly political role as *haseki*—may well have coincided with their sons' assumption of their provincial posts.[52] But when, under seniority, princes lost access to public adulthood, their mothers lost *their* public roles as well. It went against the protocol of dynastic politics to publicly honor the mother of a son who had yet to achieve public identity. The position of *haseki* as a true favorite of the sultan was thus incompatible with the practice of seniority.

Because of the fragmentary nature of our information, it is difficult to be precise about the reproductive alliances of the sultans after Selim II and Murad III. The following pages can therefore present only a brief catalogue. We have very little information about the sultans' concubines, and we tend to have biographical information about the *valide sultan* only if she had been a *haseki*. Sometimes we do not even know the number and names of princes and princesses born to a particular sultan. This silence is in part a result of the general anonymity of the dynastic family once it was gathered into the imperial palace. With the princes' loss of stature came the anonymity of their mothers. While still potentially important figures in dynastic politics, since the death of other princes might render their own sons principal candidates for the succession, these women no longer engaged in visible public activity, such as the endowment of charitable institutions or the construction of tombs for their sons or themselves, that would allow them to penetrate either public awareness or the historical record.

Mehmed III (r. 1595–1603) did not have a *haseki,* unlike his grandfather, his father, or his son and heir Ahmed I.[53] Mehmed had several sons, none of whom was publicly privileged through assignment to a provincial governorate. He may have followed the one mother-one son policy, since his eldest surviving son, Mahmud, and the future sultans Ahmed and Mustafa—all born before Mehmed's accession—each had a different mother.[54] The absence of a *haseki* and reinstitution of polyconcubinage was probably influenced by two factors: Mehmed's experiences as prince and his mother's strong personality. As noted above, Mehmed's aim in avoiding the public designation of an heir was probably to save himself from having to compete with a rival son for the loyalty of his subjects. Furthermore, Mehmed's reign was dominated by the *valide sultan* Safiye, who may well have warned him against endowing any one of his sons and that son's mother with special status. Here her aim would have been not only to avoid a challenge to her hold over the compliant sultan but also to prevent any challenge to his authority. As mother of the prince, Safiye had protected Mehmed from his father; as mother of the sultan, she would naturally want to prevent a prince from acquiring the status that would enable him to rival his father.

Mehmed III was the last sultan to father children during his princedom. Of the four subsequent sultans, three came to the throne as children, and one, Mustafa, was emotionally disturbed and refused to have intimate contact with women. By the time the sultanate was again inherited by an adult male—İbrahim, who ascended the throne in 1640—the transition to succession by seniority had largely been accomplished and with it the practice of denying princes the possibility of parenthood. Succession by seniority meant that much of the purpose of the reproductive politics of previous generations was no longer relevant. In theory, a sultan was no longer concerned with the threat of overthrow by one of his sons or civil war among them, or with taking measures to ensure the succession of a favored son. As a consequence, sultans may have enjoyed more latitude of choice in their private lives, as long as they met the vital requirement that they produce heirs to carry on the dynasty and did not violate the protocols of sultanic etiquette (as the notorious İbrahim was to do).

The career of Mehmed III's son and successor, Ahmed I (r. 1603–17), was very much like that of Süleyman: he chose as his *haseki* his second or third concubine, Mahpeyker Sultan, known popularly as Kösem. While Hurrem was the woman of the Ottoman dynasty best known in Europe, it is Kösem who is remembered by Turks as the most powerful. Kösem's career was similar to that of Hurrem in important respects. She had a large number of children and may have ultimately become the sultan's only sexual partner. She was the mother of the sultans Murad IV and İbrahim, of the prince Kasım, and perhaps of the prince Süleyman; her daughters included Ayşe, Fatma, Hanzade, and perhaps Gevherhan, whose husbands she relied on in her political dealings. In 1612 the Venetian ambassador Simon Contarini described Kösem as a woman of "beauty and shrewdness, and futhermore . . . of many talents, she sings excellently, whence she continues to be extremely well loved by the king. . . . Not that she is respected by all, but she is listened to in some matters and is the favorite of the king, who wants her beside him continually. . . ."[55] According to Cristoforo Valier in 1616, Kösem was the most powerful of the sultan's intimate associates: "she can do what she wishes with the King and possesses his heart absolutely, nor is anything ever denied to her."[56] Contarini noted, however, that Kösem "restrains herself with great wisdom from speaking [to the sultan] too frequently of serious matters and affairs of state."[57] Her circumspection was probably aimed at avoiding the displeasure of the sultan, who was determined to avoid giving the appearance of being dominated by a woman, as his father had been.

Unlike Hurrem, Kösem's greatest influence occurred not as *haseki* but as *valide sultan*. She held this position for twenty-eight years during the reigns of her sons Murad IV and İbrahim and the early years of the reign of her grandson Mehmed IV. It is even possible that Kösem played a role in the transformation of the succession system: the Venetian ambassador stated that she lobbied to spare Mustafa the fate of fratricide with the ulterior goal of saving her own sons from the same fate.[58] Like Hurrem, Kösem is blamed for acting to preserve her own power rather than that of the sultan or of the dynasty.[59] It is certainly worth noting that the two women of the dynasty to suffer the harshest judgment by history had two things in common: the absence of a *valide sultan* during most of their career as *haseki* and an unusually large number of sons. What appears to have earned them their unsavory reputation was their power to influence the fate of the empire by favoring one of their sons over another. As we have seen, the political heritage of the Ottomans viewed the succession as a domain governed by divine will.

Kösem was the last of the colorful and influential *haseki*s of the "sultanate of women." Henceforth, the position of *haseki* would lose its special status. Osman II (r. 1618–1622), who succeeded his father Ahmed at the age of fourteen, after the reproductively barren reign of his uncle Mustafa, had a concubine with *haseki* rank for most if not all of his reign, but all that can be determined about her is that her name was Ayşe.[60] As was the custom with *haseki*s, Ayşe Sultan continued after Osman's death in 1622 to reside in the imperial palace and receive the *haseki*'s large retirement stipend.[61] We do not know whether Osman had other concubines in addition to Ayşe, or who gave birth to his children, none of whom seems to have survived infancy.

The domestic politics of Osman's reign did not lack drama, however. The young sultan made the most radical alliance of this period by contracting a legal marriage with Akile, the daughter of the *müfti* Esad Efendi.[62] Esad Efendi was the son of the esteemed Sadeddin Efendi, royal tutor, *müfti*, historian, and founder of a veritable dynasty of prominent religious officials (two of his four sons and three of his grandsons held the post of *müfti*, while his other two sons held the post of chief justice). This marriage appears to have taken place only a few months before Osman's death in 1622. Acting as the sultan's proxy in the marriage was the prominent Jelveti sheikh Üsküdarî Mahmud, among whose followers figured Esad Efendi.[63] Nevizade Atai, compiler of a seventeenth-century *ulema* biography, described Esad Efendi as "a second Edebali" because he was "honored by the tie of marriage to the dynasty and foremost among the Ottoman *ulema*."[64] This comparison may tell us less about popular reception of the marriage than it does about the degree to which the memory of Edebali and the marriage of his daughter to the first sultan (and the first Osman) remained alive. In fact, Esad Efendi's relations with the sultan cooled, in part at least because of the marriage.[65] Osman's marriage was a sharp break with the dynasty's tradition of avoiding legal alliances, especially with highborn Muslim women, and it contributed to the popular discontent that culminated in his deposition.[66]

Privy purse accounts suggest that Akile never entered the harem of the imperial palace. Certainly, this freeborn Muslim woman of great status would have been an anomaly in a household composed of slaves, and her presence disruptive of the harem's established hierarchies. An incident related by the Venetian ambassador Simon Contarini in his 1612 report suggests that the prospect of the *müfti*'s daughter residing within the imperial harem may have been an important element in the unpopularity of the marriage. According to Contarini, when roughly a decade earlier the daughter of the grand vezir Kuyucu Murad Pasha had wanted to enter the harem of Osman's father, the harem stewardess had discouraged her by arguing that she would lose her mind among so many slaves and that her sons would probably be killed through the practice of fratricide.[67] Demonstrated here is a paradox of the royal harem: it gave birth to and nurtured the most powerful and august family of the empire, perhaps even of the entire Islamic world, yet it was beneath the dignity of a freeborn Muslim woman to enter it.

As with Osman, very little is known about the concubines of his brother Murad IV, principally because neither sultan left sons who survived their father's death to reach the throne, thereby bringing their mothers to public attention as *valide sultan*. Privy purse registers record the presence of a single *haseki*, Ayşe,[68] until the very end of Murad's seventeen-year reign, when a second *haseki* appears.[69] It is possible that Murad had only a single concubine until the advent of the second, or that he had a number of concubines but singled out only one as *haseki*. If Ayşe was his only concubine, it is possible that it was fear of lack of male issue that prompted the sultan to take another, for his sons all died in infancy.

When the emotionally disturbed İbrahim, the only royal male to survive Murad, inherited the throne in 1640, there was considerable concern that the dynasty would face extinction. For the first year or more of his reign, fears that İbrahim would resemble his uncle Mustafa in his inability to perform sexually seemed confirmed. Fortunately for the Ottoman house, İbrahim ultimately proved quite capable of fathering children. He had eight *haseki*s, of whom the first three—Hadije Turhan, Saliha Dilaşub, and Hadije Muazzez—each had one son.[70] Unfortunately, attempts to interest İbrahim in performing his procreative duties led to an abnormal interest in sex on the part of the sultan. An unfortunate outcome of the lurid stories of İbrahim's sexual excesses and the squandering of public funds on palace orgies is that the eight-year reign of this incompetent sultan, the first four years of which were relatively orderly, has become emblematic of dynastic life throughout the seventeenth century.

The presence of more than one *haseki* was a significant change in the reigns of Murad and İbrahim, signaling that the age of the favorite was coming to an end. In this period the meaning of the title *haseki* begins to shift from a single "favorite" to something more general like "royal consort," similar to the earlier *khatun*. This title deflation was a sign of the return of an earlier principle of royal reproduction, that of a number of concubines roughly equal in status. That other concubines were no longer consigned to languish in the shadow of a favorite is suggested not only by the fact that each was endowed with the title *haseki* but also that their stipends were on the whole equal.

While the contrast between the stipend of Nurbanu, Selim II's *haseki*, and that of the mothers of his other sons was enormous (at the end of Selim's reign Nurbanu received eleven hundred aspers a day but the others a mere forty aspers), Murad's two *haseki*s and İbrahim's eight *haseki*s received roughly equal stipends at the one-thousand-asper level and higher.[71]

For the most part, subsequent sultans continued this pattern of having a number of formally recognized concubines.[72] By the end of the seventeenth century the title *haseki* was falling out of official use and was being replaced by the less elevated title *kadın*.[73] A set hierarchy was emerging according to which the sultan's first concubine (or the mother of his first child, but not necessarily his first son) was known as "head consort" (*baş kadın*) and subsequent concubines as "second consort" (*ikinci kadın*) and so forth.[74] A distinctive feature of this settled pattern of the late seventeenth and eighteenth centuries is that the one mother–one son principle continued to be observed virtually without exception.[75]

Changes in official titulature reflect not only the eclipse of the *haseki* and its replacement by a more regularized system in which royal concubines enjoyed greater equality but less prestige, but also an increase in the prestige of the *valide sultan*. The hierarchical and ceremonial gap between the sultan's mother and his concubines was symbolized by the fact that by the end of the seventeenth century the title "sultan" was denied to royal concubines and permitted only to the *valide sultan* and to princesses of the royal blood. Royal concubines were now demoted, so to speak, to the shared title of *kadın*, related to the title *khatun*, which they had held before the emergence of the *haseki* in the reign of Süleyman.[76]

The idea of a principal or favorite concubine, however, did not disappear immediately or completely. One of İbrahim's *haseki*s, Saliha Dilaşub, consistently received a slightly larger stipend than the others.[77] To bestow special honors and recognition on the favorite of his final years, a concubine named Hümaşah, İbrahim married her in an elaborate ceremony of state, much as Süleyman had used marriage to elevate Hurrem's status. Hümaşah became known as "Telli Haseki" because of the silver and gold thread (*tel*) used to adorn a bride's hair. The marriage was described by the historian Naima:

> In accordance with the imperial command, the vezirs of the imperial council each gave the gift of a moon-faced slave girl bedecked with jewels. Then they escorted [the bride] in a well-ordered procession from the gardens of Davudpasha to the imperial palace. The ceremony was performed with the chief black eunuch acting as proxy for the bride and the grand vezir for the sultan. Robes of honor were bestowed on the vezirs and the *ulema*, and others received honors according to custom.[78]

İbrahim's son and successor, Mehmed IV (r. 1648–1687), was extremely attached to one concubine, Rabia Gülnüş Emetullah, the mother of his two sons, although he had other concubines.

The idea of a favorite perhaps lingered on in the status of "head concubine," since the *haseki* was so often the first concubine of the prince or sultan.

The ban on a prince's fathering children that went along with confinement to the palace and the transition to seniority did not preclude his enjoying the company of slave women, and it seems likely that a new sultan would choose as his first full sexual partner a woman to whom he was personally attracted.

The Rise of the *Valide Sultan*

Over the course of the seventeenth century, the sixteenth-century phenomenon of the *haseki* was gradually assimilated to the older traditions of Ottoman reproductive politics: a multiplicity of concubines and rough parity among princes. Why, then, the interlude of the *haseki,* if it was incompatible with the fundamental constitution of the dynastic family? When we take a broad view of the dynasty's reproductive politics in the sixteenth and seventeenth centuries, the institution of the *haseki* appears to be one of several inextricably related developments: the end of the period of conquest, the demise of the princely governorate, the consolidation of the entire royal family in the capital, and the transition to succession by seniority with its corollary of the lapse of royal fratricide. Certainly, the *haseki* was a key development in the transformation of the system of succession. This is not to say, however, that the structural changes within dynastic politics, particularly intense in the late sixteenth and early seventeenth centuries, were the result of a deliberate and sustained plan. As noted in the previous chapter, while control of the power exercised by its various members was a constant concern of the dynasty, particularly of the reigning sultan, structural changes seem to have been as much the result of ad hoc decisions determined by the press of momentary issues as of deep thinking about the optimal constitution of the family.

There were strong forces behind the persistence of concubinal polygyny and against the notion of a single, privileged consort. Given the dangers of infant and child mortality or death through illness and on the battlefield, there was a conviction that the survival of the dynasty was more secure if not pinned to the capacity of one woman to produce healthy sons. There was also the tradition inherited from earlier Islamic dynasties that it was more appropriate for the august ruler to avoid the limitations of a legal marital alliance or any encumbering relationship; it was this tradition that had been a principal motivation behind the Ottomans' earlier abandonment of interdynastic marriage. The paradox of Süleyman's marriage to Hurrem was that it simultaneously exemplified the sultan's supreme authority to violate tradition, yet, in the eyes of his subjects, introduced limits on his autonomy. The legacy of ill feeling toward Hurrem stemmed largely from popular belief that the sultan was unfittingly and unnaturally dominated by her. Finally, there was a sense that each prince required the tutorial and guardian functions performed by his mother; until the transition to seniority was fully accomplished, the vagaries of dynastic politics meant that every prince still had a potential chance to defeat or outlive his male relatives for the succession.

It was this importance of the mother to the prince and then to the sultan that was perhaps the ultimate reason for the failure of the *haseki* to become a permanent feature of the dynasty's sexual politics. The structure of the Ottoman dynastic family and its reproductive arrangements yielded pride of place to the mother, not the consort. Even when a prince or sultan designated a favorite, he had primary ties to two women: his mother and his *haseki*. While the mother was alive, the *haseki* was subordinate to her. Furthermore, the *haseki* also had a dual allegiance: to her sovereign and spouse, and to her son. It was the second bond that was ultimately the more vital. The solution to this tension among primary loyalites was to transfer the important function that Hurrem had played in shaping the public image of female sovereignty to a figure who would not infringe on the authority of the sultan. This figure was the mother of the reigning sultan.

Among the reasons why it was in the late sixteenth century that the institution of the *valide sultan* emerged, two should be highlighted. The first is the consolidation of the multiple households of the royal family into a single household. As I argued in Chapter 2, the basic relationship upon which the pre-Süleymanic princely household was founded was that of mother and son. The mother's function in the provincial court was not only to head the prince's domestic household but also to act as a public exemplar in the provincial capital of the dynasty's solicitude for its subjects. However, through the reign of Süleyman, when the prince became sultan, the domains of mother and son separated, with the queen mother becoming head of the Old Palace household and the sultan head of the imperial household resident in the New Palace. But in the post-Süleymanic period, with the integration of the harem into the sultanic household, the mother once again became preeminent as the senior member of the royal household, with claim to certain generational prerogatives over her son. The Old Palace became the home of retired queen mothers, whose careers formally ceased at the death of their sons.

The fact that the dynastic family was now housed under one roof meant that women of considerable status and political influence pursued their own careers and promoted those of their sons in close proximity to one another. Heretofore the mothers of princes and the sultan's mother had each presided over a separate royal household. Now they faced the task of articulating separate spheres of influence within a single physical domain. In this highly charged and competitive environment a hierarchy of power was required. The solution that emerged at the end of the sixteenth century was to bolster the authority of the *valide sultan*. Further evidence of the need felt for the presence of a female elder at the head of the domestic household is the institutional prestige acquired in this period by the harem stewardess and the sultan's childhood wet nurse, the two members of the harem institution who might assume the functions of the *valide sultan* in the event of her death.

The second development underlying the prominence acquired by the *valide sultan* in the late sixteenth century is the prominence acquired by the *haseki* in the reign of Süleyman. As we shall see in Chapter 7, Hurrem established precedents in several arenas that formed the foundation of the *valide sultan*'s prerogatives. Not only did the advent of the *haseki* in the person of Hurrem prepare the way for the advent of the *valide sultan* in the reign of Murad III, but in addition the persistence of the *haseki* for at least a half century after Süleyman's death enabled the political prestige and power of the *valide sultan* to become virtually institutionalized. The sultan's favorite—this description was clearly merited by Hurrem, Nurbanu, Safiye, and Kösem—was able to marshall many resources that enabled her, first, to work toward achieving her son's enthronement, and second, to maintain her son in power once enthroned and thus to perpetuate her own role. These resources included material ones (wealth, children, servants dependent upon and therefore devoted to the survival of the *haseki* and her son) as well as intangible ones (status, political experience from close exposure to the problems of government, and sometimes direct political power). The greater the sultan's affection and esteem for the *haseki*, the more extensive all of these resources were likely to be. *Valide sultan*s who had not been *haseki*s were hampered in their exercise of authority. They had fewer material resources and sparser networks of contacts within and without the palace. The mother of Sultan Mustafa, for example, who had lived in relative obscurity as a minor concubine and mother of a prince who was deemed incapable of governing, seemed quite unable, when suddenly elevated to the position of *valide sultan*, to work out means of sustaining her son's and her own authority.

If a career as *haseki* was the springboard for a powerful *valide sultan*, the prestige of the *haseki*'s position was conversely a serious problem for the *valide sultan*. Three of the four most prominent *valide sultan*s of this period— Nurbanu, Safiye, and Kösem—had themselves been *haseki*s. Aware of the power they had enjoyed as *haseki,* these *valide sultan*s appear to have been anxious to curb the power of their daughters-in-law in order to preserve their own authority, not only over their sons but also over the resources of government. The advantages of becoming the sultan's favorite were no secret; we can only imagine that it was the goal of every ambitious concubine.

By the end of the sixteenth century, the *valide sultan* was head of a household in which her daughters-in-law were present and moreover theoretically subordinated to her. The prerogatives and imperatives of her role enabled her to constrict the political arena in which the *haseki* might act. As the female elder of the dynastic family, the *valide sultan* enjoyed control of the marriage alliances created both for her own daughters and for her granddaughters; she was thus able to usurp the opportunity of her son's concubines to create politically strategic alliances with royal *damad*s. Since one of the primary duties of the *valide sultan* was to protect her son and his sultanate, she inevitably clashed with the *haseki*, who was manuvering under the same roof to defend and promote *her* son (or sons). As the sultans scrutinized the behavior of the prince, so the *valide sultan* scrutinized the potentially subversive activities of her daughter-in-law the *haseki*.

The tension between *valide sultan* and *haseki* was in some ways similar to that between the grand vezir and his immediate subordinates—other vezirs and particularly the lieutenant grand vezir (*kaymakam*) who was appointed to remain in the capital when the grand vezir was absent on military duty. This problem was given expression by Sinan Pasha, five times grand vezir and four times dismissed from the post, in his attempt to persuade Mehmed III to take up the *ghaza* in person, Sinan argued that when the grand vezir led a military expedition, the lieutenant grand vezir would fail to send supplies to the front, thus hoping to bring about the downfall of the grand vezir and his own appointment to that office. When a vezir other than the grand vezir was put in command, the grand vezir would act just like the lieutenant grand vezir, for fear that the commander might otherwise be sufficiently successful to be rewarded with the grand vezirate.[79] For both grand vezir and *valide sultan*, holders of the highest offices to which the sultan's male and female slaves might aspire, the principal political challenge lay in maintaining their authority in the face of other claims on the sultan's favor. The most effective tool of the monarch is the arbitrariness of favor; only the sultan could overturn established hierarchies within the ruling elite, and, indeed, that is how he ultimately protected himself.

Modern accounts of this period tend to suggest that the *valide sultan* was intent on the aggrandizement of her power merely in her own interest.[80] Self-interest was surely one motive, but it is important to recognize that the *valide sultan* did not exercise power in a vacuum. She was the heart of a number of different factions and networks of influence in whose collective interest she can be said to have acted. In addition, hierarchies of status and power clearly placed the *valide sultan* above the *haseki*. To allow the ordained relationship between the two to be disrupted was to court social and political disorder, particularly in the Ottoman conception of a just society, whose foundation was the maintenance of the boundaries of each individual's proper role. Many of the *valide sultan*'s actions which resulted in the curtailment of the *haseki*'s power appear to have been aimed at upholding either the power of the sultan or dynastic custom. By the same token, however, there were limits to the contraints that could be imposed on a *haseki*. While the *haseki*'s relationship with the sultan might be undermined, her status as the mother of a prince rested on an unassailable foundation.

In the years between 1520, the beginning of Hurrem Sultan's career, and 1651, when Kösem Sultan died, the Ottoman Empire was influenced in diverse ways by dynastic women whose power derived to a significant extent from their experience as *haseki*. But this new source of power carried the seeds of its own destruction because the *haseki*, unless she predeceased her son, would go on to exercise even greater power as *valide sultan*. As the authority of *valide sultan* became institutionalized, the success of a particular queen mother became less dependent upon her previously acquired status and resources. The last of the great *valide sultan*s of this period, Turhan Sultan, had in some ways been a weak candidate: spurned by her spouse İbrahim and dominated by her mother-in-law Kösem, she had been *haseki* in name only. Moreover, when she became *valide sultan,* she was a very young woman rather than a female elder. Turhan's power rested basically on two factors: her long experience within the imperial harem and, more important, popular acceptance by the mid-seventeenth century of the *institutional* legitimacy and necessity of the *valide sultan*.

5

The Imperial Harem Institution

The Seraglio I saw as farre as Strangers use, having accesse into the
second Court . . . the inside I saw not; but an infinite swarme of officers
and attendants I found, with a silence, and reverence, so wonderfull, as
shew'd in what awe they stand of their soverayne.

> Henry Blunt,
> *A Voyage into the Levant,* 1638

I include a chapter on the quarters of the women only to demonstrate to
the reader the impossibility of knowing it well. . . . Entrance is forbidden
to men with greater vigilance than in any Christian convent. . . .

The nature of the sultan's love life is kept secret, I will not discuss it
and I was unable to learn anything about it. It is easy to compose a fantasy
on this subject but exceedingly difficult to speak accurately.

> Jean-Baptiste Tavernier,
> *Nouvelle Relation de l'interieur*
> *du serrail de Grand Seigneur,* 1675

I can, my dear brother, more easily than any other, satisfy your curiosity
about the Seraglio of the Ottoman Emperors, for, having been confined in
it more than twenty years, I have had the time to observe its beauties, its
way of life, its discipline. If one believed the many fantastical descriptions
of various foreign travellers, some of which have been translated into our
language, it would be difficult not to imagine that this Palace was an
enchanted place. . . . But its principal beauty lies in the order which one
observes within it and the education of those who are destined for the
service of the powerful who inhabit it.

> François Petis de la Croix,
> *Etat General de l'empire otoman,* 1695,
> speaking through his Ottoman informant

Penetrating the Harem: The Problem of Sources

Very little is known about the internal functioning of the harem and of relationships among its residents in the period under study. Ottoman narrative
sources are virtually silent with regard to life within the harem. Just as the
harem was hidden from a man's eyes, so was talk of life within it meant to be

beyond the reach of his ears. In the absence of indigenous descriptions of the workings of the harem institution, we must turn to accounts written by European observers of the Ottomans, our only contemporary sources. In the sixteenth and particularly the seventeenth centuries, many works providing comprehensive descriptions of the Ottoman Empire and its court were written by European travelers and ambassadors as well as by captives and renegades who had served in the sultan's palace. Descriptions of the harem and the sexual practices of the sultans clearly helped to sell books about the Ottomans and were therefore featured prominently. A mix of fact, hearsay, and fantasy, these works frequently conflate various descriptions of harem life that appear to have their origins in different stages of its evolution.

As the enterprise of writing about the lands and peoples of the Near East, and about the palace of the Ottoman sultan in particular, developed in the sixteenth and seventeenth centuries, European writers themselves recognized the limits of a foreigner's ability to accurately comprehend and describe the private aspects of the society he contemplated. At least this was an idea to which lip service was paid: it became routine for a writer to preface his own account by asserting that, particularly with regard to women, his predecessors had described things of which they could have had no experience and had therefore proffered descriptions that were nothing more than fantasy.[1] Lady Mary Wortley Montagu, woman of letters and wife of the English ambassador to the Ottoman court in 1717–1718, was eloquently cynical about her male predecessors:

> Tis certain we have but very imperfect relations of the manners and Religion of these people, this part of the World being seldom visited but by merchants who mind little but their own Affairs, or Travellers who make too short a stay to be Able to report any thing exactly of their own knowledge. The Turks are too proud to converse familiarly with merchants etc., who can only pick up some confus'd informations which are generally false. . . . Tis a particular pleasure to me here to read the voyages to the Levant, which are generally so far remov'd from Truth and so full of Absurditys I am very well diverted with 'em. They never fail giving you an Account of the Women, which 'tis certain they never saw, and talking very wisely of the Genius of the Men, into whose Company they are never admitted, and very often describe Mosques, which they dare not peep into.[2]

Writing in the second half of the seventeenth century, François Petis de la Croix, secretary to the French embassy and one of the more sober and thoughtful observers of the Ottomans, drew attention to the dubious nature of previous accounts of the royal harem and of the sultan's relations with his women. Speaking through the voice of his Ottoman informant, he wrote: "It appears that these writers would have [the harem] pass as a stage for numerous amorous scenes and gallant stories, which they report with such certainty that one would think they had been eye witnesses, so as to present all according to the tastes of their own country, which are not ours, where love is naught but the slave of nature for its satisfaction. . . ."[3]

The corollary to this critical dimension of the travel literature of this period, artificial though it may have been, was the rote assertion by each writer of the originality of his own work. Jean Baptiste Tavernier, a seventeenth-century author who made six voyages to the Levant, made this assertion in the very title of his best-selling work on the sultan's palace: "Nouvelle Relation de l'interieur du serrail du grand seigneur, contenant plusieurs singularitez qui jusqu'icy n'ont point esté mises en lumiere."

As important as his claim to originality was a writer's insistence on his faithfulness to "truth"—the rigor of his research, the integrity of his informers, the reliability of his own experience. There were, however, two fundamental limits to the foreign observer's ability to achieve "truth" with regard to the harem—the one a limitation imposed by his own culture, the other a barrier created by Ottoman society. Beginning in the second half of the sixteenth century and increasingly during the seventeenth century, currents within European thinking about the nature of political society transformed the prevalent image of the Ottoman sultanate from that of a powerful enemy admired for the discipline it exacted from its subjects into the embodiment of depraved tyranny, in whose moral degeneration the seductive and corrupting features of the harem figured prominently.[4] Writers on the Ottoman Empire were caught in the tension between the growing emphasis in the seventeenth century on eye-witness accuracy and the legacy of humanistic history-writing of the sixteenth century, with its permissiveness toward the bending of truth in order to provide a moral lesson accessible and acceptable to readers—in this case the exposure of the mechanisms of Oriental absolutism, with its subtext of implied criticism of European monarchy.[5] It was this need to pay homage to the quest for truth as well as to satisfy the expectations of readers—the tension between the *vrai* and the *vraisemblable,* the demonstrable and the plausible—that accounts for the fact that in these works the ritual debunking of earlier travelers' accounts and the assertion of the superior validity of one's own information are so often followed by the facile repetition of old stories and the creation of new fantasies. Thus, while Lady Mary replaces the theme of the oppressive seclusion of women with her repeated insistence on the freedom bestowed on Turkish women through the anonymity provided by their veil, she embellishes the theme of the libidinous Turk, describing the countless adulterous assignations in which veiled women are able to engage.[6]

The second limitation was the physical impenetrability of the imperial harem and the cordon of silence regarding life within the walls that surrounded it. In his three-volume study of the Ottomans, Paul Rycaut, secretary to the English ambassador in the 1660s, admitted this limitation in his caveat regarding his ability to offer a description of the harem: "I ingenuously confess my acquaintance there (as all my other conversation with Women in Turky) is but strange and unfamiliar."[7] Rycaut attempted to overcome this limitation by employing as informant "an understanding *Polonian,* who had spent nineteen years in the *Ottoman* Court."[8] This "Polonian" was most probably Albertus Bobovius, a music page trained in the inner palace school, whose own account of the sultan's palace is one of the best we have for the seventeenth century.[9] But even Bobovius missed crucial details of harem organization. For example, although he understood the nature of the queen mother's power very well, he incorrectly assigned her title to the mother of the sultan's firstborn son.[10] The problem in relying on Christian captives who, as servants of the sultan in the inner palace, could be expected to know more about its functioning than almost any other contact a European traveler might court, was suggested by Tavernier. In order to impress his readers with the impossibility of obtaining inside information about the harem, he pointed out that one of his two informants, a Sicilian who had spent fifty-five years in the palace service and had been employed in the suite of the head treasurer, one of the principal eunuch officers of the inner palace, could describe the functioning of the third courtyard with exquisite detail but could not supply a single fact about life within the women's apartments.[11]

For both of these reasons, the difficulty of achieving accurate representations of the harem was exacerbated as time went on. As the focus of their own political and social world shifted from the battlefield to the court—a process that accelerated, like that of the Ottomans, in the second half of the sixteenth century—Europeans became more preoccupied with the problems of sovereignty and royal absolutism. When they considered the Ottoman sultan, they were less concerned than their predecessors with the elements of his military might and instead cast their gaze increasingly upon the palace and its private domains, the closest equivalent of their own courts. But while European absolutism was exemplified by Louis XIV's representation of himself as the Sun King, the power of the Ottoman sultan was demonstrated through his seclusion.[12] His very hiddenness impeded the quest for "truth." The frustration of European inquiry thus created a fertile climate for speculation and the propagation of fanciful, even lurid, tales. Moreover, the European reading of changes in the Ottoman sultanate may well have been influenced, to some degree at least, by that current of late sixteenth- and early seventeenth-century Ottoman opinion, eloquently expressed in a number of writings, that greeted the increasingly sedentary and secluded sultanate with dismay (see Chapter 6). These Ottoman writers could agree with their European counterparts that the sultanate more and more embodied the quality of tyranny, although the specific content of that "tyranny" was differently defined.[13]

However, among the numerous sixteenth- and seventeenth-century European works on the Ottoman Empire, some stand out as providing more reliable information about the harem institution and its highest-ranking members. These works tend to be of two kinds: the accounts of captives who served as pages in the imperial palace,[14] and the reports, dispatches, and letters of ambassadors resident in Istanbul, their secretaries, and other members of their suites.[15] The best of these works have the advantage over those written by less well informed travelers of their authors' direct experience of Ottoman institutions and acquaintance with prominent persons, and the linguistic competence necessary to exploit these resources. In particular, ambassadorial writings—the formal "relations" composed for home government consumption, dispatches, formal and informal letters, and memoirs—form an excellent complement to Ottoman narrative sources for the political activities of harem women, if less so for the structure of the harem. Recognizing the importance of palace-based networks and factions and the importance of royal women in their formation, ambassadors strove not only to acquire information about these women but to establish ties to them. The sources of information tapped by ambassadors would appear to have been no less highly placed than those of which Ottoman writers availed themselves (the question of motivation in sharing information is of course another matter). It is primarily from these sources that popular reaction to the influence of harem women can be gauged. Of the ambassadorial writings for the sixteenth century, those of the Venetians surpass all others in their volume, comprehensiveness, sophistication, and accuracy.[16]

One touchstone for the reliability of an account of the harem institution is its treatment of the *valide sultan*. Mention of her is omitted in a number of influential European descriptions, which instead pay much attention to the sultan's concubines. Frequently such works accurately describe aspects of the *valide sultan*'s authority but attribute them to the principal concubine.[17] This confusion certainly owed something to the real importance of the *haseki*. However, it must also be ascribed in part to the apparent cultural blinders of these European observers who, in this case, sought the counterparts of their queens and so were unprepared to recognize that it was the queen *mother* who enjoyed the greatest power and status in the Ottoman harem. A further reason for this inaccuracy is that writers tended to be heavily influenced by earlier accounts of the palace and indeed on occasion indiscriminately incorporated portions of them into their own works. One wonders how the Venetian ambassador Ottaviano Bon, whose tenure in Istanbul overlapped with the career of the extraordinarily powerful *valide sultan* Safiye, could omit mention of her office in his lengthy account of the Ottoman court. Even Rycaut, who was well aware of the importance of the *valide sultan,* for he recounted in a long chapter the murder of Kösem Sultan, neglects the *valide sultan*'s central role in his description of the harem institution.[18] Perhaps writers such as Bon and Rycaut, while appreciating the distinction between *valide sultan* and *haseki,* conflated the two in the expectation that their readers would find it more satisfying to believe that power lay with the sultan's concubine rather than with his mother.

The example of Rycaut illustrates the fact that even the most reliable of European descriptions of the harem partook to some degree of the body of hearsay and fantasy circulated among foreign observers. Even the page Bobovius's detailed accounts of the sexual practices and mores of the royal family clearly fall into this category. Since Bobovius probably wrote his memoir for circulation among the foreign embassies in Istanbul, it may be that he was simply describing what his audience wanted to hear. On the other hand, it may be that the body of hearsay and fantasy about the harem so popular among European writers was shared by the male establishment within the palace, or perhaps even originated there. Bobovius himself exemplifies the links between the lore of the palace and that of the European community— and perhaps of Ottoman observers as well, though they did not dare to record it. Like all slaves of the sultan, Bobovius was converted to Islam; however, after expulsion from the palace for excessive fondness for drink, he abandoned his Muslim name of Ali, returned to his original faith, and wrote his memoir. In addition to acting as Rycaut's informer, Bobovius may well have served Petis de la Croix in the same capacity, either through oral testimony or by means of his memoir.[19] That writers, no matter how well intentioned or devoted to unearthing the "truth," were inescapably tied to the dictates of what had become a fixed genre is suggested by the fact that, in his *Etat general de l'empire otoman,* intended for a public audience, Petis de la Croix repeats the standard exposition of the harem, concentrating on the sultan's chief concubine rather than on the *valide sultan,* while in his memoirs he gives a detailed description of the latter's commanding presence and authority over even her son.[20]

In attempting to give an account of the harem institution in the sixteenth and seventeenth centuries, we thus find ourselves on the horns of a dilemma: do we reject everything European accounts tell us and thus retain only the fragments that can be acquired from Ottoman sources, or do we risk compounding the errors of European writers by admitting their evidence? The problem is exacerbated by the fact that the few modern scholarly accounts of harem life tend to make indiscriminate use of the writings of European travelers, ambassadors, and captives who served in the sultan's palace.[21] Modern studies suffer from another limitation: they conflate the accounts of women who lived in the harem in the nineteenth and twentieth centuries with the earlier descriptions written by Europeans. While the accounts of harem women, some of them members of the dynasty, are perhaps accurate for the period they describe, they cannot be presumed valid for a period two or three hundred years earlier. Despite areas of continuity, the harem was, as we have seen, an institution that experienced continuous change. An example of inappropriate projection into the past of a later pattern is the assumption that the system of formally ranked royal concubines that existed from the end of the seventeenth century and its accompanying titulature—head *kadın,* first *kadın,* and so on—was a timeless feature of the harem institution; as a consequence, the sixteenth- and seventeenth-century phenomenon of the *haseki* has been overlooked.[22]

Fortunately, Ottoman archival materials can assist us in making judicious use of European sources and the fragments contained in Ottoman narrative sources. Most useful are privy purse registers (*masraf-ı şehriyari/harc-ı hassa defteri*) covering the century from the 1550s to the 1650s. These registers of royal income and expenditure provide information that enables us to understand the structure of the harem institution, to chart its tremendous growth in this period, and to reconstruct the careers of individual women of the dynasty. The portrait of the harem institution that can be drawn from these registers, when joined with the more complete knowledge we have of the structure of the third courtyard, can serve as correctives to the deficiences and excesses of European accounts.

At the Heart of Empire:
The Integration of the Harem into the New Palace

The transformation of the imperial harem into a coherent and highly articulated institution was a principal feature of post-Süleymanic dynastic politics. This transformation was the result of changes that occurred during the reigns of Süleyman and his successors, in particular the consolidation of the royal family in the capital. As the sultan became an increasingly sedentary palace ruler, the members of his family, heretofore scattered among provincial capitals, were gradually relieved of their public duties and gathered into the imperial capital. By the end of the sixteenth century, no member of the royal family—male or female—left the capital, with the exception of the sultan himself. Sons as well as mothers became permanent inhabitants of the inner world of the palace. As the sixteenth century progressed, the ranks of the royal residence steadily grew, first absorbing the suites of royal concubines and then those of princes, and adding service staff to accommodate the needs of the harem's increased population. The soaring of palace expenses in the late sixteenth century, generally thought to be the result of the devotion of post-Süleymanic sultans to a life of pleasure, was primarily the result of the dynastic family's consolidation into a single household.

The rise to power of the imperial harem was due not just to the presence of the royal family in the capital but also to the integration of the domestic (and principally female) side of the royal household into the imperial residence. Until Süleyman's reign, the principal quarters of the harem were the royal residence known as the Old Palace (*saray-ı atik*), the first palace constructed by Mehmed II after the conquest of Istanbul. By 1468 Mehmed had taken up residence in the splendid New Palace (today called the Topkapı Palace) that was being constructed on the most dramatic site in Istanbul: the point of land at the confluence of the Sea of Marmara, the Golden Horn, and the Bosphorus. However, the harem remained behind in the Old Palace for nearly another century. It did not begin to be incorporated into the New Palace (*saray-ı jedid*) until Hurrem Sultan took up residence there. After the reign of Süleyman, the harem not only grew rapidly but acquired organizational and functional characteristics befitting its new role as a principal division of the imperial residence. The enormous growth in the population of the harem created the need for greater hierarchical organization and differentiation of function than had previously been necessary. It is this expanded harem that we can appropriately call "the harem institution." It consisted of the female members of the dynastic family and the extensive household that served them. The basic outlines of the harem institution were set by the first decade of the seventeenth century, although it continued to grow and mature in succeeding decades.

As the primary residence of the sultan's family until the reign of Süleyman, the Old Palace housed princes and princesses and their mothers, and it was there that the sultan's own mother, the individual with the greatest status and authority in the harem, resided. The sultans visited the Old Palace frequently, presumably to observe the progress of their children, to enjoy the company of their consorts, and to pay their respects to their mothers and consult with them. At least one mother of a sultan, Gülbahar Khatun, the mother of Bayezid II, believed that her son did not visit her frequently enough, for in a letter to him she wrote plaintively: "My fortune, I miss you. Even if you don't miss me, I miss you. . . . Come and let me see you. My dear lord, if you are going on campaign soon, come once or twice at least so that I may see your fortune-favored face before you go. It's been forty days since I last saw you. My sultan, please forgive my boldness. Who else do I have beside you . . . ?"[23] Because it housed all members of the royal family except the sultan himself, the Old Palace played a prominent role in royal ceremonial. Celalzade Mustafa, imperial chancellor to Süleyman and historian, described in great detail the 1530 celebration of the circumcision of Süleyman's three elder sons, Mustafa, Mehmed, and Selim. When it came time for the princes to join the festivities, they were formally escorted from the Old Palace:

> On the fourteenth day the aghas of the inner and outer service of the most noble royal household, all on horseback, arrived at the Old Imperial Palace and mounted the blessed princes on horses. . . . The princes proceeded in imperial glory to the Hippodrome, [where] the most exalted of the pashas greeted them on foot. They descended from horseback at the entrance to the hall of the imperial council, filling the *padishah* [who awaited them] with abundant happiness.[24]

Although the sultan maintained an apartment in the Old Palace,[25] his principal residence was the third courtyard of the New Palace, where he was attended by eunuchs and pages in training. From its initial construction, the New Palace also contained quarters for women, but on a limited scale.[26] According to Iacopo de Promontorio de Campis, a Genoese merchant whose description of the court of Mehmed II is one of the earliest that makes mention of the royal harem, 150 of "the most splendid, well-kept, and beautiful women that could be found in the world" were lodged at the New Palace, while the Old Palace housed 250 women.[27] It seems likely that these New Palace quarters functioned primarily to house the young women who were the sultan's current favorites and the staff to serve them; fittingly, the harem area was known in this period as "the palace of the girls."[28] Given the one mother-one son policy, such an arrangement was a logical one: a concubine would be a candidate for the sultan's sexual attentions until she became pregnant, after which time she would be lodged in the Old Palace in preparation for the royal birth, and would continue to reside there with her child (if she gave birth to a daughter, she might still be eligible for the sultan's sexual attentions). The source of new concubines for the sultan was the Old Palace, where certain carefully selected young girls were given the training appropriate to a royal consort. Luigi Bassano described the custom by which a concubine chosen by the sultan was brought from the Old Palace to the New Palace:

> The Grand Turk has a palace of women at quite a distance from his own. There he keeps a great number of young Christian slave girls. . . . From

these the Grank Turk chooses whoever pleases him the most, and keeps her separate for two months, and amuses himself with her as he pleases; if she become pregnant, he takes her as his consort, otherwise he marries her to one of his men. . . .[29]

According to Guillaume Postel, a richly caparisoned carriage, accompanied by four or five eunuchs, would transport a newly chosen concubine to the sultan's residence.[30] Even after the integration of the sultan's domestic household into the imperial palace, the Old Palace continued to be a source of concubines for the sultan. Describing the Old Palace, John Sanderson, a member of the English embassy at the end of the sixteenth century, commented that "the virgins of the Grand Sig[no]r remaine ther. Thether he goeth many tims upon pleasure. . . ."[31]

The fact that extensive repair and expansion took place in the New Palace harem quarters in the late 1520s[32] suggests that Süleyman was planning at that time to move at least some part of his harem to the New Palace. Hurrem Sultan was probably the first female of consequence to live in the sultan's palace. As we have seen in Chapter 3, she and her children appear to have been living there by 1534. Süleyman's mother Hafsa Sultan may also have taken up residence in the New Palace before her death in March 1534, although there is no evidence to demonstrate this. Following his father's precedent, Selim II kept his *haseki* Nurbanu in the New Palace.[33] Since Selim's younger sons also lived at the palace,[34] it is likely that their mothers lived there as well. In 1573, a year before Selim's death, Costantino Garzoni reported that the harem quarters in the New Palace were small (housing 150 women) in comparison with the Old Palace (whose female population he sets at 1500, a gross exaggeration). The harem under Selim II was indeed small—a palace salary register at the time of Selim's death shows a harem population of forty-nine women in the New Palace and seventy-three in the Old Palace (not counting members of the royal family).[35] Garzoni also noted that the sultan entered the harem at night, suggesting that his formal residence was still the third courtyard.[36]

From the beginning of Murad III's reign in 1574, privy purse registers record steadily growing numbers of women present in the New Palace. Over the course of Murad's twenty-one year reign, the population of the New Palace harem grew to several times the size of Selim II's harem (see table). Because of the extensive renovation and expansion of the harem that took place during his reign, the New Palace was better able to accommodate a larger harem population than before. An eyewitness account of the departure from the New Palace of Murad's concubines at his death in 1595 suggests that the entire royal family was then resident in the New Palace:

> Directly after these poor princes [Murad's nineteen executed sons] . . . had been buried, the populace waited at the gate to witness the departure from the Seraglio of their mothers and all the other wives of the king, with their children and their goods. All the carriages, coaches, mules, and horses of the court were employed for the purpose. Besides the wives of the king and the 27 daughters, there were 200 others, consisting of nurses and slaves and they were taken to the Eschi Seraglio [the Old Palace]. . . .[37]

Growth of the Harem as Reflected in Privy Purse Registers

	New Palace		Old Palace		Total	
Date of register	Harem Population	Monthly stipend expenditure (in aspers)	Harem Population	Monthly stipend expenditure (in aspers)	Harem Population	Monthly stipend expenditure (in aspers)
1552	—*	—*	167	24,360	167	24,360
1575	49	12,510	73	7,470	122	19,980
1581–1582	104	27,180	146	19,320	250	46,500
1600–1601	275	52,373	298	52,740	583	104,113
1603–1604	276 (10	64,855 10,500)	334	65,330	610	130,185
1612	—† (10	56,913 15,342)	—† (8	107,031 16,500)	—† (18	163,944 31,842)
1622	295 (47	112,570 61,900)	411 (17	128,520 26,130)	705 (64	241,090 88,030)
1633	433 (65	136,470 59,970)	412 (19	120,450 36,420)	845 (84	256,920 96,390)
1639–1640	—† (102	169,037 77,760)	—† (18	125,010 34,700)	—† (120	294,047 112,460)
1647–1648	—† (147	233,916 133,408)	—† (21	142,827 30,612)	—† (168	376,743 164,020)
1652	436 (142	206,258 131,085)	531 (16	128,505 25,050)	967 (156	334,763 156,135)

Figures do not include active or retired *valide sultan*s, *haseki*s, harem stewardesses, or nurses. Figures in parentheses indicate the portion of the harem population represented by the household staff, the *Dar üs-Saade*.

*Although Hurrem Sultan and her suite were living in the New Palace, the register lists them as resident in the Old Palace.

†No figures are given in the register.

The information in this table is drawn from the following registers in the Prime Ministry Archives: Maliyeden Müdevver Nos. 487 (1575), 422 (1581–1582), 5633 (1600–1601), 843 (1612), 847A (1622), 2079 (1633), 1692 (1647–1648), 774 (1652); Ali Emiri, Kanuni No. 24 (1552); Kamil Kepeci No. 7104A (1639–40). The data for 1603–1604 is from an unidentified register published by Barkan ("İstanbul Saraylarına ait Muhasebe Defterleri," 155).

As this account indicates, once it became accepted practice for the extended family of the sultan to reside with him in the New Palace, the Old Palace became the home principally for retired harems. Henceforth, upon a sultan's death, the women associated with him—his servants, his mother (should she outlive him), and his concubines, as well as their servants and suites—would be transported to the Old Palace. A sultan's unmarried daughters would accompany their mothers to the Old Palace, and so, presumably, would princes who were considered too young to be separated from their mothers and governesses. For many members of the harem of a deceased sultan, marriages would be arranged with suitable men in the service of the state; at the time of her marriage, a slave woman would customarily be manumitted and provided with a dowry.

As a rule, it was considered unseemly for the mother of an Ottoman prince to be married, and so she might form the center of a court whose size and influence would depend upon the status she had acquired in her career in the New Palace. At times, when it housed more than one woman of considerable status, the Old Palace was undoubtedly a place of both ceremonial and political importance. In the early years of the reign of Osman II, for example, there were resident in the Old Palace two former *valide sultans*—Safiye Sultan, the once-powerful mother of the deceased Mehmed III, and the mother of the deposed but still living Mustafa—as well as Kösem Sultan, the influential *haseki* of the deceased Ahmed I, who would become *valide sultan* in a matter of years.

The Old Palace continued to serve as one of the focal points on the map of royal urban ritual. It was from there that the daughters of the sultans were married. In the post-Süleymanic period, princesses' weddings were celebrated with great pomp. They counted among the most important of the grand occasions that enabled the urban populace to take pride in the magnificence of its sovereign house. These weddings were ceremonial events in their own right, no longer occurring as adjunct to the circumcision of a prince, as the wedding of Süleyman's only daughter Mihrimah had been to the celebration of her brother Bayezid's circumcision in 1539. Occasionally, the entire domestic household of the sultan removed to the Old Palace for the wedding celebrations. During the festivities leading statesmen and religious dignitaries as well as their harems were formally received and feasted.[38]

The weddings of Murad III's daughters in particular were splendid events centered on the Old Palace. It was from there that Ayşe Sultan was married in 1586 to İbrahim Pasha, governor of Egypt,[39] who would serve three times as grand vezir to Ayşe's brother Mehmed III, and that Fatma Sultan was married in 1593 to the admiral Halil Pasha.[40] The historian Selaniki described the excitement of the crowds who turned out to watch the elaborate processional that carried Fatma Sultan, who was concealed behind a screen of red satin, to the palace of her new husband. On such festive occasions, the lucky onlooker might receive one of the coins distributed as tokens of the dynasty's beneficence (and perhaps also as a means of ensuring a sizeable and appreciative audience); Selaniki wrote that at the wedding of Fatma Sultan "skirtfulls of shiny new coins were distributed . . . those who did not receive any sighed with longing."[41] The ceremonial importance of the Old Palace continued into the seventeenth century: when Ahmed I's daughter Hanzade Sultan was married in 1623 to Bayram, agha of the Janissaries, she was escorted from the Old Palace by the vezirs, who walked on foot at the head of the bridal procession.[42]

The Old Palace was also one of the several places in Istanbul to which the sultans were in the habit of going periodically for what Selaniki called a "change of air." Sanderson noted that it was not only the presence of his concubines that drew Mehmed III frequently to the Old Palace, but also its "faire lodginges, great orchards, many banias [baths], cleare fountayns."[43] Selaniki tells us that in 1597 Mehmed moved to the Old Palace in "perfect spendor and magnificence," where he spent the month of October in pursuit of "tranquillity and repose," although his sojourn there began with a great show of fireworks "the resounding echo of [whose] dreadful crashing caused commotion to the farthest point in the heavens."[44] Gradually, however, the Old Palace seems to have diminished in status, although it continued through the seventeenth century to house larger numbers of women than did the New Palace: in 1622, there were 411 women in the Old Palace harem and 295 in the New Palace; in 1652, the numbers were 531 and 436, respectively.[45] An official memorandum written at midcentury by the *valide sultan* Turhan to the grand vezir scolded him for neglect of the Old Palace: "There is not enough firewood in the Old Palace to boil soup! What's the reason for this? Is it not a royal palace?"[46]

A question that must be asked is why Mehmed the Conqueror separated the residence of the sultan's family from his own and why Süleyman and his successors reintegrated the two royal households.[47] The answer may lie, in part at least, in the system of dynastic reproduction followed in the fifteenth and early sixteenth centuries. This system created a structural separation between the sultan and the mothers of his children, whose roles were defined through their relation to their children, in particular their sons. This separation was echoed in the structuring of the royal family's residences. The New Palace was the center of government and a world of men, the second courtyard publicly devoted to affairs of the empire, and the inner sanctuary of the third courtyard—an all-male *harem*—devoted to preparing youths for service to the empire. In the fifteenth century the function of the sultan's residence was increasingly defined by the expanding apparatus of government—which, because of the central role created for the household slaves of the sultan (*kapıkulu*) by Mehmed II, meant the expansion of the imperial residence. The function of the Old Palace was to house, nurture, and educate the sultan's family and its female servants. The fact that the sultan's formal role in sustaining the dynasty—fathering its sons and daughters—was accomplished in the New Palace highlights the functional separation of the two royal households.

The phases of a concubine's career could be marked by her passage between the two households. During her training in the Old Palace, she was defined by her subordination to its senior female members and the yet undecided nature of her future career. If she was chosen by the sultan for his bed, she was transported to the New Palace. There, for a brief period, she was defined solely by her relationship to the sultan: she was his sexual partner. If she became pregnant, she acquired a functional role that required her return to the Old Palace, where she was endowed with her own quarters and attendants. If her child was male, she and he would eventually leave the Old Palace to form a new shared household in a provincial capital. If the concubine did not become pregnant, the sultan would marry her off to one of his slaves, an indication that there was no role within the dynastic household for a childless, therefore functionless, concubine. Süleyman's singling out of one woman as *haseki* extended the sexual phase of the concubine's career into a permanent relationship; her residence in the sultan's palace was a corollary of that relationship. Correspondingly, the rule for residence in the Old Palace in the post-Süleymanic period became the absence of a relationship with the sultan: it was the home of the harems of deceased rulers and a training school for young slave women.

The integration of the harem into the New Palace was completed with the transfer of the sultan's primary residence from the third courtyard into the harem precinct. While Süleyman and especially Selim II undoubtedly spent considerable time within the harem, their principal quarters were the privy chamber in the third courtyard, where they were attended by the elite of the pages in training. The transfer occurred in a definitive fashion when Murad III had constructed within the harem precinct exquisitely decorated quarters for himself and a majestic hall where receptions and entertainments could be held with the inhabitants of the harem. The fact that, while the new royal quarters were undergoing construction, Murad removed to the Old Palace together with his harem[48] rather than to the third courtyard, underlines the degree to which the female rather than the male harem had become the primary residence of the sultan.

It was necessary that the harem provide an environment suitable for the monarch. Much of its growth and structural development in the reign of Murad and subsequent sultans came about for this reason. The sultan's new residence—the second imperial harem—was styled after the first, especially with regard to the functional definition of the sultan's personal servants. In addition, the harem acquired its own corps of eunuchs. By 1594 the black eunuchs had been removed from the jurisdiction of the agha of the Gate of Good Fortune (*Bab üs-Saade*), white eunuch head of the third courtyard. They were structured into a hierarchy of offices under their commanding officer, the agha of the Abode of Good Fortune (Dar üs-Saade), and occupied quarters that formed a boundary between the harem and the second, semi-public, courtyard.[49]

Hierarchy of the Harem Institution: The Family Elite

In the privy purse registers of the period under study, harem residents were listed in three categories, which we can assume represented the broad divisions within the institution. The first of these was the elite of the harem: those carrying the title "Sultan" (the *valide sultan*, the *haseki sultan*, and princes and princesses) and, after 1620 or so, the sultan's wet nurse (*daye khatun*), and the harem stewardess, chief officer of the institution (*ketkhüda khatun*). The second was a middle group composed of the harem's administrative and training staff and other women of some status. The final, and largest, group was the rank-and-file service corps. The outstanding revelation of these registers is the extraordinary status within the dynastic family of the *haseki* and especially the *valide sultan*.

The hierarchy of the harem institution was recognized and symbolized by the daily stipends (*mevacib*) paid to each of its members from the imperial treasury. Nearly every member of the governing elite, including members of the dynasty, received a stipend from the empire's treasuries. Even the sultan, who in theory held the empire's wealth as his personal possession and for whom a stipend would thus not be appropriate, was assigned "pocket money." In some cases *mevacib* constituted one's wage, remuneration for actual service, while in other cases it was an honorary stipend (as in the case of an infant prince or princess). The *mevacib* of a high-ranking Ottoman, male or female, did not represent his or her total wealth, which might consist also (and in some cases exclusively) of land grants, tax concessions, and the like. But while one's *mevacib* was not a reliable index of total monetary worth, it was a reliable index of status, and it is as such that the stipends of harem members will be considered in the following discussion. Information in the privy purse registers, especially stipend figures, forms the basis for this discussion of the harem hierarchy, which begins with the family elite.

The *Valide Sultan*

The supreme position of the *valide sultan* was the keystone of the harem institution. She was invested with guardianship of the royal family as well as with administrative control of the day-to-day functioning of the harem household. The *valide sultan*'s superior status as the most important and powerful member of the dynastic family within the harem was acknowledged by her stipend, the highest in the empire. Nurbanu Sultan, mother of Murad III and the first *valide sultan* to govern the harem institution in the post-Süleymanic period, was assigned a daily stipend of 2,000 aspers.[50] Mehmed III raised this stipend to 3,000 aspers for his mother Safiye Sultan, Nurbanu's daughter-in-law and successor as *valide sultan*. This increase was awarded on the eve of Mehmed's departure from Istanbul on the Erlau campaign, about a year and a half after his accession,[51] and was no doubt meant to signal the authority the sultan delegated to his mother in his absence. Safiye's stipend appears not to have been reduced upon Mehmed's return to the capital; privy purse registers indicate that she continued to receive 3,000 aspers a day throughout her son's reign.[52] In contrast, the highest stipends of leading public officials listed in the privy purse registers are those of the *müfti* (750 aspers a day), the chief justices of Rumeli and Anatolia (572 and 563 aspers, respectively), and the Janissary agha (500 aspers).[53] The stipends of the members of the imperial council are not listed in these registers, but if the information of John Sanderson is correct, the vezirial stipend at the end of the sixteenth century was 1,000 aspers a day. According to Sanderson, the sultan allowed himself only 1,001 aspers.[54] This 1:3 ratio between the stipends of the sultan and his mother is the same as that between Süleyman's princely stipend in Manisa and the stipend of his mother Hafsa, suggesting that it may have been a standard multiplier within the dynastic family.[55]

The *valide sultan*'s stipend remained at this extraordinarily high level with two brief exceptions. These two exceptions suggest that not all *valide sultans* were equal and that a powerful *valide sultan* could extend her influence beyond her natural term of office—the reign of her son—thus confining the status of her successor. The extraordinary prestige of Safiye, who dominated the sultanate of her son, was reflected in the fact that she continued to receive a daily stipend of 3,000 aspers after her removal to the Old Palace following

Mehmed's death in 1603,[56] while her successor in office Handan Sultan, mother of the new sultan, Ahmed I, received only 1,000 aspers.[57] Handan Sultan is a pale figure in this period of colorful women. Her inferior status as *valide sultan* was no doubt a result, in part at least, of her inferior status as concubine; Mehmed had elevated none of his concubines to the status of *haseki*, and so Handan was deprived of the kind of recognition enjoyed by Nurbanu and Safiye before their sons' sultanates. Furthermore, Handan died two years after her fourteen-year-old son Ahmed I took the throne, and therefore did not have much opportunity to develop an influential presence as *valide sultan*. In reaction to his grandmother Safiye's domination of his father, Ahmed appears to have deliberately downplayed the *valide sultan*'s role, and perhaps lowered his mother's stipend accordingly.

When Ahmed's brother Mustafa became sultan in 1617, his mother—whose name is lost to history[58]—received 3,000 aspers as *valide sultan*[59] although her mother-in-law Safiye was still alive.[60] However, she received only 2,000 aspers during her retirement in the Old Palace between her son's two reigns;[61] during the first months of Mustafa's mother's retirement Safiye was still alive, perhaps a neighbor in the Old Palace, receiving 3,000 aspers a day. While Mustafa's mother, as a concubine of Mehmed III, had suffered the same obscurity as Handan, she was clearly able to command greater status as *valide sultan* than her fellow concubine had. This was probably in large measure because she exercised power more directly, acting as regent for her mentally incompetent son.

Like Safiye, Kösem Sultan's prestige as *valide sultan* overshadowed that of her daughter-in-law, Turhan. Kösem, who had enjoyed considerable status as the favorite of Ahmed I, was for twenty-five years a powerful *valide sultan* to her sons Murad IV and İbrahim. In 1648, when Mehmed IV succeeded his father İbrahim at the age of seven, his grandmother did not retire to the Old Palace as custom required, but stayed on as "great *valide sultan*." Mehmed's own mother Turhan received the title *valide sultan*, but was distinctly subordinate to her mother-in-law, a state of affairs underlined by the fact that Kösem continued to receive her stipend of 3,000 aspers while Turhan received only 2,000 aspers.[62] When, after Kösem's death in 1651, Turhan became head of the harem institution, her stipend was immediately raised to 3,000 aspers.[63]

The *Haseki*

According to the criterion of stipend, the *haseki*, or favorite concubine, enjoyed the greatest status in the imperial harem after the *valide sultan*. The *haseki*, a slave concubine and no blood relation to the reigning sultan, ranked higher than the sultan's own sisters and aunts, the princesses of the dynasty. Her elevated royal status derived from the fact that she was the mother of a potential future sultan. In 1575, just after Murad III's accession, his *haseki* Safiye Sultan received a stipend of 700 aspers a day, while his sister İsmihan Sultan, wife of the esteemed grand vezir Sokollu Mehmed Pasha, received only 300 aspers, and his sister Gevherhan Sultan, wife of the vezir Piyale Pasha, 250 aspers. Murad's aunt, Mihrimah Sultan, daughter of Süleyman and

Hurrem Sultan, widow of the grand vezir Rüstem Pasha, and an extremely powerful woman in her own right, received 600 aspers in her retirement in the Old Palace, the highest stipend awarded any princess in the period covered by this study.[64] Even later, when sharp distinctions of rank ceased to be made among the sultan's concubines and the title *haseki* no longer meant "favorite," royal concubines continued to rank higher than princesses: in 1643, the two concubines of İbrahim received 1,000 and 1,300 aspers a day, respectively, while the maximum stipend for princesses, including İbrahim's sisters Ayşe, Fatma, and Hanzade, was 400 aspers.[65]

When Süleyman was princely governor and clearly his father's heir, his mother Hafsa received a stipend of 200 aspers a day.[66] Süleyman's *haseki,* Hurrem, received a stipend of 2,000 aspers a day, at least toward the end of her career.[67] After her death, this extraordinary sum was granted only to the *valide sultan,* while the standard *haseki* stipend in the following century was only half that amount: 1,000 aspers a day. Only two departures from this practice appear to have occurred. First, Safiye Sultan received only 700 aspers as *haseki,* whereas her predecessor Nurbanu had received 1,000 aspers.[68] While this would seem unusual in view of Murad's intense devotion to his favorite concubine, it may represent a scaling down of the *haseki*'s stipend in relation to that of the *valide sultan,* for there had been no *valide sultan* when Nurbanu was *haseki.* The second departure from the norm occurred in 1633, when Murad IV raised the *haseki* stipend to 2,000 aspers, where it remained throughout his reign.[69] This increase was most likely linked to a general increase in stipends throughout the palace during Murad's reign, described by Koçi Bey,[70] and was accompanied by a marked growth in the size of the harem. These changes were probably an aspect of Murad's dramatic assertion of personal control of government after nine years of his mother's regency. Curiously, despite İbrahim's notorious squandering of the empire's treasury on extravagances of the harem, the *haseki* stipend was returned to 1,000 aspers during his reign.[71]

The rule seems to have been once a *haseki,* always a *haseki:* a favorite maintained her status even in retirement (which could occur only after the emergence of seniority as a principle of succession, when a prince's mother might mark time in the Old Palace between the death of her master and the accession of her son). Kösem continued to receive the *haseki*'s standard stipend of 1,000 aspers[72] for the five years of her retirement between the death of Ahmed I and the accession of her eldest son Murad IV. Even Ayşe, the relatively obscure *haseki* of Osman II, received this amount for more than eighteen years after the sultan's death, despite the fact that she had no sons to lend her prestige as a potential *valide sultan.*[73] The fact that the *haseki*s of Murad IV and İbrahim received only 100 aspers in retirement[74] is further evidence that the special status of the *haseki* began to disappear toward the mid-seventeenth century.

The Royal Concubine of Non-*Haseki* Status

Concubines who were not favorites of the sultan in the century following the deaths of Süleyman and Hurrem tend to be the forgotten women of the harem. We are aware of them only when the vagaries of succession catapulted them into the public eye. Their status relative to their favored colleagues, as reflected in their stipends, was distinctly inferior. They were often not listed among the family elite of the harem, and are discussed here principally to demonstrate the unusual status of the *haseki*.

While Hurrem received a daily stipend of 2,000 aspers toward the end of her career,[75] the customary stipend for the concubine mother of a prince at that time was 30 or 40 aspers.[76] At the end of Selim II's reign, the *haseki* Nurbanu received 1,000 aspers a day, while Selim's other consorts, each the mother of a son, received only 40 aspers.[77] The mother of Mustafa I, concubine of Mehmed III, received 100 aspers a day between Mehmed's death and Mustafa's accession, while the *haseki* Kösem received 1,000 aspers a day at a parallel point in her career.[78] With respect to stipend, mothers of princes before the reign of Süleyman probably did not enjoy a status much greater than that of these women: in 1513, as the mother of the heir apparent (Süleyman), Hafsa Sultan received a stipend of 150 aspers a day.[79] The gap between Hafsa's stipend and Hurrem's stipend of 2000 aspers a day at a parallel point in her career only forty years later further underlines the exceptional nature of Süleyman's treatment of Hurrem.

The manner in which the sultan's concubines were listed in privy purse registers sheds light on the manner in which they must have been perceived in the hierarchy of the harem. Favorites were listed as "haseki sultan" or, in retirement, "*haseki* of the deceased Sultan X"—suggesting that the individual's fundamental relationship was with the sultan himself. Other concubine mothers of sons were listed as "the mother of Prince X" (*valide-i Sultan X*)— suggesting that the individual had no special relationship with the sultan, but only with a potential sultan, her son. Concubines who were the mothers of daughters only were not even listed individually in the privy purse registers, suggesting that they were perceived as enjoying no empowering relationship within the dynastic family.

The fact that so little is known about these concubines of non-*haseki* rank should not lead us to assume that they were completely deprived of status and power, however. That they enjoyed the prerogatives of a member of the royal family is suggested by the fact that Şemsiruhsar Khatun, one of the many concubines of Murad III and the mother of a daughter, created an endowment for the recitation of the Qur'an in the mosque of the Prophet in Medina.[80] These women, especially the mothers of princes, were surely not political ciphers, since their sons were the magnets around which factions opposed to the sultan or the heir apparent gathered. The popularity of Mahmud, son of Mehmed III, outside the palace, which led to his own and his mother's execution on grounds of suspected treason, testifies to the possibility of such political leverage; had Mahmud not been executed, his mother might have played an important role as *valide sultan*.

As we have seen, toward the middle of the seventeenth century the special status of the *haseki* and the gross salary differences that had characterized the harem hierarchy of previous reigns began to disappear. What emerged was a system in which royal concubines began to enjoy roughly equal status, diminished from the lofty level of the *haseki* but improved over the neglected position of the non-*haseki*. At midcentury, seven of İbrahim's eight concubines received stipends of 1,000 aspers a day and the other concubine 1,300 aspers.[81] Toward the end of the century, in 1690, the six *kadın*s of Süleyman II, including the head *kadın,* received gifts of equal amounts—one purse plus 100 *kuruş*—on the occasion of the court's departure for a sojourn in Edirne;[82] the same amount was given to the four princes and one princess resident in the palace, suggesting an improvement in the status of royal offspring vis-à-vis that of royal concubines. Unfortunately, Süleyman's mother, Saliha Dilaşub, had died the previous year, so we do not know how much larger the *valide sultan*'s gift would have been; however, a gift of five purses was awarded the harem stewardess, who had replaced the deceased *valide sultan* as head of the harem institution.[83]

We must not, however, exaggerate the equitability of the pattern that emerged as the age of the *haseki* drew to a close. In all likelihood absolute equality never obtained among royal concubines—at the very least the head consort must have enjoyed some privileges, and a sultan must have been able in some way to enhance the status of a particular favorite, perhaps through promotion to a vacancy created by the death of a woman with greater seniority. That there was some variation among concubines is suggested by the sizes of the suites of the six consorts (*kadın*) of Mahmud I toward the mid-eighteenth century: the head consort (*baş kadın*) had twenty attendants, the second *kadın* eleven, the third fourteen, the forth eight, the fifth ten, and the sixth twelve.[84]

Princess and Prince

The Ottoman princess of this period appears to have enjoyed little status within the harem. It was only with marriage to high-ranking statesmen that princesses were able to play a role of any significance and thus to acquire recognition. This change of status was reflected in their stipends: until they left the imperial palace as married women, they received 100 aspers a day, but upon their marriage they would begin to receive 300 or 400 aspers a day in addition to a generous household allowance. From the point of view of stipend, princesses were not worse off than their brothers: princes resident in the palace also received only 100 aspers a day in this period. These stipends of the royal offspring were strikingly small in comparison to the stipends of other harem residents, including those of nonfamily members of the royal family household. Nor, while they were resident within the palace, were their stipends supplemented by the income from land grants or other such sources. Perhaps this lack of status resulted from a view of the royal offspring as not yet in the actual service of the dynasty. Once a princess proved useful to the dynasty through her marriage, her status improved considerably; a key factor here was that she was now mistress of a household. The actual service of a prince of course raised him to the loftiest station in the empire. The low stipend status of princes and princesses was not peculiar to the late sixteenth century: as princely governor in Manisa and heir apparent, Süleyman received a stipend of 67 aspers and an unmarried sister who accompanied her brother and mother to Manisa 40 aspers.

The *Daye Khatun*

The sultan's relationship with his wet nurse was considered one of filiation. When a sultan's mother predeceased him, his *daye* assumed a ceremonial role as maternal mentor. The importance of the *daye khatun* was not just a phenomenon of the expanded harem in the post-Süleymanic period. Ümm Gülsüm Khatun, the *daye* of Mehmed II, conqueror of Constantinople, was sufficiently endowed with income by the sultan to undertake the construction of two mosques in Istanbul and one in Edirne; the neighborhood surrounding the latter came to bear her name.[85] Her importance may have been due to the fact that Mehmed's mother died three years before he became sultan. The *daye* of Osman II performed the role of maternal stand-in during the last two years of the reign of the young sultan, after his mother died; during this time she received a stipend of 1,000 aspers a day, five times the *daye*'s normal stipend.[86]

Befitting her status, the *daye khatun* was usually married to a high-ranking state official. Like princesses of the dynasty, she thus functioned as a potential link between the dynastic family and its servants. The Venetian ambassador Garzoni reported in 1573 that Selim II "spends the greater part of his time playing chess with the mother of Ahmed Pasha, an elderly woman who was formerly his nurse, and delighting in witticisms that she is accustomed to telling him."[87] Selim and his *daye* had other ties: she was married to the son of one of Bayezid II's daughters, and her son, Şemsi Ahmed Pasha, was a royal confidant of the sultan. The daughter of Mehmed III's *daye* was married to Lala Mehmed Pasha, who rose to serve as grand vezir, although only for a matter of days before he suddenly died.[88] The husband of Murad IV's *daye* rose to the positions of head chancellor (*nişancı*) and governor of Egypt.[89]

The *Ketkhuda Khatun*

While she had no family tie with the sultan, by the second decade of the seventeenth century the harem stewardess was also listed in privy purse registers among the family elite. This was in part because of her exalted position as the senior administrative officer of the harem institution and her role in training the women who personally served the sultan. Like the *daye khatun*, the *ketkhüda khatun* (or *kâhya kadın*) had been an important figure in earlier times: the position appears in registers from the reigns of Bayezid II and Selim I.[90]

The prestige of this office in the post-Süleymanic period was boosted by the career of Janfeda Khatun, the powerful harem stewardess during the reign of Murad III. According to the historian Mustafa Ali, the *valide sultan* Nurbanu had Janfeda brought from the Old Palace and put in charge of the training of forty slave women, including those destined for the sultan's personal service. On her deathbed Nurbanu enjoined her son to place control of the harem in Janfeda's hands, which Murad proceeded to do.[91] Janfeda Khatun was in all likelihood the first official *ketkhüda khatun* of the New Palace harem. The responsibilities of this office appear to have expanded to include management of the assignment of jobs, and the training and the promotion of all women in the harem household. Its principal function, however, seems to have remained the training of the select group who personally served the *valide sultan* and the sultan.[92]

Like the *daye khatun*, the *ketkhüda khatun* also possessed the status and the wherewithall to undertake public works: Janfeda Khatun built a mosque and a public fountain in Istanbul as well as another mosque and public bath in a village in the suburbs of the city.[93] Janfeda's retirement stipend was a handsome 100 aspers a day, but when this amount proved insufficient for the public works she wished to undertake, it was doubled.[94] Janfeda's mosques were constructed after the death of Nurbanu Sultan, suggesting that the *ketkhüda khatun* could, like the *daye khatun*, assume the *valide sultan*'s prerogatives in the event of her death. It is no doubt this role as stand-in for the *valide sultan*, in her capacity both as mother of the sultan and as head of the harem institution, that allowed the *daye khatun* and the *kethüda khatun* to be counted as members of the family elite.

The Hierarchy of the Harem: The Household

As the number of high-ranking members of the royal family resident in the imperial harem increased, so perforce did the household required to maintain this organization of growing complexity. Privy purse registers list the harem household in two divisions, which we might term the household staff and the household domestics. The latter consisted of the women and girls who performed the menial tasks of the harem—the preparation and service of food, the laundry, the cleaning, the tending of fires, the maintenance of the baths, and so forth—and who, as the lowest ranking members of a particular individual's suite, did the bidding of their superiors. In the official hierarchy of the harem, they were known as *jariyes*.[95] While the technical meaning of the term *jariye* is "female slave," it, like the term *kul* for men, could also be used loosely to refer to any female subject of the sultan, including the women of his family.[96] In a context such as that of the harem hierarchy, however, where an office or position of any status tended to be marked by a title, the *jariye* was clearly a person who lacked status.

The term "household staff" is used here to refer to those nonfamily harem residents holding a position in the harem that was dignified by a title and, usually, by a stipend greater than that of the rank-and-file *jariye*. This group begins to emerge as a distinct and significant element in the harem hierarchy at the beginning of the seventeenth century, when privy purse registers refer to it as the *Dar üs-Saade*, literally, the "Abode of Good Fortune."[97] *Dar üs-Saade* is a term with several layers of meaning, denoting variously the imperial capital, the imperial palace, and the harem quarters within the palace. Each of these is a space that constitutes an "abode of good fortune" because it is inhabited by the person of the sultan. In privy purse registers of Süleyman's reign, the term *Dar üs-Saade* is used to refer inclusively to all residents of the harem, family and household alike.[98] The later restriction of the term to the household staff suggests that the emergence of this specially identified group was stimulated not only by the sheer growth in numbers of the harem population but also, and more important, by the harem's transformation into a division of the imperial palace and its growing importance as a training school. The similarities between the structure of the household staff and that of the staff of the privy chamber, the sultan's residence in the third courtyard, provide further support for the hypothesis that the elaboration of this element of the harem institution was a result not only of the harem's growth in general but also of the sultan's presence within it. The special title of this group, *Dar üs-Saade,* suggests that it was the core, or defining, group of the harem institution.

The *Dar üs-Saade* was not an unprecedented element in the harem hierarchy that emerged at the turn of the century. A special group of "distinguished" persons (*jemaat-ı müteferrika*) had existed under Süleyman—and perhaps earlier. These were individuals of some status who were grouped separately in privy purse registers, neither with the family (princes, princesses, their mothers, and their governesses and wet nurses), nor with the rank-and-file *jariyes*. This group may have been a parallel to the *müteferrika* corps in the palace outer service, a kind of miscellaneous group of persons of some status.[99] In a 1552 register, this group, which included two men, consisted of Gülfem Khatun (an individual with considerable status in Süleyman's harem whose precise function is unclear—perhaps she was the harem stewardess),[100] the nurse of Süleyman's deceased son Mehmed, the mother of Mehmed's daughter, the tutor of Süleyman's youngest son Jihangir, and the imam of the palace. Their stipends ranged from Gülfem Khatun's 150 aspers a day to the imam's 10 aspers, at a time when the average *jariye* stipend was 6 aspers.[101] In 1599–1600 the *Dar üs-Saade,* or household staff, consisted of ten unspecified individuals, all of whose stipends were 40 aspers a day—a group not much larger than the *müteferrika* of Süleyman's day.[102] However, although the *müteferrika* may have formed a precedent for the *Dar üs-Saade,* the fact that the latter expanded rapidly during the first half of the seventeenth century suggests that it was a body constituted with a different, or at least a more consciously dignified, purpose. This is supported by the appearance in privy purse registers of 1612 of a group of the same name—Dar üs-Saade—in the Old Palace harem, a dozen years or more after the group's emergence in the principal harem.[103]

The household staff grew not only in size but in range of personnel. By 1612, it still consisted of ten persons, but there were now three levels of stipend: 100, 60, and 40 aspers a day.[104] By 1620 it consisted of forty-seven persons, with six stipend levels: 200, 100, 60, 40, 20, and 15 aspers.[105] By 1640, the end of the reign of Murad IV, the household staff had doubled to 102 persons,[106] and by the mid-seventeenth century it consisted of approximately 140 persons at twelve different stipend levels ranging from 200 to 13 aspers.[107] Throughout the period, the stipends of greatest frequency were 40, 20, and 15 aspers, while the number of persons receiving stipends greater than 40 aspers typically ranged between eight and ten until the very end of the period, when it grew to sixteen. While the range of *Dar üs-Saade* stipend increased, there appears to have been no rise in stipend during this period, although an individual might work her way up the household hierarchy; from the beginning to the middle of the seventeenth century, the average *jariye* stipend, however, increased by 25 percent from 6.8 to 8.5 aspers. The multiplicity of stipend levels suggests that the household staff was characterized by an increasingly well-defined functional or status hierarchy.

Unfortunately, privy purse registers after the reign of Süleyman do not indicate who the members of the household staff were. The group most certainly included the administrative/supervisory officers, those high-ranking women who personally served the sultan and his mother and who were responsible for training promising young *jariyes*. It is likely that it also included women who had attained a certain status through a personal relationship with the sultan but had not been sufficiently honored to be regarded officially as a member of the royal family. Some idea of the composition of this group is suggested by an important document of the mid-eighteenth century: a list of the nonfamily members of the New Palace harem by office or name and stipend.[108] The size of the harem as demonstrated in this document—444 women—and the stipend range—5 to 100 aspers a day—with 73 women receiving stipends at the *Dar üs-Saade* level (15 aspers or more) and 371 at the *jariye* level (10 aspers or less), are so close to the situation that existed in the previous century as to suggest that the harem underwent little change in its basic structure after an initial period of adjustment to its new location and role in the New Palace.[109]

The women receiving the highest stipends at the time the list was drawn up were the chief administrative/supervisory officers of the harem. The mistress of the palace (*saray ustası*), the mistress of the laundry (*çamesuy usta*), and mistress of the pantry (*kiler usta*) all received 100 aspers a day; the head scribe (*baş katibe*) and the "great mute coiffeur mistress" (*büyük dilsiz berber usta*) received 80 aspers; the second treasurer (*ikinci hazinedar*), the tasting mistress (*çaşnigir usta*), the coffee mistress (*kahveci usta*), and the mistress of the ablutions ewer (*ibrikdar usta*) received 50 aspers. This list of the top echelon of the eighteenth-century household staff is remarkably similar to a description, provided by Petis de la Croix in his memoirs, of the *valide sultan*'s attendants in the mid-seventeenth century: this group included the treasury mistress, the scribal mistress, the laundry mistress, the mistress of the box (whose office was probably connected with the royal bath), the bath mistress, the bath attendant, the tasting mistress, the coffee mistress, the pantry mistress, and the mistress of the ablutions ewer (Figure 5-1).[110]

Next in rank after the chief administrative/supervisory officers came four *ikbals*, who each received 40 aspers; *ikbals* were women singled out as favorite companions, perhaps concubines, of the sultan who were in line for promotion to the rank of *kadın*.[111] Also at the 40-asper rank were the stewards of six princesses living outside the New Palace,[112] as well as the second scribe, the

Figure 5-1 The *valide sultan* attended by her suite. Enjoying a leisurely moment in one of the palace kiosks, the *valide sultan* takes a cup of coffee from one of her servants. Another fans her, while yet another holds an ornamented receptacle. A black eunuch stands in attendance at the right. From *Costumes Turcs de la cour et de la ville Constantinople, f.4. (Courtesy of the Bibliothèque Nationale, Paris)*

head *jariye* of the personal suite of the harem stewardess, and the assistant mistress of the pantry. At lower ranks within the household staff were women in the personal suites of the various officers mentioned above or assigned directly to different service divisions within the harem, such as the pantry and the boiler room (*külhane*). For example, the mistress of the pantry had a *jariye* assigned to her personal service, while several other *jariye*s were assigned directly to the pantry. Also in the lower ranks of the group were governesses and wet nurses of the younger princes, *jariye*s in the suites of the older princes,[113] and women assigned to the chief officers of the black eunuch corps and other eunuch court companions of the sultan.

Simply listed by name in the document, with no function or assignment specified, are 167 *jariye*s (those receiving stipends of 10 aspers or less). Presumably this group was made up of those who performed the menial housekeeping tasks in the harem and perhaps also included newly acquired slave girls and women in the first stages of training. Another 185 *jariye*s are listed in the suites of various individuals or assigned directly to service divisions; while these women also received a maximum stipend of 10 aspers, it is possible that they were more advanced than the previous group in the training and service hierarchy of the harem. Of the suites to which these *jariye*s were assigned, those of the princes and the sultan's concubines (*kadın*s) were the largest, with the former ranging from nineteen to seven women and the latter ranging from twenty to eight women. The suites of the *ikbal*s ranged from six to four women. The harem officers also had women assigned to their personal service: the harem stewardess had four, the second treasurer three, while other leading officers—the tasting mistress and the mistresses of the palace, the laundry, and the pantry—had only one servant each. An interesting feature of the document is evidence that, at least at this time, the leading members of the black eunuch corps had members of the harem assigned to their service, perhaps to act as their deputies, since they ordinarily did not enter the harem proper. The chief black eunuch had five, while the second-in-command of the black eunuch corps had two, and the agha of the treasury four.

Several high-ranking harem women do not appear in this list. Indeed, its heading—"Names and daily wages of the *jariyes*"—suggests that it contains only the names of those who might be thought of as servants of the royal family. Its omissions are consonant with the bookkeeping traditions observed in seventeenth-century privy purse registers, where the three basic divisions among harem women are the royal family, the household staff, and the rank-and-file servants. Predictably, absent from the list are the six *kadıns*, the chief concubines of the sultan. Also absent are the harem stewardess and the wet nurse of the sultan. The latter two individuals were the members of the harem with the greatest status after the sultan's chief concubines. Their standing is revealed by the size of their stipends throughout most of the period in this study—200 aspers a day—as well as by the fact that around 1620 they began to be listed in privy purse registers together with family members rather than with the household staff.

The Hierarchy of the Harem Institution: The Physical Structure

The physical layout of the New Palace harem quarters provides another dimension for understanding the hierarchical and functional divisions of the harem and the relationships among the women who lived there.[114] Unfortunately, because the harem underwent continual expansion, restructuring, and reorganization, it is hard to deduce from the structure of the palace as it exists today just what uses were made of some rooms and complexes of rooms in the sixteenth and seventeenth centuries.[115] The area of the harem housing the majority of women was destroyed by fire in 1665 and quickly rebuilt by Mehmed IV over the next few years. While in subsequent decades and centuries, accretions in the form mainly of additional stories and partitioning of existing rooms altered the appearance of much of the harem quarters, the basic structure of this area would seem to remain as it was when rebuilt in the 1660s, when Turhan Sultan was *valide sultan*.[116] The area of the harem inhabited by the women was bounded on its four sides by the quarters of the black eunuchs, a passageway separating the harem from the third courtyard, chambers constructed by individual sultans for their own use, and the outer wall of the harem, which looked down onto the sloping palace grounds and out to the mosque of Süleyman and the upper Golden Horn.

Figure 5-2 External view of the *valide sultan*'s apartments. This photo, taken from the kiosk of Osman III within the harem section of the palace, shows the "tower of justice" atop the imperial council hall in the background and, on the right, the dormitories of harem servants and women in training. (*Photo by B. Dianne Mott*)

Dominating the women's quarters was the suite of the *valide sultan*. It was rivaled in size and splendor only by the apartments constructed by Murad III for his personal use (Figure 5-2). It consisted of a large salon and other smaller rooms, including a bedroom and a prayer room. It had three principal entrances: a corridor leading to a double bath (with one side for the *valide sultan* and the other for the sultan) and on to the great hall of the harem built by Murad III; an entrance from the corridor leading from the black eunuchs' innermost guardpost to the "courtyard of the *jariyes*," and an entrance from the large, centrally located, paved courtyard known as "the courtyard of the *valide*" (this courtyard and the rooms opening off it were probably the first structures in the New Palace harem).[117] In addition to these architecturally prominent entrances, the *valide sultan* also had access from within her apartment to what is thought to have been a detention area or prison, located partially below her suite. Another route from her rooms to the quarters of the sultan led through a series of second-story rooms above her own; whoever occupied this series of linked rooms could be closely supervised by the *valide sultan*.[118]

The centrally located suite of the *valide sultan* divided the harem into two distinct areas. Between her rooms and the quarters of the black eunuchs lay the quarters of the *jariye*s, while on the other side of her rooms were situated the apartments of the sultan and of the young princes. The *valide sultan*'s suite can thus be thought of as dividing the harem into a "service wing" and a "family wing." Her central location allowed her to keep a watchful eye on both. Her means of access to all corners of the harem are concrete evidence of her roles as executive of the harem institution and guardian of the royal family. The physical structure of the harem suggests that it was the *valide sultan* rather than the sultan who was its dominant resident.

Each "wing" of the harem had a small number of elegant suites, clearly for women of distinguished status, although these in no way rivaled the splendor of the *valide sultan*'s suite or the rooms and pavilions constructed by the different sultans. In the "service wing," there were three such apartments, each consisting of a central salon with a balcony-like sleeping area and several secondary rooms, probably for the personal servants of the suite's mistress. These were the only suites in the harem of this period, in addition to those of the sultan and *valide sultan*, to have windows with a view of the outside world. Although it is not clear who occupied these suites, it seems likely that they belonged to the harem stewardess, who was in charge of the girls' training, and other leading administrative officers with supervisory duties. The "family wing" also contained elegant apartments, though with no outside view.[119] Since they are located under the quarters of princes and princesses, it seems likely that they belonged to the children's nurses and/or to the sultan's *hasekis*. Rooms with no outside view would have been appropriate for the sultan's concubines, who would have been the most strictly guarded of the harem's inhabitants; visual access to the outside world could more properly be permitted older women whose harem careers were devoid of a sexual component, such as the *valide sultan*, the harem stewardess, and other leading administrative officers. This is, however, only speculation.

Some residential features of the harem remain unexplained. Where, for example, did widowed or divorced princesses returning to the palace live? Perhaps the elegant suites were used by them on occasion. What is clear is that those residents of the harem who were not high-ranking concubines or officers lived a far less comfortable life than those who were more successful in their harem career. Descriptions of the harem as a congeries of cramped, dark rooms and corridors are inappropriate with regard to these successful women but accurate for the rank-and-file staff. In this respect, however, the imperial harem was probably very little different from any family in the empire wealthy enough to possess domestic slaves.

The Harem as a Training Institution: Purpose and Organization

For the members of the dynastic family, the harem served as residence. For the servants of the royal family, it might best be described as a training institution. Young women were trained with the goal not only of providing suitable concubines for the sultan and attendants for his mother and other prominent harem women, but also of providing suitable wives for men near the top of the military/administrative hierarchies (the highest ranking officials would marry Ottoman princesses and their daughters). Just as the inner court-yard school prepared men through personal service to the sultan within his palace for service to the dynasty outside the palace, the harem prepared women through personal service to the sultan and his mother to take up their roles in the outer world. Manumitted and married to inner palace graduates and other officials, these women would in turn form harems that comple-mented the male households formed by their husbands. Marrying male and female slaves was an ancient practice that appears to have originated with the institution of elite slavery itself: the ninth-century Abbasid caliph Mu'tasim, whose Turkish slave guard was the earliest instance of the Islamic practice of elite slavery, married his soldiers to slave women of the same ethnic origin.[120] An example of an Ottoman slave alliance was that made for Pilak Mustafa Pasha, a minor vezir under Süleyman. A product of the inner palace school, Mustafa Pasha received a career boost through his marriage to a harem gradu-ate: according to the historian Peçevi, "after he rose to the rank of governor general, he was married to a lady named Şahhûban, one of the slave women of the imperial harem, and because of this he was graced with the vezirate."[121]

Through these slave marriages, the organizational and educational pattern established by the sultan's household was replicated to form the social and political foundation of the Ottoman ruling class.[122] The palace system of training—for both men and women—had as one of its fundamental goals the inculcation of loyalty to the ruling house. Because women as well as men sustained the ties that bound the empire's elite, the focus of the latter's loyalty was not only the sultan himself but also the women of his household, that is, the dynastic family as a whole. Thus, when we examine the organization of the imperial harem and the relationships among its inhabitants, we observe not an isolated body but a matrix for the formation of a vital element of the ruling class.

A striking feature of the organizational elaboration of the harem after its move to the New Palace is its similarity to the organization of the pages and eunuchs who inhabited the third courtyard.[123] The sultan's new residence within the harem appears to have been tailored to resemble the old, with the crucial difference that the gender of his personal servants had changed. There were many parallels between the two organizations.[124]

A principal similarity was the multiplicity of ranks within each institution. According to Bobovius, whose informant was a woman who was married to an imperial cavalry officer of his acquaintance and who had served in the harem in the suite of the *valide sultan* Kösem, "the women are separated in the palace into the same number of chambers as are the pages . . . and they observe the same degrees of rank as obtain among the men."[125] As the ranks of female and male slaves-in-training were parallel, so were the career paths through the two institutions. Entry-level trainees in both organizations were grouped in two chambers known as the Greater Chamber (*büyük oda*) and the Lesser Chamber (*küçük oda*). Trainees would proceed to work their way up through the training/service divisions—in the third courtyard, the Campaign, Pantry, and Treasury Chambers, and in the harem the Pantry, Boiler, and Treasury Chambers.[126] Those who were not transferred out of the two institutions at intermediate levels—the men through assignment to a post in the outer palace service or to one of the imperial military forces, the women through marriage to these very men—rose to the top echelon of their respective institutions: the Privy Chamber and the *Dar üs-Saade*. The highest ranking members of these privileged groups carried similar titles, titles denoting service to the person of the sultan (in the case of the harem, to the person of the *valide sultan* as well): in the Privy Chamber, the keepers of the sultan's sword, garments, and linen, his stirrup-holder, and his private secretary, and in the harem the coiffeur, tasting, and coffee mistresses, the mistress of the ablutions ewer, and the scribe.

The similarity between the hierarchies of the two inner-palace institutions is underlined by the similarity in their stipend levels. It appears that the "horizontal cross-referencing of ranks between the professional branches" in the outer administration noted by Cornell Fleischer extended through the two inner worlds of the palace.[127] In 1664 the average stipend of the pages in training in the five chambers—the Greater and Lesser chambers and the Pantry, Treasury, and Campaign Chambers (excluding the Privy Chamber)— was 8.5 aspers a day;[128] in 1652 the average stipend of the *jariyes* in the New Palace (excluding the *Dar üs-Saade* group) was 8.7 aspers a day.[129] The four highest ranking pages of the Privy Chamber (the *arz ağaları*) received stipends equivalent to those of the principal members of the *Dar üs-Saade* group: according to Bobovius, the sultan's stirrup-holder received 140 aspers a day, his sword-bearer 100 aspers, the keeper of his garments 80 aspers, and the keeper of his linen 50 aspers.[130] For most of the period in this study, the harem stewardess—the highest paid officer in the harem—received a stipend of 200 aspers a day, which was paralleled in the palace outer service only by that of the keeper of the standard,[131] a position to which were promoted the highest-ranking pages and aghas of the Privy Chamber.[132]

Another similarity between the third courtyard and the harem institutions was the seriousness of the educational enterprise undertaken in each. The ambitious program of study followed by the third courtyard pages was paralled in the harem by training in skills that were deemed appropriate to the women at the various levels of its hierarchy. Angiolello, a page in the palace during the reign of Mehmed II, described the training of the women in the sultan's harem: "[T]he most senior [women], who are trained, teach the new and unrefined to speak and read and instruct them in the Muhammadan law, and also teach them to sew and embroider, and to play the harp and to sing, and instruct them in all their ceremonies and customs, to the degree that [these girls] have the inclination to learn."[133] Nearly two centuries later, Bobovius described a similar situation:

> Among all these Slaves, those who occupy elevated ranks in the service of their mistress [the *valide sultan*] are obliged to do no work at all, but the others are made to perform all necessary services such as cleaning the rooms, sewing, embroidering, and bleaching, and they are even made to work on the clothing of the pages, which tailors, after having cut the cloth, send to them to be sewn.[134]

Both institutions were characterized by enforced industriousness and a strictness of discipline, and were compared by foreigners to monasteries. As in the third courtyard, a rule of silence prevailed in the harem, where there were female mutes, lending it an air of serious and solemn endeavor.[135]

Needlework appears to have been the principal skill imparted to the ordinary harem inhabitant. Menavino, a page in the palace of Bayezid II and Selim I, related that ten teachers of embroidery would come to the Old Palace every morning to instruct the young recruits.[136] According to Postel, who was writing in the mid-sixteenth century, those who were trained in the arts of the needle were the many who, because of "lack of beauty and grace," failed to rise to higher status. However, commented Postel, the sultan had them trained with such diligence that one would think they were his daughters.[137] There was little leisure time for ordinary residents of the harem, for, according to Bobovius, "[their] occupation, when they are not employed in domestic duties, is to work embroidery in gold or silk thread on cotton cloth, which they make into handkerchiefs or turbans which they wrap around their heads."[138] Their skill at needlework seems to have stood these women in good stead, however, for when they were transferred to the Old Palace at the death of the sultan they served, they were able to generate some income from the sale of their handiwork through the intermediacy of Jewish tradeswomen.[139]

Bobovius's claim that those who occupied elevated ranks in the harem were obliged to do no work no doubt referred to their freedom from domestic service. Women who made their way up the harem hierarchy by appointment to the training/service divisions or to the suites of high-ranking family or household staff members presumably spent their time acquiring and perfecting the skills and manners appropriate to their new station. Those who showed an aptitude for instrumental music, singing, or dance were trained in these arts. The *valide sultan* selected the most talented and beautiful of these more highly trained women for her own suite. According to Paul Rycaut, secretary to the English embassy in the 1660s,

> Out of these, the Queen Mother chooses her Court, and orderly draws from the Schools such as she marks out for the most beauteous, facetious [witty], or most corresponding with the harmony of her own disposition, and prefers them to a near attendance on her Person, or to other Offices of her Court. These are always richly attired and adorned with all sorts of precious stones,

fit to receive the adresses and amours of the *sultan:* over them is placed the *Kadun Kahia* or Mother of the Maids, who is carefull to correct any immodest or light behaviour amongst them, and instructs them in all the Rules and Orders of the Court.[140]

Waiting on the *valide sultan,* while it did not involve hard labor, was undoubtedly a full-time occupation, similar to the constant attendance on the sultan by the pages of the Privy Chamber and similarly reserved for the select of the trainees. These women were instructed with an eye to their eligibility for the highest position to which a harem resident might aspire. According to Bobovius, the sultan almost always chose his concubines from among the attendants of his mother, who trained them for just that purpose: "[S]he takes care to keep them splendidly outfitted and to have them instructed in all that they can learn so that they might be capable of inspiring in the Grand Seigneur the love which might allow them to become concubines, and perhaps one among them the favorite and the honored mother of his eldest son, or else to be married to persons of quality outside the palace."[141]

To sum up, the career of a *jariye* might culminate in one of three ways: entry into the dynastic family as the mother of an Ottoman prince, promotion to one of the administrative offices of the harem institution, or manumission and entry into the Ottoman ruling elite as the wife of a male servant of the dynasty. It is not clear at what point the harem career bifurcated, but it seems likely that the concubinal career was accessible only to those women at the very peak of the training process. A successful career as concubine, as with the pages, depended on character, intelligence, and accomplishment as well as on physical appeal. Women at this level of training who did not become royal concubines most probably went on to occupy the highest offices in the administrative/supervisory staff of the harem or to marry men high in the sultan's service.

Titles that came into official use at the end of the seventeenth century (and were probably used informally before then) suggest that the training of a talented *jariye* prepared her for both a concubinal and an administrative career.[142] A woman who became the sultan's *ikbal*—a favorite companion, perhaps concubine, of the sultan, who ranked below the senior concubines (*kadıns*) and was in line for promotion to the rank of *kadın*—also carried the title *kalfa* ("assistant master/mistress"), a rank below that of *usta* ("master/mistress"), the title of the leading administrative/supervisory officers of the harem.[143] The titles *usta* and *kalfa* belong to the terminology of Ottoman guild organization and other hierarchically organized corporate bodies. That these women were known simultaneously as *ikbal* and *kalfa* suggests that they were eligible for both kinds of high-level harem career.

A final way in which the two inner palace organizations were similar is the slave status of their personnel. While it was not impossible for freeborn Muslims to be trained as pages in the third courtyard of the palace—indeed, their access to this education increased in the seventeenth century[144]—the great majority of the inhabitants of the third courtyard were slaves. If we knew more about the inhabitants of the harem, perhaps we would find a similar presence of Muslim women within its ranks. Current evidence, however, suggests that the imperial harem was composed exclusively of slave concubines. One of the key features of dynastic politics—reproduction through concubinage rather than through legal marriage—suggests that the freeborn Muslim woman was an anachronism in the harem. The protest against Osman II's marriage to the daughter of the *müfti* was inspired largely by the inappropriateness of such a free Muslim woman joining the sultan's harem. The only inhabitants of the harem who were not slaves were the *valide sultan*, freed automatically upon the death of her master, and the princesses of the royal family. The one, however, had risen as a slave concubine to her lofty position and the others were insignificant figures in the hierarchy of the harem.

Harem Networks of Power

Despite their considerable influence, high-ranking women of the imperial harem were for the most part confined to the palace. If they left the royal residence, it was under the tight surveillance of the black eunuch guards of the harem. Only the *valide sultan* appears to have had mobility outside the confines of the harem: in public ceremonials she might make herself visible from within her carriage or palanquin as she cast coins to onlookers or acknowledged their obeisances. She might also meet with high-ranking government officials in private conference if she were carefully veiled or screened. On a routine basis, however, even she did not have face-to-face contact with men. Thus it was essential that women of the harem develop links with individuals or groups in the outside world. There was no lack of parties eager to cooperate, for as the harem became an ever more important locus of imperial authority not only did its residents require outside channels through which they might accomplish their political goals, but outsiders were anxious to form ties with potential patrons within the palace.

Like the sultans during this period, women of the harem built much of their networking on family-based relationships. As I have noted, the family was not limited to blood relationships but included the entire royal household, the vast majority of which was composed of slaves. Within the imperial harem, it was the sultan's mother and his favorite concubine or concubines who were best positioned to build for themselves or for their sons factional support bridging the palace and the outer world. For one thing, they might be mothers of princesses as well as of the sultan or potential sultans. For another, their status and wealth permitted them to control the careers of a large number of personal attendants and to influence the careers of the harem's administrative officials. The manumission of a slave, a meritorious act for a Muslim, worked to the practical benefit of the former owner, who enjoyed the loyalty of the ex-slave in a clientage relationship. The seventeenth-century historian Mustafa Naima praised the generosity of the *valide sultan* Kösem, who appears to have taken pains to cultivate close ties of patronage with her freed slaves:

> [S]he would free her slave women after two or three years of service, and would arrange marriages with retired officers of the court or suitable persons from outside, giving the women dowries and jewels and several purses of money according to their talents and station, and ensuring that their husbands had suitable positions. She looked after these former slaves by giving them an annual stipend, and on the religious festivals and holy days she would give them purses of money.[145]

Manumitted slaves might act as agents for their former mistresses, just as princess daughters, when married, could help their mothers, who remained within the imperial compound. Because both daughters and freed slaves might be counted on to influence their husbands to act as advocates, *valide sultan*s and *haseki*s strove to exert as much control as possible over the choice of those husbands.

Perhaps the most dramatic example of the transfer of loyalty from the palace to the outside world is the career of Meleki Khatun, who served both Kösem Sultan and her successor Turhan. Meleki was originally a member of Kösem Sultan's suite. In 1648 Kösem's second sultan son, İbrahim, was deposed for mental incompetence, an event that should have brought her twenty-five year career as *valide sultan* to an end. However, instead of retiring and relinquishing her office to the mother of İbrahim's successor, she was asked by leading statesmen to stay on as regent to the new sultan, her seven-year-old grandson Mehmed IV, because of the youth of his mother, Turhan. When, however, Turhan began to assert what she saw as her rightful authority, Kösem reportedly planned to depose the young sultan and replace him with another prince, whose mother she believed more tractable. At this point Meleki deserted Kösem and betrayed her plans to Turhan, thus enabling the latter to eliminate her mother-in-law (Kösem was murdered in a palace coup led by Turhan's chief black eunuch). Meleki became the new *valide sultan*'s loyal and favored retainer. She was eventually manumitted and married to Şaban Khalife, a former page in the palace training school. The couple established residence in Istanbul, where, as a team, they were ideally suited to act as channels of information and intercessors on behalf of individuals with petitions for the palace. Şaban received male petitioners, Meleki female petitioners; Şaban exploited contacts he had formed while serving within the palace, while Meleki exploited her relationship with Turhan Sultan. The political influence of the couple grew to such a point that they lost their lives in 1656 when troops stationed in Istanbul rebelled against alleged abuses in government.[146]

The links established through family and household connections of high-ranking harem officers outside the palace might be of a quite high level. Particularly important were the connections of the sultan's former wet nurse and the harem stewardess; in terms of stipend and ceremonial prestige, these two were the highest ranking women in the harem after members of the royal family. A *valide sultan* might turn to one of these women to form a political bridge to the outside world, as did the mother of Mustafa I. No one had expected that Mustafa, who suffered from severe emotional problems, would become sultan, and so his mother had not enjoyed a position of much status within the imperial harem.[147] As *valide sultan* she had a potential ally in her daughter's husband, Kara Davud Pasha, but during Mustafa's first reign, which lasted only three months, she was unable to exploit this relationship by appointing Davud Pasha vezir. Indeed, she may not have *wished* to challenge existing authority: the incumbent grand vezir had, after all, allowed the violation of the centuries-old tradition of father-son succession in favor of Mustafa. Nevertheless, the *valide sultan* worked to build alliances loyal to her son and herself: the sultan's sword-bearer Mustafa Agha, a high-ranking inner palace officer, was brought out of the palace and awarded the prestigious and strategically vital post of governor of Egypt on condition that he marry the sultan's wet nurse.[148] When, four years later, Mustafa was suddenly catapulted to the throne for a second time at the deposition of his nephew Osman II, the *valide sultan*'s first choice for grand vezir was her son-in-law, Davud Pasha. When he became a political liability and had to be removed from office, the *valide sultan* had the former sword-bearer appointed grand vezir at the first opportunity.[149] The political bond created through the marriage of the wet nurse and the sword-bearer was doubly strong, since both had been intimate personal servants of the sultan.

The most important links with centers of power outside the palace were forged by harem women through the marriages of their daughters, the princesses of the dynasty, to leading statesmen. As we have seen in Chapter 3, becoming a royal son-in-law, a *damad*, was a mark of high honor, conferred generally on the highest-ranking government officers or on promising younger officers. The weddings of princesses and *damad*s were lavishly celebrated state occasions, serving in the sixteenth and seventeenth centuries to demonstrate imperial magnificence and munificence, as the weddings of princes, now confined to the palace and forbidden to marry, had done in the fourteenth and fifteenth centuries.

The dynasty had always used the marriages of princesses for political ends; what stands out in this period is the frequency with which they occurred. By the seventeenth century, serial marriages of princesses were common. Serial marriage was possible because princesses might first be engaged or married at the age of two or three (this practice of engaging or marrying small children was not confined to the royal family; such marriages appear in sixteenth-century Anatolian records).[150] By the time a princess reached puberty, she could be in her third or fourth marriage, since her husbands encountered many risks in high office, including death in battle or by execution. Perhaps the most extreme example of this practice, Kösem's daughters Ayşe and Fatma were each married at least half a dozen times. They were well along in years at their final betrothals: Ayşe was approximately fifty and Fatma sixty-one.[151]

A rare inside view of these marriages is made possible by Evliya Çelebi's frequent mention in his *Book of Travels* of Melek Ahmed Pasha, his patron and twice an imperial *damad*.[152] In 1644 Melek Ahmed, who was then in his mid-fifties, was married to Kaya Sultan, the thirteen-year-old daughter of Murad IV, the most heroic and the most autocratic of the seventeenth-century sultans. Kaya refused to allow the pasha near her on her wedding night—when she even struck him with a dagger—and for seven years thereafter (Evliya attributes her fear of her husband to a prophesy that she would die were she to bear him a daughter). Eventually, however, their marriage became a very happy one, although the princess died in childbirth at the age of twenty-six. Melek Ahmed was so devastated that he flung himself on Kaya's coffin during her funeral and wept uncontrollably, scandalizing the assembled grandees of the empire.[153]

Kaya's support of her husband was of enormous political importance. On several occasions she rushed to his aid with both strategic and financial assistance. Evliya also portrays Kaya as an extraordinarily generous patron and a most pious woman. Praising her many good qualities, he writes: "It is a fact that, of the seventeen sultanas who were alive in those days, none got on with her husband so well as Kaya with Melek. She was, too, very clever and prudent in managing her household. She was a true daughter of Sultan Murad IV, a raging lioness, and a benefactress to all the other sultanas."[154] While Evliya's account is no doubt colored by his multiple ties to the household of Kaya and Melek Ahmed, through patronage (he was a retainer of the pasha and his sister was a retainer of the princess), kinship (his mother and the pasha were first cousins), and ethnic solidarity (both Evliya and Melek were Abkhasian), it is evident that Kaya exemplified the dynasty's duty of beneficence.

Melek Ahmed Pasha's subsequent marriage to Fatma Sultan, daughter of Kösem and aunt to Kaya, was another story. At the time of their wedding, Fatma, who had been married several times already, was in her late fifties, the pasha in his seventies. According to Evliya's account, Melek Ahmed was miserable over the marriage, which he blamed on the antagonism of the late grand vezir Köprülü Mehmed Pasha ("I gave Melek an elephant, let him feed her," remarked Köprülü). On the couple's wedding night, the princess gave the pasha a peremptory account of the support she expected him to provide for herself and her large household. When he pleaded that such sums were impossible, she answered that divorce was the only solution and he should prepare to return her dowry, which amounted to a year's tax revenues from Egypt.[155] When the pasha died shortly thereafter, Fatma Sultan immediately sealed the rooms of his residence, claiming his treasury and all his possessions as her dowry; it took the grand vezir's intervention to set the situation aright. Were the story to be recounted from the princess's point of view, however, it might be that Fatma Sultan was as unhappy with the marriage as Melek Ahmed.

With the greater seclusion of the sultan in the post-Süleymanic period, the strong personal bonds that had earlier existed between the ruler and his leading subjects, forged as they fought side by side and sat together in the imperial council, were no longer possible. The frequency of princess-*damad* marriages in the late sixteenth and seventeenth centuries no doubt reflected the greater importance of these alliances as a kind of political cement sealing the loyalty of statesmen to their sovereign. Bringing a pasha into the royal family as *damad* might even serve to control sedition, as in the case of the rebel vezir İbşir Mustafa Pasha, who became the final husband of the six-times-married Ayşe. When İbşir amassed a huge number of troops in Anatolia and began to defy imperial orders on the grounds of avenging the deposition of Sultan İbrahim and assuming the neglected defense of the empire against the "heretical" Safavids, the young sultan Mehmed IV and the *valide sultan* Turhan adopted the strategy of appointing him grand vezir and making him imperial *damad*. The marriage served to honor and symbolically to reunite the disaffected pasha with his sovereign house, but it also had the more practical outcome of forcing İbşir to come to the capital and fixing his location (the palace of his wife). Soon after his arrival in Istanbul, İbşir was executed.[156] But while the "honor" of becoming a royal son-in-law may have limited a statesman's maneuverability, it also continued, as in the sixteenth century, to enhance his status: as governor of Van, Melek Ahmed Pasha couched an ultimatum to a rebel Kurdish leader under his jurisdiction in the following words: "[M]y khan and brother, I do request that you keep this in mind: I am a grand vezir of the Ottoman sultans. In particular, I am the son-in-law of Sultan Murad IV. And now I am governor of the province of Van."[157]

Obviously, not only sultans but their mothers and consorts as well bene-fited immensely from the practice of princess-*damad* marriage (the first exam-ple of a powerful harem-*damad* alliance was that of Süleyman's favorite Hurrem and his grand vezir Rüstem). Married princesses enjoyed relatively easy access to the imperial harem, their parental home, and could serve as informants, couriers, and political strategists. Because the interests of prin-cesses and their mothers in the harem were harmonious—the goals of the former being to prolong the political careers, indeed the lives, of their hus-bands, and of the latter to secure loyal allies on the outside—the networks formed by the marriages of princesses were extremely vital ones. It is surely no coincidence that the most powerful *valide sultan*s were those with several daughters: Nurbanu (*valide sultan* from 1574 to 1583) had three and possibly four, Safiye (1595–1603) had two, and Kösem (1623–1651) had at least three. Indeed, it was largely the efforts of *valide sultan*s that resulted in the fre-quency of princess-statesman alliances in this period. Such political links were vital to sustaining the regencies frequent in the first half of the seventeenth century.

While the *valide sultan* was not alone in deciding who princesses would marry, the significant influence she exerted in these arrangements gave her considerable opportunity to shape the networks and alliances that cemented the loyalty of the dynasty's most important servants. She arranged the mar-riages not only of her own daughters but also of the daughters of her son and his concubines. It was in the *valide sultan*'s interest to marry off her granddaugh-ters so that she might reap the political benefit of claiming their husbands as her political allies. The Venetian ambassador reported in 1583 that Nurbanu planned to marry her son Murad III's second daughter to the head of the palace guards.[158] Kösem's long career gave her considerable opportunity to forge family-based alliances. In 1626 or thereabout she wrote to the grand vezir Hafız Ahmed Pasha proposing marriage to one of her daughters: "Whenever you're ready, let me know and I'll act accordingly. We'll take care of you right away. I have a princess ready. I'll do just as I did when I sent out my Fatma."[159] Hafız Ahmed became the third husband of Ayşe. In the early 1640s Kösem emerged victorious from a conflict with a concubine of her recently deceased son Murad IV over the marital fortunes of the thirteen-year-old Kaya, daughter of the concubine and granddaughter of Kösem. The concubine was anxious for Kaya to marry one of her own political allies, the former sultan's sword-bearer, but Kösem's candidate, Melek Ahmed, won out.[160] However, because of the practice of serial marriage, a princess's mother might eventually profit from alliances to be made through her daughter.

The importance the dynasty attached to princess-*damad* alliances was not without its critics. Karaçelebizade Abdülaziz Efendi objected to the monies allotted to child princesses betrothed or married to prominent statesmen (the future brides remained in the imperial harem until they reached the age when the marriage might be consumated). He asserted that the extraordinary sums alloted in 1648 to two four-year-old daughters of the deposed İbrahim were being diverted from the public treasury in contravention of the Sharia.[161] On the other hand, Evliya Çelebi's account of the seizure immediately following Kaya Sultan's death of her treasury and household goods at the order of the grand vezir Köprülü Mehmed Pasha[162] suggests that princesses were treated no differently from other members of the ruling elite in terms of their financial status. Money and material goods accumulated by powerful individuals in the service of the state (including members of the dynasty) were viewed as property on loan, the temporary or usufruct use of which ceased when the owner left office or died. Increasingly during the seventeenth century, systematic confiscation of the estates of deceased notables became a principal means of filling the imperial treasury;[163] estates were inventoried immediately upon the death of an individual and often ruthlessly seized, as in the case of Kaya Sultan. As always, we need to evaluate criticism of the dynasty and its practices in the context of the partisan factionalism that was the political milieu of the times. Karaçelebizade, for example, was a notoriously contentious and outspoken member of the *ulema* and an enemy of the *valide sultan* Kösem, who was undoubtedly instrumental in the allotment of funds to the two child princesses. Nevertheless, his criticism underlines the extraordinary concentration of wealth and power in the dynasty and in the capital. Now that princes no longer played public roles or headed courtly households, it was the females of the royal family who served alongside the sultan in demonstrating the dynasty's wealth and distributing its largesse.

In conclusion, it is clear that a *valide sultan* or a powerful concubine could work different sectors of public government by creating and utilizing the variety of networks described above. Through the marriages of princesses or the imperial wet nurse, alliances could be formed with the most powerful of statesmen. Through clientage ties with former slaves, contacts could be created with a wide range of middle-level public officials. It is important to recognize that this establishment of a constellation of contacts outside the palace was by no means surreptitious. Nor was it a uniquely "female" or "harem" paradigm for the organization of political patronage and the creation of political influence. The governing class of the Ottoman Empire in this period operated not so much on the basis of institutionally or functionally ascribed authority as through a complex of personal bonds and family and household connections. Functionally ascribed authority—authority devolving from one's office—certainly existed, but more important was the web of individual relations—of patronage and clientage, of teacher and student, of kinship and marriage—that brought one to that office and that one used in the exercise of one's official power. Men as well as women sustained their careers by means of such networks, and men and women played significant roles in the formation of each other's networks.

Only when the paradigm of rigidly separate public/male and private/female spheres is discarded can we begin to appreciate the ways in which the structure of the Ottoman ruling class enabled women to participate in the political life of the empire. Conversely, by understanding how women were able to acquire and exercise power, we obtain a clearer picture of the structure of Ottoman politics and society in the early modern period. That the household was the fundamental unit of Ottoman political organization in this period is widely recognized, but the role of women in the construction and maintenance of the household system has been ignored. Whether the essential role played by women in the Ottoman dynastic household was reflected in the organization and operation of households of lesser status is a subject for future research.

II

WOMEN AND SOVEREIGN POWER

6

Shifting Images
of Ottoman Sovereignty

The Ottomans created a political culture that drew on the multiplicity of options available in the early modern Islamic world. The unparalleled longevity of the Ottoman dynasty among Islamic dynasties was in part the result of its ability to accommodate and manipulate different political traditions, different concepts of sovereignty, and different bases of legitimation. This process did not end with the establishment in the early sixteenth century of the Ottoman state as the dominant Islamic power and a major world empire. Indeed, the process of adjustment to these new circumstances—in particular, the expectations generated by Ottoman preeminence—presented the dynasty with a challenge it had not previously encountered.

As long as the empire could continue to score victories over its European and Muslim antagonists, its status was largely intact. But the slowing down of expansion in the second half of the sixteenth century and the consequent inability of the empire to sustain the image of the Ottoman sultan as an ever-victorious world conqueror made a shifting of emphases among the images of sovereignty promoted by the dynasty both necessary and inevitable. It is not that the Ottomans experienced military decline in this period: in the 1580s they made major advances in the Caucasus at the expense of the Safavids, and in 1600 they were sufficiently strong that the Hapsburgs feared a second campaign to take Vienna was imminent.[1] Not until the end of the seventeenth century did the Ottomans have to begin to confront the implications of substantial territorial loss. However, by the late sixteenth century, warfare no longer consisted of swift, one-season campaigns in which large territories would fall to victorious sultans. Now, protracted operations that lasted a decade or more might result in the gain of a few strategic border positions or simply maintenance of the status quo. The long war with the Hapsburgs, which lasted from 1593 to 1606 and made enormous demands on the economic and military capabilities of the empire, was a crucible in which much change was forged. The events of the late sixteenth century demonstrated that former military/administrative institutions were outmoded. The emergence of new institutional arrangements, however, led inevitably to economic and social strain as old hierarchies were displaced and new fiscal measures imposed to meet the urgent demands of warfare conducted increasingly on a cash basis. If there was a "crisis" at the turn of the century, it consisted essentially of the natural anxiety generated by the rapid transformation of institutions and the attendant adjustments in the nature of relationships among different groups in the society.

Until the last decade or so, historical writing about this period was dominated by the categories of analysis set forth by political commentators and historians of the late sixteenth and early seventeenth centuries who rued contemporary developments and believed that Ottoman society should be returned to the conditions that had prevailed under Süleyman and its vigor thus restored.[2] From the early nineteenth century on, modern historians have taken the jeremiads of certain writers of this period and constructed from them a scenario of precipitous Ottoman decline in the decades following the death of Süleyman.[3] It has suited the biasses of some Western historians as well as some modern Turkish historians to perpetuate the idea of an Ottoman Empire stagnant and unable to respond to the post-Renaissance rise of Europe.

The seventeenth century *was* a time of ups and downs for the Ottomans, with some very bad moments: the sociopolitical uprisings in Anatolia known as the Jelali rebellions; the Safavid advance under Shah Abbas which came on the heels of the war with Austria; fiscal, military, and political disorganization resulting from four accessions in the years between 1617 and 1623 and suffered again between 1644 and 1656, as the empire endured and recovered from the utter incompetence of the sultan İbrahim; and finally the disastrous consequences at the end of the century of the failure of the second Vienna campaign and its political aftermath. But equally, if not more, notable is the fact that there was recovery and even periodic prosperity in the face of these obstacles. While it is certainly true this was a period in which Ottomans confronted serious challenge both externally and internally, recent scholarly work has demonstrated the means that they devised to adapt to changing circumstances and the ways in which responses that had their genesis in times of crisis resolved themselves into permanent solutions. Major structural changes took place in the dynasty (as we have seen), the military, the religious institution, and provincial administration, while the financial bureaucracy, which experienced consolidation rather than significant change, emerged as a stabilizing element in the polity.[4] Discarding the vocabulary of decline, recent studies employ terms such as "transformation," "reform," and even "modernization" to describe institutional developments in this period.

One aspect of the preoccupation with decline that has not received sufficient discussion is the effect it has had of distorting our view of the pre-Süleymanic period. It has encouraged a romanticization of Ottoman history up to and through the reign of Süleyman, as if this period were one long march to glory, a heroic age. We have therefore tended to lose sight of the many and severe strains experienced by the empire in its formative phase. The rise of the Ottoman Empire was in fact slow in the context of Near Eastern history. The Ottoman state grew up out of soil cultivated for the first time for Islam. It experienced a prolonged phase of conquest. The empire was assembled gradually, element by element, in contrast to most earlier Muslim states,

whose dynasties simply took over conquered states and installed themselves
on foundations and institutions already established.[5] Moreover, at the beginning of the fifteenth century, the nascent Ottoman state suffered near collapse
at the hands of the conqueror Timur and was reassembled at great cost. In the
fourteenth and fifteenth centuries the Ottomans faced numerous challenges
by the European holy alliance (Murad II was unable to retire to a life of
spiritual contemplation because European powers moved immediately to exploit the weakness of his successor, the adolescent Mehmed II). The sultans
struggled to gain control simultaneously over the warlords who had done so
much to build the empire and over popular religious figures such as Sheikh
Bedreddin and Shah Kulu who challenged the dynasty's legitimacy and revealed the fragility of many subjects' allegiance to their Ottoman overlords.[6]
Nor were the costs of conquest so easily met during this period: the financial
straits experienced during Mehmed the Conqueror's reign led to widespread
confiscation of private property and pious foundations. This is to say nothing
of the ravages of succession wars and the challenges of pretenders, which
repeatedly and for years on end tied up internal and external programs of
government (the Jelali rebellions of the seventeenth century can be seen in
part as a continuation of endemic opposition to the imperial center earlier
expressed in the rebellions of dissident princes and popular leaders). The
celebration of *ghazi* ideology and the conquests of the sultans through
Süleyman have tended to obscure the fact that there was near-constant warfare in the fourteenth and fifteenth centuries, a good deal of it taking place on
Ottoman territory. While many became rich as a result of the booty of conquest, many—subjects of the conquerors as well as of the conquered—
suffered impoverishment or loss of life.

One problematic outcome of this interpretation of the so-called classical
period is that the institutional arrangements that obtained in the "heyday" of
this period—the reign of Süleyman—are generally regarded as the exemplary
institutions of the Ottoman polity, which began to "degenerate" after his
death. This view ignores the constant evolution that Ottoman institutions
underwent. There is no one moment in the history of Ottoman state and
society that can be frozen and labelled "the classical empire." Recent work
has suggested that the late-sixteenth-century spate of reform treatises criticizing post-Süleymanic developments should be viewed as only one episode in
the periodic manifestations of the literary genre of advice-to-kings treatises
and the topos of the failure of the state to meet an ideal construct of justice.[7]
Excessive concern with the reform literature, most of which was written by
members of the scribal bureaucracy, has also had the effect of obscuring other
voices of criticism, which opposed the administration of the state for its failure
to observe Islamic norms.

One aspect of these writings and the historiography built on them that
needs to be challenged, particularly with regard to the dynasty, is overempha-
sis on the role of individuals. The notion has persisted that developments after
Süleyman's death—new centers of power, new means of coping with political
and economic problems—were corruptions of mature institutions, which, if

they had not been undermined by incompetent or venal persons, would some-how have continued to maintain the vigor of the empire. In relation to the dynasty and its women, this period has been dismissed as one characterized by the personal incapacity of its sultans, in contrast to the vigor and ability of their ancestors, and by the "meddling" of harem women who exploited their influence over weak-minded sultans to satisfy their selfish hunger for power and wealth. As a consequence, little attention has been paid to the changed environment in which the authority of the sultans was exercised and that of dynastic women expanded. Nor has it been sufficiently noted that what mod-ern scholarship has viewed as manifestations of a weakening of the dynasty were frequently perceived by contemporaries as symptoms of its growing and excessive power.

This chapter briefly surveys the evolution of public images of Ottoman sovereignty. The shifting emphasis among the public faces of the dynasty is the context that determined the sources and shape of women's power in this period, discussed in subsequent chapters. This chapter also examines two major aspects of sultanic conduct that caused concerned subjects to question whether their sovereign was behaving as traditional conceptions dictated: the decline in the sultan's participation in war and his seclusion in the imperial palace. While critical analysis of the reform literature of this period is beyond the scope of this work, we need to look briefly at its concerns not only because it expressed the reactions of an important element in Ottoman society to changes in that society, but also because it articulated the most vocal critique of women's public roles.

Ghazi, Sultan, Khan:
The Faces of Ottoman Sovereignty

The conquest of Baghdad in 1258 by Mongol forces and the demise of the Abbasid caliphate ushered in a period of great political fluidity that permitted dynasties established subsequently, including the Ottomans, to assert multiple claims to legitimacy.[8] Even after the Abbasid caliphate's loss of military and political predominance in the ninth and tenth centuries, it had continued to provide legitimation for Muslim rulers who came to power not, as had the Umayyad and Abbasid dynasties, as successors to the Prophet (that is, descen-dents of the tribe of Quraysh), but rather through forceable conquest or internal usurpation of power.[9] The demise of the caliphate deprived the Is-lamic world of this unifying force, however tenuous it might have been in its final years, and opened the way for new formulations of legitimacy. Simulta-neously, through the establishment, after the Mongol conquest, of Muslim states based to a greater or lesser degree on Turco-Mongol political traditions, different models of sovereignty and different principles of legitimacy received greater emphasis than they had before the mid-thirteenth century.

The discontinuity between pre- and post-Mongol political organization and theory should not, however, be overemphasized. Central Asian traditions had been penetrating the Islamic political and social world for more than two hundred years, through the practice of dynasties of Turkish origin and their military commanders, themselves frequently of Turkish origin. These traditions had to a significant degree been absorbed into Islamic political theory and practice before the fall of the caliphate. Furthermore, political ideas and institutions that have been associated with the nomadic steppe peoples—the notion of sovereignty as the possession of the entire dynastic family, for example, and the division of the patrimony into appanages assigned to family members[10]—existed independently among peoples indigenous to the Middle East.[11] Indeed, it is difficult to separate out a distinctively Turco-Mongol strand from Islamic political culture in the early thirteenth century. The latter was above all a synthesis, an accommodation of Muslim religious prescriptions contained in the Qur'an, prophetic traditions, works of jurisprudence, and so forth, to the political forms and ideals of the three imperial traditions already encountered by Islamic civilization: the Persian, the late Roman/Byzantine, and the Turco-Mongol. Nonetheless, the renewed and more direct experience of Turco-Mongol political traditions that began with the Mongol conquest, occurring as it did in the vacuum created by the demise of the caliphate, necessitated renewed efforts at synthesis.[12]

From the perspective of the Ottoman dynasty's claims to political legitimacy and the images of sovereignty it projected, its history—at least for the first three hundred years—reflects the accommodation of the various traditions that constituted the political currency of the fourteenth, fifteenth, and sixteenth centuries.[13] By the reign of Süleyman, the Ottoman sultanate had come to represent many things to many people. It was a multifaceted institution that could be manipulated to reflect now one, now another of the legitimating images it had assimilated in the more than two centuries of its existence. Representing the ideals of the different classes which served it, different aspects of the dynasty's persona might be invoked for particular audiences or to meet particular sets of circumstances. At times, this process seemed to result more in an agglomeration than in a synthesis of legitimating traditions.[14]

The first set of images enabled the nascent state to justify its local power. The Ottoman state was formed in the politically decentralized Anatolian environment of the late thirteenth and early fourteenth centuries. It was one of several principalities (*beylik*) that grew up as the power of the Anatolian Seljuk dynasty and then its Mongol overlords waned. Before the family of Osman became the House of Osman, that is, before it asserted its independent sovereignty, it probably received recognition as frontier lords (*uc beyi*) from the Anatolian Seljuks. According to a tradition recounted in the early histories of the Ottomans, Osman (or in some accounts his father Ertuğrul), was awarded the insignia of rulership by the Seljuk sultan for his victories as *ghazi,* warrior for Islam against the infidel enemy.[15] *Ghaza,* the pursuit of the holy war, was an ideology that fit a frontier state of nomadic origin; it was an Islamic calque that suited a tribal society given to raiding and seeking booty, yet it provided a moral code and Islamic legal justification that could rally other elements in what was rapidly becoming an increasingly complex society. The nascent dynasty's assumption of the title "sultan" marked its claim to local sovereignty; the title appeared on coins minted by Orhan, the second ruler of the dynasty. *Ghazi* and *sultan* were thus early established as twin faces of Ottoman sovereignty: an inscription of 1337 on the mosque constructed by Orhan in the first Ottoman capital of Bursa describes its builder as "Sultan, son of the sultan of the *ghazis, Ghazi,* son of the *Ghazi,* the valiant [defender] of government and religion, warden of the horizons, champion of the world, Orhan son of Osman."[16] It was their successful pursuit of *ghaza* that the Ottoman sultans were to make the basis of their claims to preeminence in the Muslim world. Their devotion to *ghaza* was articulated by Mehmed II when asked why he underwent such extreme hardship in order to take the Byzantine city of Trebizond (Trabzon); according to the historian Neşri, the sultan replied: "These tribulations are not for Trabzon but for God's sake. The sword of Islam is in our hands. If we did not choose to endure these tribulations, not only would we not be worthy to be called *ghazis,* we would be ashamed to stand in God's presence on the Day of Resurrection."[17]

Because in the post-Mongol world the title "sultan" was available to virtually any local Muslim power with a claim to sovereignty based on Islamic legitimizing principles (however tenuous that claim might be) and backed up by sufficient military force, more grandiose titles would need to be found as Ottoman pretensions to greater status developed after the collapse of Seljuk-Mongol rule in Anatolia.[18] The third sultan, Murad I, styled himself *sultan-ı azam* (the most exalted sultan), and *hudavendigâr* (emperor), the first a title used by the Anatolian Seljuks and the second by the Mongol Ilkhanids.[19] At the end of the fourteenth century, Bayezid I, the fourth Ottoman sultan, adopted the title "Sultan of Rum" (Rum being an old Islamic name for Anatolia, which had belonged to the "Roman" Byzantines); he thereby laid claim to successorship to the Anatolian Seljuks and challenged the claims of other Anatolian principalities.[20]

By midcentury, Mehmed II, conqueror of Constantinople, was emboldened to claim parity with the Mamluk sultan in Cairo. Before his reign, the Ottoman ruler had addressed the Mamluk sultan as "my father, Sultan of the two noble sanctuaries"; Mehmed, however, addressed him as "my brother, the Sultan of Egypt" and "Servitor of the two noble sanctuaries."[21] The latter's principal role in the service of the Muslim community was, Mehmed asserted, the protection of the pilgrimage routes to the holy cities of Mecca and Medina, while it was the Ottomans' victorious *ghaza* that justified their claims to eminence. In 1485 Mehmed's son Bayezid refused to campaign in person against the Mamluk sultan on the grounds that it was unfitting for the Ottoman sultan to lower himself to the level of "a Circassian slave."[22]

The Ottomans' fifteenth-century claim to overlordship of Anatolia brought them into conflict with a number of counterclaimants. The Ottoman response to these challenges was, in part, to augment their repertoire of legitimizing images. From the east came an Islamicized Turco-Mongol challenge. It was represented first by Timur and his successors, whose vast empire claimed as its foundation both Islamic holy law, Sharia, and Mongol customary law, the *yasa* of Chinggis Khan.[23] The challenge took its second form in the Turkman

Akkoyunlu dynasty, the Ottomans' principal rival in eastern Anatolia, who appealed not to the Mongol tradition of dynastic legitimation and law, but instead based their claims to sovereignty on descent from the ancient Turkish khans of Central Asia, in particular the legendary Oghuz Khan.[24] The Ottomans, themselves of Turkman origin, found it expedient in the mid-fifteenth century to bolster the legitimacy of their dynasty by elaborating their own claim to descent from Oghuz Khan.[25] This synthesis of the Islamic and Central Asian heritages of the Ottomans was perhaps most readily exemplified by the title that became the standard designation for the Ottoman sultan: "Sultan [Mehmed] Khan."[26]

Historiographic tradition of the fifteenth century was careful to disassociate the Ottomans from Mongol tradition. Chinggis Khan was at best a ruler whose polity, governed by customary law or the discretionary law of the ruler, was inferior to a polity regulated by Sharia;[27] at worst he was a "merciless infidel."[28] Even the Muslim Timur was denigrated.[29] Ahmedi, the author of the early fifteenth-century epic *The Book of Alexander,* whose final section is probably the earliest historical account of the Ottomans, warned of the dangers of applying the ruler's law (which he termed *kanun* rather than *yasa*) outside of the context of Sharia, as the Mongols had done. In the introduction to his section on the Ottomans, Ahmedi spoke as follows of the Mongol Ilkhanid rulers of Iran, the last of whom converted to Islam, and their Muslim Jalayirid successors:

> What were they like, those Mongol sultans? Come, listen to their story.
> They did not openly tyrannize the people [the Muslims] as Chinggis Khan did.
> They tyrannized through the law, they did not stain their hands with blood.
> Tyranny, when it comes in the guise of law and order, is easily mistaken by the people for justice. . . .
> Now that we have recounted the story of those masters of cruelty, let us tell of the masters of justice [the Ottomans].
> Let us celebrate those rulers who were both Muslim and just.[30]

In the introduction to Neşri's late-fifteenth-century history of the Ottomans, this new basis of legitimacy—the Central Asian Turkish khanate—was enhanced and accommodated to the Ottomans' principal identity as Muslim sovereigns through the claim that Oghuz was the first Turkish khan to convert to Islam. According to Neşri, Oghuz's father, like Chinggis Khan, was a "tyrannical pagan infidel," although his grandfather possessed the material requisites and admirable qualities of rulership: "many lands, sovereignty, power, awesome majesty, and many soldiers." The anachronistic aspect of these genealogical claims is exemplified by Neşri's assertion that Oghuz Khan's conversion (to monotheism) took place in the lifetime of the prophet Abraham.[31]

The Caliph of Islam

These numerous images of sovereignty projected by the Ottoman sultans in the fourteenth and fifteenth centuries were not seen as incompatible or competing. They appear side by side in the histories of the dynasty that began to be written in the second half of the fifteenth century. Indeed, a characteristic feature of this period, not only among the Ottomans, is the elaboration of multiple claims to legitimacy based most overtly on Muslim religious principles but drawing on other political traditions as well. At the same time that Mehmed the Conqueror was claiming superiority to the Mamluk sultans, his Akkoyunlu counterpart to the east, the conqueror and ruler Uzun Hasan, was declaring himself free of Mamluk overlordship.[32] Sophisticated political rationales to justify the pretensions of the two dynasties were constructed in the second half of the fifteenth century from Islamic religious texts, Greco-Islamic political philosophy, traditions of ancient Persian statecraft, and eschatological and esoteric doctrines. The most influential formulation was that of Jalal al-Din Davani in his *Akhlaq-i Jalali* (The Jalalian Ethics), composed for Uzun Hasan and his son in the 1470s; an Ottoman version of this ideological synthesis is contained in the introduction to Tursun Beg's *Tarih-i Ebü-l'Feth* (History of the Conqueror), written for Mehmed's son Bayezid II around 1490.[33]

At the start of the sixteenth century, the first Safavid ruler, Ismail, Uzun Hasan's grandson and heir to his empire, created an even more grandiose synthesis than that of his Akkoyunlu predecessors or his Ottoman contemporaries.[34] Ismail bolstered his Akkoyunlu heritage by adding his role as charismatic spiritual leader, *pir* of the Safavi sufi order and saint to large numbers of Anatolian Turkmans. While claiming *ghazi* status, he differentiated himself from the Ottoman and now-defunct Akkoyunlu sultanates by formally adopting the title *shah,* thus appealing directly to the heroic tradition of the Persian kings. Ismail's principal claim to Muslim legitimacy was radical for his times: he installed Twelver Shi'ism as the religious and juridical basis of the Safavid state and, asserting descent from the Prophet Muhammad, claimed eligibility to act as representative of the Hidden Imam of Twelver tradition.

The brief but spectacular career of Selim I (r. 1512–1520) equipped the Ottomans to meet the formidable challenge posed by the Safavid synthesis. The rapid rise of this powerful Shi'i state and Selim's determination to combat its threat through military confrontation and a bloody purge of Safavid sympathizers from the Ottoman realm initiated what became a permanent geographic division of the Middle Eastern Islamic world into Sunni and Shi'i.[35] Selim's defeat of Shah Ismail at Chaldiran in 1514 contained Safavid pretensions in Anatolia and endowed the Ottoman sultan with the prestige of being the first to halt the advance of this militant new political and religious force. However, it was Selim's conquest of the Mamluk empire in 1516–1517 that was of greater significance for Ottoman standing in the Islamic world. In addition to gaining territories strategically located and rich in revenue, the Ottoman sultans could now claim the prestigious title *hadım ul-harameyn,* "servitor of the two sanctuaries"—guardian of the holy cities of Mecca and Medina and of the pilgrimage routes that led to them.[36]

When Süleyman mounted the throne in 1520, he was the first Ottoman sultan to begin his reign as the most powerful sovereign in the Islamic world. In the eyes of most of his subjects, the sultan was now the principal upholder of Sunni Islam and the foremost guardian of the Muslim community. Rival Oghuz Turkman pedigrees no longer figured overtly in ideological discourse, since the principal Muslim powers of the sixteenth century—the Ottomans, the Safavids, the Uzbeks, and the Mughals—all claimed Central Asian political traditions in either their Mongol or Turkish form. By the sixteenth century, the terms of ideological discourse had become almost exclusively religious and followed the new cleavage between the sunnism of the Ottomans and the shiʻism of their principal rivals, the Safavids.

Toward the end of Süleyman's reign, the former grand vezir Lutfi Pasha argued that the Ottoman sultan was entitled to be called "caliph" as well as "the imam of the age." His reasoning was contained in a treatise he composed to answer a query that had been put to him, namely, who was entitled to claim spiritual leadership of the Muslim community since the demise of the Abbasid caliphate.[37] Defining the terms of his argument, Lutfi wrote: "What is meant by 'the Sultan' according to the *Sharia* is the oath of allegiance [sworn by subjects], conquering power, and power of compulsion. . . . What is meant by the Imâm is one who maintains the Faith and governs the kingdom of Islâm with equity. . . . What is meant by the Khalîfa [caliphate] is he who commands to the good and prohibits the evil. . . ."[38] If all of these conditions are present in one person, continued Lutfi, then that person is a sultan who can justly claim to be the imam of the age and the caliph. This person, of course, was the Ottoman sultan, whose superior claim among Muslim sovereigns lay in the fact that the dynasty was unequalled in its maintenance of the Sharia and its defense of the territories of Islam.[39] Lutfi accused the Safavids of distorting religious tradition by asserting that the imamate was reserved for descendents of the Prophet.

In this discussion, it was the "imam of the age" that was probably the more important title to which claim was laid, for two reasons. First, it more effectively countered the Safavid claim to preeminence: as Shiʻis, the Safavids would claim not the caliphate, a title that had become associated with Sunni Islam, but the imamate, a title that referred both to the spiritual leadership of the Shiʻi community and also, more generally, to supreme authority in Islam (Lutfi Pasha's usage). Second, the title of caliph no longer signified preeminence in the Islamic world.[40] As the result of a process similar to the earlier scaling down of the title of sultan, it could be arrogated by any powerful ruler who governed, or claimed to govern, on the basis of the Sharia. The title of caliph had earlier been claimed by the Akkoyunlu Uzun Hasan and also by the founder of the Central Asian Uzbek dynasty, Muhammad Shaibani Khan, upon his conquest of Herat in 1507 from the last Timurids. It had even been applied by the Persian vezir and historian Rashid al-Din at the end of the thirteenth century to the first member of the Mongol Ilkhanid dynasty (founded by Hulegu, the extinguisher of the Abbasid caliphate) to convert to Islam.[41] That the title of caliph was in common use by the reign of Mehmed the Conqueror is suggested by the inscription on a Manisa mosque built by a member of Mehmed's government: "The builder of this blessed mosque is the founder of pious establishments, Sinan Bey son of Abdullah, the freed slave of Sultan Mehmed son of Murad Khan, in the time of his caliphate, the middle of the month of Rejeb in the year 879 [1474]."[42]

The Safavids were not the only contemporaries of Süleyman who claimed descent from the Prophet as grounds for legitimacy. In Islamic religious tradition, there was a strong idealization of the family of the Prophet Muhammad and his descendants—especially his daughter and only surviving child Fatima, his cousin and son-in-law Ali, and their sons Hasan and Husain—who were known and revered as "the people of the House" (ehl-i beyt). Not only were the Prophet and members of his family emulated as paragons of moral virtue and social propriety, but many rulers and would-be rulers bolstered their claims to legitimacy by producing genealogies demonstrating their blood descent from them (including, in the latter part of the twentieth century, the Iraqi president and invader of Kuwait, Saddam Husain).

It was blood descent from the Prophet Muhammad that was made the basis of the claims to legitimacy of the Moroccan Sa'di dynasty, which took over the throne in 1548, and following it the 'Alawi dynasty.[43] M. E. Combs-Schilling has argued that these legitimizing claims were imprinted on popular consciousness through elaboration of public rituals identifying the monarch with the Prophet, most notably celebrations of the Prophet's birthday and the reenactment of Abraham's sacrifice of Ismail that is the central feature of the Feast of Sacrifice, the most important Muslim holiday.[44] As John Woods has shown, even the successors of Timur had asserted descent from the house of Ali, and in so doing laid claim to a joint Muslim-Mongol pedigree: a genealogical inscription placed in Timur's mausoleum proclaimed that the "radiant being" of Mongol mythology, who had impregnated the legendary ancestress of the lines of both Chinggis Khan and Timur, was a descendant of Ali.[45] Shaun Marmon has argued that earlier, the Mamluk sultans, while not claiming descent from the Prophet, sought to enhance their stature through assimilation to the charisma of the Prophet. They did this primarily by elaborating a set of rituals around the tomb of the Prophet which they replicated in their own tombs.[46] The Safavid rulers, especially in the early decades, encouraged a view of themselves as the "vicar of God" (vali Allah) and the equal of Ali, the charismatic representative of the Prophet's family in Shi'i Islam. The polemical poetry of Shah Ismail, which circulated in Anatolia and inspired the allegiance of many, declared that Ismail was the incarnation of Ali and even of the Godhead.[47]

While over time the Ottoman dynasty put forth various claims to legitimacy and did not hesitate to manufacture genealogies when this seemed an opportune thing to do, it did not claim descent from the Prophet. Nor did the sultans attempt through public ceremonies or institutions to assimilate themselves to the charisma of the Prophet. In the classic formulation of din ü devlet, "religion and government," they embodied the devlet, a term that connoted at once the state, the dynasty, and the divine grant of secular dominion.[48] They might be the defenders and patrons of Islam, and as the "imam of the age" the supreme authority in the Muslim world, but their legitimacy did not stem from any inherited religious capacity. *Din* in the Ottoman polity was represented by the *ulema,* the official hierarchy of judges, jurisprudents, theologians, and teachers trained in the Islamic sciences, and by Sufi sheikhs and their orders. The closest the Ottomans ever came to assimilating themselves to the Prophet and the events of the early Muslim community was to assert that their legendary ancestor Oghuz Khan and his descendents were Muslim from the very beginning and were in contact with early Muslim leaders.[49]

The value of links to the Prophet and to the first generation of Islam was not, however, lost to the Ottomans. For example, sultans made use of the Prophet's relics in times of crisis, both military and dynastic. But it is significant that the most directly articulated links between the Prophet and his family and the Ottoman dynasty in the sixteenth and seventeenth centuries were forged between the women of these households. Princesses as well as slave concubines and mothers of the sultans, nonblood members of the Ottoman dynasty, were likened to the females of the Prophet's family, especially his wives, nonblood members of his household. Even if they were not included among "the people of the House," the Prophet's wives had been honored by a revelation from God to Muhammad in which they were named "mother of the believers." The honorific titulature employed for Ottoman royal women and often their names quite consciously recalled the women of the Prophet's family, particularly Khadija, the first wife of the Prophet, his third and beloved wife 'A'isha, and Fatima, Muhammad's daughter by Khadija. While the sultan was the "imam of the age," royal women might be the "'A'isha of the age" or "the Fatima of the era." The 1663 foundation deed for the pious endowments established by the mother of Mehmed IV referred to her as "the illuminating light of the household of the greatest caliphate, the Khadija of the times"; this allusion was all the more powerful because one of the queen mother's names was Khadija.[50] (By a quirk of history that could not have been known at the time the queen mother acquired her name, all future sultans were to descend from her, just as the Prophet's wife Khadija was the progenetrix of "the people of the House," a connection that seventeenth-century Ottomans may well have recognized.) This means of linking the dynasty to the household of the Prophet is only one example of the ability of royal women to serve functions not available to or perhaps even avoided by the males of the dynasty. In the case of royal concubines, this form of assimilation of the dynasty to the family of the Prophet may have been available precisely because they were not blood members, not people of the Ottoman house, so to speak. There may even have been tacit reference to the fact of conversion—Ottoman concubines were converts to Islam as of course were the Prophet's wives.

Like their Moroccan counterparts of the sixteenth century, the Ottomans certainly used public ceremonial as a legitimating device, but they used it to celebrate themselves, that is, to aggrandize the dynastic house. The major public events and celebrations involving the sultans and other members of the royal family were not specifically religious in focus. Ottoman royal ceremonial moved according to the rhythms of the dynasty rather than the religious calendar. It marked important events in the royal life cycle: births, circumci-

Figure 6-1 Mehmed III's victorious entry into Istanbul. Hailed as "Sultan Ghazi Mehmed Khan" for his victorious 1596–1597 campaign in Hungary, the sultan (the stout figure with two plumes in his turban) makes his triumphal entry into Istanbul. At the upper right, women are depicted watching the victory parade. From Talikizade, *Şahname-i Mehmed Han,* fs. 68b–69a. (*Courtesy of Topkapı Palace Museum Library, Istanbul*)

sions, weddings, funerals, the departure of a prince for his provincial post, and the sword-girding ceremony marking the accession of a new sultan. To be sure, there was significant religious content in these public events, but the subject of the ceremony was the royal person. The major religious holidays occasioned a good deal of public, communal celebration, but the sultan was not a featured presence; his attendance at prayer services was eagerly awaited and observed, but his own marking of the event was a hand-kissing ceremony conducted within the palace and confined to the elite of the ruling classes. Only the festivities surrounding the *ghaza*—the ceremonious departure of the sultan on campaign and the (hopefully) triumphal return to the capital—were rituals that integrated the celebration of a central feature of Islamic doctrine and the legitimacy of the dynasty (Figure 6-1). It is significant that the celebration of *ghaza* had the power to suspend one of the most fundamental of Ottoman social norms: women temporarily enjoyed the freedom to move about the city and mix with male company.[51]

While ceremonial occasions were intended primarily to aggrandize the dynasty and cement the loyalty of subjects, they had another purpose, or at least another effect: they wove an urban fabric out of the myriad and sometimes contending elements of the city of Istanbul. Paula Sanders has demonstrated in the context of Fatimid Egypt the function of royal ceremonial not only in securing political legitimacy but also in the creation of an "urban language."[52] Public celebrations offered an opportunity for generating civic pride. They featured pantomimes depicting Ottoman victories over enemies and public demonstrations of the martial skills of the royal troops. The contribution of ordinary subjects to the prosperity of Ottoman society was not neglected in these events. The most lavishly staged occasions, for example, the circumcision of Murad III's son Mehmed in 1582 and the departure of Murad IV in 1638 on campaign against the Safavids, included a great parade of the guilds. From elaborately prepared floats members of the various guilds demonstrated the practice of their craft and might distribute samples of their products to the crowd. Included in the parades were representatives not only of the standard professions and crafts but also of the empire's ethnic minorities and even of marginal elements, such as pickpockets and scavengers. Social tensions were acknowledged in these events, yet safely contained under the watchful eye of the sultan. These parades provided a survey of the creative energy of the populace yet harnessed it in the service of the dynasty. It is no coincidence that foreign ambassadors were given ringside seats at these events.

Polemic regarding the dynasty's preeminence was reflected in another vital aspect of political life: the cultivation of the image of the Ottoman sultan as the most majestic and munificent monarch of the Islamic world. As in other monarchical polities, power in the Islamic world was measured not just by military might but also by courtly splendor, lavish public ceremonial, and liberal royal patronage. It was the sultan who symbolized the empire's cultural unity and claim to cultural preeminence. Süleyman not only carried on his father's drive to extend Ottoman territorial dominion, but also assiduously cultivated imperial éclat through numerous public celebrations, extensive court patronage of cultural activity, public building on an unprecedented scale, and embellishment of the imperial palace.[53] It was for good reason that he was known by Europeans as "the Magnificent." Such imperial majesty was certainly not new in the Ottoman dynasty, but the scale of its celebration in the sixteenth century was unequaled. Şerif Mardin's observation about the mid-nineteenth-century sultanate—that its "conspicuous consumption" was probably the result of its emulation of the more lavish standards of European courts[54]—may be relevant to Süleyman's reign: the standards of courtly discourse in the sixteenth century were universally high. During the first decades of Süleyman's reign the lavishness of imperial ceremonial reached unprecedented levels, much of it centered on the celebration of dynastic rituals such as weddings of princesses and circumcisions of sons. Ottoman royal splendor continued to be cultivated by Süleyman's heirs, especially his grandson Murad III, who devoted the greatest energy of his reign to furthering his grandfather's achievements in this respect.

Despite this emphasis on the material trappings of power, there was also a discernible movement in the sixteenth century toward a greater public religious posture on the part of the dynasty. This was partly a reflection of the rhetoric of legitimacy, which was not simply empty polemic, especially after the sharpening of Sunni and Shi'i identities. As overlord of much of the Middle Eastern Islamic world, the Ottoman sultan needed to substantiate his claim to be the *imam* and to defend the integrity of Sunni belief. The enhanced religious posture of the dynasty was also partly pragmatic, a useful image to cultivate as *ghaza* became more difficult to achieve and the prestige of the Ottoman sultanate could no longer be based solely on conquest. A defense of Sunni identity was useful in other respects as well: the persecution of "heretics," which began in earnest under Selim I, was a means of eliminating political dissidents and Safavid sympathizers.

As we saw in Chapter 3, a shift of emphasis began to take place toward the middle of Süleyman's reign, more precisely, around the year 1537. After establishing his own personal legitimacy through the celebration of military victory and courtly magnificence, Süleyman began to concentrate on demonstrating his own and the dynasty's piety and charity. The sultan began to undertake a number of pious works and to observe a personal austerity more in line with the norms of Islamic piety. The religious patronage of the Ottoman sultans had always been ample, but now it encompassed the whole of the Sunni Muslim world. Moreover, it paid conspicuous attention to the historic memories of the Muslim community. In the most ancient centers of Muslim civilization—the holy cities of Mecca, Medina, and Jerusalem—Süleyman and members of his family improved physical structures and the quality of religious life: the sacred compound in Jerusalem and the walls of the city were restored as were the Meccan waterworks, for example, and a number of religious institutions were newly established (see Chapter 7).

Süleyman also addressed the tensions between the Sharia and secular or dynastic law. While it is debatable which emerged the stronger, the point is that he, together with his chief justice and then *müfti* Ebussuud Efendi, attempted to address charges of irreligion that had been leveled against Ottoman administration and to reconcile the two bodies of law.[55] Even Süleyman's activities in the codification and enforcement of secular dynastic edicts and customary practices—*kanun*—can be seen as efforts to enhance his image as the good Muslim sovereign, who, according to prevailing political thinking, was characterized by his righteousness and justice. Strengthening *kanun* in the service of Sharia, Süleyman fit the ideal put forth by fifteenth-century critics of the Mongols.

The greater religious content in the dynasty's construction of its identity may have exerted an influence on its internal structure. The pattern of succession to the throne that prevailed until the seventeenth century—contest among contending princes—was fundamentally tied to Central Asian principles of legitimation: the state belongs to him who can take it, to the conqueror. While Turco-Mongol traditions of legitimation gave a broad mandate to the ruling house, in each generation the polity was reconquered, both literally and symbolically, by one of its scions; in other words, the new sultan had to legitimate his own rule by demonstrating his personal capacity. Laws were considered to be in abeyance between the death of the ruler and the accession of his successor (thus the need to conceal the death of the sovereign lest looting and urban disorder ensue). Patents of office had to be reissued by the new ruler and foreign treaties renegotiated. So personal were the ties that formed government that when the sultan went on campaign, the entire upper echelon of the ruling elite, including the leading members of the religious hierarchy, went with him. The various offices of administration were thus symbolically attached to the person of the sultan, lacking a separate institutional identity. Such a system was compatible with a state organized for warfare and expansion and with a view of the sultanate as legitimated principally through *ghaza*. But sixteenth-century formulations such as that of Lutfi Pasha gave a broader foundation to Ottoman sovereignty, which was no longer derived solely from the "conquest and compulsion" of the "Sultanate." Significantly, Lutfi argued that princes of the dynasty possessed the qualifications for rule simply by virtue of inheritance.[56] Certainly, legitimating polemic was not the only reason for movement toward some kind of structured succession (see Chapter 4), but it provided an ideological sanction.

It might be expected that these developments would give greater power to the religious establishment. In many ways they did. Over the course of the next two centuries, leading members of the *ulema* emerged as the only aristocracy in the empire;[57] their hereditary "dynasties" were matched in the military/administrative arena only by that of the Köprülü grand vezirs of the seventeenth century. Within the empire, the influence on government policy of leading members of the *ulema,* particularly the *müfti,* increased over the course of the sixteenth century. Early in the century the authority of high-ranking members of the *ulema* was strictly limited to matters clearly falling within the jurisdiction of the Sharia;[58] by the end of the century the *müfti* was regularly called upon to advise the sultan on matters of policy beyond the scope of the Sharia. Ambassadors began to comment on the influence of the post.[59] By the end of the seventeenth century the scholar and writer Hüseyin Hezarfenn ("the polymath") could comment that the *müfti* was at least equal to the grand vezir in influence, if not greater, and in some areas clearly superior; this was because "the affairs of state are founded upon religion."[60] The *fetvas* of the *müfti,* juridical interpretations of the Sharia, became more important as one of the means subjects could resort to to exert control on the sultanate; after the transition to succession by seniority, the *müfti*'s role in depositions and accessions increased.

Yet, as Madeline Zilfi has shown, the privileges bestowed upon the religious establishment were a mixed blessing.[61] The *ulema* were administratively subordinated to the control of the throne. If they enjoyed extraordinary privilege, it existed ultimately at the sultan's sufferance. The *müfti* had the authority to make appointments, but these could be revoked by the sultan, who also enjoyed considerable latitude in introducing his favorites into *ulema* ranks. Furthermore, the sultan controlled the appointment of the *müfti.* The initial privileging of the post of *müfti* with Ebussuud Efendi was strikingly similar to the privileging of the grand vezirate with İbrahim, and even of the royal concubine with Hurrem. Like İbrahim and Hurrem, Ebussuud was endowed with extraordinary powers, public honors, and Süleyman's intimate affection, while the sultan was able to assert personal control over hierarchies of state and society that might act as checks on his authority.

The Sedentary Sultanate

In their reform treatises, Ottoman writers of the late sixteenth and early seventeenth centuries appear to have been concerned in particular about two interrelated aspects of sultanic conduct. They suspected that it was the infrequency with which Ottoman rulers now led military campaigns and their seclusion within the imperial palace that lay at the root of problems that appeared to them ever-more intractable around the turn of the century. These commentators were not entirely wrong: after the reign of Süleyman, the sultan *did* become a more sedentary ruler who spent more time in the capital and within the palace. Süleyman's son Selim II and grandson Murad III were perhaps the most remote from the public, neglecting for long periods even the traditional public appearance of the sultan for the communal Friday prayer service. But this development was neither sudden nor absolute; the sultans after Süleyman differed from one another in this respect, just as Süleyman, his father Selim, and grandfather Bayezid II had differed. Furthermore, the sedentarization of the sultanate was part of a whole web of changing circumstances and institutional accommodations, a phenomenon the commentators lacked the perspectives of time and distance to appreciate.

Lapse of Sultanic *Ghaza*

Between Süleyman's final European campaign in 1566, on which he died, and Mehmed III's European campaign of 1596, the Ottoman sultans did not participate in military activity. Then another lapse of more than twenty years occurred before the young sultan Osman II took up arms. The preference of the majority of post-Süleymanic sultans for entrusting the direction of military activities to their grand vezirs and other statesmen has been explained primarily as the result of their all-too-worldly concerns. The attractions of court life are said to have overwhelmed the sultans' devotion to the waging of holy war and their desire for glory on the battlefield and sense of solidarity with statesmen and soldiers.[62] This simplistic reading ignores a number of factors, not the least of which was the fact that the Ottomans were not alone in adjusting to the burdensome consequences of empire. In 1589, Giovanni Botero, political thinker of the Counter Reformation, posed the following question in his *The Reason of State:* "Whether it is a greater task to extend or preserve a state?", and proceeded to answer it: "Clearly it is a greater task to preserve a state, because human affairs wax and wane as if by a law of nature, like the moon to which they are subject. Thus to keep them stable when they have become great and to maintain them so that they do not decline and fall is an almost superhuman undertaking. . . . Might conquers but wisdom preserves: many are mighty but few are wise." While he regarded "the Turk" as a continuing menace to Europe, Botero resembled his Ottoman counterparts, the political critics of the late sixteenth and early seventeenth centuries, in his belief that enlightened analysis could diagnose the ills of a state, which could then be cured through a precise application of rules and procedures. John Elliott notes that Botero was widely read and discussed in Spain, where debate about the decline of the Spanish empire was starting to take taking place.[63]

Even before the role of the *ghazi* sultan became problematic for the Ottoman dynasty, the issue of military command had been a tension endemic in the polity. Earlier sultans had delegated command of the army and had sometimes been criticized for doing so. In describing Mehmed the Conqueror's delegation to the grand vezir Mahmud Pasha of preparation for the campaign against the principalities of Kastamonu and Trabzon, the historian Neşri commented, "At that time Mahmud Pasha was at the summit of his power; it was as if the *padishah* had turned the sultanate over to him and exempted himself from responsibility."[64] When in 1524, after dispatching the grand vezir İbrahim Pasha to quell disturbances in Egypt, Süleyman spent the winter hunting in Edirne and upon his return to Istanbul repaired to another leisure retreat, the Janissaries broke out in open revolt.[65]

The sultans of the post-Süleymanic period and their advisers appear to have considered it politic for the ruler to refrain from leading the Ottoman forces on campaign except in extraordinary circumstances. The legacy of Selim I and Süleyman's conquests was an empire so large that military engagements on its borders entailed lengthy absences of the sultan from his capital. In 1529 Süleyman bestowed command of the army together with unprecedented powers on the grand vezir İbrahim Pasha; to the head of his chancellery, from whom he requested the necessary order, he had said:

> Through the will of God the borders of our kingdom have expanded, and there is no end to our concerns for the welfare of the Muslim community. It is not appropriate for us to attempt to attend to every problem personally. We have appointed İbrahim Pasha commander so that he might concern himself with the affairs of the faith and the empire and implement the necessary policies. Draw up and bring me a draft of an order to all my subjects to submit to him.[66]

Antonio Erizzo, Venetian ambassador to Süleyman's court from 1554 to 1557, commented that the sultan's hold on the throne, now distant from either of the empire's fronts, was severely endangered when he campaigned, especially since he took the better part of his government with him.[67] The difficulties in protecting far-flung borders and the increasing costs of lengthy campaigns were important factors underlying the devotion of Süleyman and his grand vezirs during the last decades of his reign to a policy of peace. The comments in 1562 of the Austrian ambassador Busbecq are instructive in this regard. Busbecq defended his emperor Ferdinand against charges of weakness in failing to take the offensive against "so formidable an enemy" as the Ottoman sultan and commended the emperor's policy of devoting his resources to fortifying the frontier:

> It is now about forty years since Soleiman captured Belgrade, slew King Louis, and reduced Hungary, and so secured the prospect of possessing him-

self not only of this province but also of territory farther north. In this hope he besieged Vienna. . . . But what has he achieved by his mighty array, his unlimited resources, his countless hosts? He has with difficulty clung to the portion of Hungary which he had already captured. He who used to make an end of mighty kingdoms in a single campaign, has won, as the reward of his expeditions, some scarcely fortified citadels and unimportant towns and has paid dearly for the fragment which he has gradually torn away from the vast mass of Hungary. He has once looked upon Vienna, it is true, but it was for the first and last time.[68]

The view that the sultan might better serve his empire by remaining in Istanbul was presented in a document prepared in 1595 for Sir Edward Barton, the English ambassador to the Ottoman court. The document attributed Ottoman success in the recent decade-long conflict with the Safavids in part to Murad III's decision to stay at home:

> Sultan Murat . . . was a warrior by nature, but he always made war by means of his captains. . . . He became convinced that the Ottoman princes gained more by not going in person to the wars. Because the wars between kingdoms being lengthy affairs are not ended in one or two years; and thus the Emperors, desirous of returning home in the winter, often lost the states they had gained during the summer. But Sultan Murat remained at home and by having the places taken, fortified and not going himself with the armies, nor with his captains, he conquered the greater part of Persia.[69]

While the author of the document flattered Murad, who was far from being personally inclined toward combat, his reign did not lack aggressive military action.[70]

Grand vezirs as well came to regard this course as politic for themselves. In 1606 Lala Mehmet Pasha petitioned Ahmed I to permit him to remain in Istanbul, so that he could oversee the delicate situation on the Austrian border, rather than send him east against the Safavids. In an audience with the sultan, leading statesmen argued in his support that military victory did not depend on the presence even of the grand vezir on campaign: "All the statesmen said, 'It is prudent that commanders be sent to both fronts and that the grand vezir make decisions in the capital, his attention being devoted to the support of both fronts. . . . In the old days there were many vezirs, such as Mustafa Pasha and Ferhad Pasha who, while not the grand vezir, accomplished many glorious conquests and laudable wars for the faith. . . .' "[71]

An additional motive in the sultans' shunning of military activity was no doubt the desire to avoid association with defeat, for it was becoming increasingly evident that military stalemate or even loss were as likely outcomes of war as victory. It is perhaps noteworthy that Süleyman's delegation of full command to İbrahim Pasha occurred before the risky, and ultimately unsuccessful, siege of Vienna in 1529. The lavish public celebration of the circumcision of Süleyman's elder sons immediately after the close of the campaign suggests that the sultan was anxious to deflect attention from the Ottoman failure. Caroline Finkel has pointed out that in the prolonged siege warfare characteristic of the late sixteenth century, it was difficult to determine who the victor was from year to year or when the war might be over.[72] Given the likelihood of inconclusive results, the wiser course may well have been to avoid the greater demoralization that would follow the failure of an imperial campaign than that of one led by the grand vezir or a lesser commander.

A number of incidents in the early seventeenth century suggest that the notion that the sultan should remain in the capital was gaining currency. Both Ahmed I and Osman II were strongly advised by vezirs and leading religious dignitaries against their plans to leave Istanbul, the former desiring to campaign against the Jelali rebels, the latter to make the pilgrimage to the holy cities. Ahmed was warned that there were many disadvantages to a sultan's campaigning,[73] and a ruling sent to Osman II by the *müfti* decreed that "the pilgrimage is not necessary for sultans. It is preferable that they stay in their place and dispense justice. This is lawful since disorder might ensue."[74] Admittedly, the motivation of some of Osman's advisers was not entirely disinterested since they were opposed to his rumored intention to do away with the Janissaries under the guise of pilgrimage. Nevertheless, the incident suggests that the *müfti*'s argument carried a weight that its authors assumed the sultan would have difficulty countering. By the end of the seventeenth century, registers of campaign expenses no longer distinguished between campaigns led by the sultan and those led by the grand vezir;[75] this suggests that the issue of the sultan's military leadership had lost its importance.

Participation in military campaigns was not, however, entirely abandoned by the post-Süleymanic sultans, nor did the mystique of *ghaza* lose its power. Osman II led a campaign into Poland, and Murad IV exhibited great personal courage and martial skill in the two victorious campaigns he led to recover territory lost to the Safavids. But most sultans did not elect to participate in military campaigns, or were discouraged from doing so, as in the case of Ahmed I. When they did, or were prevailed upon to do so by their advisers, their presence was more ceremonial than functional, their leadership more symbolic than real. Mehmed III, for example, had to be persuaded to participate in the Erlau campaign of 1596. His tutor, the prominent religious scholar Sadeddin Efendi, convinced him with difficulty of "the necessity of conquest for sultans and the virtues of holy war."[76] The sultan lost courage on the eve of the battle of Mezö Kerésztés and petitioned the grand vezir to be allowed to return to Istanbul. Persuaded to endure the fray, he again lost courage in the midst of battle. Sadeddin Efendi saved the day by urging him to don the mantle of the Prophet, and soon the battle turned unexpectedly into an Ottoman victory.[77] Despite the sultan's sorry performance, he earned his laurels as *ghazi,* and was hailed by Hasan Kafi el-Akhisari, the author of one of the turn-of-the-century reform treatises, as "the world-conquering emperor, Sultan Ghazi Mehmed Khan." In this widely read treatise (completed in 1596), Hasan Kafi, who participated in the Erlau campaign, praised Mehmed for having turned the tide of battle (see Figure 6-1, p. 164).[78]

The image of a monarch skilled in the arts of war and the hunt, war's training ground, was so powerful that it continued to inform sultanic ceremonial of the most sedentary sort. A vivid example is provided by Thomas Dallam, the English organ-builder who accompanied the organ that was the accession gift of Elizabeth I to Mehmed III. In his travel memoir, Dallam described the sultan and his retinue as they awaited his performance on the organ, installed in one of the garden kiosks of the inner palace. The sultan "satt in greate state, yeat the sighte of him was nothinge in Comparrison of the traine that stood behinde him, the sighte whearof did make me almoste to thinke that I was in another worlde." In addition to two hundred pages of the inner court, the retinue included one hundred mutes, some of whom held hawks in their fists, and one hundred dwarves, each of whom held a scimitar by his side. Beside the sultan's throne lay a scimitar, a bow, and a quiver of arrows.[79]

The Palace Sultan

The second concern of the political commentators was the sultan's withdrawal from contact with his subjects and government officials. To a certain extent, they were drawing attention to a conspicuous reality, especially with regard to the long reign of Murad III, which was the inspiration for a good deal of the reform literature. Murad did not leave the capital once during the twenty-one years of his reign.[80] He even had to be persuaded by his grand vezir to leave his palace for the one communal function expected of the sultan, attending Friday prayers with his subjects;[81] at one point, two years elapsed during which he neglected this duty.[82] However, if we view the late-sixteenth-century Ottoman experience in the broader context of Islamic history rather than simply comparing Ottoman sultans of this period with earlier Ottoman sultans, the question appears to be more why the seclusion of the sultan was viewed with such distrust than why later rulers abandoned the model of the "*ghazi*" sultans (who actually spent a good deal of time in their palaces). The practice of splendid isolation did not necessarily conflict with an active military career: the most powerful conqueror encountered by the Ottomans, Timur, maintained a distance between himself and his family and court, who could not approach him without permission.[83]

The maintenance of distance between the ruler and his subjects was an accepted feature of Islamic monarchical tradition. *Heybet*, awe-inspiring majesty, was a trait to be cultivated by rulers. Despite the impulse toward austerity in the Islamic moral ideal—men were forbidden to wear silk or use gold and silver implements—the influence of ancient Near Eastern ideals of kingship persisted in the cultivation of courtly splendor and luxury as a measure of a ruler's power.[84] According to Nizam al-Mulk, vezir and author of a well-known manual for kings whose composition was requested by his Turkish sovereign, the eleventh-century Seljuk sultan Malikshah, the king should remain aloof, for "if he consorts too much with nobles, generals and civil governors, it injures the king's authority; they grow too familiar and become slack in obeying orders and defraud the state of money."[85] This is why the king has a vezir, with whom he should discuss all matters, and boon companions, with whom he can relax "without detriment to his majesty and sovereignty." On the other hand, Nizam al-Mulk, whose practical formulations expressed synthesis of Persian ideals of kingship and Islamic norms, was adamant that the sultan appear in public twice a week "for the redress of wrongs, to extract recompense from the oppressor, to give justice and to listen to the words of his subjects with his own ears, without any intermediary."[86]

The process by which the Ottoman sultan was separated from other members of the ruling elite, far from being an abrupt development of the post-Süleymanic period, began well before then. It is difficult to say exactly when the sultans began to enforce protocols that limited access to their person, but this practice was most likely in place by the time of Bayezid I (r. 1389–1402), since criticism of the inaccessibility of the sultan began during his sultanate. For example, Molla Feneri, the judge of Bursa and one of the most eminent religious figures of his day, is said to have refused to accept Bayezid's witness in court as valid because he no longer joined his followers in the communal Friday prayer service. The sultan responded, in what would seem an attitude of compromise, by building a mosque near his palace, at which he began to pray regularly, albeit in a special reserved area.[87]

As in the later sixteenth century, an integral aspect of the early critique of sultanic seclusion was the charge that "infidel" women were responsible for the corruption of the dynasty. One of the principal objects of blame for Bayezid's devotion to the pleasures of court life, especially drinking parties, was his wife Maria, daughter of the Serbian king Lazar Grebelyanovich. Maria was accused by the late-fifteenth-century historian Aşıkpaşazade of introducing drink and its social rituals to the Ottoman court: "Drinking parties and banquets were held, the infidel girl came and wine cups were passed around. . . . The House of Osman had never taken drink before. What do you expect, Osman? Many things happened because of the infidels."[88] Maria may indeed have brought certain courtly customs to the Ottoman house, but the convivial banquet (*bezm*) was a traditional feature of both Turco-Mongol and Irano-Islamic royal society. In the history of Neşri, who was more tolerant of high court life than Aşıkpaşazade, almost every description of a military campaign ends with the statement that the sultan and his companions returned to the capital to drink and enjoy the pleasures of life as well as to "dispense justice."[89] The contemporary history of one of Bayezid's Anatolian rivals, Kadi Burhaneddin Ahmed, recognized the two faces of medieval monarchy, the courtly and the martial, in its title, *Banquets and Battles* (*Bazm u Razm*).[90]

It is important to recognize that Aşıkpaşazade's critique of the moral laxity of court life, like the late-sixteenth-century critique, was emblematic of pervasive concern for a deeper transformation that was taking place in the public definition of state and society and in the practical realities of administration. More immediately, the sultan's indulgent life-style was suspect as the principal cause of military setback (in the case of Bayezid I, the ravages of Timur, and in the case of Murad III, the intractability of the European defense). It is also noteworthy that the strongest criticism came from those whose expectations were frustrated by new developments and who consequently felt themselves marginalized. Aşıkpaşazade spoke for the elements in early Ottoman society closest to the Turkish and tribal origins of the dynasty, freebooting frontier raiders (*akıncı*) and their chiefs, who were being constrained by the requirements of Islamic law and displaced by the slave elite of the royal household. As Cornell Fleischer has shown, Mustafa Ali, government bureaucrat, man of letters, and the most vocal and influential of the late-sixteenth-century critics (one is tempted to say the crankiest), was embittered by his inability to receive the professional appointments he believed he deserved, which he blamed on the misguided favoritism and uninformed patronage of the sultan, his leading officials, and other members of the dynastic family. Like Aşıkpaşazade, Mustafa Ali placed great blame on the powerful women of the dynasty.[91] In an interesting parallel, the second half of Nizam al-Mulk's work, written after his fall from favor, was a bitter indictment of weaknesses in the government, including the influence of women on political affairs.[92]

By the reign of Murad II (1421–1451), while the sultan still appeared frequently in public audiences, his distance from his subjects had increased and his presence had become more ceremonial. According to Bertrandon de la Broquière, who observed Murad in his court in Edirne, "there are few who have seen him drink or eat or who have heard him speak."[93] The conquest of Constantinople in 1453 can only have given further impetus to the process of sultanic seclusion. The traditions of Byzantine court society, with their emphasis on the sacral nature of the sovereign and the seclusion of the royal family in the eunuch-guarded inner reaches of the imperial palace, undoubtedly encouraged the tendency toward sultanic seclusion inherent in the Ottomans' Islamic heritage. The sultanic rescript (*kanunname*) prescribing imperial ceremony and protocol associated with Mehmed II, conqueror of Constantinople, detailed the few circumstances under which even the highest ranking members of the ruling elite might approach the person of the sultan. For example, no longer was anyone except a member of the royal family deemed worthy of joining the sultan as he ate: "It is my command that no one dine with my noble self except members of my family. My great ancestors are said to have eaten with their vezirs; I have abolished [this practice]."[94] Let us recall that it was around this time that the practice of interdynastic marriage was abandoned; as Menavino noted, if the sultan took a wife, "it would then be necessary that she be treated as Queen, just as he is the King."[95]

Modifications of a number of traditional practices reflected in the *kanunname* had the effect of reducing the sultan's visible presence in both the symbolic sphere and the actual mechanics of government. The *kanunname* restricted to the two major Muslim religious holidays the occasions on which the sultan would emerge from the sanctuary of the third courtyard for the customary audience with ministers and soldiers, where a ritual meal took place following the obeisance of the assembled statesmen and Janissaries.[96] During the period when Bayezid II's rebel brother Jem Sultan posed a threat to the security of Bayezid's throne, the sultan was constrained to resume this audience in the second courtyard on a daily basis; Selim I and Süleyman, however, limited their participation to once a year.[97]

As this discussion suggests, an important aspect of the ceremonial renewal of mutual pledges of sultanic beneficence and subject loyalty was the meal. Food—its preparation, its consumption, and its rejection—was a common metaphor among the Ottomans to describe the reciprocal ties of bounty and loyalty between ruler and ruled. In Central Asian Turkish tradition, the ceremonial gathering for a feast (*toy*) was an important occasion for marking this compact; refusing to attend or rejecting food was a sign of withdrawal of allegiance to the ruler.[98] Food symbolism permeated the Ottoman military/ administrative organization. One was distinguished as a member of the ruling elite if one "ate the sultan's bread," that is, received a salary; Neşri, for example, speaks of the prince Süleyman, son of Bayezid I, "eating" the province of Saruhan, that is, receiving its revenues.[99] The Janissaries were organized into units known as hearths (*ojak*), and the public square associated with them, where their mosque was located, was known as the "Meat Square" (Et Meydanı), since it was there that the weekly distribution of meat rations to the *ojak*s took place. Upsetting a cauldron of food was the symbolic gesture indicating Janissary discontent with the sultan or grand vezir. Sultans conspicuously demonstrated their piety and fulfillment of the mandatory duty of the Muslim to give alms by distributing food to the poor; when the second sultan, Orhan, established a soup kitchen in the city of Iznik (Nicea), he himself distributed the first food the day it opened, having lit the hearthfire the evening before.[100] The sultan's abandonment of the daily meal in the palace courtyard must have seemed at the time a weakening of his commitment to his subjects. That Bayezid II was forced to forego his seclusion during the period when his soldiers could wield the threat of switching allegiance to his brother suggests their resentment of their lord's inaccessibility.

The *kanunname* also implied that the sultan would no longer attend meetings of the imperial council (*divan*), where ordinary subjects might deliver petitions to the sovereign.[101] The conduct of these meetings was relinquished to the grand vezir. Thus was surrendered another of the traditional responsibilities of the ruler, one that Nizam al-Mulk had urged his sultan to uphold: monitoring the administration of justice in his realm by making himself publicly available on a regular basis to personally receive petitions from the common people. However, the sultan would preserve his role in the administration of royal justice by receiving the council members' report of the proceedings in the royal audience hall. This hall was constructed just beyond the entrance to the third courtyard, enabling the sultan to meet with select members of his government without leaving the confines of the male harem. The sultan thus separated himself not only from common petitioners but also from his own ministers, whom, according to the *kanunname,* he would receive while seated behind a curtain.[102]

Over the course of the sixteenth century, while the sultan continued to hold consultative meetings with the leading officials of the state, these were increasingly restricted to extraordinary or emergency situations. Access to the sultan by even the grand vezir and the *müfti*, the highest officials of the empire, was strictly controlled. The use of a curtain to conceal the sultan continued: the historian Selaniki noted that Mehmed III sat hidden during a private meeting in 1600 with the *müfti*.[103] This is not to say that the sultans did not display an active concern for the fortunes of the empire or play a directive role in affairs of state: Süleyman, for example, ordered the construction of a secluded post overlooking the council chamber, from which he secretly monitored council proceedings.[104] However, imperial prerogatives were increasingly exercised from a distant and inaccessible source. The public's amazement at the easy access of Süleyman's grand vezir İbrahim to the inner palace, indeed to the sultan's bedroom, expressed popular acceptance of these boundaries surrounding the royal presence.

The remoteness of the sultan from ordinary human intercourse was emphasized through extension of the enforced silence that was a marked feature of ceremonials in the second, semipublic courtyard of the imperial palace. In the private domains of the palace, a special sign language was employed in the royal presence, further emphasizing the ruler's remoteness from ordinary human intercourse.[105] The extent to which members of the governing elite—at least those who had been trained in the inner palace—were familiar with the palace sign language is suggested by the report of the Venetian ambassador, Ottaviano Bon, of the execution of the lieutenant grand vezir Mustafa Pasha in 1604: the pasha conversed in sign language with the mute who summoned him to his death.[106]

One reason modern historians have tended to accept the views of critics who blamed the post-Süleymanic sultans and sometimes Süleyman himself for the seclusion of the sultan is that it was only in the sixteenth century, with the regular presence of ambassadors who were admitted into the sultan's presence and wrote about it, that descriptions of inner palace ceremonial became available. European ambassadors and members of their suites remarked on the utter silence and immobility of the enormous royal suite that attended their reception in the second courtyard and noted the idol-like posture of the sultan, who scarcely moved or spoke as he received ambassadors in the royal audience hall. These ceremonial receptions were, of course, staged with precisely the intent of inducing an awed reaction in the foreign observer. A particularly vivid account is that of Philippe du Fresne-Canaye, a member of the suite of the French ambassador Noailles, describing the latter's audience in 1573 with Selim II:

> We observed with great pleasure and the greatest admiration the frightening number of janissaries and other soldiers lined up along the wall of this [the second] court, their hands joined in front of them in the manner of monks, in such silence that it seemed we were not seeing living men but statues. And they remained immobile in this way for more than seven hours, not a one of them uttering a sound or making the slightest movement. Certainly it is nearly impossible to imagine such discipline and obedience if one has not observed it. . . .
>
> [In his audience hall] the Grand Seigneur was seated on a sofa covered with a very rich carpet . . . and was dressed in cloth of red gold, and his feet rested on a cushion of the same material, but they were so hidden in his clothing that they could not be seen, and his hands likewise; so that one was

forced to believe that no one had ever kissed the hands of the Grand Seigneur, or that this sultan was more haughty than his predecessors and found
this courtesy unworthy of his grandeur. . . . I remember well that he did not
look directly at us; but with a troubled eye, very evil and frightening, he held
his head turned toward the hearth, with an air of unawareness of those who
had so humbly come before him. All around this chamber were hidden I
don't know how many mutes. . . . The Ambassador stated briefly the purpose of his embassy . . . and the Grand Turk himself began to answer him,
but Mehemet Pascha [the grand vezir Sokollu Mehmed Pasha], saying that it
did not become the majesty of the sovereign of so many lands to speak with
ambassadors, took it upon himself to state briefly what he had to say. . . .
[Later] as we were making our way home, what did we see but the janissaries
emerging from the palace with such fury that we were forced to make way for
them. Pressing ourselves against the wall, away from the road, we saw pass all
those thousands of janissaries, guardsmen, and others who had seemed like a
palissade of statues in the court, now transformed, not into men but into
starved animals or unchained dogs.[107]

Conflicting Images of Sovereignty

If turn-of-the-century writers exhibited a rigid view of the sultanate, one of
the most flexible of Ottoman institutions, their writings nevertheless serve to
remind us of its charismatic and symbolic power. It was to the sultan that the
Ottomans looked for both the cause and the cure of their society's ills, for
they believed that the prosperity of society was inseparable from the sultan's
zealous enforcement of social and political order. Popular metaphors for the
sovereign—the heart or head of the body politic, the shepherd leading his
flock—represented the sultan as the keystone of society. In the traditional
Muslim understanding of statecraft and kingship, to which the Ottomans were
heir, the well-being of society depended ultimately on the vigilance of the
ruler, whose duty was to ensure that the different elements or classes in
society remained in their fixed places and performed their fixed functions. It
was this, the maintenance of social harmony and order, that was the highest
expression of the ruler's "justice" (*adl*). "Tyranny" (*zulm*), the opposite of
"justice," occurred when one element, allowed to supersede its bounds, in-
fringed on the rights of others. As Tursun Beg argued in the introduction to
his late-fifteenth-century history, the sultan's principal means of ensuring order was the judicious application of summary punishment (*siyaset*); this right
of the sultan over the lives of his subjects was itself a source of tyranny,
however, if it was not exercised within the confines of the holy law, and not
tempered with forebearance (*hilm*).[108]

No wonder, then, that the shifting emphases in the image and exercise of
sultanic sovereignty were naturally the focus of Ottomans disturbed by the
very real dislocations in their society in the later sixteenth century. Unable to
recognize the more profound sources of social and political change, they
tended to see the causes of what they perceived as Ottoman slippage in the
sultan's conduct. The harm to society of the sultan's withdrawal from contact

with his subjects was a prominent theme in the several treatises that were composed in the late sixteenth and early seventeenth centuries to draw attention to what their writers perceived as flaws in the practice of statecraft and to suggest remedies. The first of these treatises was Mustafa Ali's *Counsel for Sultans,* composed in 1581. The author, the most prolific and outspoken of the end-of-the-century critics (at least in the written record that survives), decried the inability of the sultan, "isolated behind the curtain," to maintain his grasp on public affairs and to effectively supervise government officials.[109] The anonymous author of *Kitab-i Müstetab,* most probably written for Osman II (d. 1622), discusses twelve areas of weakness in government and then presents a series of questions to be posed to a kind of panel of experts made up of leading men of state; the first of these questions is whether the fact that the sultans succeeding Süleyman no longer lead the army on campaign is a factor in the repeated military defeats and losses of territory and revenue suffered by the empire since Süleyman's death.[110] Koçi Bey, in his treatise on the proper conduct of government, composed in the early 1630s for his political pupil Murad IV, cited Süleyman's withdrawal from the imperial council as the first of his failings. Koçi Bey appealed to the example of the Prophet, the first four "rightly guided" caliphs, and other caliphs and sultans, who had personally managed the affairs of the people and had not hidden themselves "behind a curtain."[111] The theme of the harm done by the ruler's isolation from his subjects was sounded even by Talikizade, an official court historian writing at the end of the sixteenth century.[112]

Yet there is a profound ambivalence toward sultanic seclusion expressed in these writings. Let us take as an example the introduction to Mustafa Ali's *Counsel for Sultans.* Despite the fact that the general thrust of Ali's argument in his treatise was the harmful effects of sultanic seclusion, in the introduction he described as the first of six divine gifts to the Ottoman dynasty the fact that the sultans "reside solitary and alone within a palace, like a matchless pearl deep within its lustrous shell, and sever all their relations with family and followers. . . ."[113] Ali's ambivalence on this point can be seen in his comments on the practice of seclusion by former sultans. He says, "it had become difficult for [Murad III's great and noble ancestors, his eminent predecessors] themselves to mix with their soldiers . . . and contrary to good practice personally to take care of the affairs of the people . . . ,"[114] and "Now in our time, the eminent sultan . . . is following the orientation of his ancestors by preferring isolation to mixing with the people and by putting the state of hiddenness before the personal management of affairs so as to remain an object of awe and veneration to the people. . . ."[115] However, he also comments, "the mighty sultan has abandoned the principle of togetherness, that was sponsored by his great ancestors, and [thus] his intercourse and close contact with high and low as well as his personal interference to stop oppression are no more feasible."[116] For Ali, as for other commentators, the issue would seem to be one of balance between the public and the secluded personas of the ruler, a balance that appeared to them to be dangerously tipped in favor of the latter.

In the view of the critics, the seclusion of the sultan led not to weakness and loss of control, as modern historians have depicted developments in the post-Süleymanic sultanate,[117] but rather to a more autocratic, because more isolated, style of rule than had obtained earlier. Detached from public institutions of authority—the imperial council, the command of the army—the sultan was thought to be less bound by traditional restraints on his power. One chapter of the section of Mustafa Ali's history describing the reign of Murad III was entitled "The Disorder of the Innovative Proliferation of Royal Rescripts"; in it Ali criticized the excessive use of this form of imperial legislation as an arrogation by the sultan of authority that had previously belonged to the grand vezir.[118] In Ali's opinion, this opened the door to the unprecedented, and thus unwarranted, influence of the companions of the sultan's isolation from public life, among them the eunuchs and women of the harem. (Yet elsewhere in his history Ali heaped praise on Gazanfer Agha, chief white eunuch, and on Janfeda Khatun, stewardess of the harem, the two most powerful individuals in the inner palace apart from members of the royal family.)[119]

Mustafa Ali's antipathy to the influence of women, most specifically and outspokenly expressed in regard to the power that had been exercised by Hurrem, her daughter Mihrimah, and the grand vezir Rüstem Pasha,[120] was echoed by some of his contemporaries. Ottoman writers were generally quite circumspect in their allusions to royal women, indeed, to any women. While a number of political thinkers of this period regarded the influence of women as a principal cause of the numerous economic, military, and political problems confronting the empire, they could only mention this in passing and in very general terms. The kind of broadside attack on women in political life that occurred in Europe, such as John Knox's *The First Blast of the Trumpet against the Monstrous Regiment of Women* (1558), directed against Mary Stuart and Elizabeth I, would have been unthinkable in the Ottoman world.[121] However, in 1599, the *müfti* Sunullah Efendi was powerful enough or bold enough to include the influence of women and eunuchs in government in a public proclamation listing abuses in government.[122]

In a widely read reform tract of the late sixteenth century, the author, Hasan Kafi el-Akhisari, urged a return to what he viewed as principled and effective government. As one of the two main causes of recent harmful tendencies in government he cited "esteeming the women and following their advice" (the other was bribery).[123] Roughly twenty-five years later, a similar view was echoed in the *Kitab-ı Müstetab*. Looking back to the early decades of Süleyman's reign as the zenith of the empire's well-being, as did most political critics, the anonymous author cast his prescription for reform in the shape of a prophecy: he related that Süleyman had asked his first grand vezir, Piri Mehmed Pasha, if there was anything that could undermine the seemingly invincible empire. The grand vezir named three things that might prove harmful if Süleyman's successors were not vigilant: appointing an incompetent grand vezir, awarding offices to ineligible persons in return for bribes, and "acting according to the wishes of women."[124]

It is worthy of note that several of these reform treatises criticize the sultan's appointment of his personal favorites to the grand vezirate. The *Kitab-ı Müstetab* places the prophecy in the mouth of the venerable statesman, Piri Mehmed Pasha, the grand vezir whom Süleyman replaced with his favorite İbrahim. Koçi Bey criticized this appointment of İbrahim to the grand vezirate directly from the inner palace service on the grounds of his inexperience. He also criticized the enormous wealth the sultan bestowed on his favorite and son-in-law, the grand vezir Rüstem Pasha, who then passed it on to members of his family; in both cases, Koçi Bey asserted, the interests of the public were harmed. It is also noteworthy that there seems to have been little or no criticism of Selim II, perhaps the least activist of the post-Süleymanic sultans, for abdicating control of government to the grand vezir and royal son-in-law, Sokollu Mehmed Pasha. What most disturbed the critics was the weakening of the hierarchies of outer administration through the arrogation of power to the sultan and his favorites.

At the heart of the unease given voice by the turn-of-the-century critics was concern about the contractual nature of relations between the sultan and his subjects, especially the military/administrative elite. The Ottoman sultan was not an absolute monarch. Apart from the religio-legal requirements for sovereignty monitored by the *ulema* and the aura of legitimacy they might lend popular protests by sanctioning or joining them, it was the military elite that traditionally set standards for the sultan's performance. Most vigilant in monitoring the sultanate and most vocal in voicing discontent were the royal troops, the Janissaries and, to a lesser extent, the imperial cavalry. These were household troops, "slaves of the Porte" (*kapıkulu*), through whom the sultan enacted his will, as he did through the most select of his officials, the vezirs and the pashas, most of whom were graduates of the palace school. The shifting orientation of the sovereign away from conquest threatened the status of this elite as the premier ruling body of the empire, the group that reaped the lion's share of the rewards of conquest. A whole series of adjustments in institutional organization, elite recruitment and recompense, and patronage relationships were set in motion by this transformation at the heart of government. To be sure, much of this change was evolving independently of the sultanate, but it could not escape being affected by the dynasty's conduct. Furthermore, the transformation in the sultan's role was perhaps the most immediately visible sign of the reorientation of the state (here I am using the term "state" as an Ottoman of the sixteenth century would have understood the term *devlet*—the dynasty and the government classes immediately dependent upon it). This reorientation was no means abrupt, and probably even the most farsighted Ottoman of the times would not have described it in these terms. It was only in the mid-eighteenth century that grand vezirs began to be appointed from the bureaucracy,[125] and only in the nineteenth century that the military and administrative bases of government were definitely separated. However, the beginnings of this process were evident by the late sixteenth century. Much of what critics perceived as bribery and favoritism at the turn of the century was in fact the operation of new social and political arrangements, which expressed less the decline of Ottoman society than its vitality.

A principal factor that affected the process of institutional adjustment and reordering of patronage relationships was the consolidation of the central dynastic household as the fixed arena of government. While Ottoman rulers had been quick to abandon the relatively egalitarian conduct of their nomad forebears and adopt the imperial style of the Turco-Islamic dynasties they succeeded, the sultan's retinue had been mobile and had consisted exclusively of men. The relative lack of a central and influential court society before the sixteenth century was underlined by the sumptuousness of the provincial courts established for princes. As the royal household evolved in the late sixteenth century, two features in particular affected the nature of the dynasty's relation with the ruling elite: the abolition of princely households and the incorporation of a second, female, harem into the imperial household.

The demise of the principate meant the disappearance of the secondary channels the princely establishments had provided for members of the ruling class to associate themselves with the dynasty. Moreover, access to the sultan himself, the principal channel, was becoming more difficult. At the same time, influence *within* the royal household was no longer the exclusive prerogative of the personnel of the male harem but was increasingly shared with the female harem. As the female harem grew in institutional stature, a kind of routinized authority accrued to the *valide sultan,* the sultan's leading concubines, the harem stewardess, and the elite of the black eunuch corps, whose top post was on its way to becoming one of the three or four most influential offices in government.

The power base of these individuals was hardly narrow or confined to the arena of the palace. They headed extensive networks within the ruling class, enjoyed broad sources of income and considerable opportunity for patronage, and, in the case of the black eunuchs, had important responsibilities in outer government. But while they may have allied themselves with traditional institutional powers, for example the grand vezirate or the Janissary command, such links could not be monitored through the earlier mechanisms that had provided a check on the central power. The grand vezirate, for example, previously the culmination of a long career in outer government, might now be filled directly from the palace (Süleyman's grand vezir İbrahim was the most conspicuous example). In addition, a tie of marriage was likely to link vezirs to the dynasty; not a new practice, admittedly, but one which was intensified over the course of the sixteenth century. What Koçi Bey may have intended but could not say explicitly in his critique of the *damad* vezir was that when a *damad* held the highest post, the grand vezir was no longer the "independent deputy" of the sultan, uncompromised in his exercise of authority.

The palace career was also becoming an important springboard to provincial military/administrative posts that had previously been acquired through upward motion along the provincial career ladder. As Metin Kunt has noted, this was a symptom of the obsolescence of the provincial career as it had operated through Süleyman's reign.[126] Certainly, the demise of the principate was another symptom of the obsolescence of the provincial career as previously constituted, and another check on sovereign authority lost.

But, in fact, the sultanate was not becoming an unchecked despotism as some critics seem to have feared, for new kinds of counterbalancing influences were emerging. Perhaps most profound but not immediately visible was the development of a bureaucratic infrastructure in the second half of the sixteenth century which, as Linda Darling has argued, acted to stabilize the balance among elements in government as well as between government and subjects.[127] A number of studies have pointed to the continued, indeed increased, strength of local initiative.[128] In addition, there were new channels of entry into the military/administrative elite, as the households of pashas and provincial governors began to parallel the imperial household as the training ground for a government career.[129] Soldiers, provincial governors, and even pashas acquired their posts through the patronage of other pashas. If the provincial career as it had been known was becoming obsolete, a balance between center and province was maintained.

Sometimes it seemed a violent see-saw whose equilibrium threatened to be tipped by successive waves of Anatolian provincial rebellions in the first half of the seventeenth century. Known as the Jelali rebellions, these movements were led by rebel pashas joined by a variety of elements, as yet not well identified, but including large numbers of the ad-hoc militia contingents that became so important in the long Hungarian war at the end of the sixteenth century.[130] The frequency and duration of these rebellions have typically been seen as signs of weakness in the dynasty, but they were arguably also—or even more so—a sign of its strength. The Jelali rebellions were in part an expression of impatience with the new forms of entry into the ruling classes, an articulation of the expectations of new legions of the sultan's servants. What is remarkable is that the powerful "rebel" pashas of the seventeenth century ultimately opted to stay within the system rather than break away. The nature of their rebellions contrasted with earlier challenges to the Ottoman dynasty, such as the defection of much of the empire to Timur, the revolt of Sheikh Bedreddin in the aftermath of Timur's invasion, or the revolt of Shah Kulu in 1511, which was supported by the emerging Safavid state. There appears to have been a recognition in the seventeenth century that membership in the Ottoman state under the Ottoman dynasty offered the only viable existence for a would-be leader. In other words, there was no real alternative to the sultan's service. This dilemma was dramatically demonstrated in the capitulation of İbşir Mustafa Pasha in 1655: architect of a large-scale rebellion originating in eastern Anatolia, İbşir was "honored" with the grand vezirate and marriage to a princess. His long delay in making his way to the capital, where he correctly feared he would be executed, was simply a prolonged last breath. This lack of alternative was largely the result of the lasting division of the Near East between the stable and powerful Ottoman and Safavid states, accomplished largely by the 1550s: any breakaway state would be crushed by the one or absorbed by the other. But the charisma of the Ottoman dynasty—at over three hundred years of age and still vigorous, the longest-lived ruling house in Islamic history—was no minor factor in its ability to weather the storms of the seventeenth century.

The idea that the ruler should remain secluded and aloof, while it provoked ambivalent reactions in the late sixteenth and early seventeenth centuries, appeared to gradually gain greater acceptance. A contemporary observer of the Ottoman political scene, Sir Thomas Roe, the English ambassador to the Ottoman court from 1621 to 1628, believed that one reason for the downfall and ultimate execution of Osman II was his lack of majesty. In one of his dispatches, he wrote:

> [E]ven yett the king had not fallen thus lowe, if first he had not lost that awe and reverence which always attendeth upon majestie, by unseemely offices done by him in the streetes and taverns, apprehending many soldiours for petty faults like a constable, making his person common, cheape, and despised among them, which was wont only to be seene and feared, as somwhat supra humanitatem.[131]

Roe was no doubt influenced in his observations by customs of the English court, but he reflected an expectation of monarchy that was shared by many of the sultan's subjects.[132] This attitude may have contributed to the unprecedented scorn heaped upon Osman's person during the events of his deposition. Osman was forced to ride through the streets on a carthorse and wear a dirty, torn turban taken from a bystander; he was reduced to tears when his legs were pinched by a member of the crowd; and he was reviled with taunts and curses which the historian Peçevi, an eyewitness to the scene, described as "unfit not only for the pen to record but for the tongue to utter."[133] The people of Istanbul were said to be pleased to see that the new ruler, Sultan Mustafa, was dressed splendidly in his first public appearance, like earlier sultans, and not, as Osman had preferred, in simple garb and on a horse with plain trappings "in the manner of a freebooter."[134] Mustafa's stature was diminished in the eyes of his vezirs, however, through his refusal to observe the rule of silence: "Sultan Mustafa, because he could not accustom himself to this silent gravity, caused the members of his Council of State to complain of him, and to say that speaking freely to his subjects, as Mustafa did, was more appropriate to a Janissary, or to a Turkish merchant, than to their emperor."[135]

Koçi Bey might have agreed with this criticism of Mustafa, for he instructed his second royal pupil, the sultan İbrahim, to speak little, refrain from looking around, and maintain a stern and fear-inspiring posture during audiences, and to give only the slightest acknowledgment of obeisances by the people during ceremonial processions.[136] However, Koçi Bey would have approved of Osman's austerity, for he regarded Süleyman's "finery and pomp" as one of the causes of the empire's undoing and urged Murad IV to avoid such wastefulness:

> Sultan Süleyman Khan, seeing that the army was strong and the treasury full, indulged in greater luxury and pomp. The vezirs copied him, and, as the proverb "the people follow the religion of the monarch" tells us, soon everyone took on the ways of luxury and pomp. Things came to such a pass that, because the income of officials and the pay of the military was not even sufficient to buy bread, they were forced to oppression and extortion, and the

country was ruined. In this exalted empire there has been no innovation [*bidat*] so harmful as pomp and luxury.[137]

In this criticism, Koçi Bey was combating powerful strains in the history of Islamic monarchy. His political students did not follow his advice. A master at manipulating royal ceremonial, Murad was responsible for a dramatic increase in the size of the palace community and in its wages;[138] İbrahim was deposed for the ravages wreaked in the imperial treasury by his excessive indulgence in luxuries.

In the introduction to his history, which bore the outlines of the classic genre of "advice to kings," Mustafa Naima, the great historian of the late seventeenth century, presented a model of the sovereign which suggests that the sedentary sultanate of the post-Süleymanic period was ultimately not only accepted but viewed as the norm. In Naima's view, great deeds were not to be expected from the ruler, indeed were not necessary. His public role was largely a ceremonial one, although, like Nizam al-Mulk and Mustafa Ali, Naima cautioned that the sultan must take care not to lose control of those to whom he delegated his authority:

> There are many benefits to rulers in refraining from speaking with the common people and in spending most of their time hidden and secluded. Behaving familiarly with the people undermines the etiquette and manners which are required in the presence of a ruler and robs him of his majesty. The people fear the dignified ruler who is concealed by the curtain of magnificence and glory; wondering what the ruler will do and when he will do it, they are always in a state of surmise. Especially when the ruler occasionally does a fine and praiseworthy deed and honors the worthy and suddenly punishes the wayward and the fearless, or from time to time performs admirable actions, then his glory and fame will increase daily. With this condition, however, that the gates of government be open at specified times to those with business, and that the affairs of the people not be neglected. Rulers who conduct themselves in this way have intimidated the people more than those who are bloodthirsty and tyrannical.[139]

The mixed reactions to sixteenth-century change in the role of the Ottoman sultanate described in this chapter were manifestations of the tension between prevailing ideals of sovereignty: the heroic warrior-ruler—be it the Central Asian khan implementing a god-given mandate of universal dominion or the Muslim *ghazi* fighting for Islam—and the distant but majestic palace emperor, an ideal that derived less from Islamic doctrine than from the traditions of Persian and Byzantine kingship embedded in the Islamic heritage. Under favorable circumstances and with sufficient time and energy, sultans such as Mehmed II and Süleyman might fully qualify as heroic warrior for the faith, arbiter of justice, and connoisseur of imperial culture. Once conquest became difficult, the cost to the dynasty and to the stability of the state of trying to attain the first of these attributes was excessive. Murad IV was able to achieve a reputation as a conqueror in the tradition of his ancestors only at the end of his reign and only after the violent suppression of opposition, which tarnished his image as a just sovereign. It was perforce the other aspects of Muslim sovereignty that were more effectively cultivated. The ideal sovereign of the post-Süleymanic Ottoman Empire was a sedentary monarch whose defense of the faith was manifested more in demonstrations of piety, support of the holy law, and endowment of religious institutions than in personal participation in battle, and whose charisma was derived more from seclusion broken by ritual ceremony than from martial glory. One result of these shifts in emphasis was that royal women enjoyed a greater latitude to participate in the various expressions of sovereignty.

7

The Display of
Sovereign Prerogative

According to Evliya Çelebi, the seventeenth-century traveler and recorder of Ottoman customs and mores, the mosque of the *valide sultan* Nurbanu was "a mountain of light."[1] This was an apt tribute to the public monument of a woman whose name meant "lady of light." Visible in other areas of the city from its location on a hill above the district of Üsküdar, this imposing structure was the only imperial mosque to be built in the capital by a member of the dynastic family between the construction of the Süleymaniye in 1557 and the mosque of Ahmet I in 1617. Completed in 1583, the year of Nurbanu's death, her large complex included the mosque, a religious college, a school for the study of prophetic tradition, a primary school, a school to teach reading to the illiterate, a dervish convent, and a hospital. It also contained a large public complex for travelers and the homeless consisting of two hostels, small heated rooms in which visitors might rest or eat, a refectory, a soup kitchen for the poor and homeless, a storehouse, and other attendant structures.[2] Nearby was located a public bath, the income from whose fees was devoted to the upkeep of the mosque and its affiliated institutions. Among the amenities of the complex noted by Evliya was the Thursday evening meal served in the soup kitchen, which featured a dish of sweetened rice colored with saffron, a treat normally reserved for weddings.[3]

Nurbanu Sultan's role as endower of public institutions was at the same time conventional and radical. Monumental building by and for royal women was a traditional feature of Islamic culture, particularly in those states influenced by a Turco-Mongol heritage. Ottoman women had always figured in the dynastic family's display of beneficence and piety. Princesses were active builders, and one of the marks of the political status of a royal concubine was the privilege of building. What was unusual in the projects of royal women from the mid-sixteenth century on was their grand scale.

The increasing visibility of royal women in the public display of sovereignty was inextricable from the increasing power they exercised. It was impossible to separate day-to-day political influence in the Ottoman Empire from the symbolic expression of political power. The status of members of the governing elite, including women of the dynasty, was communicated by such public signs as the size of their retinues, the scale and location of the mosques they were permitted to build, the gestures used by the sultan in acknowledging their obeisances, and so forth. Particularly after the sultans ceased to personally direct the conduct of war or preside over the deliberations of the imperial council, the dynasty's claim to sovereign power and legitimacy was increasingly demonstrated through the pomp of royal ritual and the monuments of dynastic largesse—in other words, through imperial magnificence and munificence. The prominence of royal women in these activities was a partial solution to two problems that faced the dynasty in the late sixteenth century; filling the ceremonial gap left by the attrition of the political and propagandistic roles of princes and bolstering the image of royal women to bring it into line with the de facto power they were in the process of accruing.

The disinclination of Ottoman society to create physical images of its rulers for public consumption—on coins, with statues, in portraits—meant that certain modes of dynastic propaganda exploited in other imperial cultures were not available to the Ottomans.[4] Europeans made use, for example, of literary and graphic representations of women both to assimilate their queens into the repertoire of politically legitimating images and to broadcast their majesty.[5] The Ottomans, by contrast, were not only unwilling to give physical representation to royal women but also refrained from writing about them. They used other means to invoke the Muslim world's mythic symbols, for example, honorific titulature. However, although inaccessible to the direct gaze of their subjects, royal women in the Muslim world could, like their European sisters, be incorporated into, and even form the subject of, royal progresses and public ceremonial; they were simply concealed within a carriage or palanquin.

The *Valide Sultan* and the Symbols of Imperial Dominion

During the reign of Murad III (1574–1595) the public persona of the *valide sultan* gained expression in a number of ways. Just as the privileges that Hurrem enjoyed created precedents for her daughter-in-law's career, Nurbanu established a paradigm for the careers of the *valide sultan*s of the century following her death. However, there were more potential avenues of expression of the *valide sultan*'s prestige and power than there were for the *haseki*, since the queen mother, as venerable elder of the dynastic family, could exploit public exposure to a greater degree than could the sultan's favorite.

Süleyman's mother Hafsa Sultan had been an honored member of the royal family. Her death was the occasion of conspicuous public mourning. In describing her funeral, the royal chancellor and historian Celalzade Mustafa honored her with a long series of formulas of praise, among which are the most exalted that can be applied to a Muslim woman, likening her to the Prophet Muhammad's first wife Khadija, his daughter Fatima, and his third and favorite wife 'A'isha: "[S]he was a woman of great asceticism and a lady of righteous thought, queen of the realm of chastity and the Khadija of the capital of purity, builder of charitable foundations and doer of pious deeds, the Fatima of the era and the 'A'isha of the age."[6] It is significant, however, that Hafsa Sultan figures in contemporary chronicles only at the time of her death. It was only after Süleyman, and in part as a result of the extraordinary role played by Hurrem, that ceremonial prestige and institutional power were overtly bestowed on the sultan's mother during her lifetime. As a result, she became an individual of such public consequence that she began to figure in the narratives of Ottoman historians with ever-greater frequency.

According to tradition, it was during the reign of Murad III that the mother of the sultan acquired a formal title, that of *valide sultan* (which is best translated as "royal mother").[7] Previously, she had been officially referred to as "the mother of Sultan X," or by a metaphoric phrase such as "the great cradle" (*mehd-i ulya*) or "the nacre of the pearl of the sultanate" (*sedef-i dürr-i saltanat*). With her formal title, the *valide sultan* joined the ranks of the most exalted officials of the empire, whose status was acknowledged by the omission of their personal names from their title. While her new title continued to emphasize that her identity (and thus the legitimacy of her authority) was derived from that of her son, it suggested that her role was not subordinate to his and was an officially sanctioned one. The acquisition of the title *haseki sultan* by Hurrem no doubt provided a precedent for the queen mother's title; indeed, it would have been unseemly for the concubine but not the mother to be so honored.

Tradition also places in Murad's reign the inception of what became in later years the processional transfer, shortly after a sultan's accession, of the *valide sultan* and other members of the new sultan's harem from the Old Palace to the harem quarters in the New Palace.[8] Known as "the procession of the *valide sultan*" (*valide alayı*), this event developed in later centuries into an elaborate ceremonial.[9] Virtually all echelons of the governing elite were represented in the procession: the palace hierarchy as well as the outer administration, the military establishment as well as the religious institution. As the procession made its way across the city of Istanbul, the *valide sultan* received the obeisance of the agha of the Janissaries and in turn distributed bonuses to his troops (much as the sultan, upon his accession, customarily granted an accession bonus to these troops). The *valide sultan* was received in the palace by her son, who awaited her on foot and greeted her with obeisance (an honor accorded by the sultan to no other person). She marked her installation in her new office and residence by dispatching to the grand vezir on the day after the procession an imperial order giving him formal notice of her arrival, which she accompanied with the gift of a ceremonial robe of honor and a dagger. The symbolism of this ceremonial suggests that its purpose was to give public sanction to the *valide sultan*'s role not only as the head of her son's private household but also as a partner in sultanic sovereignty. While this ceremonial as it was constructed for Nurbanu (if indeed it did occur as such during Murad III's reign) may not have been of the scale it later acquired, the fact that tradition accepted the *valide sultan*'s procession as having originated with her testifies to the authority she exercised.

The *valide sultan*'s enhanced status was made manifest to the populace of the empire's capital through her great mosque complex. Selim II had broken the tradition that had prevailed since the reign of the third Ottoman sultan, Murad, whereby a mosque or mosque complex of royal scale was built in the empire's capital by the sultan (in the case of Selim I, by his son, in honor of his deceased father). Selim II built his mosque in Edirne, the empire's second capital, to which the sultans frequently repaired during the winter months for a change of venue. Murad III chose Manisa, the location of his princely governorate, for his own imperial mosque. With Nurbanu's assumption of the sultanic prerogative of constructing an imperial mosque in the capital, another step toward the assimilation of women into public manifestations of dynastic sovereignty was taken. The privilege exercised by the *valide sultan* may have owed something to the tradition that the funds for a sultan's mosque should be won through *ghaza;* neither Murad nor his father Selim ever left Istanbul on campaign. Nurbanu's mosque was the first constructed in the capital by a woman of the dynasty to have two minarets, an imperial prerogative. The precedent set by Nurbanu was followed in turn by several subsequent *valide sultan*s who were responsible for imperial mosque complexes in the capital.

It was not only in life but in death as well that Nurbanu Sultan enjoyed extraordinary honors. Contrary to the custom whereby the sultan remained in the palace during a funeral, Murad accompanied his mother's coffin on foot, weeping as he walked, to the mosque of Mehmed the Conqueror, where funeral prayers were said (Figure 7-1). The choice of the Conqueror's mosque, the most distant of the sultanic mosques from the imperial palace, ensured both a maximum number of bystanders' prayers for Nurbanu's soul and maximum appreciation by the capital's residents of this display of royal piety and respect for the *valide sultan*. According to the historian Selaniki, the "whole world" crowded into the mosque for the funeral prayers. For forty days high-ranking statesmen and religious officials were required to pay their respects at the *valide sultan*'s tomb, while the Qur'an was read continuously.[10] The extraordinary nature of this funeral is suggested by the fact that in the extensive collection of the Topkapı Palace Library, the only miniature that depicts an event in the life of a female member of the dynasty is one illustrating the emergence of Nurbanu Sultan's funeral cortège from the imperial palace.[11]

Of the several ways in which Nurbanu's career broke tradition, her burial in the tomb of Selim II had perhaps the greatest symbolic import. Murad buried his mother beside his father at the head of the splendid tomb, centrally located in the courtyard of the great mosque of Aya Sofya, in which Selim II had been buried nine years before Nurbanu Sultan's death in 1583. Nurbanu was the first concubine of the dynasty to be buried together with the sultan who was her master. By linking his mother with his father in this manner, Murad emphasized his mother's place within the dynastic family and suggested that his legitimacy was derived from her as well as from his father. Because the tombs of sultans were popular sites of pilgrimage and prayer and the only place where the ordinary subject might stand close to his or her sovereign, the symbolic union of Murad's mother and father was accomplished in the most visible and lasting manner possible.

Figure 7-1   Funeral of the *valide sultan* Nurbanu. Murad III walks in front of his mother's casket as it emerges from the palace, while harem eunuchs follow it. Palace and government officials as well as ordinary subjects (including a number of women carrying small children) pray with uplifted hands. At the lower left, three Janissaries prepare to distribute coins to the crowd. From Lokman, *Şahinşahname*, II, f. 146a. (*Courtesy of Topkapı Palace Museum Library, Istanbul*)

Murad's choice of burial site for his mother would seem to be an aspect of wider change he initiatied in the politics of royal burial. From the mid-fifteenth century, Ottoman sultans had been the sole occupants of their tombs. It was Murad who ended this practice by burying other members of the dynasty beside the sultans. The five sons of Selim II whom Murad executed upon his accession were buried together with their father. When Mihrimah Sultan, Murad's aunt, died in 1578, she was buried in her father's tomb, perhaps as a tribute to the special status of this beloved only daughter of

Süleyman. Süleyman and Mihrimah lay alone in the tomb until the end of seventeenth century, when the sultans Süleyman II and Ahmed II were buried there. Burial of family members in the tombs of sultans became so routine that when several of Murad's daughters died of an epidemic disease in 1598, four years after his death, his own tomb became so full that its doors were locked to prevent any further burials.[12] When Sultan Mustafa died in 1639, his body lay seventeen hours before a decision could be made regarding his burial, for all the royal tombs were too crowded to accommodate him. Evliya Çelebi noted that it was the suggestion of his father, a court goldsmith, that Mustafa be buried "in a vaulted oil-magazine in the courtyard of Aya Sofya, which had been empty for some centuries; [he was] covered with earth brought from the innermost imperial garden."[13]

While no doubt a practical necessity of dynastic sedentarization and centralization, these group burials also emphasized the embeddedness of sovereignty in a family context. They functioned as important means by which women were associated with the power and charisma of the dynasty. The tombs of the first four sultans of the post-Süleymanic period—Selim II, Murad III, Mehmed III, and Ahmed I—reflect this image of the sultan as patriarch of an extended family: buried beside each of these sultans is the mother of his heir and around him various princes and princesses. The tomb of Ahmed housed three sultans: Ahmed I and his sons Osman II and Murad IV. Of Murad III's ancestors, only Osman I, Orhan, and Mehmed I, the first, second, and fifth sultans respectively, were similarly surrounded by members of their families. One might suggest that the emphasis on family connections in the tomb protocol of these sultans reflected a need to shore up dynastic legitimacy: Osman and Orhan confronted the task of establishing the initial legitimacy of the dynasty, Mehmed I of reestablishing legitimacy in the face of Timurid hegemony, and Murad III of establishing the legitimacy of the post-*ghazi* sedentary sultanate.

Murad was intensely devoted to his mother and would naturally have wanted his subjects to acknowledge her prestige. But the aggrandizement of the *valide sultan* was no doubt also intended to legitimize the enormous political power she wielded. Adorned with the symbols of imperial dominion—a title, an inaugural ceremony, royal building privileges, full royal burial—the *valide sultan*'s de facto power was presented as a legitimate exercise of sovereignty.

Display of the Body Sovereign: Ceremonies and Progresses

Despite the practice of female seclusion, more stringent as one moved up the Ottoman social ladder and thus most strictly enforced in the royal family, the *valide sultan*, as a female elder, succeeded in maintaining a prominent public profile. Like the sultan, she did not appear in public without ritual and retinue appropriate to her status. Her movements between the various royal residences, imperial gardens, and great mosques of the city took the form of ceremonial processions through its various districts and neighborhoods.

Public promotion of the *valide sultan* helped to compensate for the dearth of sultanic ceremonial resulting from the rapid decline in the sultan's public appearances in the post-Süleymanic period. Selim II was the first sultan to deprive his subjects of the pageantry surrounding departure for and return from military campaigns.[14] With the advent of the sedentary sultanate, the public's need to see its sovereign depended for its satisfaction principally on the elaborate processions of the sultan to one of the imperial mosques for Friday prayers or to one of the royal palaces or gardens in the capital. According to Du Fresne-Canaye, a member of the suite of the French ambassador to Selim II, the sultan left the palace for Friday prayers only twice during the three months that du Fresne-Canaye was in the city; Süleyman had done so every Friday.[15] It was against the wishes of the people and the advice of his vezirs that Murad eschewed this tradition to an even greater degree than his father had; at one point he did not leave the palace for Friday prayers for two years.[16] The Venetian ambassador Moro noted in 1590 that Murad attended Friday services only because the grand vezir Sinan Pasha urged him "to comfort with his appearance the ignorant masses, who, while they are displeased with him, nevertheless flock in great numbers to see him."[17] Nurbanu Sultan may well have appeared in public more frequently than her son. She maintained her own residence in Yeni Kapı, on the Marmara shore (it was there that she died),[18] and she probably attended prayer services at her Üsküdar mosque.[19]

The unusually prominent role played by women in the 1582 celebration of the circumcision of Murad's son Mehmed was surely an important step in the cultivation of the domestic face of the dynasty. The prince's circumcision was the greatest ceremonial event held in the capital in the decades following the reign of Süleyman, perhaps the greatest that had ever occurred in the Ottoman city. The celebration was staged as an international event: invitations to the festivities were sent to both European and Muslim sovereigns.[20] Joseph von Hammer, author of a multivolume history of the Ottomans published in the early nineteenth century, justified his long and detailed description of the event on the grounds that it was the focus of Ottoman foreign policy for many years, and that it threw light upon many aspects of Ottoman society.[21] Writing in the post-Napoleonic era, the era of the Concert of Europe, Hammer was sensitive to the political uses of ceremonial; in addition, he appreciated the importance of royal women in both the symbolic sphere and the practical mechanics of diplomatic discourse.

In contrast to Süleyman's participation in the various events of the two circumcision celebrations of his reign, Murad did not personally participate at all; instead, he was represented by the grand vezir.[22] His seclusion in the harem of his palace was re-created at this public ceremonial, with the result that the dynasty's women, while hidden from view, were important presences. In the elegant palace on the Hippodrome, which had formerly belonged to İbrahim Pasha, the favorite of Süleyman, stations for observing the festivities were established for the sultan, the prince, and the women of the royal family: the prince's grandmother Nurbanu, and his mother Safiye, his aunts and other princesses, and perhaps additional female members of the court. A European diplomatic dispatch noted that "from behind the grille on their stand, the Chief Sultanas were also able to enjoy the spectacle."[23] The arrival of the royal women at the Hippodrome palace three days after the arrival of the sultan and the prince was accompanied by an elaborate procession of sugar sculptures of exotic animals. Presumably intended to acknowledge the presence of the women, the parade of the guilds, which lasted thirty-eight days, opened with the makers of hats and shoes.

Hammer described a curious and remarkable feature of the festivities, a dramatic representation sponsored by İsmihan Sultan, the prince's aunt:

> The musicians of the sultana, widow of Sokolli, put on a kind of mythological pantomime; accompanied by the harmony of cymbals, lutes, and violins, a hired assassin approached a young child disguised as Cupid, and tried to seize him, at first using flattery, then force; but a young girl, armed with a javelin like a nymph of Diana or an Amazon, intervened at that moment, drove off the audacious aggressor, and saved the young child.[24]

Hammer's classical references aside, the theme of this representation—the female rescuing a child threatened with danger—is reminiscent of episodes in the Central Asian Turkish epic tales of Dede Korkut, familiar to the Ottomans, where women, especially mothers, take up arms to save young men unable to defend themselves.[25] The message of the pantomime may have been the vigilance of the prince's female elders in protecting and defending him from overt and covert threats as he embarked on his political career.

To the public witnessing this ceremony, its symbolism surely suggested that mothers shared with fathers the honor of acknowledging the entrance of the dynasty's heir into the public life of the empire. When the circumcision finally took place on the thirty-seventh day of the event, the *valide sultan* Nurbanu was presented with the knife with which the operation was performed, and the prince's mother, the *haseki* Safiye, received the foreskin on a gold plate.[26] The vezir who performed the operation, Jerrah ("the surgeon") Mehmed Pasha, was liberally rewarded not only by the sultan, but also by the *valide sultan,* who presented him with three thousand gold coins, ceremonial robes, valuable textiles, and items of clothing.[27] Soon after the event Mehmed Pasha was honored by marriage to the prince's aunt, the widow Gevherhan Sultan.

Another significant arena of dynastic life with which the *valide sultan* might be publicly associated was victory in war. It was an old custom for the women of the dynasty, particularly the sultan's mother, to go out from the capital to greet and honor the ruler when he returned from a victorious campaign. According to Neşri, the mother of Osman, the first sultan, went out one or two days' journey from Bilejik, together with other relatives, to greet her son upon his return from the conquest of Iznik.[28] The *valide sultan*s of the post-Süleymanic sedentary sultanate did not have much opportunity to reenact this tradition. However, the reigns of Mehmed III and Murad IV, both of whom led military campaigns, were exceptions. Describing Mehmed III's Erlau campaign of 1596, John Sanderson, a member of the English embassy, commented that when a sultan returned from war, "it is lawefull for all their women, both smaule and great, to mete him without the waules; at other tim[e]s the women of any accompt or creditt never come in multitudes emongest the men."[29] Kösem Sultan was prominent in the celebrations surrounding the triumphal return of her son Murad IV to Istanbul after the reconquest of Baghdad from the Safavids in 1638. After having processed out from Istanbul to hail Murad in Izmid, two days' journey from the capital, the *valide sultan* retraced her route while the sultan returned by sea. Preceded by the vezirs and high-ranking religious dignitaries on richly caparisoned horses, she rode in a carriage hung with gold cloth, its wheels studded and spokes entirely covered with gold. The *valide sultan*'s carriage was followed by twelve other carriages, probably carrying members of the harem.[30]

Simply by moving from one palace to another, the *valide sultan*, like the sultan himself, could create a ceremonial occasion. We know of these mini-progresses because Ottoman historians considered them worthy of inclusion in their narratives. Selaniki recorded the movements of Safiye Sultan between palaces in the capital in flowery prose perhaps intended to match the ritual of her processions: "[t]he mother of the seat of royal glory moved to the palace she caused to flourish in the gardens of Davudpasha for the purpose of festive entertainment and a change of air. She departed with the hope of enjoying rest and tranquility there until the holy Festival of Sacrifice."[31] And on another occasion, he reported that "the mother of the emperor who is the refuge of the world and the seat of royal glory (may God preserve her chastity) moved with sublime grace to the palace she built in Davudpasha, desiring a change of climate in the season of roses and cherries. She made her way by boat in royal dignity and magnificence and disembarked at the garden of Iskender Çelebi."[32]

The frequent sojourns of the court in Edirne during the reign of Mehmed IV created opportunities for lengthy progresses between the two imperial cities. The *valide sultan* was a central figure in these events. Clifford Geertz has drawn attention to the importance of the royal progress as a "ceremonial form by which kings take symbolic possession of their realm."[33] The court accompanied the sultan to and from Edirne, often in two separate processions, with the *valide sultan* leading one and the sultan the other. The opportunity for public display of royal power and magnificence was thus doubled. In September 1658 the sultan departed from Edirne in preparation for an eastern campaign; his mother Turhan Sultan preceded him, her journey under the protection of her former steward, Ali Pasha, who was released from his position as lieutenant grand vezir to serve as escort.[34] In December 1672 Antoine Galland, secretary to the French ambassador Nointel, recorded in his diary the activity surrounding the *valide sultan*'s departure from Istanbul for Edirne; she was accompanied by the sultan's favorite, the Silahdar (sword-bearer) Mustafa Pasha, and Vani Efendi, the sultan's personal sheikh and resident preacher at the *valide sultan*'s mosque.[35] A company of three thousand Janissaries escorted the *valide sultan*'s convoy.[36]

To Jean Baptiste Tavernier, a French jewel merchant in quest of treasures for his monarch Louis XIV, we are indebted for an eyewitness account of the *valide sultan*'s entry into Istanbul in 1668. Like the later trip described by Galland, this journey was placed under the protection of the Silahdar. The enormous size of the queen mother's retinue and the presence in it of high-ranking officers of state and armed soldiers served to uphold the honor and inviolability of the *valide sultan* and to symbolize her power in government. Let us examine the composition of the procession in detail.

First to enter the city were two hundred mounted men of the Silahdar's retinue, followed by the retinue of the lieutenant grand vezir. Behind them rode four hundred men of the imperial cavalry, each wearing plaited armor and a short robe of taffeta and carrying a quiver covered in green velvet embroidered with gold wire and a bow in a matching case; their horses' trappings were of rich materials of yellow, red, or purple, worked with silver thread. Behind them rode their leader, with a helmet plume three feet high, followed by six attendants. Next marched a group of Janissaries and their commander, who was also accompanied by six attendants. Twelve fools, wearing bells on their clothing and caps with donkey ears on their heads, carried silver staffs. Then came the lieutenant grand vezir, who was proceeded by one hundred guards, each carrying a spear with a banner attached, and three hundred fancily clad heralds. The vezir's party was followed by five to six hundred imperial gardeners. Next came representatives of the religious institution; two hundred judges in plain dress, wearing black boots of Morrocan leather and huge turbans, marched in strict discipline (in contrast to the disorganization of several of the groups). They were followed by sixty descendants of the Prophet, each wearing a turban of green, the color of the Prophet, and two officials dressed in white representing the *müfti*, who, according to Tavernier, never participated in such processions.

At the end of the procession, leading the *valide sultan*'s retinue, was the Silahdar himself, riding a horse whose harness was of gold studded with pearls. He was followed by fifty riderless horses with sumptuous trappings, each led by a groom. Escorting the carriages of the women was a group of colorfully dressed black eunuchs. Turhan Sultan's carriage was drawn by six horses and surrounded by six guards who carried spears with red horse tails, symbols of sovereign power. The second carriage, presumably carrying the *haseki sultan* Rabia Gülnüş, was escorted by a number of pashas. Despite the fact that each carriage door was masked by a small screen and the body of a black eunuch, enabling the women to look out but not to be seen, the crowd was instructed to look away. These two carriages were followed by twelve more carrying the female servants of the harem, and many litters and four wagons filled with ice and provisions for the women.

Even allowing for exaggeration by Tavernier, what was clearly an enormous parade took three hours to pass. Tavernier noted that several prominent Frenchmen in Istanbul had received special permission to observe the event.[37] We do not know if the sultan himself also returned to Istanbul at this time, or, if he did, whether the procession accompanying him was of similar magnitude. What is clear is that in the *valide sultan*'s procession all elements of the governing class were represented, with the exception of the members of the imperial council, the chief officers of state, who presumably remained with the sultan. Such public association with those delegated to execute the sultan's will was a profound statement of the *valide sultan*'s authority.

An extended progress of Mehmed IV's reign, which began in June 1659, was the occasion for celebrating Turhan Sultan's unstinting concern for the protection of the empire. A highlight of this progress, during which the court journeyed from Istanbul to Bursa and Edirne, honoring the three Ottoman capitals with its presence, was a state visit in September to the two fortresses on the Çanakkale Straits whose reconstruction Turhan Sultan had undertaken.[38] While the *valide sultan* herself remained in the city of Gelibolu, the eighteen-year-old sultan and his retinue, escorted by the grand vezir Köprülü Mehmed Pasha and the chief black eunuch, inspected the fortresses. The wardens, lookouts, and gunners of the fortresses, and those responsible for filling in the shore were liberally rewarded, while robes of honor were awarded to those in charge of the construction as well as to the admiral Ali Pasha (the *valide sultan*'s former steward) and the grand vezir. Cannons were fired as the sultan visited each side of the straits. After urging that the construction of the fortresses be accomplished quickly, the sultan returned by galley to Gelibolu.[39] This ceremonial visit was memorialized by the sultan's private secretary Abdi Abdürrahman Pasha, who composed both a prose narrative and a poem on the occasion. In the poem, he celebrated the pious deed of the *valide sultan:*

> It is for all to see, the custom of the House of Osman,
> It has always striven abundantly to do pious deeds.

> Especially the mother of Sultan Mehmed Khan Ghazi,
> That is, the *valide sultan,* [has striven to bestow] this gracious gift.

> With pure heart she resolved to build monuments and undertake pious
>   deeds;
> She drew spiritual succor from the friends of God. . . .

> Building two fortresses, one on either side [of the straits],
> She made the lands of the people of faith safe from the enemy.

> What grace, to fill in the sea on two sides,
> So parallel, and thus to build the straits anew. . . .

> Before now no *valide sultan* was worthy
> Of establishing such a pious monument in this world. . . .[40]

The *valide sultan*'s public appearances might represent not only the magnificence and munificence of the dynasty but also the supreme attribute of Muslim sovereignty: justice. The public appearance of the sovereign was, for his subjects, more than merely an occasion to marvel at the pomp and circumstance of monarchical display, for custom obliged the sultan to accept the petitions of his subjects on these occasions. The obligation of the ruler to personally provide justice for the humblest of his subjects was an ancient principle of Near Eastern monarchy. That the queen mother as well was viewed as a source of royal justice is suggested by the following incident related by the historian Selaniki. In October 1600, as Mehmed III, his mother Safiye Sultan, and members of the court were returning to the imperial palace from a sojourn at a suburban palace belonging to Safiye, they were approached by a group of Anatolians. These men, having completed the requisite training, were waiting for appointment to positions in the religious hierarchy; they had traveled to the capital to complain that the chief military judge of Anatolia, third highest ranking member of the *ulema*, was accepting bribes in return for bestowing appointments on unqualified persons. Their petition could only be shouted to the sultan, who was sailing down the Golden Horn in his caique. But the *valide sultan*, returning by carriage, was stopped by the petitioners, who pleaded, "Your favors to the people of the world are manifold. Accept the blessings of the clerics who pray for you, and make Ahizade Abdülhalim Efendi military judge over us." From there the petitioners proceeded to a meeting of the imperial council, where they complained vociferously to the grand vezir. Their petition was granted.[41] In this urban progress, it was the *valide sultan* who was more accessible to petitioners, while the sultan, protected by the barrier of water, was the more remote.

The events surrounding the first popular deposition of an Ottoman sultan, that of Osman II in 1622, suggest the profound faith of the dynasty's subjects in the power of their monarch and his mother to effect justice. As the political drama unfolded, the emotionally disturbed Mustafa, enthroned in Osman's place, was removed by Janissary rebels from his room in the imperial palace and transported to the Old Palace, where his mother resided.[42] Together they were taken by the rebels to a safer haven, the mosque of the Janissaries, transported there in a carriage used to carry sick women from one palace to another. The historian Peçevi provides us with an eyewitness account of the procession:

> Our windows looked out on the broad gate near the Şehzade Mosque, that is, on the street, [so we were able to observe] the strange manner in which they transported Sultan Mustafa. So many people had gathered that it was as if the Day of Judgment had arrived and the dead had come to life. That broad avenue was so crowded that if a pin had dropped from the sky, it could not have fallen to the ground. Thronging against each other, the people pressed up around the afore-mentioned carriage to hand bits of their clothing into the carriage as tokens, tearing them from their skirts, their turbans, or their sleeves. Sultan Mustafa was seated at the back of the carriage in such a way that he could not be seen. His mother, seated in the front, took the tokens and made fine promises to the people.[43]

The bits of clothing were probably intended as tokens of pledges to perform some good deed in return for the granting of a petition by the sultan or his mother or perhaps for their blessing. The popular belief that the emotionally disturbed were saintly no doubt contributed to the eagerness of the crowd to appeal to the new sultan.

The public appearances of the *valide sultan* also served as occasions for demonstrating the munificence of the dynasty through the distribution of coins to those who had gathered, perhaps to pray for her, perhaps to appeal to her, perhaps merely to observe the display of royal pomp associated with her appearance. Even her funeral provided such an occasion. The funerals of the *valide sultan*s were in some ways more suitable for these purposes than those of the sultans. Because of the lack of a regularized principle of succession to the throne for most of this period, the death of a sultan precipitated a period of crisis during which looting and other public disturbances were temporarily licensed. Moreover, the new sultan might execute his brothers—an event that never failed to arouse the discontent of the people. Because of nervous anticipation of what might ensue, popular attention might be distracted from the attempt to celebrate a deceased sultan's career. In contrast, during the funeral of a queen mother public attention could be more effectively focused, especially in this period when her piety, charity, and wisdom were so assiduously demonstrated. Coins were distributed to the poor in the hopes that they would pray for the soul of the deceased. Selaniki noted that at the funeral of Nurbanu Sultan, "the wealth of a Pharaoh and countless gifts of benefaction were distributed as alms to the poor and wretched." According to the historian Naima, at the funeral in 1605 of Handan, the mother of Murad III's grandson Ahmed I, "large amounts of food and alms were distributed for the sake of her soul."[44]

Even foreigners might be graced by the *valide sultan*'s largesse. In his journal Galland recorded a story of Turhan Sultan's generosity to one of his countrymen. One day in Edirne, a procession of fifteen or twenty carriages carrying Turhan Sultan, the sultan's two sons and two brothers, and a large part of the harem, was making its way across a bridge over the river Tunca. The French ambassador's baker happened to be standing at the far end of the bridge. When he saw that the door of the first carriage was open, he attempted to prostrate himself to avoid suspicion of trying to see the *valide sultan*. At that moment she caught sight of him and his companions, and called out, "Don't be afraid, my sons." She then had coins cast to them; the baker received 160 aspers.[45]

The Philanthropy of Royal Women

Perhaps less dramatic than public ceremonial but longer lasting in its effects was the sponsoring of monumental public works, one of the most salient symbols of royal power to which women had access in the sixteenth and seventeenth centuries. The construction of public works—usually a complex of buildings providing public services grouped around a mosque[46]—was an element of Muslim noblesse oblige. By undertaking the creation of such institutions and of endowments (*vakıf*) for their maintenance and the salaries of their staffs, members of the ruling classes individually provided much of the urban infrastructure that was the responsibility of the state in other societies. Such works, known as *hayrat*—pious deeds or establishments—were undertaken for the ostensible purpose of pleasing God through an act of piety, but they had the worldly benefit of announcing the status and wealth of the builder and of garnering the gratitude of the local population for his or her philanthropy. The size and location of the public work sponsored by an individual was usually a reliable index of his or her social and political status. Women as well as men undertook these charitable efforts. Indeed, monumental building by and for imperial women was a traditional feature of Islamic culture.

The nature of power in the Ottoman ruling class of the sixteenth century gave women of the royal family a prominent role in public building.[47] After the first two Ottoman generations, princes had been deprived of this privilege, leaving only the sultan and the female members of the royal family to carry out this mandatory activity on behalf of the dynasty. Following them in major endowments were members of the military/administrative elite, many of whom were *damad*s. It is noteworthy that men of religion, members of the *ulema,* did not endow public institutions on a large scale. Monumental building was the prerogative of dynastic power, *saltanat,* and its delegates.

The Women of Süleyman's Reign

As we might expect, it was during the reign of Süleyman that a new paradigm for women's public building took shape. Süleyman's mother Hafsa, his daughter Mihrimah, his sisters and granddaughters, and especially his *haseki* Hurrem built on a grander scale than had their predecessors and for the first time constructed major monuments in the empire's capital. These women created public-building roles that formed the standard for the *valide sultan* in future generations.

What was unusual about Hurrem as an endower of public institutions was not the endeavor itself but the location and the number of the works built by and for her. The monuments of earlier royal women were located in provincial centers, a practice consonant with the decentralization of the dynasty that characterized the pre-Süleymanic era. But Hurrem's works were located in the urban capitals of the empire. They were the most tangible evidence of the *haseki*'s prestige. For the first time in the history of the Ottoman dynasty, the building enterprise of a royal concubine can be said to constitute an architecture of power.

Precedent for Hurrem's imperial building was set by Hafsa Sultan, Süleyman's mother. Shortly after Süleyman's accession Hafsa built a mosque complex larger than that built by any concubine before her. It consisted of a mosque, a religious college, a dervish hostel, a primary school, and a soup kitchen, with provision made for the employment of a staff totalling 117; Süleyman later added a hospital and a bath in his mother's name.[48] The mosque had two minarets, an honor that had until then been reserved for the sultan. Fittingly, the complex came to be known as "Sultaniye," the imperial mosque.[49] It was endowed with the income from many properties Hafsa Sultan had acquired with the financial support first of Süleyman's father Selim I, and then of Süleyman himself. An example of the groundwork laid by Hafsa Sultan for her project was a collective purchase in 1518, carried out through her agent, of 56 ordinary shops, 11 shops with roofed fronts, and 111 booths in the market of Urla, a town in the district of Izmir, not far from the prince's post in Manisa.[50] This mass purchase consisted of 116 individual transactions in which property with a total value of 66,690 aspers was acquired by the prince's mother, who assigned the rents from the shops as well as various market tax revenues to the upkeep of her mosque complex.[51]

Not content with simply constructing a monument, Hafsa Sultan undertook to encourage settlement in the neighborhood of the mosque. Lots were made available for rent or sale, and those who constructed residences on the lots were exempted by the sultan from various taxes.[52] Here we observe an example of the Ottoman use of mosque complexes as a strategy in urban development. The complex served as a magnet around which a new neighborhood would form or as a means to inject new resources into existing neighborhoods whose renewal was deemed desirable. One of Mehmed the Conqueror's first efforts in the attempt to revitalize Istanbul after its capture from the Byzantines and to accomplish the city's transformation from a Christian to a Muslim capital was to encourage leading statesmen to undertake the construction of mosque complexes in the various neighborhoods of the city.[53]

Hafsa Sultan's monument was located not in the capital but in Manisa, the provincial post occupied by the former prince. But the two mosque complexes constructed in the name of the princess Mihrimah—one by Süleyman for his daughter and one by Mihrimah herself—were located in Istanbul. The most numerous and grandest structures, however, were built by and for Hurrem. Major philanthropic institutions existed in her name in Mecca, Medina, and Jerusalem, the holiest cities of the Islamic world, and in Istanbul and Edirne, the principal seats of the Ottoman sultanate after 1453. The earliest of these, the Istanbul complex, constructed between 1537 and 1539, consisted of a mosque, a religious college, a soup kitchen, a hospital, and a primary school.[54] The well-endowed complex in Jerusalem, completed in the early 1550s, contained a mosque, a fifty-five-room dwelling for religious pilgrims, an area devoted to charitable services for the poor (including a bakery, soup kitchen, storeroom, and public toilets), and an inn and stable for travelers.[55] The Edirne complex consisted of a mosque, soup kitchen, and inn.[56] An imperial decree of 1549 illustrates how the projects in distant cities were undertaken: Semiz Ali Pasha, the governor of Egypt (and later *damad* and grand vezir) was instructed to facilitate the work of one Selman Agha, who had been sent from Istanbul to oversee the construction of the complex that Hurrem wished to sponsor in Medina.[57]

In Istanbul, the structures bearing Hurrem's name—or rather her title of *haseki*—should be seen as part of a large-scale building program in the imperial capital undertaken during Süleyman's reign. The numerous endowments for the public welfare were visible and lasting testimony to the ruling family's piety, its solicitude for its subjects, and the sultan's victories as *ghazi* (a sultan's own mosque could only be built with war booty). Whereas the sultans before Süleyman had limited themselves to a single mosque complex, during his reign five major mosque complexes were built in the capital by members of the dynasty (six if the mosque Süleyman built for his father at the very beginning of his reign is counted). Three of the five were associated with women.

The mosque complex Süleyman endowed for Hurrem was the first of the five to be built. Completed in 1539, the Haseki complex was followed in 1547 by the Üsküdar mosque Süleyman built for his daughter Mihrimah, in 1548 by the Şehzade mosque endowed by the sultan as a memorial to his son Mehmed, in 1557 by Süleyman's own great complex, and in the early 1560s by a complex built by Mihrimah at Edirnekapı. It is significant that these mosques were built in the second half of Süleyman's reign, when it was becoming increasingly evident that visions of endless conquest were unrealistic. In contrast to the emphasis on the ceremonial pomp and splendid luxury of the court in the early decades of Süleyman's sultanate, the dynasty's wealth and might were demonstrated principally through pious works in its later decades.

Spread out over the capital, the mosques of Süleyman's reign carried into the different neighborhoods of the city the message of the dynasty's piety and concern for its subjects' material and spiritual welfare. The inscription over the main entrance to the Üsküdar mosque of Mihrimah Sultan hailed her as the

> patron of pious foundations, protector of the state and the world and the faith, the princess (may God the Almighty dedicate her to an abundance of benevolence), daughter of the khan of the khans of the Orient and the Occident, sultan of the sultans of the lands where the sun rises and sets, cultivator of justice and goodness in the inhabited world, builder of edifices of safety and security for the people of faith, the sultan, son of the sultan, Sultan Süleyman Khan, son of Sultan Selim Khan (may his caliphate endure for an eternity of time). . . .[58]

Because the mosques of women tended to have less choice locations than those of the sultan himself, they often formed the only imperial mosque in their vicinity. The Haseki complex and Mihrimah's complex at Edirnekapı were in their day, and still are, the most outlying imperial structures in the old city.

The locations of Hurrem's two monuments in Istanbul—the Haseki complex and a large public bath—appear to have been deliberately selected to shape a public image for her, and perhaps to contribute to the public image of the dynastic family as a whole. The mosque complex was constructed near the "Women's Market" (*Avrat Pazarı*), in an area far from any other imperial mosque and away from the built-up center of the city.[59] This site was perhaps chosen to serve the women of the area in which the mosque was located. The charitable endeavors of female benefactors were not uncommonly devoted to women. According to local tradition, the Üsküdar mosque built by Gülfem Khatun, a prominent member of the harem, was intended for the use of women and opened to men only in recent times.[60]

Despite its thinness, the historical record of the women of the Ottoman dynasty contains a number of stories testifying to their compassion and concern for other women, especially those who had fallen on hard times: prostitutes, convicts, captives, orphans. Süleyman's sister Şah Sultan divorced her husband, the grand vezir Lutfi Pasha, over an affair concerning his inhumane treatment of a prostitute (he punished her by having her genitals mutilated).[61] According to Mustafa Ali's account of the affair, when Şah Sultan protested, Lutfi asserted that he would continue to inflict this punishment on prostitutes, and began to beat the princess when she lost her temper at him. Süleyman granted his sister's request for a divorce and dismissed the grand vezir from office, putting an end to his official career.[62]

Another story of concern for prostitutes, on this occasion demonstrated by the *valide sultan* Safiye, was related by John Sanderson, secretary of the English embassy:

> The Queene Mother, with the Grand Sultana and other of the Grand Signiors women, walking in their serraglio espyed a number of boates upon the river [the Bosphorus] hurrying together. The Queene Mother sent to enquire of the matter; who was told that the Vizier did justice upon certain chabies [*kahpe*], that is, whoores. Shee, taking displeasure, sent word and advised the eunuch Bassa that her sonne [absent on campaign] had left him to govern the citie and not to devoure the women; commanding him to looke well to the other businesse and not to meddle any more with the women till his masters returne.[63]

Royal women also directed forms of charity toward unfortunate females. Ayşe Sultan, daughter of Murad III, bequeathed funds to ransom Muslim prisoners of war, with the condition that female captives be freed first.[64] One of the several personal charities of the *valide sultan* Kösem was to seek out orphaned girls who could not marry for lack of a dowry and provide them not only with the necessary dowry but also with lodgings and furnishings for their home.[65]

It is possible that Hurrem's mosque was intended to project the dynasty's concern for its female subjects. The historian Peçevi commented that the location of the Haseki complex in the area known as the Women's Market was a manifestation of the sultan's "utmost delicacy."[66] Evliya Çelebi emphasized the association of women with structures in the area in a humorous passage in his *Book of Travels:* matching different classes of the city's population with appropriate public baths, he assigned women to the Avrat Pazarı bath.[67] Describing the Istanbul of the mid-seventeenth century, Evliya noted that the mosque was commonly known as "Haseki Avrat," a name which suggests a fusion in the popular mind of benefactress and beneficiary.[68] The complex, which Peçevi described as "known to all humankind," eventually gave its name to the neighborhood—"Haseki"—as often happened with the areas in which mosques were located. Hurrem's mosque, which originally consisted of a single domed room with a large porch, was not built on an imperial scale, and it had only a single minaret, in contrast to the two permitted the mosque constructed by Süleyman for Mihrimah and Hafsa Sultan's mosque in Manisa; the mosque's simplicity was no doubt a reflection of the fact that Hurrem was not a blood relative of the reigning sultan. It was the scale and number of its affiliated structures that constituted the grandness of Hurrem's complex. However, the congregation of the mosque became so large and its endowment so rich that in 1612 the executor of the mosque's endowment decided to enlarge the mosque by adding another domed chamber.[69]

If Hurrem's mosque demonstrated concern for the common people, the second public work bearing her name in Istanbul spoke both of her piety and of her imperial status. Even a structure as relatively mundane as a bath could be elevated to a statement of magnificence and power through its placement. The splendid bath built in the mid-1550s by Süleyman in Hurrem's honor was located on the imperial axis formed by the royal palace, the great church-turned-mosque of Aya Sofya (Hagia Sophia)—the premier imperial mosque of the city[70]—and the Hippodrome. Fanny Davis has suggested that the Hippodrome (*At Meydanı*) was culturally and ceremonially an extension of the palace, in a sense the most public of its courtyards.[71] It was there that important dynastic events such as weddings and circumcisions were celebrated. This axis—the heart of the ancient Byzantine capital, neglected and abandoned in the empire's last centuries—reached its fullest development under the Ottomans in the early seventeenth century when Ahmed I chose the Hippodrome as the site of his imposing mosque complex. Cleared of pasha palaces to make way for the new mosque, the area was thus rendered both more public and a greater testimony to imperial piety and power. Hurrem's own pious effort in this charismatic center of the capital was represented by the bath, which was built to serve the staff and congregation of the mosque of Aya Sofya. The bath may have served as a reminder of her concern for women as well, since it was a double one, with separate sections for men and women.

The poor were the recipients of a considerable amount of the charitable effort of the dynastic family during Süleyman's reign. One of the five duties required of every Muslim, alms giving was ostentatiously undertaken by Muslim monarchs. The "two noble sanctuaries" of Mecca and Medina, brought under Ottoman dominion by his father, received much attention from Süleyman and his family. According to Peçevi, while giving alms to the inhabitants of the two cities was nothing new, Süleyman greatly increased their scope and saw that they were effectively and efficiently distributed. For example, noted Peçevi, while alms derived from the tax on non-Muslims had previously been distributed only to the most prominent of the *ulema*, under Süleyman these alms reached almost all the inhabitants of the two cities.[72] While allowance should be made for the hyberbole of Ottoman accounts, the symbolic importance of the Ottoman dynasty's munificence toward the newly won holy cities should not be underestimated. As the first Ottoman sultan to assume the responsibility for the welfare and adornment of the holy cities, Süleyman needed to establish himself as a worthy heir to the great caliphs and sultans who had held this responsibility before him.

The complexes built for Hurrem in Mecca and Medina may have been constructed with the intention that they associate her with the responsibilities of the Ottoman sultanate toward the inhabitants of its most holy possessions. Peçevi commented that in these two "rich" complexes, "every day the poor of Mecca and Medina are given food and drink."[73] The complex Hurrem herself built in Jerusalem was largely devoted to services for the poor. The government in Istanbul was vigilant about the needs of this institution, concerning itself, for example, with shortages of rice from Egypt (as much as 190 pounds of raw rice a day was used in the kitchens) and problems with the grain supply (the crop of 1559 was consumed by locusts).[74] As late as 1944 this institution was still providing nourishment to the poor.[75]

Süleyman's apparent desire to have the women of his family publicly recognized was echoed, perhaps deliberately, in the attention he paid to the memorials of two women of the first Muslim centuries. He restored the dome over the tomb of Khadija, the first wife of the Prophet, and constructed a dome over her house.[76] The first convert to Islam and mother of the Prophet's children, Khadija was posthumously honored with the title *umm al-mu'minin,* "mother of the believers."[77] In describing Süleyman's restoration of her tomb, Evliya Çelebi referred to her as "Mother Khadija, mother of the believers."[78] Like her daughter Fatima and the Prophet's other wives, especially 'A'isha, Khadija served as a model of Muslim womanhood. Her name, like theirs, was invoked in the honorific titulature assigned to Ottoman royal women. The symbolic resonance of Süleyman's gesture of respect toward this pious and powerful woman must have been considerable.

The second woman recalled by the sultan's charitable works was Zubeida, the wife of the famed Abbasid caliph Harun al-Rashid. Like Harun's mother Khayzuran, Zubeida was responsible for a large number of public works undertaken for the benefit of the Muslim community. One of these was the construction of a series of wells, reservoirs, and aqueducts that brought water directly to the sacred precinct in Mecca. During the annual pilgrimage, pilgrims from all over the Muslim world derived benefit from these waterworks and perhaps carried stories of Zubeida's charity back to their homes. During Süleyman's reign these waterworks were repaired and the water supply to Mecca expanded, a project possibly underwritten by Hurrem or Mihrimah.[79] The positive association between the women of Harun's family and those of his own must surely have struck Süleyman's subjects, and was most likely intended. An imperial order dated 1560 and attached to the endowment deed of Hurrem's Jerusalem complex describes her as "the quintessence of the queens amongst women, the Zobeida of her time and age . . . who is unique and to whom there is no second queen in prosperity and good fortune. . . ."[80]

Hurrem's Jerusalem complex recalled another great lady of the eastern Mediterranean world. Helena, mother of Constantine, the Byzantine emperor and founder of Constantinople, is said to have built a pilgrim's hospice on the site of the complex. The daughter of a pagan innkeeper, Helena was converted to Christianity by her son and proceeded to accomplish the miraculous discovery of Christian holy sites in Jerusalem. The site of Hurrem's complex had been occupied under the Mamluks by the magnificent residence of the Lady Tunsuq al-Muzaffariya, a slave convert to Islam who was living in Jerusalem as a religious pilgrim, perhaps a refugee from Timur's invasion of Iran.[81] Today the location is known as "Ladies' Hill" and the street on which the structure faces variously as the "Street of the Soup Kitchen," "Street of the Ladies," or "Street of Queen Helena."[82] The philanthropic work of sixteenth-century Ottoman women thus appears as one manifestation of a strong indigenous tradition of women benefactors, Christian and Muslim alike, in the eastern Mediterranean.

The public works undertaken by the Ottoman elite were financed through revenue generated by grants in freehold of crown lands (*mülk*) and other sources of income. The ceremonial importance attached to Hurrem's public works is highlighted by the magnificence of the deeds to such income-generating sources granted her by Süleyman. These deeds, superb examples of the arts of calligraphy and illumination, are among the most exquisitely worked documents in the royal archives of the imperial palace. Among the most beautiful documents are a group of deeds issued between December 1550 and June 1559 granting revenue to provide for the Jerusalem complex.[83] The first of these, for example, was the grant of the income derived from taxes on the village of Amyin in the province of Trablus, which provided a revenue of 97,978 aspers a year.[84]

That the granting of these income sources to Hurrem was a serious business of state is indicated by the fact that the deeds were witnessed by the highest officers of the empire. They appear to have been routinely witnessed by the ranking vezirs.[85] Some had the entire top echelon of government as witnesses: for example, a deed of 1539 was witnessed by the grand vezir Lutfi Pasha, the vezirs Hadım Süleyman Pasha, Mehmed Pasha, and Rüstem Pasha, the *müfti* Ebussuud Efendi, the chief justices of Rumeli and Anatolia, the chief finance ministers, and "other statesmen";[86] a deed issued in March 1557, granting Hurrem the income of two villages in the province of Vize, was witnessed in Edirne (where the sultan often wintered) by the grand vezir Rüstem Pasha, the vezirs Semiz Ali Pasha, Sokollu Mehmet Pasha, and Pertev Pasha (all *damad*s or *damad*s-to-be), the two chief justices, and the finance ministers.[87] The magnificence of these documents and the large assignments of revenue contained in them not only honored Hurrem personally but served to demonstrate her prestige to the leading members of both the military/administrative and religious hierarchies.

Through these various monuments and charities, which formed the most tangible expression of the ruler's benevolence toward his subjects, Hurrem was assimilated into the public image of sovereignty. The privileges allowed her were extraordinary, indeed unique in the history of the dynasty, for a woman who was not the blood relative of the reigning sultan. Hurrem's mosque complex was the only complex built for the concubine or wife of a sultan during his lifetime. The prestige and achievements of Hurrem served as precedent for future generations of dynastic women. The next century was characterized by their activities as principal purveyors of dynastic largesse through the construction of foundations for public benefit.

The Philanthropy of the *Valide Sultan*

Much of the enormous wealth of the *valide sultan*s was returned to the empire's subjects through the institutions and services they established for the public welfare. With the aggrandizement of the *valide sultan* in the reign of

Murad III, demonstration by women of the piety, munificence, and power of the dynastic family through the construction of monumental public works and acts of charity became largely her prerogative. The privileges that had been enjoyed by Hurrem and Mihrimah were allowed no other concubine or daughter of the sultan. Henceforth, royal concubines might undertake pious works, but like their persons, their charitable efforts were not publicly visible. They did not build monuments but rather established endowments for such "veiled" pious works as recitation of the Qur'an in the mosque of the Prophet in Medina (a charity of Şemsiruhsar, concubine of Murad III)[88] or the distribution of clothing to the poor of the holy cities (a charity of the powerful *haseki* Kösem).

Construction of pious foundations   With the exception of Ahmed I, who built a magnificent mosque bearing his name on the Hippodrome, the sultans of the late sixteenth, the seventeenth, and the early eighteenth centuries observed the precedent established in Murad III's reign whereby the imperial mosques constructed in Istanbul were built by or for the sultan's mother. The mosque of Nurbanu Sultan (described above) was the first of these. It was followed by that of Nurbanu's daughter-in-law Safiye Sultan. In 1597, two years into her son's reign, Safiye began the construction of a mosque complex on the shore of the Golden Horn, near its confluence with the Bosphorus. High-level government officials acted as her agents in the project. The steward of the powerful chief black eunuch of the imperial palace was appointed superintendent of the construction, and the grand vezir assumed the responsibility of keeping an eye on its progress. An area of the Jewish quarter in the midst of which the mosque was to be located was cleared through purchase and razing of houses. In December the Venetian ambassador reported that "the Sultana Mother has begun to pull down some houses belonging to Jews in order to build her mosque, which is to cost a great deal."[89] However, Safiye had to give up her project upon Mehmed III's early death in 1603 and her subsequent retirement to the Old Palace. The partly constructed mosque languished, ravaged by fire. Pietro Foscarini, Venitian ambassador to the court of Murad IV, reported in 1637 that the sultan, desiring to immortalize his name, had begun reconstruction of the mosque but abandoned the project because of its excessive cost.[90] Finally, in 1660 Turhan Sultan undertook its completion at the urging of the grand vezir, Köprülü Mehmed Pasha.[91] In addition to the mosque, the complex contained a primary school, a school to teach literacy, two public fountains, and a double market. Like the mosque of Nurbanu, the "New Valide Mosque," for so it was called, was abutted by an elegant pavilion, which was connected by means of a corridor to the imperial loge in which members of the royal family performed their prayers (Figure 7-2). Turhan Sultan was able to observe the building of the mosque from this pavilion,[92] and she and other members of the dynasty presumably used it when attending the mosque. Turhan Sultan's mosque was the first mosque built by a woman to join the ranks of the imperial mosques, those which formed the highest level of appointments in the hierarchy of the religious

Figure 7-2 A seventeenth-century view of the New Valide Mosque. The French cap·
tion reads, "The *Valide*, built by the Sultana, mother of the Grand Seigneur." The
"sultana" was Turhan Sultan, mother of Mehmed IV. On the left is the royal pavilion,
and on the right is the covered market, which generated rental income to support the
mosque complex. From G. J. Grelot, *Relation nouvelle d'un voyage de Constantinople*,
1689. (*Courtesy of Princeton University Libraries*)

institution; other mosques in this category were Aya Sofya; the mosques of
the sultans Mehmed II, Bayezid II, Selim I, Süleyman, and Ahmed I; and the
Şehzade mosque built for Süleyman's son Mehmed.[93] This is testimony to the
prestige that the office of *valide sultan* had acquired by the mid-seventeenth
century.

Perhaps the most remarkable feature of Turhan's "New Valide Mosque"
from the perspective of dynastic politics is its large imposing tomb.[94] In a
dramatic evolution of royal burial protocol, this matriarchal tomb took over
from the patriarchal tombs of Süleyman and his successors the function of
housing the royal family in death. The catafalque of Turhan Sultan occupies
the most prominent position at the head of the tomb. At its foot is that of her
son Mehmed IV, and below the catafalque of Mehmed are those of several
others, including four sultans: Mehmed's sons Mustafa II and Ahmed III, and
his grandsons Mahmud I and Osman III (who were, of course, the grandsons
and great-grandons of Turhan). The *valide sultan* Saliha, mother of Mahmud
I, and Zeynep, a concubine of Ahmed III, are also buried within Turhan's
tomb. Attached to the main tomb is an additional structure known as "The

Tomb of the Ladies," which is filled with palace women; in the garden of the tomb are buried more palace women and a number of princes and princesses. With the possible exception of the tomb of Süleyman, there appear to be more people buried in and around this tomb than at any other royal tomb in Istanbul. The importance of the tomb within the total complex and, more generally, the significant place in the religious life of Muslims occupied by tombs and their ceremonies, are suggested by the fact that the endowment deed of Turhan Sultan's complex specified 157 individuals to be employed in her tomb.[95]

Both Nurbanu and Turhan endowed their mosques with libraries. Included in the collection assembled by Nurbanu, the first woman to establish a library in Istanbul,[96] were sixteen superb Qur'ans, several of them the work of the late sixteenth century,[97] perhaps commissioned by the *valide sultan*. Turhan's Istanbul mosque as well as two smaller mosques she built on the Çanakkale Straits were supplied with books transferred by imperial command in 1662 from the palace treasury; forty-seven books were donated to the two small mosques and over three hundred to the New Valide Mosque.[98] It is probable that Turhan Sultan also commissioned works for the latter's library. The establishment of a mosque library not only benefitted the mosque's staff and students at nearby religious colleges, but in addition provided the *valide sultan* with opportunities for patronage of calligraphers, artists, bookbinders, and other skilled craftsmen.

The only mosque complex to be built by the royal family during the reigns of Murad IV and İbrahim was constructed by their mother, Kösem Sultan. It was of relatively modest scale and was located in an out-of-the-way neighborhood of Üsküdar, not far from the magnificent complex of Nurbanu Sultan.[99] One wonders why Kösem, probably the most powerful *valide sultan,* perhaps the wealthiest, and certainly the longest lived, did not built a grand mosque. It may be that Murad IV, aggressively dominant in the second half of his reign and the greatest *ghazi* sultan after Süleyman, intended to construct an imperial mosque himself, as his father Ahmed had. If so, his early death at the age of thirty-one put an end to such a plan. The ambassador Pietro Foscarini reported that Murad had entertained such an idea but did not follow through when he learned how much it would cost (the avarice of the sultans—perhaps better interpreted as fiscal restraint—was a constant theme in Venetian reports of the 17th century).[100] Murad's premature death may have impelled Kösem to hastily undertake the construction of her mosque. It was built in the first year of İbrahim's reign, when none of the concubines of this sole male member of the dynasty to survive Murad's reign became pregnant. The extinction of the Ottoman line appeared to be a serious possibility; in their reports for 1640 and 1641, the Venetian ambassadors discussed the imminent demise of the dynasty and speculated as to what might ensue.[101] The pious *valide sultan* may have wished to endow a complex before the collapse of her career, indeed of the empire.

Mosque complexes were not the only structures that might convey the charitable concerns of the *valide sultan* and bring her pious deeds to the daily attention of the users of her establishments. Other structures such as baths and *han*s (the Ottoman "office building" that provided shop, office, and storage space for numerous craftsmen, tradesmen, and traveling merchants) not only served the public but generated income to support her charitable establishments. Kösem Sultan's mosque may have been modest, but the large *han* with its own mosque, known as the "Valide Han," which she built in the center of the city's market area, was the grandest in the capital. Nurbanu Sultan established a number of baths in the city to contribute to the support of the many public services associated with her mosque: these included a double bath (with separate sections for men and women) in the vicinity of her mosque, another in the center of Üsküdar, an especially elegant double bath on the main thoroughfare leading from the mosque of Aya Sofya to the covered market, and a single bath in Yeni Kapı, where her private palace was located.[102]

A perennial charitable concern of its elite was the provision of water for the capital's residents through the construction of aqueducts, water channels, and fountains.[103] Fountains, like mosques, performed the function of making their donors known to the public, and were frequently constructed by *valide sultan*s as well as by women who could not undertake larger structures. The inscription on the fountain built in Beşiktaş by Turhan Sultan (whose full name was Hadije Turhan) drew attention to the virtue of both the sultan and his mother and to the latter's good deed:

> Hadije Sultan, who is the crown of chastity of the well-guarded and the mother of
> Mehmed Khan, sultan of the sultans, the order of sovereignty and the community, pure of character,
> Caused this sublime fountain to flow freely, so that the thirst of the whole universe might be slaked.[104]

Other charities and pious works   In addition to building, *valide sultan*s also undertook other kinds of charities and pious works that displayed their piety and generosity. Salient among them were efforts to benefit Mecca and Medina. As *haseki sultan*, at the very end of Ahmed I's reign, Kösem Sultan established a set of pious charitable services, including the furnishing of water to pilgrims making their way to the holy cities (a service that employed thirty camels, six camel drivers, and six water carriers); the annual distribution of shirts, woolen cloaks, shoes, and turban materials to the poor of the two cities and the poor among the pilgrims; and the recitation of the Qur'an in the sanctuaries of Jerusalem, Mecca, and Medina.[105] As *valide sultan* she continued to undertake personal charities, including the provision of stipends during the holy months of Rejep, Şaban, and Ramazan to two hundred descendents of the Prophet, and the provision of dowries to orphaned girls. Every year in the month of Rejep, Kösem would leave the palace in disguise and personally arrange for the release of imprisoned debtors and other criminals (except murderers) through payment of their debts or recompense for their crimes.[106]

Turhan Sultan's personal charities resembled those of her mother-in-law.

They included the annual distribution of rice, cooking oil, and wood to the poor of Üsküdar at the beginning of Ramazan, the month of fasting, and the provision of water for pilgrims to Mecca and Medina (employing sixty-five camels). She also created endowments for the recitation of the Qur'an in several places: 30 *hafız* (persons who have memorized the entire Qur'an) were to be employed in the mosque of Aya Sofya; 15 pages in the two large chambers for pages of the imperial palace; and 130 individuals each in the sanctuaries of Mecca and Medina.[107] Another kind of pious work was assumption of the responsibility for royal tombs: Safiye Sultan established an endowment for the recitation of the Qur'an in the tomb of Murad III (in which she would be buried at her death),[108] and Handan Sultan an endowment for the maintenance of Mehmed III's tomb and the salaries of its employees.[109]

Prominent religious figures might also receive the patronage and protection of the *valide sultan*. Safiye Sultan was petitioned by a sheikh named Bekir, who had been an intimate of Murad III, and honored with the position of preacher and sheikh at the mosque of Selim II in Edirne on the accession of Mehmed III. At that time, Safiye had presented him with a gift of several religious texts. Now he complained that he had lost his position, having answered the sultan's command to accompany the army on a campaign to Wallachia. He had pawned his books to assemble his own company of more than one thousand soldiers, but the new *müfti*, Sadeddin Efendi, refused to reappoint him to his former post when he returned from combat. Hence his appeal to the *valide sultan*.[110] Kösem Sultan constructed a tomb for Abdülmejid Şeyhi Efendi, better known as Sivasi Efendi. Sivasi Efendi was a sheikh of the Halveti order who was a prolific writer and the most prominent opponent of the fundamentalist cleric Kadızade, making him one of the two most widely known religious figures of Murad IV's reign.[111]

Among those for whom the *valide sultan* provided were her own servants. Nurbanu Sultan arranged for the manumission of 150 of her female slaves at her death and the provision of one thousand gold coins—a small fortune—to each.[112] According to Naima, Kösem Sultan would free her female slaves after two or three years (a short term of service), and she would arrange a marriage for each of these women, providing her with a dowry, jewels, and purses of gold. The groom, a retired palace official or an individual from outside the palace, would be selected according to the talents and accomplishments of the prospective bride; the *valide sultan* would make certain that he had a secure position. Every year on religious festivals and holy days Kösem would remember her former servants with purses of money.[113] In the endowment deed for the charitable institutions and services she established, Turhan Sultan awarded a lifetime stipend of twenty aspers a day to one Tevekkül Khatun, who was perhaps a palace servant (her title suggests that she would have been a high-ranking one).[114] It was not only the duty of responsibility placed by Islam on the master or mistress of a slave that impelled the *valide sultan* to look after her servants. The manumission of slaves and the maintenance of ties of patronage with them helped her to create a clientage network that was a vital link with the world outside the palace.

Supporting the government   The empire itself was on occasion the recipient of the *valide sultan*'s munificence. Under the title "The Valide Sultan Gives Funds for Good Deeds on the Path of Ghaza," the historian Selaniki described Safiye Sultan's donation in 1597 of funds to the war effort, which he termed "alms": "At this time the mother of the emperor, who is the refuge of the world and the seat of royal glory, donated two purses of gold of her pure wealth, with the order that it be used for holy war on the path of Allah and spent on nothing else but the refurbishment of cannon and the purchase of sufficient numbers of choice pack animals."[115] In the late 1650s Turhan Sultan undertook the reconstruction of two fortresses guarding the Çanakkale Straits. The straits had been breached by the Venetian navy at the end of the reign of İbrahim and were, until the conquest of Crete in 1669, a constant theater of naval warfare. Built by Mehmed II two centuries earlier, the fortresses had fallen into complete disrepair. Turhan's first attempt to undertake their reconstruction was abandoned when the inhabitants of the area protested, but she was convinced by the grand vezir Köprülü Mehmed Pasha to take up the project again.[116] Known as the "Imperial Fortress" (*Kale-i Sultaniye*) and the "Dam of the Sea" (*Sedd ül-Bahr*), the fortresses each contained a mosque, a primary school, a public bath, homes for the soldiers posted to the fortress, and shops and markets.[117] Funds for the construction of the fortresses, which totaled 29,595,000 aspers over the course of one year,[118] came from the income from lands held by the *valide sultan*, and were disbursed by her steward to the chief admiral, who relayed them to the *valide sultan*'s agent in charge of the construction. Every stage of the transfer of funds was marked by the issuing of receipts and recording of transactions. Even in the most insignificant of these records, the *valide sultan*'s prestige was acknowledged through the careful notation of her honorific titles: "crown of the veiled, coronet of the modest. . . ."[119]

All members of the empire's governing class, including the sultan, were expected to contribute toward the effort to protect and expand the empire's borders. Where European governments raised funds through credit advanced by an international capital market, the Ottoman state relied upon the wealth accumulated by individuals,[120] available through borrowing or through the systematic confiscation of the estates of dismissed or deceased members of the ruling elite. The sultan himself might be pressured by the grand vezir or the *müfti* to donate emergency funds from his private treasury to supply the army or navy or to cover the quarterly payments of the troops. He was not always compliant, however: when Ahmed I was urged by the *müfti* Sunullah Efendi to turn over the annual income from Egypt—the sultan's "pocket money"— to support the Persian war, he refused; when told that Süleyman had funded his last campaign personally, Ahmed tersely replied, "The times are not the same."[121]

Like the sultan, the *valide sultan* appears to have been expected to share her enormous wealth in times of crisis. And like the sultan, she was not always able or willing to respond to requests from outside the palace for funds. Answering a plea by the grand vezir early in Murad's reign for money to pay the troops,

Kösem Sultan replied that she had done all she could, although she wished she could do more. In these years the imperial treasury was still suffering from having had to pay out accession bonuses four times within the previous decade.[122] Thirty years later a similar plea was voiced by the lieutenant grand vezir Melek Ahmed Pasha to the *valide sultan* Turhan: "Yesterday . . . fifty purses were requested for the payment of stipends tomorrow, Saturday, God willing. There is no possible way of obtaining the funds outside [the palace] this week and indeed, it will not be possible to make the payment tomorrow. I am extremely distressed by the fact that we have on hand at most four or five purses. There is no other remedy for our dilemma but you. . . ."[123] The *valide sultan*'s response to this desperate plea suggests her own distress at the fiscal impasse:

> You have requested fifty purses by tomorrow. I am in tremendous debt. Still, let us suppose that I borrow fifty purses and give that amount to you by Sunday or Tuesday. What can you come up with? Have you been able to raise anything or not? Where should I find the money so that I might give it to you? You won't believe me but I swear by God that I am in debt for more than two or three hundred purses. I myself am dumbfounded . . . what can I grab hold of?[124]

This crisis appears to have occured in the spring of 1655, when the capital nervously awaited the arrival of the grand vezir İbşir Mustafa Pasha. İbşir Pasha was a powerful member of the governing elite whose rebellion in Anatolia the palace had attempted to contain by appointing him to the highest office possible and giving him a princess in marriage. According to Naima, shortly before İbşir Pasha's arrival in Istanbul, the troops in the capital were paid on his order; their refusal to accept the debased coins that they were given threatened to provoke a riot. It was perhaps at this point that the exchange between the *valide sultan* and the grand vezir occurred. Eventually one hundred purses were hastily borrowed from the pious foundations for Mecca and Medina, suggesting that the *valide sultan* may have turned for help to her ally in the palace, the chief black eunuch, who was the superintendent of the foundations of the holy cities.[125]

Sources of the *Valide Sultan*'s Wealth

The often enormous expenditures required for construction and maintenance of public institutions, acts of charity, and aid to the government suggest the extent of the financial resources of the *valide sultan*. Her income was derived from a variety of sources. The most important of these was the tax income from crown domains assigned to her or from lands granted to her in freehold by the sultan, either when she was *haseki* or during her son's reign. Such grants had been a feature of the Ottoman dynasty from the very beginning, when the first sultan, Osman, bestowed the village of Kozağaç on his wife at the time of their marriage.[126] The fourteenth-century North African traveler Ibn Battuta noted that "among the Turks and Tatars . . . each khatun possesses several towns and districts and vast revenues. . . ."[127] Ibn Battuta's observation suggests that such grants were an aspect of the Turco-Mongol tradition of sharing the patrimony among members of the dynastic family. Although the practice of granting provinces to princes lapsed at the end of the sixteenth century, land grants to women of the dynastic family became more extensive. This tendency was in some ways parallel to the accumulation of enormous wealth in the households of the most powerful statesmen of the period, many of whom were *damads*.[128]

The Ottomans often referred to these grants to dynastic women as *paşmaklık,* "slipper money." The uses to which their income was put, however, were for the most part more serious than its name would imply.[129] In the early 1630s the secretary-in-chief of the imperial council, Avni Ömer Efendi, submitted a memorandum to Murad IV that laid out in simple terms the varieties of land tenure and taxes in the empire. When he came to the subject of *hass* (a large grant from the crown domains), Avni Ömer was careful to distinguish between *paşmaklık hass* and veziral *hass,* which he explained as characterized by being assigned to the office holder only for the duration of his tenure in office:

> There is another kind of *hass* which is assigned to some royal women to cover their needs: this is called *paşmaklık.* . . . . *Hass* which is called *paşmaklık* is not like [vezirial *hass*], because royal women are not like officials in being appointed and dismissed from office; rather they possess these *hass* on a lifetime basis. Unlike the *hass* of office holders, these [*hass*] are not transferred from one individual to another; in fact, if an individual is no longer in need of her *hass,* usually that *hass* will revert to the imperial domains.[130]

In their relation to the empire's sources of income, royal women were thus similar to the sultan, who held the empire's territory as his personal domain. This is not unexpected in a polity that still retained important elements of the Turco-Mongol political heritage, particularly the notion that all members of the dynasty were entitled to a share of the patrimony.

These *hass* domains consisted principally, but not exclusively, of agricultural land. A portion of Handan Sultan's income was derived from mining production.[131] Part of Kösem Sultan's Iskenderun *hass* was the port of Iskenderun, which yielded customs duties, harbor taxes, and taxes levied on the port's market.[132] In 1629 the English were in disgrace at the Ottoman court, in part for attacking some Venetian ships anchored in the port of Iskenderun and thus "prejudicing the interests of the Sultana mother, who is mistress of the duties. . . ."[133]

The *hass* holdings of a royal woman, particularly a *valide sultan,* could be vast. According to Naima, Kösem Sultan possessed five *hass*—Menemen, Zile, Ghaza, Kilis, and Ezdin—of which the total annual income was more than 250,000 *riyals,* or 20 million aspers.[134] Archival records suggest that Kösem's possessions were more extensive than—or possibly different from—those listed by Naima.[135] As *haseki,* she had been assigned the income from twenty-three villages in the province of Eğriboz, a grant that was renewed by Osman II and Murad IV, and yielded 394,373 aspers a year at the time of

Murad's accession in 1623.[136] In the same year, the fourteen-year-old sultan granted his mother the Iskenderun *hass*, which yielded 40,000 *kuruş*, or 3,200,000 aspers a year.[137] Karaçelebizade Abdülaziz Efendi, a prominent member of the *ulema* during the career of Kösem, commented that in 1648 Kösem had a greater *hass* income than any *valide sultan* before her: 300,000 *kuruş*, or 24 million aspers, a year.[138]

It would appear that certain crown lands were reserved for use as *paşmaklık* grants to *valide sultan*s, reverting to the imperial domain upon the death of their holder to be reassigned at some future point. The *hass* of Zile, which Naima lists among Kösem's possessions, had belonged to Safiye Sultan, yielding her 1,419,750 aspers in the year of Mehmed III's death;[139] the Ezdin *hass* held by Kösem was later granted to Turhan Sultan.[140] However, a *valide sultan* might devote a significant amount of the lands granted to her to permanent endowments (in the form of *vakıf*) to support the public welfare institutions and charities she established. Early precedent for this practice was established by the wife of Osman, who endowed the income of Kozağaç to her father's dervish hospice located in the village.[141] While *valide sultan*s followed the normal practice of establishing endowments from land granted in freehold, it appears that by the beginning of the seventeenth century they were also converting *hass* possessions directly to endowments.[142] This was another instance of a sultanic privilege assumed by the sultan's mother.

The inhabitants of lands granted to members of the royal family were well treated in an effort to maximize the income generated; this was especially true if the lands were converted from freehold to endowment. When Nurbanu Sultan was granted the *hass* of Yeni İl by her son Murad, the sultan exempted the inhabitants from various non-Sharia taxes and the Christians among them from the forced levy of young boys for service to the sultan. The exemptions were reconfirmed in administrative regulations issued a few years later in 1583, when these lands had been converted to endowment for the *valide sultan*'s mosque complex. Because the lands had been converted to endowment, it was considered, according to the regulations, "even more necessary that [the inhabitants] be protected."[143]

This privileged treatment of the inhabitants of royal endowment lands led on occasion to surplus income beyond the needs of the endowment. Nurbanu Sultan's Yeni İl *hass* generally produced an income of four million aspers year, but in one year during Ahmed I's reign it yielded an additional 800,000 aspers.[144] Even a *valide sultan* as relatively insignificant as Handan Sultan, who had not enjoyed the status of *haseki* and who died two years after her young son, Ahmed I, ascended the throne, converted to endowment lands that produced an income of 1,797,933 aspers in one year. After deducting the expenses of her endowment—the upkeep of the tomb of Mehmed III and salaries for its employees, which amounted to 655,413 aspers—the chief black eunuch, superintendent of all royal endowments, turned over to the sultan the surplus: 1,142,520 aspers.[145]

However, the *valide sultan*'s income could also suffer from the hardships endured by the inhabitants of her lands. A chronic problem was the intermittent sociopolitical revolts that occurred in Anatolia; particularly acute were the so-called Jelali rebellions in the first decades of the seventeenth century. In 1606, during the height of the Jelali disorders in Anatolia, the agent in charge of collecting taxes from lands in Kütahya converted to endowment by the recently deceased *valide sultan* Handan reported that many of the villages he visited were deserted. He appended a note to the end of his account excusing his poor tax harvest:

> Before this servant arrived at the afore-mentioned villages and the arable fields belonging to them, Jelalis had many times attacked and burned them. The peasants have scattered, so that a village formerly of 100 houses now has five or ten houses at most. The peasants do not live in the villages but have moved to the mountains, without harvesting what they had planted. Many peasants fled from the Jelali oppressor called Tavil, so that there is no agricultural or mining production to yield taxes.[146]

It was to quell the rebellion of Tavil—"the tall one"—that Ahmed I set out on campaign in 1605; unfortunately, he became ill in Bursa drinking the waters of Uludağ and had to return to Istanbul.[147] The fact that Handan Sultan's endowment lands in Menemen and Kilizman produced excess income in the same period suggests that Jelali ravages were not ubiquitous in Anatolia.

Urban property and other forms of urban income also contributed to the *valide sultan*'s wealth. Indeed, in the summary endowment deed for all Turhan Sultan's charitable establishments and services, it was explicitly acknowledged that the income she had endowed was of two sorts: "The first part is made up of the real estate specified and the rental properties described below, which are situated in the abode of the sublime sultanate, Constantinople the well-protected, and the second part is made up of the lands mentioned and the estates recorded below, which are situated in Rumeli."[148] The first category of Turhan Sultan's endowment income included rents from a bakery, four shops, two establishments for roasting and grinding coffee, and six plots of land.[149] Nurbanu Sultan's mosque complex was supported in part by income from various properties in the Üsküdar neighborhood of the mosque; in a two-year period from 1616 to 1618 the sum of 220,668 aspers was generated by the complex's public bath and the rents from "rooms, shops, and the like."[150] Safiye Sultan's mosque in the village of Karamanlu was supported in part from "rents in Istanbul" and "rents from shops in Üsküdar."[151]

The *valide sultan*'s wealth also consisted of money and personal goods such as jewelry, jeweled ornaments, and rich materials.[152] Luxury items were not merely indulgences but one of the principal forms in which women invested their wealth. A primary source of cash income was the *valide sultan*'s enormous stipend of 3,000 aspers a day, which totalled over one million aspers a year. In addition, money or luxury items were received as gifts from the sultan and others on religious holidays, at the weddings of princesses and the circumcisions of princes, and after important conquests (the execution of İbrahim's former favorite, the Silahdar Yusuf Pasha, was caused in part by the displeasure of the sultan's court over the modest gifts he offered after an

important victory on the island of Crete). Foreign powers and their ambassadors also were in the habit of bestowing gifts on important figures, not the
least of whom was the *valide sultan*. It was said that after Kösem Sultan's
death in 1651, twenty chests filled with gold coins were found in the great *han*
she had built.[153] This cash wealth of the *valide sultan*s might be turned to
profit: for example, in 1664, roughly two-thirds of the income—54,750
aspers—of the endowment established for Safiye Sultan's Karamanlu mosque
came from the profit on cash investment.[154] In addition to endowing sums of
money directly, the *valide sultan*s no doubt used their money to purchase the
urban properties described above.

So great was the *valide sultan*'s wealth and so extensive her financial
dealings that her various agents—in particular her steward—might become
very rich and enjoy public prestige. When recording in his history the death of
Kösem Sultan's steward, Üsküdarlı Koja Behram, Naima commented:

> The afore-mentioned Behram Kethüda enjoyed great prestige and distinction
> and wealth. As the manager of all the affairs of the *valide sultan* and the pious
> institutions she had established, and as an extremely trustworthy man, he
> acquired a great deal of wealth and property. But his children and his grand-
> children did not maintain the high stature he had enjoyed, and his wealth and
> property were squandered.[155]

Upon his death, Behram's office was assumed by his own steward, Arslan
Agha. That a *valide sultan*'s agent might be closely associated with her public
endeavors is suggested by the fact that a street running along several of the
institutions of Nurbanu Sultan's large complex is today called "the street of
the Valide's steward." Serving as the *valide sultan*'s steward could play a vital
role in the advancement of an individual's career: Turhan Sultan's steward Ali
went on to become lieutenant grand vezir and then admiral of the imperial
navy.[156] Agents could also serve as scapegoats. In keeping with the Ottoman
tendency to blame the subordinates of prominent individuals for their faults,
critics of Kösem Sultan recorded the depredations of her "violent tax-
collectors," who, in an effort to increase their own take, were responsible for
her huge *hass* income. Naima relayed the comment of the historian Şarih ül-
Menarzade, who disapproved of Kösem's power and wealth: "The *valide
sultan*'s stewards . . . collected incalculable amounts of money. The peasants
of the Ottoman domains suffered much violence and disaster on account of
the excessive taxes, but because of their fear of the stewards, they were
unable to inform the *valide sultan* or anyone else of their situation."[157]

Conclusion

The dynasty was served in a number of ways by the prominence assumed by
royal women in the public expressions of sovereignty: its rituals, its prerogatives, its obligations. In a period when it was deemed politically useful for the
sultan to remain aloof from his subjects, public promotion of royal women
helped to compensate the populace for the paucity of sultanic ceremonial.

The vital constituency of the Ottoman dynasty was the city of Istanbul; to deprive its residents of occasions during which the mutual bonds of subject loyalty and sultanic benevolence could be renewed was politically unwise. If the sultan considered it politic to remain hidden within the palace, the function of representing the dynasty in public could with impunity be assumed by his mother. Her appearances in the public arenas and streets of the capital and in royal progresses in the countryside appear to have been deliberately orchestrated to provide a visible symbol of the legitimacy and benevolence of the dynasty and to cultivate subjects' loyalty and sense of community. Her appeal was perhaps especially useful in diverting attention from the numerous military, economic, and social problems that emerged in the last decades of the sixteenth century.

The establishment of charitable foundations and the performance of deeds of personal charity by women of the dynastic family served to broadcast not only their own piety and generosity but that of the whole dynasty as well. The munificence of royal women was felt as far away as the holy cities of Mecca and Medina, where their good works could be noted by pilgrims from all over the empire and from other Muslim states. Royal women's patronage of scholars as well as of calligraphers, artists, architects and other craftsmen had the function of enhancing the image of the court as a discriminating consumer and promoter of culture.

The various monuments sponsored by royal women contributed to the public's awareness of them in a variety of ways. Ordinary subjects might benefit from the services provided in the various institutions making up a mosque complex, or they might be employed on the staffs of these institutions. For example, Hurrem's Jerusalem foundation included a hospice housing fifty-five pilgrims and a soup kitchen feeding four hundred indigent persons a day, and employed a staff of thirty-six.[158] Or they might work the land whose revenues were consecrated to the upkeep of the complex. As noted above, peasants on royal endowment land were accorded privileged treatment: the inhabitants of the Bulgarian village of Bobosevo, which had formed part of the holdings of İsmihan Sultan, daughter of Selim II, today still remember that their village was under the protection of a princess ("under the veil of a Sultana").[159]

The names of royal women must frequently have been on the tongues of the *ulema,* if for no other reason than that the religious colleges (*medrese*) endowed by the women of Süleyman's family came to constitute the initial level of higher-ranked colleges. Appointment to these higher colleges, known as "medreses of the interior" because they were built by members of the royal family, was the first step in an elite *ulema* career.[160] The career of Molla Şemseddin Ahmed, son of the *müfti* Ebussuud Efendi, reflects both the *damad*-dynasty connection as well as the links between the dynasty and the religious establishment: Ahmed Efendi taught first at the Rüstem Pasha *medrese* and then at the Haseki *medrese* before moving up to the more prestigious *medreses* of the mosque of Mehmed the Conqueror.[161]

The charitable efforts of royal women may have served the additional purpose of setting an example that the dynasty hoped members of the ruling class would follow. The role of individual charity was vital in the development and survival of Ottoman civilization. Urban improvement, for example, was largely the result of the establishment of pious endowments for public hospitals, markets, trade centers, colleges, schools, libraries, hostels, aqueducts, fountains, and so on. Establishments for the indigent—soup kitchens, hostels, and the like—may have helped relieve the problem of the potentially rebellious urban poor. The enormous wealth bestowed on dynastic women and the expanded opportunities for its charitable uses in the sixteenth and seventeenth centuries were perhaps intended in part to spur women of the ruling elite to use their wealth for the benefit of the community; at the mid-sixteenth century, more than one-third of the founders of pious endowments in Istanbul were women, but they established proportionally fewer endowments for the public benefit than did men.[162] Similarly, the *valide sultan*'s donations to the military effort were perhaps pointed examples for the elite in a period when financial crisis was more and more frequently met out of private pockets.

8

The Politics of Diplomacy

In 1593 Elizabeth I, queen of England, sent the *valide sultan* Safiye a jewelled portrait of herself. Six years later Safiye asked the English ambassador Henry Lello if she might have another likeness of the queen.[1] Inquiring what she might give Elizabeth in return that would most please her, Safiye was told to send an outfit such as she herself might wear. Her gift included "two garmentes of cloth of silver, one girdle of cloth of silver, two handekerchers wrought with massy gould."[2] Here was an intimate yet serious moment in the business of diplomacy among monarchs in the early modern world. Particularly prominent in the diplomatic activities of the empire in the sixteenth and seventeenth centuries were four Ottoman women: Hurrem, Nurbanu, Safiye, and Kösem.

Participation in interdynastic diplomacy was not an unprecedented activity for royal women in states of Turkish origin. It was an old Turkish custom for the ruler to send a female elder of the dynastic family, especially his mother, as emissary to intercede with other rulers.[3] For example, the Akkoyunlu monarch Uzun Hasan sent his mother, Sara Khatun, to try to negotiate a peaceful compromise with Mehmed II and stall the Ottoman state's eastward expansion,[4] and in the war of succession after the death of Mehmed II, Jem Sultan sent his great-aunt, Seljuk Khatun, to try to persuade his elder brother Bayezid to divide the empire with him.[5] The increasing seclusion of the royal family, men and women alike, meant that by the sixteenth century Ottoman women no longer functioned as ambassadors, but through the exchange of letters and gifts they still could create diplomatic channels across borders. Moreover, the more regular presence of European ambassadors in Istanbul in the later sixteenth century created a local arena for diplomatic activity. The majority of royal women's contacts were with European rulers and ambassadors; their activities suggest the considerable degree to which the Ottoman Empire was a member of the greater European diplomatic community in these years.

A striking feature of Ottoman women's diplomatic contacts is the partisan nature of so much of it. The frequency with which women promoted the interests of their countries of origin is evidence that the notion that members of the slave elite were divorced from contact with their families and the land of their birth is a myth, at least for the most powerful. As Metin Kunt has demonstrated, ethnic origin was not suppressed as an aspect of a slave's identity.[6] In fact it was often the first item included in the biographical notices of male statesmen that were featured in Ottoman histories. The origins of royal concubines are often obscure, but there is some evidence to suggest that people were aware of their ethnic identity and that they participated in the formation of the ethnic blocs that were a prominent feature of seventeenth-century politics. An example of this phenomenon is the following comment of the rebel pasha Abaza Mehmed, known more simply as Abaza Pasha, "the pasha from Abkhasia" (an area in the Caucasus). Abaza Pasha disrupted the second reign of Sultan Mustafa through his attempts to avenge the execution of Osman, the previous sultan. In a letter to the second in command of the Janissary forces, whom he held responsible for Osman's deposition, he wrote: "It might have seemed that I should rejoice at Sultan Mustafa's accession, since his mother is Abkhasian and we have that affinity. But this is not important to me."[7]

The *Haseki* as Diplomat

Through the voice Hurrem was given in the diplomatic life of the empire her prestige was demonstrated to the empire's rivals. When Elkas Mirza, the rebel brother of the reigning Safavid shah, Tahmasp, was offered refuge in Istanbul in 1547, he was showered with gifts and treated to displays of Ottoman pomp. Such ostentation was not simply a sideshow in relations between rival dynasties but a central element in dynastic diplomatics. In addition to demonstrating the strength and wealth of the Ottoman sultan, it served to signal both the status in Ottoman eyes of a particular enemy or ally and its current strategic importance. The Ottomans tended to put their best ceremonial foot forward for emissaries from the Safavids, their principal Muslim rival after the 1517 conquest of the Mamluk Empire.

Prominent among the gifts offered to this princely Safavid defector were a number from Hurrem worth more than ten thousand florins, including silk shirts she herself had sewn, as well as clothes, mattresses, pillows, sheets, and quilts embroidered in gold, and some handwork designed for women (presumably for the women in Elkas Mirza's harem).[8] The political nature of the *haseki*'s efforts is evident in the fact that the entire top echelon of government was required to participate in this display of Ottoman generosity. According to Peçevi, "in order to consolidate the honor and reputation of the sultanate, all the leading figures showed extraordinary effort in giving gifts and favors." So lavish was the welcome afforded to Elkas Mirza that the public began to complain about the expense incurred by this orgy of gift giving, especially since in their view the Safavid prince, a Shi'i "carrying the virus of heresy and apostasy," was a dangerous presence among Sunni Muslims. To these rumors of popular discontent the sultan's response was, "we have done what was required to uphold the honor of the sultanate; we have entrusted his punishment to God the Almighty, should he betray us."[9] Hurrem may also have had a personal interest in courting Elkas Mirza, since she might have hoped that the Safavid prince would serve as an incentive to an eastern campaign. Such a campaign would provide an opportunity for her son-in-law Rüstem to demonstrate his military skills and for one of her sons to be posted to the defense of the European provinces in Süleyman's absence.[10]

While Hurrem never undertook a personal embassy, she acted as the sultan's voice in diplomatic correspondence. Her correspondence centered on two things: assurances of the sultan's peaceful intentions and the exchange of gifts. Since women's diplomatic roles seem to have been associated with suits for peace, it is possible that Süleyman purposely spoke through Hurrem when peace was his aim. Peace on the empire's frontiers was increasingly Süleyman's goal in the later years of his reign.[11]

Diplomatic contacts with Hurrem's native Poland were frequent during Süleyman's reign. Poland sent more embassies to the sultan—eighteen in all—than did any other power.[12] Largely because of Hurrem's influence, Sigismund I, king of Poland, was able to maintain peace with the Ottomans. Hurrem enjoyed a private correspondence with his son, Sigismund II, who became king in 1548. Upon his accession she wrote personally to congratulate him. Later, responding to a letter from Sigismund, she wrote that she had transmitted to the sultan his assurances of friendship and that, in his pleasure over this news, Süleyman had responded, "the old king and I were like two brothers, and if it pleases God the Merciful, this king and I will be like son and father." Hurrem then assured Sigismund that she would be glad to petition the sultan on his behalf if he informed her of his wishes. She closed her letter by announcing that she was sending a gift of two pairs of pajamas, six handkerchiefs, and a hand towel.[13] The contents of Hurrem's letters were mirrored in letters written by Mihrimah, and sent by the same courier, who also carried letters from the sultan and the grand vezir Rüstem Pasha, Mihrimah's husband.[14] Diplomacy with the Polish king was clearly a family affair.

Hurrem also corresponded with Sultanim, sister of the Safavid monarch Shah Tahmasp. In honor of the completion of Süleyman's mosque, the shah made a gift of carpets to cover its floor. A letter from Sultanim informed Hurrem that the carpets had been sent, and assured her that all the people of Iran prayed for Süleyman and the continuation of his sultanate. The letter then lauded the recent treaty between the two states (the Treaty of Amasya, signed in 1555) and asserted that there was no doubt that Hurrem and the grand vezir (Rüstem Pasha) were "the authors and the cause of this good deed" and "partners and associates" in bringing it about. In her reply, Hurrem thanked Sultanim for the Safavid donations to Süleyman's mosque, and stressed the sultan's devotion to the peaceful alliance between the two monarchs. She commented that Süleyman's earlier campaigns in Safavid territory had not been for the purpose of "destroying the lands of Muslims" but rather for the purpose of "repairing the houses of religion and adorning the lands of God's law" (a reference to Süleyman's conquest of Baghdad, the former seat of the Sunni caliphate, and his restoration of the tomb of Abu Hanifa, founder of one of the four Sunni schools of law). Much of the rhetoric of both letters was devoted to expressions of concern for continued peace.[15]

The *Valide Sultan* as Diplomat

The *valide sultan*s of the generations after Hurrem engaged freely in the
conduct of relations with foreign powers. This they did through contacts with
foreign ambassadors in the Ottoman capital and correspondence with heads
of state. Not only were they, as dynastic elders, freer than Hurrem had been
to initiate diplomatic contacts, but they enjoyed more opportunities to do so.
Just as the *valide sultan*'s public appearances may have helped to fill a gap left
by the increasing seclusion of the sultan, so may her contacts with foreign
powers have helped on occasion to create direct links that the sultan, deigning
to communicate with none except his most intimate advisers, could never
have accomplished himself.

The efforts of the *valide sultan*s of the late sixteenth century, like those of
Hurrem, were devoted largely to preserving peace. Their activities may have
been strategically useful in keeping options open during a period of diplomatic
difficulty for the Ottomans, who were embroiled in long and expensive campaigns on both the European and Safavid fronts in the last decades of the
century. However, the *valide sultan* did not always represent the sultan's will
and seems not to have hesitated to act in her own interest.

The involvement of the *valide sultan*s in the conduct of foreign relations
was particularly salient during the reigns of Murad III and Mehmed III.
Several notable features of this period contributed to their prominence: intense diplomatic activity between the Ottomans and the various European
powers, the presence of powerful royal women in Europe, and the extraordinary influence on political affairs permitted the *valide sultan*s Nurbanu and
Safiye. The Venetian ambassador Soranzo noted in 1581 that whoever sought
"grace and favors from the Porte" was required to appeal to the mother and
the favorite of Murad III, "or at least not to cross them."[16]

Perhaps the most constant feature of Nurbanu and Safiye's diplomatic
efforts was support of the Republic of Venice. Because Venice was the European power most often the victim of Ottoman advance during this period, the
two *valide sultan*s' promotion of Venetian interests may have been tolerated as
a useful means of conciliating the republic. Nurbanu's interest was at least
partly personal: she was the illegitimate daughter of two prominent Venetian
families, taken prisoner by the Ottoman admiral Hayreddin Pasha in 1537.[17]
According to the ambassador Contarini in 1583,

> [s]he . . . appears to have great affection for this Most Serene Republic, and
> wants to be recognized as such and to do what she can. She has done me
> many favors, and when I left, in addition to the customary honors done me as
> the representative of Your Serenity on numerous public occasions, she sent
> me [many gifts] and with affectionate words entreated me to keep them as a
> token of the esteem in which Her Highness held me, and of her extreme
> satisfaction (to use her exact words) with my conduct. . . .[18]

In the same year, perhaps at Contarini's urging, the Venetian Senate resolved
by a vote of 131 to 5 to present a gift of two thousand sequins to Nurbanu
Sultan for her good services to the republic.[19] The French ambassador,

Jacques de Germigny, complained to his sovereign of the *valide sultan*'s partiality to Venice:

> Your Majesty will have seen from several dispatches the lack of good will that she has always demonstrated toward the conservation and maintenance of this friendship [that is, past good relations between France and the Ottoman Empire], whereas on the contrary the Venetian Lords obtain many good offices from her, as much because it is said that she is from their country as because of the grand and frequent presents they give her.[20]

Shortly before her death, the *valide sultan* may have performed her greatest service to her homeland by preventing a possible Ottoman invasion of Crete, a Venetian possession. Upon learning that the admiral Kılıç Ali Pasha planned to propose such an invasion as one of a number of possible plans for the following year, Nurbanu sent word to him that under no circumstances should war be waged against Venice, since that would bring more harm than good to the sultan's realm. In addition, she warned that in no way was the admiral to raise the possibility with Murad. On his way to his audience with the sultan, the admiral dropped the paper carrying the proposal, and when one of his attendants picked it up and returned it to him, he tore it up, saying that it was no longer of any use since the *valide sultan* opposed its contents.[21]

Safiye Sultan carried on her mother-in-law's pro-Venetian efforts, receiving glowing praise and commensurate remuneration from the republic's ambassadors. In 1585, when she was still Murad's *haseki*, Morosini reported that Safiye openly favored Venetian interests.[22] Her intercession with the sultan was sought in 1588 in a petition addressed to her by the ambassador Moro: "Great favour has your Highness done me by informing me through your slave, the Chirazza, of the calumnious report to the Grand Signor. It is absolutely false that the Republic has sent galleys to the King of Spain to assist in an attack on England. . . . The Venetian Ambassador begs your Highness to point all this out to the Grand Signor."[23] In 1592 Bernardo reported that Safiye had interceded on behalf of his predecessors on several occasions, helping to appease the sultan for the loss of a galley and to obtain for the Venetians the trade in grain;[24] he remarked, "I always consider it wise to retain her good will by presenting her on occasion with some pretty thing that might invite her gratitude."[25] Reporting to the Venetian senate in 1596, Zane described Safiye as the republic's greatest support in Istanbul:

> Through her intermediacy the ambassadors of Your Serenity have in different times obtained great favors, as you have been informed. She is a woman of her word, trustworthy, and I can say that in her alone have I found truth in Constantinople; therefore it will always benefit Your Serenity to promote her gratitude, as I have many times already by presenting her [gifts]. She has introduced [the custom of] not waiting to see if presents will be given to her, but seeks from the ambassadors either by letter or by messenger what she requires.[26]

The Venetian ambassadors' assiduous cultivation of women close to the sultan continued after Safiye's retirement from active political life upon her son's death in 1603. Reporting in 1616 that Kösem, at that time the favorite of

Ahmed I, was the most valuable ally to be had in Istanbul because of her sway over the sultan, Cristoforo Valier recommended that her favors and her contribution to Venice's good standing be appropriately rewarded.[27]

Support of Venice did not, however, preclude bestowing favors on the representatives of other powers eager to maintain the Ottomans' good will or to enlist their support for a diplomatic or military initiative. In the uncertain world of diplomacy, it was good Ottoman policy to keep all options open; in the uncertain world of Ottoman politics, it was good individual policy to cultivate as many potential allies as possible, both Ottoman and foreign. *Valide sultan*s and *haseki*s were not the only persons to develop symbiotic relationships with the representatives of foreign powers. Many pages of Venetian ambassadorial reports from the last decades of the sixteenth century are taken up with a review of principal figures of the Ottoman elite with respect to their stand toward Venice. Judging from these accounts, many of the highest ranking members of the elite, including vezirs and inner palace personnel, received substantial largesse from the republic in return for political favors. Contarini reported that the grand vezir Siyavuş Pasha welcomed gifts—"the larger they are, the more willingly he takes them"—because of the high cost of maintaining his princess wife (he was married to Fatma, a daughter of Selim II).[28] Bernardo listed gifts of three thousand sequins each to the grand vezir Sinan Pasha and his successor Ferhad Pasha.[29]

Sadeddin Efendi, the private tutor (*hoja*) of Mehmed III, collected gifts not only from the Venetians, but from the French and English as well.[30] In 1587 one observer of the diplomatic scene in Istanbul noted his ability to influence the direction of Ottoman diplomacy: "[C]ontrary to all expectations, the Spanish mission has got the worst of it, and the English embassy, with five thousand ducats which it has thrust into the jaw of the Hoja of the Sultan, holds the field."[31] Money might, however, flow in the other direction: upon the death in 1599 of Sadeddin Efendi, who had become *müfti*, a member of the English embassy commented: "That the Mufti is dead we have to rejoyce, for he would have troubled us aboute that debt of the deceased ambasitor. He was of power and would have performed his pleasure, to Your Worships great losse."[32] The debt owed Sadeddin by the English ambassador, Edward Barton, was considerable: seven hundred thousand aspers.[33]

At the end of the sixteenth century the England of Elizabeth I, hoping for the sultan's aid in the contest with the Spanish Hapsburgs, was a particularly ardent suitor of the Ottoman Empire. The surprising success of their embassy, established only in 1583, was to no small extent the result of Safiye Sultan's favor.[34] Edward Barton, the second ambassador, managed to maintain himself on intimate terms with powerful Ottomans, and enjoyed the unheard-of privilege of accompanying Mehmed III on the Erlau campaign of 1596. John Sanderson, whom Barton left as his lieutenant during this absence from the capital, remarked on the "extraordinary esteme" in which Barton was held: "By meanes chefelie of the Turks mother['s] favoure, and some mony, he made and displaced both princes and patriarks, befrended viceroys, and preferred the sutes of cadies (who ar thier chefe preests and spirituall justisies)."[35]

A curious feature of Safiye's relationship with the English embassy was the fancy she took to Paul Pindar, secretary to Barton's successor, whom she met in 1599 when he delivered to her the queen's gift of a sumptuous coach. According to Thomas Dallam, an organ maker who accompanied the queen's gift of an organ to the sultan, "the sultana did Take greate lykinge to Mr. Pinder, and after wardes she sente for him to have his private companye, but there meetinge was croste."[36] The meeting was probably "crossed" by the sultan, who could not have permitted such a breach of moral as well as political etiquette (Pindar was merely a secretary). Despite the relatively greater social freedom enjoyed by the *valide sultan*—a result both of her prestige and of the generally greater mobility of older women—it was imperative that the *valide sultan,* exemplar of the dynasty, maintain absolute propriety of conduct. A fundamental rule of proper conduct was the observance of boundaries and the maintenance of the proper distance, not only between the sexes, but between persons of different status. Diplomatic contacts between foreign embassies and the *valide sultan* were accomplished principally through the intermediacy of the latter's Jewish agent, known as the "Kira" (the "Chirazza" of Moro's petition cited earlier). Like the *valide sultan*'s steward, her *kira* could acquire considerable wealth and influence.[37] Commenting on the necessity of maintaining the good will of Safiye's *kira* Esperanza Malchi, Barton noted, "because my selfe cannot come to the speech of the Sultana, and all my busines passe by the handes of the said Mediatrix, loosing her freindshippe, I loose the practick with the Sultana. . . ."[38]

The *valide sultan*'s diplomatic preferences were not always compatible with those of the sultan. The ambassador Morosini commented on the inability of Murad III's mother and others to persuade him to favor Venetian interests:

> [The sultan] has always been against my plans, despite my many efforts to win him over, and those of his mother as well, who in truth could not have done more than she did to help Your Serenity; but as he is a true Turk, and very ambitious, he fears being thought the advocate of Christians. . . . I do not think we can hope [to persuade] him, unless we could accomplish it in person, for he holds in little regard what is done through his mother and his relatives. . . .[39]

Advocating English interests in 1593, Safiye (as *haseki*) failed to persuade Murad III to allow Barton to try to negotiate a settlement to the Hungarian war that had broken out between the Ottomans and the Hapsburgs a year earlier; the Venetian ambassador Zane reported, "I hear that the Sultana has tried to persuade the Sultan to allow the English Ambassador to mediate for peace, but that his Majesty would lend no ear to her."[40] Two years earlier she had turned the grand vezir Sinan Pasha against Barton as a result of her efforts to persuade the sultan to sail against the Spanish;[41] Sinan Pasha apparently feared that a successful naval campaign might result in the admiral Çigalazade Sinan Pasha's appointment to the grand vezirate. Safiye appears to have had better luck persuading her son in Barton's favor, for it was after the death of

Murad in 1595 that Barton's career reached its peak of influence, demonstrated to all, Ottoman and foreigner alike, through his participation in the Erlau campaign. If not always able to persuade the sultans to support their own diplomatic preferences, Nurbanu and Safiye appear to have been able to stave off the most harmful of unfavorable decisions.

Several decades later Kösem Sultan and her young son Murad IV differed in their views on the wisdom of a truce with Spain. According to a Venetian dispatch of 1625, "the Imperialists and Spaniards declared that the matter was progressing favorably, being actively assisted by the Sultan's mother."[42] A year later, the Venetian ambassador reported that the sultan, "with a prudence beyond his years," was opposed to the truce, as were most leading statesmen except the admiral Rejep Pasha and Bayram Pasha, governor of Egypt, and noted that the Spanish "base their hopes on these two and the Sultan's mother and sister."[43] The ambassador was probably aware of the fact that Rejep Pasha was married to Gevherhan Sultan and Bayram Pasha to Hanzade Sultan, the latter and possibly the former a daughter of Murad's mother Kösem.

Letters written by and to Nurbanu Sultan and Safiye Sultan in the late sixteenth century provide us with another perspective on the relations between Ottoman women and foreign courts. The correspondence was carried on at the highest level: Nurbanu communicated with the Venetian doge and the French dowager queen Catherine de Médicis (and perhaps others), while Safiye was in correspondence with Elizabeth of England.[44] Nurbanu's Venetian letters are direct and brief, suggestive of an established and businesslike relationship between her and the government of the republic, in which she appears the dominant partner. The contents of the letters are confined to acknowledgment of gifts received, notice of gifts being sent to the doge or to the ambassador in Istanbul, and requests for favorable treatment of persons recommended by the *valide sultan*. Among the gifts for which Nurbanu sent thanks were a bale of silk, twenty-one robes of two-colored damask and nineteen of cloth of gold, and two dogs (about which she complained—they were too large and their hair too long). Three weeks before her death she requested cushions of gold cloth from the ambassador Morosini.[45] Nurbanu also requested favors. One of her petitions was for the freeing of a Muslim who had fallen into the hands of the prince of Palermo, probably at the battle of Lepanto in 1571; the man, Kara Ali, is identified as "the son of Yasemin Khatun the Arab," who may herself have petitioned the *valide sultan* for this favor. On another occasion she requested that Samuel Zevi, a doctor who served in the imperial palace, and several other Jewish subjects of the sultan be reimbursed for goods they had lost on a Venetian galleon. On behalf of her personal agent, the *kira* Esther Handali, she requested that the *kira*'s son Salamon be permitted to sell some jewels by lottery in Venice.[46]

Nurbanu's communication with Catherine de Médicis, the queen mother and regent for the French king Henry III, had the goal of promoting good relations between the Ottoman and French courts. Nurbanu appears to have invited Catherine to send an embassy to Istanbul for the purpose of strengthening relations between the two countries. Here again, it is possible that the *valide sultan* was given the task of promoting good relations with a country that the Ottomans otherwise were taking little care to court, as the French ambassador De Germigny's rueful comments indicate. One issue involving Catherine personally caused friction for over two decades: the French refused to return two Turkish women who had been captured at sea by Henry III's brother-in-law and made members of Catherine's court. Interceding on behalf of the Turkish women were Mihrimah and İsmihan, sister-in-law and daughter of Nurbanu; it is likely that Nurbanu as well played a part in this affair, which was settled only two years before her death.[47]

Catherine, who appears to have corresponded regularly with the sultan, wrote at least one letter to Nurbanu as well. Addressing her letter "from the Queen mother of the King to the Sultana Queen mother of the Grand Seigneur," she requested Nurbanu's help in the renewal of the Capitulations, trading privileges first granted to France in 1536:

> The very exalted, the very excellent and magnanimous Princess, the Sultana Queen mother of the very exalted, very excellent Seigneur, and our very dear and perfect friend, may God increase your grandeur with a very happy conclusion. Knowing the lofty place Your Highness holds next to His Highness the great Emperor your son because of your rare and excellent virtues, and [knowing] that [Your Highness] will always judge wisely and surely the extent to which it is necessary that the inviolable friendship which has long existed between [His Highness's] predecessors and this crown be maintained and conserved for the common good and contentment of the two Princes, we have thought to write you to request, with the greatest possible affection, that you might use all good and appropriate offices in such a commendable work; and that you might also, to the extent possible, assist in the immediate renewal of the existing Capitulations, which have formerly been established between the predecessors of His Highness your afore-mentioned son and this afore-mentioned Crown, as things very necessary for the security of the traffic between our subjects and the lands under the authority [of your son]; in which, apart from the fact that [Your Highness] will be demonstrating that love and maternal affection that you bear for your afore-mentioned son, for whom you always seek the things that can most add to his contentment, we will forever bear you gratitude, and will by means of all praiseworthy efforts cause our sincere and cordial good will to become manifest when the opportunity arises. . . .[48]

The letters of Safiye to Elizabeth, like Nurbanu's correspondence with Catherine, were concerned with the maintenance of good relations. In this they resemble the letters written by Hurrem and fall within the traditional mode of female diplomacy in the Islamic world. But Safiye's letters to Elizabeth also exhibit concern with the material, and in fact the purpose of their composition was principally to thank the queen for her gifts and to inform her of gifts being sent to her. This exchange of gifts between monarchs was a matter of no small political import. It was an aspect of the inseparability of regal consumption and display and the exercise of royal politics. The quality of a gift and the timing of its presentation could cause diplomatic comment. The four-year delay in the presentation of the English queen's gifts to Mehmed III and the *valide sultan* in honor of the sultan's accession caused difficulty for the embassy in Istanbul; the ambassador Barton informed his government of the splendid accession gifts given by the Venetians and urged that the English gifts be dispatched immediately.[49] Conversely, a ruby and pearl tiara missing from Safiye's gift to Elizabeth of an Ottoman outfit provoked the English queen's comment; the tiara's eventual arrival at the English court put an end to a minor international scandal and was noted in European diplomatic circles.[50]

In Safiye's letters to Elizabeth, she urges the queen to allow her to petition the sultan on her behalf. She will be the queen's intercessor, her voice at the Ottoman court. In 1593, when Safiye was *haseki* to Murad III, a letter that was probably the formal work of court scribes and calligraphers informed the queen that "if she will never cease from [sending] such . . . letters which foster the increase of sincerity and love, this is to be made known: . . . while striving for that illustrious princess's and honored lady's salvation and her success in her desires, I can repeatedly mention Her Highness's gentility and praise at the footdust of . . . the Padishah . . . , and I shall endeavor for her aims. . . ."[51] Letters sent in 1599, when Safiye was *valide sultan,* were probably written without the aid of a scribe; they are far less elegant in presentation and style, but more direct, written in her own voice. They suggest that Elizabeth had requested Safiye to support good relations between the two countries:[52]

> I have received your letter. . . . God-willing, I will take action in accordance with what you have written. Be of good heart in this respect. I constantly admonish my son, the Padishah, to act according to the treaty. I do not neglect to speak to him in this manner. God-willing, may you not suffer grief in this respect. May you too always be firm in friendship. God-willing, may [our friendship] never die. You have sent me a carriage, and it has been delivered. I accept it with pleasure. And I have sent you a robe, a sash, two large gold-embroidered bath towels, three handkerchiefs, and a ruby and pearl tiara. May you excuse [the unworthiness of the gifts].[53]

The very fact of communication among these four queens—Nurbanu, Safiye, Elizabeth, and Catherine—and the favors they asked of one another suggest the existence of a unique form of diplomatic contact in the last decades of the sixteenth century. These queens appear conscious of—and perhaps deliberately cultivated—their special communication as women. As mothers of rulers, Catherine, Nurbanu, and Safiye no doubt recognized the greater flexibility of power they enjoyed as influential presences at the heart of government without the restrictions of actual sovereignty. And Elizabeth may have valued the existence of this second channel of communication with the Ottomans, whom her government was so assiduously courting. Certainly the Ottoman sultan, bound by the protocols of inaccessibility, could not have communicated with another monarch with the directness displayed by the women's letters.

9

The Exercise of Political Power

From the late thirteenth century to the beginning of the seventeenth century, the Ottoman throne passed in an unbroken line from father to son for fourteen generations. While the sultan was compelled to exercise vigilance in order to protect himself from his sons' ambitions, he was also concerned with their survival and with protecting them from one another. Furthermore, it was he who was ultimately responsible for his sons' training for the imperial career. With the institution of succession by seniority, the link between father and son was weakened. Unable to father children until his accession, a sultan might well die before his sons reached maturity. Moreover, he could not regard his sons as his direct heirs since any brothers or cousins he might have would rule before them. If the ruler was still hailed as "the sultan, son of the sultan," the charismatic link between father and son that had endured for three centuries was broken. It was the relationship between mother and son that became the fundamental dynastic bond, in terms not only of its political utility—for the prince's mother had always been a vital figure in his career—but also its public celebration.

With the growing importance of the imperial palace as the locus of sovereign power, the status and authority of the *valide sultan* increased. Over time, her political role was so routinized that it came to be viewed as an office with a title. Like the holder of any position of great political influence, the *valide sultan* might arouse considerable opposition, occasionally even that of her son, the sultan. Yet, while she might be only one of several contenders in the political arena, at the same time she had the capacity to assume a supra-political role that enabled her to represent the dynasty as a whole. In moments of crisis, the *valide sultan,* as the dynasty's senior member, could act as an integrating force in the polity, smoothing over ruptures as severe even as the deposition of a sultan.

Mother of the Prince: Guardian and Tutor

One of the key political relationships of the pre-Süleymanic period was the bond between the prince and his mother. The changes in dynastic politics that occurred during the sixteenth century, while they altered the dynamics of the royal family, did not displace this fundamental relationship. Although a new

role was introduced—that of *haseki,* a role which emphasized the bond between royal concubine mother and sultan—and although princesses were
placed in a different relationship to power through their marriages to top
officials, the greatest source of authority and status for dynastic women continued to be the role of mother of a male dynast.

It would be wrong to think that princes needed their mothers less under
the system of succession by seniority. While armed contests among princes for
the succession no longer took place, the transition from the open succession
that had prevailed through Süleyman's reign to the system of seniority was not
smooth. When the heir to the throne was identified (as, for example, during
the reign of Murad III), there was mutual distrust between the sultan and the
prince, who was awaiting his own turn on the throne: the former feared
dethronement and the latter execution. Even under the system of seniority,
there was distrust, now between brothers. Princes continued to need protection. They no longer had tutors and the many other members of their princely
courts who might have an interest in securing their survival. Confined to the
palace, a prince had as his principal and sometimes only effective ally his
mother and her supporters, unless one faction or another within or without
the palace chose to support his candidacy. Indeed, such factional support was
generally brought about through the agency of his mother.

The most vital function of the prince's mother was to keep him alive. One
of the most important ways in which she did this was to guard him from the
sultan's displeasure, especially by preventing any suspicion on the sultan's
part of the prince's designs on the throne. As we have seen in Chapter 2,
Gülruh Khatun, the mother of Bayezid II's son Alemşah, was anxious to
protect her son from manipulation by members of his princely entourage and
to ensure that the sultan regarded the latter—and not the prince or herself—
as responsible for the reports he had received about Alemşah's misconduct.
According to Guillaume Postel, Süleyman's mother Hafsa saved her son from
execution at his father's hands by instructing him to deny any interest in the
succession. A few years before his death, Selim I was said to have tested his
sons' loyalty by telling them that he wished to retire from the sultanate and
inquiring which of them wanted to rule the empire. Postel related that "those
who were so bold as to respond died. The present Sultan Sulyman, admonished by his mother, who understood the Prince [Selim], refused all, and said
he was his father's Slave, and not his son, and that even after his death he
could assume that responsibility only with the greatest distress."[1] While this
story may be inaccurate in its details or even apocryphal, it illustrates prevalent conceptions of both the tenuousness of the relationship between sultan
and prince, and the vital role of the mother in preventing its complete rupture.

Busbecq, the Hapsburg ambassador to Süleyman, described Hurrem's
efforts to protect her son Bayezid from his father's wrath. Toward the end of
Süleyman's reign, when only Bayezid and his elder brother Selim remained as
potential heirs, Bayezid angered his father by supporting the claims of a
pretender to the throne. Father and son communicated their positions
through an exchange of poetry, as the Ottomans were wont to do: Bayezid's

poem concluded, "Forgive Bayezid's offense, spare the life of this slave / I am innocent, God knows, my fortune-favored sultan, my father"; in response, Süleyman wrote, "My Bayezid, I'll forgive your offense if you mend your ways / But for once do not say 'I am innocent,' show repentance, my dear son."[2] According to Busbecq, Hurrem was instrumental in dissuading the sultan from severely punishing the prince:

> Letting a few days elapse in order that his wrath might die down, she touched upon the subject in the Sultan's presence and dwelt upon the thoughtlessness of youth, and the inevitableness of fate, and quoted similar incidents from the past history of Turkey. . . . It was only fair, she said, to pardon a first offence; and if his son amended his ways, his father would have gained much by sparing his son's life; if, on the other hand, he returned to his evil ways, there would be ample opportunity to punish him for both his offences. She entreated him, if he would not have mercy on his son, to take pity on a mother's prayers on behalf of her own child. . . .[3]

In the seventeenth century, when princes and their mothers were resident in the imperial palace rather than in a distant province, they needed to be extremely discreet. They were now under the watchful eye not only of the sultan but of the *valide sultan* and of the mothers and supporters of rival princes. The *valide sultan* was the most formidable challenge to a prince's mother because she was equally intent on protecting the interests of her own son, the sultan. The clash between the two generations of mothers is most vividly illustrated in the affair of Mahmud, the eldest son of Mehmed III, whose mother was not sufficiently circumspect in her efforts to bolster the prince's candidacy. Mahmud and his mother were executed after the *valide sultan* Safiye intercepted a message sent into the palace to Mahmud's mother by a religious seer, whom she had consulted about her son's future. The message indicated that Mahmud would succeed his father within six months. Grown so fat and physically unfit that his doctors warned him against campaigning,[4] the sultan was particularly threatened by this augury because of Mahmud's popularity with the Janissaries.[5] This affair was reported at length by Henry Lello, English ambassador to the Ottoman court:

> [The sultan's] eldeste sonne beinge betwen 18 & 19 yeeres of Age begane to grieve & murmur to see how his father was altogether led by the old Sultana his Grand mother & the state went to Ruyne. she respecting nothing but her owne desire to gett money, & often Lamented therof to his mother the young Sultana his fathers weif [who was] not fauored of the Oueene mother [but] who grieved likewise but could not remedie it. yet she thought wth her self that she would send to a wiseman or fortune teller (for they are very sup[er]stitious) to know yf her sonne should be the succeeding king & how longe her husband the Emperor should liue. answeare whereof was retorned her in writinge the Messenger fayling in his messadge deliurd it to the old Sultana in steed of the yong Sultana who opening the same findeth it was directed to her daughter in lawe, wherein was sett downe that wthin six monethes her sonne should be Emperor not shewing how whether b[y] the deathe or depriuacon of his father wch the Q. mother presentlie comprehended was a plot of

Trechery & therewth incensed her sonne the Emperor who conceaued noe les (& where they ha[ve] any Ielosie they haue noe mercie) called his son(.) examined him hereof who indeed knewe nothing of his mothers action therein he was layed downe & beaten upon the feete & bellie as there faishon is to make him confesse kept him in Close prison & after two daies was beaten aga[in] having evy tyme 200. bloews. & could gett nothing from him. Then the mother was called in question & examined who confessed she did send unto a wiseman to know her sonnes fortune. but wth no intention of hurte or thought of the depriu[ation] of her husband whom she tendered so much wth many p[ro]testacons of loue to him wch would not satisfie him espially the Q. mother but was p[re]sentlie that nighte wth 30. more of her followers wch they supposed to be interested in the busines shutt vp a lyve into sacks & so throwne into the sea.[6]

Lello goes on to describe the execution of Mahmud, who was "strangled & most basely & obscurely buryed" (he was, however, honored after his father's death with burial in "a goodly tombe" by his brother, Ahmed I). Ironically, Mehmed III died in December 1603, six and a half months after Mahmud's execution. Unlike his predecessor Edward Barton, Lello disliked Safiye Sultan intensely, and this account of the affair may have been colored by his views.

Kösem Sultan, *haseki* to Ahmed I and *valide sultan* during three reigns, had a long career as guardian of princes. Not only did she, like Hurrem, have several sons, but these princes were severely threatened by the dynastic politics of the previous generations. The trend toward primogeniture in the later sixteenth century suggested that her sons might well fall victim to their elder brother Osman, who was born of another concubine. It is possible that the significant modifications in the pattern of succession to the throne set in motion during the reign of Ahmed I owed something to the efforts of Kösem.

Kösem was a very influential *haseki* at the crucial point in Ottoman dynastic history when the transition to seniority became possible. If, after producing heirs, Ahmed had executed his brother Mustafa, as custom demanded, he would have been succeeded by his eldest son Osman. The pattern of son-to-father succession thus maintained, it would have been likely that the new sultan, once he produced sons, would execute all his brothers, including Kösem's sons Murad, Kasım, and İbrahim. In 1612 the Venetian ambassador Simon Contarini reported that Kösem had prevailed upon Ahmed to spare Mustafa, with the argument that since Ahmed, not his father's firstborn son, had himself been brought to the throne purely through an act of fate, he should not harm his own brother, even if this was against the custom of the Ottoman house. Her motive, according to Contarini, was "to see if it was possible that this mercy which she displayed at the present to the brother might also be employed later toward her son, the brother of the [firstborn] prince."[7]

If Kösem's lobbying on Mustafa's behalf may have contributed to his survival and his accession after Ahmed's death, Osman's failure to capture the throne may have been caused in part by the absence of a mother to lobby in his favor. Osman's mother, Mahfiruz, was alive when her son was finally enthroned in 1618 after the deposition of the incompetent Mustafa. However, contrary to the assumptions of modern accounts,[8] she did not live in the imperial palace during Osman's reign nor did she act as *valide sultan* (privy purse registers from Osman's reign list no *valide sultan*).[9] Mahfiruz died in 1620, two years after her son's accession, and was buried in the large sanctuary of Eyüb. From the middle of 1620, Osman's governess, the *daye khatun*, began to receive an extraordinarily large stipend (one thousand aspers a day rather than her usual two hundred aspers),[10] an indication that she was now the official stand-in for the *valide sultan*. What seems likely is that Mahfiruz fell into disfavor, was banished from the palace at some point before Osman's accession, and never recovered her status as a royal concubine. Banishment in disgrace would explain both Mahfiruz's absence from the palace and her burial in the popular shrine of Eyüb rather than in her husband's tomb. The Venetian ambassador Contarini reported in 1612 that the sultan had had a beating administered to a woman who had irritated Kösem; perhaps this woman was Mahfiruz.[11] Mahfiruz's banishment would have removed a serious obstacle to Kösem's efforts to save Mustafa from execution, since the party of Osman had the greatest stake in the survival of the traditional system of succession.

Further evidence that Mahfiruz was absent from the palace as her child grew up is the positive relationship that appears to have developed between Osman and Kösem. As a small boy, Osman went for carriage rides with Kösem; he liked to make himself seen during these outings by casting coins to bystanders.[12] Eventually Ahmed interfered with this relationship between his son and his *haseki:* the ambassador Valier reported in 1616 that the sultan did not allow the two eldest princes (Osman and Mehmed) to converse with Kösem. His motive perhaps, as Valier speculated, was fear that the princes' security was threatened by Kösem's well-known ambitions for her own sons.[13] Another possible motive was the judgment that it was no longer proper for the princes, who were approaching maturity, to associate with a woman who was not, according to Islamic law, within the degree of family relationship that permitted open association among males and females. Nevertheless, after Ahmed's death, the relationship resumed: in 1619, as sultan, Osman honored Kösem with a three-day visit in the Old Palace, to which she had retired as the concubine of a deceased sultan.[14] Kösem may have cultivated this relationship with the intent that, if and when Osman became sultan, she could use her influence to persuade him to spare her sons. Indeed, when as sultan he departed on the Polish campaign of 1621, Osman executed only Mehmed, the eldest of his younger brothers, who was not one of Kösem's sons.

The factional strife that marked the second reign of Mustafa, Osman's uncle and successor, is further evidence that a prince's mother was clearly identified with her son in the competition for the throne in the early decades of the seventeenth century. Sir Thomas Roe, the English ambassador to the Ottoman court and chronicler of the dramatic political upheavals of the early 1620s, reported that the faction that supported the incompetent Mustafa and resisted the party of Murad, Kösem's eldest son and next in line for the throne, not only demanded the execution of a pro-Murad grand vezir, but "the soldiours require also the head of the mother of Moratt sultan. . . ."[15]

In addition to protecting her son from the vagaries of succession, a prince's mother continued in the seventeenth century to play an important role as political tutor. With the abandonment of the princely governorate, the education and training of princes was confined to the palace. As young boys, princes had previously received both physical and intellectual training alongside the pages in the palace's third courtyard.[16] Now, although they continued to receive training in horsemanship and the martial arts among the pages, they were taught in the "princes' school" located within the harem precinct. In his provincial capital, each prince had been surrounded by a variety of persons who contributed to his political and cultural training,[17] whereas now several princes might be placed under the tutelage of a single teacher. While Murad III appointed the prominent and highly respected Sadeddin Efendi to be imperial preceptor to his firstborn son Mehmed, on whom the succession was bestowed during his father's lifetime, four of Murad's younger sons shared the poet Nevʻi as their preceptor.[18]

As provincial governors princes had received military training in battles commanded by their father. Süleyman, for example, personally provided each of his sons with careful training in military and administrative affairs, taking them with him on campaign and assigning them to guard areas of the empire. For example, Mustafa was placed in charge of Anatolia in 1534 and 1538, when Süleyman and the grand vezir were occupied with the Persian and then Moldavian campaigns; the sultan took Mehmed and Selim with him in 1540 to spend the winter in Edirne; and Bayezid accompanied him on the 1543 campaign, the sultan's tenth, to Hungary.[19] As Süleyman crossed Anatolia in 1548 to take up arms once more against the Safavids, his eleventh campaign, he met with each of his three sons stationed in the provinces: first with Selim, who was dispatched to Edirne to protect the capital from any incursion from the west; then with Bayezid, who rode with his father for several stations before returning to his post in Akşehir; and finally, with Mustafa, whom the sultan summoned from Amasya to accompany him for several days. Süleyman also summoned his sons and his grandsons, singly and in groups, to join him in leisure activities, especially the hunt, a custom reflected in a number of miniatures that illustrate the histories of his reign (Figure 9-1).

In the seventeenth century, however, there were few opportunities for a prince to receive on-the-job training from his father. The frequent depositions meant that a prince might never even know his father. Or he might know him only as a child: Ahmed I was fourteen when his father died, Mustafa eleven, Osman II thirteen, Murad IV six, İbrahim two, and Mehmed IV seven. Furthermore, he might spend his formative years ignored by an uncle- or brother-sultan who was unlikely, in these times when a sultan's hold on his throne was tenuous, to expose a younger member of the dynasty to the public view. Were a sultan to feel secure enough to do so, he would undoubtedly be more interested in promoting the welfare of his own offspring (as did Mehmed IV).

Figure 9-1 Süleyman and his son Selim hunting. Süleyman spent time with Selim shortly after the sudden death in 1543 of the prince Mehmed, whom Selim succeeded in Manisa. Süleyman hunts on a black horse, and Selim turns to take aim at a gazelle. From Arifi, *Süleymanname*, f. 462b. (*Courtesy of Topkapı Palace Museum Library, Istanbul*)

It was natural under these circumstances that a prince's mother would assume much of the burden of his political education. Particularly if she was or had been a favorite of the sultan—as were Nurbanu, Safiye, and Kösem—she was likely to have acquired a considerable grasp of the problems and protocol of government. From the time of Süleyman, the inner palace was increasingly the central arena of government. Its inhabitants—the sultan's male favorites and eunuchs, his mother and his *haseki*s, and the harem's officers and black eunuch guards—acquired both formal and informal influence over the sultan's decisions. Far from being isolated from public events, high-ranking women of the harem lived at the very heart of political life.

The political education of royal concubines was acquired principally through the agency of other women in the harem. Turhan Sultan, for example, who bore İbrahim's first son and was the last of the great *valide sultan*s of this period, was largely ignored by the sultan, who in any case had little political experience or sense himself. However, as a new slave woman in the palace, a gift of Kör Süleyman Pasha to the *valide sultan* Kösem, she had been trained by Atike Sultan, a sister of Murad IV,[20] and groomed by Kösem, who presented her to her son. Serving in the suite of the powerful and experienced *valide sultan* before she became concubine to the sultan, Turhan was no doubt privy to discussions of affairs of state and perhaps directly instructed in her duties as a potential *valide sultan*. A letter Turhan wrote as *valide sultan* some twenty years later illustrates the kind of information to which concubines had access; in the letter, written to the grand vezir, Turhan questioned the drop in revenue received from Egypt:

> What is the reason why the [annual] revenue from Egypt has fallen to 800 purses when it used to be 1200 purses? . . . During the reign of my lord Sultan İbrahim, may God have mercy on him, and during the reign of Sultan Murad, how many times, year after year, did we see the Egyptian revenues arrive. What can they be thinking of that they send such a shortfall?[21]

However one's political education was acquired, it is clear that seclusion in the harem was not an obstacle to following public events. For example, a Venetian ambassadorial dispatch shortly after the enthronement in 1623 of Murad IV commented on Kösem Sultan's political experience: "[A]ll power and authority [is with] the mother, a woman completely different from that of Sultan Mustafa, in the prime of life and of lofty mind and spirit, [who] often took part in the government during the reign of her husband."[22] Roe, the English ambassador, writing a month before the Venetian dispatch, commented in much the same vein, predicting that the new sultan would be "gouerned by his mother, who gouerned his father, a man of spirit and witt."[23]

The *Valide Sultan:* Mentor and Guardian

The crucial role played by a prince's mother before he ascended the throne was translated into a more institutionally secure and publicly visible role when the prince became sultan and his mother *valide sultan*. The *valide sultan* continued to carry on her roles as tutor and protector of her son. Her prominence and the nearly universal esteem in which she was held, at least formally, gave her wider and more legitimate scope for exercising her power. This is a principal reason why Ottoman writers of the period mention the *valide sultan* with far greater frequency than they do the sultan's *haseki*.

The *valide sultan* continued to instruct the sultan as she had the prince. The extent to which her influence on her son's decisions or her direct influence on political affairs was publicly evident depended on a number of factors, including the sultan's independence of spirit, the number of other mentors with whom he had developed a close relationship, and the degree to which he was devoted to his political office. However, since only those politi-cal matters or events in which the *valide sultan* either appeared publicly or worked through the agency of someone outside the harem tended to enter the historical record, it is nearly impossible to know the extent to which a sultan consulted his mother's opinion on a daily basis or the degree to which she influenced events in a routine and nonpublic manner. According to Petis de la Croix, the sultan paid court to his mother on a daily basis (de la Croix was most likely describing the relationship between Mehmed IV and Turhan).[24] While the relative silence of the sources might suggest that Kösem Sultan was a less powerful *valide sultan* during the reigns of her adult sons than were Nurbanu, Safiye, or Turhan, it is hard to imagine that she was not politically active.

That the *valide sultan* would act as mentor to her son appears to have been expected by Ottomans of the sixteenth and seventeenth centuries. It was considered both her duty and her right. Earlier historical tradition attributed such a role to the mother of Osman, the first Ottoman ruler. According to the late-fifteenth-century historian Neşri, when the Seljuk sultan Alaeddin sent Osman the regalia of the sultanate, symbols of his independent sovereignty, a ceremonial assembly was held; as the Seljuk sovereign's musicians began to play, Osman's mother instructed her son to stand in respect.[25] Standing during the playing of royal music became a feature of sultanic ceremonial tradition until it was abandoned by Mehmed II, who found it no longer appropriate to the exalted station of the Ottoman house. Like many of the events he relates regarding the early history of the Ottoman dynasty, here Neşri may have been preserving legend rather than fact. Nevertheless, the fact that Osman's mother's role as guardian—or in this case initiator—of Ottoman tradition was included in a late-fifteenth-century history suggests that such behavior was considered appropriate at that time.

The historian Peçevi, a contemporary of many of the events he relates, describes as "a mother's right" the efforts of Handan Sultan, mother of Ah-med I, to counsel her son. Describing Handan Sultan's attempts to convince Ahmed to follow the advice of the admiral Derviş Pasha, Peçevi wrote:

> Sometimes the *padishah* would sit Derviş Pasha in the imperial garden and would act according to his suggestions. The next day all of a sudden a huge problem would develop. In fact . . . the *valide sultan* would get her son to swear, by her mother's right and her suckling breast, that he would not do anything contrary to [Derviş Pasha's] words and thoughts. The nature of women is well-known. She thought [Derviş] Pasha was someone free from malice and resentment, virtuous and well-intentioned.[26]

Peçevi's reservations about the wisdom of the *valide sultan*'s counsel most probably stemmed from the fact that the powerful admiral was the chief political enemy of Peçevi's patron, Lala Mehmed Pasha. But while criticizing Handan Sultan for her alleged naïveté, Peçevi legitimized her authority over her son in a way that would have invoked an immediate and positive response from his audience. He echoed an old and popular saying, "A mother's right is

God's right." As we have seen in Chapter 2, one of Gülruh Khatun's complaints about her son's tutor and other members of his court was that they had
deprived her of her "mother's right." Mother's milk was also a traditional
image, one that signified a strong bond of loyalty and obligation between
mother and son and also a source of power and healing.[27]

Of the post-Süleymanic sultans, Murad III was one of the most devoted to
his mother and dependent upon her counsel. According to Paolo Contarini,
who submitted his report to the Venetian government shortly before Nurbanu's
death in December 1583, Murad's mother was the person on whom he most
relied for guidance: "[He bases] his policies principally on the advice of his
mother, it appearing to him that he could have no other advice as loving and
loyal as hers, hence the reverence which he shows toward her and the esteem
that he bears for her unusual qualities and many virtues."[28] As Nurbanu lay
dying, the sultan loudly lamented that he would be an orphan, with no help or
counsel to support the weight of sovereignty.[29] Nurbanu's final advice to
Murad, was, in the words of the ambassador Morosini, "the most judicious and
prudent caution as regards this government that could have come from a good,
intelligent, and consummate statesman."[30] Nurbanu urged her son to be particularly heedful of three matters: ensuring that swifter and more impartial
justice be rendered to his subjects, restraining his natural avidity for gold and
money, and above all keeping watch on the conduct of his son.[31]

A powerful *valide sultan* might attempt to influence important figures
directly. According to Selaniki, Safiye Sultan, seated behind a curtain, was
present at a private consultation to which the sultan had summoned the *müfti*
Sunullah Efendi in 1600. The sultan and the müfti discussed affairs of state,
the former urging the latter to permit nothing contrary to the holy law. Then,
recounted Selaniki,

> [I]t became apparent that the *valide sultan* was listening. She hastened to
> support [the sultan's words] and said, "affairs of state have become exces-
> sively disordered, taxes imposed through harmful invention on the peasants
> of the empire have multiplied beyond bounds, and the whole world is becom-
> ing increasingly obsessed with pennies and pounds and taking bribes. All is
> being corrupted because ignorant and base persons have taken control. A
> remedy *must* be applied to these ills."[32]

Repeating the litany of criticism that late-sixteenth-century Ottomans, including Selaniki himself, were wont to direct toward the palace, mother and son
appear to have adopted the tactic of laying the responsibility for the many
problems of the empire on the shoulders of their delegates. Or, in attributing
this speech to the *valide sultan,* perhaps Selaniki was unwilling, at least in
print, to lay the blame for misgovernment directly on the sovereign.

The *valide sultan* was a principal intermediary to whom statesmen could
appeal to temper the sultan's behavior. When, in the spring of 1599, Mehmed
III showed reluctance to contribute funds from the inner treasury to the
Hungarian campaign, the grand vezir (and royal *damad*) İbrahim Pasha appealed to Sadeddin Efendi, formerly the sultan's preceptor and now the *müfti.*

Sadeddin Efendi in turn appealed to Safiye Sultan.[33] On another occasion, Safiye was directly petitioned by the governor of the Yemen, who complained that his many previous petitions to the sultan regarding the lack of troops to defend the isolated province had been ignored.[34] In 1634 it was again a *müfti* who appealed to the *valide sultan* to instruct her son. Distressed by Murad IV's execution of the judge of Iznik for a minor offence, the *müfti* Ahizade Hüseyin Efendi petitioned Kösem to advise Murad on the requirements of proper treatment of members of the religious establishment: "It is our hope that you will give counsel [*pend ü nasihat*] to him and thus receive the blessings of the *ulema*."[35] (As we shall see later in this chapter, this affair had disastrous consequences for the *müfti*.) As *valide sultan* to the lackluster Mehmed IV, whose passion for hunting increasingly overwhelmed his interest in government, Turhan Sultan was the principal stimulus encouraging the sultan to perform his kingly functions. In the words of the historian Silahdar Mehmed Agha, when Turhan died in 1683, "everyone was sad and sorrowful and wailed, saying 'Alas, the strongest prop of the state is gone.' "[36] Indeed, the sultan's utter lack of concern over the empire's crumbling European frontier led to his deposition four years later.

In works they addressed to the *valide sultan,* writers and poets might appeal to her to guide her son to better government. Mustafa Ali, historian, government official, and critic of late-sixteenth-century Ottoman society, presented to Safiye Sultan and Mehmed III a brief history, extracted from the longer work he was preparing. The purpose of the shorter work was to warn the sultan and his mother that if measures were not taken to correct defects in government, the Ottoman Empire could easily succumb to their ravages.[37] In his introduction Ali alluded to Safiye Sultan's powerful role in government and her close ties with a number of the grand vezirs of Mehmed's reign (several were her sons-in-law):

> Though the sultan does not condone oppression, his vezirs . . . bring unworthy ones into service and destroy the order of the world by bribe-taking. They do not tell the sultan the truth, excusing themselves by saying they cannot tell him such things out of fear. However, they contradict themselves. Do they imagine it will be easier for them if, fearing his anger, they tell the *valide sultan*? She would never allow such disruption of order or such affairs to besmirch the reputation of her dear son.[38]

Similarly, in one of the poems addressed to Safiye by Nev'i, preceptor to four of the sons of Murad III, the poet heaped superlatives on the queen mother, praising her as "the queen of the age, mother of the commander of the faithful." He then appealed through her to urge the sultan to take up arms against the infidel:

> My *padishah,* make prosperous the domains of this lone world,
> It does not matter that the revival of government may cause anguish to the
>   sultanate.
> Your sword has already found the scabbard of sovereignty,
> It is time that you drew it against the evil infidel.[39]

During the early years of the "mad" İbrahim's reign, when he was amenable to instruction, Kösem Sultan may have been instrumental in the preparation and presentation of advice memoranda to her son.[40] Koçi Bey, who had prepared such memoranda for Murad IV, was called upon to do so for the new sultan. Whereas for Murad, Koçi Bey had laid out the problems of the empire and suggested reforms, for İbrahim he prepared simple explanations of the structure and function of different offices and organizations within the palace and outer government.[41] It is possible that Kösem had earlier suggested the usefulness of such memoranda to Murad, for whom a number were written around the time that he began to take active control of government. At least one such work had been presented to Osman II, with whom Kösem was on friendly terms; it may have provided inspiration for those written for her sons.[42] While undoubtedly useful as a substitute for the training princes formerly received in their provincial post, these memoranda frequently urged a return to policies and institutional structures that no longer fit the realities of Ottoman administration.

In addition to counsel, the *valide sultan* continued to provide vigilant protection to her son, particularly during his absences from Istanbul. Because her tenure in office was dependent upon that of her son, she was his most trusted and watchful ally. The constant threat of sedition against the throne, particularly in this period of dynastic transition, made her efforts to guard the sultan as necessary as they had been when he was merely prince. One of the reasons the sultans of the post-Süleymanic period were reluctant to leave the capital was that princes who might be enthroned in their place were ready at hand in the palace rather than scattered in the provinces.

During the Erlau campaign of 1596 Mehmed III gave his mother Safiye Sultan virtual executive power—not surprisingly, since she was for all practical purposes co-ruler with her son. According to Selaniki, he left her in control of a treasury of a billion aspers.[43] The degree of Mehmed's deference to Safiye's authority during her interim rule is revealed in two appointments to office he made during the campaign and then rescinded. He granted the judgeship of Istanbul to the son of his preceptor, Sadeddin Efendi, but upon the appeal of the lieutenant grand vezir, Safiye Sultan decided in favor of the incumbent, and the sultan refused to override this decision when pressed by Sadeddin.[44] When Mehmed received letters from Safiye congratulating him on the Ottoman victory but criticizing his bestowal of the grand vezirate on Çigalazade Sinan Pasha, at the first opportunity the sultan reappointed the former grand vezir İbrahim Pasha, who had been largely responsible for the victory. Perhaps more important, İbrahim Pasha was Safiye's son-in-law.[45]

In 1634 Kösem Sultan moved swiftly to protect Murad IV from a threat of sedition during his absence on a royal progress in the area around Bursa. Murad's execution of the judge of Iznik for a minor offense generated such discontent among the religious hierarchy in Istanbul that rumors began to circulate that the *müfti* Ahizade Hüseyin Efendi was stirring up sentiment against the sultan and aiming at his overthrow. When accusations against the *müfti* were brought to the *valide sultan*'s attention, she immediately sent word to Murad to return to the capital as soon as possible. The unfortunate Hüseyin Efendi was strangled before proof of his innocence could reach the irate sultan. This was the first execution of a *müfti* in the history of the Ottoman state.[46]

In the sultan's absence the *valide sultan* might protect his honor as well as his throne. When the Marquis de Nointel, ambassador of Louis XIV, arrived by ship in Istanbul in 1670, he did not make the customary artillery salute when passing by the imperial palace, both because he wished to assert the superiority of the French monarchy to the Ottoman sultanate and because the sultan, Mehmed IV, was absent in Edirne. The city was scandalized and the ambassadorial community furious at the French for jeopardizing its collective standing. The diplomatic crisis was resolved when Turhan Sultan appeared one day with her retinue on the shore of the palace grounds in order to inspect a ship under construction and demanded that the French perform the royal salute in her name. The French ships were immediately decked out with multicolored banners, and their artillery began to fire, vying with the palace cannon, which were also fired in the *valide sultan*'s honor. Soon, however, the volume and duration of the French detonations began to annoy the population of the city, and the Ottoman admiral sent word that pregnant women were miscarrying because of the disturbance.[47]

Conflict: Uncertain Boundaries of Power

Despite the importance of the *valide sultan* as the sultan's ally, her expanded power and status in the second half of the sixteenth century were not without their problems. Not all sultans welcomed their mother's influence once they mounted the throne or reached an age at which they felt competent to take up the reins of government themselves. This was not surprising: as the *valide sultan* acquired public status and a claim to legitimate authority in government, the tensions that had previously existed between father and son, an inescapable feature of their shared claim to power, were transferred to the relationship between mother and son.

The most difficult task of a sultan was surely to recognize which of his intimate advisers offered counsel that was most beneficial to the stability and well-being of the empire and thus to the security of his throne. While his mother's career ultimately depended upon his own, her power was not exclusively derived from his. Her networks of influence were extensive: her daughters were married to leading statesmen (these marriages were often contracted before her son's accession), her freed slaves were important allies outside the palace, and her influence over important inner palace officials— for example, high-ranking black eunuchs or the sultan's preceptor—could be considerable. The *valide sultan*'s cultivation of these networks, which required her to reward her supporters with influential and lucrative offices, meant that she was anxious to arrogate as many of the resources of government as possible. This placed her in competition with other intimate counselors of the sultan—the vezirs, the *müfti*, the chief black eunuch, the sultan's preceptor, his male and female favorites—who were equally eager to create supporting factions within the governing elite. In an absolute monarchy such as the Ottoman Empire, political power consisted of maintaining a hold on the ear, the trust, and the good will of the sultan. In the contest for influence, the sultan's mother was a formidable competitor.

The sultan was not always willing to countenance his mother's attempts to promote her allies or her own interests, particularly when these clashed with his own. Even Mehmed III, who so often gave in to his mother, resisted on occasion. To a certain extent Mehmed had no choice but to restrain his mother because of her unpopularity with the soldiers and many statesmen. Indeed, Safiye can be said to have rivaled Hurrem as the most unpopular female member of the dynasty in this period. According to the ambassador Agostino Nani, who resided in Istanbul from 1600 to 1603, Safiye's position was tenuous:

> [A]t one time she was taken away from the palace and sent to the Old Palace by her son, the present king, but a few days later she was brought back and restored. She will succeed with difficulty in escaping being removed [again] at the petition of the soldiers, who want her sent to some faraway place, although they do not want to shed her blood. This might be accomplished by having her driven away to Edirne. They attribute many disorders to her, in particular the consumption of money for a most superb mosque she is having built; but she has halted its construction.[48]

The suspension of construction was only temporary: John Sanderson commented a few months later that "the Great sultanaes church goeth up apace, and she rayneth as before."[49] The English ambassador Henry Lello also commented on Safiye's unpopularity: "[S]he was ever in fauor & wholy ruled her sonne: notwthstanding the Mufti & souldiers had much compleyned of her to ther king for misleading & Ruling him."[50]

The most difficult crisis Safiye had to weather was an uprising in 1600 of the imperial cavalry troops in the capital. The rebellion was directed at Esperanza Malchi, one of a series of kiras, Jewish women who acted as agents for the valide sultans. The kira and one of her sons, known as "the little padishah" because of his and his mother's influence, were brutally murdered. It was with difficulty that Safiye herself was protected from the anger of the rebels, who held the valide sultan responsible for the huge fortune the kira had amassed (her assets in commercial goods and cash alone were fifty million aspers). They also blamed Safiye for the debased coins with which they were paid because of the kira and her son's control of the customs office.[51] According to Sanderson, "This was an acte of the Spahies [the imperial cavalry], in spight of [to spite] the Great Turkes mother; for by the hands of this Jewe woman she toke all hir bribes. . . ." Mehmed calmed the rebels by telling them that "he would counsell his mother and correct his servants."[52] The palace was extremely wary after this event of any appearance that Mehmed was the tool of his mother or any other. The Venetian ambassador described the precautions taken to prevent suspicion that decrees were being improperly issued in the sultan's name:

[T]he Sultan, on the persuasion of his mother has refused to issue any more signs manual [signed decrees]; [instead] the Grand Vizir in the presence of the other Vizirs, writes out the Sultan's replies, as used to be done in the days of Suleiman Sultan. In this way the Sultana and the Chief Eunuch hope to obviate the danger which threatens them from the insolent soldiery, and to free themselves from the charge of turning the Sultan round absolutely; all the same, owing to their secret influence with the Grand Vizir, everything is arranged to suit their views.[53]

The affair was not yet over. Safiye tried to have her sons-in-law, the grand vezir İbrahim Pasha and the admiral Halil Pasha, removed from office for failing to protect her interests and save her agent from the rebellious troops. Mehmed resisted her pressure. According to Selaniki,

[S]he decided on revenge, saying "my sons-in-law have become my enemies, this was not the way to protect the honor of the state and the sultanate" and "they both had a role in the troops attacking in this way." She sent a message to her son saying, "If it was determined that the Jewish woman had to be punished with death, did it have to be in such an obscene fashion? Why couldn't she have been thrown into the sea? Couldn't this have been more thoughtfully planned and carried out? If not, it's clear that they are too weak and deficient to manage the majority of the affairs of government and incapable of discharging their duties as ministers."

The sultan, however, refused to meet his mother's demands; in Selaniki's words, "the padishah of celestial dignity stated, 'The vezirs have committed no crime in this affair.' "[54]

So wary was Ahmed I of appearing to be dominated as his father had been dominated by his grandmother Safiye that he allowed his mother Handan little scope for influencing political affairs. When Ahmed was urged by his intimates to grow a beard like that of his father, he replied that he did not mind emulating his father in this respect, but wished to be like him in no other way.[55] Only fourteen when he inherited the sultanate, Ahmed asserted his control from the very beginning (he even mounted the throne himself without waiting for the customary ceremonial in which leading statesmen enthroned the sultan).[56] The execution in 1603 of the vezir Mehmed Pasha, son of the five-times grand vezir Sinan Pasha, illustrates the sultan's disregard of his mother's wishes. Sent to quell rebellious Jelali forces in Anatolia, Mehmed Pasha proved ineffective, and conducted himself so inappropriately as to arouse suspicions that he had turned rebel himself. With the *valide sultan*'s intercession, he was pardoned by the sultan and returned to Istanbul expecting to take up his duties as vezir. However, he was executed at the first sitting of the imperial council. When Handan Sultan asked Ahmed why he had not respected the pardon, he reportedly replied: "[M]y pardon permitted him to return to his place in the council; he returned and received his punishment."[57] When Handan Sultan died two years after Ahmed's accession, he refused to postpone his departure from Istanbul on campaign against the Jelalis for the customary seven days of mourning, despite the appeals of his vezirs.[58]

While Kösem Sultan had the longest career as *valide sultan,* hers is perhaps the least documented. Three reigns opened with her regency—for the
eleven-year-old Murad in 1623,[59] for the emotionally disturbed İbrahim in
1640, and for her seven-year-old grandson Mehmed IV in 1648. There was
tension in the governments of both her sons as each became impatient with his
mother's control as regent. Here we encounter one of the most important
issues in the politics of the dynasty in this period, the boundary of the *valide
sultan's* authority. The tension lay in determining just where and when her
duty to counsel became an infringement of the sovereignty of the sultan.

In some remarkably candid letters Kösem wrote to the grand vezir during
Murad's reign, we can trace the young sultan growing independent of his
mother's tutelage and her resignation to the fact that he would increasingly
manage affairs on his own.[60] His assertions of independence would appear to
date from 1628, when he was sixteen, if not earlier. Murad was certainly aware
that his father Ahmed and his brother Osman, both fourteen at their accession, had taken charge of affairs. No doubt he also knew that sixteen was the
age at which a boy was considered to pass into adulthood. It was also the age
at which many of his ancestors had taken up provincial governorates.

In one letter to the grand vezir, Kösem indicates that she is very troubled
about Murad's health. We can also sense her frustration at her inability to
exercise direct influence on important decisions:

> Letters have come from Egypt—apparently to you too—which describe the
> situation there. Something absolutely must be done about Yemen—it's the
> gate to Mecca. You must do whatever you can. You'll talk to my son about
> this. I tell you, my mind is completely distraught over this [the Yemen situa-
> tion]. . . . It is going to cause you great difficulty, but you will earn God's
> mercy through service to the community of Muhammad. How are you getting
> along with salary payments? Is there much left? With the grace of God, you
> will take care of that obligation and then take up the Yemen situation. My son
> leaves in the morning and comes back at night, I never see him. He won't stay
> out of the cold, he's going to get sick again. I tell you, this grieving over the
> child is destroying me. Talk to him, when you get a chance. He must take care
> of himself. What can I do—he won't listen. He's just gotten out of a sickbed
> and he's walking around in the cold. All this has destroyed my peace of mind.
> All I wish is for him to stay alive. At least try to do something about Yemen.
> May God help us with this situation we are in. . . . You two know what's
> best.[61]

A Venetian ambassadorial dispatch of September 1628 related that Murad
was twice ill to the degree that his life was in danger; it is possible that the
letter above dates from this period.[62] Another letter reveals the same concern
that the young sultan be counseled and disciplined, if not by Kösem Sultan
herself, then by the grand vezir. It also suggests that Kösem Sultan was acquiring some information concerning affairs outside the palace through Murad
rather than directly:

> I heard from my son that he had written you and warned you that [your
> steward] is not a man of good intentions. Is it true that he is giving you a bad

name? To a degree it is a pasha's own men who cause his bad reputation. May God give them the reward they deserve. I'm not referring to anything specific. A friend is one who tells a person his faults to his face. I wouldn't wish ill on any of you. May God protect us all from evil. I wish you would listen to me and have them stop practicing the javelin in the Hippodrome. Why can't they go play in Langa? My son loves it, I lose my mind over it. Whoever says it's good for him is lying. Caution him about it, but not right away. What can I do? My words are bitter to him now. Just let him stay alive, he is vital to all of us. I have so many troubles I can't begin to write them all. You must give him as much advice as you can—if he doesn't listen to one thing, he'll listen to another.[63]

Murad may have felt circumscribed by the close relations between his mother and the grand vezirs of his early reign. During these years the government was managed in relative harmony, principally by the grand vezir and the *valide sultan*. None of these early grand vezirs was a *damad*, although one, Hafız Ahmed Pasha, was married to the princess Ayşe shortly after his dismissal from the post. In 1628 the sultan moved to sever the *damad* tie that linked Kösem to the admiral Çatalca Hasan Pasha, husband of her daughter Fatma. Angered by his mother's excessive patronage of Hasan Pasha, Murad had the marriage dissolved. Hasan Pasha had enjoyed the protection of the powerful chief black eunuch as well as that of the *valide sultan*. He had begun his career in the saddlery of the chief black eunuch's household, whence he passed into the sultan's service as a kitchen attendant and then head courier (*çavuşbaşı*).[64] Murad's move against the otherwise successful admiral may have been the result of his growing desire to shake off the influence of his inner palace advisers and assert his control over prominent and powerful officials of the government. Kösem Sultan reportedly attempted to appease her son with a gift of elaborately outfitted horses and a banquet costing ten thousand aspers.[65]

Contemporary sources present Murad as emerging rather abruptly in 1632 to take over the government.[66] Given the present lack of research on Murad's reign, the most plausible explanation for this change seems to be that the sultan bided his time until he had acquired the resources and personal authority to assert control—a control that was then so total and relentless that it was paralleled perhaps only by that of Selim I. Murad's success in restoring the military fortunes of the empire and in filling its treasures is legendary, as is the cost in the thousands of lives exacted by the sultan.

This does not mean, however, that Murad ceased to rely on his mother for advice during the second half of his reign. As the Ahizade affair demonstrates, he trusted her to look after his interests during his absences from the capital. However, brooking no restraints on his actions, he did not permit her the degree of influence that Nurbanu and Safiye had exercised. Indeed, one must assume that every sultan after Mehmed III was aware of the harmful political consequences of the excessive exercise of power by the *valide sultan* and was vigilant in monitoring the boundaries of his mother's authority. The few indications of the relationship between Murad and his mother suggest a modus vivendi in which each respected the other's formal role. Kösem Sultan figured in public ceremonies, but she did not endow a mosque complex during her son's reign.

While İbrahim, Kösem's second sultan son, began his sultanate under the tutelage of his mother, he ultimately rejected her authority entirely. Saved by Kösem from death at the hand of his brother Murad, İbrahim had been spared because he was considered incompetent to rule. Unexpectedly brought to the throne as a result of Murad's early death and lack of heirs, İbrahim in the early years of his sultanate appears to have cooperated with his mother and the grand vezir Kemankeş Kara Mustafa Pasha. Mustafa Pasha was an able and effective statesman who had been Murad's last grand vezir. As İbrahim became increasingly disturbed, however, he began to resist their attempts to guide him. This was partly a result of the influence of individuals introduced into his company to cure him. Most notorious was Jinji Hoja, a minor religious official with a reputation for occult powers who was brought into the palace to remedy the sultan's lack of heirs. For his success, the sultan endowed Jinji Hoja with the highly inappropriate reward of a chief justiceship, the second highest of *ulema* ranks.

Jinji Hoja's appointment was only one of several instances of the overturning of hierarchies of power and protocol at court when Kösem and Mustafa Pasha lost control of the sultan. The grand vezir was executed in January 1644. İbrahim even tried to banish his mother. He planned to have her exiled to the island of Rhodes, but this indignity was resisted by his *haseki*s, and the sentence commuted to exile in one of the imperial gardens in the capital. According to the historian Naima,

> [T]he *valide sultan* would sometimes speak affectionately, giving counsel to the . . . *padishah*. But because he paid no attention to her, she became reluctant to talk with him, and for a long while resided in the gardens near Topkapı. During this time the *padişah* became angry as a result of some rumors and sent the grand vezir Ahmed Pasha to exile the *valide sultan* to the garden of İskender Çelebi, thereby breaking the hearts of all, great and small.[67]

In another assault on palace protocol, İbrahim subjected his sisters, Kösem's daughters Ayşe, Fatma, and Hanzade, and his niece Kaya to the indignity of subordination to his concubines. He took away their lands and jewels (presumably to award them to his *haseki*s), and made them serve Hümaşah, the concubine he married, by standing at attention like servants while she ate and by fetching and holding the soap, basin, and pitcher of water with which she washed her hands.[68]

The *valide sultan*'s power might also be resisted by grand vezirs. Through the sheer weight of her power she was bound to inspire opposition. Traditionally, the grand vezir was the most powerful individual in the empire after the sultan; now, with the greater influence of palace-based networks and particularly of women of the royal family, the grand vezir often found his efforts to persuade the sultan frustrated. Sinan Pasha, a distant *damad* through his marriage to a granddaughter of Selim I, was particularly resentful of Nurbanu and Safiye's influence. As we have seen, he incited Nurbanu's anger by asserting that "empires are not governed with the counsel of women."[69] Sinan blamed his dismissal from the post of grand vezir in 1591 on Safiye; according to the Venetian ambassador, he "said to the English dragoman these very words, that he knew that he had not fallen through any demerit on his part, but only because the Sovereign had allowed himself to be influenced by a whore, and this was a consolation to him. . . ."[70] When Alvise Contarini arrived in Istanbul in 1640, sent by the Venetian government on the occasion of İbrahim's accession, he gave letters of congratulation addressed to the *valide sultan* to the grand vezir Kemankeş Kara Mustafa Pasha for delivery. The latter, Kösem's rival for control of the weak İbrahim, did not forward the letters, "as if scorning them," reported Contarini, "and told me that the queen mothers of the Ottomans are slaves of the Grand Signor like all others, not partners or heads of government, like those in Christian countries."[71] In the comments of these two powerful grand vezirs is revealed the reverse side of the aggrandized image created for the *valide sultan*. Their need to deflate her image, to stain it, is a negative testimony to the challenge posed by her authority. Even though the grand vezirs themselves were slaves of the sultan, their choice of slander, based as it was on the slave concubine origin of the sultan's mothers, appears to be an attempt to undermine the aura of dynastic legitimacy cultivated for them in the post-Süleymanic period.

Damad vezirs, of course, were more likely to get along with the *valide sultan*. They were often beholden to her for their office and therefore less free to oppose her—at least openly. It is possible that recognition of the potential for open conflict between the *valide sultan*, on the one hand, and the grand vezir and other high-ranking statesmen, on the other hand, was an important reason for the intensification in the late sixteenth century and especially the seventeenth century of the practice of linking the latter to the dynastic family through marriage. Yet even a *damad* might find the queen mother's influence bothersome. Urging temperance on the rebel grand vezir İbşir Mustafa Pasha, the lieutenant grand vezir Melek Ahmed Pasha, who was married to Kösem Sultan's granddaughter, described the trials he had endured when he had held the post of grand vezir. He included the *valide sultan* in the list of those whom he had had to put up with; "I was sick of them all," he commented, "but I made a virtue of necessity, and I got through my sixteen-month stint as grand vezir unscathed." Melek Ahmed continued by advising İbşir not to make the mistake of his successor, Siyavuş Pasha, who thought he could simplify his job by eliminating his opponents, including the *valide sultan* (assassinated in a palace coup); Siyavuş's tenure lasted only fifty-four days.[72]

The *valide sultan*'s great financial wealth could also be a controversial subject. In his memoirs, Karaçelebizade Abdülaziz Efendi, a prominent member of the *ulema*, described a meeting of the imperial council in which the subject of crown lands held by royal women was being discussed. When it was reported that the *valide sultan* Kösem held lands whose annual income was three hundred thousand *kuruş*, Karaçelebizade protested, "A *valide* with so much land is unheard of!" Those who disagreed with him, he contended, did so only because of personal enmity toward him or because they were recipients of the *valide sultan*'s largesse.[73] Even such seemingly commendable deeds as charitable acts could be criticized. The historian Şarih ül-Menarzade argued that Kösem Sultan's extensive charities were misconceived since they were financed from her immense personal fortune; he viewed the wealth she had accrued as an abuse of the empire's fiscal management, especially harmful at a time when the treasury was in severe straits, the peasantry impoverished, and the soldiers unpaid. A century later, however, the historian Naima defended Kösem from the criticisms of Şarih and others. On the subject of her charities, Naima commented that, had her substantial fortune remained in the general treasury, it might well have been squandered rather than spent for the benefit of the populace, as it was through her efforts.[74]

The *Valide Sultan* as Regent

While an adult sultan could limit his mother's political role, there were few limits placed on the *valide sultan*'s exercise of power during the reign of a less than fully competent sultan. Of the six sultans to come to the throne in the first half of the seventeenth century, four were fourteen years old or younger, and two were deemed incapable of ruling by themselves. The first two, Ahmed and Osman, ruled actively from the time of their accession, but the mothers of the others took leading roles in their sons' governments. The Ottomans of the seventeenth century did not use a term such as "regency" to describe or differentiate these periods in which *valide sultans* took charge.[75] This role was simply one manifestation of the historic function of mothers as political mentors. The closest any contemporary account comes to a label is "the duty of training and supervision," a term used by Karaçelebizade Abdülaziz Efendi in recounting the appointment of Kösem Sultan as "great *valide sultan*" to her seven-year-old grandson Mehmed IV.[76]

The first sultan who required someone to act in his stead was Mustafa, who reigned for three months in 1617 and 1618 and again for a year in 1622 and 1623. During both of Mustafa's reigns, it was his mother who made decisions for her son. According to Kâtip Çelebi, "when signs of mental and physical illness became apparent in the illustrious sultan, he was committed to the care of doctors . . . , and the conduct of government was delegated to his honored mother."[77] Mustafa's mother did not exercise sole authority, but she assumed the functions that could be performed only by the sultan, for example, controlling appointments to high office. When high-ranking members of the religious establishment wanted the chief black eunuch Mustafa Agha, an extraordinarily powerful figure in the palace during the previous reign, removed from office, they made their case to the *valide sultan*. Mustafa Agha was attempting to persuade leading statesmen that the sultan's bizarre conduct necessitated his dethronement (according to his critics, the agha found his authority diminished under the new sultan). The *valide sultan,* however, "deceived by his weeping eyes and his sweet tongue,"[78] did not dismiss him, with the result that her son was soon replaced by Osman II.

When Osman II was deposed four years later, rebels removed Mustafa from his room within the imperial palace and hastily reenthroned him. Their next move was to find his mother, who from that point on assumed a central role in the stormy events of the next few days. When Osman was murdered, it was to her that his severed ear was brought as proof of his death.[79] The Janissary chiefs who had led the rebellion against Osman consulted with the *valide sultan* as to who should assume the office of grand vezir; seeing that she was inclined toward Davud Pasha, her son-in-law, they urged his appointment.[80] Three months later, when troops in the capital demanded the dismissal of Davud Pasha's successor in the grand vezirate, a royal letter was issued from the palace in the sultan's handwriting—but almost certainly dictated by his mother—naming three candidates from whom the troop leaders were to choose. Unable to agree, they threw the decision back to the palace, which named Lefkeli Mustafa Pasha, the husband of the sultan's wet nurse.[81] The readiness of the soldiers to appoint the *valide sultan*'s candidate may have reflected their recognition that the first priority was crisis management, which required a workable alliance between the *valide sultan* and the grand vezir.

One of the most pressing of the many problems that plagued Mustafa's second reign was finding money to cover the quarterly payment of the troops. The treasury had been bankrupted by the payment of three accession bonuses in six years, and the financial health of the empire further weakened by severe inflation between 1615 and 1623. Sir Thomas Roe, the English ambassador, described cooperation between the grand vezir Mere Hüseyin Pasha and the *valide sultan* in heading off a fiscal crisis occasioned by lack of funds:

> The sultana mother, with this vizier, fynding it impossible to prouide for the next pay by the ordinarie entrata, haue resolued to chandge the mynt, and to remooue it into the Seraglio; wher they now give out all the saddles, bridles, bitts, stirrups, chaynes, and ould plate of silver and gould that can bee found, to make coyne. Thus they hope to patch up their quiett for a tyme. . . .[82]

Cooperation between the two most powerful figures in government, *valide sultan* and grand vezir, continued when Kösem Sultan assumed the role of regent to Murad IV after Mustafa's second deposition in 1623. Roe noted a surprising calm following Murad's accession: "As yett all seemes serene and quiett; never appeared so great a chaunge, even in affections if not dissembled. The most disordered assume a face of obiedience (which I once thought banished this citty). . . ."[83] Nevertheless, money problems continued to be an urgent issue, especially when the troops broke their promise not to demand an accession bonus from the new sultan. Furthermore, the loss of Baghdad to the Safavids a year after Murad's accession necessitated the mounting of an expensive campaign for its recovery.

Kösem Sultan's correspondence with the grand vezir indicates that he counted on her help with the twin problems of finding enough money to furnish the army with military provisions and its soldiers with pay. In one letter the *valide sultan* wrote, "You say that attention must be paid to provisions for the campaign. If it were up to me, it would have been taken care of long ago. There is no shortcoming on either my or my son's part."[84] In another, she sends good news: "You wrote about the provisions. If I were able to, I would procure and dispatch them immediately. I am doing everything I can, my son likewise. God willing, it is intended that this Friday ten million aspers will be forwarded to Üsküdar, if all goes well. The rest of the provisions have been loaded onto ships."[85] Bayram Pasha, the governor of Egypt and Kösem's son-in-law, wrote directly to the *valide sultan* on a number of issues, and she communicated the contents of the governor's letters to the grand vezir along with her own comments on these matters. Among the problems discussed were delays in the provision of gunpowder, the troublesome situation in the Yemen, and shortfalls in the province's revenue (in 1625 Egypt sent only half of its normal revenue because of the ravages of a plague known in Egyptian annals as "the plague of Bayram Pasha"[86]).[87] The extensive cooperation between grand vezir and *valide sultan* is suggested by Kösem Sultan's frank comment to the former: "You really give me a headache. But I give you an awful headache too. How many times have I asked myself, 'I wonder if he's getting sick of me?' But what else can we do?"[88]

With the accession in 1640 of the emotionally disturbed İbrahim, Kösem Sultan was once again politically active as regent. However, she enjoyed a less compatible relationship with the powerful grand vezir Kemankeş Kara Mustafa Pasha than she had with the grand vezirs of Murad's early reign. Now entering her second regency and fourth decade of political involvement, Kösem was a shrewd and experienced politician. However, Mustafa Pasha, who had been the final grand vezir of Murad IV, no doubt also expected to exercise untrammeled power. The competition between the two was reported by the Venetian ambassador Alvise Contarini:

> In the present government, to the extent that this son's capabilities are less, she is held in greater esteem [than at the end of Murad's reign]. And thus, with her commanding affairs within the palace and the grand vezir [commanding] those outside, it happens quite often that these two rulers come up against each other and in doing so take offense at each other, so that one can say that in appearance they are in accord but secretly each is trying to bring about the downfall of the other.[89]

Nevertheless, the early years of İbrahim's reign, during which affairs were managed principally by the grand vezir and the *valide sultan,* were relatively peaceful and prosperous ones. Ten years later, Mustafa Pasha's administration was remembered as a model of sound fiscal management. Ultimately, however, İbrahim got the best of both his mother and his grand vezir, exiling the former and executing the latter in 1644. The empire's quick slide into fiscal and military disorganization soon thereafter demonstrates how dependent the Ottoman polity was on strong control at the center.

When İbrahim was deposed in 1648, it was clear that his successor, the seven-year-old Mehmed IV, would require a regent. In this case, however, there were two *valide sultan*s: Mehmed had a very young mother, Turhan Sultan, who was perhaps twenty-two or twenty-three, and a very experienced grandmother, Kösem Sultan, the "elder" *valide sultan*. According to Karaçele-bizade Abdülaziz Efendi, then the chief justice of Rumeli and a central figure in the dynastic upheavals of the time, it was considered prudent to appoint the more experienced woman regent in contravention of tradition:

> It being an ancient custom that upon the accession of a new sultan the mother of the previous sultan remove to the Old Palace and thus give up her honored office, the elder *valide* requested permission to retire to a life of seclusion. But because the loving mother of the [new] sultan was still young and truly ignorant of the state of the world, it was thought that if she were in control of government, there would result the possibility of harm to the welfare of the state. Therefore the elder *valide* was reappointed for a while longer to the duty of training and guardianship, and it was considered appropriate to renew the assignment of crown lands to the *valide sultan*.[90]

Karaçelebizade's comment is particular testimony to the degree to which the role of *valide sultan* had been institutionalized by the mid-seventeenth century, for the chief justice usually wasted no opportunity to criticize Kösem.

Kösem Sultan's interpretation of her mandate appears not to have been universally accepted, however. A seasoned politician, certainly one of the most experienced and knowledgeable of the governing elite, she now assumed direct exercise of sultanic authority. It was inevitable that Kösem Sultan would clash with the grand vezir, Sofu Mehmed Pasha, who seems to have considered himself not only regent but also a kind of temporary ruler. According to the historian Mustafa Naima, the grand vezir was misled by "certain would-be doctors of religion" who quoted legal texts to the effect that the guardian of a minor sultan was entitled to exercise the prerogatives of sovereignty. The grand vezir's mistake, in Naima's view, was that he failed to understand that "the soldiers of this exalted state respect only the honor of inherited nobility,"[91] honor to which, in Naima's view, the mother of the sultan could lay claim. In other words, government was not legitimate without some participation by the dynasty, represented in this case by the *valide sultan*.

In any event, the grand vezir was unable to resist the power of Kösem Sultan and her Janissary allies. During an imperial audience to which all leading statesmen were summoned, the sultan, with his grandmother seated at his side behind a curtain, dismissed Sofu Mehmed Pasha and appointed the Agha of the Janissaries, Kara Murad Pasha, to the vacant office. Speaking from behind the curtain, Kösem defended her role and silenced her critics in a speech the vehemence of which surprised all present. She cited the former grand vezir's shortcomings, including his plans to assassinate her, to which she commented, "Thanks to God, I have lived through four reigns and I have governed myself for a long while. The world will be neither reformed nor destroyed by my death."[92] She then berated Karaçelebizade Abdülaziz Efendi, ally of the disgraced former grand vezir, by referring to his chiding of

Mehmed IV: "When certain imperial commands have been issued, they have said [to the sultan], 'my dear, who taught you to say these things?' Such patronizing behavior towards sultans is impermissible! And what *if* the sultan is instructed?" In Naima's words, Abdülaziz Efendi "drowned in the sea of mortification."[93]

Kösem Sultan next faced a challenge from the young sultan's mother. A faction formed around the junior *valide sultan* Turhan, in which her principal supporter within the palace was Süleyman Agha, the head black eunuch in her suite. The viability of the faction's claim to legitimacy—the defense of Turhan Sultan's right to the regency—was bolstered by popular discontent with the domination of outer government by the ruling elite of the Janissary corps, Kösem Sultan's allies. Moreover, Turhan's faction was supported by the new grand vezir, Siyavuş Pasha. In a pre-emptive move, Kösem planned to over-throw Mehmed and enthrone Süleyman, the second son of İbrahim. Her aim was less to switch one child ruler for another than to replace Turhan with Süleyman's mother, Dilaşub, whom she believed to be more tractable and "not anxious to exercise the authority of the *valide sultan*'s station."[94] But one of Kösem's female servants, Meleki Khatun, betrayed her, and informed Turhan of the plot.[95] During the night of September 2, 1651, Kösem Sultan was murdered by Süleyman Agha and his followers. The murder was at least sanctioned, and perhaps instigated, by Turhan Sultan.

The death of this powerful, widely respected, and widely feared woman provoked a political crisis. When news of the *valide sultan*'s violent death became public, the people of Istanbul shut down the city's mosques and markets for three days in mourning.[96] Kösem's murder precipitated a series of reprisals. The first phase was the execution of Kösem's Janissary allies and the elimination of the faction they had led, which had controlled government during the three years of Kösem's regency to Mehmed. In the second phase, popular anger at this purge led to pressure on the new palace regime under Turhan to dismiss the grand vezir, who had carried out the executions.

This power struggle between the two *valide sultan*s illuminates a number of features of mid-seventeenth-century political life. It demonstrates that the palace was not a political monolith. It also suggests the complexity of links between inner palace politics and the outer world of administration. Further-more, the competing claims to legitimate authority by the mother as well as the grandmother of the sultan are another indication of the degree to which the role of the *valide sultan* as guardian and representative of the sultan had been institutionally secured by the mid-seventeenth century. Indeed, in this period when there were no adult male members to represent the dynasty, the intergenerational competition between the two *valide sultan*s appears to be a kind of continuation of the tension surrounding the succession that had previ-ously existed between fathers and sons.

If Turhan Sultan was swept into the position of regent by forces over which she may not have been fully in control, she found herself in command of government by virtue of her office. Only the *valide sultan* could formally represent the child sultan, even though she may at first have been extensively counseled by her allies in the palace: Süleyman Agha, who was soon promoted to the position of chief black eunuch, and the royal preceptor Hoja Reyhan Efendi. The large number of letters exchanged between Turhan and the grand vezirs of the early years of her regency testifies to the fact that it was she who ratified decisions made by officials of state and who at times even initiated policy. Once again, it was the *valide sultan* and the grand vezir who ran the government of the empire.[97]

Turhan Sultan was very concerned about custom and propriety. When she was not certain of protocol or legal procedure, she consulted knowledgeable people or the *kanunname*s (compendia of imperial edicts and traditions) in which such matters were codified. For example, in a letter concerning the death of a Crimean khan, she wrote to the grand vezir: "You've requested a sword and a robe of honor for his successor. From what I hear, it is customary rather for the Tatar Khan to send [gifts] to the sultan. It's true I've never witnessed such a thing but that's what I hear. Now you examine the *kanunname*s and act accordingly."[98] On another occasion, concerned about lack of funds for outfitting the navy, she informed the grand vezir that she had learned that the income of certain state lands was set aside for naval expenses and demanded to know where these lands were and the extent of their revenue: "Bring me all the registers [of these lands]. I have learned that there are regulations governing everything down to the cloth for sails. I must know everything in precise detail."[99] That Turhan Sultan's grasp of the reins of government became firmer as she rapidly acquired experience and widened her circle of advisers is evident in the increasingly impatient tone she takes in her letters with the incompetent Gürcü Mehmed Pasha, the second grand vezir of her regency, dismissed after nine months in office. Her communications with later grand vezirs or lieutenants are more businesslike and contain little of the rote exhortation to assiduous service characteristic of her earlier letters.[100]

When the young Mehmed IV attended important meetings of state, his mother was at his side to help him play his role, as his grandmother had been during her regency. At an imperial assembly during which the inability of the province of Egypt to pay its yearly tribute was heatedly discussed, the eight-year-old sultan turned to Turhan Sultan, seated behind a curtain, for guidance. "Did you hear what he said?" he asked, referring to the opinion voiced by Mesud Efendi, chief justice of Anatolia. "He speaks the truth," she replied, "what *he* says is right."[101] On another occasion Turhan spoke up from behind her curtain to admonish Gürcü Mehmed Pasha for boasting of the wisdom he possessed by virtue of his age (his "whitebeardedness") and to instruct him to implement the suggestions of Mesud Efendi, increasingly her trusted adviser: "Really, pasha! White beards and black beards are not the issue. Sound policy comes not from age but from intelligence. Whatever [Mesud Efendi] says, do immediately; listen to him and discuss everything with him. I warn you, do nothing contrary to his views!"[102] The combination of child-sultan and young *valide sultan* was not sufficient, however, to command the requisite etiquette, for the meeting turned into a shouting match between Mesud Efendi and Gürcü Mehmed Pasha, and had to be abruptly terminated. A letter that appears to be from Gürcü Mehmed Pasha to Turhan Sultan complains about the influence of Mesud Efendi and may have been written at this time:

> I have been dealing with military affairs for over seventy years, and I still have shortcomings. What does the honorable chief justice know about war? where can he have learned anything about it? Every area of government has its experts who know the most expedient ways of dealing with the problems they encounter. Yesterday in the imperial audience he said a hundred things, but the management of the war is not his duty. . . .[103]

As Turhan Sultan matured politically, her circle of advisers widened to include people outside the palace, such as the royal architect, Kasım Agha, who became her personal steward,[104] and Mesud Efendi, a member of the powerful *ulema* family known as "the sons of the Hoja" (*Hojazade*), descendents of the late-sixteenth-century imperial preceptor, *müfti,* and scholar Sadeddin Efendi. Nine months after assuming the regency, Turhan dismissed Gürcü Mehmed Pasha and her erstwhile ally, Süleyman Agha, whose political goals had begun to run counter to her own.[105] Turhan apparently did not regard allying herself with a single element in the ruling elite as the most effective means of implementing her decisions. She thus avoided the principal error of Kösem's final years, when the elder *valide sultan* relied almost exclusively on the Janissary leaders. Rather, Turhan resembled the younger Kösem of the early years of Murad IV's reign, attempting to work together with the grand vezir in the classic pattern of authority shared between the sovereign center and its "absolute deputy."

Indeed, Turhan Sultan appears to have struggled to find a grand vezir able and astute enough to overcome the factional strife that flourished in this period of weakened central government stemming from the ravages of İbrahim's follies and the presence of a child on the throne. Turhan's second grand vezir, Tarhuncu Ahmed Pasha, was instructed during his installation ceremony that one of his goals must be a balanced budget. The seriousness of this charge was demonstrated by the ten-year-old sultan's unusual request (no doubt engineered by his mother) that the *müfti* and the two chief justices act as guarantors that the grand vezir carry out his charge honestly. Tarhuncu requested the authority to institute austerity measures and received an imperial decree to that effect.[106] His lack of success may have been what prompted the palace to call a high-level conference on the financial crisis. Kâtip Çelebi, in a memorandom composed as a result of this conference, provides us with an eyewitness account of its proceedings:

> At the Hijri year 1063 [1652–1653], 364 years had passed since the founding of the Ottoman state. As a natural result of the divinely ordained course of events, there began to be observed change in the society which made up the Ottoman state and disagreement among its different elements. The sultan . . . commanded that experienced clerks of the council and prominent persons responsible for the problems of government come together and de-

bate these matters among themselves and resolve upon measures to relieve the distress. . . . According to the imperial command, the members of the council assembled in the presence of the *defterdar pasha,* who is the noble vezir in charge of financial affairs, and debated the problems of insufficient income, excess expenditure, the resultant impoverishment and distress of the peasants, and the excessive numbers of the military.

All the [previous] meetings that had taken place since the sultan's accession had been consumed with gossip about the past. Here is how this meeting went: a decision was made to draw up written discussions to address the following: "At the end of the grand vezirate of Kemankeş Kara Mustafa Pasha, in the year 1053 [1643–1644], income and expenditure were equal. Let the reasons for the decline of income and rise of expenditure from that time until now be determined; let each of these issues be studied in detail and then let appropriate corrective measures be prescribed." The meeting was then adjourned.[107]

According to Naima, nothing came of these efforts because no one was strong enough to enforce the necessary reforms; the would-be reformer Tarhuncu was brought down by the discontent of influential persons injured by his attempts to economize.[108] The year-and-a-half-long grand vezirate of Derviş Mehmed Pasha in 1653 and 1654 was a respite of relative solvency and harmony, but after his death matters once again began to deteriorate. The integrity of the throne was increasingly threatened both internally by rebellious pashas and externally by Venetian advances in the war over the island of Crete, as well as by chronic fiscal shortages now exacerbated by the costs of mounting campaigns against these internal and external enemies. A serious uprising of the troops in March 1656 that resulted in the execution of many palace officials demonstrated the urgent need for a political solution. It was found six months later when Turhan Sultan appointed the elderly Köprülü Mehmed Pasha grand vezir.

The End of the "Sultanate of the Women"

In agreeing to the conditions Köprülü Mehmed Pasha demanded before accepting office, Turhan Sultan willingly surrendered much of the authority she wielded as regent for her son. The new grand vezir was guaranteed virtually unlimited power in government, including the authority, generally reserved to the sovereign, to control the appointment to office of high-ranking government servants.[109] The efforts of Köprülü Mehmed Pasha and of succeeding members of the dynasty of grand vezirs that he initiated brought about a period of relative political and fiscal stability that lasted until the failure of the Ottoman siege of Vienna in 1683 and the dismissal of Köprülü Mehmed Pasha's son-in-law, Merzifonlu Kara Mustafa Pasha—perhaps the first important political error committed by Mehmed IV after his mother's death. Like the brief renaissance of Ottoman power under Murad IV, this period of stability was sustained, at least initially, by means of severe authoritarian control and large-scale execution.

Turhan Sultan has been praised by some historians who regard her appointment of Köprülü Mehmed Pasha as a recognition that women had no role in the political realm; for these historians, the appointment marks the restoration to the grand vezir of his "rightful" authority "wrongfully" usurped by palace figures, in particular the women of the harem.[110] Such a judgment is untenable for several reasons.

First, it is based on the erroneous assumption that the seclusion of women in Muslim society precluded their playing a significant public role. The institutional authority inherent in what had become by the mid-seventeenth century the "office" of *valide sultan* negates the notion that this authority was illegitimately and capriciously exercised. Turhan Sultan would certainly have regarded her exercise of power as natural and legitimate—after all, she had sanctioned the murder of her mother-in-law so that she herself might enjoy the authority of the *valide sultan*'s office. Turhan's efforts both to instruct herself in the ways of government and to find capable delegates can be interpreted as a manifestation of the role of the *valide sultan* as protector of the sultanate, since political and fiscal chaos increasingly threatened her son's security on the throne.

Second, while it is true that Turhan Sultan significantly increased the power of the grand vezir by guaranteeing Köprülü Mehmed Pasha the security in office he required to undertake unpopular measures, in so doing she was limiting not only her own authority as *valide sultan* but that of her son as well. Her efforts appear to have been aimed at restoring the traditional balance between sovereign and grand vezir that constituted the basis of Ottoman government. Turhan's political acumen was manifested not, as the view of her frequently encountered in modern histories would have it, in the admission that she as *valide sultan* had no proper place in the government of the empire, but rather in her realization that the excessive factionalism of the time could not be contained by executive power confined to the palace alone. Indeed, the bestowal in 1654 on the grand vezir of his own residence to be used for the conduct of government in place of the council chambers located within the imperial palace was an expression of the perceived need to restore the balance between inner and outer political authority.[111]

Third, Turhan Sultan did not retire from an active role as *valide sultan* upon Köprülü Mehmed Pasha's appointment. The year 1656 is a significant date not because the delegation of extraordinary power to the grand vezir was unusual: it had been tried earlier with Tarhuncu Ahmed Pasha. Furthermore, there were precedents for an independent executive authority exercised by the grand vezir, most notably that of Sokollu Mehmed Pasha, perhaps the most lauded of all Ottoman grand vezirs. The year 1656 is significant rather because Köprülü Mehmed Pasha succeeded where most of his predecessors had failed.[112] The grand vezir could have been removed from office at any time by the sultan and his mother. Köprülü Mehmed Pasha's success was due in no small measure to Turhan's continuing commitment to his appointment in the face of bitter opposition to the grand vezir both within and without the palace.

Fourth, Köprülü Mehmed Pasha was, in a sense, Turhan's man. He owed his appointment entirely to political connections that inspired her patronage and protection. Köprülü understood very well the political utility in his era of the *valide sultan*'s patronage. Sent in 1650 to execute a miscreant pasha, he instead urged him to appeal to the then *valide sultan* Kösem: "[S]eek the protection of the *valide sultan*, repent of your sins, and God willing, there is no doubt that you will be pardoned."[113] In spite of his advanced age and unspectacular career, Köprülü had been consistently recommended to Turhan as a valuable statesman and potential grand vezir by Kasım Agha, her trusted adviser and Köprülü's ally and fellow Albanian.[114] Originally skeptical of such a political unknown's ability to overcome the formidable opposition he would face, Turhan did not seriously consider his candidacy early in her regency. Nevertheless, she agreed to make him a vezir of the imperial council; for this act of patronage she suffered the consequence of having to exile Kasım Agha because of rumors that he had given her a bribe of five hundred purses of aspers to appoint his friend.[115] While Turhan could not prevent the grand vezir Gürcü Mehmed Pasha from exiling Köprülü Mehmed Pasha so that he would be out of the running as a potential replacement, she was able several months later to force his recall.[116] In 1656 Turhan ran a serious risk by appointing the unpopular (insofar as he was known) Köprülü to the grand vezirate. It was an act of daring that succeeded. Lacking daughters, Turhan did not have the opportunity of appointing a *damad* grand vezir on whom she could rely. The next best kind of tie was that of *intisab*—the mutual relationship of patronage and loyal service that had come to exist between the *valide sultan* and Köprülü Mehmed Pasha.

The year 1656 is, nevertheless, an appropriate date at which to conclude a study of the political role of dynastic women in this period, for henceforth the emphasis in Turhan Sultan's role as *valide sultan* would be altered. As her overt political involvement lessened, her ceremonial and philanthropic roles increased considerably. Indeed, the appointment of Köprülü Mehmed Pasha seems to have initiated a period of intense ceremonial aggrandizement of the dynasty. It was shortly after his appointment that Turhan undertook the construction of the Çanakkale fortresses and her great mosque—both reportedly at the grand vezir's urging. The elaborate royal progresses between Edirne and Istanbul and to Bursa and other areas near the capital also date from this period. Mehmed IV, who in the forty-five years of his reign displayed little interest in the government of his empire, nevertheless campaigned a number of times as a figurehead *ghazi* under Köprülü Mehmed Pasha's successors. It may be that these royal rituals were planned by Köprülü Mehmed Pasha, or Turhan Sultan, or both, in order to divert attention from continuing crises and the severe and bloody solutions imposed by the grand vezir. With political power and military leadership delegated to the grand vezir, the most useful function that the sovereign might perform was to furnish visible symbols of majesty and piety to maintain the subjects' loyalty and sense of community.

The year 1656 is a watershed date in the history of Ottoman dynastic women for a second reason. After Mehmed IV's reign there were no other occasions on which the *valide sultan* acted as regent to her son. It was in large part the series of dynastic accidents in the first half of the seventeenth century necessitating regencies that had endowed the *valide sultan* with extraordinary political power. Despite the fact that by the mid-seventeenth century the *valide sultan*'s role as regent was an accepted phenomenon, it was clearly considered a temporary arrangement. The choice of Mustafa over the sons of Ahmed I had been publicly justified in terms of the wisdom of avoiding child sultans. Karaçelebizade Abdülaziz Efendi's comment that at Mehmed IV's accession Kösem Sultan was delegated to act as regent "for a while longer" implies that she was expected to yield her authority as the sultan matured. Indeed, through Kösem Sultan's letters to the grand vezir during the early years of Murad IV's reign, we observe the *valide sultan* withdrawing from active control of affairs of state, despite the misgivings with which she accepted her son's independence. When the fifteen-year-old Mehmed IV was forced to meet with rebellious soldiers during the 1656 uprising, the soldiers' spokesman began his petition by thanking God that the sultan had come of age. He then urged Mehmed to assume the duties of the sultanate on his own: "Our fortune-favored padishah has reached the age of maturity and possesses the aptitude and capacity to be a perfect champion of fortune and to be able to manage all the affairs of the sultanate. Why then doesn't he take heed and show effort and solicitude regarding the order and regulation of the world?"[117] Turhan Sultan's relinquishing of direct control of government in the same year was undoubtedly in part a recognition that the natural span of her regency was coming to an end.

The *Valide Sultan* as Dynastic Matriarch

While the direct political authority of the *valide sultan* was ultimately limited both in scope and duration, she was the individual most responsible for ensuring the continuity and survival of the dynastic family. Certain aspects of her power were independent of and different in nature from that of her son. The *valide sultan* exercised a kind of authority that transcended the particular sultanate and reinforced the legitimacy of the dynasty as a whole. The sultan was the ultimate repository of political authority, but as head of the harem the *valide sultan* wielded authority over the dynastic family, particularly after it was concentrated within the imperial palace. Because the sultan's residence was also the seat of government, the authority of the *valide sultan* over the harem had repercussions in the public domain. In a system in which the household was the model of government and the basis of social organization[118] (at least for the ruling class), the structure of the dynastic household had a profound effect on the management of government. As the sultanate became more sedentary, the status of the domestic household was enhanced: not only did the *valide sultan* acquire greater authority, but her relationship with her son was transformed from an essentially private one into one that encompassed the whole of society. The *valide sultan* came to represent the royal family as a whole, providing a vital link between dynastic generations and symbolizing the continuity of the dynasty in times when it seemed perilously threatened.

Reproducing the Dynasty

At the most fundamental level, the *valide sultan* was entrusted with preventing the extinction of the dynasty. She accomplished this task both by encouraging the birth of princes and by preventing their execution. This task became ever more vital as the exigencies of dynastic politics placed the burden of reproduction on the sultan alone. It could be said that, beginning with Ahmed I, the first sultan to come to the throne childless, a new *valide sultan's* first order of business was to encourage her son to father children. Infant mortality being what it was, the birth of the sultan's first son was a welcome but not sufficient event. Moreover, while the generation of sons was obviously essential, daughters too were necessary to the dynasty for the political alliances formed by means of their marriages.

It was principally because of the importance of her son's producing heirs, rather than the alleged motive of jealousy of her daughter-in-law,[119] that Nurbanu Sultan, mother of Murad III, tried to dissuade her son from his monogamous relationship with his first concubine, the *haseki* Safiye. In the twenty years Murad remained faithful to her, Safiye had provided him with only two sons, one of whom died young. Frequent epidemics, one of which took the lives of hundreds of the Old Palace's inhabitants in the late sixteenth century, must have made the possibility of the young prince's death a constant fear. Furthermore, his own ability to produce offspring was untested. Nurbanu Sultan's attempts to interest Murad in a succession of concubines were unsuccessful until his sister İsmihan Sultan, daughter of Nurbanu and widow of the former grand vezir Sokollu Mehmed Pasha, presented her brother with two concubines, probably sometime in the early 1580s. The graphic account by the historian Peçevi of Murad's subsequent impotence, the *valide sultan's* discovery and dispelling of a hex that had supposedly been cast on the sultan by the *haseki sultan,* and his ensuing concupiscence (resulting in the birth of nineteen more surviving sons before his death in 1595) is surprising to the modern reader for what appears to be its prurient interest but more likely represents contemporary concern with a politically vital activity of the sultanate.[120]

As *valide sultan* to Murad IV, Kösem Sultan's principal effort in protecting the dynasty appears to have been dissuading the sultan from executing all his brothers toward the end of his reign. The princes Bayezid and Süleyman were executed during the celebrations over the victory at Erivan (1635) and Kasım, Kösem's own son, during the Baghdad campaign. Only Kösem Sultan's plea that the sole surviving prince, İbrahim—also her own son—was incapable of governing prevented his execution and thereby saved the dynasty from extinction. During the first two years of the hapless İbrahim's reign, the dynasty experienced its most perilous moment, for the emotionally disturbed sultan failed to produce any children. Kösem Sultan's task was to encourage the repopulation of the dynasty—an obligation İbrahim ultimately met so successfully (perhaps the only sultanic duty that he adequately discharged) that the final words he spoke as sultan were, "I am the father of a dynasty!"[121] It was the *valide sultan* who presented the sultan with his first concubine, Turhan, the birth of whose son, the future Mehmed IV, caused great rejoicing both within and without the palace.

As with Murad III, pressure on the sultan to father children, which took the form of a flow into the harem of concubines presented by leading state officials, resulted in a greater interest on İbrahim's part in the pleasures of the bed than either the palace or the outer administration might have wished. His obsession led to notorious extravagances that depleted the treasury and ultimately led to his dethronement. Kösem Sultan has been blamed for encouraging İbrahim's interest in procreation—she is alleged to have diverted him with cuncubines so she might take over the reins of government—but her motive, at least originally, was the perpetuation of the dynasty. Moreover, like others, Kösem rued the inordinate influence İbrahim's concubines came to have over public affairs. During the final chaotic weeks of İbrahim's reign, Kösem Sultan was once again cast into the role of protector of the dynasty when the Janissary aghas, planning to demand the dismissal of the unpopular grand vezir, sent word that she should take extreme precautions to ensure the safety of the princes.[122]

As he came of age, İbrahim's son and successor, Mehmed IV, wanted to invoke the practice of fratricide in favor of his sons Mustafa and Ahmed, both born of his beloved *haseki* Rabia Gülnüş Sultan. Public opinion, however, had come to regard the practice of fratricide as effectively lapsed. It was the *valide sultan* Turhan who assumed the responsibility of protecting Mehmed's brothers, Süleyman and Ahmed, neither of whom was her own son.[123] According to the French ambassador, the Marquis de Nointel, who during a visit to Edirne in 1673 had the *valide sultan* as an unexpected neighbor on the midcity island on which he was lodged, Turhan Sultan exercised constant vigilance over the two princes. She had been summoned several times to the court in Edirne (where the sultan spent much of his time) but had hesitated to go for fear that if she brought her son's two brothers, he would have them executed.[124] The *valide sultan* appears to have kept the two princes always at her side during her many migrations between Istanbul and Edirne.[125] According to Galland, de Nointel's secretary, the sultan planned to construct a separate palace in Edirne for his mother and his two brothers.[126]

Preserving Dynastic Continuity

The death of a sultan was always a time of potential dynastic crisis. Until the lapse of the princely governorate, a number of days might pass between the death of the sultan and the arrival in Istanbul of his successor. The news of the death of Süleyman, which occurred while the sultan was heading a military campaign in Europe, was concealed for more than five weeks while word was sent to his heir, Selim II, who journeyed at top speed from his post in Kütahya to meet the imperial troops and pray over his father's corpse. During the waiting period the grand vezir Sokollu Mehmed Pasha had the sultan impersonated by an official who sat dressed in the sultan's robes and turban in the imperial carriage, while another official, whose handwriting resembled Süleyman's, issued written orders.

Interregnums were periods of social disruption. Because of the personal nature of the bond between sultan and subjects, oaths of loyalty were considered to have lapsed at the death of a sultan. This led to the practice of looting and general insubordination until the next sultan had been enthroned and could demand the obedience of his subjects. At these times of potential disruption, royal women played a vital role in preserving dynastic continuity: by hiding the death of the old sultan and thus preventing social disruption, by protecting the interests of the new sultan, and by preserving the traditions of the dynasty.

The death or deposition of a sultan was the event that transformed the concubine mother of the heir into the *valide sultan*. Her very first duty was to ensure the smooth accession of her son. The responsibilities of Nurbanu Sultan toward her son Murad III and Safiye Sultan toward Mehmed III were particularly great because of the presence of the new sultans' younger brothers in the capital. According to the historian Selaniki, when Selim II died, Nurbanu had his body preserved in ice until her son Murad could arrive from his post at Manisa, see to his brothers' execution, and then bury his father. No one was informed of the sultan's death except the grand vezir Sokollu Mehmed Pasha, the courier sent to notify the prince, the admiral Kılıç Ali Pasha, who set out to transport the new sultan across the Sea of Marmara, and presumably a few others who had to be informed.[127] When Murad III died, the grand vezir Ferhad Pasha wanted to send another vezir to fetch the new sultan, Mehmed III, but, according to the ambassador Marco Venier, "the Sultanas declared that this sudden departure would waken suspicion. Accordingly they resolved to send the . . . chief gardener, in the middle-sized caique, as he was accustomed to go every day to . . . fetch water for the Sultan's use."[128] New sultans made their way to the harem at the earliest opportunity after arriving in the capital: Selim II sought his sister Mihrimah (his mother Hurrem had died eight years earlier), and both Murad and Mehmed conferred with their mothers. This urgency no doubt reflected the new sultans' need to be informed of the political situation in the capital by a trusted ally, as well as their desire to be reunited with loved ones. It also reflects the importance of female elders in the hierarchy of the imperial household.

Venier's dispatches from the days following Murad III's death provide a sense of the tension rife in the capital during this uncertain period (obviously the palace's attempt to hide the sultan's death was not entirely successful). He reported that he had hidden the embassy archives and brought in armed men to protect his house because of his fear that it might be looted or burned:

> The rumour of the Sultan's death has spread down to the very children; and a riot is expected, accompanied by a sack of shops and houses as usual. . . . In the eleven days which have elapsed since the death of the Sultan Murad, several executions have taken place in order to keep the populace in check. Inside the serraglio there has been a great uproar, and every night we hear guns fired—a sign that at that moment some one is being thrown into the sea.[129]

Venier also reported that before his death, Murad had ordered the eldest of his sons, Mahmud, to be placed in safekeeping "so that the women of the harem should not make away with him."[130] Presumably Murad feared that Mahmud's partisans within the harem would try to save him from execution or perhaps even attempt his enthronement.

The *valide sultan* might also act to preserve custom in the enthronement of a new sultan. When the group of government officers who had decided that İbrahim must be removed from office demanded that the palace send the sultan's seven-year-old son to be enthroned in a mosque, Kösem Sultan refused to comply and demanded that they come to the palace instead. She based her refusal on the grounds that no sultan had ever been enthroned in a mosque.[131] No doubt her motivation was in part to force the occasion to take place where she could have some control over the course of events. At issue was not only the preservation of her own authority but also the welfare of the new sultan, a small boy who might be psychologically harmed by suddenly being thrust into a world of which he had had no previous experience.

The role of the *valide sultan* during the crises of deposition reveals another aspect of her unique authority within the dynastic family: she provided sanction for these potential ruptures in dynastic continuity. One of the most salient features of the seventeenth-century history of the sultanate was the advent of deposition by soldiers and statesmen. Whereas no popular depositions had occurred before the reign of Süleyman, of the twenty-seven sultans following him, thirteen were forcibly deposed.[132] A number of explanations for this phenomenon can be suggested.

Of central importance were changes in dynastic politics. The increasingly sedentary nature of the sultanate brought about a transformation in the basis of sultanic legitimacy, outlined in Chapter 1. Sultans no longer established their right to rule by proving themselves victorious over their brothers and therefore, in theory, more qualified to rule, or by being designated heir by their fathers. Instead, they were passively brought to the throne as a result of dynastic accident or the new system of succession by seniority. This was particularly true in the first half of the seventeenth century, when no sultan ascended the throne as an adult possessed of full mental competence. Weak or unpopular dynasts might no longer be disqualified before coming to the throne. Deposition was the only way for subjects to rid the polity of rulers who proved to be, or were perceived to be, incompetent. Furthermore, the consolidation of the imperial family in the capital afforded discontented statesmen and soldiers easy access to princes who might be substituted for an unpopular sultan.

These changes had the effect of subtly altering the relation of subjects to their sultan. With the lapse of open succession and the princely governorate, a prince became sultan without the legitimating aura of victory over his brothers or designation by his father. Moreover, the duties of loyalty were no longer personally enjoined by the sultan through his public leadership of government, nor were the rewards of loyalty personally bestowed. From a sultan on campaign, the ordinary soldier might hope for the honor of personal recognition and recompense. On holy days during campaigns, the sultan prayed in the midst of his troops, and then, following an ancient ritual, allowed them to playfully devour his holiday meal.[133] In the capital, petitions for the redress of grievances might be pressed by the ordinary citizen on a sultan who assiduously pursued his duty of attending Friday prayers with his subjects. But the diminished public role of the sultans following Süleyman meant that there were fewer opportunities for the renewal of the mutual bonds of bounty and loyalty, of justice and service, between ruler and ruled. Loyalty of its subjects to the House of Osman appears in the seventeenth century to have become more abstract, a loyalty more to the dynasty than to the individual. Islamic norms regarding the theoretical qualifications of the ruler began to be invoked more frequently in debates about eligibility, and *müftis* became more involved in decisions as to who should rule. Noting this shift in the relationship between ruler and ruled, we can better reconcile what at first seem to be irreconcilable attitudes on the part of the people toward the sultanate: the absolute devotion of its subjects to the Ottoman dynasty, so that the substitution of another ruling house was never considered, yet absolute scorn for a deposed sultan, exemplified by the treatment meted out to Osman II as he was dragged through the main streets of the city.

Another factor in the frequency of depositions was the fact that since the second half of the sixteenth century, Janissary and imperial cavalry troops stationed in the capital had become increasingly willing to voice their grievances through uprisings.[134] The problems created by the troops and the government's difficulties in paying them form a constantly recurring theme in the histories, reform tracts, and government documents of this period. The causes and consequences of their discontent were many and complex, and will only be briefly mentioned here. Chronic fiscal problems resulted in delays in the troops' quarterly payments and sometimes failure to pay them at all; when they were paid, it was often with debased coinage that merchants would refuse to accept. Military campaigns now brought less booty, and the mercenary troops increasingly employed in warfare competed with the imperial troops for their share of what war profit could be had.[135] The numbers of troops stationed in the capital swelled enormously through the legally dubious enrollment of unqualified persons in their ranks, creating greater competition for scarce salary resources and for alternate employment in the city. In the uprising of 1656, one unpaid member of the imperial cavalry described his situation to the sultan in these words: "[W]e languish in the corners of boarding houses hungry and impoverished, and our stipends aren't even enough to cover our debts to the landlords."[136] There was no lack in the capital of potential allies in a demonstration against the sultan: merchants and tradesmen, members of the religious establishment, factions among the governing elite, both within and without the palace, and the rootless mass of immigrants to the capital.

It is in this changing political environment that the significance of the *valide sultan*'s role in depositions can best be understood. The mother of the deposed sultan performed the function of providing sanction for the rejection of the *individual* sultan, thus allowing *dynastic* legitimacy to be preserved. The mothers of three of the five seventeenth-century sultans who were deposed–Mustafa, İbrahim, and Mustafa II (r. 1695–1703)—were alive at the time of their sons' depositions. There is evidence to suggest that each of these women was formally petitioned by the highest officers of state—the grand vezir and the *müfti*—not only to approve but also to assist in the transfer of authority.

When it became clear to all that Mustafa's mental incompetence was such that his continued rule was harmful to the empire, his mother assented to the petition of *ulema* leaders that she meet with the grand vezir and *müfti* to sanction his deposition. She requested, however, that he be spared execution.[137] The deposition of İbrahim in 1648 was formally accomplished only after a long confrontation between the *valide sultan* Kösem and leading statesmen who had come to the decision that the unbalanced sultan's conduct could no longer be tolerated.[138] The lengthy and dramatic account of the event by the historian Naima is an indication of its historical importance.

The extended debate during which the assembled statesmen tried to persuade Kösem of the propriety and legality of the deposition reveals the complexity of the *valide sultan*'s role. The confrontation between Kösem and the assembled statesmen over İbrahim's deposition was actually a bit of a sham, since Kösem was by this point anxious to get rid of her son, whose disastrous administration had undone the restorative work done by his elder brother. To the grand vezir Hezarpare Ahmed Pasha she had written, "In the end he will leave neither you nor me alive. We will lose control of the government. The whole society is in ruins. Have him removed from the throne immediately."[139] Nevertheless, it was necessary that she publicly resist the deposition, since it was expected of her that she invoke her roles as protector and mentor rather than appear too eager to sanction her son's demise. When urged to carry out İbrahim's overthrow and deliver the child Mehmed to be enthroned, Kösem Sultan pleaded at great length against the deposition, giving in only after attempting to counter the several arguments adduced by the statesmen. Naima explains Kösem Sultan's efforts as stemming from maternal compassion so strong that it overrode the anger and sorrow she felt at the sultan's ruination of the state and his mistreatment of her and her daughters.[140]

The *valide sultan*'s resistance fulfilled another purpose: it allowed important political arguments to be rehearsed. Kösem reminded the politicians of the need for loyalty to the dynasty: "Wasn't every single one of you raised up through the benevolence of the Ottoman dynasty?" They countered with the imperative of the holy law: a mentally impaired individual cannot govern the *umma,* the community of Muslim believers. At a key point in the discussion, the statesmen employed a brilliant strategy: they addressed the *valide sultan* as *umm al-mu'minin,* "mother of the [Muslim] believers."[141] An honorific title that had been bestowed through Qur'anic revelation on the wives of the Prophet Muhammad, this accolade endowed Kösem with an identity that enabled her to extend her maternal role as mentor/guardian beyond her son and the dynasty to the empire, indeed to the whole Muslim community, and thus to sanction the deposition. Furthermore, it allowed her to mediate the two contending forces in the Ottoman polity: the sovereign authority of the dynasty and the law of Islam.

That this legitimizing function of the *valide sultan* became routinized is suggested by the events surrounding the deposition of Mustafa II in 1703. His mother, Rabia Gülnüş Sultan, had played a comparatively minor public role during her son's reign. Yet she was petitioned to approve and apparently to effect the deposition of Mustafa and the enthronement of her second son, Ahmed III. Sending separate replies to the petitions of the grand vezir and the *müfti*, she wrote, "All of you have requested in concord and unanimity that my majestic son Sultan Ahmed be seated on the imperial throne and that my other son Sultan Mustafa be deposed. Your petition has been complied with."[142]

The *valide sultan*'s role in these dramatic events was to some degree a formality: she was asked to ratify a decision that had already been made by leading politicians and religious dignitaries. Yet her sanction of the forcible transfer of power from one sultan to another was necessary because it symbolically prevented the rupturing of dynastic continuity. Despite the fact that Islamic legal tradition allowed rebellion against a sovereign who prevented the pursuit of the proper Muslim life (it was precisely this kind of argument that had been put forth to justify İbrahim's deposition), the devotion of Ottomans to their dynasty was so great that the rebellion of the sultan's servants against their master appeared to violate their oath of loyalty to their sovereign and to return ingratitude for the bounty he had bestowed on them (it was principally with this argument that Kösem Sultan countered the religio-legal argument). In being called upon to legitimate the subjects' withdrawal of their loyalty, the *valide sultan*, as the senior member of the royal family, was endowed with the responsibility of representing the welfare of the dynasty as a whole, even if this meant sacrificing the interest of a particular sultan.

There was another aspect to the *valide sultan*'s crucial role in the transfer of sovereignty. With the lapse of the princely governorate and the decline of sultanic *ghaza*, this transfer occurred within the palace. The new sultan no longer arrived in Istanbul after a hurried and well-guarded journey from his provincial capital, awaited by the leading officers of state who immediately performed the ritual gestures of obeisance that invested him with sovereignty. Moreover, it was not always simply a question of inaugurating the new sultan. In the case of a deposition, the former sultan had to be convinced to give up his station and the new sultan had to be brought out from his quarters. These crucial moments had to be attended to by individuals who possessed the requisite status and authority to enter the inner precincts of the palace. It would have been a violation of the sanctity of the imperial residence for statesmen to have forcibly done so. The *valide sultan*, as head of the imperial harem, was the one individual who could sanction the crossing of its boundary if necessary. In the absence of the sultan, she was the one individual who could exercise authority in both the outer and inner worlds of government.

CONCLUSION

Women, Sovereignty, and Society

The Ottoman sultans and their families mattered very much to their subjects. On both an ideological and a practical plane, their proper conduct was thought to be essential to the well-being of the empire: if the sultan's household was disordered, so the administration of the state was likely to become disordered. Furthermore, through the wide-reaching networks centered in its household, the dynasty was the ultimate source of favors. Yet the subjects of the empire were not without influence on their sovereigns. The Ottoman sultanate was not an unlimited despotism; while the sultan enjoyed the power of summary punishment, he had to operate within the parameters of public opinion. Moreover, family politics in the House of Osman were constrained by the views of ordinary subjects. While we know little about the structure and mores of the ordinary family in this period, we do know something about how people expected their rulers to behave. The subjects of the sultan appear to have accepted the fact that the dynastic household ordered some of its relationships differently from the ordinary family, but this did not prevent them from expressing their approval or disapproval. Furthermore, they were quick to protest what they perceived to be the dynasty's infringements of its own rules. In this final chapter, I would like to explore briefly the social and cultural environment that shaped the expectations and reactions of sixteenth- and seventeenth-century subjects of the dynasty to the political influence of royal women.[1]

One influential view of women and their proper roles—a view that has been uncritically accepted by many historians as representative of broad popular thinking—was the typically misogynist perspective of the *ulema,* members of the corps of scholars and clerics trained in the religious sciences. Let us return to the incident with which this book opened: the *müfti* Sunullah's public castigation in 1599 of the political activity of royal women. While the *müfti*'s objection to women's influence was in part a tactic aimed at preserving his own authority, it was framed in terms that were likely to elicit a deeper reaction in his audience. His criticism recalled an oft-quoted saying or tradition (*hadith*) attributed to the Prophet Muhammad which pointed to the harmful consequences of female sovereignty: "[A] people who entrusts its affairs to a woman will never know prosperity."[2] The Muslim feminist Fatima Mernissi has argued that this tradition was exploited by the medieval Muslim religious elite, uniformly male, to preserve its authority over society, thus

267

distorting Islam's original message of equality between the sexes.[3] Other scholars, Muslim and non-Muslim, have debated the degree to which the nascent Muslim community provided positive models for women's participation and influence in the community.[4]

The controversy in Muslim society over the public role of women took as one of its principal arenas of debate the career of Muhammad's third and much-cherished wife, 'A'isha, who was known as the "beloved of the Prophet of God."[5] It was precisely because she had the greatest public influence, through her special relation to the Prophet as well as her own piety, learning, and forceful character, that 'A'isha was the most controversial woman of the first Muslim generation. Twenty-four years after Muhammad's death, 'A'isha took to the field, indeed to the battlefield, to prevent leadership of the Muslim community from passing into the hands of Ali, the Prophet's cousin and son-in-law. Denise Spellberg argues that this partisan activism was in keeping with the prominent roles played by women of status in the seventh-century political environment in which the new religion arose.[6] Yet in the social milieu of the ninth century, when the history of Islam began to be written and religio-historical sources (such as *hadith*) scrutinized, 'A'isha's public activity was regarded as disruptive of the social and religious order. When Zubeida, the wife of the celebrated caliph Harun al-Rashid, was urged to take 'A'isha as a model and avenge the death of her son (the outcome of a civil war between Harun's two eldest sons, born of different mothers), she disdained this advice, saying, "It is not for women to seek vengeance and take the field against warriors."[7]

The theme of women's unsuitability for political action was expressed not only in the writings of the *ulema,* but also in more secular works on ethics and matters of practical etiquette frequently written by statesmen. The well-known eleventh-century vezir Nizam al-Mulk devoted a chapter of his *Book of Government,* composed to instruct his Seljuk monarch, to demonstrating the harmful effects of allowing "wearers of the veil" any influence because of their "incomplete intelligence." Nizam al-Mulk was here appealing to a stock image of women as mentally deficient that had been a feature of Near Eastern culture before the rise of Islam.[8] Once again, the focus of the argument was 'A'isha, who despite the liability of her political activity was revered in (Sunni) tradition for her Muslim learning. Nizam al-Mulk first related a *hadith* according to which the Prophet, on his deathbed, rejected 'A'isha's advice as to who should take his place as leader of the communal prayers; Nizam al-Mulk then commented, "so imagine what the opinions of other women are worth."[9] Spellberg suggests that the aim of the vezir's diatribe, in which he manipulated the positive image enjoyed by 'A'isha to discredit her entire sex, was to discredit his contemporary, Turkhan Khatun, a powerful wife of the sultan and the vezir's political foe.[10]

While scholarly works on ethics might stress the rights of ordinary women in marriage and the duties of husbands toward their wives, they often pointed to women's inferiority as the basis of these rights and duties. In the section on the etiquette of marriage in his monumental compendium of religious knowledge, the great medieval thinker Al-Ghazali enjoined men to "good conduct with [their wives] and tolerating offense from them out of pity for their mental deficiencies."[11] The dangerous power of women to bring harm to men was underlined by the thirteenth-century scholar-statesman Nasir al-Din Tusi, whose ethical treatise was frequently quoted by the Ottomans. Tusi concluded the section of his work devoted to "the chastisement and regulation of women" by stating that a man incapable of controlling his wife should remain a bachelor; "[F]or the mischief of associating with women, quite apart from its disorder, can only result in an infinite number of calamities; one of these may be the wife's intention to bring about the man's destruction, or the intention of another with regard to the wife."[12] It is important to recognize that these misogynist views were not peculiar to Islam but rather formed an aspect of the heritage of ancient Near Eastern and Mediterranean society. One common source through which such views passed into both Islamic and European political and social tradition was the writings of Greek philosophers, especially Aristotle.[13]

Many of these views of women were given new voice in the Ottoman period. Members of the Ottoman *ulema* enjoyed an especially broad arena in which to pronounce on female behavior, for they could do so in their public roles as well as in their writings. Sunullah's criticism of women in politics was just one item in a list of abuses of the Sharia and "harmful innovations" (*bid'at*) of recent times that he presented publicly. Another item in the list concerned ordinary women, who, proclaimed the *müfti*, "absolutely must not walk about openly in the markets among men."[14] Earlier in the sixteenth century, this social ideal of the segregation of the sexes was affirmed by the religious scholar and *müfti* Kemalpaşazade: a query addressed to him asked for judgment about a long list of offenses which the questioner assumed—and Kemalpaşazade affirmed—invalidated the perpetrator's ability to give legal witness: along with those who refused to attend communal prayer services, those who cheated in the marketplace, and those who sold wine from their homes, were those who socialized with women who were *nâmahrem*, that is, beyond the specified degrees of blood relationship within which men and women could freely mix, and those who did not prevent their wives from such socializing.[15] Concern with preventing contact between the sexes was most pronounced in the teachings and writings of the fundamentalist (*selefi*) *ulema*. In his work *The Way of the Prophet Muhammad* (*Tarikat al-Muhammadiye*), the scholar and teacher Birgivi Mehmed Efendi (d. 1573) listed among the "sins of the tongue" conversation between a man and a young woman or girl not within the permitted degrees of kinship; one should not even say "Bless you!" if such a young woman were to sneeze.[16] *The Way of the Prophet Muhammad* was a widely quoted manual of Muslim morals and etiquette that together with its author's *Treatise* became the handbook of a puritan movement that remained strong throughout the seventeenth century.[17]

The writings and pronouncements of the *ulema* about women and their place in the social world were obviously of considerable significance, for they reflected the opinions of an influential segment of the society. In particular, the prescriptions of the *ulema* established ideals or models of behavior that many accepted as valid, even if they found them impracticable or impossible to realize in their daily lives. But these writings offer only one window through which to view the social life of Ottomans. If we do not examine other perspectives on the dynamics of Ottoman society, we are likely to make the mistake of assuming that this literature is descriptive as well as prescriptive. In doing so, we may overlook sources of women's social and political power and erroneously arrive at the conclusion that their public influence was illegitimate, or worse, nonexistent. Fortunately, recent studies of Mamluk and Ottoman society have begun to provide a fuller, if more complex, portrait of the late medieval and early modern Muslim social world.

The segregation of the sexes did not mean that women, especially women of the elite, lacked power or were denied accomplishment. As Jonathan Berkey has shown in a study of education under the Mamluks, although Mamluk women were strictly excluded from public institutions of education (some of which they themselves founded), it is clear that many, especially the daughters and wives of the *ulema,* were well educated. While they did not excel in the religious sciences necessary for public careers, many achieved prominence as transmitters of *hadith* and were cited as authorities by male scholars. Women were taught at home (as were young boys) by their fathers, brothers, and husbands, as well as by other women; in addition, some attended the public instructional sessions commonly held in mosques.[18] Understanding this tradition of household education, which we can observe as well in Ottoman society, we can better appreciate the means by which women of the Ottoman harem (and male dynasts as well) learned politics, the business of the imperial palace.

In a treatise describing practices of which he disapproved, the conservative Mamluk religious scholar Ibn al-Hajj, spiritual ancestor of Birgivi Mehmed, was particularly disturbed by the social mixing of men and women. Huda Lutfi has used this text to show the range of public activities Cairene women managed to engage in and the means they used to overcome the barriers established by the practice of gender segregation.[19] Norms that upheld the segregation of the sexes could most easily be suspended for public activities whose objectives were perceived as more vital than those of female seclusion. Even traditionalists such as Ibn al-Hajj and Birgivi Mehmed recognized attendance at mosque teaching sessions as a legitimate reason for a woman to leave her home without her husband's permission (this was acceptable in their view, however, only if the husband did not or could not provide the religious knowledge of which his wife was in need).[20] The ubiquitous and popular custom of praying at tombs and seeking the intercession of the dead, to which both women and men were devoted, is further evidence that public expression of religious devotion could override the rules of female seclusion. Predictably, conservative *ulema* routinely denounced this custom as a "harmful innovation"; Birgivi Mehmed, for example, quoted a tradition according to which the Prophet cursed women who visited tombs.[21]

Nearly a century after Birgivi Mehmed, Kâtip Çelebi, a learned Ottoman bureaucrat, scholar, and consultant to the throne, presented his opinions on controversial issues of doctrine and popular practice in a work entitled *The Balance-Scale of Truth*. His purpose was, he stated, to free certain fanatics from "the fetters of extremism" and guide them toward "the frontier of moderation."[22] In a spirit of tolerance and pragmatic moderation, Kâtip Çelebi observed that it was impossible to keep the common people from holding beliefs and performing rituals such as tomb visiting which might be questionable from a strict doctrinal point of view, such as that adopted by Birgivi and his disciples.[23] In Kâtip Çelebi's opinion, Birgivi erred in that "he attached no importance to custom and usage," hence "he had no success with the common people."[24] It was this more tolerant view that prevailed in the seventeenth-century religious establishment, despite the sizeable following of the puritan movement led by Birgivi's spiritual heirs.

It was not only religious activity, however, that sanctioned women's public presence. The work of Ronald Jennings and Haim Gerber in the sixteenth- and seventeenth-century court records of the Anatolian cities of Kayseri and Bursa demonstrates that women were active as plaintiffs and defendants in legal suits and as participants in the economic life of the community.[25] Nor was it only among the "common people" that women could be seen outside the home. It is true that the social segregation of the sexes, and in particular the seclusion of women, was largely a class phenomenon. The social ideal that dictated that upper- and middle-class women refrain from appearing in public existed in the pre-Islamic Near East and the lands of the Christian Byzantine Empire. The segregation of the sexes rested on the availability of poorer women or slaves to perform the public chores of upper-class households (such as carrying dough to the baker) and provide services to their homes (hence the female peddler, barber, doctor, midwife, and so on).[26] Yet even among the upper classes the seclusion of women was not absolute. The judicial rulings of Ebussuud Efendi, the celebrated *müfti* of Süleyman's reign, make clear that women of the Ottoman elite went out, but were thought to place their status at risk by doing so unless they were surrounded by a retinue, that is, by a cordon of servants that symbolically represented the protection of harem walls. In Ebussuud's view, what was essential in maintaining a reputation for modesty and honor was that a woman not be seen by men other than members of her household and not conduct her affairs in person; honor was not dependent upon conformity to the prescriptions of the Sharia, stated the *müfti,* and so non-Muslim women could also enjoy an honorable reputation.[27] Seclusion was thus not simply about gender; it was to a significant degree about social status. In the introduction to this book, I argued that the same criterion for preserving status—appearing in public arenas with the requisite dignity—applied to men. It was the sultan who set the standard of conduct for all. The all-male "harem" of the inner palace courtyard was transportable: when the sultan emerged from the royal residence, he was surrounded by the pages and eunuchs of the inner court, who performed the symbolic function of representing the inner palace walls. As we have seen,

Osman II, the first Ottoman sultan to be forcibly overthrown and executed, was publicly criticized for not observing the public protocols that exalted sultanic rank and honor.

However, if women and men might be subject to the same social rules, the proclamations of Sunullah attacking the excessive visibility of both royal and ordinary women, delivered in the midst of criticisms of royal women's political influence that appeared in turn-of-the-century political tracts, suggest an acute concern over women's place in society toward the end of the sixteenth century. (Whether this concern was actually greater than at other times can be determined only through further research.) According to E.J.W. Gibb, historian of Ottoman poetry, this was "an age when a rampant and aggressive misogyny was reckoned honorable" among the learned.[28] The debate over women was no doubt in part inspired by the rapid political and social changes of the late sixteenth century. Reaction to such change was often expressed in terms of fear that social categories and moral boundaries would be jeopardized and disorder ensue. It was typical in times of stress to blame the socially subordinate and to place restrictions on their public conduct. Women were the most frequent target of social control. While calls for the control of women were voiced most vehemently by conservative *ulema,* responding to public anxiety by exerting control over the movement of women was a relatively simple means by which governments could demonstrate authority in otherwise difficult times. The Ottomans were not alone in employing such a tactic. During the famine and plague of 1438 the Mamluk sultan conferred with religious scholars about the causes of these catastrophes, and they agreed that the primary cause was the appearance of women in the streets; a decree was immediately issued ordering women to stay home.[29]

Women were not the only targets of public anxiety, however. Commoners too were seen as a potential source of social disorder, and sixteenth-century judicial rulings were attentive to maintaining distinctions of class among Muslim men. More notably, it was common for religious minorities—the Christian and Jewish subjects of the empire—to suffer scrutiny in times of stress.[30] The judicial rulings of sixteenth-century *müfti*s regulated social contact with Christians and Jews as they did with women.[31] However, it appears from the periodic decrees issued by the government to remind local authorities of these regulations that they were for the most part allowed to lapse. It was less the goal of lasting social control by the state than the *capacity* for such control that was demonstrated in these reactions to political stress.

The debate over women was thus not always *about* women; rather, they were often a metaphor for order. This role of women as a barometer of public confidence in the well-being of society is vividly illustrated in a minor incident which the early seventeeth-century historian İbrahim Peçevi included in his work. Peçevi, who heard the story first hand, related it in order to illustrate the incapacity of the government after the disastrous second reign of Mustafa (1622–1623). An Anatolian village grandee had imposed such financial burdens on a poor peasant that the latter was forced to sell him his daughter as a slave. The grandee then took the girl to the nearby city of Tokat, where he auctioned her off in the streets. At the time the incident occurred, the grand vezir, the Janissary commander, and the commanders of the imperial cavalry troops were all resident in Tokat, their winter campaign headquarters. Peçevi commented, "[T]hings had come to such a pass that even with so many great men in the city supposedly keeping order, not a one prevented this or was capable even of speaking out against it."[32] This story was not simply about the cruel fate of the peasant's daughter. The contemporary observer would have recognized that an entire hierarchy of obligations had been subverted. The father betrayed his paternal duty, the village grandee failed to protect his peasants from oppression, and the boundary between Muslim and "unbeliever" was violated (Islamic law prohibited the enslavement of a free Muslim). Underlying all of these betrayals was the sultan's failure, through his officials, to preserve justice. The supreme duty of the monarch, justice was defined as ensuring that no subject violated the rights of another by transgressing the boundaries of his or her class and role in society.

If the debate over women became particularly acute in the late sixteenth century, the increasing political power of royal women over the course of the century was surely a factor in stimulating it. The concern among political commentators of this period over the changing nature of the sultanate meant that the growing influence of royal women was inevitably drawn into the discussion. But it was not only in the treatises of thinkers and the pronouncements of the *ulema* that the reality of women's influence was reflected; ordinary people were witness to the changing politics of the royal family and the increasingly prominent display of royal women's power.

As this book has argued, the structure of Ottoman dynastic politics made that power inevitable. While the shape of women's power displayed some distinctly Ottoman characteristics, such as the exclusive reliance on concubinage in the reproduction of the dynasty and the preference for permitting a royal concubine to give birth to no more than one son, the Ottoman dynasty was not alone in producing influential women. Ann Lambton has noted the prominence of women in the dynasties that ruled the central Islamic lands in medieval times, while Carl Petry has demonstrated the influence wielded by Mamluk royal women over politics and the guardianship of property.[33] The evolution of women's roles in the dynasties of the Turco-Mongol Timurids and the Turkman Akkoyunlu, as yet unstudied, appears to have been similar, in some respects at least, to that of the Ottomans: the careers of Gawharshad Agha, wife of Timur's son and successor Shahruh, and of Saljukshah Begum, wife of the greatest Akkoyunlu sultan Uzun Hasan, suggest that the prominence of women corresponded with a period characterized by the consolidation of conquest and attention to Islamic philanthropy.[34] (The same might be said of Turkhan Khatun, wife of the Seljuk Malikshah and political foe of Nizam al-Mulk). The influence of all Muslim royal women was particularly evident in the politics of succession, hence the authority they tended to exert over their sons.

The reality of royal women's power in the Islamic Near East was reflected in another discourse about women which, because it honored their authority, stood in opposition to that of the *ulema*. This view of women was heavily influenced by Turco-Mongol political traditions, which explicitly accorded royal women important roles in government, especially in their capacity as mothers of princes and rulers. The thirteenth-century Persian statesman-historian Rashid al-Din praised the political wisdom of Mongol mothers in his world history, *The Compendium of Histories,* which was widely read in the Islamic world. Not surprisingly, he lauded in particular Sorqoqtani Beki, mother of Möngke and Kubilai, the fourth and fifth great khans of the Mongols, and of Hülegü, founder of the Ilkhanid dynasty that ruled Iran from the mid-thirteenth to the mid-fourteenth centuries and employed Rashid al-Din as vezir:

> [J]ust as when Chingiz Khan was left an orphan by his father, his mother ... trained him and all the army, sometimes even going into battle herself and equipping and maintaining them until Chingiz Khan became independent and absolute, and attained to the degree of world-sovereignty, and accomplished great things thanks to his mother's endeavors, so too Sorqoqtani Beki followed the same path in the training of her children. . . . There is no doubt that it was through her intelligence and ability that she raised the station of her sons above that of their cousins and caused them to attain to the rank of [khans] and emperors.[35]

It is interesting that Rashid al-Din felt obliged to justify to his readers his departure from the usual Muslim historigraphical practice of avoiding mention of women, explaining that he did so because the Mongols accorded women equal treatment with men.[36] However, he also ascribed to Sorqoqtani qualities that were stock attributes for Muslim women: "[S]he towered above all the women in the world, possessing in the fullest measure the qualities of steadfastness, virtue, modesty, and chastity."[37] In the *İskendername* (The Book of Alexander), a popular epic poem written in the early fifteenth century for an Ottoman prince, the author Ahmedi praised the rule of the Mongol Ilkhanid princess-sultan Sati Beg, although he simultaneously affirmed the inherent intellectual inferiority of women. Emphasizing that a woman could be the equal of a man in the qualities necessary for good government, Ahmedi played on the word *erlik,* which meant "manhood" as well as the qualities of courage, aptitude, and so on associated with the ideal man:

> Although she was a woman, she was wise,
> She was experienced, and she had good judgment.
>
> Whatever task she undertook, she accomplished,
> She succeeded at the exercise of sovereignty.
>
> There are many women who are greater than men,
> There are many men who are baser than women.
>
> What is manhood? It is generosity, intelligence, and piety.
> Whoever possesses these three things is surely a man. [38]

Sati Beg was a contemporary of Osman and Orhan, the first Ottoman rulers. The fourteenth-century North African Muslim traveler Ibn Battuta, who traveled through the Ottoman principality during the reign of Orhan, noted that "among the Turks and the Tatars their wives enjoy a very high position."[39] In Chapter 2, we saw that Ibn Battuta commented on the good qualities of Orhan's wife, who was presiding over the newly conquered city of Iznik. Crossing the Black Sea to the domain of Muhammad Uzbek Khan, ruler of the "Tatars" (the Mongol Golden Horde), Ibn Battuta was astonished by the prestige of the khan's wives; he noted that "indeed, when they issue an order they say in it 'By command of the Sultan and the Khatuns.' "[40] Ibn Battuta's comments suggest that Turco-Mongol political traditions were very much alive in the public roles of these fourteenth-century women. The similarity of these roles to those played by Arab women of the first Muslim generations as political activists and public exemplars of political virtue suggests the influence on these nascent political communities of the tribal cultures of Arabia and Central Asia. Both these cultures appear to have been more egalitarian with regard to the public roles of women and men than the sedentary cultures of the ancient Near East, which proved the dominant tradition in the evolution of Islamic society.

By the sixteenth century, the nature of political discourse had changed, and Central Asian models and traditions had lost much of their overt force. Nevertheless, the idea persisted that a woman of the royal dynasty, especially in her capacity as mother, had a vital role to play in the transmission of political values and the protection and preservation of the dynasty. As we have seen, there was a readiness among Ottomans to accept the public role of the *valide sultan* and a conviction that her counsel could help the sultan to better govern his subjects. When the *valide sultan* was criticized, it was the individual, not the office, that was perceived to be at fault. When Ottomans of the sixteenth and seventeenth centuries praised royal women, they appealed to the stock qualities of wisdom, experience, munificence, and piety which earlier Muslim writers had ascribed to Mongol and Turkish women.

While Ottoman dynastic politics in the early generations may have given women power as wives, by the end of the fourteenth century (if not earlier) the dynasty appears to have evolved its henceforth characteristic practice of basing female power on motherhood isolated from wifehood or indeed from any sexual connection with the sovereign. Even if, like neighboring Christian and Muslim states, the sultans contracted interdynastic alliances through the middle of the fifteenth century, they appear not to have fathered children with any of these royal wives, instead confining their reproductive activity to serial concubinage. Given our present lack of knowledge, it is difficult to know if there were parallels to the Ottoman practice of concubinage. There is a resemblance in the Mamluk practice of slave concubinage, but because the Mamluk state elevated the ethos of male slavery to a constitutional principle, the resemblance is superficial. An obvious precedent is the Abbasid practice of slave concubinage; however, because the Abbasids were far removed in time and space from the Ottomans, their precedent most likely served to legitimate a reproductive option rather than to provide a model. The Ottomans' immediate predecessors in Anatolia, the Seljuk dynasty of Rum, as well as their

Timurid and Akkoyunlu neighbors, appear to have combined dynastic marriage, cousin marriage, and concubinage, a practice followed by the Ottomans only in the first generations. The most we can say is that, as they did with other institutions, the Ottoman dynasty drew on a number of precedents, adapting them as they saw necessary to the goal of concentrating power in the sultanate.

The Ottoman dynasty's reproductive politics—the manner in which it produced and raised its princes and princesses—had two goals: the preservation of the House of Osman and the minimization of political challenge to the individual sultan. Until Hurrem, the favored concubine of Süleyman the Magnificent, women who figured ceremonially at the royal court—foreign brides—had little domestic political power (although they were important as diplomatic links). While the duties of royal motherhood endowed the concubine mothers of the sultan's sons with political roles, these roles were performed in the theater of a provincial capital. Especially after the reign of Murad II, when sultans no longer contracted interdynastic marriages, there were no female players on the center stage of dynastic politics. The mother of the sultan, who was to acquire immense power toward the end of the sixteenth century, appears not to have received public honors until the reign of Süleyman.

However, the aim of the dynasty's reproductive politics was not to diminish female political power as such. The controls on women were paralleled by increasing restrictions on male dynasts. When challenged, the dynasty was as ruthless toward its own male members as it could be toward members of the ruling elite. As the Ottoman state emerged, the political rights of the sultan's male relatives were gradually eliminated or their effective power restricted: uncles and brothers were barred from the succession (although challenges by uncle and brother pretenders continued through the mid-fifteenth century, and partition of the empire among brothers appears to have been a plausible consideration as late as the 1480s), and the independent power of princes was reduced. Indeed, political survival required that the sultan himself be subject to strict rules regarding family relationships. During the period of Ottoman expansion the defense and celebration of the patriline—enshrined in the oft-repeated sovereign title "the sultan, son of the sultan [who was] son of the sultan"—was the supreme dynastic goal. It was accomplished largely through the Ottoman adaptation of the traditional Islamic practice of royal or "military" slavery. From the late fourteenth century on, male and female slaves gradually took over the roles of which family members were being deprived. Thus, when the dynasty's preference for slave concubinage is considered in the context of loss of power by male dynasts, it becomes evident that the practice of slave concubinage had as its goal not so much the disempowerment of women as the preservation of the unitary dynastic state.

Raising the integrity of the male bloodline to a near sacral principle meant that slave concubinage was virtually inevitable. Interdynastic marriage entailed political obligations and circumscribed the sovereign's freedom of action. Moreover, it provided a pretext for political intervention by the royal wife's relatives, and worse, it might entitle them to a claim in the succession.

Once established as a regional power, the Ottomans no longer needed marriage. While they used the vocabulary of ancient Persian kingship and were strongly influenced in matters of sovereign etiquette by neighboring dynasties based in Iran, they did not share the latter's need to establish legitimacy by appropriating kingly genealogies through interdynastic marriage. This relative freedom from the necessity of establishing legitimacy through successorship to earlier Near Eastern states was one of the great virtues of the Ottomans' Anatolian and Rumelian base and of the conquest of Constantinople.

It is probable that Islamic law and custom also played a role in the Ottomans' preference for slave concubinage and in the lack of cousin marriages typical of Turco-Mongol and Turkman dynasties. Marriage brought certain rights to free Muslim women that would have presented obstacles to the strict controls the dynasty placed on reproduction: women had a right to children, and they could expect sexual satisfaction from their husbands and the right to refuse certain forms of birth control.[41] Ottoman reproductive politics required severe limitations on rights of mothers: the apparent restriction to one son meant that a woman's right to children was curtailed and her sexual needs disregarded after the birth of her son. Furthermore, she faced the possibility that her son would be executed in the inevitable succession battle that followed his father's death; it was this aspect of royal concubinage that was emphasized in the attempt to dissuade the daughter of the grand vezir Kuyucu Murad Pasha from her desire to enter Ahmed I's harem.[42] In the paradoxical logic of the royal harem, the sovereigns of the Ottoman House, from the sixteenth century on the greatest princes of the Islamic world, were the product of an environment that violated the dignity and the rights of a free born Muslim woman.

If the dynasty strove to subordinate the natural rights of family members to the goal of survival, the public appears to have set limits to its ability to invert the rules of family order or suppress the identity of family members. There were a number of ways in which popular opinion tempered the concentration of power and charisma in the sultan alone. One was the need to see represented in the dynasty the honor that Ottoman society accorded motherhood and female lineage. The importance of female lineage is demonstrated in the fact that, when histories of the dynasty began to be written in the late fifteenth century, they celebrated the wrong women—royal wives—in an attempt to bestow a worthy lineage on the sultans' mothers. The popularity of concubine mothers and their public stature are evident not only from the contemporary comments of foreign travelers and ambassadors, but from the fact that they are still honored today in the cities that were Ottoman capitals: the small tomb of Devlet Khatun, mother of Mehmed I, is well tended by the Bursa neighborhood in which it is situated and functions as a local pilgrimage site (Figure C-1); annual festivals in Manisa commemorate the patronage of Hafsa Sultan, mother of Süleyman.[43] It is difficult to determine the extent to which the prestige the dynasty began to accord its royal concubines toward the end of the fifteenth century was a concession to popular pressure (there were political considerations as well), but it is clear that the public did not hesitate

Figure C-1 The Tomb of Devlet Khatun. The casket of Devlet Khatun, mother of Mehmed I, lies in a simple open-air tomb in Bursa. The tombstone reads: "This is the noble tomb of the virtuous lady, Devlet Khatun, the sultan of khatuns. She is the mother of the most exalted sultan, Sultan Mehmed son of Bayezid Khan. May his dominion endure." Devlet Khatun died in 1412. (*Photo by Kerim Peirce*)

to express its respect and affection for the mothers of princes. The career of Hafsa Sultan heralded the full incorporation of the sultan's mother into the dynastic family. Hafsa's prestige was marked publicly in several ways: she was the first concubine to exercise the prerogative of building an imperial mosque, she was given an imperial funeral, and her tomb in the mosque courtyard of Süleyman's father Selim enjoyed an unprecedented architectural prominence. Hafsa is also the first royal concubine to be remembered with the title "Sultan," which recognized her as a legitimate sharer in dynastic power.

Another way in which the public limited the autonomy of the sultan was its cherishing of princes. Dynastic legends of the Turks, both Central Asian and Anatolian, sanctioned the overthrow of the sovereign by his son under justifiable conditions. In the legends preserved in histories of the early fourteenth-century Anatolian Turkman principalities, it is the sovereign's son who is the charismatic figure, the activist, while the father is remote, isolated in the "harem" of sovereignty, no longer the *ghazi* warrior. Many of the feats of Osman, Orhan, and the latter's son Süleyman that are celebrated in the early histories occurred during their father's tenure as sultan; similarly, the ruler of the Aydınoğulları principality, Mehmed Beg, is a peripheral figure in the legendary history of his son, Ghazi Umur Pasha.[44] As we have seen, Ottoman princes were enormously popular despite the controls exerted on them. So powerful was the image of the warrior prince that in 1603 Mehmed III felt compelled to execute his son Mahmud largely because of the popularity the prince enjoyed among the Janissaries despite the fact that he never left the imperial palace. The need felt by sultans to prevent their sons from usurping the role of *ghazi* hero accounts in part for their continuous campaigning. The spectacle of the aging and ailing Süleyman on his final campaign (during which he died) maintaining his seat in the saddle only with the help of his retainers surely owed something to the fact that his grandfather, who campaigned only in the beginning of his reign, was displaced by a militarily activist son.

Another arena in which broad societal norms influenced the politics of the dynasty was the tension between sexuality and authority. It is *this* interaction between popular attitudes and dynastic politics that is most central to our discussion because it affected the distribution of power among royal women when they acquired public prominence in the sixteenth century. Under the increasing influence of sedentary Near Eastern/Islamic norms, the prestige of wives in the first Ottoman generations gave way to the prestige of female elders. In the two hundred years between Ibn Battuta's meeting with Orhan's wife and the advent of "the sultanate of women," major changes had taken place in the social environment of the family. The principal differences were increasingly strict norms of gender segregation and the subordination of the childbearing generation to control by its seniors.

Female elders in medieval and early modern Muslim society typically enjoyed greater respect for their wisdom and authority and greater freedom to mix with men because they were no longer sexually active. In the Qur'an, the injunctions regarding modest dress are explicitly relaxed for women past childbearing.[45] There are many examples from the sixteenth century illustrating social distinctions between sexually active and inactive women. In his judicial decisions, Ebussuud interpreted the Sharia to permit greater public mobility to older women; for example, when presented with the query "If in some districts women come to the mosque to participate in the Friday prayers, does the Sharia prescribe that they be prevented?", the *müfti* responded, "If there are young women [among them], yes," implying that older women were free to join the Friday congregational service.[46] Birgivi's warning against "calamities of the tongue" specified that it was with a *young* woman or girl that a man must not converse. An imperial order of 1580 vividly illustrates the public distinctions made between female generations: previously taxi boats operating on the Golden Horn and the Bosphorus had been ordered to prevent young women (*taze avretler*) from boarding boats on which "virile young men" (*levendat*) were present; some "people of honor," however, had caused vexation to "elderly ladies" (*ihtiyar hatunlar*) from the poorer classes by preventing them as well from riding on the boats; now the boatmen were instructed to allow the older women to board but not to "violate the Sharia" by allowing young men and women on together.[47]

It is not simply that women past childbearing no longer threatened the integrity of their husband's patriline with illicit behavior. The social construction of sexuality identified sexual activity with a lack of full maturity stemming from the inability to control physical desires that might lead to illicit conduct.[48] Islamic ethical literature urged mastery of passions and discipline of desire.[49] The fully mature, both male and female, moved beyond active sexuality to a stage where full concentration could be marshalled for more serious matters. Male and female elders were entrusted with upholding social norms and preventing the sexually active under their guardianship from disrupting those norms. It is important to note that, just as the controllers were both male and female, so were the controlled. While it was the mobility of young women that was most strictly regulated, that of boys ("beardless youths") and young men (the "virile" and the "hotblooded") was also closely monitored; boys had to be protected from men's pederastic desires, while young men of a sexually aggressive age had to be kept away from women, girls, *and* boys.[50]

The need for the dynasty to conform to popular expectations was especially pressing once the whole royal family had settled in Istanbul. The incorporation of the harem into the imperial compound and the subsequent rise of a court society that was both male and female meant that the royal family was more exposed to scrutiny by its subjects. Births, deaths, marriages, accessions, depositions, and executions now all took in place in the capital. It is noteworthy that the most unpopular feature of Ottoman dynastic politics— the practice of fratricide—did not long survive once it began to be enacted in an urban environment.

When royal concubines ceased to accompany their sons to the provinces, they became subject to social norms that restricted the public visibility of the "wifely" or childbearing generation. Concubines before Hurrem had of course been of a "wifely" generation in relation to the sovereign, but their public role as the female elder of the princely household meant that they were no longer associated with the sultan. In other words, they clearly enjoyed the status of the postchildbearing generation. By remaining in the imperial household with Süleyman when her sons were graduated to the provinces, Hurrem could not herself graduate to the status of the postsexual woman. Hurrem's vulnerability was symbolized in the fact that, although the documents granting her income for her vast building projects identified her as "mother of the prince," her buildings were popularly known as the "mosque of the favorite" and "the bath of the favorite," broadcasting an image of her as sexual object. As we have seen, public antipathy toward Hurrem was expressed in the rumor that she bewitched the sultan with love potions. This widespread belief reflected not only popular mores but also acceptance of the dynasty's own rules separating the functions of consort and mother. Hurrem's unpopularity did not mean that concubine favorites were henceforth denied power, but never again was it so publicly demonstrated. The influence of a concubine might be considerable, but, like the childbearing woman herself, it was now "veiled." This invisible influence is symbolized in the charitable efforts of favorites after Hurrem: they did not undertake monumental building as she had done, but instead made donations to the poor or sponsored the reading of the Qur'an in major mosques.

The invisibility of concubines was affected by another aspect of dynastic consolidation in the capital. By bringing together two generations of royal mothers, the unification of the royal family into a single household in the second half of the sixteenth century made necessary the establishment of a hierarchy among women. The prominence and authority of the elder generation, which consisted of a single individual, the *valide sultan*, was inevitable, as was the expectation that she would exert control over the sultan's concubines.

There appears to have been a more or less fixed age—approximately thirty-three—at which it was considered appropriate in the sixteenth century for royal concubines to assume public roles. The earliest age at which a prince began to father children was sixteen, and royal concubines appear also to have been in their midteens when they became consort to a prince or sultan. If her first child was a son, a concubine would be thirty-three or so when he reached sixteen, the age of male maturity. It is significant that Hurrem began construction of her mosque in 1537, when her eldest child, Mehmed, turned sixteen; while she did not move to a provincial capital, she can be thought of as exercising a prerogative accruing to the mother of a prince who had come of age. The explicitly political role of Nurbanu Sultan, Hurrem's daughter-in-law, began when Nurbanu's son Murad took up his princely post; Nurbanu's acute concern as *valide sultan* with Murad's failure to end his sexual relationship with his favorite Safiye was no doubt related to the fact that their son Mehmed was approaching his graduation to the provinces.

However, dynastic accidents of the seventeenth century meant that not all *valide sultans* were safely of postsexual status. Turhan Sultan, who was probably about twenty-five when she took control of the government in 1651 as regent to her nine-year-old son, clearly presented a problem. That Turhan's youth was perceived as threatening both the polity and society at large with sexually engendered disorder is suggested by rumors that circulated about her alleged sexual misconduct: she was said variously to enjoy a lesbian relationship with Meleki Khatun, a slave woman who had become her trusted agent,[51] and, some years later, an incestuous relationship with the elder of her two stepsons.[52] Under the rubric "A Strange Event," the historian Naima related an incident that underlines the degree of discomfort aroused by Turhan's presence at the head of government. In 1653, two years after her regency began, a sheikh from the city of Diyarbakır in eastern Anatolia came to Istanbul to broadcast God's revelation to him: "[T]he reason that religion and government [had] fallen into ruin and that the Muslims [were] mired in misery," preached the sheikh, was that the holy law had been abandoned and the queen mother and her followers were running the government. As long as this continued, "disorder and depravity" would only increase. The solution, according to the sheikh, was to marry off the queen mother and remove her from the palace. When, after being warned by the grand vezir to keep silent, the sheikh continued to spread his story, an order was issued that he be placed in the lunatic asylum of the Süleymaniye mosque complex. But his fame spread, and the people of the city, revering him as divinely inspired, flocked to his cell and began to say, in Naima's words, "What a pity! See, this is what happens to someone who speaks the truth. The sheikh has revealed God's command. Why shouldn't the queen mother be married?" The situation got so out of hand that the only solution was to send the sheikh back to Diyarbakır. In his own comment on this affair, Naima, like Kâtip Çelebi in his comments on tomb visiting, drew attention to the importance of custom and precedent. In Naima's view, the necessary role that the queen mother had come to play overrode the issue of her age:

> Those who say that the marriage of the queen mother is proper do not [ask whether], given the established usage of the state, it is even possible. Nor do they take into sufficient account considerations of its possible benefit or harm to this exalted state. . . . The truth is, those who do not recognize the power and dignity of the sublime station of the most magnificent sultanate and the most exalted cradle [the queen mother] are ignorant. . . . In my opinion, the aforementioned sheikh from Diyarbakır belonged in the lunatic asylum.[53]

The unease provoked by the rule of the socially immature female had its male parallel. The transition to succession by seniority in the early seventeenth century was inspired in large part by the fear of an underage prince coming to the throne. There had not been a minor on the throne since the first reign of Mehmed II (1444–1446), and that had proved a disaster. But more important, the whole constellation of qualities that defined the active sexuality of the young male was clearly a source of unease in late-sixteenth-century Ottoman society, and doubtless influenced the transformations that took place in the dynastic career. It was the "virile young male" who was the ideal of the military state, for it was his energy and his prowess which determined its destiny. In Central Asian Turkish lore, a youth did not receive his manhood name until he successfully performed his first warlike feat; he was then by definition socially and politically mature. It was such a man, the *ghazi* hero, that the succession system which prevailed among the Ottomans until the end of the sixteenth century aimed to identify. In the early years of his reign, Süleyman appears to have employed his very person to symbolically display the achievement of maturity through military victory, or at least so he is represented by the historical record: the miniature paintings that illustrate the celebratory history of his reign by Arifi, the official court historiographer, suggest that it was not until the return march from his first, victorious, military campaign into Hungary in 1521 that the twenty-seven-year-old sultan grew a beard, a traditional sign of political maturity among the Ottomans.[54] It is noteworthy that it was only after a second victory, the successful seige of the island of Rhodes, that the young sultan felt able to dismiss Piri Mehmed, Mehmed "the Elder," the grand vezir he had inherited from his father.

But in the environment increasingly shaped by urban norms, it was the sober householder who won out. In the transformed succession system, seniority was the criterion that established eligibility. This was of course not an absolute change: the survival of the Ottoman state through Süleyman depended upon its successful containment of the tension inherent in open succession: how to give rein to princes in fraternal combat so as to determine the fittest, while preventing them from tearing the state apart. Moreover, the symbolic value of prowess on horseback continued in the seventeenth century to inform dynastic ritual in small ways: for example, the celebration of the hunt in which the child-sultan Mehmed IV bagged his first prey, a turtledove, was an occasion that warranted the composition of panegyric poems by "the finest minds of the times," as the historian Naima put it.[55] But increasingly in sixteenth-century legitimating polemic centering on the Ottoman sultan's duty to defend Islam, it was less the extension of its borders that was emphasized than the defense of its holy law, or, to use the terms Lutfi Pasha employed in his defense of Ottoman superiority, less the "conquering power" of the Sultan than the Imam's "maintainence of the Faith and government of the kingdom of Islam with equity."[56]

As dynastic politics evolved toward the system of seniority, princes became subject to ever greater controls. In fact, with the demise of the principate, the stage of development that had been characterized by the display of martial prowess and youthful ardor, albeit carefully limited, was suppressed entirely as a part of the dynastic career, and replaced by the more sedate training of princes within the confines of the royal household. In the process, active sexuality, a defining feature of this life stage symbolized in the function of captured wives of rival rulers as markers of military superiority, was also suppressed. At first, the prince's traditional responsibility for repopulating the dynasty was narrowed from the practice of multiple concubinage to the limited goal of producing a single son with a single concubine. Finally, the sexuality of princes was symbolically suppressed altogether, as they were denied the mutually dependent marks of social maturity: fathering children and establishing an independent household.

An interesting question is why the seventeenth-century regencies of young *valide sultan*s such as Turhan and Kösem (who was probably in her early thirties when her son Murad IV became sultan at the age of thirteen) were not challenged to a greater degree. The reluctance of statesmen to let Turhan assume the office of *valide sultan* in 1648 when her seven-year-old son Mehmed IV became sultan and the consequent retention of his experienced grandmother Kösem in the office show that the youth of a regent mother was an issue among the ruling elite. Why then, for instance, was the institution of the *lala,* the male guardian assigned to a prince to oversee his political training, not adapted to meet the need for a regent? The answer seems to be the power of the notion that sovereign authority, which a regent could claim, had to be exercised by a member of the dynastic family. There were strategic factors at issue. For example, the history of earlier Islamic dynasties showed that *lala*s could not be trusted with the destiny of a dynasty, for too often they arrogated sovereignty to their own bloodline. But more important, as Naima commented on the vain hope of the grand vezir Sofu Mehmed Pasha that it would be he and not the boy's grandmother who would act as regent to the young Mehmed IV, "the soldiers of this exalted state respect only the honor of inherited nobility."[57]

It might seem odd that a woman whose career had begun as a slave concubine should be thought to bear "the honor of inherited nobility." In part, this "honor" was the result of the rise in status of royal slaves from the mid-fifteenth century on and the standing they acquired through association with the royal household. As we have seen, slave *damad*s—royal sons-in-law—came to hold the most prestigious offices in the military/administrative hierarchy. However, as concubine the female slave could establish a stronger link with the dynasty than the male slave could through marriage. Her blood tie to her son provided her with a kind of retroactive lineage, and it is in this way that she was endowed with "inherited nobility."

As mother of a prince, the concubine could appropriate the discourse that legitimated women's political authority. Ordinary concubines, however, were vulnerable to the discourse that discredited women's intelligence and refused to see them as legitimate political actors. Discretion prevented Ottoman writers from criticizing royal mothers (they did not record the hostile barbs directed by Ottoman statesmen at queen mothers and favorites which made their way into European accounts), but they did not hesitate to employ invective in the case of lesser women of the sultan's harem. Naima, so careful to defend the young queen mother Turhan, criticized other concubines of the "mad" İbrahim with relish. He recounted the frustration of the grand vezir, when, in 1648, Ibrahim threatened to stuff his skin with straw if he did not recover from Medina all the precious items ever sent by İbrahim's ancestors. Naima related the angry complaint of the vezir, himself a slave: "[I]t is at the instigation of a passle of mentally deficient slave girls, daughters of Russian, Polish, Hungarian and Frankish infidels, that I am subjected to such violent propositions."[58]

The *valide sultan*s of the late sixteenth and seventeenth centuries succeeded in their exercise of power largely because it was based on a relationship—that of mother and son—that strengthened rather than threatened the social order.

The politically harmonious relationship that had characterized the princely governorate, with the mother heading her son's domestic household, counseling him and tempering his excesses, and in addition, carrying out the responsibility for royal patronage and charity, was now transferred to the imperial household. The prominence of the *valide sultan*s was in part a result of their capacity to function as a secure and reliable center of gravity during a period of profound reorientation in dynastic family relations. They eased the transition to succession by seniority by functioning as a symbolic link between sultanic reigns, thereby mitigating the loss of the charismatic connection between father and son.

But while the *valide sultan* might share in inherited nobility, there were limits to her sovereign role. Her extraordinary power was tolerated only so long as it was employed in the interest of her son; otherwise, it was an infringement of sultanic autonomy. However, relinquishing power to her son did not put an end to the *valide sultan*'s influence, for the status within the family attendant upon motherhood—especially motherhood of mature children—provided her with other sources of authority and other channels of influence. She utilized networks based on her daughters, sons-in-law, retainers, and slaves, drawing from her vast wealth in their support. As the female elder of the royal household, she functioned as exemplar of such sovereign attributes as justice, piety, munificence, and devotion to the defense of the faith. This book has argued that the principal tension within the dynastic family was generational competition for power. In considering the limits to the sovereign influence of the *valide sultan*, emphasis should be placed less on her femaleness than on her function as family elder charged with the timely handing over of power to the maturing heir. That the distribution of political power in the Ottoman dynasty was determined as much by generational as by gender distinctions becomes clearer when we remember that the generation to which the *valide sultan* handed over authority consisted not only of her son, the sultan, but also of the mothers of future rulers.

Because the household was the fundamental unit of political as well as social organization in the early modern Ottoman world, one's power in the polity derived principally from one's role within the household (a role that changed as one moved through the life cycle). The household functioned as the matrix for a complex network of relationships that transcended the public and the private, the personal and the institutional. In these networks, the interests of men and women combined to create a variety of factions that cut across the dichotomy of gender. This was nowhere more evident than in the dynastic household, which formed the model for the negotiation of political power.

APPENDIX

Genealogical Charts

The Ottoman Sultans through the Seventeenth Century

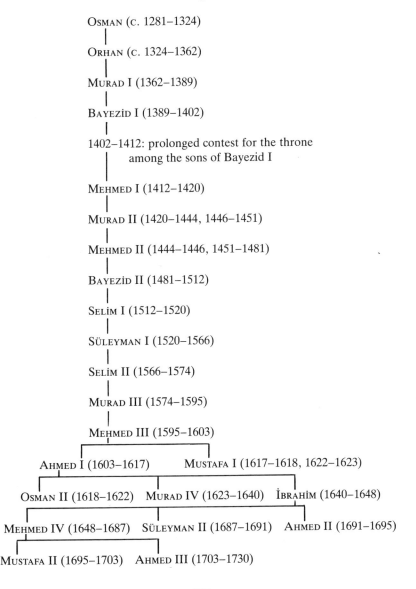

OSMAN (C. 1281–1324)

ORHAN (C. 1324–1362)

MURAD I (1362–1389)

BAYEZİD I (1389–1402)

1402–1412: prolonged contest for the throne
among the sons of Bayezid I

MEHMED I (1412–1420)

MURAD II (1420–1444, 1446–1451)

MEHMED II (1444–1446, 1451–1481)

BAYEZİD II (1481–1512)

SELİM I (1512–1520)

SÜLEYMAN I (1520–1566)

SELİM II (1566–1574)

MURAD III (1574–1595)

MEHMED III (1595–1603)

AHMED I (1603–1617)   MUSTAFA I (1617–1618, 1622–1623)

OSMAN II (1618–1622)   MURAD IV (1623–1640)   İBRAHİM (1640–1648)

MEHMED IV (1648–1687)   SÜLEYMAN II (1687–1691)   AHMED II (1691–1695)

MUSTAFA II (1695–1703)   AHMED III (1703–1730)

Sultans and *Valide Sultan*s of the Sixteenth and Seventeenth Centuries

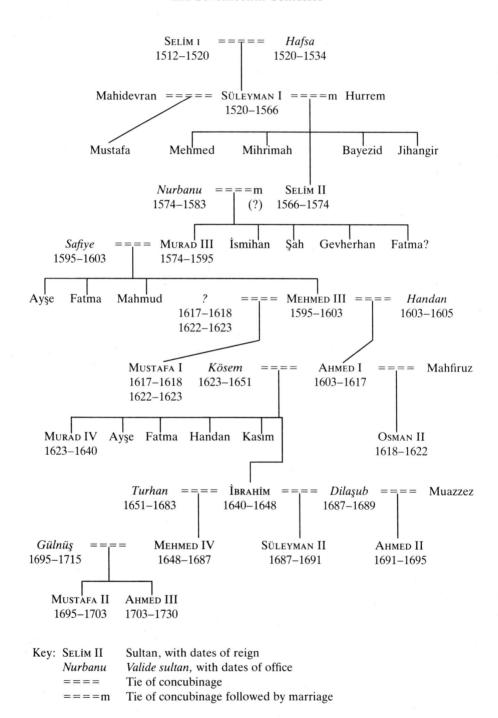

Key: SELİM II   Sultan, with dates of reign
      Nurbanu   *Valide sultan,* with dates of office
      ====   Tie of concubinage
      ====m   Tie of concubinage followed by marriage

NOTES

Abbreviations

TSMA   Topkapı Saray Müzesi Arşivi (Topkapı Palace Museum Archives)
E   Evrak (single document)
D   Defter (register)
BA   Başbakanlık Arşivi (Prime Ministry Archives, Istanbul)
AE   Ali Emiri Tasnifi (Ali Emiri Classification)
CEV   Cevdet Tasnifi (Cevdet Classification)
IE   İbn ül-Emin Tasnifi (İbn ül-Emin Classification)
KK   Kâmil Kepeci Tasnifi (Kâmil Kepeci Classification)
MM   Maliyeden Müdevver (Transferred from the Finance Ministry)
SL   Süleymaniye Library

EI(1)   *Encyclopedia of Islam*, 1st ed.
EI(2)   *Encyclopedia of Islam*, 2d ed.
IA   *İslam Ansiklopedisi*

Mustafa Ali, *Künh ül-Ahbar* Nuruosmaniye Library MS. 3406
Künh ül-Ahbar, vol. 1 Volume 1 of the printed edition
Neşri, *Kitab-ı Cihan-Nüma:* *Gihannüma: Die Altosmanische Chronik*, edited by F. Taeschner
Neşri Tarihi *Kitab-ı Cihan-Nüma: Neşri Tarihi*, edited by F.R. Unat and M.A. Köymen

Preface

1. Selaniki, *Tarih-i Selânikî*, ed. and trans. İpşirli, 826.
2. Alberi, *Relazioni degli ambasciatori veneti al senato*, 3:235.
3. Dispatch of the ambassador Gianfrancesco Morosini, December 13, 1583, cited by Spagni, "Una Sultana veneziana," 333.
4. The term "the sultanate of women" (*kadınlar saltanatı*) first appeared as the title of a four-volume history of Ottoman royal women written by Ahmed Refik, a popular historian of the early twentieth century. Refik's distinctly misogynist account has influenced subsequent readings of the lives of royal women.
5. For a discussion of the construction of gender in medieval Islamic law, see Paula Sanders, "Gendering the Ungendered Body: Hermaphrodites in Medieval Islam."

Introduction

1. See Ch. 5 for further discussion of this theme.
2. For a discussion of the term "harem," see Marmon, *Eunuchs of the Holy Cities*, ch. 1.

3. Meninski, *Lexicon Arabico-Persico-Turcicum,* 2:464–65.

4. For the legal and social status of slave concubines, see Marmon, "Concubinage, Islamic," and Brunschvig, "ʿAbd."

5. Barkan, "Edirne Askerî Kassamı'na Ait Tereke Defterleri (1545–1659)," 13–14; Gerber, "Social and Economic Position of Women in an Ottoman City, Bursa, 1600–1700," 232.

6. The size of the imperial harem was exaggerated by Western travelers and scholars: in the mid-sixteenth century it consisted of approximately 150 women and in the mid-seventeenth century approximately 400 women (BA: AE Kanunî 24; KK Saray 7098; MM 774, 1509, 1692).

7. Withers, "The Grand Signiors Serraglio," 330ff.; Baudier, *Histoire géneralle de serrail,* 19; Tavernier, *Nouvelle Relation de l'interieur du serrail de grand seigneur,* 541.

8. On the origins of a gendered public/private dichotomy in Western political thought and its persistence in contemporary theory and practice, see Okin, *Women in Western Political Thought* and *Justice, Gender, and the Family;* and Pateman, *The Sexual Contract.* For an overview of evolving—and increasingly critical—approaches of feminist scholarship in the United States toward the notion of a public/private dichotomy, see Helly and Reverby, eds., *Gendered Domains: Rethinking Public and Private in Women's History,* introduction, 1–17.

An example of the persistence of the idea of an a priori, universal, and gendered division of public and private can be found in the comments of Georges Duby in the Foreward to volume 1 of *A History of Private Life,* gen. eds. P. Ariès and G. Duby: "We started from the obvious fact that at all times and in all places a clear, commonsensical distinction has been made between the public—that which is open to the community and subject to the authority of its magistrates—and the private. In other words, a clearly defined realm is set aside for that part of existence for which every language has a word equivalent to "private," a zone of immunity. . . . This is the place where the family thrives, the realm of domesticity; it is also a realm of secrecy."

9. The first, and still the most detailed, treatment of this issue for this period in Ottoman history is Jennings, "Women in Early Seventeenth Century Ottoman Judicial Records: the Sharia Court of Anatolian Kayseri."

10. N. Z. Davis ("Women on Top," *Society and Culture in Early Modern France,* 126) argues that the public roles and legal rights of women in France and England decreased from the sixteenth to the eighteenth centuries.

11. Among those who have made positive contributions regarding the historical roles of Ottoman royal women, İ. H. Uzunçarşılı and M. Ç. Uluçay tend to regard the political influence of women as illegitimate (especially in the post-Süleymanic period); however, other historians, notably M. Cavid Baysun and Bekir Kütükoğlu, do not exhibit this bias.

12. An interesting beginning has been made by Marcus in his work on eighteenth-century Aleppo: "Privacy in Eighteenth-Century Aleppo: The Limits of Cultural Ideals" and *The Middle East on the Eve of Modernity: Aleppo in the Eighteenth Century,* ch. 8.

13. On the Turkish family, see Duben, "Turkish Families and Households in Historical Perspective." On the influence that Turkic tribal women today derive from their separate social organization, see Tapper, "Matrons and Mistresses: Women and Boundaries in Two Middle Eastern Tribal Societies."

14. On the subject of visiting among the female Ottoman elite, see Lady Mary Wortley Montagu, *The Complete Letters of Lady Mary Wortley Montagu,* 1:347–52, 380–87; F. Davis, *The Ottoman Lady: A Social History from 1718 to 1918,* 131–55.

15. For a brief exposition of the legal position of women, see Esposito, *Women in Muslim Family Law*, 13–48.

16. See Gerber, "Social and Economic Position of Women"; Jennings, "Women in Early Seventeenth Century Ottoman Judicial Records"; Marcus, "Men, Women, and Property: Dealers in Real Estate in Eighteenth-Century Aleppo."

17. Meninski, *Lexicon*, (4:428), s.v. "muhaddere," def. 2. See also some pertinent responses to queries on points of Islamic law (*fetva*) of the late-sixteenth-century Ottoman chief *müfti* Ebussuud (*Ebussuûd Efendi Fetvaları Işığında 16. Asır Türk Hayatı*, ed. M. E. Düzdağ, 55).

18. On the distinction between *hass* and *amm* (*khâṣṣ* and *'âmm* in Arabic transcription), see Beg, "Al-Khâṣṣa w'al-'Âmma"; Mottahedeh, *Loyalty and Leadership in an Early Islamic Society*, 115–29, 154–55. See also B. Lewis, *The Political Language of Islam*, 67.

19. For definitions of these words, see Meninski, *Lexicon*, 2:530, 3:673; Redhouse, *A Turkish and English Lexicon*, 821, 1279. Meninski's and Redhouse's lexicons reflect, respectively, seventeenth- and nineteenth-century Ottoman usages.

20. Meninski, *Lexicon*, (2:530), s.v. "hass," def. 2: "quod princeps sibi domesticum aut familiare habet."

21. See Pakalın, *Osmanlı Tarih Deyimleri ve Terimleri Sözlüğü*, 1:750ff., for other similar designations.

22. Meninski, *Lexicon*, (2:530), s.v. "hass," def. 4: "sanctitas."

23. B. Lewis, *The Political Language of Islam*, 11–13, 22–23.

24. Andrews, *Poetry's Voice, Society's Song*, especially ch. 5.

25. Mehmed Halife, *Tarih-i Gılmani*, 13.

26. See Vryonis, *The Decline of Medieval Hellenism in Asia Minor*, esp. 463–475; Cahen, *Pre-Ottoman Turkey*, esp. ch. 6. M. F. Köprülü has argued against a significant Byzantine influence on Ottoman state and society while acknowledging Byzantine influence on Islamic society in earlier centuries ("Bizans Müesseselerinin Osmanlı Müesseseleri Üzerine Te'siri"). Cahen (216–17) makes some useful remarks on this historiographical controversy.

27. Mustafa Ali, *Künh ül-Ahbar*, quoted in Miller, *Beyond the Sublime Porte* (29–30). The prince was Uğurlu Mehmed, who, after his unsuccessful rebellion against his father, the Akkoyunlu ruler Uzun Hasan, sought refuge at the Ottoman court; Mehmed II betrothed one of his granddaughters to the prince.

28. On the history and meaning of the palace see Miller, *Beyond the Sublime Porte;* F. Davis, *The Palace of Topkapı in Istanbul;* Eldem and Akozan, *Topkapı Sarayı: Bir Mimari Araştırma;* C. G. Fisher and A. Fisher, "*Topkapı Sarayı* in the mid-Seventeenth Century: Bobovi's Description," 5–16; Necipoğlu, "The Formation of an Ottoman Imperial Tradition: The Topkapı Palace in the Fifteenth and Sixteenth Centuries."

29. See Ives, *Anne Boleyn*, 5–15, 122–124, for interesting comments on the nature of Tudor monarchy, which for the most part are apt for the Ottoman case.

30. Marmon, *Eunuchs of the Holy Cities*.

31. Mustafa Ali, *Künh ül-Ahbar*, 290a–b; Süreyya, *Sicill-i Osmani*, 3:619.

32. For similar constellations of power in a European monarchy, see Elias, *The Court Society*, on the French court of Louis XIV.

33. For explanation of career path relationships among the inner and outer palace hierarchies and military/administrative service, see İnalcık, *The Ottoman Empire: The Classical Age, 1300–1600*, 79–84, and Kunt, *The Sultan's Servants: The Transformation of Ottoman Provincial Government, 1550–1650*, ch. 4, especially the diagram on page 68.

Chapter 1

1. See the Appendix for a genealogy of the Ottoman dynasty. Although it contains many errors, the most comprehensive genealogical study of the dynasty is still Alderson, *The Structure of the Ottoman Dynasty*. See also Oransay, *Osmanlı Devletinde Kim Kimdi?*, an updated version of the section dealing with the dynasty in vol. 1 of Süreyya's late-nineteenth-century Ottoman biographical dictionary, *Sicill-i Osmanî*.

2. Doukas, *Decline and Fall of Byzantium to the Ottoman Turks*, 136.

3. Roe, *The Negotiations of Sir Thomas Roe in his Embassy to the Ottoman Porte*, 46.

4. At issue here are not abstract concepts or ideals of sovereignty such as those current in the Europe of Süleyman's contemporaries: the notion of a national sovereignty inhering in a territorial base, embodied in, for example, "the king of France"; the notion of sovereignty derived from an historic precedent, such as rulership of the Holy Roman Empire; or the legal-constitutional notion articulated in sixteenth-century England of "the king's two bodies"—the abstract, legal quality of kingship and the flesh-and-blood monarch, which might at first seem analogous to Ottoman allegiance to the dynasty as a whole over an individual sultan. (On the sixteenth-century revival of the Holy Roman Empire, see Yates, *Astrea: The Imperial Theme in the Sixteenth Century*, pt. 1: "Charles V and the Idea of the Empire"; on English constitutional theory, see Kantorowicz, *The King's Two Bodies*, 12–23 and throughout.)

5. Roux, "L'Origine céleste de la souveraineté dans les inscriptions Paléo-Turques de Mongolie et de Sibérie," esp. 234–39.

6. See ch. 2, n. 18.

7. Aşıkpaşazade, *Tevarih-i Al-i Osman*, ch. 4; Neşri, *Kitab-ı Cihan-Nüma*, 1:26; [Anonymous], *Die Altosmanischen anonymen Chroniken: Tevarih-i Al-i Osman*, 6–7; Uruc, *Tevarih-i Al-i Osman*, 8–9 (in Uruc's version of the story, Ertuğrul, Osman's father, has the dream about Osman); Kemalpaşazade, *Tevarih-i Al-i Osman*, 1:92–94; Lufti Paşa, *Tevarih-i Al-i Osman*, 20–21; Solakzade, *Tarih*, 8; Sadeddin, *Tac ul-Tevarih*, 1:29–30.

8. This is argued by M. Fuad Köprülü (*Osmanlı Devleti'nin Kuruluşu*, 6–9), who points out two notable thirteenth- and fourteenth-century versions: the dream of the late-tenth-century founder of the Ghaznavid dynasty, Sebüktigin, about his son Mahmud, perhaps the most legendary of Muslim sovereigns (included in the *Tabaqât-i Nâsirî* of the historian Juzjânî); and a version included by the great Persian historian Rashid al-Din in his world history, *Jâmi' al-Tawârîkh*, as an example of the traditions of the Central Asian Oghuz Turks (from whom the Ottomans claimed descent). A similar dream experience opens the *Zafarnama*, the celebratory biography of the Central Asian conqueror Timur (Tamerlane) by Sharaf al-Din Yazdi; in this dream the portent of Timur's sovereignty is a brilliant star rising from the breast of one of his ancestors (Woods, "Timur's Genealogy," 91).

9. Tekin, *A Grammar of Orkhon Turkic*, 234–35, 267 (from the Kül Tigin inscription); I have made slight alterations in Tekin's translation.

10. However, a marriage alliance with a powerful dynasty might enhance the status of a lesser prince; Timur acquired legitimacy by marrying a princess from a branch of the Mongol dynasty founded by Chinggis Khan (on the sources of Timur's legitimacy, see Manz, "Tamurlane and the Symbolism of Sovereignty"). There were rare instances of Muslim Turkish or Mongol women ruling, but they were usually replaced as soon as possible with a male dynast, or married and their husband elevated to the throne; on these women see Üçok, *İslam Devletlerinde Kadın Hükümdarlar*.

11. On the roles of Mongol women, see Rossabi, "Khubilai Khan and the Women in His Family."

12. "*hizmet-i terbiye ve nezaret,*" in Karaçelebizade Abdülaziz Efendi, *Ravzat ül-Ebrar Zeyli,* 10r–v. Karaçelebizade was a high-ranking member of the *ulema* in the mid-seventeenth century.

13. Kramers, "Sultan," *EI(1).*; B. Lewis, *The Political Language of Islam,* 51ff.

14. In an imperial gift register covering the years 1503–23 (Ceyb-i Hümayun Masraf Defteri, Atatürk Library, Muallim Cevdet 0.71), the sons of Bayezid II carry the title *bey* (as well as *sultan*), but toward the end of the register, the title *bey* is given only to lesser male members of the dynasty, such as the sons of princesses. In a royal order sent to the prince Selim in 1491, both titles were used simultaneously: the prince was addressed as "Sultan Selimşah Bey" (Gökbilgin, *Edirne ve Paşa Livası,* 159). While it fell out of fashion for royal women, the title *khatun* continued to signify status, being given for example to the harem stewardess and the royal wet nurse, as well as to other women of the elite.

15. However, if in general reference the ruler was not known as "sultan," by the sixteenth century other members of the royal family were: princes and princesses were known as *şehzade sultan* (royal son/daughter), principal concubines as *haseki sultan* (royal favorite), and the reigning sultan's mother as *valide sultan* (royal mother).

16. Wittek advanced the idea that the function of *khan* in this title (*Sultan X Khan*), which was used only by the monarch, was to signify his supreme position in the dynastic family, his rulership ("Notes sur la Tughra ottomane," 329–34).

17. On these titles, see ch. 4, n. 76.

18. Quoted in Kunt, *The Sultan's Servants,* 41–42.

19. According to the *fetvas* of Ebussuud, the leading Ottoman jurisconsult of the sixteenth century, if there were clear signs of puberty, it could begin as early as twelve years of age; in the absence of physical changes, it began at eighteen for males and seventeen for females (*Ebussuûd Efendi Fetvaları,* ed. Düzdağ, 33).

20. Imber's recent work, *The Ottoman Empire, 1300–1481,* makes thorough use of non-Ottoman sources in addition to the early Ottoman histories in order to rectify this historiographical problem. Imber devotes his efforts to the construction of an accurate chronological narrative and deliberately eschews analysis.

21. Deshayes de Courmenin, *Voyage de Levant,* 176; Pakalın, *Osmanlı Tarih Deyimleri ve Terimleri Sözlüğü,* 3:331. Growing a beard was a common symbol of political maturity: the young men in training in the imperial palace were not permitted to grow beards until their formal promotion from palace training to their first appointment. A miniature illustration in the *Süleymanname* by Arifi, the court historiographer of Süleyman's reign, indicates an exception to this rule: in a scene in which Süleyman converses with his eldest son, Mustafa, the prince has a beard (Atıl, *Süleymanname: The Illustrated History of Süleyman the Magnificent,* plate 48; see ch. 3, fig. 3-1 of this volume). Süleyman's father, Selim I, appears to have been an exception to the customary growing of a beard by the sultans, or so at least miniature representations of him suggest.

22. In Iznik Süleyman Pasha, son of Orhan, endowed a religious college (*medrese*), the first in the Ottoman domain. Yakup Bey, the son of Murad I, built a mosque in Iznik.

23. İnalcik, "Osmanlılarda Saltanat Veraset Usulü ve Türk Hakimiyet Telakkisiyle İlgisi." See also Giese, "Das Seniorat im osmanischen Herrscherhause," 248–50.

24. See Chejne, *Succession to the Rule in Islam,* 139–42 and *passim.*

25. The Germiyanid princess Devletşah, who married Bayezid I, brought as her dowry the greater part of her father's possessions.

26. The earlier mosque complex in Üsküdar associated with Mihrimah had been built for her by her father.

27. Mustafa Ali, *Künh ül-Ahbar,* 220b.

Chapter 2

1. Male dynasts may have made marriages with the daughters of Ottoman notables as well, but claims for such alliances are weakly attested, if at all, given the present state of historical knowledge.

2. Bellefonds, "Kafâ'a," 404.

3. In 1450 Murad II married his son Mehmed (II) to Sitti, a princess of the House of Dulkadır, a principality on the Ottomans' southeastern frontier; Mehmed in turn married his son Bayezid (II) to Ayşe, another Dulkadır princess, in 1467 (most probably to secure the neutrality of the Dulkadır rulers in anticipation of his eastern campaign against the Akkoyunlus in 1468); and Bayezid married his son Mehmed to the daughter of the vassal Crimean khan Mengli Giray in 1504.

4. Alderson, *The Structure of the Ottoman Dynasty,* esp. the genealogy of Mehmed II, table 27.

5. Taken after Mehmed's defeat of her father, David Komnenus, in 1461, Anna was given to Zaganos Mehmed Pasha, one of the sultan's closest counselors (perhaps after spending time in the imperial harem), and eventually married to another Ottoman official (Doukas, *Decline and Fall of Byzantium,* 322, n. 321). Sphrantzes's wife and children were captured at the fall of Constantinople and sold to the sultan's master of the stable; the latter, who, according to Sphrantzes, "amassed a great fortune by selling many other beautiful noble ladies," retained Sphrantzes's wife but sold his children to the sultan. Sphrantzes was able to ransom his wife, but Thamar died in 1455 in the sultan's palace of an infectious disease at age fourteen (Sphrantzes, *The Fall of the Byzantine Empire,* 70–71, 75). According to contemporary Greek sources, Mehmed the Conqueror demanded Helena, the daughter of Demetrios Paleologus, ruler of the Greek Morea, to seal the latter's capitulation in 1458. There is disagreement about the outcome of the negotiations that took place: the marriage project may have been abandoned (Alderson, *The Structure of the Ottoman Dynasty,* table 27, n. 10), while according to Sphrantzes, Helena died in 1467 in Istanbul from the plague.

6. Menavino, *I Cinque Libri della legge religione et vita de' Turchi della corte,* ch. 34, 134.

7. For example, Uluçay, the principal historian of the Ottoman harem, describes the reign of Bayezid II (1481–1512) as "a transition period" between interdynastic marriage and concubinage, the period when the royal offspring "began" to be born through concubinage ("Bayezid II.in Ailesi," 105–6).

8. On the Muslim concubine, see Marmon, "Concubinage, Islamic"; Schacht, "Umm Walad"; Brunschvig, "'Abd."

9. This assertion must for now remain a hypothesis because of the lack of studies of other dynasties' reproductive politics.

10. To my knowledge the only exception is the short history of Şükrullah, *Behçet ül-Tevarih.*

11. Hammer, *Histoire de l'empire ottoman,* 2:187. On the Byzantine ceremonial that preceded Theodora's departure, see Bryer, "Greek Historians on the Turks: The Case of the First Byzantine-Ottoman Marriage."

12. BA, Mühimme Defteri 31, f. 217, quoted in Uzunçarşılı, *Osmanlı Tarihi,* 1:561, n. 1.

13. For a concise treatment of the role of dervish leaders in the early Ottoman period, see Beldiceanu-Steinherr, "Le Règne de Selîm Ier: Tournant dans la vie politique et religieuse de l'empire ottoman," 35–42; see also the important article by Barkan, "İstila Devirlerinin Kolonizatör Türk Dervişleri ve Zaviyeler," esp. 284–85. For the religio-political influence of dervish sheikhs in Central Asia and Anatolia, see Köprülü, *Türk Edebiyatında İlk Mutasavvıflar*, 195–200, 253–54, and "Ahmed Yesevi." The military role of dervishes can be observed even as late as the Turkish War of Independence following the collapse of the Ottoman Empire in World War I: concerning popular belief in their role in the victorious war, see the memoirs of Aziz Nesin, *Istanbul Boy*, vol. 1, 66–67.

14. Like the Ottomans, other Muslim sovereigns who appealed to Turco-Mongol legitimizing principles sought the blessing of popular religious leaders: for the efforts of Timur, see Barthold, *A Short History of Turkestan*, and Manz, *The Rise and Rule of Tamerlane*, 17–18; for the Akkoyunlu ruler Uzun Hasan, see Woods, *The Aqquyunlu: Clan, Confederation, Empire*, 94–96, 101, 119–20.

15. Uzunçarşılı, "Gazi Orhan Bey Vakfiyesi," 282, 284–85.

16. Uzunçarşılı suggests that the Umur Bey of the endowment deed was of Pachymeres's Amouri ("Gazi Orhan Bey Vakfiyesi," 285). Other scholars have suggested that the Amouri (notably Muzaffer al-Din Yavluk Aslan) were the descendents of Çoban, a Seljuk amir (Togan, *Umumi Türk Tarihine Giriş*, 326–327; İnalcık, "The Emergence of the Ottomans," 266–67; Zachariadou, "Pachymeres on the 'Amourioi' of Kastamonu"; Yücel, *Çoban-Oğulları, Candar-Oğulları Beylikleri*, 47); Cahen (*Pre-Ottoman Turkey*, 310–12) reserves judgment.

17. The fact that Edebali's daughter is called by different names in the sources, for example, Rabia and Bala, suggests that these may have been the names of other wives. Sheikh Edebali's daughter is referred to as "Rabia" in the history of Uruc (*Tevarih-i Al-i Osman*, 9, 12), and as "Malhun" in those of Aşıkpaşazade (*Tevarih-i Al-i Osman*, ch. 4) and Neşri (*Kitab-ı Cihan-Nüma*, 1:26, 2:32). The latter tradition has proved dominant, and Orhan's mother Mal Khatun (daughter of Umur Bey) is commonly thought to be Sheikh Edebali's daughter.

18. Neşri, *Kitab-ı Cihan-Nüma*, 1:24; Kemalpaşazade's history contains a much longer and more dramatic and romantic rendering of the story (*Tevarih-i Al-i Osman*, 1:68 ff.).

19. Kepecioğlu (*Bursa Kütüğü*, 2:10–11) states, perhaps on the basis of the land grant record he cites, that Eftendize was the daughter of an Akbaşlu Mahmud Alp, but does not posit any family relationship between Orhan and his wife. In the endowment deed published by Uzunçarşılı ("Gazi Orhan Bey Vakfiyesi"), Efendi is listed as the daughter of Akbaşlu. This was the name, or probably the *lakab* (nickname), of Orhan's uncle, and it is on this basis that Uzunçarşılı concludes that Efendi was Orhan's cousin; further possible evidence is that Süleyman's daughter Efendi, probably named after her mother, had a son named Gündüz, who was probably named after this ancestor. Uzunçarşılı is not aware that Efendi/Eftendize was Orhan's wife.

20. Sultan ibn Orhan was the first of the sons to sign the deed, suggesting that he was the eldest, or the eldest of those present at the witnessing of the deed (the other sons signing were Süleyman and İbrahim, Murad being too young to be a witness or perhaps not even born). Sultan was still alive in the summer of 1347, when John VI Kantakuzenos dined with his son-in-law Orhan and his four sons, including Sultan (Bryer, "Greek Historians on the Turks," 479).

21. Yanki İskender Hoci, "Şehzade Halil'in Sergüzeşti," 442–43; Kepecioğlu, *Bursa Kütüğü*, 1:183–84. In the late seventeenth century a woman named Saliha

appeared in the Bursa court to defend her claim as a descendant of Asporça to her share of this inheritance (TSMA, E 7386/2,3). This endowment deed is said to be the earliest to survive in Ottoman records.

22. Aşıkpaşazade, *Tevarih-i Al-i Osman*, ch. 12, 13; Neşri, *Kitab-ı Cihan-Nüma*, 1:30–31. See also Baysun, "Nilüfer Hatun," 284. Aşıkpaşazade gives 699/1299–1300 as the date for Nilüfer's capture at the victory at Bilejik.

23. Turgut, *İznik ve Bursa Tarihi*, 180.

24. This is the hypothesis of Kepecioğlu (*Bursa Kütüğü*, 10–11), who bases it on the fact it was common for Turkish families of this period to name their children after their (the children's) grandparents; Süleyman had a daughter named Eftendize, as his younger brother Murad, son of Nilüfer, had a daughter named Nilüfer.

25. All manuscripts of Ibn Battuta's work give Balayun Khatun as the name of Orhan's wife. H.A.R. Gibb, editor and translator of the work into English, suggests that this may be an error for Nilüfer Hatun, introduced because of the similarity of the Arabic orthography of the two names (*The Travels of Ibn Battuta*, 2:453, n.149). Baysun ("Nilüfer Hatun," 284) discusses the controversy surrounding the name of this wife of Orhan.

26. Ibn Battuta, *The Travels*, 2:454.

27. For example, Bülbül (nightingale), Hüma (mythical bird of paradise), Kumru (dove), Gülruh (rose-cheeked), Gülbahar (rose blossom), Gülşah (rose monarch), Çiçek (flower).

28. İnalcık, "Servile Labor in the Ottoman Empire," 35.

29. Ibn Battuta, *The Travels*, 2:441.

30. According to early histories (Neşri, *Kitab-ı Cihan-Nüma*, 1:35, 2:48, and Uruc, *Tevarih-i Al-i Osman*, 13), command of one of the two fortresses constructed for the seige of Bursa was given to Osman's slave (*kul*) "Balabancık bahadırı" (Osman's nephew held command of the other). In variant versions of the text, Balaban is said to be Osman's brother's slave (Neşri, *Neşri Tarihi*, 1:116). Perhaps Balaban and others like him were considered to be in the service of the ruling family as a whole, thus presaging the *kapıkulu*.

31. Aşıkpaşazade, *Tevarih-i Al-i Osman*, ch. 29; Neşri, *Kitab-ı Cihan-Nüma*, 1:43, 2:64–65. The simplicity of Osman's household was probably exaggerated by later historical tradition, which was critical of later sultans' accumulation of wealth.

32. Aşıkpaşazade, *Tevarih-i Al-i Osman*, ch. 22.

33. Doukas, *Decline and Fall of Byzantium*, 71–72.

34. Uzunçarşılı, "Gazi Orhan Bey Vakfiyesi," 279–81. A later *vakfiye* of 1360 was witnessed by one Evrenkuş Hadım, who was probably also a eunuch (Uzunçarşılı, "Orhan Gazi'nin, Vefat Eden Oğlu Süleyman Paşa İçin Tertip Ettirdiği Vakfiyenin Aslı," 442).

35. For example, Arnakis, "Gregory Palamas among the Turks and Documents of His Captivity as Historical Sources," 113.

36. Ibn Battuta, *The Travels*, 2:452.

37. Kepecioğlu, *Bursa Kütüğü*, 2:145–47.

38. Yakhşi's small underground tomb is located near Gülçiçek's larger tomb in Bursa (Baykal, *Bursa ve Anıtları*, 45). It is today a local pilgrimage site, for Yakhşi is remembered as a holy man.

39. Gülçiçek's endowment deed mentions two relatives named Mihal and Todoros (Kepecioğlu, *Bursa Kütüğü*, 2:145).

40. G. Lewis, trans., *The Tales of Dede Korkut*.

41. Doukas, *Decline and Fall of Byzantium*, 241.

42. Taçlu Khatun was given to Tajizade Jafer Bey, the chief military judge of Anatolia (Sadeddin Efendi, *Selimname*, 75r). According to a variant tradition, it was not Taçlu Khatun but Bihruze Khatun, another wife of Shah Ismail, who was taken by Selim; Taçlu Khatun, "the shah's beloved," was also captured, but managed to bargain her way to freedom by giving up a valuable pair of earrings.

43. TSMA, E 5038 (in Uluçay, *Osmanlı Sultanlarına Aşk Mektupları*, 42–43).

44. Khunji, *Târîkh-i 'Alam-âra-yi Amînî*, trans. V. Minorsky, 20.

45. The exception was the daughter of the *müfti* Esad Efendi, whom Osman II married in 1621 (see ch. 4, 106).

46. Busbecq, *Turkish Letters*, 29; Baudier, *Histoire générale du serrail*, 53. Petis de la Croix rejected this explanation, although acknowledging that it was widespread, and went on to endorse the second explanation (*Etat general de l'empire otoman*, 106).

47. Withers, *The Grand Signiors Serraglio*, 342; Deshayes de Courmenin, *Voyage de Levant*, 164; Baudier, *Histoire géneralle*, 53; Rycaut, *The Present State of the Ottoman Empire*, 155.

48. Brunschvig, "'Abd," 34; Marmon, "Concubinage, Islamic," 528.

49. Ménage, "Some Notes on the *Devshirme*," 72–77.

50. See Ménage, "Some Notes on the *Devshirme*," 66, and Kunt, *The Sultan's Servants*, 41–42, for a discussion of the ambiguous meaning of the term *kul* (slave, servant), which can refer not only to those legally of slave status, but also to other members of the ruling class, and even to the lowliest of the sultan's subjects.

51. See ch. 5 for development of this idea.

52. "Al-mulk 'aqîm," quoted in Mottahedeh, *Loyalty and Leadership in an Early Islamic Society*, 190. The Ottoman historian Peçevi quoted a version of this proverb in speaking of Selim I's anger at his milk-brother's presumption that the sultan would favor him: "Hükümdarlarda vefa olmaz" (There can be no loyalty in a monarch) (Peçevi, *Tarih*, 1:455).

53. Menavino, *I Cinque Libri*, 134.

54. There is little evidence, and none of a conclusive nature, that royal wives bore children. There is a possibility that Hadije Halime, the Jandarid wife of Murad II, was the mother of the younger of his two sons named Ahmed (see Kemalpaşazade, *Tevarih-i Al-i Osman*, 7:6). The birth of a son to Murad II late in his career may have been prompted by fear that the dynasty was in jeopardy, since the only living males were the sultan himself, his eighteen-year-old son Mehmed, and one grandson. Murad may have hoped that Mehmed would not execute Ahmed upon his accession since the small child would presumably present no challenge to Mehmed, who was guaranteed the succession. One assumes nevertheless that Hadije Halime and Murad were alert to the possibility that Ahmed would meet a violent end.

55. Reasonably effective methods of birth control were known to the medieval Muslim world and their use sanctioned; see Musallam, *Sex and Society in Islam*, esp. ch. 5.

56. Sphrantzes, *The Fall of the Byzantine Empire*, 61.

57. See Musallam, *Sex and Society in Islam*, esp. ch. 5.

58. Şükrullah, *Behçet ül-Tevarih*, 58, 62.

59. Uzunçarşılı ("Osmanlı Tarihinin İlk Devirlerine Aid Bazı Yanlışlıkların Tashihi," 185–87) has shown that the mother of Mehmed I was a slave woman named Devlet (an unusual name for a slave in this period since it was often used for princesses from one dynasty married into another). That Devlet Khatun was a slave can be deduced from her endowment deed, in which her patronymic appears as *bint 'abd Allah,* the typical patronymic of a convert to Islam. Murad II's mother has

traditionally been taken to be Emine Khatun, daughter of the Dulkadıroğulları ruler Süli Bey. According to Şükrullah (*Behçet ül-Tevarih*, 62), not only Murad's mother but the mothers of all Mehmed I's sons were slave women; Şükrullah (58) says the same of the mothers of all Bayezid I's sons. See Uluçay, *Padişahların Kadınları ve Kızları*, 14–15, for Mehmed II's mother Hüma Khatun, and 21–23, for Selim I's mother Gülbahar Khatun.

60. Uluçay, *Padişahların Kadınları*, 7–8.

61. Imber, *The Ottoman Empire*, 64–67.

62. For a serious history that almost uniformly asserts Muslim royal identity for the sultans' mothers, see Mustafa Cezar et al., *Mufassal Osmanlı Tarihi*, Istanbul, 1957–60.

63. See Uzunçarşılı, *Osmanlı Tarihi*, 1:70; Uluçay, *Padişahların Kadınları*, 8–9.

64. Uluçay, *Padişahların Kadınları*, 19–20; Gökbilgin, *Edirne ve Paşa Livası*, 318. Sitti Khatun's mosque may have been finished by another Dulkadır princess, Ayşe Khatun, who was Sitti's niece and married to Mehmed's son Bayezid II (Babinger, *Mehmed the Conqueror and His Time*, 58).

65. Kemalpaşazade, *Tevarih-i Al-i Osman*, 7:236ff.

66. For the Akkoyunlu view, see Khunji, *Târîkh-i 'Alam-ârâ-yi Amînî*, trans. V. Minorsky, 20, n.2; for the Ottoman view, see Tursun Beg, *Tarih-i Ebü'l-Feth*, 209.

67. Doukas, *Decline and Fall of Byzantium*, 190.

68. Sphrantzes, *The Fall of the Byzantine Empire*, 62.

69. Bryer, "Greek Historians on the Turks," 488.

70. Babinger, *Mehmed the Conqueror*, 66, 149, 162ff., 276ff., 289; Ménage, "Seven Ottoman Documents from the Reign of Mehemmed II."

71. Bassano, *Costumi et i modi*, ch. 15, folio 18r, and ch. 17, folio 21r.

72. Alberi, *Relazioni*, 1:115–16.

73. "In his grandfather's time, Orhan Ghazi performed this task [of commander], and in his father's time, his brother Süleyman Pasha did. Because he himself had no such relative to appoint, he appointed Lala Şahin. Lala Şahin was the first commander who was not of Ottoman descent" (Müneccimbaşı, *Sahaif ül-Ahbar fi Vekayi ül-A'sar*, 3:292).

74. This is an estimate based on undocumented dates in the historical tradition. Assuming Murad was born around 1326, the traditional date, his eldest son could have been born in 1343 (figuring Murad would receive his first consort at the age of sixteen).

75. See Imber, *The Ottoman Empire*, 26–27, 37, for the reigns of Murad I and Bayezid I.

76. Neşri, *Kitab-ı Cihan-Nüma*, 1:138.

77. İnalcık, *The Ottoman Empire*, 59.

78. Fleischer, "From Şehzade Korkud to Mustafa Ali: Cultural Origins of the Ottoman *Nasihatname*," 4–5.

79. M. Arif, ed., *Kanunname-i Al-i Osman*, 27.

80. Neşri, *Kitab-ı Cihan-Nüma*, 1:153.

81. Kemalpaşazade, *Tevarih-i Al-i Osman*, 7:238ff.

82. Amasya had been the capital of the Eretnid state, which passed into the hands of Kadı Burhaneddin, from whom the Ottomans took it; Konya had been the capital of the principality of Karaman and earlier capital of the Anatolian branch of the great medieval dynasty of the Seljuks; and Manisa was the capital of the principality of Saruhan; other capitals and their former ruling houses included Kastamonu (Jandar), Kütahya (Germiyan), Antalya (Hamid), and Trabzon (a branch of the Byzantine Comnenos dynasty).

83. İnalcık, "Murad II," 598.

84. The eldest son was generally given command of the right "arm" (*kol*) and the next eldest of the left "arm"; leading officers holding command of the right and left "wings" (*cenah*) presumably backed up the princes. At the battle of Kosovo in 1389, Murad I's eldest son Bayezid commanded the right arm and his second son Yakub the left arm. At the battle of Başkent, the Akkoyunlu right wing was commanded by the Akkoyunlu sultan Uzun Hasan's third son Zeynal, who died in battle, and the left wing by Uzun Hasan's nephew Murad b. Jihangir. Uzun Hasan's second son Uğurlu Muhammad, also on the left, led the charge on the Ottoman camp.

85. The asper, or *akçe*, was the silver coin that formed the basis for most financial transactions in this period. See Pakalın, "Akça," *Osmanlı Tarih Deyimleri ve Terimleri Sözlüğü*, 1:32–35.

86. TSMA, D 10052 (a register of household staff and expenses for March–May 1513) and D 8030 (a similar undated register, but clearly of a later date). These registers have been partially transcribed by Uluçay ("Kanuni Sultan Süleyman ve Ailesi ile İlgili Bazı Notlar ve Vesikalar," 243–49); Uluçay's transcriptions contain a number of errors as well as omissions.

87. The female doctor (*hekime*) certainly could have complained of salary discrimination: she was paid two aspers a day while the male Jewish doctor Sinan earned fifteen aspers a day (TSMA, D 8030, folio 3a).

88. Peçevi, *Tarih*, 2:89.

89. See Fleischer, *Bureaucrat and Intellectual in the Ottoman Empire: The Historian Mustafa Ali (1541–1600)*, 54–55, for Ali's attempts to win favor at the princely court of Murad (III).

90. Report of the Venetian ambassador, March 4, 1533, in Hammer, *Histoire*, 5:489.

91. Peçevi, *Tarih*, 2:90.

92. Angiolello, *Historia Turchesca*, 128.

93. Doukas, *Decline and Fall of Byzantium*, 115. On the campaign, see Imber, *The Ottoman Empire*, 78–79. The earlier capture of Bayezid I by Timur may offer indirect evidence that concubines were separated from the sultan: it was Bayezid's wife Maria who was with him at the time of his capture, suggesting she must have accompanied the sultan on campaign.

94. Gülşah Khatun may have been a party to illicit relations between the prince and the wife of the grand vezir Mahmud Pasha; see Uzunçarşılı, "Fatih Sultan Mehmed'in Vezir-i Azamlarından Mahmud Paşa ile Şehzade Mustafa'nın Araları Niçin Açıktı?" Angiolello denied any role for Mahmud Pasha in Mustafa's death (*Historia Turchesca*, 66).

95. Neşri, *Kitab-ı Cihan-Nüma*, 1:221.

96. See Yınanç, "Ahmed Paşa, Gedik," 196.

97. However, princes—at least seasoned princes—may have been able to exert some control over the choice of their *lalas*. Selim I, while at his post in Trabzon, refused to accept appointees who were not to his liking (Uzunçarşılı, *Osmanlı Devletinin Saray Teşkilatı*, 125).

98. TSMA, E 5499; reproduced in Uluçay, *Haremden Mektuplar*, 36–40.

99. TSMA, E 5432, in Uluçay, *Haremden Mektuplar*, 23–24.

100. "La Madonna vecchia." This was probably Angiolello's approximation of a Turkish title. In salary registers, the prince's mother was listed as "hazret-i khatun-ı mu'azzama," "the most exalted Lady" (TSMA, D 8030, 1b; D 10052, 1b).

101. Angiolello, *Historia Turchesca*, 69–70; the "maidens" were most likely the

slave women in Mustafa's harem who served as ladies-in-waiting to the prince's mother; his concubines would presumably have been among those sent to the imperial palace and married out, unless they had children, as in the case of Nergisşah's mother, when they would have remained in the imperial harem to raise them. Angiolello also describes the funeral oration delivered by Nergisşah, whom he describes as well educated.

102. Uluçay, *Padişahların Kadınları*, 22.

103. Especially at their accession and during military campaigns, the sultans visited the tombs of their ancestors and the tombs of warriors and holy men associated with the *ghazi* enterprise. This was an important public royal ritual and a means of maintaining the moral and political authority of the dynasty. In addition to visiting tombs, restoring the tombs of earlier Islamic and Ottoman heroes was a major aspect of the endowment of public works undertaken by most sultans. Tomb restoration provided another means by which the sultans could remind their subjects of their heritage and of their duties as loyal Muslims and servants of the Ottoman dynasty. Other than caring for the tombs of their dynastic ancestors, the sultans put most of their effort into caring for the tombs of important religious figures, thereby enhancing their own charisma and winning or cementing the loyalty of the followers of those figures.

104. Aşıkpaşazade, *Tevarih-i Al-i Osman*, ch. 5. The tomb of Aydoğdu, son of Osman's brother Gündüz, also martyred in battle, became known as a place where injured horses might be cured through circumambulation of the tomb (Aşıkpaşazade, *Tevarih-i Al-i Osman*, ch. 17; Neşri, *Kitab-ı Cihan-Nüma*, 1:34; Uruc, *Tevarih-i Al-i Osman*, 13).

105. Bates, "Women as Patrons of Architecture in Turkey," 245–46.

106. Since the tomb of Osman and the neighboring tomb of Orhan were constructed in 1868 to replace a single tomb housing both sultans that was destroyed by earthquake and fire (Turgut, *İznik ve Bursa Tarihi*, 141), it is not possible to determine the placement of family catafalques before the reconstruction or indeed to determine their original placement. Asporça Khatun's catafalque is today located in the tomb of Osman, but was presumably, like the several other catafalques housed in the two tombs, located in the single pre-1868 tomb. On Nilüfer's death and burial, see Aşıkpaşazade, *Tevarih-i Al-i Osman*, ch. 13.

107. Baykal, *Bursa ve Anıtları*, 45, 142. Today (1991) the small tomb of Devlet Khatun is well cared for and marked as a (minor) tourist site, whereas the somewhat larger tomb of Gülçiçek Khatun is not as well marked; it must be known to the local population, however, since the nearby underground tomb of her son Yakhşi is a pilgrimage site.

108. With the exception of Gülbahar Khatun, concubine of Bayezid II and mother of Selim I, who died in Trabzon during her son's princely governorate there and was buried there. Since the identity of Murad II's mother is not certain, it cannot be determined where she is buried.

109. TSMA, E 3058.

110. TSMA, D 8030, 1b.

111. TSMA, D 8030, 1b. Hafsa Khatun is thought to have been the mother of more than one daughter of Selim I; since the register does not identify the princess by name, it is not clear which one is meant. The princess appears as "the sister of His Majesty the Prince" (*hemşire-i hazret-i mir*).

112. Ibn Battuta, *The Travels*, 2:480–89.

113. Ibn Battuta, *The Travels*, 2:340.

114. "Bcg" and "bey" (as well as "bek") are variant renderings of the Arabic spelling; the core meaning of *bey* is one who exercises executive power: lord, governor, prince, ruler, and so on.

115. On the Seljukid atabegate, see Cahen, "Atabak"; Lambton, *Continuity and Change in Medieval Persia,* 229–33.

116. Lambton, *Continuity and Change in Medieval Persia,* 246.

117. See the chapter devoted to Shajar al-Durr in Üçok, *İslam Devletlerinde Kadın Hükümdarlar.* I am grateful to Michael Winter for his comments on this discussion.

118. Even the stipend of the mother of a prince was linked to that of her son: as Süleyman's princely stipend increased, so did that of Hafsa (TSMA, D 8030, 1b; D 10052, 1b).

119. TSMA, D 8030, 1b.

120. Alberi, *Relazioni,* 3:102.

121. Bassano, *Costumi et i modi,* folio 19r.

122. Alberi, *Relazioni,* 1:77.

123. Alberi, *Relazioni,* 3:102.

124. Alberi, *Relazioni,* 1:173.

125. Kepecioğlu, *Bursa Kütüğü,* 3:165–66; and "Tarihi Bilgiler ve Vesikalar," 405 ff.

126. The endowment consisted of the rent from forty-two houses in Bursa and the interest from cash loans. A record of income and expenditure of the endowment for the six-year period 1761–67 shows income of 17,372 aspers a year and expenditures of 27,000 aspers; the administrator of the tomb complains to the chief black eunuch, to whom the record was sent, of his inability to function with such a shortfall (TSMA, D 5290).

Chapter 3

1. Mustafa Ali, *Künh ül-Ahbar,* 7a–b.

2. There is at present no comprehensive scholarly study of Süleyman's reign. Gökbilgin, in his "Süleyman I," concentrates on conquest and diplomacy. The best short treatment of the period is Veinstein, "L'Empire dans sa grandeur (XVIe siècle)."

3. Sokolnicki, "La Sultane Ruthène," 229–30. The author cites a seventeenth-century Polish use of the term "Roxolanes" to mean "Ruthenian maidens." See also Hammer, *Histoire,* 5:487.

4. Alberi, *Relazioni,* 3:78. Until the middle of Süleyman's reign, his female household was lodged in a residence (known as "the Old Palace") separate from his own (known as "the New Palace"). On the transfer of residence of the harem, see ch. 5.

5. Alberi, *Relazioni,* 3:96.

6. Alberi, *Relazioni,* 3:102.

7. Bassano, *Costumi et i modi,* 18r.

8. Sanuto, *I Diarii,* 41:534–35.

9. In Bragadin's words, *carne venduta.* Since Mahidevran herself was a slave, this is a case of the pot calling the kettle black, unless Hurrem had been purchased in the slave market while Mahidevran had been presented to the sultan as a gift.

10. Alberi, *Relazioni,* 1:74–75.

11. On the training of ambassadors and the role they played in the political culture of the Venetian Republic, see Valensi, "Judith," *Venise et la Sublime Porte: La Naissance du despote.* The ambassadorship to Istanbul was the most prestigious post in a form of service to the state that was required of the educated elite (19).

12. Süleyman received the news of the death of Murad, who was about one or two years old, as he returned from the conquest of Belgrade. Shortly after his return to Istanbul, he lost his eldest son Mahmud, nine years old, and a daughter (who may be the "Raziye" identified in Uluçay, *Padişahların Kadınları,* 39). These deaths may have occurred from an infectious disease making its way through the residence of the sultan's family (according to Hammer, *Histoire,* 5:20, Mahmud died of smallpox). It is not known who the mothers of these children were.

It has been alleged that the mother of Mahmud and Murad was Gülfem Khatun, a woman who maintained considerable status in Süleyman's harem throughout his reign (Skilliter, "Khurrem," 69). While having been the mother of princes would account for Gülfem's continued prestige in Süleyman's harem, it seems unlikely that this was so since she would have been referred to as such (that is, as "mother of the deceased Sultan *X*"/*valide-i merhum Sultan X*) in official documents; see a privy purse register from 1552, where the mothers of princes and princesses are listed as "the mother of X" and Gülfem is simply listed as "Gülfem Khatun." She is referred to simply as "Gülfem Khatun bint Abdullah" on her tombstone, and as "Gülfem Khatun" in an account register of the endowment she established for her Üsküdar mosque (BA, MM No. 15920, folio 1v, an account for the year 1013/1604–5). Moreover, Gülfem does not appear as a slave concubine member of Süleyman's princely staff in Manisa. It is seems likely that Gülfem was the stewardess of the harem or some other high-ranking administrative official.

13. Alberi, *Relazioni,* 3:78.

14. Alderson, *The Structure of the Ottoman Dynasty,* table 30, lists an unnamed daughter who may have married the admiral Müezzinzade Ali Pasha. It is hard to imagine that a daughter of Süleyman could have led such an obscure life; even if she were the daughter of an insignificant concubine, it is likely that she would have had some royal lands assigned to her and therefore left a documentary record.

15. Manisa Mahkeme-i Şer'iye Sicilleri (Manisa Sharia Court Registers), no. 1, folio 57; these *tarih*s ("notable dates") are transcribed, with some omissions and small errors, in Uluçay, "Notlar Ve Vesikalar," 249–50. Presumably visits to Bayezid would be recorded in similar registers in the cities to which he was posted, principally Kütahya.

16. TSMA, E 5038, transcribed in Uluçay, *Aşk Mektupları,* 42–43.

17. For example, Uluçay, *Padişahların Kadınları,* 36.

18. Alberi, *Relazioni,* 1:117.

19. TSMA, E 6056.

20. The fact that Süleyman had married Hurrem in contravention of Ottoman custom was noted by the ambassadors Navagero and Trevisano (Alberi, *Relazioni,* 1:74, 115). Ottoman sources do not describe the wedding, but Mustafa Ali (*Künh ül-Ahbar,* 125a) notes that Süleyman and Hurrem were married. See also Peçevi, *Tarih,* 1:269: "the wife [*halile*] of the fortune-favored sultan and the mother of the princes and princesses, noble of reputation. . . ."

21. Young, *Constantinople,* 135. This entry in the archives of the bank, which Young describes as containing a record of the bank's correspondence with Galata beginning in 1346, is apparently undated.

22. Busbecq, *Turkish Letters,* 118.

23. Alberi, *Relazioni,* 1:29 ("il Gran-Signore . . . l'ha sposata per moglie al modo loro"); De'Ludovici's report to the Venetian senate was delivered on June 3, 1534.

24. This view is expressed by Miller, *Beyond the Sublime Porte,* 89, and Gökbilgin, "Hurrem Sultan," 593.

25. Alberi, *Relazioni*, 1:29.

26. Bassano, *Costumi et i modi*, 17v.

27. BA, AE Kanuni 24; KK Saray 7098. These two registers, from the years 1552 and 1555, respectively, show the entire salaried harem, including Hurrem Sultan, as resident in the Old Palace.

28. Necipoğlu, *The Topkapı Palace*, 437.

29. Alberi, *Relazioni*, 3:148.

30. Bassano, *Costumi et i modi*, 18v.

31. Busbecq, *Turkish Letters*, 49.

32. The letters can be roughly dated by the names of the children in whose name Hurrem sends greeting (for example, TSMA, E 5426 and 5656 were probably written before 1526, the year of Bayezid's birth, since his older brothers and sister are mentioned but he is not). These early letters also contain poetry. Since it is most unlikely that Hurrem was the author of these poems, her reputation as a poet is probably undeserved (see Uluçay, *Padişahların Kadınları*, 35 and 67, for references to Hurrem's poetic talents).

33. Alberi, *Relazioni*, 3:101.

34. Sanuto, *I Diarii*, 42, quoted by Hammer, *Histoire*, 5:87.

35. Celalzade Mustafa, *Tabakat ül-Memalik ve Derecat ül-Mesalik*, 239a–b; Mustafa Ali, *Künh ül-Ahbar*, 41b.

36. TSMA, E 5662 (in Uluçay, *Aşk Mektupları*, 31–32).

37. TSMA, E 5662 (in Uluçay, *Aşk Mektupları*, 31).

38. TSMA, E 5426 (in Uluçay, *Aşk Mektupları*, 36).

39. TSMA, E 5662 (in Uluçay, *Aşk Mektupları*, 31).

40. TSMA, E 5038 (in Uluçay, *Aşk Mektupları*, 37).

41. TSMA, E 6036 (in Gökbilgin, "Hurrem Sultan," 594).

42. TSMA, E 5038 (in Uluçay, *Aşk Mektupları*, 37, 39).

43. Bayezid was stationed in Edirne to guard the European front during the sultan's absence from the capital.

44. TSMA, E 5038 (in Uluçay, *Aşk Mektupları*, 42–43). Uluçay dates this letter to 1548, but the fact that the sultan was wintering in Aleppo and that Jihangir was with him (Hurrem sends her love to him in the letter) makes it clear that it was written in 1553–54.

45. See TSMA, E 5859 (in Uluçay, *Aşk Mektupları*, 45) for Süleyman's request that Hurrem forward to Selim a letter he had sent her. She replied that she had already dispatched a royal courier before the sultan's letter arrived (presumably informing the prince of the same matter), but would send the letter on as he requested.

46. See Mihrimah's letters to Süleyman in Uluçay, *Aşk Mektupları*, 46–47, and *Haremden Mektuplar*, 84–95.

47. Very little work has been done on the royal *damad;* see Mordtmann, "Damad."

48. Mustafa Ali, *Künh ül-Ahbar*, 5a; Koçi Bey, *Risale*, 61. On Mustafa Ali, see Fleischer, *Bureaucrat and Intellectual;* on Koçi Bey, see Imber, "Koçi Bey," and Uluçay, "Koçi Bey."

49. The following discussion depends principally on the following: an imperial gift register covering the years H. 909–29/1503–23, *Ceyb-i Hümayun Masraf Defteri* (Atatürk Library, Muallim Cevdet 0.71); Gökbilgin, *Edirne ve Paşa Livası;* Uluçay, *Padişahların Kadınları*, and "Bayezid II.in Ailesi"; Alderson, *Structure of the Ottoman Dynasty;* Uzunçarşılı, *Osmanlı Tarihi*, vols. 1 and 2.

50. For example, Hafsa, daughter of Mehmed I, married Mahmud Çelebi, son of the Çandarlı grand vezir İbrahim Pasha (Uzunçarşılı, *Çandarlı Vezir Ailesi*, 97).

51. The only exception (which actually proves the rule) would seem to be the

marriage of Gevherhan, daughter of Mehmed the Conqueror, to the Akkoyunlu prince Uğurlu Mehmed, son of the great Akkoyunlu ruler Uzun Hasan; an exile from his own land and refugee at the Ottoman court, the Akkoyunlu prince might be considered a kind of adjunct member of the Ottoman royal household. Bayezid II's daughter Ayşe married Ahmed Mirza, son of Gevherhan and Uğurlu Mehmed.

52. The only *damads* of Bayezid II who were vezirs (of which I am aware) were Bali Bey (d. 1494), married to Hüma; Yahya Pasha (d. 1506), married to Ayşe (her second husband); and the five-times grand vezir Hersekzade Ahmed Pasha (d. 1518), married to Hundi.

53. Of Selim's daughters married during his lifetime, Hafsa was married to İskenderzade Mustafa Pasha (d. 932/1525–1526), not a vezir; Beyhan to Ferhad Pasha (executed in 1524), third vezir; Şehzade to Çoban Mustafa Pasha (d. 936/1529–1530), second vezir; and another princess, probably Hadije, to İskender Pasha (d. 1515), a vezir.

54. On Hersekzade Ahmed Pasha, see Uzunçarşılı, *Osmanlı Tarihi*, 2:535–37.

55. Dukakinzade Ahmed Pasha was married to Ayşe, the daughter of Bayezid's daughter Ayşe and Güveyi Sinan Pasha; Yunus Pasha was married to the daughter of Bayezid's daughter Seljuk and her husband Mehmed, who was himself the son of Koja Mustafa Pasha, Bayezid's last and Selim's first grand vezir.

56. Of Bayezid's grand vezirs, Hadım Ali was a eunuch and Çandarlı İbrahim was from the leading Turkish family of statesmen; of Selim's grand vezirs, Hadım Sinan was a eunuch and Pir Mehmed Pasha was of Turkish origin.

57. Only Bayezid's first grand vezir, İshak Pasha, appears not to have been linked through marriage to the dynasty. The *damad* sons of grand vezirs included Davud Pasha's sons Mehmed and Mustafa, Mesih Pasha's sons Ali and Ahmed, and Koja Mustafa Pasha's sons Mehmed and Muhîeddin.

58. There is controversy over whether Hadije Sultan was in fact İbrahim Pasha's wife. Uzunçarşılı argues she was not ("Kanuni Sultan Süleyman'ın Vezir-i Azamı Makbul ve Maktul İbrahim Paşa Padişah Damadı Değildi"); but Uluçay ("Notlar ve Vesikalar," 231–37) would seem to successfully counter this argument. A further point to add to Uluçay's argument is that, in view of the fact that Lutfi Pasha was married to a princess before İbrahim's marriage and before his own grand vezirate (see Uluçay, *Padişahların Kadınları,* 33), it would seem unlikely that the much-honored İbrahim, already grand vezir, would not be given a princess in marriage. The letters of İbrahim to his wife while he was absent from Istanbul offer a good deal of circumstantial evidence that his wife was a princess.

59. According to Mustafa Ali (*Künh ül-Ahbar,* 123a), Ayas Pasha was abnormally interested in sex. There were said to be, at one time, forty-five cradles rocking in his home, and more than twenty children survived him. See also Peçevi, *Tarih,* 1:20–21.

60. TSMA, E 7859.

61. Peçevi, *Tarih,* 1:31; Süreyya, *Sicill-i Osmanî,* 4:16.

62. Hadije, as one of the three daughters of Süleyman's mother Hafsa, was almost certainly older than Süleyman, and was unlikely to have remained unmarried until 1524 (the year of her marriage to İbrahim), when she would have been at least thirty. Hadije may have been married to İskender Pasha, the *beglerbegi* of Eğriboz and later admiral who was executed in 1515 (Uzunçarşılı, "İbrahim Paşa Padişah Damadı Değildi," 358; Uluçay, *Padişahların Kadınları,* 32). According to Uluçay, Fatma was first married to Mustafa Pasha, the governor (*sanjakbegi*) of Antalya; she was divorced from her husband when it turned out that he was homosexual and had no interest in her (*Padişahların Kadınları,* 31).

63. Alberi, *Relazioni,* 3:107–8; Hammer, *Histoire,* 5:60–61.

64. Peçevi, *Tarih*, 1:81.

65. Celalzade Mustafa, *Tabakat ül-Memalik*, 116a.

66. Hammer, *Histoire*, 5:306.

67. TSMA, D 7859. This document also contains a list of items that made up the the princesses' trousseaus (*çeyiz*); these were primarily jeweled ornaments (belts, tiaras, rings, and so on).

68. Hammer, *Histoire*, 5:53.

69. TSMA, D 7859. This practice continued: in 1586 the admiral Kılıç Ali Pasha was best man to İbrahim Pasha, and in 1593 the vezir Jerrah Mehmed Pasha was best man to the admiral Halil Pasha.

70. Alberi, *Relazioni*, 1:117, 404–7; 2:354–58; 3:239–42, 288–93, 366–74.

71. Hammer, *Histoire*, 6:154.

72. Uluçay, *Padişahların Kadınları*, 41.

73. Altundağ and Turan, "Rüstem Paşa," 803; Gökbilgin, "Mehmed Paşa, Sokollu," 605 (Gökbilgin gives a list of the grand vezir's monuments).

74. It was a holy site because Ayyub, the companion and standard-bearer of the Prophet, was reputedly buried there.

75. Gökbilgin, "Mehmed Paşa, Sokollu," 605.

76. Koçi Bey, *Risale*, 61.

77. For the tie between Zaganos and Oruç Bey, see Kepecioğlu, *Bursa Kütüğü*, 4:169 (on Oruç, see Uzunçarşılı, *Osmanlı Tarihi*, 1:395–96, 573–76); for the tie between Zaganos and Mahmud, see Gökbilgin, *Edirne ve Paşa Livası*, 56, 451; for the tie between İshak and Gedik Ahmed, see Uzunçarşılı, *Osmanlı Tarihi*, 2:534.

78. With the exception of one marriage with the Çandarlı family: Hafsa, the daughter of Mehmed I, was married to Mahmud Bey, the son of the grand vezir Çandarlı İbrahim Pasha (Uzunçarşılı, *Çandarlı Vezir Ailesi*, 97).

79. Mottahedeh, *Loyalty and Leadership in an Early Islamic Society*, 178.

80. The exceptions among grand vezirs were Karamanî Mehmed (1477–81), Çandarlı İbrahim (1498–99), and Piri Mehmed (1517–23).

81. On the military/administrative career paths, see İnalcık, *The Ottoman Empire*, 80ff., and Kunt, *The Sultan's Servants*, 33ff.

82. Mustafa Ali, *Künh ül-Ahbar*, 5a.

83. For the career of İbrahim Pasha, see Gökbilgin, "İbrahim Paşa."

84. Koçi Bey, *Risale*, 63.

85. Gökbilgin, "İbrahim Paşa," 908.

86. For a glowing firsthand account of İbrahim's talents, see the history of Celalzade Mustafa, who had been İbrahim's personal secretary (*Tabakat ül-Memalik*, 277b–78a); see also Mustafa Ali, *Künh ül-Ahbar*, 9b–10a, 121a–b.

87. Mustafa Ali, *Künhül-Ahbar*, 121a; Peçevi, *Tarih*, 1:20; Müneccimbaşı, *Sahaif ül-Ahbar*, 3:480.

88. Peçevi, *Tarih*, 1:20.

89. Alberi, *Relazioni*, 3:103.

90. Necipoğlu, "Süleyman the Magnificent and the Representation of Power in the Context of Ottoman-Hapsburg-Papal Rivalry."

91. Solakzade, *Tarih*, 446; Hammer, *Histoire*, 5:130ff.

92. Peçevi, *Tarih*, 1:154.

93. In Alberi, *Relazioni*, see the reports of Zen (1524), 3:95; Bragadan (1526), 3:103; Minio (1527), 3:116; Zen (1530), 3:121; De'Ludovisi (1534), 1:28–29.

94. Alberi, *Relazioni*, 3:104.

95. According to one tradition, İbrahim was buried in a dervish convent located

behind the imperial dockyard, his grave marked by a single Judas tree (Mustafa Ali, *Künh ül-Ahbar,* 122b); this tradition is repeated in Ayvansarayi, *Hadikat ül-Cevami,* 2:39. According to another tradition, he was buried in Okmeydanı (Süreyya, *Sicill-i Osmanî,* 1:94).

96. Naima, *Tarih,* 2:122–30.

97. On the existence of local forms of power, see Faroqui, "Political Initiatives 'From the Bottom Up' in the Sixteenth- and Seventeenth-Century Ottoman Empire." Faroqui notes İlber Ortaylı's discussion of the absolute power of nineteenth-century sultans in *İmparatorluğun En Uzun Yüzyılı* (Istanbul, 1983); this work was unavailable to me.

98. Mustafa Ali, *Künh ül-Ahbar,* 122b (*be hasb ul-tarîk*).

99. Alberi, *Relazioni,* 1:12, 28.

100. Peçevi, *Tarih,* 1:428.

101. Heyd, *Studies in Old Ottoman Criminal Law,* 183–84; see also Repp, *The Müfti of Istanbul: A Study in the Development of the Ottoman Learned Hierarchy,* 278ff.

102. Mustafa Ali, *Künh ül-Ahbar,* 124a; Peçevi, *Tarih,* 1:21–22.

103. Alberi, *Relazioni,* 1:12.

104. Mustafa Ali, *Künh ül-Ahbar,* 124a; Peçevi, *Tarih,* 1:22.

105. Alberi, *Relazioni:* Navagero in 1553 (1:74); Trevisano in 1554 (1:117); and Cavalli in 1560 (1:295).

106. Alberi, *Relazioni,* 3:90.

107. Busbecq, *Turkish Letters,* 29.

108. Alberi, *Relazioni,* 1:89; see also the report of Erizzo (1557), who commented on Rüstem's enormous power (*Relazioni,* 3:135–36).

109. Altundağ and Turan, "Rüstem Pasha," 801–2.

110. Alberi, *Relazioni,* 1:175–76.

111. Busbecq, *Turkish Letters,* 30; on Rüstem's economies, see also Y. Yücel, ed., *Kitab-ı Müstetab,* 21; Peçevi, *Tarih,* 1:22.

112. Ives, *Anne Boleyn,* 123–24.

113. Report of Andrea Gritti, ambassador extraordinary in 1503, in Alberi, *Relazioni,* 3:23–24; Uğur, *The Reign of Sultan Selim I in the Light of the Selim-Name Literature,* 179ff.

114. Alberi, *Relazioni,* 3:102.

115. The letters are contained in Manisa Mahkeme-i Şer'iye Sicilleri, no. 1 (Manisa Sharia Court Register), and are published in Uluçay, "Kanuni Sultan Süleyman ve Ailesi ile İlgili Bazı Notlar ve Vesikalar," 255–57.

116. These letters are housed in the Topkapı Palace Archives collection (E 5860, E 12316).

117. TSMA, E 5860/11.

118. For the impoverishment and loss of status of Mahidevran after Mustafa's execution, see Kepecioğlu, "Tarihi Bilgiler ve Vesikalar," 405–6; *Bursa Kütüğü,* 2:165–66.

119. Alberi, *Relazioni,* 1:77–78. Navagero's report was delivered in February 1553, eight months before Mustafa's execution.

120. Mustafa Ali, *Künh ül-Ahbar,* 5b–6a; Peçevi, *Tarih,* 1:19.

121. Kemalpaşazade, *Tevarih-i Al-i Osman,* 7, pt. 2, 523–24.

122. Hammer, *Histoire,* 5:328–29, 538.

123. This break with tradition was noted by the ambassador Trevisano (Alberi, *Relazioni,* 1:115).

124. Mustafa was buried in Bursa, and Bayezid, with four of his five sons, in the central Anatolian city of Sivas.

125. Peçevi, *Tarih*, 1:300.

126. Alberi, *Relazioni*, 1:77.

127. Navagero (1553), in Alberi, *Relazioni*, 1:77.

128. See Gökbilgin, "Rüstem Paşa ve Hakkındaki İthamlar," 20–26.

129. Bayezid II and Süleyman reigned to a much older age than did other sultans: Bayezid I and Mehmed I were probably in their forties when they died (their precise birth dates are not known, historical tradition positing that each was born during the year of his father's accession), Murad II reigned until he was forty-seven, Mehmed II until he was forty-nine, Selim I until he was fifty, but Bayezid II until he was sixty-four and Süleyman until he was seventy-two.

130. Alberi, *Relazioni*, 3:102–3.

131. Togan, *Oğuz Destanı*, 17–19 (this is a Turkish translation of the relevant section of the *Jâmi' al-Tawârikh*, the world history of the thirteenth-century Persian statesman and historian Rashîd al-Dîn).

132. Peçevi, *Tarih*, 1:300–301.

133. Peçevi, *Tarih*, 1:300; Peçevi relays the account of Şemsi Agha (later Şemsi Ahmed Pasha), one of the messengers sent by Rüstem Pasha to the sultan.

134. Busbecq, *Turkish Letters*, 158.

135. Busbecq, *Turkish Letters*, 226–28.

136. Busbecq, *Turkish Letters*, 33.

137. TSMA, E 5038, in Uluçay, *Aşk Mektupları*, 43.

138. Mustafa Ali, *Künh ül-Ahbar*, vol. 1, 34.

139. See Fleischer, *Bureaucrat and Intellectual*, 258–59, for the significance of Mustafa's execution in Ali's reading of the empire's history.

140. Mustafa Ali, *Künh ül-Ahbar*, 126b.

141. Busbecq, *Turkish Letters*, 33.

142. Alberi, *Relazioni*, 3:48, 54.

143. Alderson, *The Structure of the Ottoman Dynasty*, table 29, shows three other sons, Abdullah, Mahmud, and Murad, without giving any source. Could this be an error, since these are also the names of the three sons of Süleyman who died in infancy and were buried in the tomb of Selim?

144. Danişmend, *İzahlı Osmanlı Tarihi Kronolojisi*, 2:5, where he gives an incomplete citation for this information.

145. For example, Nizam al-Mulk, *The Book of Government*, trans. H. Darke, 88–89, and in the Ottoman period Lutfi Pasha, *Asafname*, 9.

146. Busbecq, *Turkish Letters*, 65.

147. Alberi, *Relazioni*, 1:73–74, 89.

148. Alberi, *Relazioni*, 3:58. I thank John Najemy for helping me with the translation of this passage.

149. For the honors done to Ebussuud Efendi, see Baysun, "Ebüssu'ûd Efendi"; Repp, *The Müfti of Istanbul*, 290ff.

150. On the concept of *siyâsa*, see B. Lewis, "Siyâsa."

151. Murad I executed his son Savcı for intended insurrection. The date of Savcı's execution is uncertain; the sources suggest dates ranging from 1373 to 1385. Savcı had joined forces with Andronicus, the disaffected eldest son of the Byzantine emperor John Paleologus. Savcı and Andronicus were preparing a rebellion against their fathers when the latter preempted their sons' bid for power. According to tradition, Savcı's rebellion was the reason why princes were never again appointed to provinces in the European border area but were confined to Anatolia. On this rebellion, see Hammer, *Histoire*, 1:254–57; Uzunçarşılı, "Murad I," 592.

152. Alberi, *Relazioni*, 3:164.

153. (*mazhar-ı gazb-ı padişahî*) Peçevi, *Tarih*, 1:303.

154. I thank Michael Cook for this observation.

155. Hammer, *Histoire*, 5:91–92, 195.

156. For İbrahim's household, see Alberi, *Relazioni*, 3:104; for Rüstem's, see Mustafa Ali, *Künh ül-Ahbar*, 125a.

157. This view of Hurrem stems primarily from the judgment, perhaps first put forth by Mustafa Ali, that the execution of Mustafa was a disaster for the Ottoman state, that Hurrem was responsible for it, and that Süleyman was helpless in the face of her intrigues. Even such serious scholars as Baysun and Gökbilgin regard the Hurrem-led triumvirate as pursuing illegitimate actions. Baysun states that "especially in [Süleyman's] old age [Hurrem, Rüstem, and Mihrimah] incited him to improper actions," and speaks of Mihrimah Sultan's "distasteful" role in the succession struggle ("Mihrümah Sultan," 307). Gökbilgin cites "the damaging advice advanced for years by Hurrem Sultan and her daughter" ("Hurrem Sultan," 595). Uluçay states that Süleyman "was forced to marry Hurrem against custom" and that "as he got older, he was even more under her influence and did everything she said" (*Padişahların Kadınları*, 34–35). Ignoring the custom of the princely governorate, Uluçay speaks of the "banishing" of the then eighteen-year-old Mustafa from the palace in 1533 ("Mustafa Sultan," 690). Altundağ and Turan state that "after the success of Hurrem Sultan, to whom [Süleyman] was extremely bound, in having her rival, the mother of Prince Mustafa, banished from the palace, she resorted to every kind of trick in her inordinate ambition to secure the Ottoman throne for her son Selim" ("Rüstem Paşa," 800–801). Shaw presents Hurrem Sultan as being in complete control of the government but gives no source for this extreme interpretation (*History of the Ottoman Empire and Modern Turkey*, 1:90, 98, 104, 108–10). For a similar view, see Uzunçarşılı, *Osmanlı Tarihi*, 2:357–58, 401ff. Skilliter ("Khurrem") does not question this traditional interpretation of Hurrem.

158. See TSMA, E 7816/1, 4–6, imperial deeds of property to Hurrem dating from the 1550s, in which she is referred to as "the mother of my son, Selim."

159. Busbecq, *Turkish Letters*, 29.

Chapter 4

1. Alberi, *Relazioni*, 3:234–35.

2. The identities of Nurbanu Sultan and her daughter-in-law Safiye Sultan are often confused. On this confusion and the proper identity of Nurbanu, see Spagni, "Una Sultana veneziana," and Rossi, "La Sultana Nûr Bânû (Cecilia Venier-Baffo) moglie di Selim II (1566–1574) e madre di Murad III (1574–1595)." Spagni presents an extensive biographical account of Nurbanu Sultan based on Italian sources; for a brief account in English, see Skilliter, "The Letters of the Venetian 'Sultana' Nûr Bânû and Her Kira to Venice," 515–20.

3. Alberi, *Relazioni*, 1:116 (according to the 1554 report of Trevisano, Selim was "addicted to wine and women"); 2:25, 97; 3:166, 180.

4. Şah Sultan and Gevherhan Sultan were born in 951 (1544/1545), İsmihan Sultan in 952 (1545), and Murad in 953 (1546).

5. Fatma was married in 1574, after Murad's accession (Uluçay, *Padişahların Kadınları*, 42). Uluçay asserts that she was the daughter of Nurbanu, but offers no proof for this statement. See n. 52 below.

6. Alderson, *The Structure of the Ottoman Dynasty*, 23. The grandsons' posts were

close to those of their fathers: Orhan went to Çorum at the same time his father was transferred to Amasya, and Murad went to Akşehir when his father was transferred to Konya.

7. Alderson (*The Structure of the Ottoman Dynasty*, table 31) shows Abdullah, Jihangir, Mustafa, Osman, Süleyman, and Mehmed as the six sons; Mehmed predeceased his father, while the others were executed by their elder brother Murad upon his accession. The dates of the births of these sons is uncertain; the report of the ambassador Barbaro (1573) suggests that three sons were born around the time of Selim's accession (Alberi, *Relazioni*, 1:318), while that of Badoaro (also 1573—Badoaro was extraordinary ambassador for peace negotiations) suggests that three sons, the first of Selim's sultanate, were born in 1570 or 1571 (*Relazioni*, 1:362).

8. BA, MM 487, 3r. The women were the mothers of Mehmed, Mustafa, Süleyman, and Abdullah; the mothers of the other two princes, Osman and Jihangir, had probably died. I am grateful to Dr. Gülru Necipoğlu for making copies of the relevant pages of this register available to me. According to Alderson (*The Structure of the Ottoman Dynasty*, table 31, n. 2, with no source given), the mother of Süleyman committed suicide at his execution.

9. Alderson (*The Structure of the Ottoman Dynasty*, table 30) shows six or possibly seven sons of Bayezid (four of whom were executed at the time of their father's execution) and four daughters; these children were born within a period of fifteen years or so. Nothing is known about the mothers of Bayezid's children; since his offspring were born in a period of not more than fifteen years, he probably had more than one consort.

10. Dispatch of Soranzo, October 26, 1566, cited in Spagni, "Una Sultana veneziana," 284.

11. Alberi, *Relazioni*, 1:362.

12. Alberi, *Relazioni*, 2:97; see also the report prepared for the English ambassador in Rosedale, *Queen Elizabeth and the Levant Company*, 23. *Chebin* is the ambassador's rendering of the Turkish *kâbin*, a popular term for the settlement made by a Muslim husband to his wife at the time of their marriage (the legal term is *mihr*). Ragazzoni was wrong regarding Nurbanu's origin; as stated above, she was of Venetian, not Circassian, origin.

13. L. Soranzo, *L'Ottomanno* (Venice, 1600), 2, quoted in Rossi, "La Sultana *Nûr Bânû*," 28, and in Rosedale, *Queen Elizabeth and the Levant Company*, 72. For a brief biographical sketch of Safiye, see Skilliter, "Three Letters from the Ottoman 'Sultana" Safiye to Queen Elizabeth I," 144.

14. On Murad's impotence, see Mustafa Ali, *Künh ül-Ahbar*, 289a–b; Peçevi, *Tarih*, 2:4–5.

15. Alberi, *Relazioni*, 3:284–85; see also the report of Giovanni Moro (1590), 3:328.

16. Reports of the Venetian ambassadors Jacopo Soranza (1581), in Alberi, *Relazioni*, 2:237; Paolo Contarini (1583), 3:234; Gianfrancesco Morosini (1585), 3:284; Giovanni Moro (1590), 3:328; Lorenzo Bernardo (1592), 2:359; Matteo Zane (1594), 3:439; and of Agostino Nani (ca. 1603), in Barozzi and Berchet, *Le Relazioni*, 1:39.

17. Alberi, *Relazioni*, 3:328.

18. Alberi, *Relazioni*, 2:360; Bernardo's report was delivered in 1592.

19. (*menkuha-yı memduhaları Safiye Sultan*) Mustafa Ali, *Künh ül-Ahbar*, 287a.

20. Alberi, *Relazioni*, 3:283; what I have translated as "wife" is in the Italian "la sultana moglie," which was most probably the ambassador's rendering of *haseki sultan*.

21. Rosedale, *Queen Elizabeth and the Levant Company,* 23. See n. 12 above. On the identity of Salomone, see ch. 6, n. 69. Morosini and Salomone may have used the same informant, Safiye's Jewish agent (*kira*), Esther Hanbali.

22. BA, MM 487, 2v. The ambassador Costantino Garzoni reported in 1573, a year before Murad's accession, that he had "two sons from a slave woman" (Alberi, *Relazioni,* 1:403).

23. BA, MM 442.

24. Rosedale, *Queen Elizabeth and the Levant Company,* 20.

25. Alberi, *Relazioni,* 3:180.

26. Estimates of Mahmud's age at his execution range from sixteen to twenty-one (Oransay, *Osmanlı Devletinde Kim Kimdi?,* 1:205).

27. Alberi, *Relazioni,* 1:37.

28. See the reports of Contarini (1583) in Alberi, *Relazioni,* 3:232; Moro (1590), 3:332; Bernardo (1592), 3:352; Zane (1594), 3:439.

29. Alberi, *Relazioni,* 3:439.

30. Süreyya, *Sicill-i Osmanî,* 1:72.

31. Peçevi, *Tarih,* 2:281; Naima, *Tarih,* 1:312–13. Ahmed related this story to Hafız Ahmed Pasha, later grand vezir and husband of one of his daughters; Peçevi learned it from the pasha.

32. See ch. 9, 231–32.

33. The stipend of *şehzades* (the term appears to refer to princesses as well as princes) was one hundred aspers a day.

34. Barozzi and Berchet, *Le Relazioni,* 1:131.

35. Giese, "Das Seniorat," 249. In Giese's opinion, the "riddle" of this succession defied solution (255).

36. Peçevi, *Tarih,* 2:360–61. Distance from the event appears to lessen the amount of detail recounted by historians. Kâtip Çelebi simply remarks "the princes being young, the masters of loosing and binding deemed it proper that [Sultan Ahmed's] brother Sultan Mustafa take his place. . . ." (*Fezleke,* 1:385). Karaçelebizade Abdülaziz Efendi, making no allusion to the problems of this succession, merely reports the fact of Mustafa's accession: "[A]ppointed by the decree of God's will, [Sultan Ahmed's] younger brother Sultan Mustafa, the fortune of the realm, ascended the throne of the House of Osman. . . ." (*Ravzat ül-Ebrar Zeyli,* 535). Naima, writing at the end of the seventeenth century, appears to repeat Peçevi's account, although he omits the role of Mustafa Agha (*Tarih,* 2:160).

37. Purchas, *His Pilgrimes,* 9:407–8; the letter appears as an addendum to Withers's *The Grand Signiors Serraglio.*

38. Naima, *Tarih,* 2:160.

39. Danişmend, *İzahlı Osmanlı Tarihi Kronolojisi,* 3:270.

40. Koçi Bey, *Risale,* 65. According to Evliya Çelebi, but no doubt a gross exaggeration, Murad had thirty-two children, of whom only one survived (*Narrative of Travels in Europe, Asia, and Africa,* trans. J. von Hammer, 118).

41. Giese, "Das Seniorat," 255.

42. Silahdar, *Silahdar Tarihi,* 2:295ff.

43. Naima, *Tarih,* 2:187.

44. Osman either chose not to, or was not permitted to, execute his other brothers; presumably he did not execute his uncle since it must have been thought inconceivable that Mustafa would rule again, and furthermore, he was considered to be a saint.

45. Vandal, *Les Voyages du Marquis de Nointel (1670–1680),* 107.

46. This Turco-Mongol tradition was recalled by the historian Yazıcıoğlu Ali, writ-

ing under the influence of Central Asian traditions during the reign of Murad II (r. 1420–52). In his description of Osman's acquisition of leadership, he says: "The Turkish begs of the frontier gathered together and held an assembly (*kurultay*). When they had discussed the customs (*türe*) of the Oghuz, they appointed Osman Beg, son of Ertuğrul from the tribe of Kayı, khan" (*Tarih-i Al-i Selçuk,* quoted in İnalcık, "Osmanlılarda Saltanat Veraset Usulü," 78). On the principle of election in Islamic tradition, see Chejne, *Succession to the Rule in Islam,* esp. chs. 3 and 4.

47. Giese, "Das Seniorat," 253.

48. Rosedale, *Queen Elizabeth and the Levant Company,* 27–28.

49. *Calendar of State Papers, Venice,* vol. 9, item 328. This passage is quoted in Sanderson, *The Travels of John Sanderson in the Levant 1584–1602,* 58, and in Rosedale, *Queen Elizabeth and the Levant Company,* 39 (with errors).

50. Naima, *Tarih,* 2:187.

51. Alderson, *The Structure of the Ottoman Dynasty,* 33.

52. The birth of Fatma to Selim II in 1559, which appears as an anomoly in the reproductive politics of the times as I have reconstructed them, may make some sense from this perspective. Nurbanu's son Murad left for the provinces in 1558; if her sexual role ceased at that point, Fatma may have been the result of Selim's new relationship with another concubine. This was probably an unintended birth, since no other children appear to have been born between 1546 (the year of Murad's birth) and Selim's accession in 1566. The attempt to induce Murad III to give up his monogamous relationship with Safiye seems to have intensified around the time Safiye's son Mehmed took up his post (1582).

53. Privy purse registers of Mehmed III's reign stand out from those before and after by not listing a *haseki sultan* (BA, KK Saray 7102; MM 5633, 5530). The reign of Mehmed III is particularly obscure with regard to women of the dynasty: we lack records of the names of his concubines (with the exception of Handan Sultan, whom we know only because she became *valide sultan*), and even the names of his daughters, even though they, like previous princesses of the dynasty, were married to prominent statesmen.

54. Mahmud's mother was executed, and the mothers of Mustafa and Ahmed became *valide sultans;* Alderson is mistaken in assuming that Ahmed and Mustafa were uterine brothers (*The Structure of the Ottoman Dynasty,* table 33).

55. Barozzi and Berchet, *Le Relazioni,* 1:133–34.

56. Barozzi and Berchet, *Le Relazioni,* 1:302.

57. Barozzi and Berchet, *Le Relazioni,* 1:134.

58. See ch. 9, 232.

59. The Turkish playwrite A. Turan Oflazoğlu has drawn an extremely negative portrait of Kösem Sultan in his plays *Deli [The Mad] İbrahim* (1967), *IV. Murat* (1980), and *Kösem Sultan* (1982).

60. A 1620 register of lands held by her lists her and her holdings as *"hashâ-yı hazret-i haseki Ayşe Sultan damet ismetüha ber vech-i paşmaklık"* (TSMA, D 2895).

61. Osman's *haseki* is listed in various privy purse registers from 1619 through 1640: BA, MM, 855, 1606, 672, 847, 954, 403, 859, and KK Saray 7104.

62. This marriage is well attested in foreign sources: it is mentioned by Deshayes de Courmenin (*Voyage de Levant,* 161), Baudier (*Histoire géneralle du serrail,* 53), Rycaut (*The Present State of the Ottoman Empire,* 155–56), Petis de la Croix (*Etat general de l'empire otoman,* 105), and also by d'Ohsson (*Tableau géneral de l'empire othoman,* 7:63).

63. Naima, *Tarih,* 2:232; Nev'izade 'Ata'i, *Hada'ik ül-Haka'ik,* 691.

64. Nev'izade 'Ata'i, *Hada'ik ül-Haka'ik*, 692.

65. Naima, *Tarih*, 2:232.

66. Petits de la Croix, *Etat general de l'empire otoman*, 105.

67. Barozzi and Berchet, *Le Relazioni*, 1:131.

68. Privvy purse registers from the reigns of İbrahim and Mehmed IV give the name of Murad's *haseki*: "Ayşe Sultan, the *haseki* of the deceased Sultan Murad" (*Ayşe Sultan haseki-yi merhum Sultan Murad*) (BA, MM 906, 1692, 774). Receipts from quarterly stipend payments to this *haseki* in 1671 and 1678–79 also give her name: *Ayşe Sultan haseki-yi merhum Sultan Murad Han Gazi* (İE Saray 914/1, 939/2).

69. BA, KK Saray 7104.

70. For the use of the title *haseki* for all of İbrahim's concubines, see BA, MM 5653, 906, 1692, and Uluçay, *Padişahların Kadınları*, 59–62, especially the notes. Turhan, the mother of İbrahim's eldest son and successor, Mehmed IV, may also have been the mother of Fatma Sultan (1642–1657), to whose soul she dedicated the merit (*sevab*) acquired by the reading of the Qur'an by thirty individuals in the mosque she built (SL, Turhan Hadice Sultan 150, 43a).

71. For the stipends of Selim II's concubines, see BA, MM 487. Murad's second *haseki* started her career at a stipend of 2,571 aspers a day, while the first *haseki* received 2,000; seven months later, however, the stipend of the second had been reduced to 2,000, the level at which both remained until Murad's death (BA, KK Saray 7104, parts A and B). İbrahim's *hasekis* each received 1,000 aspers a day except for the second, Saliha Dilaşub, who consistently received 1,300 (BA, MM 5653, 906, 1692).

72. Sometimes the numbers were very large—for example, Ahmed III (r. 1703–30) had seventeen, although not simultaneously (Uluçay, *Padişahların Kadınları*, 79–83).

73. A reference by the ambassador Simon Contarini (1612) to Kösem, the *haseki* of Ahmed I, as "the Bas Cadin [head *kadın*], principal favorite of the sultan" suggests that this title was in use by the early seventeenth century, although as far as I can determine, it did not become official usage until the end of the century.

74. For the use of the title *kadın*, see TSMA, E 7005/5, where the six consorts of Süleyman II appear in a list of those receiving gifts on the occasion of the removal of the court from Istanbul to Edirne in 1691: Hadije Kadın, Zeynep Kadın, Behzad Kadın, Şehsuvar Kadın, Süylün Kadın, and İvaz Kadın. A document from the mid-eighteenth century that enumerates all *jariyes* in the imperial palace (that is, all women below the rank of *kadın*) lists the women in the suites of the *baş kadın* and five other *kadıns* (TSMA, D 8075); for a detailed analysis of this document, see ch. 5.

75. This statement is based on the genealogical data presented in Alderson, *The Structure of the Ottoman Dynasty*, and Uluçay, *Padişahların Kadınları*. Ahmed II's two sons by his concubine Rabia were twins, and the second son of Ayşe Sineperver, concubine of Abdülhamid I, was born after the death of her first son. I have not considered reproductive and sexual patterns after the reign of Mahmud II (1808–39).

76. On the title *khatun*, see Boyle, "Khatun," 1133, according to whom it was of Soghdian origin and was borne by wives and female relations of various Turkish rulers; it was displaced in Central Asian Turkish states in the Timurid period by the title *begum*. According to Meninski (*Lexicon Arabico-Persico-Turcicum*, 2:527) and Redhouse (*A Turkish and English Lexicon*, 818), the term *kadın* is a corruption of the older term *khatun*.

77. See n. 31.

78. Naima, *Tarih*, 4:243.

79. Peçevi, *Tarih*, 2:189; Naima, *Tarih*, 1:135–36.

80. Uzunçarşılı, *Osmanlı Tarihi*, 3 (pt. 1):43; Shaw, *History of the Ottoman Empire and Modern Turkey*, 1:190, 191, 200, 203; Itzkowitz, *Ottoman Empire and Islamic Tradition*, 75; Uluçay, *Padişahların Kadınları*, 40, 58.

Chapter 5

1. See, for example, Deshayes de Courmenin, *Voyage de Levant*, "Advertissement"; Rycaut, *The Present State of the Ottoman Empire*, "The Epistle Dedicatory" and "The Epistle to the Reader"; Tavernier, *Nouvelle Relation*, "Dessein de l'auteur"; Petis de la Croix, *Etat general de l'empire otoman*, "Au Roi."

2. Lady Mary Wortley Montagu, *The Complete Letters of Lady Mary Wortley Montagu*, 1:315–16, 368.

3. Petis de la Croix, *Etat general de l'empire otoman*, 1:342–43.

4. On this process, see Grosrichard, *Structure du sérail: La Fiction du despotisme asiatique dans l'Occident classique*, and Valensi, *Venise et la Sublime Porte*.

5. On this tension and the changing nature of historical truth in this period, see Harth, *Ideology and Culture in Seventeenth-Century France*, 134ff.; I am grateful to Mary Harper for suggesting this work to me. See Chew, "Epilogue," in *The Crescent and the Rose: Islam and England during the Renaissance*, for the difficulties this tension produced for English writers on the Levant.

6. Montagu, *Complete Letters*, 1:327–29.

7. Rycaut, *The Present State of the Ottoman Empire*, 38.

8. Rycaut, "The Epistle to the Reader," *The Present State*.

9. For Bobovius's description of the palace, see C. G. Fisher and A. Fisher, "Topkapı Sarayı in the Mid-Seventeenth Century: Bobovi's Description."

10. Bobovius, *Mémoire sur les Turcs*, folio 239.

11. Tavernier, *Nouvelle Relation*, 541.

12. On the court of Louis XIV, see Elias, *The Court Society*, and Ladurie, "Versailles Observed: The Court of Louis XIV in 1709."

13. Valensi, who dates the advent of the Venetian view of the Ottoman sultanate as "tyrannical" to 1575 (*Venise et la Sublime Porte*, 96, 102), draws attention to the parallels between Venetian and Ottoman critiques of the sultanate at end of the sixteenth century (114).

14. For example, Iacopo de Promontorio de Campis, Giovanni Maria Angiolello, and Giovanantonio Menavino in the late fifteenth and early sixteenth centuries; Luigi Bassano da Zara in the mid-sixteenth century; and Albertus Bobovius in the mid-seventeenth century.

15. Among the most informative are the writings of Ogier Ghiselin de Busbecq, the Flemish ambassador of the Holy Roman Empire at the mid-sixteenth century; Henry Lello, English ambassador at the end of the sixteenth century; John Sanderson, secretary to Lello and his predecessors; Sir Thomas Roe, English ambassador in the 1620s; Paul Rycaut, secretary to the English ambassador in the 1660s; Philippe du Fresne-Canaye, a member of the French embassy of 1573; Antoine Galland, secretary to the French ambassador in the early 1670s; François Petis de la Croix, secretary to the French ambassador in the late 1670s; and many of the Venetian ambassadors of this period.

16. See Valensi, "Judith," *Venise et la Sublime Porte*, for the education and training of the Venetian ambassadors and the role of their ambassadorial writings in the intellectual and political life of the republic.

17. Authors who appear to have been ignorant of the *valide sultan*'s role include Bon, Deshayes de Courmenin, and Baudier.

18. Rycaut, *The Present State:* ch. 4 contains the account of Kösem Sultan's death, and ch. 9 the description of the harem.

19. Petis de la Croix states in his introduction to *Etat general de l'empire otoman* that his informant was "a solitary Turk with a long residence at the imperial palace"; if Bobovius was his informer, the French writer may have referred to him as a "Turk" because of his Muslim identity as a palace slave. Parts of Petis de la Croix's work closely follow Bobovius's manuscript (for example, the description of the consummation of an Ottoman princess's marriage, 1:411ff.) On Bobovius, see Miller, *The Palace School of Muhammad the Conqueror,* 47–48.

20. Petis de la Croix, *Etat general de l'empire otoman,* 1:107, 374ff.; *Mémoirs du Sieur de la Croix,* 356ff.

21. For example, Uzunçarşılı, *Saray Teşkilatı;* Uluçay, *Harem.*

22. Mouradgea d'Ohsson's account of the harem as it existed in the early nineteenth century appears to be the principal source for modern descriptions (*Tableau géneral de l'empire othoman,* 7:62–95).

23. TSMA, E 10292.

24. Celalzade Mustafa, *Tabakat ül-Memalik,* 199v–200r; see also Mustafa Ali, *Künh ül-Ahbar,* 34r–36v; Peçevi, *Tarih,* 1:154. For a brief English summary of this pageant, see F. Davis, *The Palace of Topkapı,* 9–10.

25. Menavino, *I Cinque Libri,* 134; see also the sources cited in Miller, *Beyond the Sublime Porte,* 25.

26. Eldem and Akozan, *Topkapı Sarayı,* 67; Necipoğlu, "The Formation of an Ottoman Imperial Tradition: The Topkapı Palace in the Fifteenth and Sixteenth Centuries," 172. Anhegger-Eyüboğlu, "Fatih Devrinde Yeni Sarayda Da Harem Dairesi (Padişahın Evi) Var Mıydı?" [Was there a harem suite (the sultan's residence) in the New Palace in the reign of Mehmed the Conqueror?], argues on the basis of the lack of archaeological remains that no women were resident in the New Palace until after the mid-sixteenth century; I am grateful to Hülya Tezcan for the observation that this lack of evidence can be explained if the early quarters for women were wooden structures that disappeared leaving no trace, before the more permanent construction of the sixteenth century.

27. Campis, *Die Aufzeichnungen des Genuesen Iacopo de Promontorio de Campis über den Osmanenstaat um 1475,* 44; Campis's figures may be exaggerated.

28. (*saray-ı dukhteran*) Necipoğlu, "Formation of an Ottoman Imperial Tradition," 432–34.

29. Bassano, *Costumi et i modi,* 18v.

30. Postel, *De la republique des Turcs,* 32.

31. Sanderson, *The Travels of John Sanderson,* 72–73.

32. Necipoğlu, "Formation of an Ottoman Imperial Tradition," 433–34.

33. Report of Andrea Badoara (1573), in Alberi, *Relazioni,* 1:359, and of Costantino Garzoni (1573), 1:395, 403.

34. Report of Garzoni, in Alberi, *Relazioni,* 1:403.

35. BA, MM 487.

36. Alberi, *Relazioni,* 1:395.

37. Salomone, quoted in Rosedale, *Queen Elizabeth and the Levant Company,* 28–29.

38. Selaniki, *A Year in Selaniki's History: 1593–1594,* ed. and trans. Peachy, 304–7, 496–99.

39. Selaniki, *Tarih,* 207.

40. Selaniki, *A Year in Selaniki's History,* ed. and trans. Peachy, 304–7, 496–99.

41. Selaniki, *A Year in Selaniki's History,* ed. and trans. Peachy, 304–11, 496–503.
42. Naima, *Tarih,* 2:206.
43. Sanderson, *The Travels,* 73.
44. Selaniki, *Tarih-i Selâniki,* ed. and trans. İpşirli, 702, 708.
45. BA, MM 847A, 774.
46. TSMA, E 7001/21.
47. Miller suggests that Mehmed II's intention in constructing the New Palace was, at least in part, to separate his private from his official household (*Beyond the Sublime Porte,* 25); this simply begs the question.
48. Necipoğlu, "Formation of an Ottoman Imperial Tradition," 445–46.
49. On the organization of the black eunuchs, see Uzunçarşılı, *Saray Teşkilatı,* 172–83.
50. BA, MM 422.
51. Hammer, *Histoire,* 7:318.
52. BA, KK Saray 7102; MM 5633, 5530.
53. BA, MM 5965 (a register covering the year 1038/1628–29). The stipends of the vezirs and other members of the imperial council do not appear in the salary registers I consulted.
54. Sanderson, *The Travels,* 82.
55. See ch. 2, 52.
56. Barkan, "İstanbul Saraylarına ait Muhasebe Defterleri," 155; BA, MM 397, 843, 858, 861.
57. Barkan, "İstanbul Saraylarına ait Muhasabe Defterleri," 155.
58. The name of Mustafa's mother has not appeared in any document or chronicle of which I am aware, although she was a very important figure in her son's two brief reigns. She was of Abkhasian (*Abaza*) origin (Naima, *Tarih,* 2:313).
59. BA, MM 858, 861.
60. The Ottoman biographical dictionary *Sicill-i Osmanî* indicates that Safiye Sultan died in 1605 (1:48). The registers, however, indicate that she died sometime in 1618 or 1619; she appears in a register covering the period May–October 1618, but does not appear in a register covering the period October 1619–January 1620.
61. BA, MM 861, 1606, 672, 847.
62. BA, MM 1692, 1509.
63. BA, MM 774.
64. BA, MM 487.
65. BA, MM 5653.
66. TSMA, E 8030, 1b.
67. BA, AE Kanuni 24 (register for 1552); KK Saray 7098 (register for 1556–58).
68. BA, MM 487, 422.
69. BA, MM 403, 859; KK Saray 7104.
70. Koçi Bey's recommendations to İbrahim detailed the stipend increases that Murad IV had awarded to members of the inner palace establishment (*Risale,* 80).
71. BA, KK Saray 1704; MM 5653, 906, 1692.
72. BA, MM 855, 1606, 672, 847, 954.
73. BA, MM 954, 403, 859; KK Saray 7104.
74. BA, MM 906, 1692, 774, 1082; İE Saray 939/2,3, 914/1.
75. BA, AE Kanuni 24; KK Saray 7098.
76. Menavino, who served as a slave under Bayezid II and Selim I, until about 1514, gives thirty aspers as the standard stipend (*I Cinque Libri,* 135).
77. BA, MM 487.

78. BA, MM 397 (for the mother of Mustafa), 1606 (for Kösem).

79. TSMA, D 10052, cited by Uluçay, "Notlar ve Vesikalar," 243. A register of gifts from the reign of Bayezid (909/1503–4) suggests that princesses enjoyed greater status than mothers of princes—princesses received larger cash gifts and were listed before mothers of princes (Barkan, *Muhasebe Defterleri*, 296–380 [a transcription of part of Atatürk Library, Muallim Cevdet 0.71], *passim*, especially 356–57); this is by no means conclusive evidence, however, since gifts may have been a less important source of income for mothers.

80. TSMA, D 7025.

81. BA, MM 906, 1692.

82. At this time the purse consisted of five hundred *kuruş;* the *kuruş* was a silver coin worth 80 aspers in the mid-seventeenth century and 120 aspers in 1720.

83. TSMA, E 7005/5.

84. TSMA, D 8075. This document can be dated to 1740–54 (see n. 108 below).

85. Gökbilgin, *Edirne ve Paşa Livası*, 54–55, 323–25; Ayvansarayı, *Hadikat ül-Cevami*, 1:69, 139.

86. BA, MM 1606, 672, 847.

87. Alberi, *Relazioni*, 1:402.

88. Peçevi, *Tarih*, 2:283.

89. Naima, *Tarih*, 4:66.

90. TSMA, D 8003, 9629, 10184, cited in Uluçay, *Harem*, 136, n. 287.

91. Mustafa Ali, *Künh ül-Ahbar*, 291a–b.

92. Deshayes de Courmenon, *Voyage de Levant*, 158; Rycaut, *Present State*, 39.

93. Ayvansarayı, *Hadikat ül-Cevami*, 1:183. In the city of Istanbul, in the neighborhood of the customs office, Janfeda Khatun built a mosque with a primary school (1584), and in the neighborhood of Saraçhane a public drinking fountain (*sebil*) and water pump (*çeşme*); the second mosque and public bath were built in the Beykoz village of Akbaba (1593). She also received permission from the sultan to repair and enlarge a water transport system originally constructed by Bayezid II in order to bring water to her Istanbul mosque and the nearby bath built by Gedik Ahmed Pasha (TSMA, E 7953).

94. Mustafa Ali, *Künh ül-Ahbar*, 291b–92a.

95. This is the manner in which they are listed in privy purse registers, where they appear collectively as *cemaat-ı cevari-i saray-ı cedid/atik*.

96. Even after her marriage, Hurrem Sultan referred to herself as the sultan's "insignificant *jariye*" (TSMA, E 5038). In an earlier letter she referred to her daughter Mihrimah as her father's *jariye;* in the same letter she described her sons as their father's slaves (*bende*) (TSMA, E 5662).

97. The *Dar üs-Saade* appears as a distinct group with this name (*cemaat-ı Dar üs-Saade-i saray-ı cedid/atik*) in a privy purse register from 1599–1600, when it consists of ten persons (BA, KK Saray 7102); it does not appear in a register from 1581–82 (BA, MM 422). Since I have seen no registers for the intervening years, I cannot establish with greater precision its first appearance in the registers.

98. BA, AE Kanuni 24; KK Saray 7098.

99. On the *müteferrika* corps, see Kunt, *The Sultan's Servants*, 39–40.

100. On the identity of Gülfem, see ch. 3, n. 12.

101. BA, AE Kanuni 24. In a register of 1556, the nurse of Jihangir, who had died in the interim, was listed as a sixth member of this group (BA, KK Saray 7098).

102. BA, KK Saray 7102.

103. BA, MM 843.

104. BA, MM 843.

105. BA, MM 1606.

106. BA, KK Saray 7104.

107. BA, MM 906 (1645), 1692 (1647–48), 774 (1651–52).

108. TSMA, D 8075. This undated document is catalogued as belonging to the sixteenth or seventeenth century, but internal evidence makes clear that it is from the reign of Mahmud I (1730–54). The document includes *jariyes* assigned to six princes, whose names are given; only in Mahmud's reign were there princes with this particular configuration of names. Furthermore, *jariyes* are listed as being in the suites of Mahmud's *kadıns* and *ikbals*, titles not used officially before the end of the seventeenth century. Since Mahmud's mother died in 1739 and there is no reference to the *valide sultan* in the document, it must date from 1739 or later.

109. A significant difference that should nevertheless be pointed out is the reduction in the size of the household staff from the mid-seventeenth century to the period from which this document dates, from roughly 140 women to 73. This may, however, simply be a feature of the normal fluctuation in size of the harem household from one reign to the next or during the course of a reign; the fact that Mahmud, the sultan at the time the document was prepared, had no children would account for some part of the reduction in staff. One wonders how extensive the household staff might have been under Mahmud's predecessor, Ahmed III, who had an extraordinarily large number of concubines and children.

110. Petis de la Croix, *Mémoirs,* 356–57. He gives the titles of these women as "Boulla" rather than *usta. Bula* ("elder sister" or "wife of one's paternal uncle") was a title used for high-ranking members of the household staff. Selaniki, for example, notes that "the *bulas* of the harem" (*harem-i muhterem bulaları*) received gifts during the wedding celebrations of Fatma Sultan in 1593 (Selaniki, *A Year in Selaniki's History,* ed. and trans. Peachy, 307); in the payment record of the purchase of a house for Şekerpare, the notorious *ketkhüda kadın* of İbrahim's reign, the latter is referred to as "Şekerpare Bula" (BA, AE İbrahim 403).

111. The rank of *ikbal* first appeared during the reign of Mustafa II (1695–1703) and would seem to be a feature of the regularization of the status hierarchy of royal concubines.

112. Important royal women had stewards (*ketkhüda*), male agents who looked after their financial interests outside the harem. It is possible that the six stewards listed in the document were such agents; however, they might also have been female agents or representatives living in the palace who looked after the interests of the princesses within the harem.

113. Of the six princes, only the elder two, Osman and Mehmed, had *jariyes* with stipends in the *Dar üs-Saade* range. Osman, son of Mustafa II and born in 1699, would have been forty years old in 1739, the earliest possible date for this document; Mehmet, son of Ahmed III and born in 1717, would have been twenty-two in 1739. Each had one *jariye* at a stipend of twenty aspers a day and one *jariye* at fifteen aspers; other *jariyes* in their suites (Osman had a total of nineteen *jariyes* and Mehmed fourteen) received stipends of ten aspers or less. That the next two elder princes, Mustafa and Bayezid, sons of Ahmed III and both born in 1718, did not have *jariyes* at the higher stipend levels may have been a mark of respect for Ahmed III's eldest son Mehmet.

114. The following discussion is based largely on personal observation of the harem as it stands today. I am grateful to Güngör Dilmen, head of the Harem Department of the Topkapı Palace Museum, for allowing me the opportunity to see parts of the harem outside the public tour area and plans representing architectural reconstructions of the

harem. Very helpful to understanding the development of the harem (as well as other parts of the palace) is Eldem and Akozan, *Topkapı Sarayı: Bir Mimarî Araştırma,* which contains reconstructed plans of the harem at different periods in its development.

115. However, the date of construction of particular areas can be established by means of inscriptions generally found above the entrances to rooms.

116. For a description of the harem quarters in the late sixteenth century, see Necipoğlu, "The Formation of an Ottoman Imperial Tradition," 457ff.

117. Eldem and Akozan, *Topkapı Sarayı,* 67.

118. One cannot be certain when these rooms and hence this route came into being; they may date from a period later than Mehmed IV's reconstruction. On the other hand, concealed in the wall running along the staircase leading from the *valide sultan*'s suite to these upper rooms is a ladder that opens out to lead up to a hidden entrance to a very small room on the left and a closet on the right. I was told that this was the closet in which Kösem Sultan hid from the black eunuchs dispatched by her daughter-in-law Turhan Sultan to murder her (a piece of her dress protruding from under the closet door revealed her presence). This event took place in 1652, before the fire of 1665, making this account somewhat suspect; one might, however, speculate that Turhan Sultan, mother of Mehmet IV, appreciated the value of this concealed area (which could well have been the repository of the *valide sultan*'s personal treasury) and had her apartment and its attendant quarters reconstructed as they had been.

119. F. Davis, *Palace of Topkapı,* 226.

120. Sourdel, "Ghulam," 1079.

121. Peçevi, *Tarih,* 1:30–31. See also Süreyya, *Sicill-i Osmanî,* 4:372.

122. The letters of Lady Mary Wortley Montagu, who arrived in Istanbul in 1717 as wife of the English ambassador, provide glimpses of the domestic households of high-ranking government officials (*Letters,* 1:342–44, 347–52, 380–87).

123. This similarity between the structures of the harem and the training school in the third courtyard has been briefly noted by İnalcık (*The Ottoman Empire,* 85), who says: "[The harem's] organization complemented the slave system, an aspect of its character forgotten amidst a proliferation of fanciful tales, and paralleled the page organization."

124. On the organization of the personnel of the third courtyard, see İnalcık, *Ottoman Empire,* 78–80, 82; Miller, *Beyond the Sublime Porte,* ch. 3, and the sequel to this work, *The Palace School of Muhammad the Conqueror.*

125. Bobovius, *Mémoire,* 257.

126. The existence of the Pantry and Furnace Chambers as service divisions is attested by the document described above ("Names and daily wages of the *jariyes*"), and the existence of the Treasury Chamber by Bobovius, who says of the Agha of the Treasury (*hazine ağası*), one of the *valide sultan*'s principal eunuchs, "he commands the girls who serve in the Treasury Chamber" (*Mémoire,* 18).

127. Fleischer, *Bureaucrat and Statesman,* 196.

128. BA, CEV Saray 1834. Koçi Bey noted that Murad IV raised salaries in the pages' organization: the stipend of members of the Greater, Lesser, Campaign, and Pantry Chambers was raised from eight to ten aspers a day, that of the Treasury Chamber from ten to twelve, and that of the Privy Chamber from twenty to twenty-five (*Risale,* 80).

129. BA, MM 774.

130. Bobovius, *Mémoire,* 214. Bobovius's figures reflect the situation at the mid-seventeenth century.

131. The keeper of the standard's stipend is listed as two hundred aspers a day in registers from the reign of Süleyman (TSMA, D 7843), and from 1628–29 (BA, MM 5965).

132. See İnalcık, *The Ottoman Empire*, 82, and Kunt, *The Sultan's Servants*, 34, 68, for the relationship between inner and outer palace offices.

133. Angiolello, *Historia Turchesca*, 128.

134. Bobovius, *Mémoire*, 246–47.

135. Withers, *The Grand Signiors Serraglio*, 363; Baudier, *Histoire générale du serrail*, 37.

136. Menavino, *I Cinque Libri*, 135.

137. Postel, *De la republique des Turcs*, 33.

138. Bobovius, *Mémoire*, 37.

139. Withers, *The Grand Signiors Serraglio*, 390.

140. Rycaut, *The Present State*, 39.

141. Bobovius, *Mémoire*, 259.

142. While these titles fall outside the scope of this study, it is useful to examine them briefly; the fact that the harem has generally been treated as a monolith rather than a constantly evolving and changing institution—whose members' titles also changed—has led to confusion with regard to these titles.

143. TSMA, D 8075 (see n. 108). The four *ikbals* of Mahmud I are listed immediately after the three leading *ustas* of the harem and immediately before the remaining *ustas*, who were more highly paid than they; they are listed as "*baş ikbal Meyyase (?) kalfa, ikinci ikbal Fehmi kalfa, ikbal Sırrı kalfa, ikbal Hübabe kalfa.*" That these women appeared in this list of *jariyes,* which did not include the sultan's *kadıns* or the *ketkhüda kadın* or *daye hatun,* emphasizes their identity as part of the household rather than family. In the nineteenth century the term *kalfa* appears to have been used exclusively for members of the household staff (Pakalın, *Osmanlı Tarih Deyimleri ve Terimleri Sözlüğü*, 2:150).

144. Kunt, *The Sultan's Servants*, 96.

145. Naima, *Tarih*, 5:113.

146. For the career of Meleki Khatun, see Naima, *Tarih*, vols. 5 and 6, *passim*.

147. On the eve of her son's accession in 1617, Mustafa's mother's daily stipend was only one hundred aspers, while the newly deceased sultan's favorite concubine (the future *valide sultan* Kösem) received one thousand and the former *valide sultan* Safiye, now in retirement, two thousand. (BA, MM 397).

148. Naima, *Tarih*, 2:159.

149. Naima, *Tarih*, 2:393.

150. Ortaylı, "Anadolu'da XVI. Yüzyılda Evlilik İlişkileri Üzerine Bazı Gözlemler," 37–38.

151. Alderson, *The Structure of the Ottoman Dynasty*, table 34; Uluçay, *Padişahların Kadınları*, 50–52.

152. Evliya Çelebi, *The Intimate Life of an Ottoman Statesman: Melek Ahmed Pasha (1588–1662) as Portrayed in Evliya Çelebi's Book of Travels*, trans. Dankoff, *passim*.

153. Evliya Çelebi, *The Intimate Life*, 233–34.

154. Evliya Çelebi, *The Intimate Life*, 234.

155. Evliya Çelebi, *The Intimate Life*, 260–61.

156. The affair of İbşir Pasha is recounted in detail in Naima, *Tarih*, 6:4–99.

157. Evliya Çelebi, *The Intimate Life*, 177.

158. Alberi, *Relazioni*, 3:243.

159. TSMA, E 2457/2.

160. Barozzi and Berchet, *Le Relazioni,* 1:370; Du Loir, *Les Voyage du Sieur du Loir,* 124–26; Uluçay, *Padişahların Kadınları,* 54–55.

161. Karaçelebizade Abdülaziz Efendi, *Ravzat ul-Ebrar Zeyli,* 6v.

162. Evliya Çelebi, *The Intimate Life,* 231–32.

163. On the practice of confiscation, see Baysun, "Müsadere."

Chapter 6

1. Finkel, *The Administration of Warfare: The Ottoman Military Campaigns in Hungary, 1593–1606,* 17.

2. For the influence of these writings in limiting historical analysis of this period, see İnalcık, "Military and Fiscal Transformation in the Ottoman Empire," 283–84. Murphey, "The Veliyyudin Telhis," 555–56, provides a succinct statement of the outlook of these Ottoman anatomists of decline. For a discussion of the reform literature, see B. Lewis, "Ottoman Observers of Ottoman Decline"; Fleischer, "From Şehzade Korkud to Mustafa Ali: Cultural Origins of the Ottoman *Nasihatname*"; Howard, "Ottoman Historiography and the Literature of 'Decline' of the Sixteenth and Seventeenth Centuries."

3. On the beginnings of this process see Howard, "Ottoman Historiography and the Literature of 'Decline,' " 173–76.

4. A number of studies have appeared in the last decade addressing aspects of institutional transformation in the late sixteenth and early seventeenth centuries. Among them are İnalcık's seminal article, "Military and Fiscal Transformation in the Ottoman Empire"; Kunt, *The Sultan's Servants: The Transformation of Ottoman Provincial Government, 1550–1650;* Finkel, *The Administration of Warfare;* Howard, "The Ottoman Timar System and Its Transformation, 1563–1656"; Darling, "The Ottoman Finance Department in a Century of Crisis." The transformation of the religious establishment in this period has not been directly addressed, although the work of Repp and Zilfi, who have concentrated on earlier and later periods, respectively, is pertinent: Repp, *The Müfti of Istanbul: A Study in the Development of the Ottoman Learned Hierarchy* and "The Altered Nature and Role of the Ulema"; Zilfi, *The Politics of Piety: The Ottoman Ulema in the Postclassical Age (1600–1800).*

5. A notable exception is the late tenth- and eleventh-century Ghaznavid state, whose political organization and evolution in many ways anticipated that of the Ottomans.

6. The work of Beldiceanu-Steinherr is of particular value on these issues: see "La Conquête d'Adrianople par les Turcs: La Pénétration turque en Thrace et la valeur des chroniques ottomanes"; her review of *Ursprung und Wesen der "Knabenlese" im osmanischen Reich,* by Papoulia; and "Le Règne de Selîm Ier: Tournant dans la vie politique et religieuse de l'empire ottoman."

7. Fleischer, "From Şehzade Korkud to Mustafa Ali," 1, 10–15; Howard, "Ottoman Historiography and the Literature of 'Decline.' "

8. See Woods, *The Aqquyunlu,* 2–7, on the political openness of the post-Mongol Islamic world. See Gibb, "Lutfi Pasha on the Ottoman Caliphate," for the problems encountered in the post-caliphal age in constructing theories of legitimacy.

9. Mottahedeh, *Loyalty and Leadership in an Early Islamic Society,* 17–19. See Bosworth, "The Titulature of the Early Ghaznavids," on the different relationships between caliph and dynastic monarchs and the images projected by the latter.

10. For steppe principles of political organization, see Barthold, *Turkestan Down*

to the Mongol Invastion, 268, 306–7; Togan, *Umumi Türk Tarihi'ne Giriş,* 59; Dickson, "Shah Tahmasp and the Uzbeks," 25–35; Fletcher, "Turco-Mongolian Monarchical Tradition in the Ottoman Empire."

11. Perhaps the most salient example is the Buyid dynasty (Cahen, "Buwayhids," 1355). See Humphreys, *From Saladin to the Mongols: The Ayyubids of Damascus, 1193–1260,* 66–75, on Kurdish and Armenian examples of this form of political organization, and Frye, "The Samanids," 149, for the suggestion that this pattern, seen even among the Samanids, may have had old Iranian roots.

12. See B. Lewis, "The Mongols, the Turks and the Muslim Polity," 194–98, for a discussion of the impact of Turco-Mongol statecraft and traditions on post-Mongol states.

13. This phenomenon is most comprehensively treated by İnalcık, "Padişah," 491–93, and "Osmanlılarda Saltanat Veraseti Usulü"; B. Lewis, *Istanbul and the Civilization of the Ottoman Empire,* 36–47; and Imber, "The Ottoman Dynastic Myth."

14. For a discussion of this issue, see Findley, *Bureaucratic Reform in the Ottoman Empire,* 8ff.

15. Ahmedi, *İskendername,* 65b; Aşıkpaşazade, *Tevarih-i Al-i Osman,* ch. 8; Neşri, *Kitab-ı Cihan-Nüma,* 1:32. On the Ottomans' *ghazi* enterprise and image, see Wittek, *The Rise of the Ottoman Empire,* and "De la Défaite d'Ankara à la prise de Constantinople"; for a critique of Wittek's arguments, see Lindner, *Nomads and Ottomans in Medieval Anatolia,* and Imber, "Paul Wittek's 'De la Défaite d'Ankara à la prise de Constantinople.' "

16. The complete inscription is given in Wittek, *The Rise of the Ottoman Empire,* 53, 27: *sultân ibn sultân al-ghuzât, ghâzî ibn al-ghâzî, shujâ' ad-daula wa'd-dîn, marzbân al-âfâq, bahlavân-i jihân, Orkhân ibn 'Othmân.*

17. Neşri, *Kitab-ı Cihan-Nüma,* 1:194.

18. See Humphreys, *The Ayyubids,* appendix A (The Ayyubid Concept of the Sultanate), on the scaling down of the title *sultan* even before the Mongol conquest.

19. İnalcık, "Padişah," 492, and *The Ottoman Empire,* 56. Kramers ("Sultan") notes that the first Muslim ruler to use the title "sultan," the Seljuk Toghril, enhanced it with the addition of "al-Mu'azzam," "the esteemed."

20. B. Lewis, *Istanbul and the Civilization of the Ottoman Empire,* 37.

21. B. Lewis, "Khadım al-haramayn," 900.

22. Tursun Beg, *Tarih-i Ebü'l-Feth,* 209.

23. See Manz, "Tamurlane and the Symbolism of Sovereignty," on the multiple legitimizing claims of Timur.

24. See Woods, *The Aqquyunlu,* 4–5, on the replacement of Mongol by Turkish legitimizing principles.

25. The cultivation of aspects of the Oghuz Turkish heritage began under Murad II. The names of two of Mehmed II's grandsons, Korkud (b. 1470) and Oghuz (b. 1480), recall the two most charismatic figures of that heritage, the eponymous ruler Oghuz and the popular religious leader Dede Korkud. This coupling of temporal and spiritual power was similar to that of Osman and Sheikh Edebali in a popular myth surrounding the origins of the dynasty (see ch. 1). Jem Sultan, father of the prince Oghuz, commissioned an epic history of Oghuz Khan and his tribe (*Oghuzname*). Jem's own name—that of the legendary first king of the Persians—illustrates his father's claim to multiple sources of legitimacy.

26. This title was used by the Mongol Ilkhanids (Boyle, "Dynastic and Political History of the Il-Khans," 409). Among the Ottomans, the title appears as early as the reign of Bayezid I, in inscriptions as well as *vakfiye*s (Yınanç, "Bayezid I," 390).

According to İnalcık ("Padişah," 491), Ottoman use of the title *khan* before the advent of the Timurid and Turkman challenge was not consciously polemical; it was "a vague[ly invoked] title tied to a distant tradition."

27. Tursun Beg, *Tarih-i Ebü'l-Feth*, 12. Tursun Beg summarized Mongol sovereignty as *örf.*

28. Neşri, *Neşri Tarihi*, 1:56–59.

29. Aşıkpaşazade, *Tevarih-i Al-i Osman*, ch. 67; Neşri, *Kitab-ı Cihan-Nüma*, 1:97.

30. Ahmedi, *Dastan ve Tevarih-i Müluk-i Al-i Osman*, ed. Atsız, 6; *İskendername*, 65b.

31. Neşri, *Kitab-ı Cihan-Nüma*, 2:4.

32. Woods, *The Aqquyunlu*, 115.

33. Tursun Beg, *Tarih-i Ebü'l-Feth*, 10–30; for a brief English summary, see İnalcık and Murphey, eds. and trans., *The History of Mehmed the Conqueror*, 20–24. Both Tursun Beg's and Davani's works drew heavily on the thirteenth-century *Akhlaq-i Nasiri* of Nasir ad-Din Tusi, written under the Mongol Ilkhanids. H.A.R. Gibb credits Davani with the definitive theoretical justification for the post-Abbasid caliphate ("Some Considerations on the Sunni Theory of the Caliphate," 144–45). A similar argument was advanced by Davani's student Fazlullah b. Ruzbihan Khunji in the early sixteenth century for the Uzbek dynasty newly established in Transoxania and Khorasan. See Woods, *The Aqquyunlu*, 114ff., on the Akkoyunlu formulation of imperial dominion.

34. On this subject, the most valuable source I have used is notes from the classes taught by the late Professor Martin B. Dickson of Princeton University. See also Savory, *Iran under the Safavids*, 2–3, 19–30; Woods, *The Aqquyunlu*, 180–84; and Frye, "The Charisma of Kingship in Ancient Iran," 52–53. On the background of the Ismailian synthesis, see Mazzaoui, *The Origins of the Safawids, Shi'ism, Sufism, and the Gulat.*

35. For a succinct treatment of this problem, see Beldiceanu-Steinherr, "Le Règne de Selîm Ier."

36. See B. Lewis, "Khadim al-Haramayn." The title appears to have originated with the Ayyubid Salah ad-Din and was taken over upon the Ayyubid demise by the Mamluk sultans.

37. On the incorrectness of the claim that Selim I assumed the office of caliph from the Abbasid shadow caliphs under Mamluk protection, see İnalcık, "Padişah" and *The Ottoman Empire*, 57.

38. H.A.R. Gibb, "Lutfi Pasha on the Ottoman Caliphate," 290. See also Imber's study, "Süleymân as Caliph of the Muslims: Ebû's-Su'ud's Formulation of Ottoman Dynastic Ideology," 179–80.

39. H.A.R. Gibb, "Lufti Pasha," 293–94.

40. İnalcık notes that it was the title of "protector of the two noble sanctuaries" that marked Ottoman supremacy, not the widely claimed title of caliph (*The Ottoman Empire*, 57).

41. Gibb, "Lutfi Pasha," 295, n. 3.

42. Uzunçarşılı, *Kitabeler*, 2:79–80.

43. Combs-Schilling, *Sacred Performances: Islam, Sexuality, and Sacrifice*, 9, 20, 136ff., and *passim.* The author is wrong in assuming (146) that the Moroccan Sa'di dynasty was the only one to claim the caliphate in this period; their claim, however, differed from that of the Akkoyunlu, the Ottomans, and the Uzbeks in that it was a caliphate based on blood descent from the Prophet.

44. Combs-Schilling, *Sacred Performance*, ch. 8, 12, and throughout.

45. Woods, "Timur's Genealogy," 87–88.

46. Marmon, *Eunuchs of the Holy Cities.*

47. Savory, *Iran under the Safavids,* 24; Minorsky, "The Poetry of Shah Ismail."

48. For seventeenth-century Ottoman usage of the term *devlet,* see Meninski, *Lexicon,* 2:770–80.

49. Neşri, *Kitab-ı Cihan-Nüma,* 1:97, and Imber, "The Ottoman Dynastic Myth," 20.

50. SL, Turhan Hatice Sultan 150, 8r ("çeragefruz-ı dudman-ı hilafet-ı kubra, Haticet ül-zaman").

51. See the comments of John Sanderson, secretary to the English embassy at the end of the sixteenth century, quoted in ch. 7, 193–94.

52. Sanders, "From Court Ceremony to Urban Language: Ceremonial in Fatimid Cairo and Fustât."

53. See Subtelny, "Art and Politics in Early Sixteenth Century Central Asia," for a discussion of the importance of the royal court and royal patronage of cultural activity in Islamic politics. On royal patronage and court-sponsored artistic production under Süleyman, see Atıl, *The Age of Sultan Süleyman the Magnificent,* esp. 24–28, and Necipoğlu, "Süleyman the Magnificent and the Representation of Power"; on religious monuments, see Kuran, *Sinan: The Grand Old Master of Ottoman Architecture;* on the expansion and embellishment of the imperial palace, see Necipoğlu, "The Formation of an Ottoman Imperial Tradition."

54. Mardin, "Superwesternization in Urban Life in the Ottoman Empire in the Last Quarter of the Nineteenth Century," 419.

55. There is considerable literature on this issue. Among the several treatments by İnalcık are "Kanun," "Osmanlı Hukukuna Giriş: Örfî-Sultanî Hukuk ve Fatih'in Kanunları," and "Suleiman the Lawgiver and Ottoman Law." This problem has also been considered in depth by Heyd; see "Some Aspects of the Ottoman *Fetvâ*" and *Studies in Old Ottoman Criminal Law,* esp. pt. 2, ch. 1. See also Imber, "Süleymân as Caliph of the Muslims" and "*Zinâ* in Ottoman Law"; Fleischer, *Bureaucrat and Intellectual,* ch. 6. For an interesting critique of the dynasty's irreligion by one of its members, see Fleischer, "From Şehzade Korkud to Mustafa Ali."

56. Gibb, "Lutfi Pasha," 294.

57. This process is traced by Zilfi in "Elite Circulation in the Ottoman Empire: Great Mollas of the Eighteenth Century" and *The Politics of Piety,* ch. 2.

58. The stories about Selim I and the *müfti* Ali Cemali (Mecdi, *Hada'ik ül-Şaka'ik,* 305–7) and of the trial of Molla Kabız (Celalzade Mustafa, *Tabakat ül-Memalik,* 172b–175b) are vivid illustrations of this point; both stories are recounted in Repp, *The Müfti of Istanbul,* 211–12, 234–36.

59. Cf. the report of Bernardo (1592), in Alberi, *Relazioni,* 2:365.

60. Anhegger, "Hezarfen Hüseyin Efendi'nin Osmanlı Devlet Teşkilâtına Dair Mülâhazaları," 389.

61. Zilfi, *The Politics of Piety.*

62. For this view, see Parry, "The Successors of Sulaiman," 107, and "The Period of Murad IV," 135; Shaw, *History of the Ottoman Empire and Modern Turkey,* 1:170; Uzunçarşılı, *Saray Teşkilatı,* 90, and *Osmanlı Tarihi,* 3 (Pt. 1): 119–20.

63. Elliott, *The Count-Duke of Olivares: The Statesman in an Age of Decline,* 93. Botero, *The Reason of State,* trans. P. J. and D. P. Waley, 5–6; on Botero's view of the Ottomans, see Valensi, *Venise et la sublime porte,* 120–21.

64. Neşri, *Neşri Tarihi,* 2:742–43.

65. Hammer, *Histoire,* 5:61–62.

66. Celalzade Mustafa, *Tabakat ül-Memalik,* 179a.

67. Alberi, *Relazioni*, 3:131–32.

68. Busbecq, *Turkish Letters*, 240–41.

69. Rosedale, *Queen Elizabeth and the Levant Company*, 21–22. The document, an account of the death of Murad III and the accession of Mehmed III, was written by "Salomone, the Jewish man." Salomon was a Portuguese Jew named Alvaro Mendès, better known in the Ottoman world as Salomon Aben Yaèx (on his identity and on his extensive diplomatic contacts and efforts toward furthering an Anglo-Ottoman alliance, see Galante, *Don Salomon Aben Yaèche, Duc de Mételin*). Rosedale suggests that the document was solicited by the English ambassador Edward Barton, who used it to convince his government of the urgency of enhancing English interests at court by dispatching a suitable gift to the new sultan; hence the flattering portraits of both father and son, which (as Rosedale points out) are patently inaccurate in a number of particulars. However, even if the document was trumped up by Barton and/or Salomon and the portraits of the sultans altered to suit Barton's needs, there is no reason to doubt the validity of its entire contents. It was John Sanderson, Barton's secretary, who translated the document into English from Salomon's Italian (*The Travels*, 82).

70. Mustafa Ali (*Künh ül-Ahbar*, 292b–93a) speculated on the reasons for Murad's sedentariness.

71. Naima, *Tarih*, 1:422–23.

72. Finkel, *The Administration of Warfare*, 211.

73. Naima, *Tarih*, 1:452.

74. Naima, *Tarih*, 2:211. "*Padişahlara hac lazım değildir. Yerinde oturub adl eylemek evlâdır. Caiz ki bir fitne zuhur eyleye. . . .*"

75. Sahillioğlu, "The Income and Expenditure of the Ottoman Treasury between 1683 and 1740," 66, quoted in Finkel, *The Administration of Warfare*, 232.

76. Peçevi, *Tarih*, 2:189; Naima, *Tarih*, 1:136–37.

77. Peçevi, *Tarih*, 2:200–201; Naima, *Tarih*, 1:137. In his account of this campaign, the historian Peçevi relates that he saw a drawing of Sadeddin Efendi and the sultan made by an enemy commander; in the drawing "the sultan was on horseback . . . in a state of complete bewilderment and vexation; the *hoja efendi* [Sadeddin] was beside the sultan's stirrup, turned toward him with his two hands raised in prayer, as if he were reciting something and casting a spell [on him]. Below the drawing was the caption, "The *hoja efendi*'s prayer is accepted!" See also the account of the English ambassador Edward Barton, who accompanied Mehmed on the campaign (Glover, *The Journey of Edward Barton*, 320).

78. İpşirli, "Hasan Kafî el-Akhisarî ve Devlet Düzenine ait Eseri *Usûlü'l-hikem fî Nizâmi'l-Alem*," 275.

79. Dallam, *The Diary of Master Thomas Dallam, 1599–1600*, 69–71.

80. Mustafa Ali, *Künh ül-Ahbar*, 292b.

81. Report of the Venetian ambassador Giovanni Moro (1590), in Alberi, *Relazioni*, 3:332.

82. Uzunçarşılı, *Saray Teşkilatı*, 88.

83. Manz, "Tamurlane and the Symbolism of Sovereignty," 120.

84. For the influence of the traditions of Persian kingship, see Grunebaum, *Medieval Islam*, 155–56; Lambton, *State and Government in Medieval Islam*, 45, 54, 67; Frye, "Charisma," 50–54. For the influence of Byzantine traditions, see Gibb, "Arab-Byzantine Relations under the Umayyad Caliphate," 50–51, 58–60; Grunebaum, "The Sources of Islamic Civilization," 480ff., 492–97, and *passim*. For Byzantine influence on Anatolian Seljuk and Ottoman society, see the sources cited in the Introduction, n. 26.

85. Nizam al-Mulk, *The Book of Government*, trans. Darke, 119.

86. Nizam al-Mulk, *The Book of Government*, trans. Darke, 13.

87. Mecdi, *Hada'ik ül-Şaka'ik*, 50. Another anecdote recounts the attempts of the prominent sheikh Emir Sultan, one of Bayezid's sons-in-law, to discourage the sultan's drinking. When Bayezid sought Emir Sultan's opinion concerning his plans for a monumental mosque (Ulu Camii) in the heart of Bursa, the sheikh commented, "[I]t's very nice, but it's missing a tavern at each of its four corners." The sultan, surprised, responded, "[B]ut it's forbidden to have taverns near a mosque, which is God's House!" Emir Sultan's answer was, "[T]hen why do you contaminate your noble heart, which is God's house, with what is forbidden?"

88. Aşıkpaşazade, *Tevarih-i Al-i Osman* ch. 63.

89. Neşri, *Kitab-ı Cihan-Nüma,* 1:88 ("ayş u nuşa ve adl u dada meşgul oldu"), 102, 118, 119, 123.

90. Astarabadi, *Bazm u Razm.*

91. Fleischer, *Bureaucrat and Intellectual,* 258–59, 298–304.

92. See Spellberg, "Nizâm Al-Mulk's Manipulation of Tradition: ʿA'isha and the Role of Women in the Islamic Government," for a treatment of Nizâm al-Mulk's discussion of women.

93. Broquière, *Le Voyage d'Outremer,* 192.

94. M. Arif, ed., *Kanunname-i Al-i Osman,* 27.

95. See ch. 2, n. 60.

96. M. Arif, ed. *Kanunname,* 25.

97. Spandugnino, *Delle Historie, & origine de principi de Turchi, ordine della corte, loro rito, & costumi,* folio K vi.

98. See "The Tale of Bamsi Beyrek," 80–81, in G. Lewis, trans., *The Book of Dede Korkud.*

99. Neşri, *Neşri Tarihi,* 1:348–49.

100. Aşıkpaşazade, *Tevarih-i Al-i Osman,* ch. 33.

101. M. Arif, ed., *Kanunname,* 23.

102. M. Arif, ed., *Kanunname,* 23.

103. Selaniki, *Tarih-i Selânikî,* ed. and trans. İpşirli, 792.

104. See Repp, *The Müfti of Istanbul,* 234–37, for a story illustrating Süleyman's effective use of the monitoring post.

105. On the use of sign language within the palace, see Bon, *Descrizione del serraglio del gransignore,* 86–87, or Withers's translation, *The Grand Signiors Serraglio,* 363; Sandys, *A Relation of a Journey,* 158; Baudier, *Histoire géneralle du serrail,* 37–38. On the training of mutes in the use of this sign language, see Bobovius, *Mémoire,* 22–23.

106. *Calendar of State Papers, Venice,* vol. 10, item 329.

107. Du Fresne-Canaye, *Voyage du Levant,* 64–72, 237–40.

108. Tursun Beg, *Tarih-i Ebü'l-Feth,* 12–13, 17–22. See Mottahedeh, *Loyalty and Leadership,* 179, for a discussion of the meaning of *adl* and *zulm,* and B. Lewis, "Siyâsa," on the concept of *siyaset.*

109. Mustafa Ali, *Counsel for Sultans (Nushat üs-Selatin),* ed and trans. A. Tietze, 1:19. On the composition, contents, and significance of this work, see Fleischer, "From Şehzade Korkud to Mustafa Ali: Cultural Origins of the Ottoman *Nasihatname*" and *Bureaucrat and Intellectual,* 95–105; for critical reaction to the latter work, see Murphey, "Mustafa Ali and the Politics of Cultural Despair."

110. Y. Yücel, ed., *Kitab-ı Müstetab,* 36–37. According to Yücel, the anonymous author was a *devşirme* product of the inner palace school (xviii).

111. Koçi Bey, *Risale*, 61.

112. Talikizade, *Şehnâme-i Hümâyûn*, trans. Woodhead, 66–68.

113. Mustafa Ali, *Counsel*, ed. Tietze, 1:122.

114. Mustafa Ali, *Counsel*, ed. Tietze, 1:18.

115. Mustafa Ali, *Counsel*, ed. Tietze, 1:21.

116. Mustafa Ali, *Counsel*, ed. Tietze, 1:25.

117. See, for example, Shaw, *History of the Ottoman Empire and Modern Turkey*, 1:170, 184: "[I]ndividual sultans no longer played a decisive role in Ottoman affairs."

118. Fleischer, *Bureaucrat and Intellectual*, 294–95.

119. Mustafa Ali, *Künh ül-Ahbar*, 290a–292a.

120. For Mustafa Ali's comments in this regard, see ch. 3, 84.

121. Knox, *The First Blast of the Trumpet against the Monstrous Regiment of Women* (repr. Westminster, England, 1895), 50, quoted in Weil, "The Crown Has Fallen to the Distaff: Gender and Politics in the Age of Catherine de Médici," 5.

122. See preface, n. 1.

123. İpşirli, "Hasan Kafî," 250.

124. Y. Yücel, ed., *Kitab-ı Müstetab*, 31.

125. Itzkowitz, "Eighteenth-Century Ottoman Realities," 85–89.

126. Kunt, *The Sultan's Servants*, 95–97.

127. Darling, "The Ottoman Finance Department in a Century of Crisis," 304–8.

128. See Faroqhi, "Political Initiatives 'From the Bottom Up' in the Sixteenth- and Seventeenth-Century Ottoman Empire," and a number of the sources cited in this article. See also Darling, "The Ottoman Finance Department," *passim*, and Howard, "The Ottoman Timar System and its Transformation, 1563–1656," 122–23, 242. Singer (*Palestinian Peasants and Ottoman Officials: Rural Administration in the Sancak of Jerusalem in the Mid-Sixteenth Century, passim*) argues that peasants could resist the demands of the state and mount self-interested initiatives in a number of ways.

129. Kunt, *The Sultan's Servants*, chs. 4 and 5.

130. İnalcık, "Military and Fiscal Transformation," esp. 296–303. Finkel (*The Administration of Warfare*, 39–46), argues for modification of this argument, pointing out that many militia members remained mobilized in garrisons or were redirected toward combat with the Safavids; she also notes that most peasant recruits for the Hungarian campaigns came from Bosnia and Albania rather than Anatolia.

131. Sir Thomas Roe, *The Negotiations*, 50.

132. See Mottahedeh, *Loyalty and Leadership*, 177–78, for a discussion of the central role of "awe of authority" in the conception of Islamic kingship.

133. Peçevi, *Tarih*, 2:389; Tugi, *Tugi Tarihi*, 501–2.

134. Naima, *Tarih*, 2:235.

135. Baudier, *Histoire généralle*, 37–38.

136. Koçi Bey, *Risale*, 110–11.

137. Koçi Bey, *Risale*, 63–64.

138. BA, MM 1515, 3634, 859; KK Saray 7101A.

139. Naima, *Tarih*, 1:53–54.

Chapter 7

1. Evliya Çelebi, *Narrative of Travels*, trans. J. von Hammer, 2:83.

2. Kuran, "Üsküdar Atik Valide Külliyesinin Yerleşme Düzeni ve Yapım Tarihi Üzerine," 232.

3. Evliya Çelebi, *Seyahatname*, 1:474.

4. On the use of female images in the political propaganda of Roman and late Roman dynasties, see Susan Wood, "*Memoriae Agrippinae:* Agrippina the Elder in Julio-Claudian Art and Propaganda," and Kenneth Holum, *Theodosian Empresses: Women and Imperial Dominion in Late Antiquity.* I am grateful to Peter R. Brown for drawing the latter work to my attention. The striking parallels between the Theodosian and Ottoman dynasties in the incorporation of women into dynastic propaganda during their "sedentarizing" stages suggests a continuity in women's roles in the imperial traditions played out in the city of Constantinople/Istanbul.

5. For a variety of images to which Elizabeth I and Catherine de Médicis were linked, see Yates, *Astrea*, 29–87, 133–35, 144. Clifford Geertz examines the symbolism of the royal progresses of Elizabeth I, where, for example, Deborah was featured in tableaux to provide an example of a woman who had ruled wisely and effectively ("Centers, Kings, and Charisma: Reflections on the Symbolics of Power," 125–29).

6. Celalzade Mustafa, *Tabakat ül-Memalik*, 239a. See Spellberg, "The Politics of Praise: Depictions of Khadija, Fatima and ʿAʾisha in Ninth-Century Muslim Sources," for a discussion of the use of these formulas of praise in the early Islamic period.

7. Uzunçarşılı, *Saray Teşkilatı*, 154.

8. Tayyarzade Ataullah, *Tarih-i Enderun*, 3:65. For a discussion of this ceremonial procession, see Uzunçarşılı, *Saray Teşkilatı*, 154–56.

9. See Silahdar Fındıklılı Mehmed Aga, *Silahdar Tarihi*, 2:298, for a description of the *valide alayı* of Saliha Dilaşub Sultan, mother of Süleyman II (1687); Davis, *The Palace of Topkapı*, 37–38 for that of Mihrişah Sultan, mother of Selim III (1789); and Tayyarzade Ataullah, *Tarih-i Enderun*, 3:65–66, for that of Nakşidil Sultan, mother of Mahmud II (1808).

10. Selaniki, *Tarih*, 173–74.

11. I am grateful to Dr. Filiz Çağman, director of the Topkapı Palace Library, for pointing out this miniature and its unique nature to me. The miniature is reproduced in Atasoy and Çağman, *Turkish Miniature Painting*, plate 30.

12. Selaniki, *Tarih-i Selânikî*, ed. and trans. İpşirli, 761.

13. Evliya Çelebi, *Narrative of Travels*, trans. Hammer, 2:12.

14. For a description of the ceremonial exit from and return to the capital during one post-Süleymanic sultanic campaign, that of Mehmed III to Erlau in 1596, see Sanderson, *The Travels*, 59–60.

15. Du Fresne-Canaye, *Le Voyage du Levant*, 120–21.

16. Uzunçarşılı, *Saray Teşkilatı*, 88.

17. Alberi, *Relazioni*, 3:332.

18. Selaniki, *Tarih*, 173. According to the Venetian ambassador Morosini, Nurbanu had a palace near the Topkapı Gate, in the vicinity of the old Byzantine city walls (Dispatch of December 13, 1583, cited by Spagni, "Una Sultana veneziana," 331).

19. Abutting the side of the mosque on which the imperial loge (*hünkar mahfili*) is located is a structure with large rooms, currently used as a residence by the imam of the mosque. It is possible that this structure, or earlier forms of it, were used by Nurbanu or other members of the royal family when they visited the mosque. Because of the mosque's distance from the imperial palace, a visit might have required some rest or perhaps an overnight stay before the return to the palace.

20. Selaniki gives a list of the rulers invited to the circumcision (*Tarih*, 164–65).

21. Because Ottoman sources do not mention the participation of women in the circumcision ceremony, the following discussion is based primarily on Hammer, *Histoire*, 7:146–63, who relied on both Ottoman and foreign accounts of the event.

22. Peçevi, *Tarih*, 2:74.

23. *The Fugger News-Letters, 1568–1605*, 65.

24. Hammer, *Histoire*, 7:157.

25. See G. Lewis, trans., *The Book of Dede Korkut*, especially "Boghach Khan Son of Dirse Khan" and "How Prince Uruz Son of Salur Kazan Was Taken Prisoner." On the subject of women in these tales, see Mehmed Kaplan, "Dede Korkut Kitabında Kadın," 103–6 ("In the *Book of Dede Korkut*, . . . devotion and love of mother for son and son for mother give rise to the greatest acts of heroism," 103).

26. Hammer, *Histoire*, 7:160, who gives no source for this information.

27. Peçevi, *Tarih*, 2:72.

28. Neşri, *Neşri Tarihi*, 1:106–7.

29. Sanderson, *The Travels*, 60.

30. Hammer, *Histoire*, 9:349.

31. Selaniki, *Tarih-i Selânikî*, ed. and trans. İpşirli, 696–97.

32. Selaniki, *Tarih-i Selânikî*, ed. and trans. İpşirli, 747.

33. Geertz, "Centers, Kings, and Charisma," 125.

34. Naima, *Tarih*, 6:359.

35. On Vani Efendi, a partisan of the followers of Kadızade Mehmed Efendi, see Zilfi, "The Kadızadelis: Discordant Revivalism in Seventeenth-Century Istanbul," 263–65.

36. Galland, *Journal*, 1:215.

37. Tavernier, *Nouvelle Relation*, 158–61.

38. The following description of the visit is drawn from the account of Abdi Abdürrahman Pasha (TSMA, E 2477).

39. Naima, *Tarih*, 6:418.

40. TSMA, E 2477.

41. Selaniki, *Tarih-i Selânikî*, ed. and trans. İpşirli, 826–27.

42. According to Tugi (*Tugi Tarihi*, 499), Mustafa's mother was resident in the imperial palace and was taken together with the sultan, two of his *jariyes*, and a male slave to the Old Palace.

43. Peçevi, *Tarih*, 2:383.

44. Selaniki, *Tarih*, 174; Naima, *Tarih*, 1:415.

45. Galland, *Journal*, 2:71–72; Vandal, *Les Voyages du Marquis de Nointel*, 108.

46. A mosque complex (*külliye*) might include any or all of the following: a hospital (*dar üş-şifa*), a lunatic asylum (*bimarhane*), a hostel for dervishes (*hankah*), an inn for travelers (*kervansaray*), a soup kitchen (*imaret*), one or more religious colleges (*medrese*), a library (*kütüphane*), a primary school (*mektep*), and the tomb (*türbe*) of the builder of the complex or of the person in whose honor the complex was built. Associated with the complex might be a bath (*hamam*) and/or a market (*pazar, çarşı*), the income from which would go to the upkeep of the charitable services of the complex.

47. For a discussion of the projects undertaken by Ottoman women and the connections between these undertakings and their political careers, see Bates, "Women as Patrons of Architecture in Turkey."

48. On this complex and its endowment deed (*vakfiye*), see Konyalı, "Kanunî Sultan Süleyman'ın Annesi Hafsa Sultanın Vakfiyyesi ve Manisa'daki Hayır Eserleri."

49. Uluçay, *Manisa'daki Saray-ı Amire ve Şehzadeler Türbesi*, 9, and "Notlar ve Vesikalar," 230–31.

50. TSMA, E 2629. See TSMA, E 3079, for Hafsa Sultan's purchase in 1516 of a property in Mudanya and its attendant structures (including five buildings and a stable).

51. Konyalı, "Hafsa Sultanın Vakfiyyesi," 51.

52. Uluçay, "Notlar ve Vesikalar," 231.

53. İnalcık, *The Ottoman Empire,* 142–43. On the reconstruction of the capital, see also B. Lewis, *Istanbul and the Civilization of the Ottoman Empire,* ch. 5.

54. Ayvansarayî, *Hadikat ül-Cevami,* 1:101.

55. See Stephan, "An Endowment Deed of Khâsseki Sultân, Dated the 24th May 1552," 182–83.

56. Mustafa Ali, *Künh ül-Ahbar,* 121a.

57. TSMA, E 5404/13.

58. Ayvansarayî, *Hadikat ül-Cevami,* 2:186–87.

59. Skilliter ("Khurrem," 66) would appear to be mistaken in construing the *Avrat Pazarı* as the women's slave market and in suggesting that the site was chosen because of Hurrem's slave origins. Numerous travelers' accounts attest to the female slave market's location next to the male slave market, between the mosque of Bayezid II and the covered market (*bedestan*) at the center of the city. The Women's Market is mentioned in some accounts; for example, Sanderson, secretary to the English embassy at the end of the sixteenth century, speaks of the "Aurat Bazar, which is as much to say, the markett place of women, for thither they come to sell their wourks and wares" (*The Travels,* 77). The confusion may stem from the possibility that the female slave market was also known as *Avrat Pazarı* (see Du Loir, *Les Voyages,* 58).

60. This was told to me in 1985 by the custodian of the mosque, which is located in the market area of Üsküdar.

61. In some versions of the Ottoman criminal code drawn up under Süleyman, physical deformation of a person's genitals was the most severe of punishments, imposed in cases of abduction, seemingly the worst offense in the category of *zina* (illicit sexual activity): the castration of a man was the punishment for the crime of abducting a woman, girl, or young boy, and the branding of a woman's vulva was the punishment for willing consent to abduction (Heyd, *Studies in Old Ottoman Criminal Law,* 97–98). On the possibility that the compilation of the criminal code may have been ordered by Lutfi Pasha, see Heyd, 26–27.

62. Mustafa Ali, *Künh ül-Ahbar,* 123a–b; Evliya Çelebi, *Seyahatname,* trans. Parmaksızoğlu, 1:129 (this passage does not appear in the printed edition of 1314/ 1896–97).

63. Sanderson, "Sundrie the Personall voyages," 436, note. The "Vizier" in question was the eunuch grand vezir Hadım Hasan Pasha.

64. TSMA, D 6932, quoted in Uluçay, *Padişahların Kadınları,* 45.

65. Naima, *Tarih,* 5:113.

66. Peçevi, *Tarih,* 1:425. This comment was repeated by Evliya Çelebi, *Seyahatname,* 1:165.

67. Evliya Çelebi, *Narrative of Travels,* trans. Hammer, 1:179–80.

68. Evliya Çelebi, *Narrative of Travels,* 1:83.

69. Ayvansarayî, *Hadikat ül-Cevami,* 1:101–2. Today a medical facility, know as the "Haseki Hospital," is located in that part of the original complex (*Dar üş-Şifa*) used for the same purpose.

70. The mosques of Aya Sofya, Fatih Mehmet, and Bayezid II were the three most important imperial mosques until those of Süleyman and Ahmed I joined their ranks. Closer at hand, the mosque of Aya Sofya tended to be more associated with royal religious ceremony. It was the highest-ranking mosque with regard to *ulema* appointments (Zilfi, "The Kadızadelis," 253).

71. Davis, *The Palace of Topkapı,* 9.

72. Peçevi, *Tarih*, 1:426.

73. Peçevi, *Tarih*, 1:427.

74. Heyd, *Ottoman Documents on Palestine*, 128, 130–33.

75. Stephan, "An Endowment Deed of Khâsseki Sultân," 173.

76. Peçevi, *Tarih*, 1:427; Evliya Çelebi, *Seyahatname*, 1:161.

77. Spellberg, "The Politics of Praise."

78. "Umm ul-mu'minin Hadije Ana," Evliya Çelebi, *Seyahatname*, 1:161.

79. There is some disagreement over who actually undertook this project. Peçevi (*Tarih*, 1:426–27) and Evliya Çelebi (*Seyahatname*, 1:161) present it as Süleyman's effort. The Venetian ambassador Costantino Garzoni reported that Mihrimah planned to construct an aqueduct from Cairo to Mecca [!] and had requested two hundred thousand measures of steel from which to make chisels to carve the stonework of the aqueduct (Alberi, *Relazioni*, 1:400); according to Baysun ("Mihrümah Sultân," 308), it was Mihrimah who undertook the repair and expansion of Zubeida's water works (quoting Eyyub Sabri, *Mir'ât al-Haramayn, Mir'at Makka*, 740–56). Another tradition holds that Hurrem undertook this project; see Abbott, *Two Queens of Baghdad*, 255, quoting F. Wüstenfeld, *Die Chroniken der Stadt Mekka*, 3:341ff. and 4:309ff.).

80. Stephan, "An Endowment Deed of Khâsseki Sultân," 171, n.2.

81. Burgoyne, *Mamluk Jerusalem*, 485–87.

82. Stephan, "An Endowment Deed of Khâsseki Sultân," 173.

83. TSMA, E 7816/1–11.

84. TSMA, E 7816/1. The income from the village was broken down as follows: 35,000 aspers *mal-ı dimus*, 30,000 aspers *mezraa*, 882 aspers *rüsum-ı saire*, 1,200 aspers *bad-ı hava*, 30,896 aspers *cizye* (253 individuals at 122 aspers a head).

85. For example, a 1539 deed witnessed by Mehmet, Lutfi, and Ayas Pashas (TSMA, E 9517), and a group of deeds issued between 1550 and 1553 witnessed by Ahmet, İbrahim, and Ali Pashas (TSMA, E 7816/1, 5, and 6).

86. TMSA, E 9099.

87. TSMA, E 765.

88. She also made provision for a former halberdier of the Old Palace who had retired to Medina (see her endowment deed of 1613, TSMA, D 7025).

89. Dispatch of the ambassador Girolamo Capello, December 31, 1597, *Calendar of State Papers, Venice*, 9:304.

90. Barozzi and Berchet, *Le Relazioni*, 2:95.

91. Silahdar, *Tarih*, 1:218–19. Ayvansarayî, *Hadikat ül-Cevami*, 1:20–21, is wrong in attributing the initial construction of the mosque to Kösem Sultan. A study of this mosque is being prepared by Lucienne Thys-Şenocak.

92. Bates, "Women as Patrons," 255.

93. Zilfi, "The Kadızadelis," 253.

94. I am grateful to Mr. Cenk Alpak, Director of Tombs, for making it possible for me to see the tomb of Turhan Sultan in 1985 and again in 1990, as well as the tombs of the Şehzade complex, all of which were closed to the public during my period of research in Istanbul. The tomb of Turhan Sultan is currently being restored.

95. SL, Turhan Hadice Sultan 150, 53a–57a. The 157 were the keeper of the tomb, 30 guards, 90 readers of the Qur'an, 20 reciters of the litanies of God's unity and his praise, 4 persons to recite certain verses of the Qur'an and to pray for Turhan Sultan's soul, a *hafız* (one who recited the Qur'an by heart), a person to burn incense, and 10 custodians.

96. Bayraktar, "*Üsküdar Kütüphaneleri*," 49.

97. Bayraktar and Kut, *Yazma Eserlerde Vakıf Mühürleri*, 48–49. I am grateful to

Dr. Filiz Cağman, Director of the Topkapı Palace Library, for drawing this work to my attention.

98. TSMA, D 4155. Among the books for the New Valide Mosque were thirty volumes of *tefsir* (Qur'an commentary), seven *şerh ül-tefsir* (explication of Qur'an commentary), sixteen *ilm ül-hadis* (science of Prophetic tradition), nineteen *şerh ül-hadis* (*hadith* commentary), fourteen *ilm usul ül-fıkh* (science of the bases of jurisprudence), thirty-eight *ilm ül-fıkh* (science of jurisprudence), thirty-one collections of *fetva;* thirteen *ilm ül-kelam* (science of Qur'anic theology); nineteen *ilm ül-lugat* (lexicology); twenty-six *tarih ve siret* (history and biography of the Prophet); nine *tıbb* (medicine); twelve *tasavvuf* (mysticism); thirteen *ilm ül-belagat* (rhetoric); five *ilm ül-sarf* (grammar); and many *şerh ül-Safiye* (commentary on the first verse of the Qur'an).

99. The complex contained a primary school, a school for the study of prophetic tradition, a double bath, a fountain for drinking water, and a fountain for household use; its mosque, while small, was lavishly decorated with tiles (Ayvansarayî, *Hadikat ül-Cevami,* 2:184–85). Kösem also built a small mosque for the fortress at Anadolu Kavağı, on the Asian shore of the upper Bosphorus; her daughter-in-law Turhan built a mosque for the fortress of Rumeli Kavağı on the opposite shore (Ayvansarayî, *Hadikat ül-Cevami,* 2:144). Turhan's mosque was built in honor of her brother Yusuf Agha, and its site—looking north across the Black Sea—may have been chosen to commemorate their Russian origins.

100. Barozzi and Berchet, *Le Relazioni,* 2:95.

101. Barozzi and Berchet, *Le Relazioni,* 1:372–73, 2:110.

102. Ayvansarayî, *Hadikat ül-Cevami,* 2:183.

103. Fountains were of two types: the *sebil,* an enclosed structure from which an attendant would furnish drinking water to passersby, and the *çeşme,* from which water could be drawn for use in the home or workplace.

104. Ayvansarayî, *Hadikat ül-Cevami,* 1:22.

105. İlgürel, "Kösem Sultan'ın Bir Vakfiyesi," 86–92; this article presents a transcription of the 1617 endowment deed with introduction.

106. Naima, *Tarih,* 5:113.

107. SL, Turhan Hadice Sultan 150, 58b–60b, 61a–64b, 69a–77b.

108. TSMA, E 4074.

109. TSMA, D 3990.

110. Orhonlu, *Telhisler (1597–1607),* no. 11, pp. 10–11.

111. Uzunçarşılı, *Osmanlı Tarihi,* 3 (pt 1): 350, n. 2. On the conflict between the factions formed around Sivasi and Kadızade, see Kâtip Çelebi, *The Balance of Truth,* trans. G. Lewis, ch. 21: "The Controversy between Sivasi and Qadızade"; Zilfi, "The Kadızadelis."

112. Spagni, "Una Sultana veneziana," 332.

113. Naima, *Tarih,* 5:113.

114. SL, Turhan Hadice Sultan 150, 58a. Tevekkül Khatun was the only individual provided for in the endowment deed; the provision for her is the first item to follow the stipulations concerning Turhan Sultan's mosque complex.

115. Selaniki, *Tarih-i Selânikî,* ed. and trans. İpşirli, 790. Selaniki later describes the exact uses to which the *valide sultan*'s funds were put (808–9).

116. Naima, *Tarih,* 6:409.

117. SL, Turhan Hadice Sultan 150, 15a.

118. BA, MM 1372, folio 8.

119. See the register of income and expenses for H. 1069–70/1658–59 (BA, MM

1372), and a copy of one entry in the register, issued as a receipt (BA, İE, Saray Mesalihi 152).

120. Finkel, *The Administration of Warfare*, 261.

121. Naima, *Tarih*, 1:428.

122. TSMA, E 7001/4. The letter is undated and unsigned, but probably belongs to the grand vezirate of Hafız Ahmed Pasha (January 1625–December 1626).

123. TSMA E 7001/42. At the mid-seventeenth century, the purse was worth forty thousand aspers; the sum requested by the grand vezir was thus two million aspers.

124. TSMA E 7001/42. This letter from the lieutenant grand vezir to the *valide sultan*, which carried the latter's response written directly on it, is undated and unsigned. However, internal evidence suggests that it belongs to the end of Melek Ahmed Pasha's term as lieutenant grand vezir, which lasted from November 1654 to May 1655.

125. Naima, *Tarih*, 6:30–31.

126. BA, Mühimme Defteri 31, folio 217, quoted by Uzunçarşılı, *Osmanlı Tarihi*, 1:561, n. 1; the village was in the district of Bilejik, where the dervish hospice of Osman's wife's father, Sheikh Edebali, was located.

127. Ibn Battuta, *The Travels*, 2:340.

128. Kunt, *The Sultan's Servants*, 91–93.

129. For this term, see Gökbilgin, "Başmaklık."

130. Avni Ömer Efendi, *Kanun-i Osmanî Mefhum-ı Defter-i Hakanî*, ed. Uzunçarşılı, 386.

131. TSMA, D 5114.

132. TSMA, D 3831.

133. Dispatch of the Venetian ambassador Sebastian Venier, *Calendar of State Papers, Venice*, vol. 21, item 686.

134. Naima, *Tarih*, 5:112; Naima drew this piece of information from one of his principal sources, Şarih ül-Menarzade; for the important role played by the latter as a source for Naima's history, see Thomas, *A Study of Naima*, 136–39. At the mid-seventeenth century, the *riyal*, or *kuruş*, was worth eighty aspers.

135. Menemen would appear to have been held by Handan Sultan and converted by her to *vakıf* land (TSMA, D 1830/10, 17). However, it is possible that only a part of Handan's Menemen *hass* was converted to *vakıf* and the rest later transferred to Kösem Sultan, or, more likely, that Menemen supported more than one *hass*. According to Naima (*Tarih*, 3:290), in 1636 "the Menemen *hass* became the Haseki Sultan's *paşmaklık*, having been the *arpalık* ["barley money"—a name used for grants to state officials] of Riyazi Efendi, dismissed from his office in Egypt."

136. TSMA, E 7905, and E 5222/2, a copy of the former.

137. TSMA, E 7927.

138. Karaçelebizade Abdülaziz, *Ravzat ul-Ebrar Zeyli*, 7r.

139. TSMA, D 4124.

140. SL, Turhan Hadice Sultan 150, 27a. This land was granted to Turhan as freehold, and was converted by her to endowment.

141. See n. 39.

142. This is suggested by a group of documents (TSMA, D 1830) relating to excess income from the *vakıf* and *hass* lands of members of the royal family. In various documents relating to the *valide sultan*'s possessions, her *vakıf* lands are called *vakıf/ evkaf hasları*: cf. no. 17—"vakıf haslarından . . ."; no. 25—"Handan Sultan vakf-ı şerifleri zevaidinden Menemen ve Kilizman hasları mahsulu . . ."; no. 37—"*valide sultan* [Nurbanu] evkafı zevaidinden Yeni İl hasları mahsulundan. . . ." See also BA, MM 4905 (an *evkaf muhasebe defteri* of royal *vakıf*s from 1630–1632): "hasha-yı Yeni İl

'an evkaf-ı cami'-i şerif-i merhume . . . valide sultan" (folio 28), and "hasha-yı Surkenar [?] 'an evkaf-ı merhume . . . valide Handan Sultan" (folio 37). More research is required, however, before this hypothesis can be verified.

143. Ménage, "Some Notes on the *Devshirme*," 71–72. These lands had belonged to Mihrimah Sultan before they were granted to Nurbanu, another example of the transfer of certain crown lands from one member of the imperial family to another. The peasants on lands that were endowed to Mecca and Medina (*harameyn evkafı*) were exempt from *avariz* taxes in the sixteenth century (Cohen and Lewis, *Population and Revenue in the Towns of Palestine in the Sixteenth Century,* 42).

144. TSMA, D 1830/37.

145. TSMA, D 1830/17. This document gives an account of the income and expenditure of the endowment for the year H. 1015/1606–7, the year following the death of Handan Sultan.

146. TSMA, D 5114. "Tavil" was the nickname of several *Jelalis* in this period; the individual referred to was Tavil Halil, a former lieutenant of the Jelali Kara Yazıcı, whose home base was Tokat and Amasya; Tavil Halil was appeased with the governor-generalship (*beylerbegilik*) of Baghdad and twelve provincial governorates for his top officers (Griswold, *The Great Anatolian Rebellion, 1000–1020/1591–1611,* 52–55, 180, 192).

147. Lello, *The Report of Lello,* 23.

148. SL, Turhan Hadice Sultan 150, 24b.

149. SL, Turhan Hadice Sultan 150, 25a–26a.

150. BA, MM 5705.

151. TSMA, D 4323.

152. For a list of the personal possessions of one *valide sultan,* Muazzez Sultan, one of the *haseki*s of İbrahim, see TSMA, D 7704.

153. Naima, *Tarih,* 5:113.

154. TSMA, D 4323.

155. Naima, *Tarih,* 4:222.

156. Naima, *Tarih,* 6:359.

157. Naima, *Tarih,* 5:112.

158. Stephen, "An Endowment Deed of Khâsseki Sultân," 187–91.

159. Kiel, *Art and Society of Bulgaria in the Turkish Period,* 109–10; Kiel quotes a 1978 study by E. Floreva.

160. Nev'izade 'Ata'i, *Hada'ik ül-Haka'ik fi Tekmilet iş-Şaka'ik, passim.* On the levels into which *medreses* were organized, see Uzunçarşılı, *Osmanlı Devletinin İlmiye Teşkilatı,* 11–12; İnalcık, *The Ottoman Empire,* 168–71.

161. Peçevi, *Tarih,* 1:62.

162. Baer, "Women and Waqf: An Analysis of the Istanbul *Tahrir* of 1546," 10, 26–27.

Chapter 8

1. The portrait was one of a number of gifts sent by Elizabeth to Safiye in 1593; the inventory given by Wrag, a member of the English delegation, lists "a jewel of her majesties picture, set with some rubies and diamants, 3 great pieces of gilt plate, 10 garments of clothe of gold, a very fine case of glasse bottles, silver & gilt, with 2 pieces of fine Holland" (from Wrag, *A Description of a Voiage to Constantinople and Syria,* quoted by Rosedale, *Queen Elizabeth and the Levant Company,* 16). For Safiye's request in 1599 to see Elizabeth's portrait, see Skilliter, "Three Letters," 151.

2. Skilliter, "Three Letters," 147–48. Safiye's accompanying letter was adorned with a "shell of gould which couered the seale of her lettere to her Magestie uppon which was sett ii smale sparkes of Dyamondes and ii small sparkes of rubies."

3. Lambton, *Continuity and Change in Medieval Persia*, 290.

4. Tursun Beg, *Tarih-i Ebü'l-Feth*, 109; Neşri, *Neşri Tarihi*, 2:161–62; Babinger, *Mehmet the Conqueror*, 193ff. See Lambton, *Continuity and Change*, 290, n. 167, for the employment of women as intercessors among the Seljuk successor states and the Ilkhanids.

5. Sadeddin Efendi, *Tac ul-Tevarih*, 3:195–96. Seljuk Khatun was the daughter of Mehmed I.

6. On the importance of ethnic origin in the slave elite, see Kunt, "Ethnic-Regional (*Cins*) Solidarity in the Seventeenth-Century Ottoman Establishment."

7. Naima, *Tarih*, 2:313.

8. Mustafa Ali, *Künh ül-Ahbar*, 69a–b; Peçevi, *Tarih*, 1:268–69. See also Hammer, *Histoire*, 6:8.

9. Peçevi, *Tarih*, 1:269.

10. Hammer, *Histoire*, 6:8–9.

11. See the report of Navagero (1553) in Alberi, *Relazioni*, 1:73, 80, 90; and Busbecq's 1560 report of his personal conversations with Rüstem Pasha, in *Turkish Letters*, 86.

12. Sokolnicki, "La Sultane Ruthène," 236.

13. For these letters, see Askenazy, "Listy Roxolany," 115–17; Uçtum, "Hürrem ve Mihrümah Sultanların Polonya Kıralı II. Zigismund'a Yazdıkları Mektuplar," 712–13. For reproduction and discussion of three of these letters (by Giles Veinstein), see Bernus-Taylor et al., *Soliman le Magnifique*, 48–50.

14. For Mihrimah's letters, see Uçtum, "Hürrem ve Mihrümah Sultanların . . . Yazdıkları Mektuplar," 712–14.

15. For Sultanım's letter to Hurrem, see *Shah Tahmasb-e Safavi, Mujmu'a-yi Asnad va Mukatibat-i Tarikhi*, 343–46; I am grateful to Kathryn Babayan for bringing this letter to my attention and translating it for me. For Hurrem's letter to Sultanım, see Feridun Beg, *Münşeat üs-Selatin*, 2:65–66.

16. Alberi, *Relazioni*, 2:237.

17. Report of Contarini, (in Alberi, *Relazioni*, 3:235). See also Spagni, "Una Sultana veneziana," 275–82. Presented along with other captives to Süleyman, Nurbanu presumably entered the imperial harem, where she may have been trained under the eye of Hurrem Sultan and presented to Selim when he was dispatched in 1543 to his provincial governorate.

18. Alberi, *Relazioni*, 3:235–36.

19. Spagni, "Una Sultana veneziana," 327–28.

20. Letter of December 13, 1583, in *Négotiations de la France dans le Levant*, vol. 3: *Correspondance de Jacques de Germigny, ambassadeur de France à Constantinople*, n.p., cited in Spagni, "Una Sultana veneziana," 334, n.1.

21. Dispatch of G. Morosini, December 13, 1583, in Alberi, *Relazioni*, 3:309. The ambassador was informed of this event by a renegade from the admiral's service, who had been present when the proposal was destroyed.

22. Alberi, *Relazioni*, 3:298.

23. *Calendar of State Papers, Venice*, vol. 8, item 665, May 18, 1588.

24. Strict prohibitions on the export of wheat had been in effect since 1564 because of grain shortages; the market began to reopen around 1591 (Maurice Aymard, "Venise, Raguse et le commerce du blé pendant la seconde moitie du XVIe siècle,"

cited in İnalcık, "Impact of the *Annales* School on Ottoman Studies and New Findings," 80–81).

25. Alberi, *Relazioni*, 2:360.

26. Alberi, *Relazioni*, 3:439–40.

27. Barozzi and Berchet, *Le Relazioni*, 1:302–3.

28. Alberi, *Relazioni*, 3:239.

29. Alberi, *Relazioni*, 2:409.

30. According to the ambassador Zane (1594), Sadeddin Efendi favored the interests of these three countries, but was opposed to Spanish interests (Alberi, *Relazioni*, 3:435–36).

31. *The Fugger News-Letters, 1568–1605* (Second Series), 131.

32. Letter to Nicholas Salter, November 3, 1599, in Sanderson, *The Travels*, 183.

33. See Sanderson's letter to Thomas Simonds, September 21, 1599 (*The Travels*, 181): "The Muftie dead one Thursdaye and buryed a Fryday. Now I knowe there wilbe no more words of the seven loade of money he demanded. . . ." A "loade" was the equivalent of 100,000 aspers.

34. On the establishment of the English embassy, see Skilliter, *William Harborne and the Trade with Turkey 1578–1582;* Kurat, *Türk-İngiliz Münasebetleri.*

35. Sanderson, *The Travels*, 61. For a specimen of Barton's charm, persuasiveness, and familiar tone with the *valide sultan*, see his petition to her in May 1592 (*Calendar of State Papers, Venice*, vol. 9, item 12).

36. Dallam, *The Diary*, 63. Kurat, *Türk-İngiliz Münasebetleri*, 86, says that Safiye visited with Pindar many times.

37. On the *kiras*, see Mordtmann, "Die Jüdischen Kira im Serai der Sultane."

38. Skilliter, "Three Letters," 148.

39. Alberi, *Relazioni*, 3:298–99.

40. *Calendar of State Papers, Venice*, vol. 10, item 240, dispatch of Zane to the doge and senate, December 4, 1593.

41. *Calendar of State Papers, Venice*, vol. 7, item 1134.

42. *Calendar of State Papers, Venice*, vol. 19, item 271.

43. *Calendar of State Papers, Venice*, vol. 19, item 475.

44. See Weil, "The Crown Has Fallen to the Distaff," on the political careers of Elizabeth and Catherine.

45. Skilliter, "The Letters of the Venetian 'Sultana,' " documents 1, 2, 7, and 10, respectively.

46. Skilliter, "The Letters of the Venetian 'Sultana,' " documents 3, 6, and 8, respectively.

47. Skilliter, "Catherine de' Médici's Turkish Ladies-in-Waiting: A Dilemma in Franco-Ottoman Diplomatic Relations," 199–200.

48. Bertaud, *L'Illustre Orbandale* (binder's title for de Germigny, *Recueil des pieces choisies, extraites sur les originaux de la negotiation de Mr. de Germigny, de Chalon sur Saône*), n.p., cited in Spagni, "Una Sultana veneziana," 320–21.

49. Rosedale, *Queen Elizabeth and the Levant Company*, appendix E.

50. See the entry in the Fugger News-Letter, March 3, 1600 (*The Fugger News-Letters, 1568–1605* [Second Series], 324). For a possible solution to the mystery of the missing tiara, see Skilliter, "Three Letters," 154: the author proposes that it was surreptitiously withheld by Safiye's *kira* from the set of gifts sent by the *valide sultan* in 1593 and offered by the *kira* as her own gift to Elizabeth when another set of Ottoman gifts to the queen was dispatched in the winter of 1599.

51. Skilliter, "Three Letters," document 1, 125–26, 132–33; the translation is essen-

tially Skilliter's, although I have made minor changes. A loose rendering of this letter in English is given in Rosedale, *Queen Elizabeth and the Levant Company*, 2–4.

52. According to Kurat, *Türk-İngiliz Münasebetleri*, 87, Elizabeth requested in her letters to both the sultan and his mother that the treaty of 1593 be renewed.

53. Skilliter, "Three Letters," document 11, 134–35, 138–39; I have made slight changes in Skilliter's translation.

Chapter 9

1. Postel, *De la Republique des Turcs*, 60. This is the only source of which I am aware for this story. The story tends to support the tradition that Selim executed all his sons except Süleyman before the Persian campaign of 1514 (see ch. 3, 85).

2. Turan, *Kanunî'nin Oğlu Şehzâde Bayezid Vak'ası*, 208–10.

3. Busbecq, *Turkish Letters*, 83 (Letter 11, July 1556). See also Turan, *Şehzâde Bayezid Vak'ası*, 42–43.

4. *Calendar of State Papers, Venice*, vol. 9, item 563; dispatch of Girolamo Capello to the doge and senate, March 1597.

5. Peçevi, *Tarih*, 2:281; Naima, *Tarih*, 1:312–13; Uzunçarşılı, "Üçüncü Mehmed'in Oğlu Şehzade Mahmud'un ölümü," 263–67. See ch. 4, 97–98, for additional details of this affair.

6. Lello, *The Report of Lello*, 14–15.

7. Barozzi and Berchet, *Le Relazioni*, 1:132. Contarini appears to assume that Kösem's eldest son Murad was Ahmed's secondborn son; he was in fact the third eldest, after Osman and Mehmed. See also Danişmend, *İzahlı Osmanlı Tarihi Kronolojisi*, 3:270.

8. Altundağ, "Osman II," 444; Shaw, *History of the Ottoman Empire and Modern Turkey*, 1:192; Uluçay, *Padişahların Kadınları*, 48 (the document Uluçay cites as evidence of Mahfiruz's role as *valide sultan* is not to be found in the Topkapı Palace Museum Archives under the number he cites).

9. BA, MM, 855, 861, 1606.

10. BA, MM, 1606, 672, 847.

11. Barozzi and Berchet, *Le Relazioni*, 1:134.

12. Barozzi and Berchet, *Le Relazioni*, 1:133.

13. Barozzi and Berchet, *Le Relazioni*, 1:294.

14. Venetian report of April 17, 1619, in Hammer, *Histoire*, 8:186, n.4.

15. Roe, *The Negotiations*, 62.

16. Spandugino, *Delle Historie, & origine de principi de Turchi*, folio m ii (v); Bobovius, *Mémoire*, 104.

17. Uzunçarşılı, *Saray Teşkilatı*, 124–25.

18. Nev'i mourned both father and sons in the same elegy (E.J.W. Gibb, *A History of Ottoman Poetry*, 3:175ff.).

19. Hammer, *Histoire*, 5:327, 363.

20. Ahmed Resmi, *Hamilet ül-Kübera*, folio 15r. Atike Sultan is referred to as Turhan's "governess" (*mürebbiye*).

21. TSMA, E 7001/32. This undated letter appears to have been written in 1651 or 1652.

22. Venetian dispatch, 10 September 1623, in Hammer, *Histoire*, 9:2, n.1.

23. Roe, *The Negotiations*, 176.

24. Petis de la Croix, *Mémoirs*, 357.

25. Neşri, *Kitab-ı Cihan-Nüma*, 1:32.

26. Peçevi, *Tarih*, 2:316. Peçevi heard this story from Jivan Bey, the brother of Derviş Pasha, when they worked together on a tax survey of Eğriboz.

27. See, for example, the tale "Boghach Khan Son of Dirse Khan" in G. Lewis, trans., *The Book of Dede Korkut.*

28. Alberi, *Relazioni*, 3:234.

29. Spagni, "Una Sultana veneziana," 333.

30. Dispatch of December 13, 1583, cited in Spagni, "Una Sultana veneziana," 331.

31. Letter of the French ambassador de Germigny, December 13, 1583, cited in Spagni, "Una Sultana veneziana," 332.

32. Selaniki, *Tarih-i Selânikî*, ed. and trans. İpşirli, 857–58.

33. Naima, *Tarih*, 1:207.

34. Telhis no. 82, in Orhonlu, *Telhisler (1597–1607)*, 72–74.

35. Naima, *Tarih*, 3:182.

36. Silahdar, *Tarih*, 2:116–17.

37. Fleischer, *Bureaucrat and Intellectual*, 176–78.

38. Fleischer, *Bureaucrat and Intellectual*, 177.

39. Nev'i, *Nev'i Divanı*, 22–23. The *valide sultan* was only one of many influential persons to whom Nev'i addressed his poems; others included the various grand vezirs and vezirs of his age, the *müfti*, and of course the sultan and his son. I am grateful to Dr. Gülru Necipoğlu for drawing this poem to my attention.

40. According to Uluçay ("Koçi Bey," 834), Koçi Bey enjoyed Kösem Sultan's patronage and was requested by her to prepare memorandums for İbrahim.

41. Koçi Bey, *Risale*, 77–127, *passim.*

42. In addition to Koçi Bey's *Risale*, the works written for Murad included Aziz Efendi's *Kanunname-i Sultanî* and the head chancellor Avni Ömer Efendi's *Kanun-ı Osmanî Mefhum-i Defter-i Hakanî.* The work presented to Osman II was *Kitab-i Müstetab.* These works have been edited by, respectively, R. Murphey, İ. H. Uzunçarşılı, and Y. Yücel.

43. Cited in Hammer, *Histoire*, 7:320, n. 1.

44. Naima, *Tarih*, 1:140. Safiye Sultan's decision against Sadeddin Efendi was probably not a personal one, since it was she who had interceded on his behalf, getting him reappointed to his former position as the sultan's tutor.

45. Hammer, *Histoire*, 7:330–32. See also Lello, *The Report*, 1–2.

46. Naima, *Tarih*, 3:182ff.

47. Vandal, *Les Voyages*, 52–54.

48. Barozzi and Berchet, *Le Relazioni*, 1:39.

49. Sanderson, *The Travels*, 204.

50. Lello, *The Report*, 2.

51. Selaniki, *Tarih-i Selânikî*, ed. and trans. İpşirli, 853–57.

52. Sanderson, *The Travels*, 86, 201.

53. *Calendar of State Papers, Venice*, vol. 9, item 950, dispatch of January 21, 1601.

54. Selaniki, *Tarih-i Selânikî*, ed. and trans. İpşirli, 861–62.

55. Barozzi and Berchet, *Le Relazioni*, 1:129.

56. Naima, *Tarih*, 1:356–57.

57. Peçevi, *Tarih*, 2:31.

58. Peçevi, *Tarih*, 2:313; Naima, *Tarih*, 1:415.

59. There is some disagreement about the date of birth of Murad IV. The confusion may stem from the fact that the Ottoman biographical compendium, *Sicill-i Osmani*, gives two dates for his birth. In the text (1:77), it is given as Cemaziyelevvel 28, 1021 (July 27, 1612), whereas in the table of corrections (4:892), it is given as 1081, almost

certainly an error for 1018 (1609). Naima, who drew on contemporary sources, gives 1612 as Murad's birthdate (2:95), as does Cavid Baysun ("Murad IV," 625). I have accepted the later date as more plausible.

60. The correspondence between Kösem Sultan and the grand vezir consists of seven undated letters written by the *valide sultan* to the grand vezir (TSMA, E 2457/1,2,3; E 7001/1,4,5,6,8; there are probably more such documents, for example, E 7001/2,3, and 7, which I was unable to see). Internal references—for example, to Bayram Pasha, the governor of Egypt from 1625 to 1627—and indications in the letters that Murad IV was still fairly young at the time of their writing suggest that the letters were written sometime between 1623 and 1628. There are other documents grouped under these two catalogue numbers that have been classified by archival scholars as belonging to Kösem Sultan, but on the basis of handwriting and internal evidence I believe they belong to the early years of the regency of Turhan Sultan (1651–56).

61. TSMA, E 2457/3.

62. Hammer, *Histoire*, 9:128, n.1. The Venetian ambassadors believed that Murad suffered from epilepsy; if so, there was probably a constant concern with his health.

63. TSMA, E 7001/8.

64. Naima, *Tarih*, 2:394.

65. Venetian ambassadorial report, 2 September 1628, in Hammer, *Histoire*, 9:127, n.3.

66. See the reports of the ambassadors Giovanni Cappello (1634) and Pietro Foscarini (1637) for comment on this change in Murad's personality (Barozzi and Berchet, *Le Relazioni*, 2:33–34, 89ff).

67. Naima, *Tarih*, 4:290.

68. Naima, *Tarih*, 4:317.

69. Alberi, *Relazioni*, 3:234–35 (report of Paolo Contarini, 1583).

70. *Calendar of State Papers, Venice*, vol. 8, item 1082.

71. Barozzi and Berchet, *Le Relazioni*, 1:374.

72. Evliya Çelebi, *The Intimate Life*, trans. Dankoff, 138.

73. Karaçelebizade Abdülaziz Efendi, *Ravzat ül-Ebrar Zeyli*, 7a.

74. Naima, *Tarih*, 5:112ff. Şarih ül-Menarzade's history was a principal source for that of Naima. Naima relays Şarih's view in his obituary notice of Kösem Sultan, in which he evaluates various judgments of her career.

75. However, the nineteenth-century biographical dictionary of the Ottoman ruling class, *Sicill-i Osmani*, refers to both Kösem Sultan and Turhan Sultan as "regent" (*naibe-i saltanat, naibe-i hükumet-i seniyye*) (Süreyya, *Sicill-i Osmanı*, 1:27).

76. Karaçelebizade Abdülaziz Efendi, *Ravzat ül-Ebrar Zeyli*, 10a–b.

77. Kâtip Çelebi, *Fezleke*, 1:387 (the term I have translated as "conduct of government" is *tedbir-i umur*). Mustafa's mother's name does not appear in any of the sources; in the privy purse registers she is listed as *valide-i Sultan Mustafa* or *valide sultan* (BA, MM, 397, 672, 847, 858, 861, 954, 1606).

78. Naima, *Tarih*, 2:160.

79. Peçevi, *Tarih*, 2:389.

80. Naima, *Tarih*, 2:222.

81. Naima, *Tarih*, 2:236.

82. Roe, *The Negotiations*, 150.

83. Roe, *The Negotiations*, 178–79.

84. TSMA, E 2457/1.

85. TSMA, E 7001/4.

86. Hammer, *Histoire*, 9:65, who cites a Venetian ambassadorial dispatch of Sep-

tember 1625: "Only half the treasury, 300m. chequins, has arrived from Cairo, to the great displeasure of the King."

87. See TSMA, E2457/1 and 3, for reference to the letters of Bayram Pasha.

88. TSMA, E 7001/4.

89. Barozzi and Berchet, *Le Relazioni*, 1:374.

90. Karaççlebizade Abdülaziz Efendi, *Ravzat ül-Ebrar Zeyli*, 10a–b.

91. Naima, *Tarih*, 4:348. Naima refers to "soldiers" most likely because of the role of the troops in the capital and their leaders in making and unmaking grand vezirs – and sultans as well.

92. Naima, *Tarih*, 4:395. Kösem Sultan had actually lived through six reigns: those of Ahmed I, Mustafa, Osman II, Murad IV, İbrahim, and Mehmed IV; she was probably counting the reigns in which she had figured; those of Ahmed, Murad, İbrahim, and Mehmed IV.

93. Naima, *Tarih*, 4:395.

94. Naima, *Tarih*, 5:107.

95. On Meleki Khatun, see ch. 5, 144.

96. Evliya Çelebi, *The Intimate Life*, trans. Dankoff, 89.

97. The correspondence between Turhan Sultan and the grand vezir consists of approximately 110 formal letters (*telhis*) from the latter or his deputy (the *kaymakam*) to the *valide sultan*, each of which carries her response written in space at the top of the letter (in Ottoman scribal terms, *beyaz üzerine*, or "on the white") deliberately left empty for this purpose, and approximately 30 letters written by the *valide sultan* directly to the grand vezir (TSMA, E 2457, 5948, 7001, and 7002; see n. 60 for attribution of these documents to Turhan Sultan). The majority of this undated correspondence appears to belong to the grand vezirate of Gürcü Mehmed Pasha (September 1651–June 1652) and thus to the earliest months of Turhan Sultan's regency.

98. TSMA, E 7001/25.

99. TSMA, E 7001/37.

100. For further analysis of these letters, see my forthcoming study of the correspondence of Turhan Sultan's regency.

101. Naima, *Tarih*, 5:203.

102. Naima, *Tarih*, 5:210.

103. TSMA, E 5948. The letter is unsigned and undated, but internal evidence indicates that it belongs to the grand vezirate of Gürcü Mehmed Pasha.

104. On Kasım Agha, see Eyice, "Mimar Kasım Hakkında," 783ff.

105. Ahmed Resmi, *Hamilet ül-Kübera*, 14b–15b.

106. Naima, *Tarih*, 5:222.

107. Kâtip Çelebi, *Düstur ül-Amel li Islah ül-Halel*, 134.

108. Naima, *Tarih*, 5:279.

109. See Kunt, "The Köprülü Years: 1656–1661," ch. 3, for a discussion of the appointment of Köprülü Mehmed Pasha to the grand vezirate.

110. See, for example, Uluçay, *Padişahların Kadınları*, 58; Uzunçarşılı, *Saray Teşkilatı*, 156–57.

111. B. Lewis, "Diwan-i Humayun," 339.

112. See Kunt, "The Köprülü Years," 59–60, for the judgment that Naima's account exaggerates the significance of the contractual agreement between Köprülü Mehmed Pasha and the sultan and *valide sultan*. Naima's patron was the fourth of the Köprülü grand vezirs, Amcazade Hüseyin, which may have led him to glorify the first Köprülü vezir's appointment.

113. Naima, *Tarih*, 4:454.

114. On Köprülü Mehmed Pasha and Kasım Agha's Albanian origins, see Eyice, "Mimar Kasım Hakkında," 767ff.

115. Naima, *Tarih*, 5:169–77.

116. On the exile of Köprülü Mehmed Pasha to Köstendil, see TSMA, E 2457/7; on his recall, see E 5948 and E 7001/13.

117. Mehmed Halife, *Tarih-i Gılmani*, 38; see also Naima, *Tarih*, 6:147.

118. See Findley, *Bureaucratic Reform in the Ottoman Empire*, 7ff., for a discussion of the patrimonial nature of the Ottoman sultanate.

119. For one such allegation, see Uluçay, *Padişahların Kadınları*, 40.

120. Mustafa Ali, *Künh ül-Ahbar*, 289b; Peçevi, *Tarih*, 2:4–5. For another account of these events, see the dispatch of Gianfrancesco Morosini cited in Spagni, "Una Sultana veneziana," document 3, 342–45.

121. Naima, *Tarih*, 4:323.

122. Naima, *Tarih*, 4:298.

123. Indeed, it was Süleyman whom Kösem Sultan was reputed to have planned to enthrone in Mehmed IV's place, thereby denying Turhan Sultan the position of *valide sultan*.

124. Vandal, *Les Voyages*, 107. De Nointel remarks that there was a widespread rumor (probably limited to the foreign community in the capital) that the *valide sultan*'s interest in the elder of the two princes was more than maternal: "c'est l'intrigue de Phèdre," he comments (242).

125. Kütükoğlu, "Süleyman II," 156.

126. Galland, *Journal*, 2:49.

127. Selaniki, *Tarih*, 124–25.

128. *Calendar of State Papers, Venice*, vol. 9, item 324.

129. *Calendar of State Papers, Venice*, vol. 9, item 326.

130. *Calendar of State Papers, Venice*, vol. 9, item 324.

131. Naima, *Tarih*, 4:314.

132. See Alderson, *The Structure of the Ottoman Dynasty*, ch. 10. In the pre-Süleymanic period, the first reign of Mehmed II ended in deposition, but this was much different from post-Süleyman depositions because of the important political presence of Murad II during this premature rule of his son.

133. Busbecq, *Turkish Letters*, 161–63.

134. The problem of rebellions by the imperial troops is explored in the ongoing work of Cemal Kafadar.

135. İnalcık, "Military and Fiscal Transformation," esp. 297–99; Finkel, *The Administration of Warfare*, 67.

136. Naima, *Tarih*, 6:141.

137. Aktepe, "Mustafa I," 694.

138. Naima, *Tarih*, 4:315ff.

139. Naima, *Tarih*, 4:303.

140. Naima, *Tarih*, 4:317.

141. Naima, *Tarih*, 4:318.

142. The petition of the *müfti* to the *valide sultan* and her reply to both the former and the grand vezir are reproduced in Tuğlacı, *Osmanlı Saray Kadınları*, 321, 323.

Conclusion

1. I am indebted to discussions with Professor Halil İnalcik on two major issues discussed in this chapter: the important role played by subjects in circumscribing the

autonomy of the sultanate and the unreliability of the writings of Ottoman scholars as a reflection of popular thinking about women.

2. This *hadith*, or prophetic tradition, is given by Bukhari, *Sahîh*, ed. Krehl (Leiden, 1862–1908), 4:376ff.; Ibn Hanbal, *Musnad* (Cairo, 1313/1895–96) 5:38ff., 43, 47, 50, 51 (cited in Abbott, *Aishah the Beloved of Mohammed*, 175–76).

3. Mernissi, *The Veil and the Male Elite: A Feminist Interpretation of Women's Rights in Islam*, trans. Lakeland.

4. For a summary of the views of some of these scholars, see Spellberg, "Political Action and Public Example: 'A'isha and the Battle of the Camel," 45–46.

5. On the career of 'A'isha, see Abbott, *Aishah the Beloved of Mohammad;* Denise Spellberg has discussed the career and subsequent religio-historical representations of 'A'isha in several publications.

6. Spellberg, "Political Action and Public Example," 49–50.

7. Spellberg, "Political Action and Public Example," 55.

8. On views of women in pre-Islamic (Sasanian) Iran, see Nashat, *Women and Revolution in Iran*, 8–11.

9. Nizam al-Mulk, *The Book of Government*, trans. Darke, 185–92.

10. Spellberg, "Nizam al-Mulk's Manipulation of Tradition," 117.

11. Farah, *Marriage and Sexuality in Islam: A Translation of al-Ghazâlî's "Book on the Etiquette of Marriage from the Ihyâ'*,'" 94.

12. Tusi, *The Nasirean Ethics*, 166.

13. An interesting exercise is to compare relevant sections of Aristotle's *Nichomachean Ethics* and *Politics* with the *Ethics* of Nasir al-Din Tusi. On the influence of Aristotle on Western political tradition, see Okin, *Women in Western Political Thought*, ch. 4.

14. Selaniki, *Tarih-i Selânikî*, ed. and trans. İpşirli, 826.

15. Kemalpaşazade, *Fetava-yı Ibn Kemal*, 78b–79a.

16. Birgivi Mehmed, *Tarikat-ı Muhammadiye*, trans. Yıldırım, 398.

17. On the influence of Birgivi's writings, see Zilfi, "The Kadızadelis," esp. 260–61, and *The Politics of Piety*, 143–46.

18. Berkey, "Women and Islamic Education in the Mamluk Period"; see also Lutfi, "Al-Sakhâwî's *Kitâb al-Nisâ'* as a Source for the Social and Economic History of Muslim Women during the Fifteenth Century A.D."

19. Lutfi, "Manners and Customs of Fourteenth-Century Cairene Women: Female Anarchy versus Male Shar'i Order in Muslim Prescriptive Treatises."

20. Lutfi, "Manners and Customs of Fourteenth-Century Cairene Women," 101; Birgivi Mehmed, *Tarikat-ı Muhammadiye*, trans. Yıldırım, 399.

21. Birgivi Mehmed, *Tarikat-ı Muhammadiye*, trans. Yıldırım, 462.

22. Kâtip Çelebi, *The Balance of Truth*, trans. G. Lewis, 137.

23. On the subject of tomb visiting, Kâtip Çelebi quoted a tradition according to which the Prophet revoked his earlier condemnation of this religious activity: "I had forbidden you to visit tombs, but now you may visit them" (*The Balance of Truth*, trans. G. Lewis, 92).

24. Kâtip Çelebi, *The Balance of Truth*, trans. G. Lewis, 130–31.

25. Gerber, "Social and Economic Position of Women"; Jennings, "Women in Early Seventeenth Century Ottoman Judicial Records."

26. 'Abd ar-Raziq, *La Femme au temps des Mamlouks*, 42; Lutfi, "Manners and Customs of Fourteenth-Century Cairene Women," 105–6.

27. *Ebussuûd Efendi Fetvaları*, ed. Düzdağ, 55–56.

28. E.J.W. Gibb, *A History of Ottoman Poetry*, 2:180.

29. Lutfi, "Manners and Customs of Fourteenth-Century Cairene Women," 101.

30. On this subject, see Seni, "Ville ottomane et représentation du corps féminin," 71–75. Lutfi points out that Ibn al-Hajj considered religious minorities as well as commoners to be sources of social chaos ("Manners and Customs of Fourteenth-Century Cairene Women," 102).

31. The form of headdress, cloak, and shoes as well as the colors and materials used were prescribed, with careful distinctions made between Christians and Jews: for example, Jews were to wear red hats and Christians black hats, and both groups were forbidden to wear the Muslim turban (Refik, *On Altıncı Asırda İstanbul Hayatı* (*1553–1591*), 47–48, 51–52, and *Hicri On Birinci Asırda İstanbul Hayatı* (*1000–1100*), 20, 53).

32. Peçevi, *Tarih*, 2:402.

33. Lambton, *Continuity and Change in Medieval Persia*, ch. 8; Petry, "A Paradox of Patronage during the Later Mamluk Period" and "Class Solidarity versus Gender Gain: Women as Custodians of Property in Later Medieval Egypt."

34. On Gawharshad, see Khwandamir, *Habib al-Siyar*, trans. Thackston, and Barthold, *Ulugh Beg*, trans. V. Minovsky and T. Minovsky, *passim;* on Saljukshah Begum, see Khunji, *Târîkh 'Âlam-ârâ-yi Amînî*, trans. V. Minorsky, *passim.*

35. Rashid al-Din, *Jâmi' ul-Tavârîkh*, trans. Boyle, 168–70.

36. Rashid al-Din, *Jâmi' ul-Tavârikh*, 1:133, cited by G. Nashat, ed., *Women and Revolution in Iran*, 12. On the roles of Mongol women, see Rossabi, "Khubilai Khan and the Women in His Family."

37. Rashid al-Din, *Jâmi' ul-Tavârîkh*, trans. Boyle, 168.

38. Ahmedi, *İskendername*, 63a. I am grateful to İsenbike Togan for drawing this passage to my attention. Ahmedi calls this woman Oljaytu, which was actually the name of her father.

39. Ibn Battuta, *The Travels*, 2:340.

40. Ibn Battuta, *The Travels*, 2:340.

41. Al-Ghazali, *Marriage and Sexuality in Islam*, trans. Farah, 93–126; Musallam, *Sex and Society in Islam*, ch. 2, esp. 28–32.

42. See ch. 4, n. 66.

43. My information about the Manisa festivals comes from a verbal communication with Evelyn Kalças.

44. Enveri, *Düstûrnâme*, trans. Mélikoff-Sayar, 45–50, 60, 77. The same holds true of the Central Asian Turkish legends of Dede Korkut, where the ruler, Bayindir Khan, remains in the background, occasionally presiding over ceremonial feasts and making executive decisions, while the tales tell of his son-in-law Salur Kazan, who controls affairs, or of the adventures of various young men.

45. Surah 24, v. 60.

46. *Ebussuûd Efendi Fetvaları*, ed. Düzdağ, 60.

47. Refik, ed., *On Altıncı Asırda İstanbul Hayatı*, 41.

48. On medieval Islamic notions of gender as expressed in the law, see Sanders, "Gendering the Ungendered Body."

49. Kai Ka'us ibn Iskandar, *A Mirror for Princes*, trans. Levy, 70–78, 117–26; Meisami, "Kings and Lovers: Ethical Dimensions of Medieval Persian Romance," 2 and throughout.

50. As was common throughout the ancient Mediterranean world, pederasty was tolerated, if uneasily, among the Ottomans (see Andrews, "The Sexual Intertext of Ottoman Literature: The Story of Me'âlî, Magistrate of Mihalich," 44–45); however, fathers and guardians of boys were exhorted to protect their wards, and pederasts could be heavily fined.

51. Rycaut, *The Present State,* 10.

52. Vandal, *Les Voyages,* 242.

53. Naima, *Tarih,* 5:315–16.

54. Atıl, *Süleymanname: The Illustrated History of Süleyman the Magnificent,* plates 1, 6–9, 10.

55. Naima, *Tarih,* 5:260.

56. See ch. 6, 161.

57. See ch. 9, n. 91.

58. Naima, *Tarih,* 4:195–96.

BIBLIOGRAPHY

Dictionaries, Encyclopedias, Catalogues, and Other Reference Works

Babinger, Franz. *Die Geschichtsschreiber der Osmanen und ihre Werke.* Leipzig, 1927.

Bacharach, Jere L. *A Middle East Studies Handbook.* Seattle, 1984.

Clauson, Sir Gerard. *An Etymological Dictionary of Pre-Thirteenth Century Turkish.* Oxford, 1972.

Çetin, Atilla. *Başbakanlık Arşivi Kılavuzu.* Istanbul, 1979.

Danişmend, İsmail Hami. *İzahlı Osmanlı Tarihi Kronolojisi.* Vols. 2 and 3. Istanbul, 1961.

Encyclopedia of Islam. 1st ed. 4 vols. and supplement. Leiden and London, 1912–1942.

Encyclopedia of Islam. 2d ed. 5 vols. Leiden and London, 1954–.

İslam Ansiklopedisi. 12 vols. Istanbul, 1940–1986.

İstanbul Kütüphaneleri Tarih-Cografya Yazmaları Katalogları, Vol. 1: Türkçe Tarih Yazmaları. Istanbul, 1943.

Meninski, Francisci. *Lexicon Arabico-Persico-Turcicum.* 4 vols. Vienna, 1780–1802.

Oransay, Gültekin. *Osmanlı Devletinde Kim Kimdi?* Vol. 1. Ankara, 1969.

Öz, Tahsin. *Arşiv Kılavuzu.* 2 vols. Istanbul, 1938–1940.

Pakalın, Mehmed Zeki. *Osmanlı Tarih Deyimleri ve Terimleri Sözlüğü.* 3 vols. Istanbul, 1946–1954.

Pitcher, Donald E. *An Historical Geography of the Ottoman Empire.* Leiden, 1972.

Redhouse, Sir James W. *A Turkish and English Lexicon.* Istanbul, 1890.

Sertoğlu, Midhat. *Muhteva Bakımından Başvekalet Arşivi.* Ankara, 1955.

Süreyya, Mehmed. *Sicill-i Osmanî.* 4 vols. Istanbul, 1308–1315/1891–1897.

Unat, Faik Reşit. *Hicrî Tarihleri Miladî Tarihe Çevirme Kılavuzu.* Ankara, 1974.

Uzunçarşılı, İ. H., İ. K. Baybura, and Ü. Altındağ. *Topkapı Sarayı Müzesi Osmanlı Saray Arşivi Katalogu.* Ankara, 1985–.

Ottoman Documents

Unpublished Documents

Prime Ministry Archives
  Ali Emiri Tasnifi
    Süleyman: 24
    Ahmed I: 45, 49, 598
    Murad IV: 487
    İbrahim: 73, 75, 76, 283, 403, 443, 485, 520
  Cevdet Tasnifi: Saray, 1834
  İbnülemin Tasnifi: Saray, 125, 914, 924, 938/3, 939/2–3, 1159
  Kamil Kepeci Tasnifi: Saray, 7098, 7102, 7104
  Maliyeden Müdevver Defterleri: 397, 403, 422, 646, 672, 774, 843, 847, 855, 858,

BIBLIOGRAPHY

859, 861, 906, 954, 1372, 1509, 1515, 1606, 1692, 1756, 2079, 3634, 4905, 5530, 5633, 5653, 5705, 5965, 15920, 17881
Mühimme Defteri: 71.
Topkapı Palace Archives
Evrak: 2455/10 + 106, 2629, 2457, 2477, 3058, 3079, 4074, 5038, 5199,5222/2, 5426, 5859, 5948, 6425, 6590, 6702, 7001, 7002, 7005, 7008, 7022/540 + 588, 7112, 7386, 7702, 7787, 7816, 7905, 7927, 7953, 9274, 9618, 10292, 11186
Defter: 1830, 2895, 3831, 3990, 4124, 4155, 4323, 5114, 5290, 7025, 7704, 7843, 7859, 8030, 8075, 10052
Atatürk Library (Istanbul): Muallim Cevdet 0.71
Süleymaniye Library: Turhan Hadice Sultan 150
Manisa Museum: Şer'i Sicil No. 1

Published Documents

Ateş, İbrahim, ed. *İstanbul Yeni Cami ve Hünkâr Kasrı* ("Hatice Turhan Sultan'ın Yeni Cami Vakfiyesi," 71–93), Ankara, n.d.
Barkan, Ömer Lutfi, ed. "Edirne Askerî Kassamı'na Ait Tereke Defterleri (1545–1659)," *Belgeler* 3, nos. 5–6 (1966): 1–472.
———, ed. "İstanbul Saraylarına ait Muhasebe Defterleri." *Belgeler* 9, no. 13 (1979): 1–180, 296–380.
Gökbilgin, M. Tayyib. *XV–XVI. Asırlarda Edirne ve Paşa Livası*. Istanbul, 1952.
İlgürel, Mücteba. "Kösem Sultan'ın Bir Vakfiyesi." *Tarih Dergisi* 16, no. 21 (1966): 83–84.
Mehmed Arif, ed. *Kânûnnâme-i Al-i Osmân* [*Kanunname* of Sultan Mehmed II]. *Tarih-i Osmanî Encümeni Mecmuası,* Supplement 3. Istanbul, 1330/1902.
Orhonlu, Cengiz. *Telhisler (1597–1607)*. Istanbul, 1970.
Refik, Ahmet [Altınay], ed. *On Altıncı Asırda İstanbul Hayatı (1553–1591)*. Istanbul, 1953.
———, ed. *Hicrî On Birinci Asırda İstanbul Hayatı (1000–1100)*. Istanbul, 1931.
Uluçay, M. Çağatay. *Haremden Mektuplar*. Istanbul, 1956.
———. *Osmanlı Sultanlarına Aşk Mektupları*. Istanbul, 1950.

Works by Ottoman Writers and Their Neighbors

Ahmed Resmi. *Hamilet ül-Kübera*. Topkapı Palace Library, MS. EH 1403.
Ahmedî, İbrahim Taceddin. *Dastan ve Tevarih-i Müluk-i Al-i Osman*. In *Osmanlı Tarihleri,* ed. N. Atsız, 1–35. Istanbul, 1947.
———. *İskendername: İnceleme-Tıpkıbasım*. Edited by İ. Ünver. Ankara, 1983.
Ali, Mustafa. *Künh ül-Ahbar*. Vol. 1. Istanbul, 1277/1860–1861.
———. *Künh ül-Ahbar*. Nuruosmaniye Library, MS. 3406.
———. *Nushat üs-Selatin*. Edited and translated by A. Tietze. *Mustafa Ali's Counsel for Sultans of 1581*. 2 vols. Vienna, 1978–82.
[Anonymous]. *Die Altosmanischen anonymen Chroniken: Tevarih-i Al-i Osman*. Edited and translated by F. Giese. Breslau, Germany, 1922.
Astarabadi, Aziz b. Ardashir. *Bazm u Razm*. Edited by Kilisli Rıfat. Istanbul, 1928.
Aşıkpaşazade, Derviş Ahmed. *Die Altosmanische Chronik des Aşıkpaşazade*. Edited by F. Giese. Leipzig, 1929.
———. *Tevarih-i Al-i Osman*. In *Osmanlı Tarihleri,* ed. N. Atsız, 79–319. Istanbul, 1947.
Atsız, Çiftiçioğlu N., ed. *Osmanlı Tarihleri*. Istanbul, 1947.

Avni Ömer Efendi. *Kanun-ı Osmanî Mefhum-ı Defter-i Hakanî*. Edited by İ. H. Uzunçarşılı. *Belleten* 15 (1951): 381–399.

Ayvansarayî, Hafız Hüseyin. *Hadikat ül-Cevami*. 2 vols. Istanbul, 1281/1864–1865.

Aziz Efendi. *Kanun-name-i Sultanî li Aziz Efendi/Aziz Efendi's Book of Sultanic Laws and Regulations: An Agenda for Reform by a Seventeenth-Century Ottoman Statesman*. Edited and translated by R. Murphey. Harvard University, 1985.

Birgivi Mehmed. *Tarikat-ı Muhammediye*. Translated by C. Yıldırım. Istanbul, 1981.

Celalzade Mustafa. *Tabakat ül-Memalik ve Derecat ül-Mesalik*. Edited by P. Kappert. Wiesbaden, Germany, 1981.

Derviş Abdullah. *Risale-i Teberdariye fi Ahval-i Aga-yı Dar üs-Saadet*. Köprülü Library, MS. II. Kısım, 233.

Doukas. *Decline and Fall of Byzantium to the Ottoman Turks*. Translated by H. J. Magoulias. Detroit, 1975.

Ebussuud Efendi. *Ba'z ul-Fetava*. Süleymaniye Library, MS. Yeni Cami 685/3.

———. *Ebussuûd Efendi Fetvaları Işığında 16. Asır Türk Hayatı*. Edited by M. E. Düzdağ. Istanbul, 1983.

Enverî. *Düstûrnâme [Le Destân d'Umûr Pacha]*. Edited and translated by I. Mélikoff-Sayar. Paris, 1954.

Evliya Çelebi. *Evliya Çelebi Seyahatnamesi*. Vols. 1–5. Istanbul, 1314/1896–1897.

———. *The Intimate Life of an Ottoman Statesman: Melek Ahmed Pasha (1588–1662) as Portrayed in Evliya Çelebi's Book of Travels*. Translated with commentary by R. Dankoff. Albany, N.Y., 1991.

———. *Narrative of Travels in Europe, Asia, and Africa*. Translated by J. von Hammer. London, 1834.

———. *Seyahatname (Giriş)*. Edited and transcribed into modern Turkish by İ. Parmaksızoğlu. Ankara, 1983.

Feridun Ahmed Beg. *Münşeat üs-Selatin*. 2 vols. Istanbul, 1247/1831–1832.

Al-Ghazali, Abu Hamid. *Marriage and Sexuality in Islam: A Translation of al-Ghazâlî's Book on the Etiquette of Marriage from the Ihyâ*. Translated by M. Farah. Salt Lake City, Utah, 1984.

Ibn Battuta. *The Travels of Ibn Battuta*. Edited and translated by H.A.R. Gibb. Hakluyt Series No. 117 (Second Series). Cambridge, England, 1962.

İpşirli, Mehmed. "Hasan Kafî el-Akhisarî ve Devlet Düzenine ait Eseri *Usûlü'l-hikem fî Nizâmi'l-Alem*." *Tarih Enstitüsü Dergisi* 10–11 (1979–80): 239–78.

Kai Ka'us ibn Iskandar. *A Mirror for Princes: The Qâbûs Nâma*. Translated by R. Levy. New York, 1951.

Karaçelebizade Abdülaziz Efendi. *Ravzat ül-Ebrar*. Bulaq, 1248/1832–1833.

———. *Ravzat ül-Ebrar Zeyli*. Süleymaniye Library, MS. Hekimoğlu Ali Paşa 747.

Kâtip Çelebi. *The Balance of Truth*. Translated by G. L. Lewis. London, 1963.

———. *Düstur ül-Amel li Islah ül-Halel*. Istanbul, 1280/1863–1864.

———. *Fezleke*. 2 vols. Istanbul, 1286–1287/1869–1870.

Kemalpaşazade, Şemseddin Ahmed. *Fetava*. Süleymaniye Library, MS. Dar ul-Mesnevi 118.

———. *Tevarih-i Al-i Osman*. Books 1, 2, and 7. Edited by Şerafettin Turan. Ankara, 1957 (Bk. 7), 1970 (Bk. 1), 1983 (Bk. 2).

Khunjî, Fadlullâh b. Rûzbihân. *Târikh-i 'Alam-ârâ-yi Amînî*. Abridged and translated by V. Minorsky. *Persia in A.D. 1478–1490*. London, 1957.

Khwandamir, Ghiyas al-Din. *Habib al-Siyar fi Ahbar Afrad al-Bashar*. Partial translation in *A Century of Princes: Sources on Timurid History and Art*, comp. and trans. W.M. Thackston, 101–235. Cambridge, Mass., 1989.

Kınalızade, Alaeddin Ali. *Ahlaq-ı Ala'i*. Bulaq, 1248/1832–1833.

Kitab-ı Müstetab. Edited by Y. Yücel. Ankara, 1983.

Koçi Bey. *Risale*. Edited by Ali Kemali Aksüt. Istanbul, 1939.

Kritovoulos. *History of Mehmed the Conqueror*. Translated by C. T. Riggs. Princeton, N.J., 1954.

Lutfi Pasha. *Asafname*. Edited and translated by R. Tschudi. Berlin, 1910.

———. *Tevarih-i Al-i Osman*. Istanbul, 1341/1922–1923.

Mecdi, Muhammad el-Edirnevi. *Hada'ik ül-Şaka'ik* (Translation of Ahmed Taşköprüzade's *Al-Shakâ'ik al-Nu'mâniyya fî 'Ulamâ' al-Dawlat al-'Uthmâniyya*). Istanbul, 1269/1852–1853.

Mehmed Halife. *Tarih-i Gılmani*. Edited by A. Refik [Altınay]. In *Türk Tarihi Encümeni Mecmuası*, Supplement, 1924.

Müneccimbaşı, Ahmed ibn Lutfullah. *Sahaif ül-Ahbar fi Vekayi ul-A'sar*. Translated by A. Nedim. Vol. 3. Istanbul, 1285/1868–1869.

Naima, Mustafa. *Tarih*. 6 vols. Istanbul, 1280/1863–1864.

Neşri, Mevlana Mehmed. *Gihannüma: Die Altosmanische Chronik*. 2 vols. Edited by F. Taeschner. Leipzig, 1951–1955.

———. *Kitab-ı Cihan-Nüma: Neşri Tarihi*. 2 vols. Edited by F. R. Unat and M. A. Köymen. Ankara, 1949.

Nev'i, Yahya. *Nev'i Divanı*. Edited by M. Tulum and M. A. Tanyeri. Istanbul, 1977.

Nev'izade 'Ata'i. *Hada'ik ül-Haka'ik fi Tekmilet iş-Şaka'ik*. Istanbul, 1268/1851–1852.

Nizam al-Mulk. *The Book of Government or Rules for Kings: The Siyar al-Muluk or Siyasat-nama of Nizam al-Mulk*. Translated by H. Darke. London, 1978.

Osmanzade Ahmet Taib. *Hadikat ül-Vüzera*. Istanbul, 1271/1854–1855.

Peçevi (Peçuyi), İbrahim. *Tarih-i Peçevî*. 2 vols. İstanbul, 1281–1284/1864–1867.

Rashid al-Din. *Jami' al-Tawarikh*. Partially translated by J. A. Boyle, *The Successors of Genghis Khan*. New York, 1971.

Sadeddin Efendi. *Selimname*. Bibliothèque National, MS. Suppl. Turc 524.

———. *Tac ul-Tevarih*. 3 vols. Istanbul, 1279–1280/1862–1864.

Selaniki, Mustafa. *Tarih*. Istanbul, 1281/1864–1865.

———. *Tarih-i Selânikî*. Edited and transliterated by M. İpşirli. 2 vols. Istanbul, 1989.

———. "A Year in Selaniki's History: 1593–1594." Edition and translation by W. S. Peachy of a portion of the unpublished segment of Selaniki's *Tarih*. Ph.d. diss., Indiana University, 1984.

Shah Tahmasb-e Safavî, Mujmu'a-yi Asnad va Mukatibat-i Tarihî. Edited by A. H. Navaii. Tehran, 1350/1931–1932.

Silahdar Fındıklılı Mehmed Aga. *Silahdar Tarihi*. 2 vols. Istanbul, 1928.

Solakzade, Mehmed Hemdemi. *Tarih*. Istanbul, 1298/1881.

Sphrantzes, George. *The Fall of the Byzantine Empire*. Translated by M. Philippides. Amherst, Mass., 1980.

Sunullah Efendi. *Fetava-ı Sunullah Efendi*. Süleymaniye Library, MS. Hasan Hüsnü Paşa 502.

Şükrullah. *Behçet ül-Tevarih*. In *Osmanlı Tarihleri*, ed. N. Atsız, 39–76. Istanbul, 1947.

Talikizade, Mehmed ibn Mehmed el-Fenari. *Şehname-i Hümayun*. Introduced and transcribed into modern Turkish by C. Woodhead, *Ta'lîkî-zâde's Şehnâme-i Hümâyûn: A history of the Ottoman campaign into Hungary 1593–94*. Berlin, 1983.

Tayyarzade Ataullah. *Tarih-i Enderun*. Vol. 3. Istanbul, 1874–75.

Tugi, Hüseyin. *Tugi Tarihi*. Edited by M. Sertoğlu. *Belleten* 43 (1979): 489–514.

Tursun Beg. *Tarih-i Ebü'l-Feth.* Edited by M. Tulum. Istanbul, 1977.

————. *The History of Mehmed the Conqueror.* Edited and translated by H. İnalcık and R. Murphey. Minneapolis and Chicago, 1978.

Tusi, Nasir al-Din. *The Nasirean Ethics.* Translated by G. M. Wickens. London, 1964.

Uruc ibn Adil. *Tevarih-i Al-i Osman.* Edited by F. Babinger. Hanover, Germany, 1925.

Contemporary European Documents and Writings

Alberi, Eugenio, ed. *Relazioni degli ambasciatori veneti al senato.* Series 3. 3 vols. Florence, 1840–1855.

Angiolello, Giovanni Maria [Donado da Lezze]. *Historia Turchesca (1300–1514).* Edited by I. Ursu. Bucharest, 1909.

Barozzi, Nicoló and Giglielmo Berchet, eds. *Le Relazioni degli stati Europei.* Series 5: Turkey. 2 vols. Venice, 1871–1872.

Bassano, Luigi da Zara. *Costumi et i modi particolari della vita de' Turchi.* Munich, 1963.

Baudier, Michel. *Histoire géneralle de serrail, et de la cour de grand seigneur, empereur des Turcs.* Paris, 1631.

Blunt, Henry. *A Voyage into the Levant.* London, 1638.

Bobovius, Albertus. *Mémoire sur les Turcs.* Harvard University, Houghton Library, MS. Fr 103.

Bon, Ottaviano. *Descrizione del serraglio del gran signore.* In *Le Relazioni degli Stati Europei*, ed. N. Barozzi and G. Berchet, 1:59–124. Series 5: Turkey. Florence, 1871.

Botero, Giovanni. *The Reason of State.* Translated by P. J. and D. P. Waley. New Haven, Conn., 1956.

Broquière, Bertrandon de la. *Le Voyage d'Outremer.* Edited by C. Schefer. Paris, 1892.

Busbecq, Ogier Ghiselin de. *Turkish Letters.* Translated by E. S. Forster. Oxford, 1927.

Calendar of State Papers and Manuscripts, Venice. Vols. 8–10, 19, 21. Edited by H. F. Brown, A. B. Hinds, et al. London, 1894–1916.

Campis, Iacopo de Promontorio de. *Die Aufzeichnungen des Genuesen Iacopo de Promontorio de Campis über den Osmanenstaat um 1475.* Edited by F. Babinger. *Sitzunberichte der Bayerische Akademie der Wissenschaften,* 1956, Heft 8. Munich, 1957.

Dallam, Thomas. *The Diary of Master Thomas Dallam, 1599–1600.* Edited by J. T. Bent. Hakluyt Series no. 87. London, 1893.

Deshayes de Courmenin, Louis. *Voyage de Levant, fait par le commandement du roy en l'année 1621.* Paris, 1629.

Du Fresne-Canaye, Philippe. *Le Voyage du Levant.* Edited by M. H. Houser. Paris, 1897.

Du Loir, Sieur. *Les Voyage du Sieur du Loir.* Paris, 1654.

The Fugger News-Letters, 1568–1605. 2 vols. (1st and 2nd series). Translated by P. de Chary (1st series) and L.S.R. Byrne (2nd series). Edited by V. von Klarwill. London, 1924–1926.

Galland, Antoine. *Journal d'Antoine Galland pendant son séjour à Constantinople (1672–1673).* 2 vols. Edited by C. Schefer. Paris, 1881.

Glover, Sir Thomas. "The Journey of Edward Barton Esquire." In S. Purchas, *His Pilgrimes,* 8:304–20. Glasgow, 1905.

Lello, Henry. *The Report of Lello/Lello'nun Muhtırası.* Edited by O. Burian. Ankara, 1952.

Menavino, Giovanantonio. *I Cinque Libri della Legge Religione et Vita de'Turchi della corte, & d'alcune guerre del Gran Turco.* Venice, 1548.

Montagu, Lady Mary Wortley. *The Complete Letters of Lady Mary Wortley Montagu.* Vol. 1. Edited by R. Halsband. Oxford, 1965.

Nicolay, Nicolas de. *The Navigations, Peregrinations and Voyages Made into Turkie.* London, 1585.

Petis de la Croix, François. *Etat general de l'empire otoman.* Paris, 1695.

———. *Mémoirs de Sieur de la Croix.* 2 vols. Paris, 1684.

Postel, Guillaume. *De la Republique des Turcs & là ou l'occasion s'offrera, des Meurs et loys de tous Muhamedistes.* Poitiers, [1560].

Purchas, Samuel. *Hakluytus Posthumus or Purchas His Pilgrimes.* 20 vols. Glasgow, 1905–1907.

Roe, Sir Thomas. "The Death of Sultan Osman, and the setting up of Mustafa his Uncle, according to the Relation Presented to His Majestie." In S. Purchas, *His Pilgrimes,* 8:343–59. Glasgow, 1905.

———. *The Negotiations of Sir Thomas Roe in His Embassy to the Ottoman Porte.* London, 1740.

Rycaut, Paul. *The Present State of the Ottoman Empire.* New York, 1971.

Sanderson, John. "Sundrie the Personall Voyages." In S. Purchas, *His Pilgrimes,* 9:411–86. Glasgow, 1905.

———. *The Travels of John Sanderson in the Levant 1584–1602.* Edited by Sir W. Foster. Hakluyt Series no. 67 (Second Series). London, 1931.

Sandys, George. "A Relation of a Journey Begunne, Anno Dom 1610." In S. Purchas, *His Pilgrimes,* 8:88–248. Glasgow, 1905.

Sanuto, Marino. *I Diarii.* Vol. 36. Venice, 1893.

Spandugnino, Theodoro. *Delle historie, & origine de Principi de Turchi, ordine della Corte, loro vita, & costumi.* 1550.

Tavernier, J[ean] B[aptiste]. *Nouvelle Relation de l'Interieur du Serrail de Grand Seigneur contenant plusiers singularitez qui jusqu'icy n'ont pas esté mises en lumiere.* Paris, 1681.

Withers, Robert. "The Grand Signiors Serraglio" [Translation of Ottaviano Bon, *Descrizione del Serraglio del Gran Signore*]. In S. Purchas, *His Pilgrimes,* 9:322–406. Glasgow, 1905.

Secondary Sources

Abbott, Nabia. *Aishah the Beloved of Mohammed.* Chicago, 1942.

———. *Two Queens of Baghdad: Mother and Wife of Harun al-Rashid.* Chicago, 1946.

———. "Women and the State in Early Islam." *Journal of Near Eastern Studies* 1 (1942): 106–26.

ʿAbd ar-Raziq, Ahmad. *La Femme au temps des mamlouks en Egypt.* Cairo, 1973.

Aktepe, Münir. "Mustafa I." *IA.*

Alderson, A. D. *The Structure of the Ottoman Dynasty.* Oxford, 1956.

Altundağ, Şinasi. "Osman II." *IA.*

Altundağ, Şinasi, and Şerafettin Turan. "Rüstem Paşa." *IA.*

Andrews, Walter. *Poetry's Voice, Society's Song.* Seattle, 1985.

———. "The Sexual Intertext of Ottoman Literature: The Story of Meʾâlî, Magistrate of Mihalich." *Edebiyat* 3 (1989): 31–56.

Anhegger, Robert. "Hezarfenn Hüseyin Efendi'nin Osmanlı Devlet Teşkilâtına Dair Mülâhazaları." *Türkiyat Mecmuası* 10 (1953): 365–93.

Anhegger-Eyüboğlu, Mualla. "Fatih Devrinde Yeni Sarayda Da Harem Dairesi (Padişahın Evi) Var Mıydı?" *Sanat Tarihi Yıllığı,* 8 (1979): 23–36.

Ariès, Philippe and Georges Duby, gen. eds. *A History of Private Life.* Vol. 1: *From Pagan Rome to Byzantium,* ed. P. Veyne, trans. A. Goldhammer. Cambridge, Mass. 1987.

Arnakis, G. Geordiades. "Gregory Palamas among the Turks and Documents of His Captivity as Historical Sources." *Speculum* 26 (1951): 104–18.

Askenazy, Szymon. "Listy Roxolany." *Kwartalnik Historyczny* 10 (1896): 113–17.

Atasoy, Nurhan, and Filiz Çağman. *Turkish Miniature Painting.* Istanbul, 1974.

Atıl, Esin. *The Age of Süleyman the Magnificent.* Washington, D.C., and New York, 1987.

———. *Süleymanname: The Illustrated History of Süleyman the Magnificent.* Washington, D.C., and New York, 1986.

Babinger, Franz. *Mehmed the Conqueror and His Time.* Translated by R. Manheim. Edited by W. Hickman. Princeton, 1978.

Baer, Gabriel. "Woman and Waqf: An Analysis of the Istanbul *Tahrir* of 1546." *Asian and African Studies: Journal of the Israel Orient Society* 17, nos. 1–3 (November 1983): 9–28.

Barkan, Ömer Lutfi. "İstila Devirlerinin Kolonizatör Türk Dervişleri ve Zaviyeler." *Vakıflar Dergisi* 2 (1942): 279–396.

———. "The Price Revolution of the Sixteenth Century: A Turning Point in the Economic History of the Near East." *International Journal of Middle East Studies* 6 (1975): 3–28.

Barthold, V. V. *A Short History of Turkestan.* Volume 1 in *Four Studies on the History of Central Asia,* trans. V. Minorsky and T. Minorsky. Leiden, 1956.

———. *Turkestan Down to the Mongol Invasion.* London, 1968.

———. *Ulugh Beg.* Volume 2 in *Four Studies on the History of Central Asia,* trans. V. Minorsky and T. Minorsky. Leiden, 1958.

Bates, Ülkü. "Women as Patrons of Architecture in Turkey." In *Women in the Muslim World,* ed. L. Beck and N. Keddie, 245–60. Cambridge, Mass., 1978.

Baykal, Kâzım. *Bursa ve Anıtları.* Bursa, Turkey, 1950.

Bayraktar, Nimet. "*Üsküdar Kütüphaneleri.*" *Vakıflar Dergisi* 16 (1982): 45–49.

Bayraktar, Nimet, and Günay Kut. *Yazma Eserlerde Vakıf Mühürleri.* Ankara, 1984.

Baysun, M. Cavid. "Ebüssuʿûd Efendi." *IA.*

———. "Kösem Sultan." *IA* and *EI(2).*

———. "Mehmed IV." *IA.*

———. "Mihrümah Sultan." *IA.*

———. "Murad IV." *IA.*

———. "Müsadere." *IA.*

———. "Nilüfer Hatun." *IA.*

Beg, M.A.J. "Al-Khassa w'al-ʿAmma." *EI(2).*

Beldiceanu-Steinherr, Irène. "La Conquête d'Adrianople par les Turcs: La Pénétration turque en Thrace et la valeur des chroniques ottomanes." *Travaux et mémoires* 1 (1965): 439–61.

———. "Le Règne de Selîm Ier: Tournant dans la vie politique et religieuse de l'empire ottoman." *Turcica* 6 (1975): 34–48.

———. Review of *Ursprung und Wesen der "Knabenlese" im osmanischen Reich,* by B. D. Papoulia. *Révue des études islamiques* 37 (1986): 172–76.

Bellefonds, Y. Linant de. "Kafa'a." *EI(2).*

Berkey, Jonathan. "Women and Islamic Education in the Mamluk Period." In *Women* in *Middle Eastern History: Shifting Boundaries in Sex and Gender,* ed. N. Keddie and B. Baron, 143–160. New Haven, Conn., 1991.

Bernus-Taylor, Marthe, et al. *Soliman le Magnifique.* Paris, [1990].

Bombaci, Alessio. "Qutlugh Bolzun! A Contribution to the History of the Concept of 'Fortune' among the Turks." *Ural-Altaische Jahrbücher* 36 (1964): 284–91, and 38 (1966): 13–43.

Bonnac, Le Marquis de. *Memoire historique sur l'ambassade de France à Constantinople.* Paris, 1894.

Bosworth, C. E. "The Titulature of the Early Ghaznavids." *Oriens* 15 (1962): 210–33.

Boyle, J. A. "Dynastic and Political History of the Il-Khans." In *The Cambridge History of Iran,* ed. J. Boyle, 5:303–421. Cambridge, 1968.

——. "Khatun." *EI(2).*

Brunschvig, R. "'Abd." *EI(2).*

Bryer, Anthony. "Greek Historians on the Turks: The Case of the First Byzantine-Ottoman Marriage." In *The Writing of History in the Middle Ages,* ed. R.H.C. Davis and J. M. Wallace-Hadrill, 471–94. Oxford, 1981.

Burgoyne, Michael. *Mamluk Jerusalem.* London, 1987.

Cahen, Claude. "Atabak." *EI(2).*

——. "Buwahids." *EI(2).*

——. *Pre-Ottoman Turkey.* London, 1968.

Cezar, Mustafa, Midhat Sertoğlu, et al. *Mufassal Osmanlı Tarihi.* Vols. 1–4. Istanbul, 1957–1960.

Chejne, Anwar. *Succession to the Rule in Islam.* Lahore, 1960.

Chew, Samuel C. *The Crescent and the Rose: Islam and England during the Renaissance.* New York, 1937.

Cohen, Amnon, and Bernard Lewis. *Population and Revenue in the Towns of Palestine in the Sixteenth Century.* Princeton, N.J., 1978.

Combs-Schilling, M. E. *Sacred Performances: Islam, Sexuality, and Sacrifice.* New York, 1989.

Darling, Linda. "The Ottoman Finance Department in a Century of Crisis." Ph.D. diss., University of Chicago, 1990.

Davis, Fanny. *The Ottoman Lady: A Social History from 1718 to 1918.* Westport, Conn., 1986.

——. *The Palace of Topkapı in Istanbul.* New York, 1970.

Davis, Natalie Zemon. "Ghosts, Kin, and Progeny: Some Features of Family Life in Early Modern France." *Daedalus* 106 (April 1977): 87–114.

——. "Women on Top." In *Society and Culture in Early Modern France,* 124–51. Stanford, Calif., 1975.

Dengler, Ian C. "Turkish Women in the Ottoman Empire." In *Women in the Muslim World,* ed. L. Beck and N. Keddie, 229–44. Cambridge, Mass., 1978.

Deny, J. "Walide Sultan." *EI (1).*

Dickson, Martin B. "Shah Tahmasp and the Uzbeks." Ph.D. diss., Princeton University, 1958.

Dilmen, Güngör. "Harem." *Sanat* 7 (April 1982): 44–52.

Duben, Alan. "Turkish Families and Households in Historical Perspective." *Journal of Family History* 10 (Spring 1985): 75–97.

——. "Household Formation in Late Ottoman Istanbul." *International Journal of Middle East Studies* 22 (1990): 419–35.

Eldem, Sedad H., and Feridun Akozan. *Topkapı Sarayı: Bir Mimarî Araştırma.* Ankara, n.d.

Elias, Norbert. *The Court Society.* Translated by E. Jephcott. Oxford, 1983.

Elliott, John H. *The Count-Duke of Olivares: The Statesman in an Age of Decline.* New Haven, Conn., 1986.

Esposito, John. *Women in Muslim Family Law.* Syracuse, N.Y., 1982.

Eyice, Semavi. "Mimar Kasım Hakkında." *Belleten* 43 (1979): 767–808.

Faroqui, Suraiya. "Political Initiatives 'From the Bottom Up' in the Sixteenth- and Seventeenth-Century Ottoman Empire." *Osmanistische Studien zur Wirtschafts- und Socialgeschichte,* ed. H. G. Majer, 24–33. Weisbaden, Germany, 1986.

———. "Town Officials, *Timar*-Holders, and Taxation: The Late Sixteenth-Century Crisis as Seen from Çorum." *Turcica* 18 (1986): 53–82.

Findley, Carter V. *Bureaucratic Reform in the Ottoman Empire: The Sublime Porte, 1780–1922.* Princeton, N.J., 1980.

Finkel, Caroline. *The Administration of Warfare: The Ottoman Military Campaigns in Hungary, 1593–1606.* Vienna, 1988.

Fisher, C. G. and A. Fisher. "Topkapı Sarayı in the Mid-Seventeenth Century: Bobovi's Description." *Archivum Ottomanicum* 10 (1985–1987): 5–81.

Fleischer, Cornell H. *Bureaucrat and Intellectual in the Ottoman Empire: The Historian Mustafa Ali (1541–1600).* Princeton, N.J., 1986.

———. "From Şehzade Korkud to Mustafa Ali: Cultural Origins of the Ottoman *Nasihatname.*" Paper presented at the Third International Congress on the Economic and Social History of Turkey, Princeton, N.J., 1983.

Fletcher, Joseph. "Turco-Mongolian Monarchical Tradition in the Ottoman Empire." *Harvard Ukranian Studies* 3–4 (1979–80): 236–51.

Frye, Richard. "The Charisma of Kingship in Ancient Iran." *Iranica Antiqua* 4 (1964): 36–54.

———. "The Samanids." In *The Cambridge History of Iran,* ed. R. Frye, 4:136–61. Cambridge, England, 1975.

Galante, Abraham. *Don Salomon Aben Yaèche, Duc de Mételin.* Istanbul, 1936.

Geertz, Clifford. "Centers, Kings, and Charisma: Reflections on the Symbolics of Power." In *Local Knowledge: Further Essays in Interpretive Anthropology,* 121–46. New York, 1983.

Gerber, Haim. "Social and Economic Position of Women in an Ottoman City, Bursa, 1600–1700." *International Journal of Middle East Studies* 12 (1980): 231–44.

Gibb, E.J.W. *A History of Ottoman Poetry.* 6 vols. London, 1900–1907.

Gibb, H.A.R. "Arab-Byzantine Relations under the Umayyad Caliphate." In *Studies on the Civilization of Islam,* ed. S. J. Shaw and W. R. Polk, 47–61. Princeton, N.J., 1962.

———. "Lutfi Paşa on the Ottoman Caliphate." *Oriens* 15 (1962): 287–95.

———. "Some Considerations on the Sunni Theory of the Caliphate." In *Studies on the Civilization of Islam,* ed. S. J. Shaw and W. R. Polk, 141–50. Princeton, N.J., 1962.

Gibb, H.A.R., and Harold Bowen. *Islamic Society and the West: A Study of the Impact of Western Civilization on Moslem Culture in the Near East.* One vol. in two parts. Oxford, 1950–1957.

Giese, Friedrich. "Das Seniorat im Osmanischen Herrscherhause." *Mitteilungen zur Osmanischen Geschichte* 2 (1923–26): 248–56.

Goody, Jack. *The Oriental, the Ancient, and the Primitive: Systems of Marriage and the Family in the Pre-Industrial Societies of Eurasia.* Cambridge, England, 1990.

————, ed. *Succession to High Office*. Cambridge Papers in Social Anthropology, no. 4. Cambridge, England, 1966.

Gökbilgin, M. Tayyib. "Başmaklık." *IA*.

————. "Hurrem Sultan." *IA*.

————. "İbrahim." *IA*.

————. "İbrahim Paşa." *IA* and *EI(2)*.

————. "Köprülü Mehmed Paşa." *IA*.

————. "Mehmed III." *IA*.

————. "Mehmed Paşa, Sokollu." *IA*.

————. "XVII. Asırda, Osmanlı Devletinde Islahat İhtiyaç ve Temayyülleri ve Katip Çelebi." In *Katip Çelebi: Hayatı ve Eserleri Hakkında İncelemeler*, ed. B. Kütükoğlu, 197–218. Ankara, 1952.

————. "Rüstem Paşa ve Hakkındaki İthamlar." *Tarih Dergisi* 18, nos. 11–12. (1968): 11–50.

————. "Süleyman I." *IA*.

Gökçen, İbrahim. *Manisa Tarihinde Vakıflar ve Hayırlar (Hicri 954–1060)*. Istanbul, 1946.

Gökyay, Orhan Şaik. *Dedem Korkud Kitabı*. Istanbul, 1973.

Grabar, Oleg. *The Formation of Islamic Art*. New Haven, Conn., 1973.

Griswold, William J. *The Great Anatolian Rebellion 1000–1020/1591–1611*. Berlin, 1983.

Grosrichard, Alain. *Structure de sérail: La Fiction du despotisme asiatique dans l'Occident classique*. Paris, 1979.

Grunebaum, Gustave von. *Medieval Islam*. Chicago, 1953.

————. "The Sources of Islamic Civilization." In *The Cambridge History of Islam*, ed. P. M. Holt, B. Lewis, and A.K.S. Lambton, 2B: 469–510. Cambridge, England, 1970.

Hammer, Joseph von. *Histoire de l'empire ottoman*. Vols. 1–11. Paris, 1835–1837.

Harth, Erica. *Ideology and Culture in Seventeenth-Century France*. Ithaca, N.Y., 1983.

Helly, Dorothy O. and Susan M. Reverby, eds. *Gendered Domains: Rethinking Public and Private in Women's History*. Ithaca, N.Y., 1992.

Heyd, Uriel. *Ottoman Documents on Palestine 1552–1615: A Study of the Firman According to the Mühimme Defteri*. Oxford, 1960.

————. "Some Aspects of the Ottoman *Fetvâ*." *Bulletin of the School of Oriental and African Studies* 32, no. 1 (1969): 35–56.

————. *Studies in Old Ottoman Criminal Law*. Edited by V. L. Ménage. Oxford, 1973.

Holum, Kenneth G. *Theodosian Empresses: Women and Imperial Dominion in Late Antiquity*. Berkeley and Los Angeles, Calif., 1982.

Howard, Douglas A. "Ottoman Historiography and the Literature of 'Decline' of the Sixteenth and Seventeenth Centuries." *Journal of Asian History* 22, no. 1 (1988): 52–77.

————. "The Ottoman Timar System and Its Transformation, 1563–1656." Ph.D. diss., Indiana University, 1987.

Humphreys, R. Stephen. *From Saladin to the Mongols: The Ayyubids of Damascus, 1193–1260*. Albany, N.Y., 1977.

————. *Islamic History: A Framework for Inquiry*. Princeton, N.J. 1991.

Imber, Colin. "Koçi Bey." *EI(2)*.

————. "The Ottoman Dynastic Myth." *Turcica* 19 (1987): 7–27.

————. *The Ottoman Empire, 1300–1481*. Istanbul, 1990.

————. "Paul Wittek's 'De la Défaite d'Ankara à la prise de Constantinople.' " *Osmanlı Araştırmaları* 5 (1986): 65–81.

———. "Süleymân as Caliph of the Muslims: Ebû's-Su'ûd's Formulation of Ottoman Dynastic Ideology." In *Soliman le magnifique et son temps*, ed. G. Veinstein, 179–84. Paris, 1991.

———. "Zinâ in Ottoman Law." In *Contributions à l'histoire économique et sociale de l'empire ottoman*, ed. J.-L. Bacqué-Gramont and P. Dumont, 59–92. Leuven, Belgium, 1983.

İnalcık, Halil. "The Emergence of the Ottomans." In *The Cambridge History of Islam*, ed. P. M. Holt, A.K.S. Lambton, and B. Lewis, 1A: 263–91. Cambridge, England, 1970.

———. "Ghulam." *EI(2)*.

———. "Impact of the *Annales* School on Ottoman Studies and New Findings." *Review* 1, nos.3/4 (1978): 69–96.

———. "Istanbul." *EI(2)*.

———. "Kanun." *EI(2)*.

———. "Mehmed I." *EI(2)*.

———. "Mehmed II." *IA*.

———. "Military and Fiscal Transformation in the Ottoman Empire." *Archivum Ottomanicum* 6 (1980): 283–337.

———. "Murad II." *IA*.

———. "Osmanlı Hukukuna Giriş." *Siyasal Bilgiler Fakültesi Dergisi* 13, no. 2 (1958): 102–26.

———. "Osmanlılarda Saltanat Veraset Usulü ve Türk Hakimiyet Telakkisiyle İlgisi." *Siyasal Bilgiler Fakültesi Dergisi* 14, no. 1 (1959): 69–94.

———. *The Ottoman Empire: The Classical Age 1300–1600*. Translated by C. Imber and N. Itzkowitz. New York, 1973.

———. "Örf." *IA*.

———. "Padişah." *IA*.

———. "The Rise of Ottoman Historiography." In *Historians of the Middle East*, ed. B. Lewis and P. M. Holt, 152–67. London, 1962.

———. "Servile Labor in the Ottoman Empire." In *Mutual Effects Between the Islamic and Judeo-Christian Worlds*, ed. A. Archer, T. Halasi-Kun, and B.K. Király, 25–52. New York, 1979.

———. "Suleiman the Lawgiver and Ottoman Law." *Archivum Ottomanicum* 1 (1969): 105–38.

———. "Tursun Beg, Historian of Mehmed the Conqueror's Time." *Wiener Zeitschrift für die Kunde des Morgenlandes* 69 (1977): 55–71.

Itzkowitz, Norman. "Eighteenth-Century Ottoman Realities." *Studia Islamica* 16 (1962): 73–94.

———. *Ottoman Empire and Islamic Tradition*. Chicago, 1972.

Ives, Eric. *Anne Boleyn*. London, 1986.

Jardine, Lisa. *Still Harping on Daughters: Women and Drama in the Age of Shakespeare*. Sussex, England, and Totowa, N.J., 1983.

Jennings, Ronald C. "Women in Early Seventeenth Century Ottoman Judicial Records—the Sharia Court of Anatolian Kayseri." *Journal of the Economic and Social History of the Orient* 18 (1975): 53–114.

Kantorowicz, Ernst. *The King's Two Bodies: A Study in Medieval Political Theology*. Princeton, N.J., 1957.

Kaplan, Mehmed. "Dede Korkut Kitabında Kadın." *Türkiyat Mecmuası* 9 (1946–51): 99–112.

Keddie, Nikki and Beth Baron, eds. *Women in Middle Eastern History: Shifting Boundaries in Sex and Gender*. New Haven, Conn., 1991.

Kepecioğlu, Kamil. *Bursa Kütügü.* 4 vols. Bursa (İnebey) Yazma ve Eski Basma Eserler Kütüphanesi Genel Bölüm, nos. 4519–22.

———. "Tarihi Bilgiler ve Vesikalar." *Vakıflar Dergisi* 2 (1942): 405–6, 418.

Kiel, Machiel. *Art and Society of Bulgaria in the Turkish Period.* Assen and Maastricht, The Netherlands, 1985.

Konyalı, İbrahim Hakkı. "Kanunî Sultan Süleyman'ın Annesi Hafsa Sultanın Vakfiyesi ve Manisa'daki Hayır Eserleri." *Vakıflar Dergisi* 8 (1969): 47–56.

Köprülü, Mehmed Fuad. "Ahmed Yesevi." *IA.*

———. "Bizans Müesseselerinin Osmanlı Müesseseleri Üzerine Te'siri." *Türk Hukuk ve İktisad Tarih Mecmuası* 1 (1931): 165–313.

———. *Osmanlı Devleti'nin Kuruluşu.* Ankara, 1984. (Originally published in 1935 as *Les Origines de l'empire ottoman.*)

———. *Türk Edebiyatında İlk Mutasavvıflar.* Istanbul, 1919.

Kunt, İ. Metin. "Ethnic-Regional (*Cins*) Solidarity in the Seventeenth-Century Ottoman Establishment." *International Journal of Middle East Studies* 5 (1974): 233–39.

———. "The Köprülü Years: 1656–1661." Ph.D. diss., Princeton University, 1971.

———. "Kulların Kulları." *Boğaziçi Üniversitesi Dergisi: Beşeri Bilimler* 3 (1975): 27–42.

———. *The Sultan's Servants: The Transformation of Ottoman Provincial Government, 1550–1650.* New York, 1983.

Kramers, J. H. "Sultan." *EI(2).*

Kuran, Aptullah. *Sinan: The Grand Old Master of Ottoman Architecture.* Washington, D.C., and Istanbul, 1987.

———. "Üsküdar Atik Valide Külliyesinin Yerleşme Düzeni ve Yapım Tarihi Üzerine." In *Suut Kemal Yetkin'e Armağan,* 231–48. Ankara, 1984.

Kurat, A. N. "The Reign of Mehmed IV." In *A History of the Ottoman Empire to 1730,* ed. M. Cook, 157–77. Cambridge, England, 1976.

———. *Türk-İngiliz Münasebetlerinin Başlangıcı ve Gelişmesi, 1553–1610.* Ankara, 1953.

Kütükoğlu, Bekir. *Katip Çelebi "Fezleke"sinin Kaynakları.* Istanbul, 1974.

———. "Murad III." *IA.*

———. "Süleyman II." *IA.*

———. "Valide Sultan." *IA.*

Ladurie, Emmanuel LeRoy. "Versailles Observed: The Court of Louis XIV in 1709." In *The Mind and Method of the Historian,* 149–73. Translated by S. Reynolds and B. Reynolds. Chicago, 1981.

Lambton, Ann K. S. *Continuity and Change in Medieval Persia: Aspects of Administrative, Economic and Social History, Eleventh to Fourteenth Centuries.* New York, 1988.

———. *State and Government in Medieval Islam.* Oxford, 1981.

Lewis, Bernard. "Askeri." *EI(2).*

———. "Diwan-i Humayun." *EI(2).*

———. *Istanbul and the Civilization of the Ottoman Empire.* Norman, Okla., 1963.

———. "Khadim al-Haramayn." *EI(2).*

———. "The Mongols, the Turks, and the Muslim Polity." In *Islam in History: Ideas, Men and Events in the Middle East,* 179–98. London, 1973.

———. "Ottoman Observers of Ottoman Decline." *Islamic Studies* 1 (1962): 71–87.

———. *The Political Language of Islam.* Chicago, 1988.

————. "Siyâsa." In *In Quest of an Islamic Humanism: Arabic and Islamic Studies in Memory of Mohamed al-Nowaihi*, ed. A. H. Green, 3–14. Cairo, 1984.

Lewis, Bernard and P. M. Holt, eds. *Historians of the Middle East.* London, 1962.

Lewis, Geoffrey, ed. and trans. *The Book of Dede Korkut.* London, 1974.

Lindner, Rudi Paul. *Nomads and Ottomans in Medieval Anatolia.* Bloomington, Ind., 1983.

Lutfi, Huda. "Al-Sakhâwî's *Kitâb al-Nisâ'* as a Source for the Social and Economic History of Muslim Women during the Fifteenth Century A.D." *Muslim World* 71 (1981): 104–24.

————. "Manners and Customs of Fourteenth-Century Cairene Women: Female Anarchy versus Male Shar'i Order in Muslim Prescriptive Treatises." In *Women in Middle Eastern History: Shifting Boundaries in Sex and Gender*, ed. N. Keddie and B. Baron, 99–121. New Haven, Conn., 1991.

Mantran, Robert. *La Vie quotidienne à Constantinople au temps de Soliman le Magnifique et de ses successeurs (XVIe et XVIIe Siècles).* Paris, 1965.

Manz, Beatrice F. *The Rise and Rule of Tamerlane.* Cambridge, England, 1989.

————. "Tamurlane and the Symbolism of Sovereignty." *Iranian Studies* 21, nos. 1–2 (1988): 105–22.

Marcus, Abraham. "Men, Women, and Property: Dealers in Real Estate in Eighteenth-Century Aleppo." *Journal of the Economic and Social History of the Orient* 26 (1983): 137–63.

————. *The Middle East on the Eve of Modernity: Aleppo in the Eighteenth Century.* New York, 1989.

————. "Privacy in Eighteenth-Century Aleppo: The Limits of Cultural Ideals." *International Journal of Middle East Studies* 18 (1986): 165–183.

Mardin, Şerif. "Superwesternization in Urban Life in the Ottoman Empire in the Last Quarter of the Nineteenth Century." In *Turkey: Geographical and Social Perspectives*, ed. P. Benedict and E. Tümertekin, 403–46. Leiden, 1974.

Marmon, Shaun. "Concubinage, Islamic." In *Dictionary of the Middle Ages*, ed. J. Strayer et al., 3:527–29. New York, 1982–89.

————. *Eunuchs of the Holy Cities.* Oxford University Press, forthcoming.

Mazzaoui, Michel. *The Origins of the Safawids, Shi'ism, Sufism, and the Gulat.* Wiesbaden, Germany, 1972.

Meisami, Julie Scott. "Kings and Lovers: Ethical Dimensions of Medieval Persian Romance." *Edebiyat* n.s. 1, no. 1 (1987): 1–27.

Mélikoff, Irène. "Ghazi." *EI(2).*

Ménage, V. L. "The Beginnings of Ottoman Historiography." In *Historians of the Middle East*, ed. B. Lewis and P. M. Holt, 168–79. London, 1962.

————. "Devshirme." *EI(2).*

————. "Seven Ottoman Documents from the Reign of Mehemmed II." In *Documents from Islamic Chanceries*, ed. S. M. Stern, 81–118. Columbia, S.C., 1965.

————. "Some Notes on the *Devshirme.*" *Bulletin of the School of Oriental and African Studies* 29 (1966): 64–78.

Mernissi, Fatima. *Beyond the Veil: Male-Female Dynamics in Modern Muslim Society.* Bloomington, Ind., 1987.

————. *The Veil and the Male Elite: A Feminist Interpretation of Women's Rights in Islam.* Translated by Mary Jo Lakeland. Reading, Mass., 1991.

———— [Sabbah, Fatna A.]. *Women in the Muslim Unconscious.* New York, 1984.

Miller, Barnette. *Beyond the Sublime Porte.* New Haven, Conn., 1931.

————. *The Palace School of Muhammed the Conqueror.* Cambridge, England, 1941.

Minorsky, Vladimir. "The Poetry of Shah Ismail I." *Bulletin of the School of Oriental and African Studies* 10 (1940–43): 1006a–53a.

Mottahedeh, Roy P. *Loyalty and Leadership in an Early Islamic Society.* Princeton, N.J., 1980.

Mordtmann, J. H. "Damad." *EI(2)*.

———. "Die Judischen Kira im Serai der Sultane." *Mitteilungen des Seminars für Orientalische Sprachen* 32 (1929): 1–38.

Murphey, Rhoads. "Mustafa Ali and the Politics of Cultural Despair." *International Journal of Middle East Studies* 21 (May 1989): 243–55.

———. "The Veliyyuddin Telhis: Notes on the Sources and Interrelations between Koçi Bey and Contemporary Writers of Advice to Kings." *Belleten* 43 (1979): 547–71.

Musallam, Basim F. *Sex and Society in Islam.* Cambridge, England, 1983.

Nashat, Guity, ed. *Women and Revolution in Islam.* Boulder, Col., 1983.

Necipoğlu, Gülru. "The Formation of an Ottoman Imperial Tradition: The Topkapı Palace in the Fifteenth and Sixteenth Centuries." Ph.D. diss., Harvard University, 1985.

———. "Süleyman the Magnificent and the Representation of Power in the Context of Ottoman-Hapsburg-Papal Rivalry." *Art Bulletin* 71, no.3 (September 1989): 401–27.

Nesin, Aziz. *Istanbul Boy: The Autobiography of Aziz Nesin, Part I.* Translated by J. S. Jacobson. Austin, Tex., 1977.

d'Ohsson, M[ouradgea]. *Tableau géneral de l'empire othoman.* Vol. 7. Paris, 1824.

Okin, Susan. *Justice, Gender, and the Family.* New York, 1989.

———. *Women in Western Political Thought.* Princeton, N.J., 1979.

Orhonlu, Cengiz. "Hass." *EI(2)*.

Ortaylı, İlber. "Anadolu'da XVI. Yüzyılda Evlilik İlişkileri Üzerine Bazı Gözlemler." *Osmanlı Araştırmaları* 1 (1980): 33–40.

Parry, V. J. "The Reign of Sulaiman the Magnificent, 1520–1566," "The Successors of Sulaiman, 1566–1617," "The Period of Murad IV, 1617–1648." In *A History of the Ottoman Empire to 1730,* ed. M. Cook, 79–157. Cambridge, England, 1976.

Pateman, Carole. *The Sexual Contract.* Stanford, Calif., 1988.

Peirce, Leslie P. "Beyond Harem Walls: Ottoman Royal Women and the Exercise of Power." In *Gendered Domains: Rethinking Public and Private in Women's History,* ed. D. O. Helly and S. M. Reverby, 40–55. Ithaca, N.Y., 1992.

———. "The Family as Faction: Dynastic Politics in the Reign of Süleyman." In *Soliman le magnifique et son temps,* ed. G. Veinstein, 105–16. Paris, 1992.

———. "The Imperial Harem: Gender and Power in the Ottoman Empire, 1520–1656." Ph.D. diss., Princeton University, 1988.

———. "Shifting Boundaries: Images of Ottoman Royal Women in the Sixteenth and Seventeenth Centuries." *Critical Matrix* 4 (Fall–Winter 1988): 43–81.

Penzer, N. *The Harem.* Philadelphia, 1937.

Petry, Carl F. "Class Solidarity versus Gender Gain: Women as Custodians of Property in Later Medieval Egypt." In *Women in Middle Eastern History: Shifting Boundaries in Sex and Gender,* ed. N. Keddie and B. Baron, 122–42. New Haven, Conn., 1991.

———. "A Paradox of Patronage during the Later Mamluk Period." *Muslim World* 73, nos. 3–4 (1983): 182–207.

Refik, Ahmed (Altınay). *Kadınlar Saltanatı.* Istanbul, 1332/1913–1914.

Reindl-Kiel, Hedda. "*damet ismetûha*—immer währe ihre Sittsamkeit: Frau und Gesellschaft im Osmanischen Reich." *Orientierungen* 1 (1989): 37–81.

Repp, Richard. "The Altered Nature and Role of the Ulema." In *Studies in Eighteenth-Century Islamic History,* ed. T. Naff and R. Owen, 277–87. Carbondale, Ill., 1977.

———. *The Müfti of Istanbul: A Study in the Development of the Ottoman Learned Hierarchy.* London, 1986.

Riasanovsky, V. A. *Fundamental Principles of Mongol Law.* Tientsin, China, 1937.

Rogers, J. M., and R. M. Ward. *Süleyman the Magnificent.* London, Trustees of the British Museum, 1988.

Rosedale, H. E. *Queen Elizabeth and the Levant Company.* London, 1904.

Rossabi, Morris. "Khubilai Khan and the Women in His Family." In *Studia Sino-Mongolica: Festschrift für Herbert Franke,* ed. W. Bauer, 153–80. Wiesbaden, Germany, 1979.

Rossi, Ettore. "La Sultana *Nûr Bânû* (Cecilia Venier-Baffo) moglie di Selim II (1566–1574) e madre di Murad III (1574–1595)." *Oriente moderno* 33, no. 11 (1953): 433–41.

Rouillard, Clarence Dana. *The Turk in French History, Thought, and Literature (1520–1660).* Paris, 1940.

Roux, J. P. "L'Origine céleste de la souveraineté dans les inscriptions Paléo-Turques de Mongolie et de Sibérie." In *The Sacral Kingship,* supplement 4 to *Numen,* 231–41. Leiden, 1959.

Sanders, Paula. "From Court Ceremony to Urban Language: Ceremonial in Fatimid Cairo and Fustât." In *The Islamic World from Classical to Modern Times: Essays in Honor of Bernard Lewis,* ed. C. E. Bosworth et al., 311–21. Princeton, N.J., 1989.

———. "Gendering the Ungendered Body: Hermaphrodites in Medieval Islam." In *Women in Middle Eastern History: Shifting Boundaries in Sex and Gender,* ed. N. Keddie and B. Baron, 74–95. New Haven, Conn., 1991.

Savory, Roger. *Iran under the Safavids.* Cambridge, England, 1980.

Schacht, J. "Umm Walad." *EI(1).*

Scott, Joan W. *Gender and the Politics of History.* New York, 1988.

Seni, Nora. "Ville ottomane et représentation du corps féminin." *Le Temps modernes* 41, nos. 456–58 (1984): 66–95.

Shaw, Stanford J. *History of the Ottoman Empire and Modern Turkey.* Vol. 1. Cambridge, England, 1976.

Singer, Amy. *Palestinian Peasants and Ottoman Officials: Rural Administration in the Sancak of Jerusalem in the Mid-Sixteenth Century.* Cambridge University Press, forthcoming.

Skilliter, S. A. "Catherine de' Médici's Turkish Ladies-in-Waiting: A Dilemma in Franco-Ottoman Diplomatic Relations." *Turcica* 7 (1975): 188–204.

———. "Khurrem." *EI(2).*

———. "The Letters of the Venetian 'Sultana' Nûr Bânû and Her Kira to Venice." In *Studia Turcologica Memoriae Alexii Bombaci Dicata,* ed. A. Gallotta and U. Marazzi, 515–36. Naples, 1982.

———. "Three Letters from the Ottoman 'Sultana' Safiye to Queen Elizabeth I." In *Documents from Islamic Chanceries,* ed. S. M. Stern, 119–57. Columbia, S.C. 1965.

———. *William Harborne and the Trade with Turkey 1578–1582: A Documentary Study of the First Anglo-Ottoman Relations.* Oxford, 1977.

Sokolnicki, Michel. "La Sultane Ruthène." *Belleten* 23 (1959): 229–39.

Sourdel, Dominique. *La Civilization de l'Islam classique.* Paris, 1968.

———. "Ghulam." *EI(2).*

———. "Questions de cérémonial 'abbâside.' " *Révue des études islamiques* 28 (1960): 121–48.

Spagni, E. "Una Sultana veneziana." *Nuovo Archivio Veneto* 19 (1900): 241–348.

Spellberg, Denise. "Nizâm Al-Mulk's Manipulation of Tradition: 'A'isha and the Role of Women in Islamic Government." *Muslim World* 78, no.2 (April 1988): 111–17.

———. "Political Action and Public Example: 'A'isha and the Battle of the Camel." In *Women in Middle Eastern History: Shifting Boundaries in Sex and Gender,* ed. N. Keddie and B. Baron, 45–57. New Haven, Conn., 1991.

———. "The Politics of Praise: Depictions of Khadija, Fatima and 'A'isha in Ninth-Century Muslim Sources." *Literature East and West* 26 (1990): *Images of Women in Asian Literature,* ed. A. F. Sjobery, 130–48.

Stephan, St. H. "An Endowment Deed of Khâsseki Sultân, Dated the 24th May 1552." *Quarterly of the Department of Antiquities in Palestine* 10 (1944): 170–99.

Subtelny, Maria Eva. "Art and Politics in Early Sixteenth Century Central Asia." *Central Asiatic Journal* 27, nos. 1–2 (1983): 121–48.

Sümer, Faruk. *Oğuzlar (Türkmenler): Tarihleri, Boy Teşkilatı, Destanları.* Istanbul, 1980.

Tapper, Nancy. "Matrons and Mistresses: Women and Boundaries in Two Middle Eastern Tribal Societies." *Archives européennes de sociologie* 21 (1980): 59–79.

Tekin, Talat. *A Grammar of Orkhon Turkic.* Bloomington, Ind., 1968.

Thomas, Lewis. *A Study of Naima.* New York, 1972.

Togan, A. Zeki Velidi. *Oğuz Destanı.* Istanbul, 1982.

———. *Umumi Türk Tarihi'ne Giriş.* Istanbul, 1946.

Tuğlacı, Pars. *Osmanlı Saray Kadınları.* Istanbul, 1985.

Turan, Şerafettin. *Kanuni'nin Oğlu Şehzade Bayezid Vak'ası.* Ankara, 1961.

Turgut, A. Memduh. *İznik ve Bursa Tarihi.* Bursa, Turkey, 1937.

Uçtum, Nejat R. "Hürrem ve Mihrümah Sultanların Polonya Kıralı II. Zigsmund'a Yazdıkları Mektuplar." *Belleten* 44 (1980): 697–715.

Uğur, Ahmet. *The Reign of Sultan Selîm I in the Light of the Selîm-Nâme Literature.* Berlin, 1985.

Uluçay, M. Çağatay. "Bayezid II.in Ailesi." *Tarih Dergisi* 10 (1959): 105–24.

———. *Harem.* Ankara, 1985.

———. "Kanuni Sultan Süleyman ve Ailesi ile İlgili Bazı Notlar ve Vesikalar." In *Kanuni Armağanı,* 227–58. Ankara, 1970.

———. "Koçi Bey." *IA.*

———. *Manisa'daki Saray-ı Amire ve Şehzadeler Türbesi.* Istanbul, 1941.

———. "Mustafa Sultan." *IA.*

———. *Padişahların Kadınları ve Kızları.* Ankara, 1980.

Uzunçarşılı, İsmail Hakki. *Çandarlı Vezir Ailesi.* Ankara, 1974.

———. "Fatih Sultan Mehmed'in Vezir-i Azamlarından Mahmud Paşa ile Şehzade Mustafa'nın Araları Niçin Açıktı?" *Belleten* 28 (1964): 719–28.

———. "Gazi Orhan Bey Vakfiyesi." *Belleten* 5 (1941): 277–88.

———. "Kanuni Sultan Süleyman'ın Vezir-i Azamı Makbul ve Maktul İbrahim Paşa Padişah Damadı Değildi." *Belleten* 29 (1965): 355–61.

———. *Kitabeler.* Vol. 2. Istanbul, 1347/1929.

———. "Orhan Gazi'nin, Vefat Eden Oğlu Süleyman Paşa İçin Tertip Ettirdiği Vakfiyenin Aslı." *Belleten* 27 (1963): 437–43.

———. *Osmanlı Devletinin Saray Teşkilatı.* Ankara, 1945.

———. *Osmanlı Tarihi.* 3 vols. 4th ed. Ankara, 1983.

———. "Osmanlı Tarihinin İlk Devirlerine Aid Bazı Yanlışlıkların Tashihi." *Belleten* 21 (1959): 173–88.

———. "Sancağa Çıkarılan Osmanlı Şehzadeleri." *Belleten* 39 (1975): 659–96.

———. "Uçüncü Mehmed'in Oğlu Şehzade Mahmud'un Ölümü." *Belleten* 24 (1960): 263–67.

Üçok, Bahriye. *İslam Devletlerinde Kadın Hükümdarlar.* Ankara, 1965.

Valensi, Lucette. *Venise et la Sublime Porte: La Naissance du despote.* Paris, 1987.

Vandal, Albert. *Les Voyages du Marquis de Nointel (1670–1680).* Paris, 1900.

Veinstein, Gilles. "L'Empire dans sa grandeur (XVIᵉ siècle)." In *Histoire de l'empire ottoman,* ed. R. Mantran. Paris, 1989.

Vryonis, Spyros. *The Decline of Medieval Hellenism in Asia Minor and the Process of Islamization from the Eleventh through the Fifteenth Century.* Los Angeles, Calif., 1971.

Weil, Rachel. "The Crown Has Fallen to the Distaff: Gender and Politics in the Age of Catherine de Médici." *Critical Matrix* 1, no. 4 (1985): 1–38.

Wittek, Paul. "De la Défaite d'Ankara à la prise de Constantinople." *Révue des études islamiques* 1 (1938): 1–34.

———. "Notes sur la Tughra ottomane." *Byzantine* 18 (1948): 311–34.

———. *The Rise of the Ottoman Empire.* London, 1938.

Wood, Susan. "*Memoriae Agrippinae:* Agrippina the Elder in Julio-Claudian Art and Propaganda." *American Journal of Archaeology* 92 (July 1988): 409–26.

Woods, John. *The Aqquyunlu: Clan, Confederation, Empire.* Minneapolis, 1976.

———. "Timur's Genealogy." In *Intellectual Studies on Islam: Essays Written in Honor of Martin B. Dickson,* ed. M. Mazzaoui and V. Moreen, 85–125. Salt Lake City, Utah, 1990.

Yanki İskender Hoji. "Şehzade Halil'in Sergüzeşti." *Tarih-i Osmanî Encümeni Mecmuası* 2: 434–45.

Yates, Frances A. *Astrea: The Imperial Theme in the Sixteenth Century.* London and Boston, 1975.

Yınanç, Mükrimin Halil. "Ahmed Paşa, Gedik." *IA.*

———. "Bayezid I." *IA.*

Young, George. *Constantinople.* London and New York, n.d.

Yücel, Yaşar. *XIII–XV. Yüzyıllar Kuzey-batı Anadolu Tarihi: Çoban-Oğulları Candar-Oğulları Beylikleri.* Ankara, 1980.

Zachariadou, Elizabeth. "Pachymeres on the 'Amourioi' of Kastamonu." In *Roumania and the Turks (c. 1300–c. 1500),* II. London, 1985. Originally published in *Byzantine and Modern Greek Studies 3,* 57–70. Oxford, 1977.

Zilfi, Madeline C. "Elite Circulation in the Ottoman Empire: Great Mollas of the Eighteenth Century." *Journal of the Economic and Social History of the Orient* 26 (1983): 318–64.

———. "The Kadızadelis: Discordant Revivalism in Seventeenth Century Istanbul." *Journal of Near Eastern Studies* 45, no. 4 (1986): 251–69.

———. *The Politics of Piety: The Ottoman Ulema in the Postclassical Age (1600–1800).* Minneapolis, 1988.

INDEX